Pete Moulton

with Jeremy Moulton
and the staff of the Moulton Company

A+
Certification

Prentice Hall PTR, Upper Saddle River, NJ 07458
http://www.phptr.com

Editorial/Production Supervision: *Kathleen M. Caren*
Acquisitions Editor: *Mary Franz*
Editorial Assistant: *Noreen Regina*
Marketing Manager: *Lisa Konzelmann*
Development Editor: *Jim Markham*
Indexer: *Bill and Nancy Lively*
Manufacturing Manager: *Maura Goldstaub*
Cover Design Direction: *Jerry Votta*
Cover Design: *Talar Agasyan*
Series Design: *Gail Cocker-Bogusz*

Prentice-Hall International (UK) Limited, *London*
Prentice-Hall of Australia Pty. Limited, *Sydney*
Prentice-Hall Canada Inc., *Toronto*
Prentice-Hall Hispanoamericana, S.A., *Mexico*
Prentice-Hall of India Private Limited, *New Delhi*
Prentice-Hall of Japan, Inc., *Tokyo*
Simon & Schuster Asia Pte. Ltd., *Singapore*
Editora Prentice-Hall do Brasil, Ltda., *Rio de Janeiro*

This book is dedicated to
Jenna Rose, Jared and Jacob, the grandchildren.
They will never know a world without PCs that serve them.

And it is dedicated
as well to and Doug and Helene, the great grandparents,
that never really knew a world with PCs.

CONTENTS

Preface   *xix*

1

PC Components and Subsystems   *1*

Hardware Components   *2*
  Main Chassis   3
  Mouse   29
  Keyboard   30
  Video   32
  Printers   37
  Scanners   39
  Video Camera   40
  Microphone and Speakers   41

Software Components   *42*
  DOS Components   43
  Windows Components   44
  Windows NT Features and Components   48

PC Boot Process   *50*
  The role of CONFIG.SYS   52
  The role of AUTOEXEC.BAT   52

2

PC Installation and Upgrade   *57*

PC Component Replacement Summary   *58*
Removing and Adding FRUs   *60*
  Removing the Chassis Cover   61
  The Pin One Rule   62
  Main Logic Board   64

v

Disk Drives   66

Power Supply   72

CPU Chip   73

Random Access Memory   76

Device Controllers and I/O Cards   77

Common PC Reassembly Mistakes   81

Hardware Configuration Parameters   *83*

Common I/O Port Addresses   84

Standard IRQ Settings   86

Upper Memory Used by PC Hardware   87

PC Direct Memory Access Channels   89

I/O Cabling and Connectors   *90*

Peripheral Port Connector Types and Cabling   91

Serial versus Parallel Cables   93

Selected Cable Pin Connections   94

Installing IDE/EIDE Fixed Disks and CD-ROMs   *107*

Master versus Slave Designation   107

IDE Devices Per Channel   108

Installing and Configuring SCSI Devices   *108*

Bus Termination Basics   109

SCSI Types   110

Device Addresses   110

Cabling   111

Typical Switches and Jumpers   112

Installing Common Peripheral Devices   *114*

Keyboards and Mice   114

Video Card and Monitor   114

Modems   115

Upgrading Your PC   *117*

RAM   117

Fixed Disk   118

Display   118

BIOS Upgrades   119

CPU   120

CPU Cache Memory   121

3

Troubleshooting and Problem Resolution *127*

Determining the Source of Problems   *129*

Troubleshooting PC Hardware   *130*
Power On Self-Test   130
Audio Beep Error Codes   131
Video Error Messages   132
IBM Numeric Error Codes   133

Diagnosing Error Symptoms and Problems by Subsystem   *134*
Power Supply   135
Main Logic Board   136
CPU   141
RAM—Random Access Memory   142
Video and Monitor   146
Keyboard and Mouse   148
Sound Cards   162
Communications   164
Slot Covers   168

Troubleshooting Tools   *170*
Troubleshooting Diskettes   172
Multimeter   174
Spare Parts or "Swap Until You Drop"   174

Troubleshooting Procedures and Practices   *176*
Problem Isolation and Determination Procedures   177
User Questions   186

4

Maintenance and Safety Practices *197*

Preventive Maintenance Products and Procedures   *199*
Cleaning Compounds   200
The PC Cleaning Process   209

PC Power and Other PC Operating Environment Hazards   *215*
Power Problems and How to Spot Them   216

Surge Suppression 217

Uninterruptible Power Supplies (UPS) 220

Radio Frequency Interference (RFI) 221

Storing Electronic Components 222

Safety Procedures for High Voltage and Laser Equipment 223

Laser Safety 224

High Voltage Components and Safety Procedures 226

PC Power Supply Safety 228

Monitor Voltages and Safety 229

Hazardous Waste Disposal 230

Batteries 230

CRTs 230

Laser Toner Cartridges 231

Solvents 231

Other 231

Electrostatic Discharge (ESD) Procedures 232

ESD Damage 233

Protecting from ESD 234

Common ESD Environments 236

5

CPUs, RAM, and Main Logic Boards 243

CPU Chips and Their Operating Characteristics 244

Intel CPU Chips 245

*Other CPU Chips—AMD, Cyrix, Motorola, and
Alpha 272*

Random Access Memory 276

Types of RAM 276

RAM Operating Characteristics and Parameters 282

Main Logic Boards 289

Types of Main Logic Boards 290

MLB Components 296

PC Bus Architectures 301

ISA 303

EISA 305

VESA Local Bus or VL-Bus   306
Micro-Channel Architecture Bus   306
PCI   307
Small Form-Factor PCI   308
Hot-Pluggable PCI   308
Advanced Graphics Port Bus   308
PC Card or PC-MCIA Bus   309
Zoomed Video   310
USB   311
IEEE 1394 or FireWire   312

CMOS Setup   *313*
Basic Settings   314
Advanced Settings   318
Passwords and Security   323
Exit   324

6

Printers   *329*

Printing Concepts, Components, and Operation   *330*
Laser Printers (Page Printers)   332
Inkjet Printers   336
Dot Matrix Printers   337
Paper Feeders   338

Printer Connections and Configurations   *340*
Parallel Port   341
Serial Port   342
LAN   343
Infrared Link   345

Resolving Common Printer Problems   *347*
Paper Feed and Output   348
Paper Jams   349
Error Indications   350
Print Quality   353
Safety Considerations   354

Printer Servicing and Preventative Maintenance   *355*

7

Laptop PCs   *363*

Laptop Configurations and Components   *364*
    LCD—Liquid Crystal Display   368
    Battery   371
    AC Adapter   373
    PC Card Bus—Type I, II, and III Cards   375
    CD-ROM Drives   378
    Docking Stations   379
    Fixed Disk Drive   380
    Networking Cards   381
    RAM   382

Common Laptop Problems   *384*
    Dropping the Computer   385
    Temperature Extremes   385
    Exposure to X-rays   386
    Unexpected Configuration Problems   386
    Windows Configuration Problems   387
    Power Management Problems   388
    Damage to Connectors   388
    Display Problems   388
    Clocking Problems   389

8

LANs and Communications   *395*

LAN Concepts   *396*
    Data Format Compatibility   397
    Networking Compatibility   400
    Types of Local Area Networks   402
    Network Interface Cards   405
    Network Protocols   407

Full versus Half Duplex   *411*
Network Cabling   *411*
Peer-to-Peer versus Client-Server Networks   *420*
Windows 3.11   *421*

Internet Access   *441*

Installing and Configuring Network Interface Cards   *445*
Jumpers   *445*
Software Setup   *446*
Board versus IP Address   *449*

Network Problem Manifestations   *453*
Reduced Capacity—Bandwidth Loss   *453*
Data Loss   *454*
Reduced Performance—Slow Networks   *455*

9

DOS Architecture   *461*

DOS Functions   *462*
PC System Management   *465*
Disk Management   *465*
File Management   *469*
Managing Applications   *470*

DOS Components   *473*

Key System Files   *476*
IO.SYS   *476*
MSDOS.SYS   *477*
COMMAND.COM   *477*
CONFIG.SYS   *478*
AUTOEXEC.BAT   *484*
ANSI.SYS   *490*
HIMEM.SYS   *490*
EMM386.EXE   *491*

10

Windows 3.x Architecture   *497*

Windows 3.x Functions   *498*
  Managing Applications   500
  Managing Disks and PC Components   505
  Managing Files   514
  Printing   516

Windows 3.x Components   *524*
  Driver Programs   525
  Dynamic Link Libraries   526
  The Kernel   526
  GDI.EXE and USER.EXE   527
  Resource Heaps   528

Key Windows 3.x System Files   *529*
  INI Files   532
  WIN.INI   532
  SYSTEM.INI   542
  USER.EXE   561
  GDI.EXE   562
  WIN.COM   562
  PROGMAN.EXE and PROGMAN.INI   563
  KRNLxxx.EXE   564
  PIF files   565

11

Windows 95/98 Architecture   *571*

**Windows 3.x versus
Windows 95/98**   *571*

Windows 95/98 Functions   *576*
  Managing Disks and Files   576
  Managing PC Components   578
  Managing Applications   578
  Managing Printing   580
  Networking   581
  Administrative Functions   582

Windows 95/98 Components   *583*
> *Device Drivers   583*
> *Virtual Machine Manager   585*
> *Installable File System   585*
> *Windows Core Operating System   586*
> *Windows 95/98 32-Bit Shell   586*
> *DLLs   586*
> *EXEs   587*
> *The Registry   587*

Windows 95/98 Key System Files   *592*
> *SETUP.EXE   592*
> *IO.SYS   592*
> *MSDOS.SYS   594*
> *COMMAND.COM and AUTOEXEC.BAT   595*
> *REGEDIT.EXE   597*
> *SYSTEM.DAT   597*
> *USER.DAT   598*
> *WIN.COM   599*

12

Disk Navigation Procedures and Management   *607*

File System Basics   *608*
> *Binary versus Text Files   608*
> *File Naming Conventions   609*
> *File Attributes   616*

DOS File Operations   *620*
> *Editing TXT and BAT Files   620*
> *Launching Programs   621*

Windows File Operations   *623*
> *Windows 3.x File Manager   624*

Disk Management Procedures   *636*
> *Partitioning   636*
> *Formatting   641*
> *Repairing   643*

Defragmenting   643

Disk Management Utilities   644
FDISK   644
FORMAT   647
SCANDISK   648
The FAT System and Directories   650
DEFRAG   654
SYS   656

13

DOS and Memory Management   *663*

Types of Memory   664
Conventional   667
Extended Memory (XMS)   669
High Memory (HIMEM)   669
Upper Memory Blocks (UMBs)   670
Expanded Memory (EMS)   673
Shadow ROM   674
Virtual Memory   675
CONFIG.SYS Memory Control Statements   676

Memory Conflicts and Their Resolution   678
DOS versus Windows Memory Conflicts   678
General Protection Faults and Illegal Operation Errors   679
Resolving Windows Problems   680
System Monitor   685
System Resource Meter   686
MEMMAKER   686
HIMEM.SYS   689
SMARTDRV   690
EMM386.EXE and Upper Memory Blocks   693

PC DOS Memory Setup   696

14

Software Installation, Configuration, and Upgrade   *713*

Operating System Installation Procedures   *715*

File Systems   716

Disk Preparation   718

DOS Installation   728

Windows 3.1x Installation   729

Windows 95/98 Installation   740

Software Upgrades   *754*

System Requirements   756

General Upgrade Procedure   757

DOS to Windows 95/98   760

Windows 3.1x to Windows 95/98   760

Booting Procedures   *764*

Booting DOS   764

The Windows 3.1x Boot Process   768

The Windows 95/98 Boot Process   768

Loading and Adding Device Drivers   *782*

Device Drivers and Windows 3.1x   782

Device Drivers and Windows 95/98   782

Windows Configuration   *790*

Changing Installed Options   790

Installing and Configuring Printers   791

Launching Windows Applications   *797*

15

DOS and Windows Software Problem Diagnosis and Resolution   *803*

Common Software Error Messages   *804*

Safe Mode   804

Incorrect DOS Version   808

Missing Operating System   809

Error in CONFIG.SYS Line xx   810

Bad or Missing COMMAND.COM   811
Bad or Missing HIMEM.SYS   812
Missing HIMEM.SYS   812
Swap File Error Messages   813
Cannot Find a Device File Needed to Run Windows   816

Resolving Frequent Software Problems   *819*
Application Program Errors   820
System Freezing or Application Programs Hang   822
Low Resources   823
Missing Floppy or CD-ROM   826
Invalid Working Directory   827
Critical Hardware Errors or
the "Option will not function" Message   829
Application Does Not Load or Start   829
Cannot Log onto Network   831

DOS and Windows Utilities   *835*
FDISK.EXE—Fixed Disk   835
SCANDISK—Scan Disk Files and Directories   836
DEFRAG.EXE—Fixed Disk Defragment   837
MEM.EXE—Memory Check Program   839
ATTRIB.EXE—Change Attributes   840
EXTRACT.EXE—Cabinet File Extraction Tool   841
EXPAND.EXE—File Expansion Tool   842
EDIT.COM—The Microsoft Text Editor Program   843
SYSEDIT.EXE—System Configuration Editor   843
MSD.EXE—Microsoft Diagnostics Program   844
The Control Panel—System—Device Manager   845
MSINFO32.EXE—MS System Information   847
ERU.EXE—Emergency Recovery Utility   850
Tweak User Interface—Tweak UI   852
MKCOMPAT.EXE—Make Compatible Utility   852

Viruses and Virus Protection   *854*
Viruses versus Trojan Horse/Worm programs   855
Sources of Viruses   859
Detecting Viruses   860
Virus Removal Procedure   863

16

Windows Networking 869

LAN Networking Functions 870
Disk Sharing 870
File Sharing 871
Print Sharing 871

LAN Types and Cards 873
Ethernet 873
Token Ring 875
ATM 877
ARCnet 878

Configuring for Internet Access 880
Dial-Up Configuration 880
TCP/IP 886
The World Wide Web (WWW) 891
Universal Resource Locators (URLs) 892
HyperText Markup Language (HTML) 892
HyperText Transfer Protocol (HTTP) 893
File Transfer Protocol (FTP) 893
Domain Names (Web Site Designations) 893
Internet Service Providers (ISPs) 894
Email 895

17

Customer Satisfaction 903

Communicating with the Customer 904

Face-to-Face 905
Telephone Communications 906

Understanding Customer Problem Descriptions 907
Verbal and Nonverbal Cues 908
Helping with Problem Identification 909

Communicating at the Appropriate Technical Level 909

Establishing Customer Rapport 910

Professional Conduct 911

Punctuality   912
Avoiding Conflicts   913

Responding to and Closing Service Calls   *914*

Handling Customer Complaints   *915*

Empathy for Customer Problems   *916*
Sense of Urgency   917
Flexibility   917

18

Y2K and Other PC Tales   *921*

PCs and Y2K   *922*
BIOS Compatibility   922
Operating System Compatibility   924
Applications Compatibility   924
General Y2K Protection   927

Other PC Tales   *928*
Tools in a Pinch   928
What Happens When?   932

Index   *939*

PREFACE

This book is the work of the team at The Moulton Company. Without the writing of Jeremy Moulton and Phil Crouse and the help of Jason Moulton, Julie Labra, Melissa Clawson, Phil Lowry and Drew Thomason the book would not have been completed. Each played an important role.

As for the final book itself, Jeremy covered Windows 95 and NT, Phil Crouse covered customer service, Jason did Internet research, and Pete worked it all into a single book. Jeremy, Jason and Pete all have A+ Certifications. The basic materials were developed from the PC Troubleshooting course attended by thousands of PC administrators and technical support personnel and taught by the people working at Moulton, Minasi & Company in the 1980s. Pete's troubleshooting experiences and mistakes made back at the dawn of IBM PC time (1981) when he began selling and building PC's also contributed to the content. Jeremy started his PC experience with Apple II PCs, and Jason teaches a network server repair and maintenance class for Compaq.

The people at Prentice-Hall publishers including Mary Franz, Miles Williams, Jim Markham, Kathleen Caren, and others have made this process as painless as it can be. They are largely responsible for keeping and improving some of the tidbits of nerd humor found throughout the book.

We hope you enjoy this book and find it a useful reference even after you have achieved your A+ certification.

—Pete and Jeremy

PC Components and Subsystems

▲ **Chapter Syllabus**

A+ 1.1 Hardware Components

A+ 1.2 Software Components

A+ 1.3 PC Boot Process

PCs are comprised of several core components and ancillary subsystems. The core components provide the basic functionality of the PC. Ancillary subsystems enhance the basic functionality to support different applications such as graphics imaging, multimedia applications, and more. PCs are a package of matched components.

The components are matched for speed (somewhat tuned) to provide the best overall performance. It makes little sense to have a super fast Central Processing Unit (CPU chip) and a slow fixed disk drive or slow Random Access Memory (RAM). Such a combination produces a slow system. PCs are as fast as their most used and slowest component. Often, fixing PC problems is making sure that the PC components are properly matched for speed.

1

The PC core components ranked from fastest to slowest are:

1. CPU Chip—fastest
2. RAM
3. Display Adapter
4. ROM
5. Fixed Disk Drive
6. Universal Serial Bus
7. Network Adapter
8. CD-ROM Drive
9. Floppy Disk Drive
10. Parallel Port
11. Serial Port
12. Mouse
13. Keyboard
14. The Nut behind the keyboard—slowest

Components and subsystems fall into three categories: hardware, software, and network. Hardware components are those components physically installed in the PC or connected to it.

They are the core and ancillary subsystems examined in this chapter. Software components are covered in later chapters. Network connections are common components of most PC systems today.

Network connections are either dial-up or Local Area Network (LAN). The connections are attached to PC hardware components and involve networking hardware residing somewhere on the attached network. We discuss networking as it impacts the PC hardware and software components and subsystems, but networks and external networking components are beyond the scope of this book.

A+ 1.1   Hardware Components

PC hardware is the focus of this section. PC hardware core components include: the Central Processing Unit (CPU chip); the Read Only Memory (ROM); the Random Access Memory (RAM); chip sets and buses; the power supply; serial and parallel input/output (I/O) ports; the floppy disk controller and drive; the fixed disk controller and drive; the CD-ROM drive; the display adapter and monitor; the keyboard; and the mouse. See Figure 1–1. These components provide all basic PC functions. Ancillary subsystems are sound cards, LAN adapters, video cameras, etc.

Figure 1–1   *Typical PC System*

The main PC chassis contains the central component for all PCs, the main logic board (MLB). This is sometimes referred to as the system board or motherboard.

The main logic board is based on a specific CPU and supporting chip set. It has a specific bus configuration and mounts the CPU, the ROM, and the RAM. Serial and parallel interfaces as well as the keyboard interface, bus mouse interface, floppy disk controller, fixed disk integrated drive electronics (IDE) controllers, Universal Serial Bus (USB) ports, and sometimes video graphics adapter (VGA) display controllers are typically built into the main logic board. Other controllers are bus-connected cards inserted into the bus of the main logic board.

Main Chassis

The main chassis or case is the box containing most PC components today. In the future this may change. Components may be connected to the main chassis using Universal Serial Bus connections. Then the main chassis would contain the PC's core components and the ancillary subsystems would occupy desktop space.

The main chassis for the PC AT contained the main logic board, its installed Intel 286 CPU chip, ROM, and RAM. The supporting chip sets provided Industry Standard Architecture (ISA) 8-bit and 16-bit connectors for installing adapter cards. Adapter cards typically installed in the AT were serial and parallel input/output controllers, display adapters, and disk controllers. The typical AT style PC chassis contained the floppy drive(s) and a fixed disk. The primary user input was via a keyboard. This was the typical 1985 PC.

In the early 1990s PCs changed. At that time Microsoft Windows made a successful entrance into the PC marketplace. It pressured PC manufacturers to change main chassis components more rapidly than before. Similar to the 1980s PCs, most main logic boards had an installed Intel 386 or 486 CPU chip—some supported American Micro Devices (AMD) CPU chips—external CPU cache RAM, ROM, and RAM. The main logic board also included the serial and parallel port I/O controllers and IDE fixed disk and floppy disk controllers. The bus connections were mainly ISA 8-bit and 16-bit connectors. Some systems had specialized connectors to speed up display and disk access. The Video Electronics Standards Association (VESA) bus and Extended Industry Standard Architecture (EISA) main logic boards had connectors that supported higher speed transfers than the ISA bus connectors.

Today's PCs incorporate both these evolutionary changes and revolutionary changes.

Their MLB typically has Intel Pentium chips, external CPU cache RAM, RAM, ROM, and built-in serial/parallel, floppy disk, IDE fixed disk, USB, bus mouse, and keyboard controllers. They often include a VGA controller as well. The chip sets and BIOS support plug-and-play controller installation and a combination of ISA and Peripheral Component Interconnect (PCI) bus connectors. This is moving rapidly to all PCI bus and USB main logic boards. This just means that it will not be your father's PC anymore. Also, maintenance and troubleshooting procedures will change to accommodate the new types of problems posed by these newest PC technologies.

SYSTEM BOARD—MAIN LOGIC BOARD

The main logic board, system board, or motherboard is the physical foundation of a computer. Baseboard, planar board, or main boards are other terms used to identify the MLB. It is the central PC building block because all other components must either plug into it or be physically mounted on it. Without a system board, there is no electrical interconnectivity that allows the PC's hardware components and subsystems to communicate.

System boards come in different configurations. The early boards emulated an IBM PC XT configuration, then the IBM PC AT configuration. As chip sets incorporated greater functionality, MLBs shrank in size and, at the same time, incorporated more functions. The next generation of system boards had a standardized "Baby AT" form factor. This meant that they had one dimension that was from 8.6 to 8.8 inches and specially placed mounting holes for plastic standoffs and bolts. Brand name PC manufacturers used proprietary system board configurations. Such proprietary configurations necessitated that replacement MLBs be provided from the PC manufacturer. They limit the ability to upgrade PCs with faster CPU chips, RAM, and other capabilities. Some limited upgradability is designed into these proprietary main logic boards, but this does not offer the same increased capabilities that can be achieved when an entire main logic board is replaced. See Figure 1–2. For more detail on main logic boards, see Chapter 5.

Today's PC clones use main logic boards that have an ATX form factor. This means that they have installed on the board external connectors for PS2-style keyboard and mouse, as well as serial, parallel, and USB connections. Generally one dimension of an ATX main logic board is 12 inches with specially placed mounting holes for standoffs and bolts. See Figure 1–3.

Viewing any of the main boards, you see sockets for the CPU chip (or the Intel Slot 1 carrier); sockets for RAM; and PCI, Advanced Graphics Port (AGP), and ISA bus connectors. Plugs for the power supply cables are also on the main board.

To examine a system board, a PC's cover must be removed. Once inside, the system board typically is the largest sheet of green or brown fiberglass mounted directly to the metal frame or chassis. In older desktop chas-

Figure 1–2 *Baby AT Socket 7 main logic board*

Figure 1–3 *ATX Slot 1 main logic board*

sis, it was typically mounted on the bottom. With newer tower configuration chassis, it is mounted vertically. System boards are multilayer boards with four to seven or more layers of connections sandwiched between the layers of fiberglass. All layouts have keyboard and mouse connectors in the right rear corner of the board. (If you were facing a desktop PC, the connections would be in the rear on the right.) See Figure 1–4.

Looking more closely, you will find a number of lines running across the system board in an organized pattern, connecting different areas of the system board together. Physically mounted on the system board should be a few different types of connectors and chips.

Figure 1–4 *Mini-tower chassis*

CPU • The CPU or the central processing unit is a computer on a chip. The CPU chip acts as the hands or heart of the computer. No brains here because computers are dumb. They only do what they are told. They are the hands that perform the work as directed and the heart pumps the data to all PC components.

Processors are classified by their interface to the main logic board and by processing horsepower. MLB interfaces are a socket interface or a slot interface. The socket interfaces are Socket 7 (Intel Pentium CPUs) and

Socket 8 (Intel PentiumPro CPUs). Intel introduced the Single Edge Contact (SEC) or slot interfaces in 1998. Most slot interfaces are Slot 1, but newer Intel chips can use the Slot 2 interface. Processing horsepower is mostly defined by clock speed. CPU purists would argue that point vigorously. However, general users would only notice performance improvements when clock speeds increase by greater than 50%.

Other components in the CPU also determine its performance, including the amount of Level 1 and Level 2 CPU cache incorporated into the chip configuration.

Starting with the 486 chip, CPUs had internal Level 1 CPU cache memory to speed up processing performance. Both Level 1 and Level 2 cache are a storage area used by processors to increase performance. Level 1 is a small, high-speed cache right on the chip, to hold recently used data and instructions from memory. Level 2 is larger in size and until recent years has been located outside the chip on the motherboard. PentiumPro chips were among the first to include the Level 2 CPU cache in the chip package.

Cache memory is a means of speeding up computer processing. Cache works on the 80/20 rule of computers. This is similar to the 80/20 rule of the IRS—they keep 80% of what you earn and you get 20% of what you earn. In computers the next piece of information that you need is 80% of the time right next to the last piece of information that you used. This means that if information is contained on a device, like a disk drive, that is slower than the component where the information is going to be used next, like RAM, then it makes sense to bring the information into a temporary holding area—the cache—that is faster than the disk drive. In this case, 80% of the time the data is retrieved from the cache and 20% of the time directly from the slower disk drive. This is disk cache operation.

To really envision cache operation, think of baking cookies. You go to the cupboard and get flour, then go back to get sugar, and go again to get chocolate chips, and finally go to get spices. Next it is on to the refrigerator to get milk, then butter and, finally, eggs. How much would it speed up cookie baking if you went to the cupboard and got the flour, sugar, chocolate chips, and spices all at once and put them on the counter top, the cookie baking cache? You could then get the milk, butter, and eggs and also place them on the counter top as well.

CPU cache performs similar functions between the faster CPU and the slower RAM. RAM is from three to ten times slower than the CPU. Even Level 2 CPU cache external to the CPU chip is half the speed of the CPU. Anything external to the CPU chip requires a relatively long time for the electrical signals to travel from it into the chip; that makes it much slower than anything inside the chip. It is similar to communication via satellite vs. terrestrial links. Electrical signals must travel 44,000 miles over some satellite links vs. 3,000 miles over a terrestrial link. It means that they require approximately 11 times longer to complete the trip via satellite.

Most PC chips today are based upon the x86 instruction set developed by Intel. Manufacturers like American Micro Devices and Cyrix produce chips that emulate the instruction set of the Intel chip. This is possible because of cross licensing of technology and patents between manufacturers. All of these competing chips run PC software equally well. See Table 1.1.

Table 1.1 *CPU chip summary*

Chip	MMX—Cache	Comment
Intel Pentium III	MMX, Streaming Single Instruction Multiple Data (SIMD) instructions, and internal level 2 cache inside the cartridge	Best performance chip
Intel Pentium II	MMX and external level 2 cache inside the cartridge	Last generation chip
Intel Celeron 266/300	MMX but no level 2 cache	Cheap Intel—slow performer
Intel Celeron 300a/333/ 366/400/433/466	MMX and 128 Kb inside chip level 2 cache	Cheap Intel—competitive performer
Pentium MMX	Initial MMX and external level 2 cache	End of life
Pentium Pro	No MMX and large internal level 2 cache	NT server Chip—end of life
Xeon Pentium III	MMX, Streaming Single Instruction Multiple Data (SIMD) instructions, and large internal level 2 cache	New NT server chip
AMD-K6	Initial MMX and external level 2 cache	Good Pentium MMX competitor
AMD-K6-2	3D—improved MMX and external level 2 cache	Good Pentium II competitor
AMD-K6-3	3D—improved MMX and internal level 2 cache	Best Pentium II competitor
AMD-K7	3D—improved MMX and inside the cartridge level 2 cache	Slot A design competitor to Slot 1 coming in '99
Cyrix M II	MMX and external level 2 cache	Good for business applications but poor for imaging and CAD

ROM • The Read Only Memory contains the start up code and the 16-bit Basic Input/Output System (BIOS) programs for the PC. ROM is divided into System ROM installed on the main logic board and adapter ROM installed on adapter cards.

System ROM is first accessed during the boot process. It performs the initial PC setup, loads the PC's cold boot loader program from the fixed disk master boot record, and handles the PC's input/output operations under DOS. Most PCs have 64 KB of ROM. The addresses are mapped into the last 64KB memory page below the memory boundary. Some PCs have more system ROM. The most notable was the Micro Channel Architecture (MCA) IBM PS-2. To operate the MCA bus and its jumperless hardware installation, 128 KB of ROM were used. The MCA bus PC was the predecessor to the Peripheral Component Interconnect (PCI) bus plug-and-play designs we have today. Plug-and-play PCs use special ROM code to implement plug-and-play. This ROM code does not, however, increase the system ROM size beyond 64 KB.

Other PC cards also contain ROM. Adapter ROMs perform special adapter card operations. They handle I/O operation or, in the case of some Small Computer System Interface (SCSI) adapters, they perform setup and diagnostic operations. Adaptec has ROM on its SCSI adapters; SCSI Select software configures the adapter, functions as a diagnostic program, and formats the SCSI drives attached. Virtually all display adapters have some type of video ROM. This ROM is about 32 KB in size. It is placed in the PC address range 832 K to 864 K (C000-C7FF). More details on memory addressing and ROM locations are provided in Chapter 9, "DOS and Memory Management."

RAM • Random Access Memory is the working area of the PC. All data must flow into and out of RAM. It holds both programs and data. When a program is running (executing), and working on data, the program and most often the data reside in RAM. In a Windows environment, RAM is virtualized. The operating system has 4 GB of virtual memory where components and applications can reside. Windows translates the virtual address space into a combination of disk accesses and memory paging and allocation, translating the virtual address space into real physical PC RAM and disk addresses.

When any PC is running, most of its electronic activity involves swapping data between RAM and the CPU. When the PC is powered down, the data in RAM is lost. The PC's maximum RAM capacity has moved from 1 MB to 16 MB and up to 4 GB or more today for many servers. Most PC RAM is comprised of DRAM's (Dynamic Random Access Memory) chips that must be continually refreshed. DRAM is comprised of thousands of capacitors acting like leaky buckets. SRAM (Static Random Access Memory) acts like small switches that once set do not need to be refreshed. SRAM is very fast and more expensive than DRAM. SRAM is used for external CPU cache.

Older forms of RAM employed a parity chip for error checking. It created an extra bit depending upon just how many ones are in the byte or character stored. When the character is read from memory, the parity is recomputed and compared to the originally stored value. If they match, everything is OK. If they did not match, older PCs signaled "201" or "Parity Check 2."

Newer memory chips are placed on modules that are minicircuit boards called Single In-line Memory Modules (SIMMs) or on Dual In-line Memory Modules (DIMMs). SIMMs and DIMMs provide an entire bank of memory on the miniboard. Replacement involves replacing the entire miniboard instead of a single bad chip.

RAM is rated and classified by access time. The slowest RAM chips were 250 Ns (nanoseconds), and the fastest is around 10 Ns. Typically RAM chip speeds are about 50 to 70 Ns. For more details on RAM, see Chapter 5.

Other types of RAM are Synchronous Dynamic Random Access Memory (SDRAM) and Extended Data Out (EDO) RAM. These are both dynamic random access memory that need refreshing. They are, however, more tuned to the CPU chip's clocking and memory refresh operations and therefore speed up the PC by reducing CPU-memory transfer times.

There is also Non-Volatile RAM (NVRAM). This is similar to ROM in that it does not lose its contents when the PC is powered off. Like RAM, NVRAM can also be written into. However, writing into NVRAM requires special software. Hence, NVRAM is used to hold ROM BIOS code that may need to be updated or changed. PHLASH programs update this information.

BIOS • The Basic Input/Output System (BIOS) is implemented in ROM. It is the code in the PC that boots the PC and controls input/output operations under DOS. Windows substitutes 32-bit driver software for BIOS routines. The original PC BIOS had a built-in BASIC interpreter program for the BASIC programming language. Around 1990, that BASIC interpreter code disappeared from even the IBM PC's BIOS. BIOS could be considered as only that part of ROM controlling input/output functions in the PC. However, a broader view would define BIOS functions as:

- Hardware setup—During boot, the PC allows you to enter hardware setup options and configure the PC's standard and advanced hardware options.
- Power-On Self Test (POST) diagnostics—Performs cursory hardware testing to assure that the PC hardware matches the setup parameters. These diagnostics are only effective in detecting major PC component malfunctions.
- Cold boot loading functions—Loads DOS from a diskette or the cold boot loader program from the fixed disk's master boot record. It also loads the initial disk drive parameters from the fixed disk partition table.

- DOS input/output operations—Controls basic floppy diskette, keyboard, display, and fixed disk input/output operations.

With Windows, these BIOS functions are used during the initial system start-up and then replaced by Windows 32-bit driver software.

FIRMWARE • Firmware is PC component driver programs installed in ROM or NVRAM. Firmware was initially used to store hardware setup and BIOS routines because it was easier to update than hardware. In contrast, software stored on disk is the most flexible and easy to change. Firmware typically controls a PC when it is first switched on. Typical firmware would perform cold boot loading of the operating system from a fixed disk or from a network and then pass control to the operating system.

CMOS • Complementary Metal Oxide Silicon (CMOS) really describes a chip technology that uses low power. This technology was originally employed in the PC AT to store hardware configuration information in a nonvolatile battery-powered memory chip. A three or six volt lithium battery powered the CMOS memory chip. Today, CMOS technology is used in chips in almost all PCs to reduce power consumption. "CMOS" as a term is used to identify the PC's nonvolatile parameter storage memory, initially implemented with CMOS technology.

When the PC is booted, the setup software implemented in ROM changes the PC operating parameters in CMOS memory. These parameters and the CMOS memory addresses are mapped into the first 64KB memory bank. CMOS is much smaller than 64KB.

ON-BOARD CONTROLLERS • Main logic boards have built-in controllers for the keyboard, a bus mouse, serial ports, parallel ports, floppy disk drives, Integrated Drive Electronics (IDE) fixed disk drives and CD-ROMs, and Universal Serial Bus (USB) ports. Some servers have on-board SCSI controllers as well.

The first on-board controllers were for the keyboard and the serial and parallel ports. Next, systems incorporated bus mouse ports and floppy and fixed disk drive controllers. These ports were initially routed to outside the PC chassis by pigtail connectors that fit into the expansion slot board covers at the rear of the PC. Such pigtail connections were used on "Baby AT" system boards. Disk drive controllers had parallel cables attached directly to the stake pin connectors on the main logic board. Today, these on-board controllers have their ports directly routed to a special connector area at the right rear of the main logic board. This is an ATX main logic board configuration.

EXPANSION SLOTS • Expansion slots implement the PCs system bus. The system bus connectors allow other circuit cards to be plugged into them.

Because they are board edge connectors, they are called expansion slots. The cards inserted in the edge style bus connectors are referred to as daughter boards or expansion boards. The daughter board label was used because the cards were inserted into the motherboard.

The expansion slots had different configurations depending upon the bus supported by the system board. The simplest configuration was the 8-bit Industry Standard Architecture (ISA) Bus used in the original PC. These bus expansion slots evolved to a 16-bit ISA bus and then on to a 32-bit EISA configuration. The physical size of the EISA slots was the same as the 16-bit ISA slots except they permitted the expansion cards to plug deeper into the connector. Thus EISA slots could support 8-bit, 16-bit, and 32-bit I/O transfers. Table 1.2 identifies expansion slots found in different PC systems.

Table 1.2 *Expansion slot versus PC system*

Expansion Slot or Bus	PC System
ISA 8 bit	PCs and XTs
ISA 16 bit	ATs
EISA	386 and 486
ISA 16 bit + **VESA** Local (VL) Bus	386, 486, and Pentium
EISA + **VESA** Local (VL) Bus	386, 486, and Pentium
ISA 16 bit + **PCI**	Pentium
EISA + **PCI**	Pentium—Servers
PCMCIA or **Card Bus**	Laptops
Micro-Channel Architecture 16 bit	PS/2—old
Micro-Channel Architecture 32 bit	PS/2—new
AGP—Advanced Graphics Port	Late 1990s Pentium

In early PCs, expansion slots were used for virtually all upgrades to the PC's basic capabilities, including RAM expansion. We had a PC AT that had 12 MB of RAM installed on several RAM expansion cards. The maximum RAM supported by the PC AT 80286 chip was 16 MB. This is not possible with today's PCs because RAM transfer to the CPU chip is at much higher speeds than the expansion slots and their buses can run. The top bus clock speed has moved from 8 MHz to 66 MHz and finally to 100 MHz. This is slow when compared to the 400 MHz and higher clock speeds of CPU chips.

Expansion slots are used to install disk controllers, display controllers, modems, video capture, and local area network adapter cards in the PC. Each type of adapter card enhances the functionality of the basic PC system. These adapters typically run at speeds that match the bus clock speed.

POWER SUPPLY

The PC power supply converts 120/240 volts Alternating Current (AC) into the 5 and 12 volts Direct Current (DC) used by the PC. Power supplies are rated by wattage. They range from 85 watts for the original PC to 300 watts for high-end PC power supplies. A watt is a power measurement that is voltage times the amperage delivered by the supply. Since voltage is the same for all supplies, a higher wattage translates into more current being delivered by the supply.

The original PC chips operated using TTL logic requiring 5 volts DC. Today's PCs can have lower voltage levels used by the CPU chips. Typically these chips employ special voltage regulation incorporated into the main logic board.

The original PC power supplies had built-in power on/off switches and power connectors for the main logic board and the disk drives. As the PC changed, so did the power supplies. Current power supplies are typically 230 to 250 watts. They have power connectors for either an AT style or an ATX style MLB. Additional power connectors support fixed disk drives, 3.5-inch floppy drives, and front panel lights. Each such connector has a different physical configuration. Furthermore, the power on/off switch is no longer on the side of the supply, but rather mounted on the front of the PC. This necessitates an insulated power connection to a front panel PC power switch. For further discussion on the types of connectors, see Chapter 5.

FIXED DISK DRIVES AND CONTROLLERS

The fixed disk drive is the file cabinet of the PC. It is the device that holds all software and data while the PC is running and once the PC is powered down.

Fixed disks are described by their capacity, speed, physical size (form factor), and controller interface. Fixed disk capacities run from several hundred megabytes to over 25 gigabytes. The largest IDE drives are 20 to 25 gigabytes in capacity.

Fixed disk speed is measured by the time it takes for the disk drive read/write heads to seek the data on the disk and the time it takes to transfer data from the disk to the PC's disk controller. Head seek times are influenced by the physical size of the drive, with smaller drives having better seek times because the read/write heads have shorter distances to travel. Typical seek times range from 8 milliseconds to just over 10 milliseconds. Fixed disk transfer rate is largely determined by the rotational speed of the disk. Disk drives originally rotated at 3,600 RPM.

Today's disk drives range in rotational speed from 4,500 RPM to 10,000 RPM. The higher the rotational speed, the higher the disk drive transfer rate.

The physical size of the disk drives ranges from 1 to 2.5-inch quarter height drives, to 3.5-inch third or half height drives, and on to 5.25-inch full height drives. Other form factor combinations exist as well. The form factor describes the size of the disk 1 inch, 2.5 inches, 3.5 inches, and 5.25 inches and the height of the drive, with a full-height drive being 3.25 inches high.

Fixed disk drive interfaces are Integrated Drive Electronics (IDE), Enhanced IDE (EIDE), or Small Computer System Interface (SCSI).

IDE AND EIDE • Disk drive interfaces started with the Modified Frequency Modulation (MFM) interfaces that were standardized by the Seagate ST-402 and ST-512 specifications. These interfaces required two cables to the disk drive from the disk controller board. One cable (the wide one) handled 8 bits of data and the drive control signals and the other (the narrow one) handled the second 8 bits of data. The data and control cable was an extension of the floppy disk interface. It was a 34-conductor cable. The second data-only cable was a 16-conductor cable.

MFM drives were displaced within a few years by Integrated Drive Electronics (IDE) interface disk drives having the drive controller built on the drive. This integration of controller and drive greatly simplified the control interface in the PC. The IDE interface is used today for both fixed disks and CD-ROM drives. It employs a single 40-conductor cable. Enhanced IDE (EIDE) controllers provide improved transfer speeds and the ability to interface to four drives.

Today IDE and EIDE interfaces can burst transfer data at 33 megabytes per second. The largest IDE drives are around 37 gigabytes, with their size expected to increase over the next few years. IDE and EIDE drives are the most commonly installed drives in PCs.

SCSI • Apple pioneered the Small Computer System Interface (SCSI). It was used to connect peripherals to the Apple computers. This was the SCSI-I interface that transferred data at 5 MB per second. SCSI became the interface of preference for large-capacity drives. SCSI was relatively expensive because not only were the drives expensive, they required the addition of SCSI interface card.

The great advantage here besides the increased drive capacity was the ability to connect up to seven drives on the same SCSI interface. This made it possible to build much larger disk volumes and to implement Redundant Arrays of Independent Disk (RAID) drives. The first CD-ROMs employed SCSI interfaces, but they have since migrated to the EIDE interface.

Most SCSI drives used a single 50-conductor parallel cable with terminating resistors at each end of the bus (often this is the end of the cable). This cable has changed as the SCSI interface speed increased. SCSI started with the Apple SCSI-I speed of 5 MB per second. Early PC SCSI drives operated at this speed. Since the SCSI bus was shared, the transfer speed increased rapidly to provide adequate PC performance. The SCSI bus was changed to fast operation, increasing the transfer speed to 10 MB per second. The fast SCSI set the basic clock rate for the SCSI interface at 10 MHz. The SCSI-II PC controllers operated at this speed. They transferred one byte at a time at 10 MHz, thus producing the 10 MB per second transfer rate.

The SCSI interface was upgraded to the fast wide SCSI that transferred 16 bits, increasing SCSI bus speed to 20 MB per second. The next enhancement was to improve the fast operating speed to 20 MHz with the 16-bit ultra-wide SCSI bus, thus providing 40 MB per second transfers. Finally, we have Ultra-2 SCSI capable of 80 MB per second transfers, accomplished using a 40 MHz bus or a 32-bit bus operating at 20 MHz. The SCSI cables changed from the original 50-conductor cable to a 68-conductor cable and finally to fiber optic SCSI channels.

SCSI drives and interfaces are prevalent and preferred in high-end PC and network servers requiring RAID and high-capacity drives. Since the SCSI bus is shared, the transfer speeds of the fastest SCSI buses are divided among the drives attached to the controller. Depending upon the PC use, such a division might enhance overall PC performance. Such enhanced performance, while measurable, is not likely noticeable by most users.

Table 1.3 provides a summary of these interfaces, their characteristics and differences.

Table 1.3 *Interface types and characteristics*

SCSI Type	Bus Speed	Bus Width	Connector	Throughput	Distance of Cable Single Ended	Number of devices
Regular SCSI	5 MHz	8 bit	50 pin	5 mb/sec	6 meters	8
Wide SCSI	5 MHz	16 bit	68 pin	10 mb/sec	6 meters	16
Fast SCSI	10 MHz	8 bit	50 pin	10 mb/sec	3 meters	8
Fast Wide SCSI	10 MHz	16 bit	68 pin	20 mb/sec	3 meters	16

SCSI Type	Bus Speed	Bus Width	Connector	Throughput	Distance of Cable Single Ended	Number of devices
Ultra-Wide SCSI	20 MHz	16 bit	68 pin	40 mb/sec	1.5 meters	16
Ultra-2 Wide SCSI	40 MHz	16 bit	68 pin	80 mb/sec	12 meters but must be LVD cabling	16

There are three types of cabling most used with SCSI: single ended, differential, or LVD (low voltage differential). Single ended has been the most commonly used over the years because of its low cost in comparison to differential. Now with the higher speeds, single ended is very limited in the distance of cabling. Differential cabling is more expensive then single-ended but can do all speeds up to 25 meters, so it is used in long runs of external cabling. LVD is relatively new on the market and is supposed to have the best of both worlds because it can run all speeds of SCSI up to 12.5 meters at a much lower cost than differential. Remember, do not mix your SCSI cabling; they are electrically incompatible.

JAZ

Iomega developed JAZ drive technology. JAZ drives are floppy disks that rotate at high speeds (5,394 RPM versus 300 RPM for floppy disk drives). They employ the Bernoulli principle (fast moving air has less pressure than static air—this is what causes planes to fly) to permit the read/write heads to get very close to the floppy disk medium. As a result they can store substantial amounts of data on 3.5-inch floppy disk cartridges. Because their rotational speed is high compared to floppy drives, they have performance that resembles fixed disks. The newest JAZ drives are capable of storing 2 gigabytes of data on a single removable floppy disk cartridge. JAZ drives interface to the PC using SCSI. JAZ drives can be installed internally or attached externally to the PC. External drives can be moved from PC to PC, provided the PCs each have an SCSI interface. In these cases the PC's parallel interface can be transformed into SCSI interface using a special Trantor interface cable.

JAZ drives provide removable media storage for PC backups. The benefit of such backup is that the JAZ drive's operation is similar to random access disks and not like linear access tape backups. Random access can make data accessibility faster than with tape. The limitation here is that each cartridge stores only a maximum of 2 gigabytes of data. JAZ cartridges can be compressed, but this presents problems for the 2-gigabyte capacity cartridges. Since JAZ drives look like older DOS fixed disks to the PC, they are limited to effectively storing a maximum of 2 gigabytes of data. Thus, when a 2-gigabyte cartridge is compressed, it produces a 2-gigabyte drive and 1-gigabyte hidden drive. The 1-gigabyte drive is useable but not conveniently so. It is much more effective to compress a 1-gigabyte JAZ cartridge to provide about 2-gigabytes of storage. The 2-gigabyte JAZ drive works with the 1-gigabyte JAZ cartridges.

OPTICAL REWRITABLE DRIVES

Optical storage drives are similar to JAZ drives. They have an equivalent 2-gigabyte capacity, and they rotate at higher speeds than floppy drives (from 2,400 RPM to 3,755 RPM). Rewritable optical drives use SCSI interface like the JAZ drives.

Optical rewritable drives store data using a magneto-optical storage process. Magnetism is used to permit laser recording of data on the disk media. Once recorded, the data is read using a laser. The main benefit here is that the recording medium is durable and lasts a long time. Where data over time can be corrupted on JAZ floppy media, it is good for 30 years on rewritable optical media. The rewritable optical cartridges use 5.25-inch media. This is larger than the JAZ 3.5-inch media.

The rewritable optical technology has migrated from the original rewritable optical drives to rewritable CD drives (CD-E or compact disc—erasable) and rewritable Digital Versatile Disk (DVD) drives. The rewritable CD drive provides more flexibility and storage capacity at a reduced cost than the original rewritable optical drives, using a 5.25-inch media similar to a CD. It has the CD recording capacity of 600 to 700 megabytes. The media does not require a special carrier (container for the media) as does the optical rewritable drive. Performance is similar to a slower CD-ROM.

Rewritable DVD drives provide greater storage capacity than other rewritable drives. Similar to a normal DVD drive, they use a blue laser to enhance storage capacity of the 5.25-inch media. They can read and write DVD media and read CD-ROM media. The interface to the PC is typically SCSI for these devices.

FLOPPY DISK DRIVES

Floppy disk drives have been the original PC storage media. From 1981 through 1983, there were no PC fixed disk drives. The first fixed disk drive that we saw for a PC was a 5-megabyte drive that cost $5,000. Months later IBM marketed the PC XT with its 10-megabyte fixed disk for $1,000. In the

1981 to 1983 time frame, we used first single sided, then double-sided floppy drives as the only permanent data storage for the PC. Of course everything was smaller then. A large file was 30 KB because it contained ASCII text-only information.

5.25 INCH FLOPPY DRIVES • The original PC diskette drives stored 160 KB of data on a single sided 5.25-inch diskette. They used 40 tracks with 8 sectors per track with each sector storing 512 characters (bytes) of data. The total capacity then was 40 times 8 times .5 K, equaling 160 KB total capacity. At one time we were so desperate for storage space that we attached four double-sided floppy disks to a PC. It was the ultimate machine at the time because of its active 1.44 megabyte storage capacity.

These diskettes were soon replaced by double-sided drives, then 9 sector-per-track drives and, finally, by high density 5.25-inch drives. Each diskette drive enhancement increased the storage capacity. The high density drives appeared with the PC AT. They stored data on 80 tracks with 15 sectors per track on two sides of the floppy. As always, the sectors contained 512 characters of data. Their capacity was (80 tracks) X (15 sectors per track) X (2 sides) X (.5 K), equaling 1.2 megabytes per diskette.

The diskettes came in a plastic holder that provided the necessary mechanical support for inserting them into and removing them from the floppy disk drive. A paper sleeve protected the floppy media by covering the read/write window of the diskette.

3.5 INCH FLOPPY DRIVES • The 3.5-inch floppy drives came out with the first IBM PS-2 PCs in 1987. They were about two-thirds the width and one-half the height of the 5.25-inch drives. They had new power connections requiring special power supply pigtail adapters to provide power to the drives. Today, all power supplies provide specific 3.5-inch disk drive power connections. The 5.25-inch drives used both 5 volt and 12 volt DC power, while the 3.5-inch drives used 5 volt DC power alone. Some 3.5-inch drives were even smaller in height and combination 3.5-inch and 5.25-inch drives were developed that fit into a single 5.25-inch half-height drive bay.

The 3.5-inch diskette media is mounted in a permanent plastic sleeve with a special sliding door protecting the disk drive media. The sliding door is one of the greater hazards for 3.5-inch drives. They are typically made out of aluminum or plastic that is easily bent or broken. Any bending makes the aluminum door catch on the inside of the 3.5-inch drive, causing destruction of the diskette and sometimes damage to the drive itself.

The 3.5-inch diskettes store data on 80 tracks with 18 sectors per track. This gives a total capacity calculated by multiplying (80 tracks) X (18 sectors per track) X (2 sides) X (.5 K), equaling 1.44 megabytes per diskette. These diskettes have become in the late 90's the basic DOS boot and initial software installation mechanism for PCs. Their capacity today remains adequate for hardware diagnostics, but it is fast becoming insufficient for installing any software. Software installation is largely from CD-ROMs. Newer PCs can boot directly from the CD-ROM to facilitate direct software installation.

The latest floppy diskette drives rotate at about twice the speed of older floppy drives. This significantly enhances their performance. Their capacity has not been increased, only their data transfer and seek time performance. Newer super disk drives, resembling floppy drives, do enhance both disk capacity and performance.

SUPER DISK (LS-120 OR LASER SERVO-120) DRIVES • The Imation, Inc. Super Disk or LS-120 drives can store 120 MB of data on special floppy diskettes. They accomplish this by increasing the track density and the sectors-per-track storage density on the floppy media. A more precise laser servo head positioning mechanism makes this possible. The Super Disk 3.5-inch diskettes store data on 1736 tracks with 69 sectors per track. This gives a total capacity calculated by multiplying (1736 tracks) X (69 sectors per track) X (2 sides) X (.5 K), equaling 119.784 megabytes per diskette.

Super disk drives interface to the PC using either the IDE/ATAPI interface, similar to CD-ROMs, or the parallel port, similar to ZIP drives. Their performance is similar to parallel interface ZIP drives. Super disk drives rotate at 720 RPM, about twice the speed of the older floppy disk drives. The higher rotational speed improves disk drive performance, making super disks faster than floppy drives but somewhat slower than ZIP or JAZ drives.

In spite of their increased capacity, super drives still lack the storage space to act as an effective installation medium for most Windows applications programs. Newer applications occupy several hundred megabytes of disk storage space, thus requiring the storage space on CD-ROMs to contain the software being installed.

Other manufacturers are about to introduce similar high capacity floppy drives. These can have storage capacities between 100 MB and 200 MB (Sony's product) with higher speed access and transfer rates as compared to existing floppies. It is likely that several floppy manufacturers will fight it out for high-capacity floppy drive market dominance in the next several years. We may ultimately have a fragmented market there, although our guess is that the manufacturer with the highest capacity, fastest drive backward compatible with 3.5-inch floppies is most likely to be the ultimate market share winner.

ZIP DRIVES • ZIP drives, similar to super disk drives, store 100 MB of data. There are ZIP 250 drives that store either 100 MB or 250 MB of data. ZIP drives interface to the PC using either a parallel port or SCSI connection. A new USB 100 MB ZIP drive is also offered. The ZIP 250 drive operates using the original ZIP SCSI or parallel port connection. The ZIP drives, just like JAZ drives, work based upon the Bernoulli principle, permitting the read/write heads to move close to the floppy recording media and thus providing the ability to store more information and provide high performance without damage to the media.

ZIP drives rotate at 2,945 RPM. Their performance is better than the super disk drives due largely to their rotational speed.

CD-ROM • CD-ROMs (Compact Disc—Read Only Memory) have become a standard part of every PC. They are about to be displaced by the newer higher-capacity Digital Versatile Disk drives because of the growing need for more information storage capacity on PCs. Such increased information storage capacity will be used to store video (movies) and large databases. For example, The AAA Map 'n Go software that stores road maps of the USA and Canada on a single CD-ROM is limited by the capacity so that detailed street maps are only provided for specific areas surrounding major cities. The DVD version can have detailed street maps for virtually the entire USA.

Typical CD-ROMs store about 650 MB of data (or 74 minutes of audio recording) on a read-only 5.25-inch plastic media. They have become the primary distribution mechanism for Windows operating and application software. With the advent of high speed Internet connectivity, the software distribution and update methodology will change to an Internet focus because of the convenience. This will extend to upgrading NVRAM of different hardware devices. For example, we recently upgraded a 3Com-USRobotics modem to the current firmware release by connecting to the 3Com site through the Internet and then dial-up communications.

The 1x speed, 2x speed, and higher speeds are measured relative to the original speed of audio CDs. The audio CDs specifications are the basis for all CD standards. The higher the "x" speed, the faster the writing speed. When reading, access and seek times are higher for higher "x" speeds.

CD-ROMs interface to the PC using the IDE/ATAPI interface. They occupy a single 5.25-inch half-height drive bay. CD-ROMs perform at different speeds and with different data buffering capabilities. The top speed CD-ROM drives are 48X drives as compared to the original 1X and 2X speed drives. Some drives advertise higher speeds. They accomplish the higher speeds through buffering of data read from the CD-ROM drives. CD-ROMs rotate at variable speeds depending upon the track being read. The rotational speed varies from 500 RPM to 200 RPM, with the inside tracks being read at the higher rotational speed.

Different types of CD-ROMs have different CD storage formats. CD-ROM formats differ for CDs storing audio only, data, CD-R (Compact Disc-Recorders) data, and CD-RW (Compact Disc-Rewritable) data. There are also variations for storing photos (Kodak Photo CDs) and video.

CD-RECORDERS

Compact Disc-Recorders or CD-R drives write and read CD-ROMs. They read prerecorded CDs, both audio and data, and write and then read recordable CDs. The reading process is at higher speed than the writing process. Typically writing is performed at 2x, 4x, or 8x and reading is performed at from 6x to 24x. The first CD-R drives interfaced to the PC via SCSI bus connection. This has changed to the IDE/ATAPI interface standard used by CD-ROM drives. Special software is required to perform the CD writing operation. This software will write data and audio CDs. CD-R drives require a single half-height 5.25-inch drive bay for mounting in a PC.

The major benefit of having CD-R drives is that they can act as a backup for valuable data. In spite of their size being somewhat limited (650 MB), they are cheap (about $2 to $5 per disc), and very transportable. If properly cared for, the life expectancy can be as long as rewritable optical drives.

There are several different CD-R discs. Not every type of disc works with every CD-R drive. To assure that a disc works with a specific drive, a test of that manufacturer's media should be performed.

DIGITAL VERSATILE DISC (DVD)

DVD discs are similar in capabilities to CD-ROMs, but they are capable of storing significantly larger amounts of data. This is possible because they use a different color laser and because they can store data on both sides of the disc. This makes it possible to store 5 MB, 9 MB, 10 MB or 18 MB of data on a single DVD disc. The single-sided DVD discs store 5 MB or 10 MB. When reading DVD discs, the drives run at slower speeds than when reading normal CD-ROMs. The DVD reading speeds are 2x to 6x, while CD-ROM speeds are as high as 48x.

DVD drives support a full variety of DVD and CD formats including DVD-ROM (DVD-5, 9, 10, 18), DVD-ROM book, DVD-Video book, CD-DA, CD-G, CD Text, CD-ROM, CD-ROM XA, CD-I, Photo-CD, Video CD,

CD-R, CD-RW. This provides backward compatibility with older CD-ROMs and forward compatibility with the enhanced storage capabilities of the newer DVD CDs. There are combination DVD and floppy drives used in laptops. This dual DVD/floppy drive occupies a single laptop PC drive bay.

DISK DRIVE SUMMARY

Disk drive capabilities are summarized in Table 1.4.

Table 1.4 *PC disk drives*

Type of Drive	Media Size	Rotational Speed	Interfaces	Capacity	Drive Size
5.25-inch Floppy	5.25-inch diskette	300 RPM	Floppy disk	160 KB to 1.2 MB	5.25-inch Half-height drive 5.25-inch Quarter-height drive (combination units)
3.5-inch Floppy	3.5 Inch diskette	300 RPM	Floppy disk	720 KB to 1.44 MB	3.5-inch Half-height drive 3.5-inch Third-height drive 3.5-inch Quarter-height drive (combination units)
LS-120 SuperDisk	3.5-inch diskette 3.5 inch Super diskette	300 RPM and 720 RPM	Parallel IDE	1.44 MB and 120 MB	3.5-inch Half-height drive
Fixed Disks	1-inch to 5.25-inch	3,600 RPM to 7,200 RPM	IDE EIDE SCSI	10 MB to 37 GB	5.25-inch Full-height to 1-inch Quarter-height
CD-ROM	5.25-inch disc	720 RPM	IDE SCSI	650 MB	5.25-inch Half-height drive
CD-R	5.25-inch disc	720 RPM	IDE SCSI	650 MB	5.25-inch Half-height drive
Optical CD-E DVD-rewritable	5.25-inch disc	2,400 to 3,755 RPM 720 RPM	IDE SCSI	650 MB	5.25-inch Half-height drive
JAZ	5.25-inch cartridge	5,394 RPM	IDE SCSI	1 GB to 2 GB	5.25-inch Half-height drive
ZIP ZIP 250	3.5-inch cartridge	2,945 RPM	IDE SCSI USB	100 MB to 250 MB	3.5-inch Half-height
DVD	5.25-inch disc	2x to 6x—DVD 24x—CD-ROM	IDE	5, 9, 10, and 18 GB	5.25-inch Half-height drive

TAPE DRIVES

PCs sometimes come with tape drives for making backups of data on the fixed disk drives. These tape drives store data sequentially on tape cartridges. They can store up to 10 GB of data per cartridge. They use 4 mm or 8 mm tape cartridges, both of which can store over 10 GB. Tape drives interface to the PC using SCSI interfaces or IDE interfaces.

SOUND CARDS

All PCs today have the capability to create and record sound. Sound cards installed in the PC provide this capability. Early sound cards were mainly used to produce sounds for Windows activities and to play CDs. Today's sound cards turn a PC into a programmable stereo system when it is connected to powered speakers. With the software and music data storage formats available, the PC becomes a programmable stereo system capable of producing 3-dimensional sound. Sound stored in an MP3 format is greatly compressed. CD stereo music can be compressed by a factor of 12 compared to the files produced when sounds are directly recorded.

The original sound file format was a WAV format used by the Creative Labs SoundBlaster sound cards. A more compressed format was a MIDI format. Some early music clips were recorded using that format. Most notably, Windows 95 and 98 include several MIDI files useful in testing a PC's sound capabilities.

The original sound PC cards represented sounds with 8 bits of data. This did not give the best sound representation. They soon evolved to 16-bit, 32-bit, 64-bit, and 128-bit capabilities. CD quality sound uses 16-bits. The 128-bit sound boards are capable of studio quality sound—3-dimensional sound, if used with four speakers—and can synthetically reproduce 128 different multi-timbre sounds. Special sound effects are also possible, such as reverberation.

Most sound boards are ISA bus boards, but the newer boards use the PCI bus. Typically, they have input jacks for microphone input, auxiliary-input, and audio input that permit recording sounds at sampling rates varying from 5 kHz to 48 kHz. Output jacks are provided for line output, rear speaker output (on 3-dimensional sound boards), and amplified output.

Figure 1–5
Stereo and mono sound plugs

Oftentimes these boards support joystick ports and MIDI ports for games. See Figure 1–5.

LOCAL AREA NETWORK (LAN) ADAPTERS

Almost all business PCs are LAN connected. Soon many home PCs will be as well. A LAN provides an easy mechanism for sharing disk drives and exchanging data between PCs. Once someone works with a LAN, they rarely want to go back to operating without the LAN. LAN connections will be used to bring high speed Internet connectivity to the home. The bad news with local area networks is that when problems occur, the PC looks like it was frozen using liquid nitrogen. Because the PC's operating system gives high priority to communications activities, it can become locked when the communications software connections disappear.

Local Area Network connection requires a LAN card in the PC, cabling to other PCs with LAN cards, and networking software installed in all inter-connected PCs. LAN cards are referred to as Network Interface Cards or NICs. Cable modems connect into PCs using Ethernet LAN adapter cards.

There were three early PC LANs: Datapoint's ARCnet, the IBM Token Ring, and the Xerox-Intel-Digital Ethernet. Of these, today Ethernet is dominant and quickly evolving to meet the demand for increased transmission speeds that new applications place upon it. ARCnet has all but disappeared.

LANs implement the electrical signaling on the LAN wiring and facilitate data transfer between equivalent NICs. Digital Equipment Corporation (now Compaq) marketed Ethernet LANs in 1982. It was one of the first LANs to interconnect PCs. In 1987, IBM delivered its token ring LAN. The first token rings were focused on IBM's mainframe computers and PCs. The token ring still holds a significant market niche today. It is moving to higher speeds, but may be displaced by newer technology LAN and telephony NICs in the next few years as Asynchronous Transfer Mode (ATM) technology takes root.

Ethernet dominates the PC LAN market today. It uses unshielded twisted-pair wiring to interconnect PCs. This wire is classified by its electrical characteristics, with different types of wire capable of higher transmission speeds. The initial Ethernet wiring was a coaxial cable bus.

This was not the same coaxial cable used for television, but a version having different electrical characteristics. Television coaxial cable was 75-ohm cable while Ethernet cable was 50-ohm cable. PCs using coaxial cable were connected in a simple bus configuration with coax cable running from one PC to another.

Unshielded twisted-pair cable soon replaced coaxial cable. Twisted-pair cable required that each network PC be wired into a hub. The hubs electrically isolated each individual LAN-attached PC from the others so that if a PC malfunctioned electrically, it did not crash the remaining PCs and the LAN. This improved overall network reliability.

Ethernet uses a Carrier Sense Multiple Access with Collision Detection (CSMA-CD) media access protocol. Each PC connected to the Ethernet broadcasts as needed. When its broadcasts collide with broadcasts from other stations, the Ethernet NIC detects this by an excess voltage drop on the cable and then computes a new time to attempt a rebroadcast of the corrupted packet. The new time is based upon previous collisions and is randomized within the rebroadcast time window.

Unshielded twisted-pair wire is classified into categories with ordinary twisted-pair telephone wire being classified as Category-3 wire, capable of transmission speeds of 10 MBPS. Most new wiring installations use Category-5 unshielded twisted-pair wire, capable of speeds up to 100 MBPS. New Ethernet LAN installations use Category-5 data grade cable or Category-6 cable, which supports speeds up to 155 MBPS. Other cable categories will support speeds up to 1 GBPS. The general rule is that the higher the speed, the shorter the wire run between the hub and the PC.

Ethernet PC network interface cards are ISA 8-bit, ISA 16-bit, and PCI bus cards. The newer Ethernet NIC cards are all PCI bus cards that operate at either 10 MBPS or 100 MBPS.

The token ring network also uses hubs to interconnect the networked PCs.

Similar to Ethernet, the hub isolates each station from the other stations on the token ring network so that PC and NIC malfunctions do not impact the other network stations. Different from Ethernet, the token ring design must have hubs to work normally while Ethernet works in a simple bus configuration or in a hub configuration. Furthermore, the token ring hubs must be configured as a closed loop to form a ring and function properly. In the token ring token passing protocol or Medium Access Control (MAC) operation, a token frame circulates from station to station. When a station has data to transmit, it marks the token frame as busy and appends data to the frame. The frame then circulates around the token ring; the destination station copies the data from the frame as it passes. If the data is copied successfully, the receiving station signals success by setting bits at the end of the frame. As the frame again passes the transmitting station, the transmitting station removes it from the ring and then re-issues a free token so that succeeding stations may use it to transmit data they have.

Token ring networks operate at 4, 16 or 100 MBPS and soon at 155 MBPS. The NIC cards have ISA 8-bit, ISA 16-bit, and PCI bus interfaces. Token ring cabling is specified by IBM as types with the preferred token ring cabling being Type-1 or Type-2. The data-carrying pairs in these cables are two shielded twisted pairs. IBM Type-3 is equivalent to Category-3 unshielded twisted-pair cable. Other token ring manufacturers use the Category-3 and Category-5 unshielded twisted-pair (UTP) cable equivalent to that used for Ethernet.

Asynchronous Transfer Mode NICs are beginning to emerge. The ATM technology promises to effectively integrate LAN functionality and video telephony into a single network connection. ATM uses hubs to switch data between interconnected PCs like a LAN, as well as between interconnected Wide Area Network switches like telephony. ATM NICs transmit data at 25 MBPS, 155 MBPS, and 622 MBPS over Category-5, Category-6, or fiber optic cable connections. ATM network interface cards interface to the PC through the PCI bus. Windows 98 comes with driver software and other software supporting ATM.

MODEMS

Dial-up networking using modems provides Internet connectivity for most home PCs. A modem is basically a telephone for a computer. Modems modulate and demodulate digital data, converting it to analog voice-grade (0 Hz to 4,000 Hz) signals that travel across telephone channels. Modems are specified by their signaling technology that in turn determines their maximum transmission speed. Table 1.5 lists the signaling specifications and related modem maximum transmission speed.

Table 1.5 *Modem transmission speed versus signaling technology*

Modem Transmission Speed	Signaling Specification
300 BPS	WE 103/113 (WE—Western Electric)
1,200 BPS	CCITT V.22 CCITT V.22bis Bell 212A (most used in U.S.)
2,400 BPS	CCITT V.22bis
4,800 BPS	CCITT V.32
9,600 BPS	CCITT V.32
7,200 BPS to 14,400 BPS	CCITT V.32bis
28,800 BPS 33,600 BPS	CCITT V.FAST CCITT V.34 CCITT V.34 +
33,600 BPS-up and 57,600 (really about 53,000 BPS) BPS-down	V.90 or K-Flex—USR-X2

The speeds listed are the maximum theoretical speeds. At 28,800 BPS and above such speeds are seldom realized over most telephone circuits.

Modems can be internal or external. When a modem is an external device, it connects to the PC using a serial port conforming to the EIA 232D specification (RS-232 interface). Typical PCs have 9-pin connectors for their serial ports while modems use 25-pin connectors. This necessitates a 9-pin to 25-pin connector cable. Each wire in the cable has a specific function on controlling data transmission across the cable. For example, pin 2 is transmit data while pin 3 is receive data in the 25-pin modem connector. This is reversed for the 9-pin PC connector.

The modem behaves as though there were a cable when it is used. Modems are sophisticated microprocessor-controlled systems in themselves. They perform not only the modulation/demodulation of the data signal but also perform data compression and flow control handshaking with the PC and the remote modem. Data compression specifications for modems are listed in Table 1–6.

The flow control handshaking between modems and PCs should always be set to hardware handshaking or Request To Send/Clear To Send (RTS/CTS) handshaking. The modem-to-modem handshaking is software-controlled. An example of software handshaking is XON/XOFF handshaking. XON/XOFF handshaking is not used for PC-to-modem flow control.

Table 1.6 *Modem data compression*

Compression Specification	Error Detection Compression	Remarks
CCITT V.42bis	Error Detection and Correction Data Compression up to 4:1	Little compression and speed increase for compressed files such as ARC, ZIP, and LZH. Some compression and speed increase for binary files such as EXE, COM, DLL, etc. Maximum compression and speed increase for text and tabular files. Transmission speed can increase as much as 400% over modem speed.
CCITT V.42	Error Detection and Correction	Error correction only. Uses synchronous transmission to increase effective data rate to as much as 120% of the rated modem speed.
MNP Class 5	Error Detection and Correction Data Compression up to 2:1	Similar to V.42bis with less effective data compression. Transmission speed can increase as much as 200% over modem speed.
MNP Class 4	Error Detection and Correction	This protocol includes adaptive packet sizing and data optimization, producing improved data transfer speeds. Maximum improvement on clear telephone lines is 120%.
MNP Class 3	Error Detection and Correction	Uses full duplex synchronous transmission to increase effective data rate. Maximum transmission speed increase is about 108%.
MNP Class 2	Error Detection and Correction	Uses full duplex asynchronous transmission to increase data rate. Maximum transmission speed increase is about 84% of modem speed.

Modems interface to the telephone circuit using the standard RJ-11 telephone jack. Typically, there are two jacks on each modem, permitting the phone line to be connected to the modem and then a phone. One jack is marked line and the other phone for those connections, respectively. Bad things happen when the phone jack is connected into the line and the line jack is connected to the phone.

The modem card interface in the PC is typically an ISA bus connection. It can be an 8-bit or a 16-bit connector because modems are relatively slow devices compared to the other PC peripherals. Some modems are plug-and-play compatible, but such ISA bus modems more often than not create installation and configuration problems.

Mouse

The mouse is the Windows pointing device of preference for most PCs. It is a rubber ball that rotates sensors on two right-angle axes. In this manner, the mouse movement is translated into vertical and horizontal pointer movement on the PC's display screen. A mouse is connected to the PC using a 9-pin serial port or through a PS-2 mouse port. Using a PS-2 interface with its small form factor, for the mouse frees up the limited serial ports for other uses. Different driver software is required for each type of connection. Windows 95/98 and Windows NT come with all needed serial and PS-2 mouse driver software.

A PC mouse has two or three buttons. The left mouse button is the most used. It performs all the selecting and dragging operations with a single click, click hold, or double click. The right mouse button expands the mouse functionality to perform specific operations. The middle expands function-ality in certain cases and can also accommodate left-handed usage.

The mouse has been revamped in several different configurations. There is the upside down mouse or trackball. In this case the user's thumb moves the ball and not the entire mouse. Trackballs are supposed to be more reliable because dirt from a mouse pad is not sucked into the movement-sensing mechanics. Of course thumbs are greasy and sweaty and dirt can fall down into the trackball mechanism. The trackball is formed to fit a hand. They have several strategically placed buttons to make clicking options easy. Some trackball buttons are configured to automatically provide double clicks. This can be as troublesome as it can be helpful.

More interesting is the hand-held mouse. It can be used a distance from the PC. It is held in the hand and not on any pad. Movement of the hand and arm is sensed by the mouse and translated into pointer movement on the PC's display screen. A simple flick of the wrist in this case moves the screen pointer. It also has buttons for selecting items and performing drag and drop operations.

Newer pointing devices include glide pads. They have a touch sensitive pad area that serves as the mouse. By moving a finger across the pad, the PC's screen pointer moves. Tapping the pad serves as a right mouse button click, and double tapping serves as a double click. A tap and hold performs selecting and dragging an item. Touch pad mice are popular for laptop computers. They can be attached to desktop PCs as well. Several buttons are included on glide pad mice to perform both right and left mouse button functions. See Figure 1–6.

Figure 1–6 *Glide pad and three-button mouse*

Finally, we have the wheel mice. A wheel mouse is a traditional mouse with a wheel mechanism mounted between the right and left mouse buttons. The mouse operates normally until a page is selected using an Internet browser of some other desktop publishing application software. When pointing to the page, the wheel permits scrolling the text up and down the display screen. This is very convenient if you work with large text documents or surf the Internet. Wheel mice can be Microsoft compatible or they can require added software to activate the wheel scrolling function.

Keyboard

The keyboard remains the primary input mechanism for the PC. Maybe it will be displaced by direct voice input devices. This will not be a total replacement, however. There are many styles of keyboards. They can be broken down into 84-key keyboards like those delivered with the first PC or into 101-key keyboards like those delivered with the PC AT.

Most keyboards today have 104 keys. These are a variation on the 101-key keyboard with three special keys assigned to Windows functions. See Figure 1–7.

Figure 1–7 *101-key keyboard with special keys assigned to Windows functions*

Important in keyboard layout is the placement and size of the RETURN and the BACKSPACE keys. In my case, these keys get the most use. A small backspace key means lots of mistakes because I tend to hit two keys at one time when they are small. The keys are laid out in a standard QWERTY arrangement with twelve function keys (F1 through F12) across the top of the keyboard. The cursor movement keys (this is somewhat different from the mouse pointer even though in some cases they perform identical item selection functions) are an inverted "T" arrangement to the immediate right of the main typing area. Above that are the other cursor control keys including INSERT, DELETE, HOME, END, PAGE UP and PAGE DOWN. To the far right is a numeric keypad area that emulates an adding machine keyboard but not a telephone keypad. Adding machines have the low numbers on the bottom of the numeric pad while telephones have them at the top. See Figure 1–8.

Some keyboards have built-in touch pads or trackballs to provide mouse functions. Many laptops use button or eraser heads or glide pads for their mouse interface. These features, while seemingly convenient, are really gimmicks that are of little effective use.

When a trackball or touch pad feature is installed in a keyboard it is connected to the built-in keyboard connector and a serial connector on the PC. The keyboard connector can be the older PC/XT/AT style DIN plug or the newer and much smaller PS-2 plug.

If a keyboard breaks, there is no effective repair. In the best scenario, broken keys can be replaced with good keys from another broken keyboard.

Figure 1–8 *Keyboard with built-in trackball*

Video

There are three components that make up the display system: the monitor, the video cable, and a display controller. The video adapter card (display controller) and the monitor determine PC video capabilities. They work in conjunction with each other. The monitor must be capable of producing the image output by the PC video card. Monitors vary in capabilities as well as video cards. The trend is to produce higher resolution (more pixels—dots—spots) images that have more colors. These images then look closer to photographs and movies.

MONITOR

The monitor or display is our window into the PC. Through it we see the information inside the PC. Displays have different resolutions or levels of visibility. This is expressed in the number of displayable dots (referred to as "pixels" for "picture elements"), dots per inch (DPI), or spots per inch (SPI). The more dots the better the image. Displays vary from 320 by 200 resolution to 1,800 by 1,440 resolution and higher. Most monitors are multiscan or multisynch monitors supporting a range of display resolutions. Display clarity also depends upon the dot pitch (from .21 mm to .31 mm) and the number of colors (or gray scale levels) displayed.

The following is display terminology:

- Monochrome display—is a one-color green, amber, or white on black background display.
- Monographic display—is a single color that displays text and graphics.
- Display—is the device producing the image. It may be a CRT (Cathode Ray Tube), LCD (Liquid Crystal Display), or gas plasma display.
- Refresh Rate—is measured in Hz and it is how frequently your monitor redraws its screen. The higher the refresh rate, the better.
- Interlaced—is a technique used by monitors to produce higher resolution at lower costs. The actual monitor will only draw the odd horizontal lines on screen in one cycle and then the even horizontal lines in the next cycle.
- Non-Interlaced—is a technique used by monitors where all the horizontal lines are redrawn every cycle.
- Monitor—is the display and supporting electronics. Monitor and display are synonymous.
- RGB (Red Green Blue)—are the primary colors forming a color display. This is used to identify the CGA monitor digital interface.

Monochrome and monographic monitors used a TTL (Transistor to Transistor Logic) interface.

- Analog RGB—is a Video Graphics Array (VGA) monitor interface producing an image with more colors and greater resolution.

- Raster versus vector graphics—are display techniques for creating images. Vector displays draw the images on the screen while raster displays create the images from dots scanned on the display screen. PC displays are raster graphics displays.

The original PC monitor was monochrome or CGA with at least 24 useable lines and 80 columns of text. The original PC display was either a monochrome display for text or a Color Graphics Adapter (CGA) display. Today virtually all PCs use a VGA color display. Monochrome displays had a high persistence phosphor, one that left a bright green spot on the display after the monitor was turned off. The display resolution was 720 by 350 dots. They could not display graphics, only text characters. This was soon changed by an after-market product, the Hercules Graphics Adapter or often called the monographics adapter. This could display graphics and text on a monochrome monitor.

The CGA could display 320 by 200 dots. The resolution here was about half that of a monochrome display. The colors presented were limited to four colors. With the AT came the Enhanced Graphics Adapter. Color was now beginning to provide the resolution of a monochrome display. The EGA display could project 640 by 350 dots using 16 colors. The Enhanced Graphics Adapter's higher resolution permits it to display up to 43 lines of text on the screen.

With the announcement of the PS-2 in 1987 came the Video Graphics Array (VGA) display. It could display 640 by 480 dots in 64 colors. At first these displays were expensive, but by 1990 the price had dropped to a very competitive level. See Figure 1–9 and Figure 1–10 for display resolution comparisons.

Today's monitors are largely CRT displays capable of displaying 1,600 by 1,200 resolution with dot pitches around .22 mm–.28 mm. Very high-resolution monitors are made for Computer Aided Design (CAD) workstations and graphic designers.

PC monitors vary in size from 14 inches diagonal to 21 inches diagonal.

Gateway makes a combination TV and PC with a 35-inch monitor. The large monitor has low resolution and a big dot pitch. Their interface to the video graphics card is a 9-pin analog RGB interface. Newer monitors will connect to PCs using USB connections.

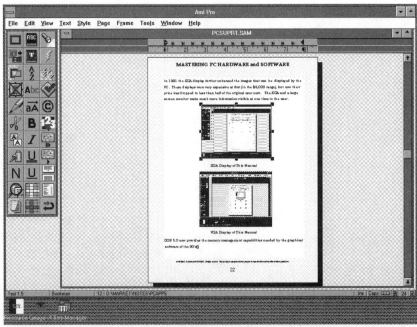

Figure 1-9 *Display image with 1024 by 768 resolution*

Figure 1-10 *Display image with 640 by 480 resolution*

Images are constructed on the CRT screen by an electron beam that is scanned across the screen and switched on and off during the scanning. The electron beam is scanned across special color phosphors to create color images on the CRT screen.

Monitors are changing to flat panel full color displays. The new Liquid Crystal Display (LCD) flat panels have a very crisp image because their pixels are more precisely formed. They use horizontal and vertical connections to precisely illuminate a single pixel on the screen. The top resolution is 1,600 by 1,024 with a .23 mm dot pitch, but this will improve in the near future. Within the next several years, virtually all monitors will be flat panel displays. Some flat panel monitors interface to the PC with the standard analog RGB 9-pin connector. Others require a special connection.

Monitor safety is an important area. Monitors contain high voltages and consequently should be treated with respect. It is not a good idea to disassemble a monitor and power it on because of the danger of electrical shock. Monitors and water definitely do not mix. Some hospital employees playing with a Uzi water pistol one Friday accidentally squirted a monitor that promptly died in flames. It is a wonder that no one was electrically shocked.

CONTROLLER

The display controller drives the monitor. The display must be matched with the correct controller to produce the proper resolutions.

If we were to use a display that had only 320 by 200 resolution with a controller that was capable of 1,024 by 768 resolution, we could only display 320 by 200 resolution. Most display controllers today have on-board video coprocessors that speed up screen refreshes.

The industry moved from VGA display controllers to the next level called Super VGA. Super VGA provided a display of 800 by 600 dots and 64 colors. In 1990, IBM announced the next level display controller, the eXtended Graphics Array (XGA). Its resolution was 1,024 by 768 dots and 256 colors. By 1992, most SVGA adapters provided a display mode with that resolution. This required so much processing to put information on the screen that the display was beginning to slow.

The speed up of the display comes with the latest VGA video coprocessor and a special Advanced Graphics Processor (AGP) bus connection. This evolved from earlier Video Electronics Standards Association (VESA) local bus boards. They perform the display processing and speed up the screen transfer rate.

All video boards have display RAM holding the video information we see on the screen. The video display information is first written to the board using a PC video memory swapping area. The more memory on the display board, the more colors and dots it can display. Super VGA and XGA displays require 512 KB video RAM. Newer 3D AGP display boards use 4 MB RAM but work much better with 8 MB or 16 MB. Most flat panel and laptop displays provide XGA resolution. See Table 1.7 for a monitor and controller feature comparison.

Table 1.7 *Display Summary*

Display Controller Type	Resolution	Colors	Monitor Interface	Connector	Monitor Scan Rate
Mono-chrome	720 by 350	2	TTL	9-pin female	18.4 KHz
Mono-graphics	720 by 350	2	TTL	9-pin female	18.4 KHz
Color Graphics Adapter	320 by 200	4 from palette (choice) of 16 colors	Red Green Blue (RGB)	9-pin female	15.7 KHz
Enhanced Graphics Adapter	640 by 350	16	RGB	9-pin female	21.8 KHz
Video Graphics Array	320 by 200 640 by 480	256 (Standard VGA with 320 by 200 resolution) 16 (Standard VGA with 640 by 480 resolution)	Analog RGB	15-pin high density female	35 KHz
Super VGA (SVGA)	800 by 600 to 1,600 by 1,20068	256	Analog RGB	15-pin high density female	50 to 70+ KHz for Non-interlaced
Extended Graphics Array (XGA)	1,024 by 768	256	Analog RGB	15-pin high density female	70+ KHz for Non-interlaced
Advanced Graphics Port (AGP) Adapters	1,800 by 1,440 and higher	32-bit color (multimillions)	Analog RGB	15-pin high density female	75+ KHz and higher

Display controllers are providing more on-board capabilities to enhance images. The movement is towards higher resolutions with more colors to produce 3-dimensional visual effects. They employ on-board graphics processors coupled with high speed AGP bus transfers to speed up display refresh.

Printers

There are several different printer technologies used by PCs today. These vary from impact printing, to color inkjet printers, to laser printers, to color laser printers. The market is moving to provide all PCs with high-speed affordable color printing capabilities.

The oldest printers were dot matrix impact printers. This type of printer formed images from small hammers hitting a printer ribbon to deposit ink on a piece of paper. These impact printers are now disappearing. They remain the only printer type able to produce multipart forms. However, with laser printers becoming cheaper and faster, it is just as easy to print a form two or three times as it is to print on multiple forms simultaneously by impact. Dot matrix printers can produce color images by using multicolored ribbon. They do not effectively print transparency film.

Most low-cost printers are color inkjet printers. They have two ink cartridges that carry black and colored inks. They print by spitting drops of ink at the paper. The ink drops vary in size to produce 360 to 1,440 dots per inch images. The ink deposited upon the paper dries to produce the printed image. Inkjet printers can print on plain paper, high density paper for excellent image reproduction, and special transparency film for presentations.

Humans can discern a maximum resolution of 600 dots per inch. Above that is not really distinguishable by the human eye. The goal for high-resolution printers is to print pictures with photographic quality. Having a relatively low 360 dots per inch resolution image print at a higher 1,440 dots per inch resolution does not noticeably improve image quality because your original image has only 360 dots per inch. However, printing a high-resolution image (600 dpi) at high-resolution print quality (600 dpi) provides an excellent printed image.

Laser printers use xerographic printing to produce black and white images on plain paper. The latest laser printers print at high speed on both sides of the paper. See Figure 1–11.

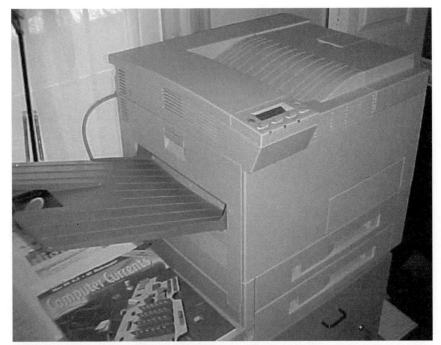

Figure 1–11 *High-speed laser printer*

This process means that laser printers are page printers, not line printers. Dot matrix ribbon and ink jet printers are line printers that print a single line at a time. When printing to a laser printer, the printer does not start printing until an entire page of data has been sent to the printer. In contrast, dot matrix and inkjet printers print each line as it is received from the PC. To see this, just do Print Screen to a laser printer several times. Laser printer page printing often confuses people. They send a printout to the laser printer and nothing happens. They again send the printout to the laser printer, only to discover that they have printed it twice and run both printouts together.

This problem is solved by making sure that your software sends a Form Feed character to the laser printer at the end of each document printed. The Form Feed character causes the laser printer to print all data it has in its buffer.

Color laser printers use multicolored dyes to produce color printouts on plain paper. They employ a variety of printing technologies to produce the images. These printers are becoming much cheaper in price and consequently much more prevalent.

Printers interface to the PC using the parallel port. Some new printers are directly attached to a network to permit sharing between multiple workstations. Some printers utilize infrared links and others USB ports to connect to PCs.

Scanners

Scanners scan paper and photographic images and convert them to digital images and text. Photos scanned in are processed by PC software to enhance image quality. Computer software can be sophisticated or relatively simple when handling images. Special Optical Character Recognition software converts a scanned image into a formatted text file.

Several types of scanners are popular. These include:

- **Flatbed scanners**—These scanners operate like a standard copy machine. The document to be scanned is placed on a flat glass panel and a light is run under it. They can scan single sheets, photos or books. They're usually the most popular choice today. See Figure 1–12.

- **Sheet-fed scanners**—These scanners handle full size paper fed through a slot. In this case, the paper moves and not the light. Until recently, sheet-fed scanners cost less than flat bed scanners, but prices are almost the same today.

- **Specialty scanners**—These scanners come in a variety of sizes and shapes. They can be hand-held or sheet-fed models modified for a specific task or ease-of-use. Some are built into keyboards; others into PCs. This category includes dedicated devices designed to handle nothing but business cards or slides.

- **Multifunction units**—This is a combination scanner, printer and fax in one space-saving unit.

Today all scanners scan color images. Some early scanners only scanned black and white images. They all have a set of specific scanning resolutions they can produce. The specialty scanners and multifunction scanners are aimed at specific tasks like scanning business cards or family photographs. These are typically sheet-fed scanners. Document scanners are mostly flatbed scanners. Some sheet-fed and flatbed scanners scan multiple sheets automatically. Hand-held scanners are best for mobile applications. A few scanners were even designed to scan multidimensional images. They used a camera mounted up away from the image placement area. Scanners most often attach to the PC using SCSI adapters or USB connections.

Figure 1–12 *Flatbed scanner*

Video Camera

Video cameras are used to capture single frame images or continuous video streams for the PC. They help turn any PC into a video telephone with the appropriate communications and software. Otherwise they are capable of capturing single frame images for transmitting with e-mail and other communications. See Figure 1–13.

Figure 1–13 *Pete from video camera*

These are simple Charge Coupled Device (CCD) imagers with varying resolution and color capabilities. They interface to the PC via the parallel port, a special video capture card, or a USB connection. Video cameras will become part of every PC system.

Microphone and Speakers

Sound capabilities are an important part of every PC today. Soon they will replace the audio systems used in most homes because the PC provides the capability to produce CD-quality surround sound with precise control of the music selections played. To provide these audio capabilities, the PC uses a good sound card attached to speakers. These speakers are stereo high-frequency speakers and a subwoofer speaker to produce the bass sounds. The PC speakers are self-powered—they do not get their power from the PC sound board, but rather from powered amplifiers built into the speakers themselves. The speakers plug into the stereo outputs from the sound board.

Some sound boards have a separate output for the subwoofer speaker while others have outputs for four-speaker surround sound. The audio quality rivals that of an expensive stereo system for most people. Only the most discerning audiophile would detect the difference between a PC-driven stereo system and a receiver-driven system. The only real advantage of a conventional system over a PC-driven sound system is that the conventional system connects to tape deck, FM radio receivers, and a multitude of other audio components. PC systems can connect to such components as well, but they typically have limited output jacks on their sound board. It is almost easier to connect them to a conventional stereo receiver and connect that receiver to the other audio components than to attempt to directly connect the PC to the audio components today.

Microphones permit sound input to the PC. The standard run-of-the-mill microphones provided with most sound boards do not provide sufficient quality for voice recognition and for broadcast audio use. Sound boards work with high-quality microphones. Such microphones reduce background noise and produce studio-quality sound. We recently used a high-quality microphone to record some audio material for our radio show that was stored in an MP3 compressed audio format, sent to a Diamond RIO MP3 player, and from there input to the radio station's control panel for broadcast. This worked quite well and provided near studio-quality sound.

MP3 stands for Motion Picture Executive Group (MPEG) 1 Layer 3. MP3 is a sound file storage format. Music and sound files are stored on a computer disk in such a way that the file size is relatively small, but the recording sounds near perfect. MP3 files typically have file names with an MP3 extension.

Study Break

Adjusting Monitor Resolution

Let's try adjusting our current monitor resolution and color depth. Find the controls for your display inside your control panel in Windows 95 or Windows 98. Click on the settings tab of your display controls.

View your current color and screen area settings. The color setting could range from 16 colors to 32-bit True Color and the screen area from 640 by 480 to 1600 by 1200.

Adjust your color settings to the 16 colors and save the settings. You may have to power off and then power on to properly display color setting.

Adjust your screen area to the highest possible setting. This causes your icons and images on the screen to become smaller because there are more dots per inch.

A+ 1.2   Software Components

PC software components depend upon the operating system (OS) installed. The operating system is a set of programs coordinating all work activity in the PC. Without it and other software, the PC does nothing but heat the room. The most common PC operating systems are:

- **DOS**—The original PC operating system is used to set up and sometimes troubleshoot PCs. DOS makes the functionality of the computer hardware accessible for running the Windows setup. DOS is the basic set of computer instructions that manages the flow of information in the PC.
- **Windows**—There are two major iterations of Windows, Windows 3.x and Windows 95/98. Windows 95/98 is the operating system delivered with most new PCs today. It provides a graphical user interface and multitasking capabilities.

- **Windows NT**—This is the network server and industrial strength operating system for PCs. It provides a similar graphical user interface to Windows 95/98. Windows NT is a more robust operating system than Windows with better isolation of DOS, Windows, and NT applications from each other. This makes for a more reliable operating environment.

Each operating system has several major components.

DOS Components

The PC Disk Operating System (DOS) components are:

- **COMMAND.COM**—This is the command interpreter for DOS. Commands typed in the keyboard at the DOS user command prompt are processed first by COMMAND.COM. It interprets the command and initiates the other software activities to complete the command. COMMAND.COM interfaces to MSDOS.COM through the DOS Application Program Interface (API).
- **MSDOS.SYS**—This performs the tasks and schedules the programs required to accomplish the DOS commands. This component is the heart and hands of DOS.
- **IO.SYS**—This DOS component handles the detailed input/output activities of DOS. It interfaces to device driver programs that perform the most detailed hardware operation and control activities. IO.SYS works in conjunction with device driver software for standard and special PC hardware.
- **Device Drivers**—Device drivers tell DOS how to properly interface with an external device. Specified by DEVICE= statements in CONFIG.SYS. Some DOS device drivers are:
  - **SMARTDRIVE.EXE**—manages the disk cache and double buffering for SCSI drives.
  - **HIMEM.SYS**—provides access to extended memory.
  - **EMM386.EXE**—manages the upper memory area and creates expanded memory from extended memory.
- **Application Programs**—Application program software interfaces with DOS to use the PC hardware to perform useful work for us. It is through the application program that we see the PC. Under DOS, the application program may have its own device drivers and command interpreter functions. Applications were typically a single large program loaded entirely into memory along with the data being worked upon.

Windows Components

Windows 3.x expanded upon DOS. It used the basic DOS disk and memory driver programs to perform input/output operations. Windows 3.x substitutes a multitasking KRNL.EXE program for MSDOS.SYS and adds to it graphical user interface components, GDI.EXE and USER.EXE. In this manner, Windows 3.x expands on the foundation laid with DOS to provide the cooperative multitasking operating system with a graphical user interface. See Figure 1–14.

Windows 3.x components are:

- Windows Virtual Machine—The virtual machine program manages the execution of all Windows applications, performing the cooperative multitasking between them.
- KRNL.EXE—The kernel is the scheduling program managing the DOS and Windows virtual machines.

Figure 1–14 *Windows 3.x structure*

- GDI.EXE—The graphical device interface program is one half of the graphical user interface. It handles the PC display and other graphical devices.
- USER.EXE—The user graphical interface program monitoring user mouse operations and similar tasks. This is the Windows equivalent to the DOS COMMAND.COM.

Windows 95/98 components are generally the same as those for Windows 3.x. However, they function differently to provide improved multitasking and GUI features. The improved features are due to Windows 95 being based upon new Windows 95 file management, networking, virtual machine manager, and device drivers as shown in Figure 1–15.

The Windows 95 overall architecture has the same basic components. These are:

- *The system virtual machine* managing execution of both Windows 16-bit and 32-bit applications. Multitasking has been changed from cooperative multitasking to preemptive multitasking. In preemptive

Figure 1–15 *Windows 95 system structure*

multitasking, no application program can dominate the virtual machine as was possible with cooperative multitasking.

- *The applications program interface* (API) layer, consisting of the Windows kernel, the graphical device interface (GDI), and user interface programs. The KRNL386.EXE still manages DOS and Windows virtual machines. The DOS virtual machines are not shown in Figure 1–15 above. The GDI.EXE (graphical device interface) program supports font scaling, color management, printing, and all the drawing on the screen. And finally the USER.EXE program creates windows and controls mouse movement, dialogue boxes, and message handling and similar functions.

- *The base system* functions support the system virtual machine and the API layer. The base system is responsible for handling key functions implemented in the Windows 95 operating system.

A powerful feature of Windows 95 is its virtual machines. Under Windows 3.x, virtual machines used the 80386 CPU virtual 8086 operating mode. In virtual 8086 mode, a VM (Virtual Machine) emulated an 8086 processor with 1 MB of RAM, I/O ports, and CPU registers. Windows 95 virtual machines are different. A Windows 95 virtual machine contains a memory map of the memory allocated to the application program, identifies any Windows resources allotted the application, and tracks hardware registers.

Under Windows 95, there are the system virtual machine and DOS virtual machines. The system virtual machine operates in the 80386 CPU's protected mode. All Windows programs, 16-bit or 32-bit, execute from this area and tie themselves into Windows through the API layer. This linkage between the application and the Windows subsystem is made during the program's load sequence. Within this virtual machine, all 16-bit applications share a common address space, a common message queue and memory heaps. This means if one 16-bit application crashes, it often corrupts one of these shared areas.

Within this system virtual machine, 16-bit Windows applications are cooperatively multitasked. Windows 32-bit applications do not use shared areas and resources. Each 32-bit application gets its own memory address space from the system virtual machine. Within its memory address space reside the application message queue and the memory heaps. The separate memory address spaces for 32-bit applications make them more reliable than 16-bit applications.

MS-DOS virtual machines are very much like a PC running DOS with 1 MB of memory. The applications running in DOS virtual machines make service requests of the system, just like they would under DOS, via INT21H (the hexadecimal interrupt 21). These requests, however, are intercepted and passed on to protected-mode code tying into system services. This is similar to the 32-bit file access function of Windows 3.11. Each DOS virtual machine is formed from an invisible virtual machine created during the Windows boot process. This virtual machine contains the global environment for all DOS virtual machines, including information such as which terminate-and-stay-resident (TSR) programs were loaded from the AUTOEXEC.BAT file. Similarly to Windows 3.x, each DOS application runs in its own virtual machine.

The Windows 95 application program interface is designed to maintain backward compatibility to Windows 3.x. Most programs first used with Windows 95 were Windows 3.x applications (Windows 16-bit applications). Windows 95 is a 32-bit operating system so it also has a 32-bit application API. This 32-bit API is compatible with the Win32 API of Windows NT. Three main components, the GDI (graphical device interface), the user graphical interface program, and the kernel, support the Windows 95 API. All Windows applications use these same modules. The modules additionally have been designed to handle both 32-bit and 16-bit operations.

The Windows 95 base system is comprised of several components including:

- Device Drivers—Windows 95 uses DOS device drivers as well as newer 32-bit device drivers. Some older DOS applications must have the older drivers loaded in order to function with the PC's hardware components. Windows 95 provides a number of these drivers in the 32-bit form, including those for PCMCIA cards, CD-ROMs, and the mouse.

- Virtual Machine Manager System—This is likely the most important base system component, providing a central core of virtual services. Windows 95 has over 700 services in the base system, and over half of those are provided by the VMM. The VMM is a Virtual anything Driver (VxD) that resides in the file DOS386.EXE. It is responsible for handling event coordination (thread supervision), interrupt handling, memory management (virtual and physical), scheduling (time slicing), and controlling the virtual machines.

- Operating System Services—This area performs many of the miscellaneous functions of the operating system including fulfilling date and time requests and the plug-and-play configuration system.

- The Network Subsystem—The network subsystem is the latest version of the peer-to-peer network, released with Windows for Workgroups. This version uses the file management system as a way to coordinate file access across the network. Because of the IFS manager, the network subsystem can also provide access to other network systems simultaneously. With the network subsystem comes support for Novell, TCP/IP, and SMB.

- File Management System—In Windows 3.1, DOS performed the fixed disk file management functions. This caused most disk operations to be performed in real mode, not in protected mode. Such switching between real and protected mode was inefficient but necessary because DOS controlled disk operations. In Windows 95, Windows controls disk operations with a new file system manager. The Installable File System (IFS) manager provides interfaces for local fixed disks, CD-ROMs, and networks.

Windows NT Features and Components

Windows NT components carry the same nomenclature as Windows 3.x and 95/98 components. Their functionality differs from Windows 95/98. From a user perspective, the GUI appears nearly identical, but the virtual machine, API, kernel and driver programs provide capabilities beyond those of Windows 95/98. The NT functionality includes:

- **Large Platform Support**—Windows provides support for a wide array of CPU chip platforms, from Intel 386 to RISC processors like the MIPS R4000 and Digital's Alpha AXP.
- **True 32-Bit Preemptive Multitasking**—NT allows preemptive multitasking to DOS, Windows 16-bit and Windows 32-bit, OS/2, and POSIX applications. The user only has to learn how to use another application, not another operating system.
- **Easy Networking**—Windows NT comes with its own networking component built in. It comes with support for Banyan VINES, DEC Pathworks, IBM LAN Server, MS LAN Manager, Windows for Workgroups, Novell NetWare, and Apple Talk.
- **Multiprotocol Support**—Windows NT supports most network protocols including TCP/IP, NETBEUI, and SPX/IPX.
- **Large Capacities**—Windows NT supports 4 gigabytes of RAM and 16 exabytes of disk space. Disk drive capacity terminology is presented in detail in Disk Preparation in Chapter 14, but be assured an exabyte is much larger than a gigabyte.
- **Broad File System Support**—Windows NT provides support for the DOS file allocation table (FAT), the OS/2 high performance file system (HPFS), the NT file system (NTFS), and the CD-ROM file system (CDFS).

These capabilities are provided by the same basic architecture as Windows 95/98, including a system virtual machine, an applications program interface, and base system functions supporting the system virtual machine and the API. At this point the similarity ends. Windows NT was written from the ground up to be both a client and a server operating system. Its program code is not an improvement on existing Windows programs but rather all new code designed to be run on high-end PCs and servers. Windows NT 4.0 provides a user interface nearly identical to Windows 95 and the Windows NT 5.0 user interface incorporates the Windows 98 interface improvements. Windows NT 4.0 lacks the plug-and-play capabilities of Windows 95 and is more limited in the PC hardware it supports. The plug-and-play capabilities and hardware support are expanded with NT 5.0, narrowing the gap between it and Windows 98. This broadens the variety of PC systems supporting Windows NT 5.0. Finally, NT was developed without regard for backwards compatibility. This means that some Windows 16-bit applications do not run on NT, while they run just fine on Windows 95 and 98. In contrast, Windows 95/98 is not designed to run as network server software. Windows 95/98 only supports peer-to-peer networking and is not robust enough to operate under heavy networking loads.

Windows NT is designed to be augmented by additional server applications software to customize its functionality to specific networking needs. Microsoft's structured query language (SQL) and exchange server programs are examples of such server-centric applications.

Study Break

Finding USER.exe and GDI.exe

It is time to find key components inside Windows. The two files that we are looking for are USER.exe and GDI.exe.

1. Click on the start menu, then drag to find and finally click on find files or folders.

2. Type in the User*.* and then click find.

3. Next type in GDI*.* and then click find.

Both of these files should come right up as they are key components of the Windows operating systems.

A+   1.3   PC Boot Process

The PC boot process varies depending on the operating system being loaded. For DOS, Windows 3.x,and Windows 95/98, booting requires some form of DOS. Windows NT loads differently using a separate NTLDR (NT loader) program.

The DOS loading sequence is:

1. POST in ROM
2. BOOT Program on Fixed Disk
3. IO.SYS (or IBMBIO.COM)
4. MSDOS.SYS (or IBMDOS.COM)
5. CONFIG.SYS
6. COMMAND.COM
7. AUTOEXEC.BAT
8. WIN.COM or DOS User Application Programs
9. SYSTEM.INI
10. WIN.INI
11. Windows 95/98 Registry

During a DOS/Windows boot, the PC first performs the Power-On Self Test (POST) procedure. This mainly determines which PC components are installed and quickly checks their basic operation. POST does not, however, perform a comprehensive system test.

The next step is to either load the cold boot loader program from the master boot record of the fixed disk or to run the ROM cold boot loader to load DOS from a floppy diskette. The cold boot loader program is a very simple program that loads the IO.SYS program from the diskette or from the fixed disk. (Some viruses use this cold boot loader program to infect PCs.)

The main loading and input/output functions are performed by IO.SYS. It first loads MSDOS.SYS and then processes the CONFIG.SYS file commands. Device driver programs are loaded and matched to the PC hardware components. Once the CONFIG.SYS file has been processed, IO.SYS loads the DOS command interpreter program. Control is turned over to COMMAND.COM and it then processes the AUTOEXEC.BAT file. AUTOEXEC.BAT loads programs establishing the DOS operating environment. Terminate-and-stay-resident (TSR) programs like DOSKEY.EXE are loaded in AUTOEXEC.BAT. After the commands in AUTOEXEC.BAT have been processed, applications programs are run.

When DOS is being used to boot into Windows, the first application run is WIN.COM, the Windows loader program. WIN.COM processes the commands in the SYSTEM.INI file to load the hardware drivers for Windows. Finally, WIN.COM processes the commands from the WIN.INI file to load Windows TSR programs and set up the Windows applications environment.

When loading Windows 3.x, all memory resident and network software are loaded first before starting Windows. It is the same with other hardware components used by a Windows PC workstation. For example, our PC workstation that is on a network and runs a scanner must have both the scanner and the network software started before Windows is initiated.

Windows 95/98 changes this because it loads the networking and other driver programs as part of Windows 95/98. Windows 95/98 can use CONFIG.SYS and AUTOEXEC.BAT for backward compatibility with older DOS and Windows software. However, CONFIG.SYS and AUTOEXEC.BAT are not required for newer Windows 32-bit applications and often can be eliminated from the booting process. Similarly, WIN.INI and SYSTEM.INI provide backward compatibility for Windows 16-bit applications. They are still used to load and configure a small portion of the Windows 95/98 operating environment. The registry controls the main loading functions for Windows 95/98. The registry loads device drivers and completes the Windows 95/98 operating environment configuration. It is responsible for configuring the user's desktop display, determining virtual memory configuration, allocating disk cache, and much more.

The Windows NT loading procedure differs from the DOS/Windows loading procedure because DOS is not required to load NT. This provides enhanced security for Windows NT because it is possible to better control and limit access to fixed disk drive files. The NT loading sequence is:

1. POST in ROM
2. BOOT Program on Fixed Disk
3. NTLDR
4. NT Kernel and other drivers
5. The NT Registry

Similarly to DOS/Windows, NT uses the cold boot loader program on fixed disk to load the NTLDR.EXE program. It is in some ways equivalent to the DOS IO.SYS program. It in turn loads the NT kernel program and basic hardware drivers. Finally, NT uses its registry to complete the boot process.

The role of CONFIG.SYS

The CONFIG.SYS file loads the basic hardware driver programs used by the PC. It tailors DOS to the specific hardware in the PC. It also is used to establish the memory management programs DOS and Windows use in accessing the HIMEM, UPPER MEMORY BLOCKS and EXTENDED/EXPANDED memory areas of the PC.

The role of AUTOEXEC.BAT

The AUTOEXEC.BAT file loads terminate-and-stay-resident programs and configures the operating environment for DOS and Windows software. It points to the subdirectories where temporary files are stored for both Windows and DOS. Windows uses temporary files for both programs and temporary data storage.

Study Break

Stepping through the AUTOEXEC.BAT

> Here is a neat trick where you can step through each different component that loads from your AUTOEXEC.BAT.
>
> Simply reboot your machine and, as your machine is booting, hold down the F8 key.
>
> If your machine has an AUTOEXEC.BAT, you will be able to choose if you would like to load the statement or not.

■ Summary

This chapter has identified a variety of PC components and subsystems. The PC hardware core components that were described in detail included: the Central Processing Unit (CPU chip); the Read Only Memory (ROM); the Random Access Memory (RAM); chip sets and buses; the power supply; serial and parallel input/output (I/O) ports; the floppy disk controller and drive; the fixed disk controller and drive; the CD-ROM drive; the display adapter and monitor; the keyboard; and the mouse.

Software components that were covered included the common PC operating system types including DOS and the Windows family, their features, and key file components.

The final section covered the booting process for the DOS/Windows operating systems, which perform similar boot functions, and Windows NT that has a distinct boot process. This section discussed the role of key file components in booting these two types of systems.

▲ CHAPTER REVIEW QUESTIONS

1. *What disk is used to COLD boot a PC?*

    A. Setup diskette

    B. System disk

    C. Diagnostic diskette

    D. Program diskette

    Answer: B. System disk

2. *What is not a typical PC system component?*

    A. Floppy drive

    B. Monitor

    C. Sound card

    D. SCSI disk

    E. IDE disk

    Answer: D. SCSI disk

3. *Fixed disk drives rotate at what speed?*

    A. 300 RPM

    B. 1,200 RPM

    C. 2,741 RPM

    D. 7,200 RPM

    Answer: E. 7,200 RPM

4. *CD-ROM drives connect to a PC using what?*

    A. Fiber cable

    B. IDE interface cable

    C. SCSI connector

    D. Floppy cable

    Answer: B. IDE interface cable

5. *IDE drives store a maximum of ___ GB.*

   A. 2

   B. 4

   C. 25

   D. 37

   Answer: D. 37

6. *What file plays an important role in booting DOS?*

   A. DOSKEY.EXE

   B. MSCDEX.EXE

   C. CONFIG.SYS

   D. DRIVER.SYS

   Answer: C. CONFIG.SYS

7. *Multimedia PCs contain what?*

   A. Scanner

   B. Power supply

   C. LAN card

   D. Sound card

   Answer: E. Sound card (all PCs contain a power supply)

8. *CD-ROM drives have a top speed of?*

   A. 48X

   B. 2X

   C. 4X

   D. 32X

   Answer: A. 48X

9. *Top monitor resolution is?*

   A. 1,024 by 768

   B. 1,600 by 1,024

   C. 1,800 by 1,440

   D. None of the above

   Answer: C. 1,800 by 1,440

10. *Storage devices are?*

   A. LAN cards

   B. Monitors

   C. Sound cards

   D. RAM

   E. Disk drives

   Answer: E. Disk drives

11. *Which device stores the most data?*

   A. Floppy diskette

   B. Fixed disk

   C. CD-ROM

   D. DVD drive

   Answer: B. Fixed disk

12. *The central component of a PC is?*

   A. Disk drive

   B. Main logic board

   C. LAN board

   D. CD-ROM

   Answer: B. Main logic board

13. *What is the fastest PC component?*

   A. Disk drive

   B. CPU chip

   C. Display controller

   D. RAM

   Answer: B. CPU chip

14. *What is the first step in the boot process?*

   A. Run POST in ROM

   B. Test the floppy drive

   C. Test the fixed disk

   D. Load the OS

   Answer: C. Run POST in ROM

15. *What does POST stand for?*
    A. A wooden pole
    B. Power-On Standard Test
    C. Power-up Original Self Test
    D. Power-On Self Test
    Answer: D. Power-On Self Test

16. *What does MLB stand for?*
    A. Major Logic Board
    B. Mother Logic Board
    C. Main Logic Board
    D. Motherboard
    Answer: C. Main Logic Board

PC Installation and Upgrade

▲ Chapter Syllabus

A+ 2.1   PC Component Replacement Summary

A+ 2.2   Removing and Adding FRUs

A+ 2.3   Hardware Configuration Parameters

A+ 2.4   I/O Cabling and Connectors

A+ 2.5   Installing IDE/EIDE Fixed Disks and CD-ROMs

A+ 2.6   Installing and Configuring SCSI Devices

A+ 2.7   Installing Common Periphal Devices

A+ 2.8   Upgrading your PC

Installing a PC can be as simple as plugging the monitor, keyboard, mouse, printer, and speakers into the main chassis; connecting the PC to AC power; and turning the power on. Yet, even in the simplest case attention should be paid to providing adequate AC power; providing good ventilation and avoiding direct sunlight for cooling; and proper user ergonomics. From a support and maintenance viewpoint, these considerations are important. However, equally important or perhaps more important is PC component installation basics. This can vary significantly between PCs, depending on their mechanical configuration. Some components are very standardized, while others are not. In this chapter, we examine the procedures for removing and installing almost all PC components.

57

Before beginning, adequate grounding and static electricity discharge precautions should be taken. This means that the PC and the service person should both be attached to a common ground to minimize the chance of static electrical discharge into sensitive electronics. A PC assembled is relatively safe from damage from static discharge because most such discharges are conducted to ground by the outside of the PC's case. There has been many a time when traveling and carrying my portable PC on a metal cart with rubber wheels during the depths of winter that, upon reaching my hotel room after traveling across miles of wool carpets, I have shot blue sparks for several inches. Even when feeling the pain and hearing that audible snap of the static discharge, I felt secure in the knowledge that only I was mildly damaged and not my PC, because it was fully assembled and riding on the metal cart. In this case, the cart conducted the static charge to ground, bypassing the PC.

A+ 2.1   PC Component Replacement Summary

Over the last decade and a half, significant changes have occurred to the PC and to PC system troubleshooting and repair. The PC components have increased their reliability by placing more functions into custom chips, and lowered manufacturing costs by using surface mount technology.

Today repair of any PC board is not within the reach of the PC user because it requires special diagnostic equipment and repair tools. Furthermore, board repair is not cost effective when compared to the purchase cost of new components providing in most cases increased reliability and functionality. With the introduction of five-hundred-dollar PC systems, PC troubleshooting and repair now assumes another dimension. Whenever repair costs exceed half the cost of a new PC, the question "Repair or replace?" must be asked.

Effective PC troubleshooting focuses on identification of a malfunctioning PC subsystem or software component, and reconfiguration or replacement of that component. PC hardware subsystems, their malfunction rate, the type of repair or upgrade, the tools required for the repair, and the approximate cost of the repair or upgrade are shown in the Table 2.1. This table is based upon our experience with various PCs that we have purchased, resold, and repaired.

Table 2.1 *PC component repair and replacement summary*

PC Subsystem	Repair	Tools	Cost	Failure Rate
System Board	RAM-ROM-CPU Replace or Upgrade	Screwdrivers	$100 to $500	Rarely—Obsolete in 12 Months
Display Controller	Replace Replace System Board	Screwdrivers	$50 to $200	Rarely—Obsolete in 12 Months
Video Monitor	Manufacturer Repair Replace or Upgrade	Screwdriver Shipping Box	$100 and up	Occasionally
Fixed Disk Controller	Replace System Board	Screwdriver	$50 to $800	Rarely
Fixed Disk Drive	Reformat Surface Scan Vendor Repair Replace or Upgrade	Software Software Hammer (satisfying temporary fix) Screwdriver	$100 to $1,000	About every 1 to 4 years
Floppy Disk Controller	Replace System Board	Screwdriver	See system board	Rarely
Floppy Disk Drive	Replace	Screwdriver	$15 up	Occasionally
RAM	Replace—Upgrade Capacity	Screwdriver	$0.70 to $4 per M	Occasionally
ROM	Flash the BIOS	Program on Diskette	$0	Obsolete
CPU	Replace	Screwdriver Special Tool	$70 to $700	Rarely or Never
Parallel Port	Replace System Board	Screwdriver	See system board	Rarely
Printer	Manufacturer Repair Vendor Repair Replace Upgrade	Shipping Box	$75 to $13,000	Somewhat Frequently
Serial Port	Replace System Board	Screwdriver	See system board	Rarely
Modem	Manufacturer Repair Replace Upgrade	Screwdriver	$55 to $170	Occasionally

Table 2.1 *PC component repair and replacement summary (Continued)*

Power Supply	Replacement from Manufacturer Replace Fan	Screwdriver	$25 to $270	Infrequently Fan failure
Keyboard	Replace	None	$8 to $50	Rarely
Mouse	Replace	None	$5 to $80	Occasionally
Option Cards	Replace	Screwdriver	$20 to $800	Rarely

Study Break

Repair or Replace?

Try to answer the ultimate question when faced with PC repairs and compare it to the chart above. What is more cost effective? To repair the broken component or replace the entire system? The following are three different scenarios with which you are confronted. Would you repair the component or replace the system?

1. Faulty power supply

2. Upgrade motherboard, processor, and memory

3. Faulty mouse

Answers:

1. Replace power supply.

2. Buy a new system; more cost effective in the long run.

3. Repair by cleaning the rollers. If this does not fix it, jump up and down on it to relieve your frustration and just replace it.

A+ 2.2 ## Removing and Adding FRUs

Replaceable PC components are called field replaceable units (FRUs). FRUs are entire modules that are replaceable in the field that repair broken systems or subsystems on a PC. For example, a fixed disk drive is a FRU while the circuit card on the fixed disk drive is not. FRUs can readily be removed and replaced as single components in the PC. Basic FRUs are the CPU chip, the main logic board, RAM SIMMs and DIMMs, the power supply, floppy and fixed disk drives, and the option cards. Almost all of these components are unbolt-and-unplug modules. Lets look in more detail at the procedures to remove and add FRUs.

Removing the Chassis Cover

In every instance the very first step is the most difficult. It is removing the PC's case. Each PC manufacturer has a different mechanism for securing the case. Generally it is held in place by three to as many as six bolts. These bolts can be hidden under the front bezel or they can be exposed on the rear of the PC cabinet. Some cases have metal slots and tabs that hold them more closely to the chassis while others slide in a tray like arrangement. Regardless, each PC is different depending upon the manufacturer.

All standard or PC clones look very similar. They first came apart just like the PC/XT/AT computers with bolts holding the cover at the rear of the PC. The front of the cover was fastened in proper position on the front of the PC by a slot into which a metal tab on the cover slid. These PCs were in a flat desktop configuration. Now most clones come in a tower configuration. The case is bolted behind the front plastic bezel. The front plastic bezel is snapped into place with plastic clips molded into the bezel. Pulling on the bottom of the bezel most often removes it, permitting access to the bolts holding the left chassis cover. Once unbolted, the cover slides forward to release it from its slot and tray-securing mechanisms. Sometimes the case cover on one side is in an inverted "L" form. When it is removed, access to the top of the chassis and the right side of the chassis is permitted. On the left side, the PC option cards and disk drives are accessible as well as the memory slots. See Figure 2–1.

Once the PC covers are removed, the remaining FRUs can be removed or added. Removing the cover is typically a very simple procedure. It requires keen observation and examination of the PC to ascertain how the cover is attached. If, when removing the cover, it gets very difficult to access a bolt, then the PC is probably being disassembled incorrectly. With my first XT computer, I was removing the fixed disk and it just would not slide out no matter what I did. I was almost to the point of prying it out with a screwdriver only to discover that there was the bottom bolt holding it into place.

Figure 2–1 *Front bezel removed*

No amount of prying would release the disk drive. If you start to pry, then reexamine the case very closely for an alternate disassembly method.

The Pin One Rule

The next general rule for installing and replacing PC components is the data cable pin one rule. Every cable has numbered pins starting with pin one. When connecting data cables, pin one always connects to pin one. The only problem is in locating pin one on the cables and on the components. Some guidelines to follow are:

Pin one is the side of the cable with the colored wire. The color is a red or blue stripe down the side of the cable. On some cables the stripe is cross-hatched.

Connectors have the pin numbers written on them. Look for the number 1 on the cable connector.

Pin one on cable connectors is marked by an offset notch, by an offset bar, or by an arrow on the pin one side of the connector. Some connectors are keyed by a tab on the outside of the connector or by a blocked pin in the connector.

Pin one is identified sometimes by a square solder pad on the bottom side of the connector. The remaining pins have round solder pads. The square solder pad is on the lower right in Figure 2–2.

Pin one on a board is often identified by a number label printed near the pin. It can be the number one, two, 34 or 50. One or two identifies the pin one side. Thirty-four or fifty identifies the opposite side of the cable.

Pin one is on the lower right side of the cable connector when the connector is horizontal. It is commonly nearest the power connector when the power connector is on the right of the drive when facing the connectors at the rear of the drive. Figure 2–3 has pin one at the lower right of the power and control cable connector nearest the power connection. Note the tab at the top of the data and control cable connector slot and the broken pin at the center on the bottom of the connector. The broken pin is for a keyed connector.

"D" shaped connectors are designed to mate pin one with pin one.

Edge connectors have a slot cut into the connector nearest pin one.

If pin one is not connected to pin one, then the components do not work. They can under some rare circumstances cause electronic components to burn out. A common symptom of not properly connecting pin one on the data cable to pin one on the drive is that the drive light stays on.

Figure 2–2 *Square solder pad*

Figure 2–3 *3.5-inch IDE drive connectors*

Main Logic Board

The system or main logic board is typically set in the bottom of the chassis or on the rightmost side of tower-style chassis.

All option cards plug into it as well as the power supply and the front panel controls. Newer system boards also have the floppy and fixed disk drive cables, the option serial port cables, and the option parallel port cables connected into the board. These must all be removed as well as the power supply to remove the system (main logic) board. Once these are disconnected, it is a matter of unbolting the board and sliding it out of its mounts. Typically the boards are mounted on plastic standoffs that slide into bottle shaped slots to hold them in place. See Figure 2–4.

The most difficult part is sliding the board out of the chassis. The newer ATX style boards have keyboard, mouse, and serial port connectors mounted on the rear of the main logic board. These are sometimes fastened to the rear of the chassis. They must be unfastened to remove the ATX style main logic board.

Installing a main logic board is just the reverse process. The plastic standoffs are inserted into the main logic board holes corresponding to the bottle shaped chassis slots. The board is slid into place so that the board mounting holes align with the bolt holes of the metal chassis. Sometimes small male-female mounting bolts must be installed to provide the proper mechanism for securing the main logic board mounting bolts. Once slid into place, the board is secured with one or two mounting bolts. These bolts ground the board to the chassis. It is possible to short the board out if there are extra mounting bolt holes that contact the main logic board in the wrong area. Placing electrical tape over extra metal mounting bolt holes averts such problems.

After the board is mounted, the power connections are put in place. Older style boards use power connections that are marked with the early PC P8 and P9 connections. To assure that the P8 and P9 connectors are not

Figure 2–4 *Plastic standoff and bottle-shaped slot*

reversed, the black (ground) wires on each connector are lined up with one another. See Figure 2–5.

On ATX style boards, the P8 and P9 connectors are combined into a single power connector that cannot be misaligned easily. Power connectors plug into sockets generally at the right rear of the main logic board.

Once power is connected to the main logic board, the front panel control signal and switch connections are made. The basic connections cover the keyboard lock (KBLCK), the reset button (RESET), the speaker connection (SPKR), and fixed disk and turbo operating light emitting diodes (LEDs). Figure 2–6 illustrates the typical MLB connections. Sometimes a turbo switch connection is included (TBSW).

Figure 2–5
Power connector alignment

Figure 2–6 *Main logic board control connections*

Disk Drives

Both fixed disk and floppy disk drives can mount in 3.5-inch or 5.25-inch mounting slots in the main chassis. Figure 2–7 shows both 5.25-inch and 3.5-inch drive mounting bays.

Disk drives are typically mounted so that the drive circuit board is on the bottom or tilted on the side. Some Compaq PCs had quantum disk drives mounted upside down—the circuit board was on the top of the drive. Certain fixed disk drives cannot be mounted in this fashion.

When drives are mounted in larger slots, a mounting kit that adapts the smaller drive to the larger slot is used. These are simple mechanical spacers. The spacers are bolted to the drive and then the drive is bolted into the chassis. There are four bolt holes on the sides as well as on the bottom of each drive. These holes sometimes take fine thread bolts or coarse thread bolts depending on the drive manufacturer. Many manufacturers provide the bolts for mounting the drive in the chassis. Once a drive is bolted into place, the data cable and power cable connections are plugged into the drive.

Figure 2–7 *Full height tower chassis drive mounting bays and slots*

FIXED DISK DRIVES

Today most internal fixed disk drives are 3.5-inch drives. In some cases, larger 5.25-inch drives and in others, smaller 2.5-inch drives can used in desktop PCs, but more frequently are found in laptops or network hubs.

All PC chassis have both 3.5-inch and 5.25-inch mounting slots for these disk drives. The 5.25-inch slots can accommodate a 3.5-inch drive with the proper mounting brackets. A 3.5-inch slot can accommodate a 2.5-inch drive again with proper mounting brackets. No 2.5-inch disk drive mounting brackets for 5.25-inch slots exist to our knowledge. However, because the 2.5-inch drives are so small and light it is possible to mount them with just two bolts into some 5.25-inch slots.

Fixed disk drives are IDE or SCSI drives. The most common 3.5-inch drives use a standard disk drive power cable providing 5-volt and 12-volt power to the drive. The 2.5-inch drives use only 5-volt power. The data cables are parallel conductor flat ribbon cables that use 40 pins for IDE and 50 pins for SCSI drives. See Figure 2–8.

In Figure 2–8, the power connector carries 12-volt power in the yellow conductor and 5-volt power in the red conductor. The black center conductors are the ground or return lines for the 5-volt and 12-volt power leads. The data cable pin one is on the left side, as indicated by the crosshatched red colored wire in the cable. Newer SCSI drives have different data cables that are described in more detail later. The 2.5-inch drives have a special drive connector combining the data and power cables together. This necessitates a special adapter on the rear of the drive to adapt the 2.5-inch drive to standard IDE data and power cables. See Figure 2–9.

Figure 2–8 *3.5-inch IDE drive cabling*

Figure 2–9 *2.5-inch drive top and bottom*

Figure 2–9 illustrates the mechanical mounting brackets for the 2.5-inch drive, enabling mounting in a 3.5-inch chassis slot. The drive is attached to a special 2.5-inch adapter that connects to both the standard 40-pin IDE cable and the power cable at the same time. Note the power connection uses only red (5-volt) and black (ground) power connections.

Most IDE controllers can handle two IDE drives if the cable has two connectors. In this configuration, one drive must be designated as the primary or master drive and the other drive as the secondary or slave drive. A jumper on the drive changes the designation from master to slave drive. The data and control cable connects from the rear of the drive to the main logic board or to an IDE drive controller board. Pin one connects to pin one precisely following the pin one rule. Most IDE drives have a slotted connector that mates with a 40-pin data cable connector with a protruding tab to assure that pin one connects to pin one. Otherwise the pin one connector pin is on the lower right hand side nearest the power connector on the right.

SCSI disk drive installation and removal is similar to IDE drives. With SCSI drives, the physical drive mounting is the same as any IDE drive. The power connection is also identical. The data and control cable connections differ. SCSI drives typically use a 50-pin cable to connect to a drive controller that is not built-in to the main logic board. The SCSI drive controller can control both the SCSI drive and floppy disk drives. The SCSI bus must be electrically terminated on both ends of the bus. With some controllers and devices, the termination can be automatic. Controller cards are usually terminated because they are at the end of the internal SCSI bus. When the SCSI bus must connect to external disk drives, the terminators on the controller card are disabled or removed. The last disk drive on each end of the SCSI bus (often the cable) must have termination enabled. If it is not enabled, you commonly have input/output errors. A quick test of proper SCSI bus and drive operation is to perform a verification of the drive using the SCSI controller card diagnostics.

One trick to use when disassembling and reassembling PCs is to use a magic marker and write everything about a component on the component in an inconspicuous spot. For example on disk drives we write the number of cylinders, number of heads, number of sectors per track and the total capacity. We also make note for IDE drives of master or slave status, and for SCSI drives of the SCSI address encoded in the switches. Sometimes it is good to mark pin one position. This is especially true if it is not obviously marked on the component or cable itself. When we have bad components, we write *BAD* on the component in big, "slap you in the face" letters. This can save so much time later when sorting frantically through old components while trying to salvage a system.

FLOPPY DRIVES

Similarly to fixed disk drives, the floppy drives mount in a 5.25-inch or a 3.5-inch drive bay slot. They also bolt in from the side. They can be mounted flat or vertical but not upside down. (See Table 2.2.)

Floppy drives are connected through a 34-pin cable to the floppy drive controller on the main logic board or the disk controller board. The 34-pin cable carries both 8 bits of data and the control signals for the floppy drive.

Table 2.2 *Floppy drive characteristics and capacities*

Type of Density	Double Density - DD	High Density - HD	Double Density - DD	High Density - HD	Extra-High Density - ED
Tracks Per Inch	48	96	135	135	135
Bits Per Inch	5,876	9,869	8,717	17,434	34,868
Disk Size and Capacity	5.25" — 360 KB	5.25" — 1.2 MB	3.5" — 720 MB	3.5" — 1.44 MB	3.5" — 2.88 MB

One key control signal is the drive select signal. There are four drive select lines in the 34-pin cable, making it possible to attach four floppy disk drives to a PC. (In the early days of PCs, I had the ultimate disk storage with four 360 KB diskette drives running off a single floppy controller. Two were internal drives and two were external drives.) The diskette drives use only drive select 1 line to activate operation while the PC signals the drives using drive select lines 1 or 2. Originally this configuration was chosen to ensure that every floppy disk drive could be plugged into any PC without performing a special jumper configuration. To make this work, the floppy disk drive control cable was twisted between the first and second drive connector. In this manner floppy drive A at the end of the cable was activated by the PC's drive select 1 signal coming into its drive select 1 signal line. Floppy drive B in the middle of the cable was activated by the PC's drive select 2 signal which also came into its drive select 1 signal line. The twist permitted the floppy drives to use drive select signal line 1 while the PC used drive select signal line 1 to activate floppy A and drive select signal line 2 to activate floppy drive B (see Figure 2–10).

Figure 2–10   *Floppy drive connector configuration*

The floppy drive signal and control cable connects to the floppy drive using either an edge connector or a push-pin style connector. Pin one on the edge connector is near a slot cut into the edge connector on the pin one side. This slot fit a cable key in the early floppy drive cables, ensuring pin-one-to-pin-one connection. Floppy cables installed backwards (that is, pin one to pin thirty-four) cause the floppy drive light to come on and stay on when the PC is first powered on. Any floppy in the drive has all its data corrupted and is not fixable.

The 5.25-inch floppy drives use the edge connector for the data and control cables, while the 3.5-inch drives use push-pin cables. The 5.25-inch drives also use the standard 5-volt and 12-volt disk drive power connector. The 3.5-inch floppy drives use a special four-pin power connector to provide the drive with 5-volt power. See Figure 2–11.

This connector is easy to plug in one pin to the left or right, shorting the 5-volt power lead directly to the chassis ground. In this case the PC cannot power up, or the power cable catches fire. In either event, you know immediately that something is wrong.

Figure 2–11
Floppy power connector

CD-ROM DRIVES

CD-ROM drives are IDE or SCSI drives. Most common CD-ROMs are IDE drives that install and uninstall like IDE fixed disk drives. They have a 5.25-inch form factor and fit neatly into a half height 5.25 drive bay slot. CD-ROMs are set typically as slave drives. In most cases they can be installed on the same IDE interface as an IDE fixed disk drive. But there has been at least one occasion where the fixed disk drive did not work in that configuration. When two IDE controllers are available on the PC's main logic board, typically the fixed disk drives are on one IDE interface and the CD-ROM is installed on the other IDE interface.

In addition to the standard power connector and the IDE data and control signal cable, CD-ROMS have an audio output cable that is tied directly to the PC's sound card. This audio cable permits playing music CDs just as with any music CD player.

Other high-density storage drives, such as Jaz and Zip drives, are installed in a fashion similar to the CD-ROM drive: they bolt into a 3.5-inch drive bay slot or a 5.25-inch drive bay slot. The power connection is a standard 5-volt and 12-volt power connector. Data and control functions run through an IDE interface. It is possible to have in any PC more than two IDE controllers and thus to support more than four IDE devices.

Power Supply

The power supply must sometimes be removed to remove the main logic board. It may be in the way or it may simply provide more maneuvering room during main logic board removal. Typically, four bolts on the rear of the supply hold the power supply in place. They bolt through the chassis to hold the supply in place. Sometimes two slots on the bottom of the supply slide into slots on the chassis to further secure the supply. See Figure 2–12.

Once unbolted, the power supply slides out of the chassis. To finish the removal, unplug the wires connecting the supply to the main logic board, the disk drives, the PC's front panel, and the AC Power switch. See Figure 2–13.

Reinstallation of the power supply is performed after the main logic board has been installed.

Figure 2–12 *Power Supply*

Figure 2–13 *Power supply cable connections*

Brand name PC manufacturers have custom-built power supplies. These supplies are designed to fit into the brand name designer chassis enclosures. Such power supplies fasten into the PC in lots of different ways. Removing them is quite challenging. However, remember when you feel the need to get out the big screwdriver and begin prying, reexamine the chassis more closely to find that hidden bolt. We promise that it is there somewhere.

CPU Chip

The Central Processing Unit (CPU) chip is typically mounted on the main logic board. It is inserted into a zero insertion force (ZIF) socket. Sockets are identified according to the number of pins they have. Older sockets are Socket-5 and newer ones are Socket-7. See Figure 2–14. The latest Intel chips are installed using a special circuit card technology called a Slot-1 cartridge.

This cartridge contains the CPU chip, level 2 cache, and power regulation components matching the chassis power to the power used by the CPU chip.

Figure 2–14 *Intel Socket-5 chip*

CPU chips are matched to the main logic board by the type of socket, the power regulation provided, and the clocking speed the main logic board provides. Chips are inserted into the ZIF socket with the chip's pin one matched to the socket's pin one. In Figure 2–14, the chip has the chip's pin one on the upper right of the figure. Notice the beveled corner of the chip and the pins beveling across the inside corner of the chip's pin area. In some sockets like the one used by our Intel chip, the pins are offset so that misinsertion is not possible. With older sockets it is possible to insert the CPU chip incorrectly. If inserted incorrectly and powered on, very bad things happen necessitating almost certain chip replacement. See Figure 2–15. Notice the upper left corner has the pin sockets beveled across the corner in comparison to the remaining corners. Pin one is in that corner.

Figure 2–15 *Socket-5*

Pin one of the chip is usually marked by a dot on the chip or a beveled corner on an otherwise very square or rectangular chip. If you are reading the writing on the chip, pin one is typically on the upper left corner of the chip. There are similar markings around the socket on most main logic boards. Also, the socket pin one is on the same side as the ZIF lever. In Figure 2–15, it is opposite the hinged part of the lever.

Slot-1 Intel chips are easier to install because they ride on a cartridge-enclosed circuit board. The board is keyed to the Slot-1 socket so that it cannot be installed incorrectly.

All CPU chips require cooling. This is accomplished by an oversized heat sink resembling the twin towers of the World Trade Center in New York City or by some kind of cooling fan that fastens to the CPU chip or Slot-1 cartridge.

If an oversized heat sink is used to cool the chip, a fan usually blows air constantly across the heat sink. See Figure 2–16.

CPU fans fail often and are one of the most frequently replaced PC components. They are clipped on to the chip, screw mounted on the chip, or sometimes glued to the chip. The CPU fan is a heat sink and fan combination. The fan uses screws to attach to the heat sink so it may be possible to leave the heat sink and just replace the CPU fan itself. The CPU fans have a power jumper cable that permits them to vampire tap into a disk drive power cable and use part of its 5-volt power to run the fan. Failing CPU fans make lots of noise. When you find a noisy PC it is most likely a CPU fan failing.

Figure 2–16 *CPU and CPU Fan*

Random Access Memory

Random Access Memory (RAM) is installed in sockets on the main logic board. RAM comes in a variety of electronic types and mechanical mounting styles. These are summarized in Table 2.3.

Table 2.3 *Common RAM Types*

RAM Type	Number of Pins	Single In-line Memory Module (SIMM) or Dual In-line Memory Module (DIMM)
Static RAM – Level 2 Cache	NA	Chip Packages
Dynamic RAM	30	SIMM
Fast Page Mode RAM	72	SIMM
Extended Data Out (EDO) RAM	72	SIMM
Synchronous Dynamic RAM	168	DIMM

RAM must be matched to the main logic board. Main logic boards support specific types of RAM. If the correct RAM is not used, the PC doesn't see the RAM and it cannot be used. RAM is installed to increase the RAM capacity of the PC. RAM modules come in different capacities and speeds. The typical speeds of RAM range from 60 nanoseconds to 80 nanoseconds. They are slower than the static RAM chips used in level 2 CPU cache. The level 2 CPU cache static RAM chip speeds vary from 10 nanoseconds to 20 nanoseconds. See Figure 2–17. The level 2 CPU cache makes it possible to use the slower dynamic RAM for main memory because it acts as an intelligent cache buffer between the slow RAM and the hyper-fast CPU.

Figure 2–17 *RAM modules*

In Figure 2–17, the top module is a 168-pin DIMM package, the middle module is a 72-pin SIMM package, and the bottom module is a 30-pin SIMM package. These plug into specific slots on the main logic board. Sometimes the order that the packages are plugged in determines whether the CPU chip can see the RAM. These topics will be discussed further in Chapter 5.

SIMMs and DIMMs are keyed so that they cannot be inserted into the main logic board sockets or clips incorrectly. If inserted incorrectly, the clips would likely break, necessitating a main logic board replacement or a chewing gum or super glue fix. Yes, I did say chewing gum. It is nonconductive and sets into a hardened, nonremovable (but dissolvable) patch.

Device Controllers and I/O Cards

PCs interface to peripherals today using option cards. These cards plug into bus connectors on the main logic board. The main logic board bus is commonly a combination of an Industry Standard Architecture (ISA) 16-bit bus and the newer Peripheral Component Interconnect (PCI) bus. Option cards installed in the ISA bus usually have hardwired interrupts (Interrupt ReQuest – IRQ) and input/output port addresses. PCI cards are plug-and-play with interrupts (IRQs) assigned when the PC first starts. Input/output controller cards can share IRQs. Installing such controller cards can be as simple as inserting the card into the appropriate bus connector, attaching external cables and restarting the PC. If resource conflicts develop in the PC, the installation process can become quite time-consuming. When replacing device controllers and I/O cards, it is a good policy to first document the existing hardware configuration and make note of any special hardware driver programs used. This can help you get back to an operating configuration in the event that the component replacement changes resource allocations for the worse. In the new Windows 95/98 machines, the control panel permits printing out all system settings for specific hardware configurations. For further detail on ISA and PCI cards, see Chapter 5.

MODEMS

Modems are installed on serial communications ports. While it is possible to have more than four COM ports in a single PC, most modems are installed on either COM1, COM2, COM3, or COM4. Typically the main logic board has both COM 1 and COM 2 hardware incorporated into it. Thus internal modem cards should be installed on COM 3 or COM 4. COM 3 shares IRQ 4 with COM 1 and COM 4 shares IRQ 3 with COM 4. The I/O port addresses differentiate COM 1 from COM 3 and COM 2 from COM 4. When installing a modem, make sure that it does not conflict with any of the main logic board serial ports. Modems most often plug into the ISA bus slots. Some modems are plug-and-play even when they plug into ISA bus slots. It is easier to disable their plug-and-play capabilities than to install them as plug-and-play devices. Once the physical installation is complete, the operating system must have drivers and software to complete the process. Windows sometimes automatically finds the new hardware but this is not always reliable.

Typical COM port settings are:

- COM1 — IRQ 4 and PORT — 3F8
- COM2 — IRQ 3 and PORT — 2F8
- COM3 — IRQ 4 and PORT — 3E8
- COM4 — IRQ 3 and PORT — 2E8

Uninstalling modem cards requires disconnecting phone and line cables, removing drivers and software, unbolting the cards, and pulling them out of their bus slot. Installation is the reverse process. Be sure that the cables to the phone and line are plugged into the correct modem ports. If not, the modem fails to work correctly.

SOUND CARDS

Almost all PCs today have some sound card installed. These cards emulate a SoundBlaster sound card because SoundBlaster dominated the PC sound card market in its infancy. Sound cards are typically ISA bus cards. They require several I/O port addresses, a Direct Memory Access (DMA) channel setting and sometimes more than a single IRQ setting. Ensuring there are no conflicts with other devices is the most difficult problem with installing sound cards. The sound cards provide high-quality output and permit both microphone and line inputs. The inputs permit creation of sound files on the PC from speaking or other sound sources. Microphone input is becoming increasingly important as better speech-to-text software comes to market. Sound cards also support game controller or joystick hardware. Some cards have connectors for CD drives and these are usually found when purchasing a multimedia kit.

Typical sound card external connections are a 15-pin "D" shaped connector for the joystick, and minijack connectors for sound output (2 channel stereo or more recently 4-channel surround sound), microphone input and line input. See Figure 2–18. Some types of cards also have connectors for other devices, like CD drives. Uninstalling a sound card is as simple as dis-

Figure 2–18
Sound Card

connecting the external cables, unbolting it from the PC chassis, and removing it from its bus slot. Installation is the reverse process.

During installation be sure that the correct minijack is plugged into the socket. There has been more than one occasion when we have repaired a sound card by just moving minijack plugs.

LAN CARDS

Home PCs do not have Local Area Network (LAN) cards as yet. However, with lowering prices and multiple PCs in a single household, they will have a LAN in the near future. Business PCs are largely LAN attached. There is nothing special about LAN cards from a PC hardware viewpoint. They act like any other I/O controller card. From a PC software viewpoint, they are quite problematic. Once a LAN card is installed, the PC can grind to a halt while talking with other network devices. It is best in this case to keep the logical network connections or drive letter mappings for any single PC to a minimum (a very, very few).

Most LAN cards are Ethernet LAN cards. Some new cards will be Asynchronous Transfer Mode (ATM) cards. There remains a niche token ring LAN market as well.

The external connection for a LAN card is generally a MOD-8 (sometimes called an RJ-45) connector with unshielded twisted-pair wiring running into a wiring hub. The MOD-8 connectors can have special mechanical configurations to differentiate them from RJ-45 telephone connectors.

Uninstalling requires disconnecting the external cable to the LAN wiring hub, unbolting the board and removing it from its main logic board bus slot. The reverse process physically installs the board. Once installed the fun begins. Now the LAN software must be configured so that the LAN board talks to the other devices on the network. We discuss this more later. LAN cards are discussed in more detail in Chapter 8.

SCSI CONTROLLERS

Small Computer System Interface (SCSI) controllers are used to connect high-capacity fixed disk drives, Zip drives, tape drives, Jaz drives, rewritable Digital Versatile Disk (DVD), rewritable CD-ROM drives and some scanners to the PC.

The disk controllers are commonly used to implement Redundant Arrays of Independent Disk (RAID) drives configurations. Some SCSI controllers provide hardware RAID support, while others let Windows NT software provide the RAID capabilities for the disks attached. SCSI controller cards have both internal and external ports. They can provide a single or multiple SCSI bus connections. Each separate bus must be electrically terminated at each end of the bus. The controller boards usually have terminations installed because the most common configurations involve only internal SCSI drives.

Each device on the SCSI bus is assigned a SCSI Target ID. ID seven has the highest SCSI bus priority. As a result, it is typically assigned to the SCSI bus controller card. ID six is the second highest priority. If two SCSI bus controller cards are on the same SCSI bus, then the second card uses ID six. Disk drives are installed starting at ID 0. CD-ROM drives can be installed at ID 3. Depending on the bus, more than eight IDs can be used. For a review of the types of SCSI devices, refer back to Chapter 1.

Uninstalling a SCSI card requires disconnecting both internal and external SCSI cables, and, when appropriate, the floppy disk cables, unbolting the card from the chassis, and removing it from its main logic board bus connector slot. Early SCSI controller boards were ISA bus boards. Newer boards are PCI slot boards. The SCSI boards have onboard ROM that sets up the attached fixed disk drives. This ROM configures the SCSI bus operation by setting parameters like transfer speed and synchronous transfer operation. It also contains programs for low-level formatting of the SCSI disk drives and for verifying the surface integrity of the drive, making it an excellent diagnostic tool. The ROM occupies an upper memory block address range and can have no conflicts with other devices installed in the upper memory area.

Reinstallation is the reverse process. Particular attention should be paid to SCSI bus terminations during installation to ensure that the SCSI controller operates smoothly once installed.

VIDEO CAPTURE CARDS

Increasingly, PCs are capturing and displaying video information, whether it is a video feed off the Internet or video camera input to still pictures for video telephony. Video capture cards provide inputs for video feeds off of small CCD video cameras or from normal VCR and camcorder inputs. They have software that translates the raw video input into compressed video or still picture files for storage on the PC's fixed disks. Video capture capability may be incorporated into the display controller card. ATI produces such a card, the ATI All-In-Wonder-Pro display controller.

Video capture cards like 3Com's big picture card share IRQ's with other I/O devices. Uninstalling them requires disconnecting them from an external camera connection, unbolting them from the chassis, and removing them from their PCI bus slot. Installation is the reverse process. The major difficulty is finding an IRQ to share with other devices installed in the PC. A good one to choose is IRQ 9.

Common PC Reassembly Mistakes

When reconnecting cables, how must each connector having pins numbered from 1 to 9, 1 to 25, etc., be mated with the opposite gender connector? To which pin does pin one on the first connector match-up to on the second connector? You remembered—pin one connects to pin one. Now it is a simple matter of finding which pin is number one. Let's review the ways for identifying pin one. They are:

- Check for the colored wire on each cable. Pin one is on the end with the colored wire.
- Most connectors have the pin numbers written on them. Look for the pin number on the cable connector.
- Often there is an arrow, a notch or a bar on the connector. This connector mark is on the pin one end of the connector.
- Cables with "D" shaped connectors can only mate with pin one going into pin one.
- The boards also identify pin one by having the pin number etched or painted on the board. The number is near the connector on the board.

- The boards with edge connectors have a slot cut into the edge connector nearest the pin one end.

- Push-pin connectors on disk controller boards have a single pin with a square solder pad. The other pins have round pads. The square-pad push-pin is pin one.

After installing the power supply, did you remember to reconnect the P8 and P9 connectors? Did the P8 connector go towards the rear of the computer and P9 towards the front? Did you remember to attach the key lock, turbo LED (light-emitting diode), speaker, and turbo switch wires to the motherboard?

Did you connect the disk drive LED cable to the LED connector on the fixed and floppy disk controller board?

Did you remember to connect the power lines to the disk drives?

As you connected the fixed and floppy cables to the stake connections on the disk controller board, did you match pin one to pin one, or did you reverse the cables?

When you installed the motherboard, did it mount flush with the chassis, or was it higher on one end than on the other? Run a finger down the outside edge to determine if the main logic board mount is flush? If you have a hard time installing your boards in the PC bus (that is, they are difficult to bolt into the PC because they stick up too high), then probably the main logic board did not properly seat.

Study Break

Finding Pin One

Let's try finding the elusive pin one. This is the pin that must match when connecting cables.

1. Dig around your computer workshop to find any extra cables used for connecting hard drives or floppies or just about any cable will do. Looking closely at the outside edge of the ribbon cable you will find red or blue, usually red, running the full length of the cable. The red edge of the cable means that pin one is located on that side of the connector. This means that side of the connector must match up with pin one on the device. Next examine the cable connector to see if the pin one side is marked with an offset slot, an arrow, or a number 1.

2. Dig around your computer workshop to find any extra floppies drives, CD drives, or hard drives lying around. If you turn them over, printed on the circuit board next to the connector should be a 1 or possibly a square pin. These both mean that pin one is located here. Now all that needs to be done is to connect pin one of the cable to pin one of the device.

A+ 2.3   Hardware Configuration Parameters

In the controller installation discussion, we alluded to the hardware configuration parameters that are used to install various PC hardware components. It is time to examine these in detail. While these hardware parameters are important today and into the near future, in the long term, hardware installation will become easier. PC hardware components may not reside in a single chassis but rather be connected through Universal Serial Bus (USB) hubs to the PC. When this transition takes place, the problems of finding free hardware resources are replaced by the problems of tuning the USB for high performance. There are always problems for us nerds to solve. PC hardware resources are:

- Input/output ports
- Interrupt ReQuest (IRQ) lines
- Upper (reserved) memory areas
- Direct Memory Access (DMA) channels.

The most critical resource is the device's input/output port assignment. This cannot be shared between devices. Next comes the IRQ line. IRQs can be shared. Virtually all PC hardware components have an I/O port and an IRQ assignment.

Some devices use the upper memory area for ROM or RAM swapping. Video display adapters are prime examples of such devices. Finally, a few devices use DMA channels for I/O transfers as well. Similar to IRQs, DMA channels can be shared. DMA channel sharing is rare.

PC resource assignments can be viewed in any Windows 95/98 PC using the control panel. By selecting control panel–system–device manager–computer–properties, Windows displays the PC's resource assignments by IRQ, I/O port, memory address and DMA channel assignment. Similar information is displayed for DOS PCs using the Microsoft Diagnostic program (MSD).

Common I/O Port Addresses

Each PC disk controller card requires an I/O address to exchange data with the CPU. The I/O address acts like mailbox for the board. These I/O addresses look like standard RAM addresses in lower memory, but they are not. Intel chips perform I/O operations using special I/O instructions. The I/O port addresses only function with the special Intel chip I/O instructions. The I/O address locations are duplicated by lower memory locations. Those lower memory locations store DOS and Windows software environment and other parameters but perform no I/O functions.

In contrast, Motorola CPU chips perform I/O operations using normal memory instructions and specially assigned memory locations. This is called memory mapped I/O.

The common I/O port addresses used in the PC are listed in Table 2.4.

Table 2.4 *Typical PC I/O port assignments*

I/O Port Address	Assignment
000-00F 081-09F	Direct Memory Access Controller
010-01F 0A0-0A1	Programmable Interrupt Controller
040-043	System Timer
060-060 064-064	Keyboard
061-061	Speaker
070-071	CMOS/Real Time Clock
0F0 – 0FF	Math Coprocessor
170-1F7	IDE Controllers
1F0 – 1F8	AT Hard Disk Controller
200 – 207	Gameport-Joystick Controller
208-20F	System Board Resources
210 – 217	Expansion Chassis
220-22F	Sound Blaster Card
274-277	I/O Read for Plug-and-Play Enumerator
294-297	PCI Bus
2A0—2A4	IBM Token Ring Network

Table 2.4 *Typical PC I/O port assignments (Continued)*

2E8—2EF	COM4 Serial Port
2F8 – 2FF	COM2 Serial Port
300 – 301	Sound Card MPU401 Emulation
320 – 32F	Hard Disk Controller—PC and XT
330 – 337	Bernoulli Box Controller
376-376	PCI IDE Controller
378 – 37F	LPT1 Printer Port
380 – 388	VGA Cards or old IBM SDLC Card
3A0—3AF	IBM—BSC Card
3B0—3BF	Monochrome Adapter—PC and XT
3C0—3CF	VGA Cards or old EGA Adapter
3D0—3DF	Color/Graphics Adapter—PC and XT
3E8—3EF	COM3 Serial Port
3F2 – 3F5	Floppy Disk Controller
3F6-3F6	PCI Primary IDE Controller
3F8 – 3FF	COM1 Serial Port
480-48F 4D0-4D1	PCI Bus
570-57F 5F0-5F7	Primary IDE Controller Alias
620-623 A20-A23 E20-E23	Sound card MIDI Port
776-776	Secondary IDE Controller Alias
778-77A	ECP Printer Port
CF8-CFF	PCI Bus
4000-403F 5000-501F	PCI Bus
D000-D0FF	VGA Board
E000-E01F	USB Host Controller
E400-E4FF	Adaptec SCSI Controller
E800-E87F	Fast Ethernet Adapter
F000-F00F	IDE Controllers

This table is not meant to be a comprehensive listing of all possible I/O port assignments. It is representative of a single PC system and some of the older IBM port assignments. It is interesting to note that available I/O addresses span the entire real mode address range of Intel CPU chips. This means that there is about 1 MB of available I/O addresses. We wonder when these will run out?

Standard IRQ Settings

The main logic board uses IRQ lines to get the CPU chip's attention. Every board must have an IRQ assignment. Some conflicts can cause boards to not operate properly. On PCs and XTs there are eight lines (0 through 7) and on AT class machines there are 16 (0 through 15). Typically, boards require you to choose IRQs 2, 3, 4, 5, 7, 9, 10, 11, or 12. IRQ 2 and IRQ 9 are linked to permit cascading interrupts from the secondary IRQ controller to the primary IRQ controller. The primary controller handles IRQs 0 through 7 and the secondary controller handles IRQs 8 through 15. Table 2.5 lists common IRQ settings.

Table 2.5 *Common PC IRQ assignments*

Device	Interrupt Line
System Timer	0
Keyboard	1
Programmable Interrupt Controller	2 (Used to cascade IRQs 8 through 15)
COM2 and COM4	3
COM1 and COM3	4
Hard Disk on PCs and XTs and LPT2 on AT Class Systems Modems	5
Floppy Disk Controller	6
LPT1 — ECP Port Sound Card (shared)	7
System CMOS — Real Time Clock	8
Networking, Video, Sound (shared)	9

Table 2.5 *Common PC IRQ assignments (Continued)*

IRQ Holder for PCI Steering SCSI Controller (shared)	10 or (A)
IRQ Holder for PCI Steering USB Host Controller (shared)	11 or (B)
IRQ Holder for PCI Steering Video Input Controller (shared)	12 or (C)
Numeric Processor	13 or (D)
Primary IDE Fixed Disk or CD-ROM	14 or (E)
Secondary IDE Fixed Disk or CD-ROM	15 or (F)

As more devices are installed into PCs, IRQ sharing has become a necessity. The new PCI bus PCs can share IRQs. USB connections can also alleviate the shortage of IRQs. However, our guess is that new performance-related problems will surface with USB bus devices. This continues the PC configuration challenge but with a new set of problems to solve.

Upper Memory Used by PC Hardware

Some PC controller cards require space set aside in the upper memory area (UMA) for buffering and ROM. Aside from video boards which have always used the upper memory area for buffering and ROM as well, the two types of boards that are most likely to use the upper memory areas are: LAN boards and fixed disk controller boards. The IBM token ring LAN adapter cards use an upper memory area for RAM buffering and another for ROM. The RAM buffering area can vary in size from 8 KB to 64 KB. The upper memory block locations used vary depending upon whether the token ring adapter card is set up as the primary token ring adapter or the secondary token ring adapter. The primary adapter uses address CC000 for ROM and D800 for RAM. Figure 2–19: illustrates common ROM and RAM swapping area assignments.

In the PC being used to write this book, some additional upper memory area assignments are:

- C800-CA7F—Adaptec SCSI Controller—Windows displays this address as 000C8000-000CA7FF.
- 10000-5FFFF—System Board Extension for the plug and play BIOS — This address is way off the scale in Figure 2–19. Windows displays this address as 00100000-05FFFFFF.

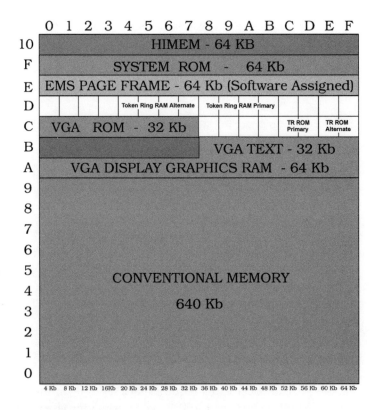

Figure 2–19 *Upper Memory Area*

- D0000000-DFFFFFFF—Pentium Processor to PCI bridge—This RAM is now way at the top of the memory address range of the memory installed in this PC system.
- E8000000-E8FFFFFF—ATI 3D Rage Pro and Pentium CPU to AGP controller.
- E9000000-E901FFFF—ATI 3D Rage Pro.
- EA000000-EA000FFF—ATI 3D Rage Pro.
- EE000000-EE000FFF—Video Capture Board Buffer.
- EE001000-EE00107F—Fast Ethernet Card.
- EE002000-EE002FFF—Adaptec SCSI controller.
- FFFE0000-FFFFFFFF—System Board Extension for the plug-and-play BIOS.

Interestingly enough, these upper memory addresses span the entire memory range in the PC. They are not restricted to the real mode memory addressing area.

PC Direct Memory Access Channels

DMA channels transfer data between a controller board and the PC's RAM by stealing memory cycles away from the CPU to perform the transfer. The value here is that the CPU can start an I/O operation, assign it to DMA (don't disturb me until you are finished), and then perform other tasks while the DMA channel handles the data transfer. Direct Memory Access channels are implemented by chips on the PC system board. These chips were fast for the original PC. Today they are slow compared to Pentium CPU chips operating at 400 MHz. A Pentium CPU running at 400 MHz can have the controller board buffering input/output data, interrupt the CPU, and tell it to transfer the data to RAM. It then transfers the data using software I/O instructions, and resumes what it was doing in less time than the data transfer could be performed by DMA. One type of device using DMA channels is a sound card.

Table 2.6 lists the PC's DMA channels and their use.

Table 2.6 *DMA assignments*

DMA Channel	Assignment
00	RAM Refresh Sound Card
01	Available
02	Floppy Controller
03	ECP Printer port Bernoulli Box
04	Direct Memory Access (DMA) Controller
05	Sound Card
06	Available
07	Available

When lots of I/O activity takes place, the CPU load skyrockets. Consequently, we find slower devices use DMA channels to reduce overall CPU load.

Study Break

IRQs

> Now it is time to view some of your IRQs. We are going to view the IRQ settings inside Windows 95/98 system information.
>
> 1. Click on the Start Button and drag up to settings. Then click on control panel. Inside control panel you find a system icon. Double Click the system icon and a window appears with four tabs. Then click on the tab Device Manager.
>
> 2. Device Manager will display all the basic information on the devices inside or connected to your PC. Expand one of the options, such as System Devices. One of the devices inside there is the System Timer. If you double click System Timer, it usually displays three tabs General, Driver, and Resources. If you click on the Resources Tab it shows the Interrupt Request 00. This corresponds to Table 2.5.

A+   2.4   I/O Cabling and Connectors

An important part of installing PC systems is the cabling. PCs use a variety of cables to connect to the peripheral components they support. These cables differ in the type of wire and the connectors used. Each cable is designed for a specific purpose. Over the next several years this will change. USB and other similar high-speed connections provide the capability to connect all PC peripheral components using one or two common wiring schemes. To achieve this, all communications to peripheral devices must be in digital form with the devices containing the electronics to convert the digital transmissions into the subsequent analog outputs. For example, there are USB speakers that receive sound information from the PC in digital form across the USB bus. They in turn transform that into amplified sound that plays over the speakers. The benefit here is that special speaker wiring is eliminated in favor of two or three digital USB connections.

USB ports were widely implemented on PCs in 1998. However, few USB PC components were available for purchase. In 1999, there will be a significant increase in USB PC components. These components will range from mice, keyboards and speakers to monitors and CD drives. The transition to USB operation should be completed in the year 2000. The USB is new PC technology for the new millennium.

Older technologies do not disappear instantly, they just fade slowly away. So let's look at some PC cabling.

Peripheral Port Connector Types and Cabling

Peripheral port connectors and cables are summarized in Table 2.7.

Table 2.7 *PC peripheral component connectors and cables.*

Component	Connector Description	Cable Description
VGA Display	Male 15-pin high-density "D" shaped connector	Shielded 12 to 15-wire round cable with a ferrite yoke. Length is about four feet.
Mouse	Male 9-pin "D" shaped connector or Male 6-pin Mini DIN connector	Unshielded 4-wire round cable about four to eight feet long.
Keyboard	Male 5-pin DIN connector or Male 6-pin Mini DIN connector	Unshielded 4-wire round cable about four to eight feet long.
Serial Port	Male 9-pin "D" shaped connector or Male 25-pin "D" shaped connector	Unshielded 9-wire or 25-wire round cable up to 50 feet long.
Parallel Port	Male 25-pin "D" shaped connector plugs into PC and Centronics style 36-pin connector plugging into printer.	Shielded 25-wire round cable up to 15 feet long.
Game or joystick port	Male 15-pin low-density "D" shaped connector	Unshielded 4-wire round cable about four to eight feet long.
Speakers	Male Mini-stereo audio plug	Shielded 2-wire round cable.
Ear Phones	Male Mini-stereo audio plug	Shielded 2-wire round cable.
Microphone	Male Mini-stereo audio plug	Shielded 2-wire round cable.
Modem	RJ-11 plug	Unshielded 4-wire "silver satin" or Category-3 twisted-pair cable.
Ethernet LAN card	Male Mod-8 plug Or RJ-45 plug Or BNC male "T" connector	Unshielded 8-wire twisted-pair Category-5 or Category-6 cable Or RG58 — 50 ohm coaxial cable.
Token Ring LAN card	Male 9-pin "D" shaped connector into the PC and IBM hermaphroditic connector or Mod-8 plug	Four wire IBM Type-1 or Type-2 shielded twisted-pair cable IBM Type-3 unshielded twisted-pair cable.
Video Camera	Male RCA plug or S-Type video connector	Shielded 2-wire round cable or S-Type connector cable.
USB Port	USB Connector	Unshielded 4-wire USB cable for 1.5 Mbps Shielded 4-wire USB cable for 12 Mbps From 2.5 to 9 feet long.
IEEE-1394 or FireWire Port	FireWire Connector	Unshielded 6-wire FireWire Cable.

Table 2.7 *PC peripheral component connectors and cables. (Continued)*

External Drives SCSI-I	Male 25-pin "D" shaped connector plugs into PC and Centronics style 50-pin connector plugging into CD-ROM	Shielded or unshielded twisted-pair 50-wire up to 3.0 meters long.
External Drives SCSI-II Fast SCSI	Male Mini-Sub-D 50-pin (miniature "D" shaped) connector	Shielded or unshielded 50-wire twisted-pair round cable from 1.5 to 3.0 meters long.
Internal Drives SCSI-I SCSI-II Fast SCSI	Male Push-pin 50-wire Ribbon cable connector	Unshielded 50-conductor ribbon cable from 1.5 to 3 meters long.
External Drives Fast-Wide SCSI Ultra SCSI Ultra-2 SCSI	Male Mini-Sub-D 68-pin high-density (subminiature "D" shaped) connector	Shielded or unshielded 68-conductor round cable 1.5 meters long.
Internal Drives Fast-Wide SCSI Ultra SCSI Ultra-2 SCSI	Male Mini-Sub-D 68-pin high-density (subminiature "D" shaped) connector	Unshielded 68-conductor high-density ribbon cable 1.5 meters long.
IDE Drives AT-Attachment (ATA)	Female Push-pin 40-wire connector	Unshielded 40-conductor ribbon cable about 18 inches long.
Floppy Drive	Edge connector or female push-pin 34-wire connector	34-conductor ribbon cable about 18 inches long.

Each cable and connector type is designed to have specific electrical characteristics tailored to the type of electrical signals carried.

Using good cables can reduce PC problems. Some quality cable features are:

- **Molded ends** provide the best end connections. There are no screws, nuts, rivets, or plastic tabs to hold the hood pieces together. These pieces can become loose and lost, causing the connector hood to fall off. Molded cables have the molding material injected directly into a mold surrounding the solder joints between the cable wires and the connector pins and the strain relief plug. This forms a single solid piece locking all components together. This prevents failure when a cable is repeatedly flexed. Assembled cables permit the solder joints to strain under continued flexing, sometimes resulting in cable failure.

- **Gold-plated contacts** provide the best connections because gold is an excellent electrical conductor, gold prevents pins from oxidizing forming a resistive coating, and gold is soft and malleable, making better connections when cables are joined together.

- **End-to-end shielding** protects the cable from external electrical signals. Such shielding should be tied to the ground wire at one end to prevent voltage from building up in the cable. Grounding both ends is not good because that permits signal (ground) loops to occur. Unused wires should be grounded as well.

- The **number of wires** in the cable is often important. Parallel printer cables need all 25 wires. Some modems require more wires than others. Asynchronous modems use nine wires. Some direct connections from PC to PC can use as few as three wires.

- **Thumbscrews** make it easy to tighten the cable to the PC. This ensures that a cable does not fall off a connector.

- **Wire gauge** (or diameter) determines the ease with which electrical signals travel through the wire. The larger the diameter (smaller gauge number 22-24 versus 26-28), the better the electrical signal at the other end. Cables longer than 15 feet should have 26 gauge or better (22-24 gauge) wire.

Follow **cable length** specifications given by the device manufacturer. Staying within the given distances ensures that the signal quality is not degraded. Cables longer than the recommended lengths can be flaky and cause errors in data transmissions.

Serial versus Parallel Cables

Printers can be connected to the PC using serial or parallel cables. Serial cables transfer data to the printer more slowly than parallel cables. Typical printing transfer speeds are 9,600 bits per second to 19,200 bits per second. The maximum transfer rate for any standard PC serial interface is 115,200 bits per second. The advantage of serial cables over parallel cables is that serial cables can run up to 50 feet or more to connect into the printer. Parallel cables are only good for much shorter distances, around a maximum of 15 feet. Some of the distance advantage is lost today because printers are attached directly to a Local Area Network (LAN). Because LAN-attached printers can be located anywhere on the LAN, it is easy to lose your output. Data is sent to LAN-attached printers for printing via the LAN. In this case, the PC requires only the LAN connection to send data to the printer. LAN-attached printers can print data from any PC attached to the LAN.

Selected Cable Pin Connections

PCs signal over cables in one of two fashions. They either activate individual wires by placing voltages on them or they send messages across a single wire. Let me illustrate with two simple hypothetical cable configurations: a single-wire cable between two devices and a three-wire cable between two devices.

For the single-wire interface devices to communicate, they must send messages down the wire. A typical conversation could be:

```
Hello anyone there?
Yep, you got me!
Great, I have data to send.
OK, send it.
Here it is --- data.
The data was received OK.
Fine, that's all I have, good-bye.
OK, good-bye until next time we send data.
```

With such a conversation there needs to be only a single wire carrying the control messages and data transfer messages. Ethernet, USB, and FireWire work in this fashion. Their cables have eight, four, or six wires that form a bus similar to the single wire above.

More common PC cables have multiple wires with some wires assigned to specific functions. This would be like our second example, the three-wire cable between the two devices. In this cable, the sending device controls wire number 1, the receiving device controls wire number 2, and wire number 3 carries the data. The device conversation would be almost identical to the previous conversation, except that some messages would be communicated by pulling on wire number 1 or wire number 2. Let me illustrate:

```
Sending device pulls wire number 1 == Hello anyone there?
Receiving device pulls wire number 2 == Yep, you got me!
Sending device pulls wire number 1 == Great, I have data to
send.
Receiving device pulls wire number 2 == OK, send it.
Sending device places data on wire number 3, while pulling
on wire number 1. As transmission finishes, sending device
stops pulling on wire number 1. == Here it is --- data.
Receiving device pulls wire number 2 == The data was
received OK.
Sending device pulls wire number 1 == Fine, that's all I
have, good-bye.
Receiving device pulls wire number 2 == OK, good-bye.
```

In this case, each wire fulfills a different communications function. Serial or COM, mouse, keyboard, parallel, IDE, and SCSI interfaces behave in this fashion. These interfaces also have message exchanges controlling data transfers as well.

Keep in mind these types of operation as we examine some PC cable interfaces. It helps us understand their function, operation and how to troubleshoot and repair them.

DB-25 AND DB-9 FOR SERIAL COM INTERFACES (RS-232)

The DB connector notation identifies a "D"-shaped connector. Twenty-five or nine is the number of wires in the cable. PC serial ports use male connectors, making the serial cables use female connectors. PC serial ports use these cables to communicate with modems, mice, or other devices such as PDAs. Their use with mice has dropped since the PS/2 connector came on the scene and most of our modems are now internal.

The original serial interface was the RS-232 interface. RS stood for Recommended Specification. The latest revision of this serial specification changed the designation to EIA-232—EIA represents the Electronics Industries Association, the group that developed and that maintains the standard. This designation is a little self-promotion.

RS-232 serial interfaces have physical, electrical and logical properties. Physically they use a 25-pin or a 9-pin connector. Electrically they use voltage signaling with voltages ranging between plus and minus 15 volts. Logically, each wire in the interface is assigned specific functions, as identified in Figure 2–20. The interface has specific operating characteristics. These characteristics are:

- **Software transparent**—it does not care about what software drivers use it.
- **Cable length**—it was designed and specified to work over 50 foot cables.
- **Low-speed data transmission**—it was designed to transmit data at 20,000 BPS or lower. Speeds up to 115,200 BPS are common over short (4-foot) cables.

In one case data was transmitted at 56 KBPS for 114 feet and 6 inches over a standard RS-232 interface. When asked how they precisely determined the speed to operate over the 114 feet and 6 inch distance, they replied that they just kept shortening the cable until it started working.

The serial connector most commonly employed today is a DB-9 connector. This is a 9-pin "D"-shaped connector. It operates like our 3-wire interface above, with specific pins having specific functions. These functions were developed with the intent of communicating between a computer and a modem. The signal lines have their functionality described in that context. Figure 2–21 identifies the pins and pin assignments for both the 25-pin and 9-pin connectors. The DB-9 connector pin designations are on the inside of the diagram. The arrow indicates the direction of the signal. For example Request to Send (RTS) goes from the PC (Data Terminal Equipment – DTE) to the modem (Data Circuit-terminating Equipment—DCE).

There are a number of alternative serial cable configurations used to interface serial printers to the PC. Figure 2–21 illustrates one possible configuration. This cable connects a PC to a printer. Both devices act as DTE.

 The pin 2 and pin 3 functions are reversed between the original 25-pin interface and the more popular 9-pin interface. The 9-pin interface was first produced on PCs with the introduction of the PC-AT in 1985. It was necessary to preserve space on the rear panel bracket of the AT.

Figure 2–20   *RS-232 interface*

Thus, pin 2 and pin 3 must be crossed so that transmit data on one side goes into receive data on the other side and vice versa. Printers know they are printers and thus do not need to think that they are talking to a modem. However, PCs always believe that the serial interface connects to a modem. Consequently, they look for approvals to transmit by signals on Data Set Ready (DSR) pin 6, Data Carrier Detect (DCD) pin 8 (or pin 1), and Clear To Send (CTS) pin 5 (or pin 8). Of these approval lines, Clear To Send is the most important.

Printer cables make the PC think it has the requisite approvals to communicate by connecting the printer's Data Terminal Ready (DTR) pin 20 (or pin 4 on the 9-pin connector) to the PC's pin 5 (or pin 8 on the 9-pin connector), pin 6 (remains pin 6 on the 9-pin connector), and pin 8 (or pin 1 on the 9-pin connector). This is illustrated in Figure 2–21.

Null modem or modem eliminator cables are used to connect PC to PC. In this instance, the PCs both need approvals to communicate. One possible cable configuration is to mirror the pin 20 to pin 5, pin 6 and pin 8 connection in the serial printer cable. In this fashion, when a PC is powered on, it pulls on its pin 20 and signals approval to the PC on the other end of the cable.

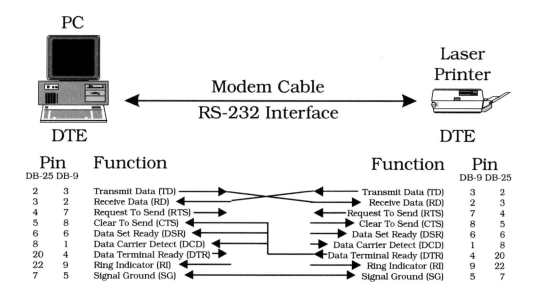

Figure 2–21   *Serial printer cable configuration*

LapLink and the DOS Interlink/Interserv programs use null modem cable configurations to communicate between two PCs at high speeds using the PCs' serial ports. EIA-232 pin functions are listed in Table 2.8.

Table 2.8 *Pin functions*

Data Leads	DTE PIN # for 25-Pin Connector	DTE PIN # for 9-Pin Connector	Abbreviation
Transmit Data	2 →	3 →	TD
Receive Data	3 ←	2 ←	RD
TIMING (CLOCK) LEADS			
Transmitter Signal Element Timing (DCE Source)	15 ←		TC
Transmitter Signal Element Timing (DTE Source)	24 →		(TC)
Receiver Signal Element Timing (DCE Source)	17 ←		RC
CONTROL LEADS			
Request to Send	4 →	7 →	RTS
Clear to Send	5 ←	8 ←	CTS
Data Set Ready (DCE Ready)	6 ←	6 ←	DSR
Data Terminal Ready (DTE Ready)	20 →	4 →	DTR
Data Carrier Detect (Received Line Signal Detector)	8 ←	1 ←	CD
Ring Indicator	22 ←	9 ←	RI
GROUND			
Signal Ground	7 ← →	5 ← →	SG
Protective Ground (Shield)	1 ← →		FG

PARALLEL PORT CABLES

Parallel port cables use a 25-pin standard "D"-shaped connector to connect into the PC. The PC port is a female port, making the cable connector a male connector. On the printer side of the cable, the connector is a Centronics style 36-pin male connector. The parallel port cables sometimes meet the IEEE-1284 specification. The pin specifications for this connector are shown in Table 2.9.

Table 2.9 Centronics parallel connector

DB-25 Pin Number	Printer Centronics Pin Number	Signal	Source	Comment
1	1	Strobe	PC	Valid Data on Pins 1 through 8
2	2	Data-1	PC	Data Bit – 0
3	3	Data-2	PC	Data Bit – 1
4	4	Data-3	PC	Data Bit – 2
5	5	Data-4	PC	Data Bit – 3
6	6	Data-5	PC	Data Bit – 4
7	7	Data-6	PC	Data Bit – 5
8	8	Data-7	PC	Data Bit – 6
9	9	Data-8	PC	Data Bit – 7
10	10	Acknlg	Printer	Data accepted by printer
11	11	Busy	Printer	Printer not ready
12	12	PE	Printer	Paper Error
13	13	Select	Printer	Printer on-line
14	14	AutoFeed	PC	Add carriage feed to each line
15	32	Error	Printer	Unspecified error
16	31	INIT	PC	Initialize Printer

Table 2.9 Centronics parallel connector *(Continued)*

DB-25 Pin Number	Printer Centronics Pin Number	Signal	Source	Comment
17	36	SLCT IN	PC	Select printer
18-25	19-30	Signal Ground		Grounds signals
	16	Signal Ground		Grounds signals
	17	Chassis Ground		Grounds to chassis
	18	+5 Volts	Printer	5-volt power

BNC LAN CABLE

The first Ethernet PC connections used coaxial cable. Similar but not identical coaxial cable is used for TV connections. The LAN coaxial cable was attached to the PC LAN card using push and twist BNC (Bayonet Neill Concelman or British Naval Connectors—we prefer Barrel Neutral Connectors—our invention) connectors. The coaxial cable was attached to the top part of a BNC "T"-shaped connector while the base of the "T" connected directly into the Ethernet LAN card. At each end of the coaxial cable bus was a 50-ohm terminating connector. The Ethernet coaxial cable bus was good for 187 meters (about 200 meters) with standard electrical signaling permitting multiple segments using repeaters or for 300 meters for boosted electrical signaling and a single segment. Such BNC cabling is designated as 10Base2 cabling. This is 10 million bits per second baseband (digital) transmission over a 200-meter cable segment. 10Base2 cabling carried the informal identification of cheapernet.

This cabling easily implemented small Ethernet networks. Its primary drawback was that any break in the cable caused the entire network to fail. In larger networks, this happened quite frequently, necessitating the move to the 10BaseT unshielded twisted-pair wiring and wiring hubs.

RJ-45 OR MOD-8 FOR LAN CABLE

Twisted-pair wiring currently dominates wiring used in facilities for both LAN and telephone wiring. Unshielded twisted-pair (UTP) wire in wide use is typically 19 to 26-gauge. Premise wire is 24 to 26 American Wiring Gauge (AWG) with two twists per foot. This wiring is designated as 10BaseT wiring—10 million bits per second baseband transmission over unshielded twisted-pair wiring. The unshielded twisted-pair wiring used can be traditional telephone wiring (Category-3 wire) or specially designed wire for higher transmission speeds (Category-5 for 100 MBPS and Category-6 for 155 MBPS).

Twisting of the wire pairs cancels out radiated energy from current flowing in any one wire by the radiated energy from the same current flowing back in the return wire of the same pair. Radiated energy is called electromagnetic radiation (EMR). Twisting effectively and inexpensively minimizes cross-talk between adjacent pairs in a multipair cable. Twisting also makes wire pairs less susceptible to external electrical noise (that is, EMR). The noise is coupled equally into each wire in the pair, causing the noise to be cancelled out when the wires are properly terminated. At voice frequencies, each pair appears to be balanced—that is, equal electrical energy is emitted from each wire within the pair to any point outside the pair of wires.

Wire can be either plenum or nonplenum cabling. Plenum cabling has Teflon insulation outside to prevent its catching fire at low temperatures and producing noxious and deadly fumes in the air plenums.

Unshielded twisted-pair LAN cables use special Mod-8 or normal RJ-45 connectors. They require two of the four pairs for communications. Most cables have all four pairs wired.

Unshielded twisted-pair cabling (UTP) is tricky to use because Ethernet and token ring use different hub-to-Network Interface Card cable configurations and different schemes to cross connect cables. Token ring and Ethernet use four wires, with each having a different set of four wires in the hub-to-NIC cable. Low-priced NIC and hub concentrators or Multistation Access Units (MAU) use RJ-45 connectors for UTP connections. This standardization allows a common cable pin configuration that works with Ethernet and token ring networks.

To determine the pin configuration for UTP, hold the RJ-45 connector by the wire with the clip down and the insertion end pointing away from you. The pin on the left is pin one. A standard RJ-45 connector has eight pins. UTP Category-3 cable uses a solid and striped wire color scheme. The wire pairs are colored: orange and orange/white; blue and blue/white; green and green/white; and brown and brown/white. This solid/striped combination identifies pairs of wires that must be twisted together in a specific sequence providing clean electrical signals. The pairs must match at the remote end of the cable to transfer the signal. Common cabling pin assignments or pin outs are:

- Ethernet 10BaseT connections use pins 1 and 2 and 3 and 6
- Token ring UTP connection uses pins 4 and 5 and 3 and 6.

- Creating a cable that works with NICs requires the following pin outs:
    - Pin 1—Orange/White
    - Pin 2—Orange
    - Pin 3—Green/White
    - Pin 4—Blue
    - Pin 5—Blue/White
    - Pin 6—Green
    - Pin 7—Brown/White
    - Pin 8—Brown

Cables with these pin outs are generally interchangeable between Ethernet and token ring networks. See Figure 2–22 for typical cable configuration.

One last word—there are two wiring schemes, an Integrated Services Digital Network (ISDN) T568A scheme or an AT&T T568B scheme. These T568A and T568B wiring specifications are used for cross-connect cables. T568A specifications use pair 3 and then 2, while T568B uses the same pairs but in the reverse order—2 and then 3. Both T568A and T568B wiring standards are compatible with 10BaseT and require no special configurations to

Figure 2–22   *Mod-8 connector*

work. As long as pin 1 connects to pin 1, pin 2 to pin 2, and so on, there should be no problems. To avoid facilitywide wiring problems, pick a single facilitywide wiring convention, T568A or T568B, and stick with it. If a building is wired to T568A, any moves, adds, or changes should be done with the T568A wiring. When T568A and T568B are mixed, wiring problems occur because they cross the signal pathways.

RJ-11 FOR MODEMS

Modems use RJ-11 modular telephone plugs connected to "Silver Satin" type telephone cable. "Silver Satin" cable runs two or four wires in parallel down a flat cable. It got its name from the silver color of the original cables produced for the telephone companies. Similar to RJ-45 connectors, RJ-11 connectors have pin 1 on the left side when viewed from the bottom of the connector. They have four wires that are often color-coded yellow, green, red, and black. Typical RJ-11 pin assignments are:

- Pin 1—Yellow
- Pin 2—Green—Tip
- Pin 3—Red—Ring
- Pin 4—Black

These wires can implement two analog phone line connections because each analog phone line uses only two wires. The center wires in the connector are red and green for the primary phone line and the outside wires are yellow and black for the secondary phone line. Modems expect to use only the center two pins, pin 2 and pin 3.

PS-2 MINI-DIN—MOUSE & KEYBOARD

The DIN connector designation comes from the Deutsche Industrie Normenauschuss (German Industry Standard, loosely translated) or Deutsche Institut fuer Normung, a German standardization body. The DIN and mini-DIN connectors are used to connect keyboards into the PC. The mini-DIN connector also connects PS-2 style mice to the PC. The original keyboard DIN connector was a 5-pin male connector. The mini-DIN connectors are 6-pin male connectors. They are round and keyed to prevent mis-insertion. See Figure 2–23.

Figure 2–23 *Pin out of a PS 2 Mouse socket*

The pin assignments are:

- Pin 1—Clock
- Pin 2—Ground
- Pin 3—Data
- Pin 4—Unused
- Pin 5—+5 volts
- Pin 6—Unused

IDE—INTEGRATED DISK ELECTRONICS

IDE (Integrated Disk Electronics or, alternatively, Integrated Drive Electronics) cables are parallel 40-conductor cables with push-pin connectors. They can run a maximum length of about 18 inches. IDE cables have connectors for the IDE disk controller and one or two connectors for the disk drives. IDE cables are also identified as AT-Attachment or ATA cables. The AT designates the original IBM PC AT (Advanced Technology—for its time) introduced in 1985.

SCSI—SMALL COMPUTER SYSTEM INTERFACE

Small Computer System Interface (SCSI) controller cards employ a wider variety of cables. The latest SCSI high-speed devices are beginning to use fiber optic connections. Such fiber connections are not discussed here beyond mentioning them at this point. The original external SCSI cables used an Apple-developed interface that connected to the SCSI PC controller using a DB-25 connector. The disk drive cables had a 50-pin Centronics-style connector. The external SCSI bus terminator was a similar 50-pin Centronics-style connector.

Internally, the SCSI cards used a 50-pin parallel cable with push-pin connectors. These cables could be quite long and could connect up to seven internal SCSI drives. We have some systems using these eight connector (one for the controller and seven for the drives) cables. The SCSI bus speed was 5 million bytes per second and the length was 3 meters or about 9 feet. PC products often identified these SCSI components as SCSI-I.

SCSI controllers were soon upgraded to higher transfer speeds. The bus clock speed was increased to 10 MHz. The resulting data rate was 10 million bytes per second because each clock cycle transferred a single byte of data. SCSI-II designated these PC SCSI components. Internal cables remained the 50-wire push-pin cables with 3 meter length. External cables changed to a high-density 50-pin "D"-shaped miniconnector. Cables providing SCSI-II to SCSI-II and SCSI-II to SCSI-I connections were used to connect newer and older external disks and CD-ROMs to the newer SCSI-II controller cards. See Figure 2–24.

These cables transferred one byte of data every clock cycle. They are also identified as "A cables." The next cable designation was a wide SCSI. Wide SCSI increased the SCSI transfer speed to 20 million bytes per second. This was accomplished using the same cables at a higher clock speed. So the wide designation only described the SCSI operating speed and not the actual cabling.

Figure 2–24
SCSI 50-pin
connector

In some cases a new 16-bit cable was used. This cable is also identified as the "P cable." Internally, this cable used 68-pin high-density "D"-shaped connectors. The cable itself was a high-density ribbon cable. Externally, the same 68-pin "D"-shaped high-density connector was used. The external cable was not a ribbon cable, but rather a round twisted-pair cable.

The next iteration moved the SCSI speed up to 40 million bytes per second. This was sold as fast and wide SCSI. Here the 16-bit interface cables were used with a higher bus speed to achieve the 40 M per second transfer speed. The bus speed was increased to 20 MHz with each clock cycle transferring two bytes of data. Provided there were proper terminations, it was possible to configure cables that were a combination of the 8-bit and 16-bit cables. The fast and wide SCSI cables were restricted to a shorter 1.5-meter (about 5-foot) length.

Current SCSI transfer speed is 80 million bytes per second. This is sold as Ultra-2-SCSI as if there would be no higher speeds. This is not very likely. This higher speed is provided by a new Q cable that transfers 4 bytes of data per 20 MHz clock cycle. Alternatively, the existing 16-bit P cable can be operated at 40 MHz clock speeds to provide equivalent SCSI transfer performance. For a review of the SCSI types and characteristics, see Chapter 1.

SCSI cables also vary depending upon the electrical signaling used. Most SCSI buses are single ended. This means that the electrical signaling is measured relative to the ground potential at each end of the SCSI bus. It is much more limited in the distance the electrical signals can travel, particularly at the higher SCSI clocking rates. Differential SCSI interfaces are not compatible with single-ended interfaces. A differential interface measures the voltage difference between two signals in the cable. Consequently, differential cables at low speeds can run at distances up to 25 meters (about 75 feet). The SCSI differential interfaces used high power and were expensive to implement. They were used for special configurations.

The newest SCSI electrical interface is the low voltage differential interface. The interface is integrated into SCSI chip sets. It supports high-speed operation with bus lengths up to 12 meters.

Study Break

Identifying Connectors

Lets try to identify classic connectors found on the PC. Below is the list of devices found in and around your PC. Find the connector that corresponds to the device using Table 2.7.

1. Ultra SCSI internal hard drive

2. Serial mouse

3. Ethernet LAN card

Answers:

1. Male Mini-Sub-D 68-pin high-density

2. Male 9-pin "D"-shaped connector

3. RJ-45 plug or BNC connector

A+ 2.5   Installing IDE/EIDE Fixed Disks and CD-ROMs

IDE and EIDE fixed disk drives—sometimes referred to as Ultra ATA (AT Attachment) drives—and CD-ROMs are easy to install. They bolt into a 3.5-inch or a 5.25-inch drive bay. Smaller drives require brackets to fit into larger bays. The brackets bolt to the drive and then are bolted to the PC chassis. CD-ROMs are 5.25-inch devices, so they must be installed in a larger bay. Fixed disks are mounted horizontally or vertically on one side. Once bolted into position the IDE drives have the data and control cable and the power cable attached. CD-ROMs have an additional audio cable that runs to the PC's sound card.

IDE drives are preformatted. All that remains to bring the new IDE fixed disk on line is to run the FDISK program and then the FORMAT program. Once completed, data and programs can be placed on the fixed disk.

Master versus Slave Designation

Some IDE data and control permit installing two drives on the same cable. In this instance one drive is designated as the master drive and one drive is designated as the slave drive. A jumper block on the rear of the drive has the master and slave jumper settings. When the settings are not clear, contact the drive manufacturer's website to obtain the appropriate documentation.

A good strategy is to keep CD-ROM drives and fixed disk drives on separate controllers. While it is possible to install fixed disks and CD-ROMs on the same controller, such configurations have on occasion not worked and could degrade slightly the PC's performance.

IDE Devices Per Channel

IDE controllers support two devices on each channel. A PC having four IDE devices would then require master and slave devices installed on both its primary and secondary IDE controllers. If additional IDE devices were installed in a PC, additional IDE controllers would need to be installed.

Study Break

Master-Slave Relationship

Let's try some basic EIDE configurations. In this instance we have a EIDE fixed disk drive and an EIDE CD drive that we would like to install. Our PC has two EIDE controllers, labeled controller A and controller B. Here are three different configuration possibilities; you must choose the correct ones:

1. Controller A EIDE fixed disk drive is set to master and controller B EIDE CD drive is set to master.

2. Controller A EIDE fixed disk drive is set to master and controller A EIDE CD drive is set to master.

3. Controller A EIDE fixed disk drive is set to master and controller B EIDE CD drive is set to slave.

Answers: Choice 1 and 3 will both work. Choice 2 is not properly configured, causing the drives to conflict.

A+   2.6   Installing and Configuring SCSI Devices

SCSI fixed disks are more tricky to install. The basics are similar to those for IDE drives. They are bolted into the PC chassis, and the cables are connected. There are both power and data/control cables to connect. In the process of cabling, the SCSI bus termination and device addressing must be set up. Similar to IDE drives, SCSI fixed disks come preformatted. This means that low-level formatting does not need to be performed. Once installed, the FDISK and FORMAT programs are all that is needed to prepare the SCSI fixed disk drive to accept data.

Low-level formatting of a SCSI drive is a way to fix corrupted drives. This low-level format is performed using the SCSI BIOS ROM on the SCSI controller board or SCSI diagnostic software provided with the SCSI controller.

Other SCSI devices like CD-RW drives and CD-ROM drives install similarly to SCSI fixed disks. They attach to the SCSI bus like any other internal or external device but with an added audio connection to the PC sound card. See Figure 2–25.

Figure 2–25 *SCSI CD-ROM connections*

The only difference from fixed disk installation is that SCSI CD devices require driver programs for proper operation. These software driver programs are special DOS drivers or are Windows drivers. SCSI scanners are similar to CD devices. They also require special driver software to operate. Scanners always install using external SCSI cables.

Bus Termination Basics

SCSI buses must be terminated at each end. Terminating resistor packs tie the bus signals to ground so their levels do not float and cause data and control errors. SCSI controller cards are typically terminated because they expect to be the last device on the bus. SCSI drives are terminated as well because they expect that they are the only device attached to the bus. This is not always the case. If the SCSI controller services both internal and external SCSI drives, then it is in the middle of the SCSI bus and needs to have the terminating resistors removed. When more than one internal or external SCSI devices are chained together, the devices at the end of the SCSI bus are the only devices terminated. The remaining SCSI devices must have their terminating resistors by-passed or removed.

SCSI terminations are typically connectors with internal resistor packs. Some terminators are active components while others are strictly passive. Both terminators dampen signal reflections on the SCSI bus. Active terminators are more resistant to noise, making the SCSI bus operation more stable. Active terminations are preferred.

SCSI Types

There are several types of SCSI buses. They vary in data transfer capabilities. The number of bits transferred and the clock rate of the bus determines SCSI data transfer speeds. These are the characteristics of each type of SCSI bus.

NARROW

The narrow SCSI bus transfers one byte of data per clock cycle. These early SCSI buses ran at 5 M per second. SCSI buses increased the clock rate to 10 MHz, improving transfer speed to 10 M per second.

WIDE

Fast SCSI was implemented first by increasing the bus clock rate from 5 MHz to 10MHz. This increased data transfer speed to 20 M per second. Doubling the bus width caused the development of 68-pin wide SCSI connectors.

Wide SCSI bus operation was accomplished by increasing the width of the data transfer from one byte to two bytes. Fast wide SCSI doubled the SCSI bus clock speed to 10 MHz and transferred two data bytes per clock cycle. Fast wide SCSI provided 20 M per second operation.

ULTRA WIDE

Similar to both fast and wide SCSI, Ultra SCSI achieved its 40 M per second transfer speed by either increasing the clock speed to 20 MHz or by increasing the bus transfers to 4 bytes. The advantage of a higher bus speed was its backwards compatibility with existing SCSI cabling and connectors. The drawback is that higher clock speeds shortened the SCSI overall bus length to 1.5 meters. To extend such SCSI buses, repeater devices were sometimes installed.

Device Addresses

SCSI devices must be assigned SCSI target IDs. The ID is the address of the SCSI device on the SCSI bus. The narrow SCSI buses can have seven devices and one controller attached. Wide SCSI buses can have fifteen devices and a controller attached. It is also possible to have multiple controllers on a single SCSI bus. With all SCSI buses, the highest priority ID is ID-7 with ID-6 being the next highest. Thus, the SCSI controllers are assigned ID-7. Table 2.10 lists the SCSI IDs in descending priority order.

Table 2.10 *SCSI IDs priorities*

Priority Level	SCSI ID Number	Device Assignment
Highest	7	SCSI Controller
	6	Second SCSI Controller
	5	DVD
	4	CD-RW
	3	CD-ROM
	2	Third Fixed Disk
	1	Second Fixed Disk
	0	Bootable Fixed Disk
	15	
	14	
	13	
	12	
	11	
	10	
	9	
Lowest	8	Scanner

The table lists some of the common ID device assignments. In multiple fixed disk installations, the additional IDs are assigned to each fixed disk drive. The fixed disk and CD-ROM devices have either switches or jumpers on them that determine their ID. These selections are made during device installation. ID conflicts cause error messages and cause the devices with conflicting IDs to not work properly. Each SCSI ID also has a subset of addresses called Logical Unit Numbers or LUNs. Every SCSI device has a unique SCSI ID plus a LUN. The LUNs range from 0 to 7. LUN 0 is the highest priority and for the most part LUN configuration is not necessary.

Cabling

SCSI cables are selected depending upon the type of SCSI controller and the SCSI fixed disk drives being attached. The biggest source of SCSI device problems is the cabling. The newer high-speed SCSI devices are particularly sensitive. Care should be exercised when removing and installing SCSI cables to assure that no pins are bent and that no cable is loosened from its connector. Cable testing is accomplished by using the SCSI controller disk software to verify all device connections and proper cable termination. Generally, high-density cables often look fine but they have poor electrical connections, causing unpredictable drive errors. Furthermore, these errors indicate that the SCSI disk drives had failed and that the cable was fine. We have seen experienced service personnel work for hours fixing bad SCSI disk drive problems that were really caused by faulty cables and had nothing to do with the drives at all.

Typical Switches and Jumpers

SCSI device switches and jumpers control the ID assignment for the device and whether the device terminates the bus. ID is generally set by a push-up or push-down switch with numbers in the center (see Figure 2–26).

Pushing up makes the ID number increase and pushing down does the reverse. Some fixed disks have jumper blocks that determine the ID number. Since the default for most fixed disks is set at 0, there are usually no jumpers installed in the fixed disk ID block. When two disks are installed the jumper needs only be set on position one. In this case it is relatively easy to guess the proper jumper setting.

Figure 2–26
SCSI Switches

Termination is set on by default. When a device is not at the end of the SCSI bus, the termination must be removed or bypassed. Here you are removing resistor packs or jumpers. Often the no termination setting is readily apparent without documentation. Note that on device boot up, the SCSI BIOS lists the devices and their IDs.

Study Break

SCSI IDs

The SCSI ID is a vital part of SCSI Bus configuration and can cause many installation and trouble-shooting headaches. In the previous section we described the common SCSI ID given to certain devices in the SCSI. Now you are given a list of devices that all must be on the same narrow SCSI bus. Your task is to give them their proper SCSI ID. Refer to Table 2.10.

1. CD drive

2. Bootable fixed disk drive

3. Second Fixed disk drive

4. Third Fixed disk drive

5. SCSI controller

Answers:

1. ID 3, 4, or 5

2. ID 0

3. ID 1

4. ID 2

5. ID 7

Remember you can not have duplicate IDs on the same SCSI bus.

A+ 2.7 Installing Common Peripheral Devices

Other PC peripheral devices are relatively easy to physically install. Most problems arise when trying to make them operate with Windows 95/98 software. This most often is a driver program issue. Obtaining the latest drivers from a manufacturer's website resolves most problems. On a few occasions a search is required to find the appropriate driver software because an older version is needed.

 One strange behavior that has been observed is that *some* IDE drives must be installed as SCSI devices. In fact, some Zip drives may require this configuration.

Keyboards and Mice

Keyboards just plug right in and work. Only when the keyboard has a built-in mouse would special drives be required. The mouse is different. Because of the variety of mouse types and manufacturers, driver software can be required to make a mouse fully functional. Logitech mouse drivers work with most all mice. So do the standard Windows mouse drivers. The Windows drivers do not provide any exciting mouse features like those provided by the Logitech mouse driver software. The wheel mouse being used on this PC works with both Logitech and Microsoft drivers, but the wheel function only works with its special driver software.

Video Card and Monitor

Video cards plug into the main logic board similar to other option cards. Newer video cards are Advanced Graphics Port (AGP) cards that must use a special AGP bus slot. This is similar to the old Video Electronics Standards Association (VESA) local bus slot. AGP slots transfer data at very high speeds. AGP boards use video memory differently from the older PCI bus graphics cards. All graphics cards require special driver software to utilize all their capabilities. When installed they start up in standard Video Graphics Array (VGA). This permits them to be used while installing their special Windows driver programs. See Figure 2–27.

Figure 2–27 *AGP video card*

Windows NT boots to a screen which permits booting into Windows NT in VGA mode as a diagnostic and recovery option in the event that the display controller drivers become corrupted. Windows 95/98 has a safe mode operation that performs a similar VGA boot option, enabling restitution of malfunctioning display adapter driver programs.

Monitors must match the display adapter refresh rate. Without a good match the display does not fill the screen properly. Displays can be too short or narrow, they can have a keystone (trapezoidal) shape, or they can have a tight girdle look (shrunk in the middle). Adjustments on the monitor can change the display scanning to make the screen fill out squarely and clearly. When the graphics board does not match the display's scanning rate, no amount of adjustment makes the display behave properly. When this happens, a monitor replacement or a display adapter downgrade usually resolves the problem.

Modems

Modems can be internal or external devices. Most modems are internal because they save desk space. Installing an internal modem is as simple as plugging it into the main logic board bus. If a modem is a plug-and-play modem, it is best to disable the plug-and-play feature (if possible) and set it to either a COM3 or a COM4 port. Modems installed on COM ports 1-4 work with virtually all communications software. If by chance the modem turns out to be on COM ports 5-8, AOL software doesn't see the modem. When the modem is on COM port 3 or 4, Windows software should install it automatically. This applies to Windows versions 95 and 98, but not on current versions of NT.

The modem then needs to be plugged into the phone line jack (and optionally a phone). Driver software, recognizing the modem manufacturer and sending setup commands to the modem, determines the transmission speed at which the modem connects. All modem setup commands contain the initial set of modem commands defined by the Hayes modems. These basic commands form the core of the modem command language. From there, two separate extensions to the modem command language have evolved. One followed the US Robotics (now 3Com) design and the other was used by Practical Peripherals and Cardinal modems. These command language variations cover the commands used to establish high-speed connectivity, error checking, and data compression functions. Fortunately, each manufacturer has default settings that make their modems perform optimally. These default settings are set into every modem using a standard Hayes &F (= restore factory defaults) command. Sometimes adding a standard Hayes command s9=1 (=set the carrier detect time to 1 millisecond) improves the ability of the modem to connect at high speeds. Also, remember to always get the latest drivers possible.

Study Break

Modem Ports

The DOS mode command can be used to determine the COM port assignments in a PC. Open a DOS Windows in Windows 95/98 and try:

1. MODE COM1

2. MODE COM2

3. MODE COM3

4. MODE COM4

The COM ports that are not installed should return "Illegal device name" or other similar error messages. The error messages vary with DOS and Windows versions.

A+ 2.8   **Upgrading Your PC**

Upgrading PCs is limited to a few basic component areas. Furthermore, the money spent to upgrade any one area should be less than $200. When the $200 figure is exceeded, it may be more practical to purchase a new PC than to perform the upgrade because a new PC would have all its components configured and tuned for optimal performance. An upgrade may only produce a minimal performance increase in a single area. The most beneficial upgrade to an old PC is increasing the RAM capacity and increasing the disk drive capacity. CPU upgrades are expensive and provide a marginal performance enhancement.

RAM

PCs today are sold with adequate RAM. Windows can run with little RAM, but when this happens it swaps data heavily between RAM and the fixed disk. There have been some Windows 95 systems sold with only 8 MB of RAM. This killed performance. It was easy to tell because the display screen refreshed slowly to the sound of the disk drive flogging itself to death.

Windows 95/98 requires a minimum of 32 MB of RAM for simple operation. If images and graphics applications are installed, more RAM is recommended. Most PC configurations would find 64 MB of RAM sufficient.

Upgrading RAM capacity is as simple as snapping in some new SIMMs or DIMMs. To upgrade RAM, first check the PC manual to determine the type of memory and the number of modules to install. Select the module capacity that, when installed, meets your minimum upgrade requirement—for instance, two 16-MB modules for a minimum of 32 MB. Selecting modules that meet your minimum capacity requirement ensures that if you must remove some RAM modules to install the upgrade, you still achieve your minimum RAM capacity. Note that SIMMs snap in at an angle while DIMMs push straight down.

Open the case and install the RAM modules in any open RAM SIMM or DIMM sockets. Power up the PC. During the Power On Self Test (POST), the PC should sense the added RAM capacity and display an error message stating "memory size mismatch." This is good because the PC found the added RAM. It then updates the memory size in the Complementary Metal Oxide Silicon (CMOS) setup memory and reboots. At this point no error message is displayed and your system RAM is upgraded.

If the RAM is not found, then install the SIMMs or DIMMs in the other main logic board sockets until the PC recognizes them.

Upgrading RAM is the most cost-effective upgrade for any PC. With the lower RAM prices we have today, it is a good policy to have at least 64 MB of RAM in any PC.

Fixed Disk

When thinking disk upgrades, most people think of replacing their existing disk drive. This is more difficult than just adding a second drive to an existing system. Most PCs have data and program files splattered across their fixed disk in a pseudorandom order. There is little thought given to organizing the data on the disk drive. This results in the disk drive becoming filled to capacity eventually causing Windows to malfunction because there is no space for swapping data to the disk drive.

A good strategy is to place all data in a special, distinct data folder. In this manner when a second disk drive is added to the PC, the data folder can be moved to it and immediately free up space on the primary disk drive.

A really good strategy is to install only Windows and Windows utility programs on the primary disk drive or disk drive partition. This partition size should be about 1 GB for Windows alone. The applications should be installed into a second partition and the data installed in a third partition. In this manner, Windows should have adequate disk space for swapping. This would make the system easy to upgrade because the applications or the data could be reinstalled or moved to the second disk drive.

Most users would find a 4 GB disk drive adequate for their Windows needs. Of course, disk drive capacity is scarce like water in a desert, not plentiful like beer in a bar. A disk drive upgrade is a worthwhile expenditure. Besides adding capacity, a disk drive upgrade can make migration to a new PC easy by providing a mechanism for moving the data files used from one PC to another. It can be particularly satisfying when a disk drive containing data is reinstalled into a new PC minimizing data transfer hassles.

Display

Display capabilities continue to evolve rapidly. A good display with 3D capabilities is important for image manipulation and games. Display upgrades are relatively painless when the correct driver programs are installed. Display upgrades are about the third most cost-effective upgrade to a PC that enhances performance.

Some graphics card upgrades are add-on boards, also known as daughter cards or boards. In this case upgrading can be somewhat more complex. For example, an ATI Rage graphics card can be upgraded with a separate 3D add-on card called Voodoo made by the 3D-FX company. The Voodoo card has been a leader in state-of-the-art 3D acceleration. It supports three different graphics Application Program Interfaces (APIs): Direct 3D, Open GL, and Glide, a proprietary API. To upgrade, the Voodoo card is inserted into a spare PCI slot and a passthrough cable is connected.

The voodoo card has two plugs on its outside. One is a traditional VGA-out connector, the other a VGA-in connector. The card comes with a jumper/passthrough cable. So to upgrade, the passthrough cable connects from the original 2D card VGA-out (this normally connects to the monitor) to the Voodoo card's VGA-in port, and finally to the monitor via the Voodoo's VGA-out port.

This type of upgrade is only an interim situation because new 2D/3D chip sets permit a single graphics card to create both types of displays. In this instance, upgrades would require replacing one graphics card with another.

Windows 98 permits installation of multiple graphics cards to drive multiple monitors. In this instance, the drivers make the monitors act like one super-wide display. Few PCs have such an upgrade because of the expense of the added monitor.

It reminds me of the days when I operated my PC XT with both monographic and CGA displays. Boy, was I cutting edge.

BIOS Upgrades

BIOS upgrades can be the cheapest to perform. They are done by updating the BIOS software installed in nonvolatile RAM (NVRAM). BIOS and other NVRAM upgrades can update the PC to more current plug and play operations. BIOS upgrades are not made to increase PC performance, but rather to solve hardware problems like Y2K compliance problems. Such upgrades are necessities and not niceties.

DETERMINING WHEN TO UPGRADE BIOS

When upgrading from one version of Windows to another (for instance, moving from Windows 95 to Windows 98), a BIOS upgrade may be required. We had a laptop that just would not run and recognize all its components under Windows 98 until the BIOS was upgraded. Determining if a BIOS upgrade is needed depends on exhaustion of other software upgrade alternatives. *If* all drivers are up to their latest revision, and the software still works improperly, then a BIOS upgrade is likely in order.

PROCEDURES FOR UPGRADING BIOS

BIOS upgrades are simple to perform. In the instance above, the PHLASH program and the new BIOS DAT file was downloaded from the PC manufacturer's website. The PC was booted into DOS, using a bootable floppy and the PHLASH program run. It found the DAT file on the floppy, determined the BIOS revision installed was older than the DAT file BIOS code, and updated the BIOS code in NVRAM. Once complete, Windows 98 installed without a hitch.

CPU

CPU upgrades are the least cost-effective upgrades. Because CPU upgrade chips cost so much relative to their impact on actual PC performance, these upgrades are really make-you-feel-good upgrades. Because the CPU is limited by the main logic board support chips, installing a faster CPU may have a 10% or 20% impact on PC performance. Such an increase is barely noticeable by humans.

CPU upgrades must be specifically matched to the PC's main logic board. Zero Insertion Force (ZIF) make popping out an old CPU a snap. Putting in the new CPU chip is equally easy, provided that no pins are bent in the process. A bent pin means no upgrade.

Slot 1 CPU cartridges are easy to replace. They are keyed and just slide on and off the Slot 1 connector.

In some cases no clocking adjustments are needed. The chip has different internal clock multipliers that function with current clock settings. In other cases, the system board base clock may have to be reset to match the multipliers of the new higher-performance CPU chip.

CPU chip upgrades do not necessarily mean that the BIOS must be upgraded as well. Generally popping in the new chip, adjusting the clock, and matching CPU chip voltages are all that is needed to complete a CPU chip upgrade, but it is always a good habit to check the manual to see if the MLB supports the new chip. Because CPU upgrades are not particularly cost-effective, in most cases it is better to purchase a whole new PC.

CPU Cache Memory

CPU cache memory can sometimes be increased. Such an upgrade is of marginal value because it has little impact on PC performance. CPU cache memory upgrade can only be performed on external level 2 CPU cache memory. Furthermore, cache memory operates with diminishing returns as the cache memory size gets larger. This means that a small amount of cache memory produces the greatest performance impact. Larger and larger amounts of cache memory provide much less performance improvement.

External CPU cache memory uses static RAM chips. These are especially sensitive to static electricity. Special attention should be paid to static when upgrading the level 2 CPU cache memory.

CPU cache memory upgrade requires adding or replacing static RAM chips on the main logic board. If chips are replaced, the older chips are replaced by faster, higher-capacity chips. Otherwise, more static RAM is added to empty sockets on the main logic board. Jumpers on the main logic board would then be changed to activate the additional level 2 CPU cache memory capacity. No special software driver or CMOS configuration changes are required.

■ Summary

This chapter described how to remove and reinstall PC components including disk drives, display cards, LAN cards, and more. The first section covered the parameters and replacement costs for typical PC components. The next section discussed in detail the procedures for adding and/or removing Field Replaceable Units (FRUs).

Hardware configuration parameters needed for installing a diverse set of PC components were covered in detail in the next section. Following the hardware configuration section, cabling and connectors for I/O devices were discussed. PCs use a variety of cables to connect to the peripheral components they support. The purpose and functions of these cables and differences in the types of wire and the connectors used was covered in detail.

Installation of IDE and EIDE fixed disk drives and CD-ROMs followed the cabling section. Installing and configuring SCSI devices was detailed in the following section.

Section 2.7 covered the installation of common peripheral components such as keyboards, mice, video cards and modems, which provided a good segue into the final section that covered upgrading your PC.

▲ CHAPTER REVIEW QUESTIONS

1. *What is the COM1 IRQ?*

   A. IRQ 4

   B. IRQ 2

   C. IRQ 3

   D. IRQ 7

   Answer: B. IRQ 4

2. *What is the COM2 IRQ?*

   A. IRQ 4

   B. IRQ 3

   C. IRQ 2

   D. IRQ 7

   Answer: B. IRQ 3

3. *What is the LPT1 IRQ?*

   A. IRQ 4

   B. IRQ 3

   C. IRQ 5

   D. IRQ 7

   Answer: D. IRQ 7 or none

4. *Identify the following connectors.*

   9 pin male

      Answer: serial port

   25 pin female

      Answer: parallel port

   50 pin Centronics

      Answer: SCSI connector

   6 pin DIN

      Answer: mouse or keyboard

   BNC

      Answer: LAN

   MOD 8

      Answer: LAN

   RJ-11

      Answer: Modem

   RJ-45

      Answer: LAN

5. *How is the SCSI ID set on a fixed disk drive?*
    Answer: Jumpers set the ID to SCSI ID 0, SCSI ID 1 or SCSI ID 2.

6. *Which ports on a PC should connect to a modem?*
    Answers: Serial Ports, COM ports, COM 3, or COM 4.

7. *Identify in Figure 2-28:*
    a mouse
    a monitor
    a system unit
    a printer
    a keyboard
    a scanner

Figure 2–28 *Question PC Components*

8. *You are using a modem. What two signals are required to accept information?*
    Answers: CTS and DSR or DCD and Receive Data.

9. *You power on your PC, the memory test runs displaying the amount of memory on the screen. What does this mean?*
    Answer: It identifies the physical RAM present in the PC.

10. *How many SCSI devices can be on a PC?*
    Answer: Seven for narrow SCSI buses or fifteen for wide SCSI buses.

11. *When selecting SCSI IDs what must be considered?*
    A. Each ID must be unique.
    B. Doesn't matter.
    C. All SCSI ID's should be the same.
    D. The SCSI controller should be on ID 0.
    Answer: A. Each SCSI ID should be unique. No SCSI IDs can be identical.

12. *Which pin is most important to remember when installing PC components?*
    Answer: Pin one—it must connect to pin one.

13. *IDE devices use a _____-pin cable.*
    A. 50
    B. 34
    C. 20
    D. 40
    Answer: D. 40-pin cable for IDE and EIDE devices.

14. *A VGA connector has how many pins?*
    A. 20
    B. 15
    C. 9
    D. 25
    Answer: B. 15 in three staggered rows.

15. *The most cost-effective PC performance upgrade is what?*
    A. Adding a new disk drive.
    B. Adding a new display monitor.
    C. Increasing floppy disk capacity.
    D. Adding RAM to increase size to a minimum of 64 MB.
    Answer: D. Adding RAM.

16. *SDRAM comes in what packaging?*
   A. 30-pin SIMM
   B. 72-pin SIMM
   C. 168-pin DIMM
   D. 20-pin chips
   Answer: C. 168-pin DIMM

Troubleshooting and Problem Resolution

▲Chapter Syllabus

A+ 3.1 Determining the Source of Problems

A+ 3.2 Troubleshooting PC Hardware

A+ 3.3 Diagnosing Error Symptoms and Problems by Subsystem

A+ 3.4 Troubleshooting Tools

A+ 3.5 Troubleshooting Procedures and Practices

This chapter describes how to diagnose and identify basic PC Field Replaceable Unit (FRU) problems. For definitions and characteristics of common FRUs, see Chapter 2.

Troubleshooting procedures using the system malfunction symptoms to identify common PC component failures are presented. PC troubleshooting requires identifying problems that fall into three key areas: PC hardware, Windows and applications software, and networks. Isolating the problem into one of these three areas is the first step in resolving PC malfunctions. Then more precise troubleshooting procedures can be applied.

This chapter discusses identifying the general malfunction area and then provides more detail on troubleshooting PC hardware problems.

Windows and application software, and networking problems are discussed in subsequent chapters.

Some fundamental guidelines for troubleshooting PCs are:

- Remember, every PC problem can be solved. The worst case scenario is to replace the PC. This guideline I learned from my ex-wife. Whenever we would argue, she would say "I will win!" and she always did.
- Make sure everything is plugged in and nothing has come loose. Check the power, display, phone lines, printer, network, and modem connections.
- Check external signs. Are the power lights on, do fixed and floppy disk drive lights flash, does the monitor come on, does the monitor display the boot program displays, is the PC making normal or strange sounds, do you smell something? Make notes of any special signs.
- Observe the POST diagnostics. Do they report any failures?
- Boot using a DOS floppy. Can you run DIR commands on all disk drives? Does FDISK indicate fixed disk errors? Can you run DOS network software?
- Check PC setup files. Are parameters correct? Have paths changed?
- Ask "Has anything changed?"
- Copy key data to backup diskettes, network, or tape.
- Disassemble the PC, clean it, reseat chips, and reassemble the PC.
- Check the nut behind the keyboard.
- Draw a picture of what connects to what. Write everything down. Try zeroing in on malfunctioning components.
- Verify working components.
- Reboot the PC by powering it off. Then, start again.
- Use any available test equipment to test components. Test equipment with identical working components, anything to verify power, or software diagnostic programs.
- Never guess. Just one setting out of thousands of possibilities is correct. The chance of hitting the exact correct setting is about the same as winning the lottery.
- Trust no one. You must fix the problem and no one will help you. Remember all PC error messages are lies.
- Observe like Sherlock Holmes. Which light comes on first, the fixed disk drive light or the floppy disk drive light? It is the fixed disk drive light.
- Wish for luck. You may need all the help you can get.

A+ 3.1   **Determining the Source of Problems**

How can a PC malfunction be quickly identified as a hardware, software or network problem? It is quite straightforward. Typically, key hardware component malfunctions are identified during the boot process by power on self-test (POST). The PC refuses to run in this case. The error messages produced are simple and obvious. At this stage, less debilitating hardware failures rarely occur. These types of failures can be spotted by simple diagnostics, programs that test the malfunctioning component, or by swapping the component with an equivalent component—the swap until you drop diagnostic approach. For example, FDISK reports that a fixed disk is unreadable, indicating that the disk itself is bad.

Software and hardware problems are manifest as Windows runs as missing VxDs and DLLs or as memory protection faults. These malfunctions are caused by incorrect driver programs for the installed hardware, or by users corrupting the software by making mistakes while using the PC. Often users install software that kills the correct Windows components, replacing them with bad software modules.

Network problems are the toughest. They can bring a PC to a grinding halt. Because networked PCs continually communicate with other networked PCs and because the network components run at a higher priority than other Windows components, they tend to stop the PC dead when the network fails. This is often hard to recognize.

Furthermore, Windows will recover from these network failures, but the time-out values are set very high so minutes may literally pass before the PC can be shut down and restarted. Sometimes the PC cannot be started because network connections cannot be made or network address conflicts exist.

Let's look in detail at the troubleshooting procedures for PC hardware components.

Study Break

Network Failure Impact

> To see the impact of network failures on PC performance, map a network drive to a drive letter and disconnect the LAN cable. This is done using the Windows Explorer.
>
> 1. Open the Explorer, expand the Network Neighborhood, find a server or a shared PC that permits you to map a drive letter to its shared drive, and map the drive letter. A drive letter should soon

appear under the My Computer icon in the Windows Explorer saying something like "DRD on Sam's PC."

2. Now click on the network drive icon to view the drive contents. How long did it take? Next click on a local drive icon. Disconnect the LAN cable from the LAN board in the PC. Now click on the network drive icon again to view the contents. Now how long did it take? Big difference.

A+ 3.2 Troubleshooting PC Hardware

Key PC components are those required for the PC to operate. They include the fixed and floppy disk drives; the main logic board with RAM, ROM, and CPU; power supply; keyboard; mouse; display adapter; and monitor. Without these components, the PC just does not run in a useable fashion. Other components are nearly as important today, including CD-ROM devices, modems, and network interface cards.

The PC will run without these, but without them the PC is less useable.

When troubleshooting these components, we are looking at a chain of components, starting with the power at the wall outlet. No power, no PC. Next is the power cord and then the power supply.

Finally, we move to the main logic board and the CPU, ROM, and RAM. If these components malfunction, you see nothing. Everything is dead and power on self-test (POST) diagnostics do not run. This is like having a person with a body but no arms and legs. They are at least able to talk, breathe, eat, circulate blood. They cannot do much else.

Power On Self-Test

The PC's power-on self-test (POST) is your primary PC hardware component-troubleshooting tool. The PC's ROM stores the POST diagnostics. They are the first programs that run when the PC boots. The POST diagnostics are loaded into the first bank of RAM to run. Without some functioning RAM, the only error indications from the POST diagnostics is beeps output to the PC's speaker. These are the audio error codes described shortly.

When there is functioning RAM, the POST proceeds to run. It displays an opening screen identifying the PC components it detected and permits entering the CMOS setup program by striking the keys displayed. See Figure 3–1. In Figure 3–1, the F2 key enters the setup program. POST tests the basic

```
PheonixBIOS 4.0 Release 6.0
Copyright 1985-1998 Pheonix Technologies Ltd.
All Rights Reserved

DELL Inspiron 7000 A366LT BIOS A00    (031A)

CPU = Pentium II 366 MHz
0640K System RAM Passed
0127 Extended RAM Passed
0256 Cache SRAM Passed
System BIOS Shadowed
UMB upper limit segment address: EB98
Mouse Initialized
Fixed Disk 0: IBM-DCYA-214000
DVD-ROM: Toshiba DVD-ROM SD-C2202




Press (F2) to enter SETUP
```

Figure 3–1   *CMOS Boot Display*

functioning of the key PC components—the CPU, RAM, floppy and fixed disk drives, the keyboard, and the display controller. The results of these tests are displayed on the PC's monitor in text format. Errors reported here identify a serious hardware problem because these tests are not comprehensive tests of any component.

For example, the POST RAM test verifies the amount of RAM installed in the PC and stored as a parameter in the NVRAM setup parameters. When there is a RAM mismatch, then POST reports that the RAM size is incorrect, adjusts the size to the new size, and causes the PC to reboot. Sometimes, RAM can be malfunctioning and pass the POST RAM test. HIMEM.SYS performs a much more thorough test. It will fail RAM when there are memory speed mismatches that often pass the POST RAM test.

Audio Beep Error Codes

Audio beep error codes are used to signal critical system errors when the PC's system board cannot display them. The actual audio beeps vary depending upon the BIOS used on the system board. The manual accompanying the board or the PC lists the beep codes and their meaning. Some of the original IBM PC beep codes are still used by system boards. These codes are:

No beep, nothing	Power supply failure or not plugged in
Continuous beep	Power supply failure
Repeating short beep	System board failure
1 long beep, 1 short beep	System board failure
1 long, 2 short beeps	Failure or lack of display adapter
1 short beep, blank screen	Missing or failed display adapter/cable
1 short beep, no boot	Floppy drive adapter failure

Because today each PC manufacturer is different, there is no guarantee that any particular system implements its beep in the same way as they were implemented by the original IBM PC.

However, all beep codes are similar. You can infer that the most probable cause of a beep code is bad RAM because there is power to the system board (enough to beep the speaker and run the ROM POST program), but the POST program cannot be run. Because it must run from RAM, the RAM is most likely bad. The beep code signals this. It is rare to encounter a system that halts and beeps. RAM today is very reliable, so the POST typically runs to completion.

Video Error Messages

POST displays video error messages. These messages are text error messages identifying the specific hardware component error. The components are those that are needed by DOS to boot the PC. Such components include:

- Random access memory (RAM)
- Serial ports on the main logic board
- Parallel ports on the main logic board
- IDE controllers on the main logic board
- Keyboard
- Floppy disk controller

Commonly, there are no error messages for failure of the CPU or the cache memories. The rationale here is direct; when they malfunction no programs run. The system is dead.

Video errors are in simple English indicating the error message rather than some cryptic code. A keyboard error states "Keyboard missing or keyboard failure" as an example. Unlike on early PCs, error codes today attempt to be self-descriptive.

IBM Numeric Error Codes

In 1981, the original IBM PC provided numeric error codes to identify component malfunctions. These error codes were a holdover from the "close to the vest" operation of IBM mainframe computers. They made knowledge of such numeric error codes essential for troubleshooting and repairing PCs. These are unnecessary today but are provided here for reference purposes. Some original IBM PC error codes are:

```
101     = Motherboard Failure
109     = Direct Memory Access Test Error
121     = Unexpected Hardware Interrupt
163     = Date and Time Not Set—CHANGE BATTERY
161,2, or 4 = PS -2 RE-RUN CONFIGURATION—CHANGE BATTERY
199     = User Response to Configuration Not Correct
201     = MEMORY
301     = KEYBOARD—HEAVY FINGERS or Stuck Key
301 8602 = PS -2 POWER OFF-ON == Mouse (RODENT) FAILURE
401     = Monochrome Adapter or Display Failure
432     = Parallel Printer Not Powered Up
501     = CGA Adapter or Display Failure
601     = FLOPPY DISK Drive or Adapter Failure
701     = Math Co-processor Test Failure
901     = Parallel Printer Adapter Test Failure
1101    = Serial Port Test Failure
1301    = Game-Control Adapter Test Failure
1302    = Joystick Test Failure
        = Printer Test Failure
1701    = Fixed DISK Drive or Adapter Failure
1702    = Controller Failure
1703    = Disk Drive Failure
1704    = Undetermined Failure—Drive or Controller
1780    = Disk Drive 0: Failure
1781    = Disk Drive 1: Failure
1782    = Controller Failure on PC AT
1790    = Disk Drive 0: Failure—Cannot read—Incorrect type
1791    = Disk Drive 1: Failure—Cannot read—Incorrect type
2401    = EGA Adapter or Display Failure
2501    = EGA Adapter or Display Failure
```

There are many PC error codes, but generally the most frequently seen are **those in bold type.** They are more than sufficient to zero in on the malfunctioning component. Furthermore, standardized PC clones do not necessarily implement any of these error codes in their ROMs. You might get "Stuck key failure" on a clone rather than the "301" that you would see on a

IBM PC. Some manufacturers attempt to maintain user dependence on their maintenance and technical support by implementing proprietary error codes. This is self-serving, designed to promote their revenue generating technical support function.

Study Break

Error Messages

To see PC component error messages shut down the PC and disconnect in sequence the keyboard, the fixed disk drive cable, and the floppy disk drive cable.

1. Exit all software and turn off the PC. Disconnect the keyboard cable. Restart the PC. What error message appears? Write It down here:

2. Now Exit all software and turn off the PC. Reconnect the keyboard cable and disconnect the fixed disk power cable. Restart the PC. What error message appears? Write It down here:

3. Now turn off the PC. Reconnect the fixed disk power cable. Disconnect the fixed disk data cable. Restart the PC. What error message appears? Write It down here:

4. Now turn off the PC. Reconnect the fixed disk data cable. Disconnect all floppy drives from the floppy data cable. Restart the PC. What error message appears? Write It down here:

5. Now turn off the PC. Reconnect all floppy drives to the floppy data cable. Restart the PC. No error messages should appears.

A+ 3.3 Diagnosing Error Symptoms and Problems by Subsystem

PC hardware error symptoms are described in these subsections. They range from the most basic of the PC acting like a rock and doing nothing to almost starting OK. Each indicates a specific type of malfunction. The key here is to think of how electrical power flows into the PC. It starts at the wall outlet. If there is no power, that must first be rectified before we can proceed further. Next is the PC's power cord. This is highly reliable, but not without an occasional failure. These failures are often caused by poor connector contacts. When these check out OK, we move on to the power supply.

Power Supply

The power supply converts 115-volts or 220-volts AC into 5-volts and 12-volts DC. Without this low voltage power the PC does nothing. When some power but not enough power is provided to the main logic board, the PC can beep to signal failure. Otherwise it is silent.

When nothing leaves the power supply, the PC is really dead on arrival (DOA). Some tests for the power supply are very simple, like listening for the fan to start. Others can require using a voltmeter to test output voltages on the power supply connectors. See Figure 3–2. Testing output voltages is great, but replacing the supply performs an equivalent test and repairs the problem in a single step. When the supply replacement does not fix the problem, then the removed supply is probably good. The removed supply can act as future power supply test equipment. It is much more elegant to test with a voltmeter, but much quicker to test with a power supply. When you have lots of service calls to close in a day, the power supply test always wins. On the A+ test, the voltmeter test is likely a better answer.

Voltmeters are good for testing cable continuity. Using the K-ohm test on a voltmeter is an effective way to determine which pins are connected to which pins at the opposite end of any cable.

Figure 3–2 *Digital voltmeter*

Main Logic Board

The next thing the power hits is the main logic board. This means that the PC begins to function. At least there are beep codes when the CPU chip functions and the RAM fails. Once we have power to the main logic board, then we verify the proper operation of the key PC components installed on the main logic board.

The key components on the main logic board are the BIOS in ROM, the CMOS or nonvolatile RAM (NVRAM), the battery, the on-board serial and parallel ports, the CPU, the RAM, the video controller, and the keyboard. A PC can function without a mouse, even within Windows. This makes the mouse an important component, but not a key component.

BIOS

The Basic Input Output System (BIOS) is software in ROM chips on the main logic board. The BIOS software performs 8-bit and 16-bit input/output functions. Chip failure here is extremely rare. A typical failure message states that there was a ROM checksum failure. BIOS upgrades were discussed in Chapter 2.

CMOS OR NVRAM

The CMOS (which stands for Complementary Metal Oxide Semiconductor) or non-volatile random access memory stores system setup and operating parameters.

Also BIOS and the initial program load setup program can be stored in the CMOS or NVRAM. A failure here would cause the setup program not to run, making the PC display nothing or possibly a checksum error message.

The CMOS setup program permits changing the PC's basic hardware settings. Entering the setup program by striking a key—commonly F1, F2 or Delete—brings up a main system setup screen. See Figure 3–3. This menu permits setting the time and specifying the fixed and floppy disk drives.

Moving one tab to the right using the right arrow key provides a system devices setup menu screen. See Figure 3–4. Here, the main logic board built-in controllers are configured. This sets the IDE, serial, and parallel interfaces as well as ancillary options like infrared communications and MPEG operation. Each option is a simple menu selection. The arrow keys move up and down and across the menu selections. Striking the Enter key permits changing the option selection with the selections often presented in a drop down menu.

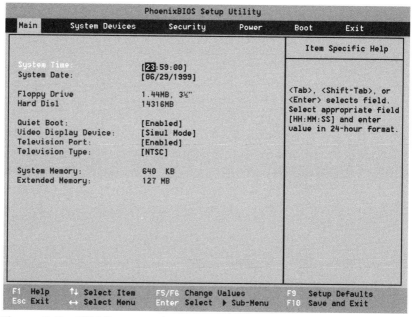

Figure 3–3   *CMOS setup main menu*

Figure 3–4   *CMOS setup system device menu*

The last tab sets the power management options that are incorporated into both the PC hardware and Windows software. See Figure 3–5. Conflicting power management settings cause many PC problems. Disabling hardware power management is one way to avoid such problems.

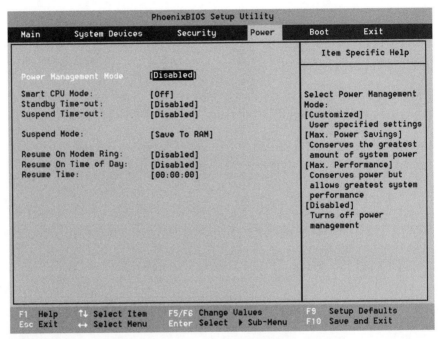

Figure 3–5 *CMOS setup power management menu*

BATTERY

On newer PCs, the NVRAM or CMOS setup parameters are stored in a Dallas chip. This Dallas chip is installed in a main logic board socket and often secured with a tie-wrap. The fix for a faulty chip is replacement of the entire Dallas chip.

This replaces both the battery and the CMOS memory.

Older PCs used a separate 3-volt or 6-volt lithium battery to power the CMOS memory. When the lithium battery failed, there were no system signs to warn the user. The system functioned normally until it was physically powered off. Once the PC was powered down, the CMOS, without its functioning battery, would loose all of its setup parameters. Most importantly, the fixed disk parameters would be lost. This would cause the PC to not recognize the fixed disk and consequently not boot. When booted from floppy diskette, the PC would appear to have lost every stitch of data on the fixed disk. Fortunately, this was not the case. To fix the problem, the setup program had to be run to restore the old fixed disk setup parameters. Once restored, the PC would be warm booted to return to normal operation. As long as the power was not removed from the PC it could be rebooted (using CTRL-ALT-DEL) without loosing the setup parameters.

PARALLEL PORT

The parallel port is not considered a critical PC operating component, and doesn't affect the PC boot process. During the boot process the PC would display the operating main logic board components. This display would include operating parallel ports and their I/O address (378 for LPT1, 278 for LPT2, or 3BC). If the parallel port was not operating or was turned off, it would not appear in the boot display. Since this display would flash briefly during the boot process, parallel port failure is only noticed when the PC fails to print to the printer. Sometimes a pause command is placed in the AUTOEXEC.BAT or CONFIG.SYS files to halt the display until the user presses a key to continue, in which case the message can be more easily seen or captured. Failure to print a document is not necessarily caused by a failure of the parallel port.

For example, when running Windows 95, the PC may become unable to print to its printer. The Windows PC displays an error message: "There was an error writing to LPT1: for TEST printer. There was a problem writing to the port. Check to make sure your printer is configured to use a valid port." This message does not necessarily indicate a printer port hardware failure, but more likely bad Windows printer drivers.

A simple test of the parallel port hardware is performed by connecting the printer to the LPT1 port, booting into DOS, and entering DIR>LPT1. This can also work from the Windows Command prompt without rebooting into DOS.

This sends the DIR command output to the parallel port and should print on any printer. To test LPT2, enter DIR>LPT2. If both ports print in the above test, the PC's port hardware is working fine. The problem is then with the driver program for the printer and how it interacts with Windows. To solve this problem, use the very latest driver programs downloaded from a support website for the printer.

SERIAL PORTS

Similar to parallel ports, a serial port is not a critical PC operating component. PCs boot without them operating. During the boot process, PCs display serial ports as operating main logic board components. The display includes operating serial ports and their I/O address (3F8 for COM1, 2F8 for COM2, 3E8 for COM3, and 2E8 for COM4). When a COM port is not operating or is disabled, it is not shown in the boot display. This display flashes briefly during the boot process, so serial port failure is only noticed if a serial device—for instance, a mouse—is attached to a serial port and that device fails to operate.

The MODE command provides a simple diagnostic capability. The MODE command has options to set up and redirect the printer and COM ports. See Figure 3–6. Other options permit setting the keyboard typematic rate, the basic display mode, and code pages for foreign language operation. We are interested in the capabilities of the MODE command to test for the presence and well being of serial and parallel ports.

The presence or absence of serial ports can be tested using the DOS MODE command. This is not a comprehensive test. Results vary depending upon the version of DOS. The MODE command test is:

```
MODE COM1 300
MODE COM2 300
MODE COM3 300
MODE COM4 300
```

This sets up the serial ports to a speed of 300 bits per second. The speed setting is not critical here. Any speed can be used, but a speed must be specified. When a serial port is present, DOS responds with messages like:

```
Microsoft(R) Windows 98
   (C)Copyright Microsoft Corp 1981-1998.

C:\WINDOWS>mode /?
Configures system devices.

Printer port:       MODE LPTn[:] [COLS=c] [LINES=l] [RETRY=r]
Serial port:        MODE COMm[:] [BAUD=b] [PARITY=p] [DATA=d] [STOP=s] [RETRY=r]
Device Status:      MODE [device] [/STATUS]
Redirect printing:  MODE LPTn[:]=COMm[:]
Prepare code page:  MODE device CP PREPARE=((yyy[...]) [drive:][path]filename)
Select code page:   MODE device CP SELECT=yyy
Refresh code page:  MODE device CP REFRESH
Code page status:   MODE device CP [/STATUS]
Display mode:       MODE [display-adapter][,n]
                    MODE CON[:] [COLS=c] [LINES=n]
Typematic rate:     MODE CON[:] [RATE=r DELAY=d]

C:\WINDOWS>
```

Figure 3–6 *Mode command options*

```
"COM1: 300,e,7,1,-
 COM1: 300,e,7,1,- "
```

Any response here means that the serial port is present. The 300, e, 7, 1,— indicate that the port speed was set to 300 bits per second, the parity detection was set to even parity, there are seven data bits, one stop bit is used, and the retry status is not set. When testing a serial port setting the speed to a slow speed e.g. 300 bits per second permits port testers with LEDs to flash when data is sent across the transmit or receive lines (pin 2 and pin 3).

If no serial port is present, the following error message is displayed:

```
"Illegal device name
COM3"
```

This is not a complete test of the serial port. The next step would be to provide a Clear to Send (CTS on DB-25 is pin 5) signal from Data Terminal Ready (DTR on DB-25 is pin 20) to the port and perform the DIR>COM1, etc. When the serial ports are working, the PC just does nothing while the directory characters are sent out the port. If an external modem with lights is attached to the port, the Transmit Data (TD on DB25 is pin 2) flickers.

Another useful and inexpensive test tool is a "minitester" that uses light signals for each of the different tests.

Once finished the PC returns to the DOS prompt. When the port malfunctions or does not have the CTS signal, the following error message is displayed:

```
"Write fault error writing device COM1
Abort, Retry, Ignore, Fail?"
```

CPU

CPU malfunctions typically result in the system lights coming on and the user being able to hear the fan turning on but nothing is displayed on the screen display. When the CPU does not work, there is no processor to perform the POST or to produce any system or error displays. Without the CPU running okay, a PC cannot even beep.

It is possible to have the PC boot and not have the CPU chip operating reliably or properly. This can be the result of a clock mismatch or bad CPU level 1 or level 2 cache. It is possible to diagnose these error conditions.

One possible cause of clock mismatches is increasing the clock rate of the CPU chip. This is called overclocking. Overclocking is a popular way to boost PC performance without paying the price for a higher speed CPU chip.

Since most CPU chips are underrated in clock speed, this often works fine—but not always. Sometimes overclocking does not work. In this case, the PC may pass the POST just fine, but it will not run any software application. As soon as Windows or applications are loaded, the PC crashes. All error messages in this instance are misleading and do not point to the root problem—the CPU chip clock mismatch.

Sometimes the overclocking failure happens well after the PC is started. This is because, when the clock frequency of the CPU is increased, it makes the CPU chip work harder and produce more heat. When insufficient cooling is provided, then the CPU chip does not fail immediately, but rather fails when the CPU chip overheats. This situation is bad and can cause the CPU chip to burn out and fail completely. Since overclocking stresses the PC and diminishes its reliability, it is never recommended by any PC manufacturer or maintenance organization. Any PC warranty is voided when overclocking is detected.

It is possible to have a CPU with a bad level 1 or level 2 cache.

These CPUs may pass POST and may load and run software. However, they are hidden landmines waiting to explode. The errors manifest themselves during I/O operations, particularly network or fixed disk I/O. Error messages will indicate a fixed disk-read or a disk-write error. The message is misleading and does not point at the root problem, a bad cache.

To test the cache, it must be disabled. The CMOS setup program may permit disabling both level 1 and level 2 cache. There is no guarantee here that any specific PC is capable of disabling its cache. Once the faulty cache is disabled, the error disappears, but the PC runs very slow. Disabling the level 1 or the level 2 cache would determine which cache is the culprit. A PC will run with level 1 and level 2 cache disabled. When a cache failure happened to me, there was a bad chip in the external level 2 CPU cache.

RAM—Random Access Memory

Memory errors may be detected by running a memory test program (that is, HIMEM.SYS—this sometimes detects a problem), getting a memory error message from POST on power-up, or having an application crash continually. When applications crash, the error message or behavior rarely looks like an obvious memory or hardware problem, however.

The early PCs employed parity to check for memory errors. An extra parity bit was added to each 8-bit byte stored in RAM. The parity was set to one or zero, depending upon the number of ones in the remaining eight bits in the byte. Parity works like a dryer, you put in an even number of socks and the dryer always produces an odd number of socks. The ones in our memory bytes are the socks. So that as data is stored away an odd (or even) number of ones are stored with each byte. Upon data retrieval, the parity is recalculated and compared to the parity stored. A mismatch is identified as an error. Today, error correcting codes use the parity bit to detect and correct single bit errors in memory.

Early PCs would display "Parity Check 1," indicating a motherboard memory problem, or "Parity Check 2," indicating an expansion card memory error. Some memory error messages allowed you to narrow the problem down to a single chip. Such detailed memory error isolation is not practical now that PCs have megabytes of RAM installed using SIMMs and DIMMs. For a review of SIMMs and their characteristics, see Chapter 2.

PCs have also stopped using parity as a memory-checking mechanism. A SIMM with parity is referred to as a 9x36 SIMM as opposed to a SIMM with no parity bits, which is an 8x32 SIMM. Common SIMM sizes and descriptions were briefly presented in Chapter 2, Table 2-3; common RAM types are covered in more detail in Chapter 5.

Older PCs have 640Kb conventional main memory. This conventional memory was divided into ten 64Kb logical banks. The logical banks are numbered 00 through 09. DOS and DOS-based application programs use conventional memory. All memory today is located on the main logic board. Each byte of memory holds one character. The PC uses hexadecimal addresses to indicate locations of memory areas or the logical banks. Portions of the memory are used as RAM and other portions are reserved for ROM or have the ROM contents copied into them (this is the shadow BIOS concept).

The original IBM PC, XT, and AT memory errors could be traced to an individual memory chip. Our worst memory error nightmare was finding a single bad RAM chip in 72 RAM chips. Needless to say this required several hours of effort because we had to swap banks of chips until the bad chip was precisely identified.

Once memory moved to SIMMs and away from chips, memory addresses were used to identify a bad SIMM. The movement to SIMMs came with the first 486 CPU PCs. SIMMs made it easier and less costly to manufacture PCs and increased the reliability of RAM. Socketed chips were a significant memory failure point.

You moved SIMMs and if the memory error address changed the SIMM moved was bad. Depending on how the address changed (it moved to higher address ranges or to lower address ranges), the SIMM could be precisely identified.

Because today's PCs have megabytes of RAM, because the RAM is typically nonparity RAM, because there are so few SIMMs or DIMMs in a PC and because RAM is inexpensive, in new PCs it is easiest to swap SIMMs or DIMMs to find memory errors. The trick is determining if the error is a hardware memory error or just something caused by Windows software. Bad memory only fails when it is used. So PCs could have bad memory installed and conceivably never have a memory failure because the bad memory was never used. The chances of this are nil—today's programs are memory hogs. Furthermore, the program just crashes when bad memory is encountered. This is very misleading as to the cause of the error. The POST does catch memory errors and sometimes PCs are configured so that the better test performed by HIMEM.SYS is not run. If the HIMEM.SYS command parameter /TEST-MEM:ON|OFF is set to OFF, HIMEM.SYS does not perform its memory test.

HIMEM.SYS has several option switches, including:

- **/A20CONTROL:ON|OFF**
  Specifies to HIMEM whether to control the A20 line. The A20 handler supports access to the High Memory Area (HMA). When /A20CONTROL:OFF is specified, HIMEM controls the A20 line only if A20 was off when HIMEM loaded. The default setting is /A20CONTROL:ON.

- **/CPUCLOCK:ON|OFF**
  Specifies whether HIMEM can affect the CPU chip clock speed. If a PC's clock speed changed when HIMEM was installed, specifying /CPUCLOCK:ON may correct the problem. Enabling this option slows down HIMEM. The default setting is /CPUCLOCK:OFF.

- **/EISA**
  Specifies allocation of all available extended memory. This switch is needed only on EISA (Extended Industry Standard Architecture) computers with more than 16 MB of memory. HIMEM automatically allocates all available extended memory on other computers.

- **/HMAMIN=m**
  Specifies how much memory in kilobytes an application must request from HIMEM for HIMEM to give that application use of the HMA. In DOS only one application can use the HMA at a time; HIMEM allocates the HMA to the first application that meets the memory-use requirements set by this option. When the /HMAMIN option is not required, the default value is zero. Omitting this option or setting it to zero causes HIMEM to allocate the HMA to the first DOS application that requests it, regardless of how much of the HMA the application is going to use. The /HMAMIN option has no effect when Windows is running in 386 enhanced mode.

- **/INT15=xxxx**

  Allocates extended memory in kilobytes reserved for the Interrupt 15h interface. Some DOS applications use the Interrupt 15h interface to allocate extended memory rather than using the XMS (eXtended-Memory Specification) provided by HIMEM. Values from 64 to 65535 can be specified; however, more memory than your system has available cannot be specified. A value less than 64 is interpreted as a value of 0. The default value is 0.

- **/NUMHANDLES=n**

  Specifies the maximum extended-memory block (EMB) handles that are simultaneously used. Values from 1 to 128 can be specified with the default value being 32. Each handle requires 6 bytes of memory. /NUMHANDLES has no effect when Windows is running in 386 enhanced mode.

- **/MACHINE:xxxx**

  Specifies computer type. Usually, HIMEM can detect the PC type successfully; however, there are a few computers that HIMEM does not detect. HIMEM uses the default system type of IBM AT or compatible. Include the /MACHINE option if a PC is a type that HIMEM cannot detect. This is indicated when HIMEM does not work properly on a PC using the default system type.

- **/SHADOWRAM:ON|OFF**

  Disables shadow RAM (SHADOWRAM:OFF) or leaves the ROM code running from RAM (SHADOWRAM:ON). Some computers make ROM code run faster by "shadowing" or copying it into RAM which uses some extended memory. Computers that use shadow RAM and have less than 2 MB of RAM cause HIMEM to disable shadow RAM and thus recover additional extended memory for Windows to use. When HIMEM disables shadow RAM, the ROM code runs in the slower ROM instead of RAM.

- **/TESTMEM:ON|OFF**

  Determines whether HIMEM performs a memory test when a PC starts. By default, HIMEM tests the reliability of a computer's extended memory each time a computer starts. This test identifies memory that is not reliable. HIMEM's memory test is more thorough than the standard power-up memory test performed by most computers. To prevent HIMEM from performing the memory test, specify /TESTMEM:OFF. Disabling the memory test shortens the PC boot time. (The default setting is /TESTMEM:ON.)

- **/VERBOSE**

  Directs HIMEM to display status and error messages while loading. By default, HIMEM does not display any messages unless an error is encountered. /VERBOSE is abbreviated as /V. Status messages are displayed without adding the /VERBOSE switch by pressing and holding the ALT key when HIMEM starts and loads.

The PC needs the first bank of RAM operational to run the POST and the NVRAM setup program. Without that first bank of RAM, a PC just beeps. One problem is determining which is the first bank of RAM and determining the number of SIMMs or DIMMs required for the RAM. Some general rules are as shown in Table 3.1.

Table 3.1 *Types and numbers of chips needed*

RAM SIMM or DIMM	CPU Chip	Number required for a bank
30-pin SIMM	386	2 or 4 SIMMs per bank
30-pin SIMM	486	2 or 4 SIMMs per bank
72-pin SIMM	386	1 or 2 SIMMs per bank
72-pin SIMM	486	1 or 2 SIMMs per bank
72-pin SIMM	Pentium	2 or 4 SIMMs per bank
168-pin DIMM	Pentium	1 or 2 DIMMs per bank

When multiple SIMMs or DIMMs are used in a bank, they should exactly match.

Malfunctioning RAM is simply replaced to correct the problem.

Video and Monitor

When a display problem occurs, possible causes are the video controller, the cable, or the monitor. Of these components, the monitor is the most fragile. Monitors are cathode ray tubes (CRTs) or flat panel displays. The CRTs tend to fail after several years of use. Flat panel displays can also fail, but they should last longer.

Display problems are typically signaled by no display. There could be several reasons that nothing is visible.

First check the power to the display. While this may seem to be an obvious check, it can be more difficult because of the power management functions built into the monitor, the main logic board, and Windows software. Any or all of them stop the power from going to the monitor when the PC is inactive. This means that the monitor is powered off. It does not lack power, but the power management functions have shut power off to the display. Lack of power to the display and power shut off by power management look the same to the PC troubleshooter.

When power management has powered down the display, hitting a keyboard key or moving the mouse sometimes brings the PC back from its sleep state and causes it to power up the monitor. In this event, the power light on the monitor lights up green. If there is power and the monitor is sleeping, the power light on the monitor is some times yellow or amber. Other times, there is just no light, period. When the power light changes to green, within several seconds (which always seem like an eternity) a display usually appears.

In some cases, when the hardware power management function is in control, the PC can be in sleep mode (think deep sleep or hibernation). Here the power switch must sometimes (particularly on laptops) be switched on to awaken the PC and have the monitor display something.

The next thing to do is check the display brightness setting. If it has been turned all the way down, nothing is visible on the display. This is a favorite A+ question.

When there is power to the monitor and no display, check the monitor cable. The easiest test is to plug in another monitor. If it works and the monitor cable is swappable, then swap the cable to determine if the failure is the cable or the monitor. Most likely it is the monitor, but you never know.

Monitor failures are also indicated by visible display problems. We have seen vertical bars (like automobile racing stripes) down the middle of the display, a loss of colors, shaking displays, and others. Bars and loss of color require a monitor repair to correct. Shaking displays could require monitor repair or repositioning of other electrical equipment farther away from the monitor. Electrical equipment that can cause a monitor to shake are fans, fluorescent lights, other monitors, electric pencil sharpeners, televisions, and more. Influence from magnets can also affect monitor performance, as can electromagnetic interference.

Spacing these three or more feet away from the monitor fixes this type of shaking.

It might also be a good idea to check the monitor type and display settings in the control panel before sending the monitor out for repair.

Other monitor shimmying may indicate failing components. For example, one time there was a lightning hit that destroyed a fuse inside a Samsung 17" monitor. After the fuse was replaced the monitor had apparently become paranoid of another lightning hit because it just shimmied all the time until finally a year later it failed. In this instance, more component replacement was needed beyond the fuse replacement.

Controller failures show themselves as weird-looking displays. Either the monitor cannot display a nice straight rectangular picture that fully fills the screen or spots are just dropped from the display. The former signals a controller scanning rate mismatch with the monitor. Reducing the display resolution down to standard VGA (640 by 480) can sometimes correct a nonstraight display. Otherwise, a monitor better tuned to the display controller is required. When spots or characters are dropped from the display, it indicates bad display controller RAM. A new display controller is typically in order when this happens.

Keyboard and Mouse

The keyboard and mouse are tested during POST. If they are found, a keyboard detected and a mouse detected messages are displayed.

Keyboard errors are the most critical. If during POST, the PC finds no keyboard, it displays a missing keyboard message with the strike F1 to continue. This seems dumb because there is no keyboard on which to strike F1, but it does provide an opportunity to plug in a keyboard if it was forgotten.

Sometimes the PC can just lose the keyboard. This happens when a keyboard is moved between PCs. To determine if a keyboard is not working with a PC, toggle the "Num Lock," "Caps Lock," or the "Scroll Lock" keys and observe the keyboard light emitting diodes (LEDs). When the keyboard LEDs turn off and on in response to toggling the keys, all is fine. When toggling the keys has no effect on the LEDs, the PC is not seeing the keyboard.

Mouse problems are obvious because the mouse produces no Windows or DOS pointer movement or the movement is erratic. Sometimes AUTOEXEC.BAT loads DOS mouse driver programs. When these programs are loaded and no mouse is found, they state "mouse not found" or similar error messages. You may want to check the cable connections first to make sure they are firmly seated.

When Windows loads, it also loads its mouse drivers. If there is a serious mouse driver versus mouse mismatch, Windows does not display a mouse pointer. When Windows senses a mouse, it displays a pointer. This is no guarantee that the Windows drivers match the mouse. Only if the mouse pointer moves as expected is the mouse OK. If there remains a mismatch, the mouse pointer jumps erratically. Erratic mouse pointer movement can be due to a dirty mouse or bad driver software. Cleaning the mouse is the easiest to check. The mouse ball is removed and cleaned and the inside of the mouse is blown out to assure no dirt remains inside. If mouse movement is still erratic, it is likely the driver software.

Sometimes mice have a switch on the bottom that changes them from a Microsoft-compatible mouse to a MouseSystems-compatible mouse. This may cause the mouse to match the driver software and fix the problem. Other mice can switch when they first get electrical power and a mouse button (generally the right one) is depressed. The button must be held down while the PC is powered up, or held down while the mouse is unplugged from the PC and then replugged into the PC. Again, if the movement stops being erratic, the problem is fixed. Otherwise call for the replacement mouse.

Serial mice connect to the serial port on the rear of the PC while PS/2 mice connect to a special Mini-DIN connector. This means that the serial mice operate with standard COM port settings. The PS/2 mice generally use the bus mouse PC resources (IRQ, I/O port, etc.).

FLOPPY DRIVES

The most common floppy disk drive problem is not being recognized when the PC boots. During POST, the PC can perform a floppy disk seek test. It tests for floppy drive A but not floppy drive B. If floppy drive B is installed and set in the NVRAM, the PC can indicate a drive mismatch when the setting is for a 1.44 MB disk drive and a 1.2 MB disk drive is installed. However, the key diskette drive is drive A because it is a potential boot drive.

NVRAM permits specifying a disk drive boot sequence. The sequence is set in the system setup area, normally entered by pressing DEL before the POST test and before Windows boots. There are several options including:
- Floppy drive A; then drive C
- Drive C; then floppy drive A
- CD-ROM drive; then drive C; then floppy drive A
- CD-ROM drive; then floppy drive A; then drive C
- Floppy drive A; then drive C; then CD-ROM

This can help speed up the booting process and can help when there is only a CD-ROM for installing software and no floppy diskettes. It does present a potential problem when the fixed disk fails. The PC doesn't boot and cannot be booted without changing the NVRAM boot option specifications.

When a floppy disk drive is not connected to the PC, misconnected to the PC, or malfunctioning, it is not seen by the POST. This means that it is not available to DOS and Windows as well. Misconnected floppy drives often have their drive light come on and stay on when the PC is started. Normally, the floppy drive light flashes briefly after the fixed disk drive is tested. The fixed disk drive light is turned on before the floppy drive light. When the floppy drive light stays lighted, the floppy cable is reversed or is not connected properly. When a bootable floppy is present in a drive with a misconnected cable, the data on the diskette is destroyed. The data cannot be recovered. The diskette is rendered useless and nonbootable.

Leaving a data diskette in the floppy drive during the boot process when the NVRAM directs the PC to boot from the floppy drive first causes nonbootable disk errors. This problem is easily corrected by removing the data floppy and striking any key to continue booting the PC from the fixed disk.

Sometimes floppy diskettes cannot be read. This is caused by a wide variety of circumstances. In such cases, the DOS COPY command should be used to copy the diskette files to the fixed disk. When read failures occur, an "Abort, Retry or Ignore" error message is displayed. When the data is important, the retry option should be used repeatedly in an attempt to recover the data. When this copies the file, the data copied is good. If this does not work, the "ignore" option can be used. It typically produces a bad file, but one time in a thousand good data can result. The DOS COPY command is used as opposed to the Windows copy command or the DOS COPY command in a DOS Window because DOS commands directly manipulate the PC's hardware. Windows commands and DOS commands in a DOS Window do not. They are much less likely to recover the data. However, if the data is really important, there are a number of recovery programs commercially available that can assist with this process.

FIXED DISK DRIVES

Fixed disk drives can have lost files or hardware failures. Both types of problems are covered in this section, with disk failures discussed first, followed by file loss.

Fixed Disks fail for a few simple reasons. The primary sources of failure are:

- **Manufacturer Design Defects**—The original IBM PC AT fixed disk drive was designed by CMI. It had defective head mechanisms that shortened its effective life considerably. The old Seagate ST-225 drives had batches of drives that failed after about one year of operation. They would get seek errors when positioning the heads to read data. Common defects include bad sectors, irregular surface flaws, etc. A few disk drive designs and manufactured batches are just plain bad. The majority of disk drives though are well designed and ruggedly built.
- **Vibration**—This is one killer of fixed disks. The greatest risk comes when they are in operation. On older disk drives, the fixed disk drive

heads were parked when the drive was powered off. This did not protect from head crashes caused by vibration when the disk is operating. Fixed disk drives today lock the heads off the surface of the disk drive unless they are actually reading data from the drive. This makes them much, much less susceptible to vibration damage. The disks and the heads themselves are designed to be more resistant to head crash damage. This is because the heads are smaller and lighter and the disk drive surface materials are more resistant to head crash damage.

- **Temperature Shock**—Computers are designed to operate in average room temperature environments. Disk drives are vulnerable to extremes in temperature—both too hot or too cold. As an example, leaving the computer off overnight and over weekends, can cause it to be chilled in winter months. When the computer is restarted in the morning, the internal temperature can climb from 40 to 60 degrees Fahrenheit to 80 to 100 degrees Fahrenheit or more within the brief period of twenty minutes. This causes internal stress and strain on fixed disk components that have very narrow tolerances (fixed disk heads fly closer to the fixed disk surface than half the diameter of a human hair). Severe strain can cause head crashes or worse. Leaving the computer on all the time helps alleviate temperature shock problems.

    After exposing the computer to any temperature extremes, it is advisable to let it come back to ordinary room temperature before turning the system on. This minimizes potential shock to the components and, consequently, damage to them.
Portable and laptop computers with fixed disks should always be kept warm. Never leave them overnight in an automobile. I lent one of my laptops to a friend who left it overnight in his truck, only to have it fail the next day when it was powered on. He swears to this day that he did nothing to make the fixed disk fail. But it failed none the less because the cool temperature caused moisture inside the drive to condense. This slight condensation crashed the disk drive heads when the laptop was started the next day.

- **Age**—Fixed disks have a limited life span. The early disks were designed to operate for 10,000 power-on hours. That is 5 years operating 8 hours per day and five days per week and fifty weeks per year. Fixed disk life now runs into 100,000 to 500,000 power-on hours. After a while, all fixed disks do fail. All my first fixed disks have all been replaced because they failed from old age. None of the recent disks have had aging problems in spite of being run 24 hours a day seven days a week (24x7 operation).

Because the directory and the FAT areas on the disk are used the most, they are likely to be the ones that lose data first. Once they are gone, the disk is unuseable. Some fixed disk preparation programs such as On-Track System's Disk Manager program allow you to move the directory and FAT to cylinders other than the beginning cylinders on the disk. This can extend the life of some disks, but eventually all disks die.

Other factors that affect the life span of a disk drive are the degree of care when moving them, conscientious preventive maintenance, and exposure to magnets (which may also include exposure of laptops to airport security equipment). No matter what the situation, the best way to protect against possible disk drive failure is to make and protect regular system backups. Then, when the inevitable occurs, there is always a solid point for recovery.

Troubleshooting the disk drives is the last key area before the PC boots. Separate problems are encountered by floppy, fixed, and CD-ROM drives.

LOST FILES • Sometimes it looks like a disk is failing when files are lost. This is not representative of a hardware failure but more likely some software operation gone awry. Recovering from lost files depends upon the software being used. Windows has the Recycle Bin which holds erased files until they are emptied from the recycle bin. Files mistakenly erased can recovered from the Recycle Bin. Some programs do not place the files they remove into the Recycle Bin. Those files cannot be recovered.

DOS also provides some file recovery capabilities. Have you been in a hurry and entered DEL C:*.*, thinking that you were killing the files in C:\TEMP? Oops! Or have you ever run FORMAT thinking that your PC is a mind reader and knows that you wish to FORMAT drive A. Before you can think to strike Ctrl Break, it has finished formatting and rewritten the directory and the FAT. Oops!

DOS provides help. It has UNDELETE and UNFORMAT commands. These commands can, within limits, restore deleted data from your fixed disk drive.

UNDELETE can be run at any time because a deleted file just has a special character placed in the first location in the file name. It also means that the chain of clusters forming the file has been released from the directory entry so that they may be reused to store new files.

Warning

This means that if you want to be sure to recover a deleted file, **DO NOT WRITE ANY MORE DATA TO THE FIXED DISK UNTIL THE FILE HAS BEEN RECOVERED.**

After deleting a file, immediately run UNDELETE for the best chance of recovering the total file. UNDELETE is menu driven and relatively simple to run. UNDELETE is equivalent to the Windows recycle bin.

Similar to UNDELETE is UNFORMAT. UNFORMAT recovers data from recently formatted fixed disk drives. Similarly to UNDELETE, it is best to use UNFORMAT immediately to recover the drive, before any new data is written to the drive. Formatting a fixed disk drive does not destroy the data on the drive but merely rewrites the directory and the FAT. Data is no longer available because, in spite of the data physically being on the disk, there is no way for DOS to tell how to retrieve the clusters that form the files. UNFOR-MAT relies on a copy of the directory and the FAT being placed on the disk by the FORMAT program. These are then used to replace the erased directory and the FAT.

The UNFORMAT command restores a disk erased by the FORMAT command or restructured by the RECOVER command. To run UNFOR-MAT you enter:

```
UNFORMAT drive: [/J]
UNFORMAT drive: [/U] [/L] [/TEST] [/P]
UNFORMAT /PARTN [/L]
```

The UNFORMAT options are given in Table 3.2.

Table 3.2 *UNFORMAT command options and actions*

Command Option	Definition
drive: .	Specifies the drive to unformat.
/J	Verifies that the mirror files agree with the system information on the disk.
/U	Unformats without using mirror files.
/L	Lists all file and directory names found, or, when used with the /PARTN switch, displays current partition tables.
/TEST	Displays information but does not write changes to disk.
/P .	Sends output messages to printer connected to LPT1.
/PARTN	Restores disk partition tables.

Both UNFORMAT and UNDELETE are useful DOS commands, when used within their capabilities. However, users misunderstand the limits of what these commands can do in recovering lost data and most often they write additional data to their fixed disk, making it impossible to fully recover their lost files. As mentioned earlier, if recovering files is crucial, there are options such as commercial data recovery programs or companies that specialize in data recovery that may help.

HARDWARE FAILURES • There are some common failure symptoms between both EIDE (IDE) and SCSI fixed disk drives. The common failure symptoms and resolutions have to do with the drive itself failing rather than the drive controller. When a drive fails, the disk becomes unreadable in one spot on its surface or in many spots on its surface. This is not necessarily a catastrophic event. The disk can still be used to store data, but should probably be replaced as soon as practical. However, surface failures in the master boot record, the root directory or the FAT areas of the disk can quickly render the drive useless. Other areas on the disk cannot be substituted for these areas. Errors in data areas on the disk can be marked as bad and bypassed when storing and retrieving new data on the disk. The SCANDISK.EXE program can perform a thorough disk surface test, moving data from bad areas to good areas as it determines a surface area is bad. It cannot recover a disk with a bad master boot record, root directory, or FAT. These problems are the same for either EIDE or SCSI drives.

Defragmenting a drive using DEFRAG.EXE on a regular basis reveals disk surface failures.

SCANDISK.EXE repairs failures in the data areas. It is possible to fix a bad disk drive with many surface failures. All disk drives use Error Correcting Code (ECC) to store and retrieve data from the disk drive. The ECC can sometimes become corrupted by bunches of errors. Returning the disk surface to its original all-zeros state can reset the ECC and make the drive appear error free. Because new data patterns are stored in the bad areas, the ECC now works, effectively making the disk appear error free. On SCSI drives, this is accomplished by performing a low-level format and surface verification on the disk drive. The SCSI adapter card typically contains the programs needed to perform the low-level format and disk surface scan. This wipes all data from the disk drive.

The drive must then be partitioned using FDISK and formatted using FORMAT. IDE drives cannot be low-level formatted without voiding their warranty. In this case, a program like the old Norton utilities WIPEINFO.EXE program that writes zeros all over the disk can be used to prepare the disk surface. Similarly to SCSI drives, the IDE drive then needs to be partitioned using FDISK and formatted using FORMAT.

Sometimes the fixed disk heads get stuck on the drive surface. This causes the disk not to rotate.

Figure 3–7 *FDISK Program*

Fixed disk controller and fixed disk drive problems can be diagnosed using the DOS FDISK program. When it is run, it provides the option to display partition information. See Figure 3–7.

When FDISK cannot read the drive, it displays an "Error reading fixed disk" message. If the fixed disk controller is bad, FDISK displays a fixed disk controller failure message. The "Error reading fixed disk" message suggests that the problem could be the cables or the fixed disk drive. Most likely it is the fixed disk drive, unless the drive is just being installed and the cables are put on incorrectly.

IDE/EIDE • Some problems unique to EIDE/IDE drives stem from the characteristics of the EIDE/IDE interface. For an EIDE/IDE drive to operate properly, its drive geometry parameters must be specified in the PC's NVRAM. These drive geometry parameters determine how the IDE controller and the driver software work with the drive to utilize its full capacity for storing data. The drive capacity is determined by the following equation:

(Cylinders) X (Heads) X (Sectors per Track) X (1/2 K) = Drive Capacity

(310) X (4) X (17) X (1/2 K) = 10,540 KB or 10 MB drive.

(620) X (4) X (17) X (1/2 K) = 21,080 KB or 20 MB drive.

This equation is referred to as the drive geometry.

A wide variety of drive geometry configurations have been employed from simple small-capacity drives defined in the ROM BIOS, to drives limited to 1,204 cylinders and drives addressed using Logical Block Addressing (LBA). As drive capacities have increased, drive geometry descriptions have evolved to accommodate these larger drive capacities.

During the power-on and POST, when the drive geometry descriptions in NVRAM do not match the IDE drive, the PC cannot read the drive. If for some reason the drive geometry descriptions are altered in NVRAM, the drive looks unuseable. Windows has crashed and in the process corrupted NVRAM. This happened with the early versions of Windows but not with Windows 95/98 or Windows NT. The problem is easily fixed by reentering the correct drive geometry or by having the NVRAM setup program auto-detect the correct drive geometry by reading it off the IDE drive.

PCs running earlier versions of DOS and Windows 95 could use large drives by subdividing them into 2 GB partitions. This 2 GB partition size limitation was due to software and not the PC's hardware. In this instance, the bootable partition had to be marked active. If the disk was partitioned and formatted with the operating system installed, it still would not boot unless the primary partition was set as active. FDISK establishes a primary partition and a secondary partition with logical drives. The primary partition and the logical drives were limited to 2 GB in size under DOS, Windows 3.x, and Windows 95 version A. Windows 95 version B and Windows 98 both supported the 32-bit FAT, permitting them to break the 2 GB partition size limitation. See Figure 3–8.

Booting from a floppy that has DOS and no large disk support will cause disk errors when trying to read or write to a 32-bit FAT drive.

Some PC manufacturers place configuration and diagnostic programs on the IDE drive in a maintenance partition. The maintenance partition contains setup information and manufacturer identification that makes automatic drive setup in CMOS possible.

This partition can be the first or the last partition on the disk drive. It is not marked as active and thus is not the bootable partition. It does however,

Figure 3–8   *FDISK large disk support*

reduce the useable disk space on the drive. FDISK reveals these partitions and can be used to remove them. They are usually shown under FDISK as non-DOS partitions. This makes them not visible under DOS and Windows. They may only be accessible when the PC is booted using a special diagnostic diskette.

IDE and EIDE drive controllers have few electronics so there is little to fail. They are installed on the main logic board and can be installed as added controllers in the PC's bus. As long as there are no IRQ and I/O port conflicts, these controllers work reliably. They support IDE fixed disks, CD-ROMs, CD-RW drives, Zip drives, Super Disk drives and DVD drives. Our focus here is on IDE fixed disk drives. Each IDE controller can support two drives. There is a primary and a secondary IDE controller on most PCs. When a controller connects to two drives, the drives must be identified to the controller as the master (primary) or slave (secondary) drive. From a boot disk perspective, it does not matter whether the primary or secondary is the bootable drive. However, when two IDE drives are marked as the master drive, disk I/O errors occur.

Generally, CD-ROM drives can be mixed with IDE fixed disk drives on the same controller, provided one is set as the master device and the other set as the slave device. However, this can also cause fixed disk I/O problems. This could be caused by DMA channel configuration, synchronous transfers for the CD-ROM drive, or other IDE configuration mismatches. When this happens, it is easier to place the CD-ROM on the second IDE controller than it is to figure out the exact cause of the incompatibility.

IDE cables must be connected pin one to pin one. It is possible to misconnect the cables, reversing the pin connections. When this happens, the fixed disk drive light comes on and stays on during the boot process. All the times this has happened to us, no data on the IDE drive has been destroyed. However, on some drives this could happen. Consequently, if, during the initial PC power-on and POST, the fixed disk light comes on and stays on, power the PC off immediately and check the cable connections at both the disk drive end and at the controller end to ensure pin one connects to pin one.

SCSI • SCSI drives require a separate controller from the IDE drive controller. This controller has ROM BIOS for operating the SCSI drives under DOS and Windows. It also contains configuration management and control, surface verification, and low-level format programs. The SCSI controller BIOS routines are entered during the boot process by striking a key combination prompted on the display screen. For Adaptec controllers this combination is CTRL A. The next menu permits working with the adapter settings or running diagnostics. See Figure 3– 9.

Figure 3–9 *SCSI select verifying a SCSI disk drive*

Adapter settings are used to set up SCSI bus operation, matching transfer speed and bus operation to the controller. If the devices attached to the SCSI bus are not matched to the controller transfer speed, the disk drives have I/O errors. This causes the PC not to run. The SCSI controller should be set at the highest priority Logical Unit Number (SCSI ID), which is 7. If it is set at a lower number, I/O errors could result. Parity checking for data transfers and host adapter termination should be enabled.

Each device must have a unique SCSI ID on the SCSI bus. Duplicate SCSI IDs cause devices to malfunction. The failure symptoms here are quite obvious. The operation of each SCSI ID is determined by the SCSI controller configuration. Parameters set include:

- Sync negotiation—to establish and perform synchronous data transfers.
- Transfer rate—the transfer speed must match here or the device fails.
- Send Start Unit command—critical for the SCSI IDs to initialize and run.
- Include in BIOS scan—makes the drive available to DOS and Windows.

The SCSI controller also provides drive geometry configuration translation for large SCSI drives. Since most SCSI drives are large drives, this is a vital feature.

When these parameters are not set properly, fixed disk I/O errors occur. These I/O errors look like the drive has failed when the problem can be corrected simply by changing to the correct parameter. Sometimes it is possible to test different SCSI bus transfer speeds with the drives attached. When the speed is set too fast, the drive has I/O errors. The PC may boot, but it doesn't run very long before failing.

The key area for SCSI disk and controller troubleshooting is the SCSI bus itself. The SCSI bus must be terminated at each end. That usually means that the controller card should have termination enabled and the last drive on the cable should also have termination set on or have a terminator attached. Any intermediate drives and devices cannot be terminated. When intermediate devices are terminated, the bus is overloaded electrically and I/O transfer errors occur. This makes the SCSI devices look like they have failed. The BIOS disk surface verification utility makes an excellent test of the SCSI bus. It shows I/O verification errors when the transfer speed and the termination are not correct on a SCSI bus. These verification errors happen almost immediately.

SCSI ID and SCSI termination are not related at all. The only concern for SCSI ID assignment is the priority assigned to the SCSI ID. The SCSI controller needs to have a SCSI ID of 7. So a SCSI device could be SCSI ID 3 and be installed at the end of the bus, thus requiring termination.

If a SCSI controller is attached to external devices, that most often means that it is installed in the middle of the SCSI bus and must not have termination enabled.

This may mean physically removing terminating resistor packs or just setting a controller configuration parameter with the setup program. In this event, the SCSI devices at the end of the external cable and at the end of the internal cable must be terminated. Many SCSI devices can be configured to terminate the SCSI bus. This is not the best configuration because they might be inadvertently moved. Consequently, it is best to terminate a SCSI bus with a terminating resistor pack.

Active terminations support higher transfer speeds. Terminations at each end of the bus should be active or passive but not mixed.

The 50-pin SCSI cables are quite reliable. The high-density 68-pin cables and connectors are much more prone to failure. Pins can be easily bent, causing some devices attached to the SCSI bus to fail and others to work properly. Usually this type of failure always happens to devices attached to a specific connector or assigned a specific SCSI ID on the SCSI bus. Bad pins in a connector may always cause the SCSI ID 5 device to fail and no others. The failure looks to be caused by the device when it is really caused by a bad cable. One of the first troubleshooting steps for any SCSI chain, and especially for high-density 68-pin SCSI buses, is to carefully examine the cables and connectors.

Any cables and connectors that are the least bit suspect should be replaced to ensure that the SCSI bus is operating properly. When cables are not available, the bus termination can be moved up and down the bus as a means of testing the cable. While this is not the most effective test procedure, it works.

No discussion of SCSI would be complete without some words on RAID. RAID or Redundant Array of Independent Disks (or Drives) uses SCSI almost exclusively. RAID is used mostly to provide redundancy to assure data recoverability in the event of a disk drive failure. The most commonly implemented types of RAID that provide redundancy are:

- RAID 1—mirroring data, and
- RAID 5—data striping with parity.

Several other types of RAID are defined and implemented, each with their own unique performance and reliability characteristics. Our discussion here focuses on RAID 1 and RAID 5. With RAID 1, mirroring, the same data is stored on two identical drives. When one fails, the other still has good data. With RAID 5, striping and parity, data and parity are stored on three or more drives. The data and parity information is spread more or less evenly across all drives. When one drive fails, the binary information on the remaining drives is used to rebuild the data on the failed drive. In this manner no data is lost. RAID can be implemented with disk controller hardware or with Windows NT or Novell Server software.

Troubleshooting RAID begins with the basic SCSI problems described above. Once SCSI bus issues are resolved, then it is a matter of working with the particular RAID controller or software. Hardware RAID drives are often called hot swappable. This really means that they are warm swappable. All activity on an SCSI bus must be halted to swap a drive with the power on.

The SCSI bus must be shut down to swap a failed RAID drive. If not, corruption of the data on the remaining drives is possible. Similarly with software RAID, the PC should be shut down before a failed drive is swapped. Swapped RAID drives are rebuilt automatically. The rebuilding is done at a binary level. Consequently, from 1 to 12 hours may be needed to rebuild a single drive. Software RAID rebuilds drives much more slowly than does hardware RAID. As drives are being rebuilt, overall system performance is diminished because of the resources devoted to rebuilding the data on the replacement drive.

CD-ROM

The most common problem with CD-ROM drives is having them not seen by DOS or Windows. CD-ROMs themselves are generally reliable. Other CD read/write devices are less reliable. Most CD-ROMs are IDE devices. CD-ROMs depend upon device drivers and the MSCDEX (Microsoft CD-ROM Extension) program to function with DOS. The device driver is loaded by CONFIG.SYS and linked to the MSCDEX.EXE program loaded by AUTOEXEC.BAT through a logical identifier. Typical CONFIG.SYS and AUTOEXEC.BAT file command lines for loading CD-ROM drivers are:

```
CONFIG.SYS
device=oakcdrom.sys /D:mscd001
AUTOEXEC.BAT
MSCDEX.EXE /D:mscd001
```

The logical identifier tying these command lines together is /D:mscd001. The MSCDEX command has several command line options including:

- /D:driver1 [/D:driver2...
  Sets the driver identifier for the CD-ROM device driver. The driver1 identifier must match the identifier specified by the /D switch on the CONFIG.SYS command that starts the corresponding CD-ROM device driver. The MSCDEX command includes at least one /D switch. Additional CD-ROM device drivers require specification of additional /D switches for each device driver.
- /E
  Permits the CD-ROM driver to use expanded memory, if available, to store sector buffers.
- /K
  Permits MS-DOS to recognize CD-ROM volumes encoded in Kanji. By default, MS-DOS does not recognize Kanji CD-ROM volumes.
- /S
  Enables CD-ROM drive sharing on MS-NET or Windows for Workgroups servers.
- /V
  Causes MSCDEX to display memory statistics when starting.

- /L:letter
  Assigns the specified letter to the first CD-ROM drive. When there is more than one CD-ROM drive, MS-DOS assigns additional CD-ROM drives the remaining available drive letters.
- /M:number
  Specifies the number of sector buffers MSCDEX can use.

If a CD-ROM drive is not accessible under Windows, the DOS commands can get the CD-ROM to work but using only the DOS mode compatibility drivers. Once this is done, forcing Windows to find new hardware or installing CD-ROM drivers can have Windows revert back to 32-bit drivers for the fixed disk drives and the CD-ROM drive. If this does not work, reinstalling Windows right over the existing Windows installation usually has Windows find the CD-ROM drive while preserving all of Windows' software settings. However, before resorting to a reinstallation of the OS, it might be worth trying the install program that comes with most CD drives or getting new updated drivers off the Internet.

Sometimes CDs are unreadable because they are not formatted correctly, their media is not compatible with the CD-ROM's laser, or they are dirty or the CD-ROM's lens is dirty. There are several storage formats for placing music and data on CD-ROMs. When your CD-ROM drive cannot understand the specific CD format, the CD is unreadable. The solution here is to try a different CD-ROM drive to read the CD. You also may want to verify that the correct software or drivers are installed. As an example, if you try to play a music CD but you don't have a player installed, you experience problems.

Different CDs work with different CD-ROM lasers. This problem occurs with CD-ROM burners and the burnable media that they use. Some CDs created on these burners cannot be read by some CD-ROM drives. This is not a formatting problem, but rather a media compatibility problem. Changing the media solves this problem and makes the CD readable.

Dirt can cause a CD-ROM to malfunction. CD-ROM lens-cleaning CDs that have small brushes can clean the CD-ROM lens. CD cleaning kits are also available to remove surface dirt from a CD. However, CD's that are scratched may not be recoverable. Smoky environments would most likely have problems with dirty CD-ROM lenses.

Sound Cards

One very obvious symptom for sound card malfunctions is a quiet PC. Several simple problems cause no sound starting with having the speakers plugged into the wrong jack. Sound cards have jacks for speaker output, microphone input, and sometimes line input. Plugging the speakers into the microphone jack and vice versa is a common error.

Another common error causing no sound is not having power to the speakers. Most speakers are powered. They must have either battery power or power from a low-wattage transformer plugged into AC power. Without power, the speakers make no sound. Not only does power have to be provided to the speakers, but they must also be turned on. The volume on the speakers must be turned up as well. There are several speaker volume controls. The most obvious are on the speakers themselves. The less obvious are the Windows software volume controls. These are available through the speaker Icon in the task bar (system tray) or through the sound-playing application program. When the PC sound card volume is set down in software, the PC is silent. Testing the sound can be performed using the Windows control panel sounds function or using multimedia programs. See Figure 3–10.

Alternatively, in the Windows media folder are several MID files that play using the Windows media player. These are an excellent sound test because they run several minutes permitting testing of jack connections, volume settings, and speaker power.

Sound cards need driver programs to operate. Installing the board in a PC is no guarantee that the driver programs are installed as well. Not only do the drivers have to be installed, but there can be no resource conflicts with other devices. To provide compatibility with other sound cards, sound cards use several I/O port addresses, a DMA channel and sometimes more than a single IRQ. If these settings are not conflict free, then the PC produces no sound.

Figure 3–10
*Control panel
sounds Icon*

Communications

The main communications devices are modems for Wide Area Networking (WAN) and Network Interface Cards (NICs) for Local Area Networking (LANs). Each PC component has its own unique problems. Most communications problems for LANs and modems are related to the communications channel. When a channel is bad, Windows becomes unstable and unpredictable.

MODEMS

Modems modulate digital data from the PC converting it into analog tones that travel through the telephone network. They convert four bits at a time into a unique token (combination) of signal phase and amplitude. Sixteen tokens are used to encode the incoming digital stream into a voice-like analog signal.

Bad telephone lines cause most common modem problems. The modem is installed in the PC and really working properly until it is time to place a phone call. The first thing that can go wrong is the phone jack being wired so that the phone line is on the yellow and black wires on the outside of the RJ-11 jack. Modems expect the red and green wires in the center of the RJ-11 jack to be the active phone line. When the line is not connected, the modem displays a "no dial tone" message. A simple test is to plug any analog phone into the phone jack to verify dial tone.

Sometimes the modem can dial the target number but has difficulty making a connection. This is due to poor line quality. Both sending and receiving modems try to match up at the top signaling rate for the given analog line quality. They dynamically adjust their signaling to compensate for changing electrical characteristics of the telephone line. Unfortunately, there are some telephone lines that are so poor, the modems just cannot communicate. The resolution here is to try different target numbers. If all the different numbers tried produce similar poor transmission quality results, then perhaps the line between your facility and the telephone company facility is at fault. Its quality can be tested by connecting an analog telephone in the line and dialing "1." This connects the phone to the long distance channel bank in the telephone company central office. When listening to this connection, the phone line should be perfectly silent. Any pops heard indicate impulse noise. A short circuit or current loss in the line causes a loud hum. These noises indicate poor line quality. Be sure that no wiring inside your facility is responsible for the poor transmission quality, otherwise it is an expensive telephone company line repair. Each telephone line has surge suppressors installed on them. Sometimes lightning destroys the surge suppressors, causing the line to be bad. The telephone company replaces faulty surge suppressors.

Another common problem is dialing a nonoperating number or a long distance number requiring a full eleven digits to complete the call. In this case the telephone company plays an error message which a caller hears but which might not be heard when using a modem because the modem speaker is set to low volume. Some programs provide a menu item for modem control. See Figure 3–11.

Using an analog phone to call the target number to verify it is a reachable number identifies and helps solve this type of malfunction. When calling the target number, you should hear the modem at the remote end answer the phone. Of course, calling people with your modem can really freak them out because you can hear them but they can only hear your modem. Dialing the correct number with the proper dialing digits solves this problem.

Some modem problems are caused by serial port conflicts. Common symptoms of this problem are the inability to talk to the modem. The software cannot communicate with the modem so it issues an error message.

In this case, the PC cannot talk to the modem at all. Adjusting the modem or serial port settings so that one or the other resides on COM3 or

Figure 3–11 *AOL program modem volume control*

COM4 fixes this problem. Generally, the serial port setting adjustment involves pointing the software to the correct serial port. In some cases it may require that PC hardware be reconfigured to COM3 or COM4. This may be done using a PC's CMOS setup program.

When your PC displays a "no dial tone message" there are no serial port conflicts and the modem is working with the PC properly. The control panel modem settings permit testing the modem. See Figure 3–12.

Test the modem by selecting diagnostics, then more info. When the modem responds, the port settings don't conflict and the modem works. Resource conflicts are resolved by using the POST setup program to change the main logic board's serial port settings or by changing the jumpers of NVRAM settings on the modem card.

Most often the conflict is caused by Windows 95/98 plug-and-play software finding conflicts between modem option cards and the main logic board built-in serial ports. This just means that Windows cannot solve the problem without someone adjusting the PC hardware.

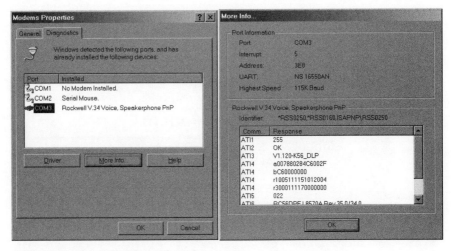

Figure 3–12   *Control panel modem test*

LAN BOARDS

Somewhat similar to modems, Local Area Network (LAN) boards may have problems with LAN cabling. The PC displays error messages like "unable to browse network" if the cable does not connect it to the LAN. Observing the lights on the wiring hub into which the LAN board is plugged is sufficient to perform simple cable verification. Bad cable connections do not light the lights. Software conflicts or bad LAN board drivers in the PC cause the wiring hub lights to be out. In this instance, it is not a hardware problem, but a software conflict that is the culprit. Powering off the PC and restarting it generally identifies hardware or software problems.

If software is causing the problem, the wiring hub lights should light and stay lit until the LAN software deactivates the LAN board. When it is a hardware problem, the wiring hub lights never light. When installing a new PC, a good hardware test is to swap cables. If the light now lights, there is a cable or a hub problem on the old port. Otherwise the LAN board is probably defective or improperly installed.

Other LAN board problems are caused by resource conflicts with other PC components. LAN boards can sometimes share IRQ resources. Good settings are IRQ 5 and I/O port address 300, 320, or 340. IRQ 9 is also a good choice. Resource conflicts are resolved using the Windows control panel. The conflicting devices are removed and Windows restarted. Its plug-and-play capability can then resolve the resource conflicts. See Figure 3–13.

PCI bus devices may sometimes be moved into different slots to fix resource conflicts. The PC has a specific resource assignment scan order. Typically main logic board resources are assigned first. Then ISA bus devices, and finally PCI bus devices according to a specific PCI bus scan order. Changing the position of the LAN board in the PCI bus can change a LAN board's resource assignments.

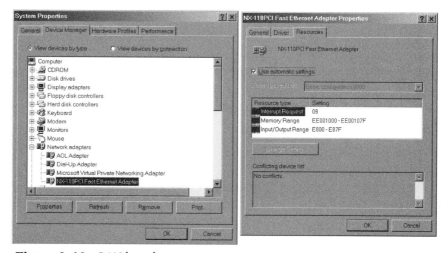

Figure 3–13 *LAN board resources*

The final network malfunction area is caused by network software. Unless the network software is configured precisely, network communications can fail. Key network software parameters for Transmission Control Protocol/Internet Protocol (or Internet Packet protocol)—that is TCP/IP—are:

- Dynamic Host Configuration Protocol (DHCP) enabled—specified as obtain an IP address automatically.
- Windows Internet Naming Service (WINS) enabled and server specified—this points to a specific server that tracks all the other devices on the network. It is like an Internet Domain Name Server (DNS).
- Default Gateway—points to a system linking networks and routing data between them.

Other settings like IP address and subnet mask settings may also be important in assuring proper network software operation. These are discussed later in Chapter 8 and Chapter 16.

When the network software is not properly configured, the PC appears frozen while it attempts to communicate with other network components.

Other network software implements Network BIOS Extended User Interface (NetBEUI) protocol and Sequenced Packet Exchange/Internet Packet Exchange (SPX/IPX or, more commonly, IPX/SPX) protocol. This software, while more automatic than Window's TCP/IP software, also has some configuration parameters that must be properly set for reliable network operation.

Whenever the network software is not configured accurately, the PC slows way down because it is looking for responses to broadcast messages from other stations on the network. The broadcast messages are network overhead identifying network devices and coordinating activity between devices attached to the network.

Slot Covers

PC boards are inserted in the bus connectors and bolted into the rear of the PC's chassis. When boards are not installed in the bus and bolted to the chassis, PC's have "L"-shaped covers for the bus connector slots. These slot covers should be installed when there are no boards in a connector slot. They assure that the cooling air is circulated around the components to provide proper cooling.

Each PC is designed to have the majority of the cooling air enter at the front of the PC, flow across the CPU and the option cards, then exit the rear assisted by the power supply fan blowing it out the rear of the PC. When this airflow is disrupted, the PC components can overheat. For example, one of the people working on this book installed a second fan in their personal PC. They had the second fan blowing air out of the PC's chassis, thinking this would increase the airflow inside the PC. It did not. What happened is that the flow of air across the CPU chip and other heat sensitive components was disrupted and reduced, causing them to overheat. The second fan should have blown air into the PC, enhancing the flow of air through the chassis, thus assisting in cooling. Slot covers keep the airflow across critical components smooth and in the flow pattern that promotes cooling. Removing them breaks up this smooth airflow, making it hotter inside the PC.

The slot covers also help reduce RF emissions from the PC. Every PC emits RF signals. The slot covers help reduce these RF emissions by covering the expansion card slot openings with chassis grounded metal covers.

Study Break

Disk Drive Geometry

To understand disk drive geometry we can use the CMOS setup to determine different disk drive capacities. Using the PC CMOS setup program:

1. Reboot the PC and hit the key (generally F1, F2 or Delete) that enters the CMOS setup program. In the main menu options, select a disk drive (first or second drive on primary IDE controller or first or second drive on secondary IDE controller). Use a drive location that does not have a physical drive installed. Cycle through the configuration options until user-defined or manual appears. Enter a cylinder—head—sector combination and record for that combination setting the disk drive capacity CMOS calculates. Try 1,024 cylinders—16 heads—63 sectors to get 504 MB. Try 1024 cylinders—64 heads—128 sectors to get a 4 GB disk drive. Try 3893 cylinders—16 heads—63 sectors. Are any of these configurations prohibited? If they are, the PC may have an older BIOS. Return the drive selection to its original configuration.

2. Go to the Advanced options and peripheral configuration. Select the serial ports and cycle through the addresses. Which options are possible? Which conform to standard COM1, COM2, COM3, and COM4 settings? Do any settings permit using COM1 on the serial ports?

Return the PC to the original settings.

A+   3.4   **Troubleshooting Tools**

Almost anything is a troubleshooting tool. In the sections above, we suggest using an analog telephone to verify telephone line operation. Stereo headphones can be used as speaker test equipment because they do not require power to produce sound and they are easy to carry. A light that works is a tool that can verify AC power to a wall outlet.

These tools seem less than professional. After all, shouldn't a service person walk in wearing a white jump suit and pulling a chest of tools. Shouldn't there be soldering irons, chip extractors, etc. Well, no, not really. If this were the case, service personnel would be quite musclebound. Also, with the low cost of PC components, by the time a chip is replaced on a defective component, the cost of that repaired component would be three times the cost of a brand new replacement component.

An effective PC troubleshooting tool kit contains both hardware and software components. Some recommended hardware parts, tools, and accessories are:

- A small flash light
- Battery packs and batteries
- A multimeter (See Figure 3–14)
- A standardized PC tool kit
- A hex-key set
- An antistatic mat
- An antistatic strap
- Compressed air
- Small vacuum cleaner
- SIMMs and DIMMs—that have been tested—30-pin, 72-pin and 168-pin configurations
- Ribbon cables for floppy, older fixed disk, IDE and SCSI controllers (both 50-pin and 68-pin high-density SCSI cables)
- Parallel cable 25-pin female to 25-pin female connectors
- Parallel cable 25-pin female to Centronics connectors
- Serial cable adapters 9-pin female to 25-pin male and 25-pin female to 9-pin male
- Power supply splitter cables that add connectors for 5.25-inch and 3.5-inch disk drives
- Power cords
- Keyboard DIN-to-IBM adapter and IBM-to-DIN adapter
- VGA extension cable

- Keyboard extension cable
- Cable ties
- Labels for I/O ports, cables, etc.
- Plastic mounts for PC mother boards
- Large and small cooling fans for power supplies
- Heat sinks and cooling fans for both socket style and slot 1 CPU chips
- Assorted screws for attaching miscellaneous hardware like mounting brackets
- A small pen magnet for retrieving dropped hardware (caution around disks!)

The most effective troubleshooting tool is careful thinking and the ability to use what is at hand to verify proper PC operation—for instance, the analog telephone.

There are a few useful tools that a service person should have on hand. Most of this is software. A virus-free DOS bootable diskette is a key tool. There should be both DOS 6.2x and Windows 98 DOS bootable diskettes. Other software tools are important as well.

Figure 3–14
Typical digital multimeter

Troubleshooting Diskettes

One procedure to use in isolating malfunctions of PC hardware or software is to use a bootable diskette.

Creating a Bootable Diskette

Create a bootable diskette using FORMAT and SYS programs. Then use the Windows 95/98 startup diskette feature to create a bootable diskette to start Windows.

1. Place a diskette in drive A: and then enter FORMAT A:/S. Once formatted, enter DIR A: /Ogn /A to see what files are installed. Is DBLSPACE.BIN or DRVSPACE.BIN installed?

2. Using the same diskette, enter SYS A:. Next enter DIR A:/Ogn /A to see the files installed. Have they changed at all?

3. Use the Windows control panel—add remove programs—start up disk to create a bootable diskette. Has Windows placed any other programs on the diskette?

The user needs to copy several key DOS programs onto the floppy, including:

- FDISK—Tests fixed disk drive and controller.
- FORMAT—Formats (creates the directory and FAT) fixed and floppy disks.
- ATTRIB—This program changes the attributes of files. They can be set or reset as Hidden, System, or Read only.
- DEBUG—Sometimes used to setup fixed disk. This program is optional.
- MODE—Used to test serial and parallel ports.
- MSD—The DOS diagnostic program.
- SMARTDRV—The DOS disk cache program.
- DOSKEY—The up arrow repeats command line.
- EDIT—Any good American Standard Code for Information Interchange (ASCII) text editor is fine here.
- COMP—Compares files.
- FC—Compares files line-by-line and shows differences.
- MSAV—The MS DOS virus scanning program.
- DEFRAG—The DOS disk defragmentation program.
- MEM—The DOS memory viewing program.
- HIMEM.SYS—Boots using memory management but no UMB space.

- EMM386.EXE—The DOS upper memory area and Expanded Memory Specification (EMS) manager program.
- UNDELETE and UNFORMAT programs to recover lost data.
  A bootable diskette should include all files and programs referenced in CONFIG.SYS and AUTOEXEC.BAT. This would mean any drivers for the CD-ROM as well as MSCDEX.EXE. All these programs may not fit on just one diskette, so several bootable diskettes may need to be prepared.

Study Break

Bootable Virus Scanning Diskette

As an exercise: Create a bootable diskette using drive A: and then place virus-scanning software on it. Next power off the PC and restart booting from the diskette and scan your PC for viruses.

Other diskettes to have handy and clearly labeled are:

- Driver program diskettes for all hardware installed in the PCs supported. This would include SCSI disk drivers, sound card drivers, video drivers, RAID configuration software, and other special hardware drivers.
- A virus scanning program diskette.
- A diagnostic program diskette for special boards—for instance, LAN boards, mainframe communication boards, and scanner interfaces.
- A diskette containing standard CONFIG.SYS and AUTOEXEC.BAT files, standard Windows WIN.INI and SYSTEM.INI files, and standard Windows for Workgroups WIN.INI and SYSTEM.INI files.
- Novell DOS LAN programs for Ethernet and token ring adapters. These can provide a handy and quick way to test adapter settings.
- A TweakUI diskette to install and then remove the Windows user interface control program.
- An ERU program diskette to make Windows Registry backups
- A diskette with a clean and simple SYSTEM.DAT Registry file. Several different SYSTEM.DAT diskettes could be created each for a specific PC hardware/software configuration supported. Because the SYSTEM.DAT file is larger than 1.44 MB, it will need to be compressed.
- A CD with the service packs for Windows 95, Windows 98, Windows NT 3.51, Windows NT 4.0, Microsoft Office, etc.
- Some performance and PC testing software like the DOS MSD program. Chapter 15 covers MSD and other programs in more detail.

These diskettes provide essential diagnostic and troubleshooting tools. The most important troubleshooting tool is a good, virus-free bootable DOS diskette and the PC's POST in ROM.

Multimeter

Multimeters test voltages and resistance. They are digital or analog. They can test for Alternating Current (AC) voltage, Direct Current (DC) voltage, and resistance.

The AC voltage test is useful in determining whether the PC has power. It is similar to plugging a lamp into a socket to determine that power is present. The multimeter can be used to trace power to and from the PC's front panel switch making it more useful than the lamp.

DC voltage tests determine whether power is being provided to the PC's main logic board, and the disk drives. The DC voltage tests also show whether both 5-volt and 12-volt power is being delivered where needed. While the multimeter can provide detailed testing inside the PC for DC power, most times a lack of power is very obvious and multimeter testing is not needed.

The resistance test determines whether there is an electrical connection or pathway between components. Often wires in cables are broken or connected to the wrong pins. The multimeter resistance check quickly verifies electrical connections and cable configurations. This type of testing is very helpful when troubleshooting PCs.

Spare Parts or "Swap Until You Drop"

The objective here is to use a duplicate system to locate the malfunctioning component. You take an identical PC and swap the malfunctioning component. The goal is to have the good PC turn bad and the bad PC to become good. This verifies that indeed the component has failed. See Figure 3–15. However, other scenarios might occur.

You swap the component and then both PCs turn into bad PCs. Bummer! This is probably caused by a setup problem in both PCs. Let's hope. This is almost your worst nightmare.

Next you swap the components back and find that both PCs remain bad PCs. Real bummer—this is your worst nightmare (kind of like realizing that you purchased the 100 million-dollar power ball lottery ticket and it was run through the wash in your shirt pocket). Fortunately, this rarely happens. In this case you cannot tell which is the killer (if there is any killer), because it could be the component or the original PC. The only to know for sure is to

Figure 3–15
Swap Until You Drop

use another PC to test the component again. If it were to then turn bad, you have the killer component. Should you perform this test? No way!

You could have things really go your way, and when the components are swapped both PC systems turn into good PCs. Should you swap back to see if they return to their old state of bad PC and good PC? If it isn't broke, then do not try to fix it.

Once a PC begins working fine, quit right there. Clean up the computer and leave. There have been several occasions where I thought that just one more step would make things better only to find myself sucked into a larger PC problem that I just created.

Study Break

PC Resources

Using the Windows 95/98 control panel, view the PC resource allocations. Print a summary of the PCs configuration.

1. Open the Windows control panel and choose the system icon. Open it by double clicking and then select the device manager tab. While computer is highlighted, click the properties button. A display of all the assigned IRQs should appear.

2. Select the Input/Output option and the assigned I/O ports are displayed.

3. Select the DMA and Memory buttons and review their assignments.

4. Exit the device manager properties and return to the main menu display. Select print and print a detailed configuration for the PC.

A+ 3.5 Troubleshooting Procedures and Practices

Oftentimes PC problems are obvious. If you cannot read from a fixed disk drive and the drive is making strange noises, chances are the drive has failed. I had a PRIAM drive that was squeaky. I fixed the squeak by periodically spraying WD-40 on the static electricity drain bearing. One day after returning from a trip, I performed a directory on my drive C: only to have my PC respond with "Failure Reading Fixed Disk." I immediately rebooted and got the message "Boot Drive Not Found." I then powered the PC off, then on. When it powered up, I could plainly hear the disk drive trying to reach its operating speed of 3,600 RPM, but it just could not quite get there. It would then fall back to a lower speed and try again.

What had happened was the WD-40 I had used to quiet the drive had gotten small particles of dust sucked up into the bearing. Those dust particles wore out the bearing so the drive could not spin at the correct speed. One dead drive and all its data lost. Oops!

As mentioned in the section under disk drive failure, your best insurance policy against system failures is a good and frequent set of backups. Your system is only as safe as the quality and reliability of your last backup, so the importance of making and storing regular backups cannot be overemphasized. It is also a good idea to keep some old backups. Being too zealous at making backups can leave you with all bad data as well.

Problem Isolation and Determination Procedures

Problem isolation and determination procedures are focused on isolating problems to a malfunctioning PC subsystem. When troubleshooting, always try to break down the problem at the highest level of subsystem. Major PC subsystems are:

- The fixed disk—the cable—the controller
- The floppy disk—the cable—the controller
- The display (monitor)—the cable—the controller
- The serial and parallel ports
- The battery
- The power supply and its fan
- The system board—RAM—ROM (BIOS and keyboard)
- Other installed boards (LANs—host connections—scanners)

For example, is the problem in the floppy or hard disk subsystem? Is it the cable? or is it the controller? Use FDISK as a diagnostic and repair tool. Does FDISK say the controller is not working? Is it the drive? Does FDISK report that it cannot find a disk drive? In this case we are looking for the failed subsystem: fixed disk, fixed disk controller, cable.

FDISK /MBR (/Master Boot Record) rewrites the disk boot record without destroying all data on the drive. This is a mechanism for fixing non-bootable fixed disks and removing viruses from the boot record. A general problem isolation procedure is:

1. Start from ground zero by powering off the PC.
2. Power up the PC and observe System Operation and any error messages or Signals. Typical Signals and Problems are:
   - No display, no fan running—power okay?
   - No display, fan running—bad power supply, bad memory in first bank, bad CPU, bad motherboard or bad display.
   - Basic or fails to boot message—bad fixed disk, lost boot sector or COMMAND.COM on fixed disk.

- Boots and hangs—bad set up with memory, bad memory, memory speed mismatch, or incorrect LAN board setup.

3. Identify the Options in the PC—RAM, VGA, disk, sound card, CD-ROM, etc.

    Most PC hardware malfunctions are nonfatal. The truly fatal system errors are failure of:

    - The power cord
    - The power supply
    - The main logic board
    - The CPU chip
    - The system ROMs
    - The first bank of RAM

4. Isolate the failing or conflicting subsystem and remove it from the PC. Does the PC reboot?
5. Try a different configuration for the failed component.
6. Try a different PC.
7. Ask did it work before? Then what changed? Change it back. Modifications in driver software can often be the culprit.
8. Review the component's documentation for any known problems.
9. Try an exact replacement component. Does it work?

The most logical troubleshooting thinking traces the power flow to the PC components that are malfunctioning. Where are the electrical power and data signals stopped or being corrupted? Answering this question usually determines the malfunctioning PC hardware.

DOS BOOT ERRORS

Some problems are simple to solve like many DOS boot problems. When DOS boots, it first loads IO.SYS and MSDOS.SYS, then the drivers specified by CONFIG.SYS, next COMMAND.COM, and finally the programs specified in AUTOEXEC.BAT. When files are missing or corrupted, DOS displays boot error messages. Some common DOS booting problems are:

- Cannot find COMMAND.COM—The COMMAND.COM file was erased from the root directory or the DOS directory of the PC. Copy the correct COMMAND.COM file to the PC's root directory to fix this problem. It is also a good precaution to use the ATTRIB command to mark the COMMAND.COM file as read only. This prevents accidental erasure.
- Invalid COMMAND.COM—The COMMAND.COM file did not match the IO.SYS and MSDOS.SYS files on the fixed disk. Replace

with the COMMAND.COM that matches. COMMAND.COM files can sometimes be found in \DOS and \WINDOWS\COMMAND subdirectories (folders). The date/time stamp identifies the COMMAND.COM file. A time of 6:22 signifies DOS 6.22 COMMAND.COM. The following times and dates are generally accurate for different DOS releases.

```
DOS 3.1 -  3/7/85 2:43 PM
DOS 3.3-- 9/16/87 1:00 PM
DOS 5.0-- 4/9/91  6:00 AM
DOS 6.0-- 3/10/93 6:00 AM
DOS 6.2-- 9/30/93 6:20 AM
DOS 6.22-- 5/31/94 6:22 AM

Windows 95a-- 7/11/95 8:50 AM
Windows 95b-- 8/24/96 11:11 AM
Windows 98-- 5/11/98 8:01 PM
Windows 98 sp#1--10/14/98 4:59 PM
```

Sometimes times are registered as 7:22 AM instead of 6:22 AM when DOS is installed. But overall these dates and times should assist in matching COMMAND.COM to IO.SYS and MSDOS.SYS. When in doubt, match the dates and times on those files.

- Nonbootable disk—Sometimes DOS cannot boot because the IO.SYS and MSDOS.SYS files have been lost. This error can be corrected by using a good bootable diskette and running the SYS C: command to reinstall IO.SYS, MSDOS.SYS, and COMMAND.COM on the fixed disk.

- Nonbootable disk or suspected virus infection—Erratic behavior or boot problems can sometimes be corrected by using the command FDISK /MBR to rewrite the fixed disk master boot record. However, if you really need this to work, it probably will not work for you.

- Lost CD-ROM drive—In this case, the CONFIG.SYS CD_ROM driver program and the AUTOEXEC.BAT MSCDEX program are not loaded or not logically linked together. Check to see that the driver program is referenced in CONFIG.SYS and is installed on the fixed disk where referenced. MSCDEX should be also present and loaded by AUTOEXEC.BAT. Furthermore, the logical identifier must correctly link the driver program to MSCDEX.

ERRORS WRITING AND READING FROM A FIXED DISK DRIVE

Under DOS the disk cache program was SMARTDRV.EXE. Some SCSI and IDE drives had problems working with SMARTDRV. To avoid trashing data on the fixed disk drive, they required double buffering of the data to help them resolve the differences between the virtual data address provided by SMARTDRV and the actual address used on the disk drive. The Device=...\SMARTDRV.EXE /double_buffer entered in the CONFIG.SYS file installs double_buffering for SCSI disk drives.

The double_buffer SMARTDRV option prevents some SCSI disk drive controllers from trashing the data they store on the fixed disk drive. It slightly diminishes (about a 4% reduction) the PC's disk performance. Double buffering ensures that the SCSI disk controller correctly translates the data address to the correct physical allocation unit (groups of sectors) address. To determine whether double buffering is required, first install SMARTDRV with double_buffer, then run SMARTDRV /S at the DOS prompt. If double buffering is not required, the buffering column states no. When double buffering may be required, a "-" is displayed. A yes indicates that double buffering should be used. See Figure 3–16.

```
Microsoft SMARTDrive Disk Cache version 5.0
Copyright 1991,1993 Microsoft Corp.
    Room for  2,048 elements of  8,192 bytes each
There have been  24,535 cache hits  and  2,208 cache misses
Cache size:  16,777,216 bytes
Cache size while running Windows:  16,777,216 bytes
        Disk Caching Status
drive  read cache  write cache  buffering
-------------------------------------------
   A:    yes       no         no
   B:    yes       no         no
   C:    yes       yes        yes <== Required
   D:    yes       yes        yes <== Required
   E:    yes       yes         -  <== Possibly Required
Write behind data will be committed before command prompt returns.
For help, type "SMARTDRV /?".
```

Figure 3–16 *SMARTDRV status display*

WINDOWS BOOT PROBLEMS

The most common Windows boot error is when Windows has just been shut down without exiting gracefully. Windows has log files and registry settings that it reads during system reboot. These files permit Windows to see that it has been shut down without closing everything properly; it then runs SCAN-DISK to verify that the directory, FAT and file structure are intact and not damaged. Once complete, Windows starts normally. (Windows trouble-shooting procedures are covered in more detail in Chapter 15.)When the Windows boot process is interrupted before it finishes, Windows displays a "boot process failure" message and indicates that it is booting with default values. Generally, the boot process completes normally in this instance as well.

Windows 95/98 has boot problems arising from plug-and-play hard-ware conflicts, lost DLL and VxD files, and corrupted registries. The error indications vary from starting directly into safe mode to a variety of error messages.

When the Windows registry is corrupted, Windows cannot start nor-mally. In some instances it locks up totally. In others, error messages indicat-ing lost or corrupted files are displayed. Sometimes lost files are referenced not by the registry, but rather by the WIN.INI or SYSTEM.INI files. Missing file messages typically identify the missing file by name and suggest searching through the Windows system files (WIN.INI and SYSTEM.INI) or the regis-try to remove references to the files. Actually, two solutions to this problem exist. First, you can remove the references to the missing files. They can be removed from the registry by scanning for the file names or by using an uninstaller program. Directly removing the file references from the registry is not recommended because it can create new problems while not fixing the old problems. Second, you can find copies of the missing files on other Win-dows PCs and copy them to the \WINDOWS\SYSTEM folder. Once the missing files are replaced, the error messages disappear. Some new ones appear in their place, necessitating copying more files. Such is the nature of PC troubleshooting.

When an irksome program is launched when Windows starts, it can be started by the Windows "startup" folder, the registry, or sometimes the WIN.INI file "run" or "load" commands. Removing the reference from the Windows "startup" folder and the Windows WIN.INI file is uncomplicated. Removing references from the registry is more difficult and an uninstaller program should be employed to accomplish this.

Corrupted registry files cause Windows to boot and display error mes-sages like "Windows memory protection fault" or "corrupted registry." The protection fault message is particularly nasty, because Windows just dies and offers no chance of recovery. The error is caused by a problem in the SYSTEM.DAT file. Replacing the SYSTEM.DAT file fixes the problem. To have a good copy of the SYSTEM.DAT file, use the Emergency Recovery Utility (ERU.EXE) program and save the backup files into a fixed disk folder and not to floppy diskette. A complete backup is only made when the files are saved to fixed disk. The old registry can be restored by then booting into DOS and running the ERD program to replace all the key Windows system files.

Hardware conflicts and corrupted registry files cause Windows to boot into "safe mode." Safe mode runs Windows with a minimal set of standard drivers as a means to fix plug-and-play hardware and other resource conflicts. Safe mode does not automatically assign hardware resources to any component or permit viewing resource assignments, but rather permits the operator to specify manual resource assignments for troublesome hardware devices. The intent is to define manual settings for conflicting components first, then have plug-and-play resolve the remaining resource allocations. Once all hardware resource conflicts are resolved, Windows boots normally. Sometimes when manually setting resources, it appears that there are no conflicts. But Windows still has the device conflicting or not working properly. In this instance, other I/O port and memory address settings should be tried, one at a time.

APPLICATION ERRORS

Similarly to Windows, application programs can have errors caused by missing components (DLL and EXE files mostly), a bad blend of old and new components that do not work together properly, and Windows garbage accumulation. These errors can result in obvious error messages like "…DLL is missing" or "system resources low" to the blue death screen and memory protection fault messages.

Missing file messages are caused by DLL and other key files being removed from the PC. This can happen when an unrelated application is uninstalled that has files used in common with an application remaining on the PC. Reinstalling the application can replace the missing files while retaining the configuration settings already in place for the misbehaving application.

A bad blend of software mixing old and new EXEs and DLLs causes a variety of error conditions in Windows but most commonly a "memory protection fault" message. To fix these problems, reinstall the software that consistently causes the error messages; apply the current published patches or service packs to the software; or restore previous registry settings.

Out-of-resource messages are caused by Windows garbage accumulation. PCs that only run a few Windows applications rarely have such problems. We have some Windows PCs that have run months without ever having such errors and being shut down. On other PCs that run lots of different applications and many of them at the same time, resource exhaustion and garbage accumulation problems force us to periodically restart the PC. See Figure 3–17.

The system resource meter program provides a means of continually monitoring Windows resource levels. Out-of-memory errors are caused by lack of disk cache memory. When disk space runs low, the Windows cache memory is reduced in size to fit into the available disk free space. When Windows needs more than is available, out-of-memory errors happen. Freeing disk space by removing junk data and programs corrects this problem. Sometimes it is just necessary to shut down Windows gracefully and restart it. Whenever there have been many Windows applications run and closed or there are lots of them open simultaneously and a memory protection error pops up, it is best to shut down the PC and restart to fix the problem. Windows applications are loaded like building a stack of pancakes or flapjacks. One is placed on top of the other. Of course what happens when you eat a flapjack off the bottom of the stack? A mess for sure. Similarly with Windows applications, those started last should be closed first and those started first should be closed last to avert Windows garbage accumulation and memory allocation problems. If Windows applications launched first are closed first, Windows does not perform a memory and resource clean up as well as it does when those are closed last. A consistent pattern of applications usage makes Windows more reliable.

Figure 3–17 *System resource meter*

VIRUSES

When weird errors occur in a PC, one should always think of viruses as a possible cause. There are three types of viruses:

- Boot-sector-infecting viruses,
- Program-file-infecting viruses,
- Macro viruses, and Trojan horse programs.

The boot-sector-infecting viruses install themselves in the boot sector and partition table of any fixed and floppy disks. They are the most commonly encountered viruses. The Stoned virus, Form-B virus, Stealth-B virus, and GenB virus have been found on rental PCs and on PCs at client sites. The most famous boot-sector-infecting virus was the Michangelo virus. Boot-sector-infecting viruses are not spread across a network because the network software prevents them from infecting boot sectors of network drives.

Program-file-infecting viruses infect programs and other files. They may be spread across networks. Some program-infecting viruses are very clever. They encrypt their code to hide from virus detection programs.

Macro viruses are dependent on the application programs supporting the macro commands. Microsoft Word was the first program to have a macro virus targeted at its macro language. As macro languages expand and are used by more applications, additional macro viruses will appear. Word currently has over seventy macro viruses targeted at it.

Trojan horse programs look like legitimate programs, but they gather information about your PC and send it elsewhere. One recent program gathered AOL passwords and other information and forwarded these to an Internet site in China. This is really twenty-first century spying.

Service personnel play a vital role in virus prevention. It is especially important for service personnel to rigorously check for viruses because their diagnostic diskettes are used in many computers. If the service diskettes become infected with a virus, that virus can easily spread to many computers in an organization. The first step in servicing any PC system should be scanning for viruses.

The F-PROT virus-detecting program is shareware and must be licensed. See Figure 3–18. Many virus programs and new definitions are available from a variety of sites on the Internet.

Figure 3–18 *FPROT*

Effective virus detection is now built into Windows and other operating environments. It is most important with all virus detection software to constantly maintain the virus signature file identifying the virus strains to the program. Only in this manner can the virus detection software detect and remove newly created viruses. See Figure 3–19.

Often virus detection software places a virus detection check code in software programs as a mechanism for discovering new viruses not listed in its virus signature file.

```
┌─ DOS ─────────────────────────────────────────────────── ▼ ◆ ┐
│ ══════════════════ F-PROT anti-virus program ═══════════════ │
│ Shareware version 2.14 - September 1994      Author: Fridrik Skulason │
│                                                              │
│  08/15           10 past 3       66A            99%          │
│  382 Recovery    405             440            499          │
│  529             621             777            800          │
│  834             1024            1024PrScr      1226         │
│  1260            1361            1600           1767         │
│  2330            4096            4870 Overwriting  A-204     │
│  Abraxas         Ada             Adolf          Advent       │
│  Agiplan         AIDS            AIDS II         Aircop       │
│  Akuku           Alabama         Alameda         Albania      │
│  Alex            Alexander       Alien           Ambulance    │
│  Amilia          Amoeba          Amstrad         Anarkia      │
│  Andryushka      Angarsk         Animus          Anna         │
│                                                              │
│ ENTER - Select   PgDn/PgUp/Home/End - Move   ESC - Cancel    │
└──────────────────────────────────────────────────────────────┘
```

Figure 3–19 *FPROT virus strains*

Most virus programs run under Windows are updated monthly via virus description files obtained from the Internet websites of the program developers. Because new virus variants emerge frequently, such updates and constant vigilance have become a part of everyday PC support.

If a virus is detected on a PC, it must be removed using a virus-free bootable floppy diskette and DOS-based virus detection and cleaning software. The PC must be completely powered off to remove the virus from memory. The bootable DOS diskette should have its write protection tab set on to prohibit writing to the diskette. This is to prevent further spreading of the virus. Once the PC has been cleaned and the virus removed, all the diskettes touched by the PC should be destroyed. It is easier to destroy them than to try to clean them while not reinfecting the PC with the same virus.

User Questions

A key part of troubleshooting PCs is having the problem described accurately by the PC user. Oftentimes they have no clue as to how to describe the nature of the problem. In part, this is because all error messages are lies. Just like the promises from politicians. The error messages mislead because they often describe a problem symptom that is several steps removed from the root source of the problem. Observing the PC's behavior and all different signs first hand is often needed to determine the true nature of a PC problem. The PC user performs such first-hand observation.

SYMPTOMS OBSERVED AND ERROR CODES

The PC user can observe some simple PC problem symptoms. They should write down if possible any error messages displayed. Other simple symptoms to check for are:

- **Lights**—Are the LED's lit? Do they light when accessing the disk drive? Are they always on when they should not be on?
- **Display**—Is it getting some kind of video signal? What does the screen look like? Are the colors correct?
- **Heat**—Does it feel very hot? Failed components give off lots of extra heat.
- **Smell**—Does it smell like Polyvinyl hot dogs cooking on the barbie? Does it have that distinctive burnt plastic electronic component smell? Where is the smell strongest?

Asking the PC user these and similar questions can help focus in on the source of the PC malfunction.

WHAT WAS GOING ON AS THE PROBLEM HAPPENED?

Problems are often related directly to the PC operations being performed. Knowing what happened the first time an error was observed can help identify the root source of the problem. Particularly, when an error is reproducible with a specific set of conditions, it can help troubleshoot the problem. Having a PC user describe what was happening when the error first occurred or when it repeatedly occurs can provide valuable troubleshooting clues. It's also important to ask the user what about the system may have changed—for example, was new software installed or has the computer been recently moved?

PC OPERATING PHYSICAL ENVIRONMENT

One key to problem-free PC operation is the physical environment. There are three major sources of potential PC environmental problems. These environmental problems can cause PC malfunctions. Checking out the PC's environment helps determine what caused a specific malfunction, what may have failed, and what must be done to correct the problem.

POWER PROBLEMS • The first thing to check for is power problems. Make sure that every PC is isolated from the power source. Trace the power line to determine if there is any heavy-duty electrical equipment on it. If there is, remove the equipment or change power lines. This is particularly important in old buildings where one power line often carries more than its rated load. At a minimum, the PC should be installed on a surge suppressor. If it is not isolated from the power source, the PC's internal components could be damaged. This would cause PC hardware component failures. It is not sufficient to just isolate the PC's power from external surges. Everything must be isolated, including printers, modems, and LAN connections.

PC COOLING • Heat is the enemy of every chip in the PC. When chips get hot working, they draw more power. When chips draw more power, they create more heat. At some point they stabilize and get no hotter, but the heat shortens the life of every chip. It can break down the electrical and chemical composition of the chip, eventually causing failures. This is like leaving a lawn chair in the sun all summer to find in the fall that the plastic is rotted and needs to be repaired. High heat shortens the life of your chips.

The best way to keep the PC cool is to provide plenty of space around the PC for air to circulate. When the office is comfortable for you, the temperature is good for the PC. The operating range for chips is from 50 degrees Fahrenheit to 140 degrees Fahrenheit. You say 140 degrees? It never reaches 140 degrees. Not necessarily true. The temperature inside the PC is from 20 to 30 degrees higher than the outside temperature. As I write this the room temperature is about 70 degrees F, and the temperature inside my PC is around 95 degrees F.

DIRT • If an environment is particularly dirty, then PC components could have heat failures, diskettes could be dirty and unreadable, and CD-ROMs could also be dirty and unreadable.

RADIO FREQUENCY (RF) AND ELECTRO-MAGNETIC INTERFERENCE • All electrical devices radiate electromagnetic signals. Some devices radiate lots more signals than others. Radiating signals means electrical and magnetic fields radiate from every wire carrying an electrical current. It is like making a magnet from a wire wrapped around a nail and a battery. The electricity passing through the wire turns the nail into a magnet.

High frequency electromagnetic signals can disrupt the PC if they get onto the signal wires traveling around inside the PC. This doesn't happen often because it takes quite a high strength signal to be picked up by the wiring inside the PC. Things to watch for are lamps next to the PC, power distribution lines in building walls, electrical transformers outside buildings, and electric pencil sharpeners.

PC's are supposed to meet FCC Class B specifications for radio emissions. To meet these RF emission requirements, all open spaces in the PC should be filled, specifically all open or unused bus slots should have a metal cover plate installed in the external board opening.

RF interference can cause monitors to misbehave, erase diskettes, and cause other PC malfunctions.

STATIC ELECTRICITY: PC SHOCK THERAPY? • One culprit in the cold dry winter months is static electricity. An assembled PC is reasonably safe from static discharge damage because the PC is attached to an earth-ground and there are many electrical pathways to dissipate the charge. The static charge heads for it rather than the chips. In the case of the cart with the PC, the static charge heads down the cart to the carpet and not into the PC on the cart.

A good preventive measure for static electricity is to make the air humid. Add a humidifier to the room. The high humidity helps drain the static charge from objects before they reach a really shocking level. There are other devices that can help like antistatic mats, and straps that tie you to your PC (as if you weren't already tied to it enough). But the easiest solution is higher humidity.

Static discharge damages PC components and erases data from magnetic media.

TEMPERATURE SHOCK OR OVERCOMING MONDAY MORNING PC BLUES • You thought that you were the only one with the Monday morning syndrome? Think of your PC. What happens to make Monday morning the prime failure time for PCs. The answer is simple—thermal shock. When you leave Friday, what do you do last to your PC? Turn it off. What happens to the building heat over the weekend? It is turned off as well. The building and the PC cool down to a nice chilly 50 degrees F over the weekend. Then Monday morning first thing you flick on your PC. The internal temperature rises from 50 degrees to 95 degrees. All the PC components huddled tightly together to get warmth suddenly are transported to Miami Beach. They expand and when they expand too much we get failures. Just think, some disk drives take a while to begin operation (they refuse to boot until warm).

How can you avoid thermal shock? Leave the PCs on. This presents a security problem (like the college student janitor playing Doom on your system with a virus-infected diskette). Is it better to just leave them on? or power on and off daily? The answer is that for most PC's in the office it does not matter because they are neither seldom used nor heavily used. For heavily used PCs, it is best to leave them on. For seldom-used PCs, it is best to power on and off every day. When you have recurring problems with thermal shock, it is probably better to leave the PCs on with a surge suppressor and some kind of key lock for security, than to be turning them on and off.

VIBRATION • Vibration is an enemy of PC components and fixed disks. The greatest risk of damage comes when the PC is being used (data is being saved on it for example) and there is some harsh vibration. When moving your computer, the heads on the fixed disk vibrate because of the jostling received during the move. If the heads can receive a significant shock between 40 to 80 times the force of gravity (40 to 80 Gs), the heads could hit the disk surface hard enough to damage a disk rotating at high speed and cause data loss. All fixed disks have heads that automatically retract to a locked position when they are not being used to read and write data to the drive.

LIQUIDS—ARE THEY CERTAIN DISASTER? • Can liquids harm your PC? What would happen if you were attacked by the office terrorist, you know the one with the Uzi water pistol? They sprayed water inside your PC. Would it live?

The electronic components inside the PC are general hermetically sealed, so that water cannot get inside and hurt them. If the PC is dried out thoroughly it should easily survive being hit with water. Mechanical components are less hardy. If water gets inside them, they may be finished for life.

I had a keyboard that got coffee spilled on it. It cleaned up OK, but was still somewhat dirty from the coffee on the inside. This bugged me so I cleaned it with water. Then some keys wouldn't work. So I dried it with a hair dryer. More keys began to work, but still not all keys. I dried those keys more and melted the key caps. Oops! It cost me $120 for a new keyboard. In that case water got into the mechanical components of the keyboard and killed them. By the way I never was able to get all the keys to operate properly even with the key caps melted.

Water is very hazardous around high power devices like monitors and power supplies. High voltages and water do not mix. One shot of water and disaster. Recall earlier in Chapter 1 the PC monitor being squirted by a water pistol. Needless to say the high voltages blew the monitor. More liquid experiences are described in Chapter 18.

MAGNETISM • Magnets destroy magnetically encoded information. They are a danger to all disk drives and diskettes. Once in class someone asked if magnets would harm the PC. So I took out my trusty magnetic screwdriver and waved it over the chips to illustrate that the PC would be unaffected. This went OK, but when I waved it over the fixed disk drive and then tried a DIR command, I got "Sector not found." Oops! Good thing it was a rental computer. The metal housing of the fixed disk is aluminum. This provides no protection from magnetism. So I scrambled up all the data on the disk.

If you really hate someone in the office and want to get even with them, here are some hints:

- Get a magnetic paper clip holder for them
- Get them an electric pencil sharpener
- Get refrigerator magnets to help them to hold their floppy disks to metal file cabinets.
- Get them a high intensity lamp for their desk
- Get them a document holder with a magnetic highlighter on the side.
- Go to their office and place their phone on top of a stack of floppy disks on their desk, then run back to your office and call them on the phone to tell them what you have just done.

Magnets, regardless of size, are a danger to your data. Observing the user environment for PC hazards is an important troubleshooting step and a means of preventing future PC malfunctions.

Study Break

Disk Destruction

1. Format a floppy diskette and copy some data onto it. Get it about half full of data. Use the COPY /V option to assure that the data is properly copied to the diskette. Put a label on it and

write Mr. Bob or Super Dave after the famous TV stunt men. Now test to see what destroys the data on the floppy. Place the floppy on a florescent desk lamp. Try several spots around the bulbs and the base. Place it in drive A and run a thorough SCANDISK test. Did it survive? If not, reformat it and copy the data to the drive again.

2. Place the floppy under an electric pencil sharpener. Oh Nooo... Now sharpen several pencils. Test it again with SCANDISK. Did it survive? If not, we can reformat and copy the data to it again. Remember to use the COPY /V option. The /V option has copy verify the data copied.

3. Now hold the floppy against a metal filing cabinet. Get one of those refrigerator magnets and Oh Nooo... hold it in place. Test it again with SCANDISK. Did any of the tests render the floppy total useless? This means that it could not be formatted and used to store data again.

The goal here is to see just what lies around the office that can destroy data on a floppy.

■ Summary

This chapter has described how to find the sources of PC hardware and software problems and presented the fixes for these problems. A proactive approach of preventing problems by creating a PC-friendly environment was also covered.

The first section covered how to determine whether a failure might likely involve hardware, software or network components.

The next section on troubleshooting discussed various methods, including the PC's Power-On Self-Test, audible beep error codes, visual and numeric error codes.

The PC hardware subsystems, which include components like the power supply, BIOS and RAM, disk drives and their respective error symptoms were described in detail in the following section.

The next section covered many various types of tools needed for troubleshooting the different types of PC problems. This section also provided a handy list of items that should be included in every PC "first aid kit."

The final section of this chapter discussed a method for troubleshooting procedures and practices. This covered problem isolation and determination procedures for identifying problems to a malfunctioning PC subsystem, methods for eliciting behavior information from users, a brief discussion of viruses and other valuable tips to help determine the source and nature of a PC's malfunction.

▲ CHAPTER REVIEW QUESTIONS

   ▲ Multiple Choice

   1. *UPS means?*
       A. Uninterruptible Power Source
       B. Uninterruptible Power Supply
       C. Usual Power Supply
       D. Unusual Power Source
       Answer: B. Uninterruptible Power Supply

   2. *When a floppy drive light comes on and stays on what is the problem?*
       A. It has no power.
       B. There is no floppy diskette in it.
       C. The cable is improperly connected.
       D. The sound cable is missing.
       Answer: C. The cable is improperly connected.

   3. *Pentium is a _____ microprocessor?*
       A. x586
       B. superconductor
       C. superscaler
       D. super486
       Answer: C. superscaler

   4. *How much conventional memory do DOS diagnostics have to use?*
       A. 320K
       B. 640K
       C. 1024K
       D. 896K
       Answer : B. 640K

   5. *What PC component contains diagnostic programs?*
       A. The display controller
       B. RAM
       C. CPU
       D. ROM
       Answer: D. ROM

6. *Windows boot problems involve what?*

    A. The fixed disk

    B. The registry and plug-and-play components

    C. DOS

    D. SCSI devices and the registry

    Answer: B. The registry and plug-and-play components

7. *A PCI bus does not have a specific scan order.*

    A. TRUE

    B. FALSE

    Answer: B. FALSE

8. *SCSI drives are an older version of IDE drives?*

    A. TRUE

    B. FALSE

    Answer: B. FALSE

9. *CD-ROMs install on what?*

    A. IDE Controllers

    B. SCSI Controllers

    C. MFM Controllers

    D. IDE and SCSI Buses

    Answer: D. IDE and SCSI Buses

10. *Modems connect to ....*

    A. The telephone

    B. The serial port and the phone

    C. The line and the phone

    D. None of the above

    Answer: C. The line and the phone

11. *An apparent modem malfunction is caused by ....*

    A. Calling the wrong number

    B. Using bad modem cable

    C. Conflicting I/O port selection

    D. All of the above

    Answer: D. All of the above

12. *CD-ROM speeds are typically*
    A. Faster than fixed disk access times
    B. Slower than fixed disk drives
    C. Equivalent to fixed disk drive access times
    D. Measured in nanoseconds
    Answer: B. Slower than fixed disk drives

13. *The first 32-bit bus was?*
    A. The PCI bus
    B. The EISA bus
    C. The MCA bus
    D. The VESA bus
    E. The AGP bus
    Answer: C. The MCA bus

14. *MMX means:*
    A. Multimegahertz
    B. Multimedia extension
    C. Maximum megahertz
    D. Multisession extension
    Answer: B. Multimedia extension

15. *PCs can boot from?*
    A. The fixed disk
    B. The floppy disk
    C. A CD-ROM
    D. All of the above
    Answer: D. All of the above

16. *Key PC environmental concerns are:*
    A. Heat, light, operator, and water
    B. Power, cooling, dirt, and RFI
    C. Magnets, dust, LAN boards, and temperature change
    D. Vibration, liquids, Modems and temperature shock
    E. None of the above
    Answer: B. Power, cooling, dirt, and RFI

17. *What program detects and corrects (when possible) fixed disk problems?*

A. DEFRAG

B. SCANDISK

C. FDISK

D. FORMAT

Answer: B. SCANDISK

18. *What program optimizes the data layout on a fixed disk to improve performance?*

A. DEFRAG

B. SCANDISK

C. FDISK

D. FORMAT

Answer: A. DEFRAG

Maintenance and Safety Practices

▲Chapter Syllabus

A+ 4.1 **Preventive Maintenance Products and Procedures**

A+ 4.2 **PC Power and Other PC Operating Environment Hazards**

A+ 4.3 **Safety Procedures for High Voltage and Laser Equipment**

A+ 4.4 **Hazardous Waste Disposal**

A+ 4.5 **Electrostatic Discharge (ESD) Procedures**

This chapter presents preventive maintenance and safety procedures for working on PCs. Preventive maintenance covers cleaning products, procedures, precautions and environmental hazard considerations. Safety practices cover safety procedures when working with lasers, high voltages, electrostatic discharge, and hazardous materials. Cleaning PCs is an important maintenance function although not quite as critical as the cleaning letter we received in 1995 suggests (Figure 4–1). Cleaning, while an important part of PC maintenance, is not actually part of the A+ exam, but is presented here in this book as an supplemental and, hopefully, valuable feature for the reader.

197

COMPUTER SERVICES, INC.

SUITE
SNOWDEN RIVER PKWY.
COLUMBIA, MARYLAND 21045
PHONE/FAX 410 NNN-NNNN

April 5, 1999

Dear Friend,

SAVE YOUR PERSONAL COMPUTER

from an early grave. Save yourself the hassle of down computers. Prevent data loss and sleep easier knowing your computer is not about to mess up your business.

We are currently offering a very special program and I wanted to be sure you knew about it.

PC Preventative Maintenance Program, this thing really works. Electro - Mechanical energy in your computer acts like a magnet attracting dust and dirt from the environment. This dirt builds up on the circuit boards in your computer and causes all kinds of problems, heat build up, short circuits, and component failure, We will come to your office and throroughly clean the interior and exterior of your computer.

Computers in this area should be cleaned at least once a year, if your computer is in an especially dry or dusty area, cleaning should be done twice a year. This can double the trouble free life of your computer.

We have reduced our normal rate of one hundred twenty-five dollars to only $75.00 for orders taken now. Call us today to get on the list.

Computer Services can also offer you complete repair and upgrading of your existing PC system. Remember, we come to you. You don't have to come to us.

Sincerely,

Laurel E.

Laurel E.
President

P.S. Call now before you forget.

(410)   or (310)   (Pager)

Figure 4–1 *Cleaning letter*

Cleaning should be performed periodically in dirty and dusty environments. A dirty environment is in a coal mine. A dusty environment is in a wood shop. While we have talked and worked on PCs in such environments, most PCs in offices are not in such severe environments so that an annual cleaning may be all that is required. The exception might be PCs installed in offices of smokers. Smoke particles like dust are naturally attracted to the PC because of the electrical charges present there. In this instance, more frequent cleaning could help maintain the PC and prevent some heat and dust related failures.

There are exceptions—for example, a digital server shut down at random times continuously over a period of several months. The service engineer came out to investigate and resolve the problem. They opened the server and found it full of half cockroaches.

What had happened was that the cockroaches were attracted to the server by the warmth and food inside. (They eat grease, plastic, and paper.) To get to this warmth and food, the cockroaches entered the server through the power supply fan opening and were cut in half by the spinning fan. This slowed the fan down which in turn caused the server to shut down because it sensed a cooling problem due to the slow fan. Of course, the fan speeded up again and the server automatically restarted when it sensed that the problem had passed. This was an unusual case, but cleaning PCs is an important part of maintenance.

A+   4.1   ## Preventive Maintenance Products and Procedures

The primary objective in cleaning a PC is to reduce heat build-up. There are two impacts from heat. The PC's electrical components can suffer from high temperatures and its mechanical components can suffer from rapid temperature changes.

High heat can destroy the electronics inside a PC. High temperatures cause the components to draw more power, creating more heat. In most cases, this process stabilizes at some reasonable operating level. Sometimes components fail.

Rapid temperature changes cause the mechanical parts to contract and expand dramatically, resulting in mismatched tolerances and component failures. Keeping the temperature stable in the PC's room prolongs the life of the PC. If the temperature varies significantly, leave the computer turned on to minimize its internal temperature fluctuations. If you leave the computer on, it must be connected to a good surge suppressor to prevent electrical damage from power surges due to storms, etc.

Radiant energy, like sunlight, can cause significant temperature variations inside a PC. It may seem cool in a room, but if the sun is beating in from a window on the PC, you can bet that its temperature is soaring, just like it was sitting on a hot sunny beach.

Even though the temperature outside may be cool, PC temperatures have moved from cool to very hot due to radiant energy from the sun. Keeping a PC clean helps mitigate heat-related problems. Regular cleaning can prevent unnecessary heat buildup inside the PC, which, ultimately, may lengthen its life. As dust and other pollutants collect on surfaces on and within the PC, normal and necessary air flow around components can become restricted. Also, dust and lint can serve as an insulator, trapping heat on or near components. It also makes the PC pleasant to work on.

Cleaning Compounds

Table 4.1 summarizes the various compounds that have been used to clean PCs, what they can clean, and how they should be stored.

Table 4.1 *Cleaning compounds and agents*

Cleaning Compound	Use	Source and Storage	Disposal
Water—sprayed on a cloth first.	Almost all PC surfaces except electronic circuitry, especially high voltage equipment.	Tap water or distilled water.	Down the drain.
Water with fabric softener (antistatic chemicals)—sprayed on a cloth first—leaves antistatic film.	Almost all PC surfaces except electronic circuitry, especially high-voltage equipment.	Tap water or distilled water. Fabric softener can be stored in almost any storage area while kept in closed container.	Biodegradable; can be washed out of cloth down any drain. Empty fabric softener containers must be disposed of in appropriate recycling container.
Spit—Yes, its here, but it is not sanitary until the equipment has sat exposed to air for several hours! We have all used this at one time or another.	Almost all PC surfaces except electronic circuitry, especially high-voltage equipment.	The mouth.	Biodegradable; can be washed out of cloth down any drain.

Cleaning Compound	Use	Source and Storage	Disposal
Alcohol (denatured isopropyl 91% or greater)—sprayed on a cloth. *Caution—highly flammable use in static free environment.*	Limited to disk drive and CD cleaning.	Temperature-controlled and fire safe room.	Evaporates. Empty containers must be disposed of in appropriate recycling container.
Glass and general purpose cleaner with ammonia— Sprayed on cloth first.	Almost all PC surfaces except electronics.	Almost any storage area while kept in closed container.	Biodegradable; can be washed out of cloth down any drain. Empty containers must be disposed of in appropriate recycling container.
Detergent cleaners	Almost all PC surfaces except electronics.	Almost any storage area while kept in closed container.	Biodegradable; can be washed out of cloth down any drain. Empty containers must be disposed of in appropriate recycling container.
Antistatic sprays	Almost all PC surfaces—must be sprayed on cloth first to coat CRTs.	Temperature-controlled room.	Carrier evaporates, coating surface. Empty spray cans must be disposed of in appropriate recycling container.
Electric circuit degreaser (hydrocarbon) *Caution—highly flammable Caution—Hazardous to breathe—high-heat produces toxic fumes.*	Cleans circuit boards and electronics.	Temperature-controlled and fire safe room.	Evaporates but must be vented to outdoors for very small quantities or into an air scrubber when used in volume. Empty spray cans must be disposed of in appropriate hazardous waste container.
Electronic contact enhancer – for instance, long polymer compounds like Tweak.	Circuit card contacts to improve electrical connectivity.	Almost any storage area while kept in closed container.	Carrier evaporates. Used in very small quantities.
High-abrasion chlorine bleach scrubbing compounds	Highly stained plastic surfaces.	Almost any storage area while kept in closed container.	Small quantities can be washed out of cloth down any drain.

Cleaning Compound	Use	Source and Storage	Disposal
Soft scrubbing chlorine bleach compounds	Stained plastic and painted surfaces and caked glass surfaces.	Almost any storage area while kept in closed container.	Small quantities can be washed out of cloth down any drain. Empty containers must be disposed of in appropriate recycling container.

Cleaning Agent or Device	Use	Storage	Disposal
Mouse Pad	Keeps grit and dirt out of mouse.	Almost any storage area.	Can be placed in the trash.
Paper tissues and towels	Wipes almost any surface—both can scratch plastic surfaces, for instance, CDs.	Almost any storage area but in large quantities they are a fire hazard.	Biodegradable. Can be placed in the paper recycle trash.
Laser printer cleaning paper	Run through laser printer to clean mechanism.	Almost any storage area but in large quantities they are a fire hazard.	Biodegradable. Can be placed in the trash.
Lint-free cloth	Wipes almost any surface but can scratch plastic surfaces e.g. CDs.	Almost any storage area but in large quantities they are a fire hazard.	Biodegradable. Can be placed in the trash.
Wipes for screen and equipment containing detergent and antistatic agents.	Most all PC surfaces except electronics.	Temperature-controlled room.	Biodegradable. Can be placed in the trash.
Tweezers	Pull loose bolts, dirt, and dust from hard to reach areas.	Almost any storage area.	Dust can be placed in the trash. Metal should be recycled.
High pressure air	Blows dust from inside PC.	Temperature-controlled room.	It is just air–no disposal necessary. Empty containers must be disposed of in appropriate recycling container.
Floppy disk drive cleaning disk—contains **alcohol** *Caution—highly flammable.*	Limited to floppy disk drive cleaning (rarely needed).	Temperature-controlled and fire safe room.	Evaporates
CD-ROM cleaning kit	CD-disk brush to clean CD lens.	Almost any storage area.	Can be placed in the trash.

Cleaning Compound	Use	Source and Storage	Disposal
CD cleaning kits—contains **alcohol**. *Caution—highly flammable.*	Limited to CD cleaning.	Temperature-controlled and fire safe room.	Evaporates.
Magnetic tape cleaning kit—contains **alcohol**. *Caution—highly flammable.*	Limited to cleaning and lubricating magnetic tape drives.	Temperature Controlled and fire safe room.	Evaporates.
Pink **pencil eraser**—acid content—not recommended as a cleaning agent.	Cleans circuit board contacts temporarily but boards become addicted to periodic erasures because of the acid in the eraser.	Almost any storage area.	Can be placed in the trash.
Plastic pencil eraser—recommended as a cleaning agent.	Cleans circuit board contacts and other surface marks where a mild abrasive is needed.	Almost any storage area.	Can be placed in the trash.
Brushes—Static discharge caution.	Loosens dust adhered to PC components for subsequent vacuuming.	Almost any storage area.	Can be placed in the trash.
Mini-Vacuum Cleaner	Sucks dust out of small areas.	Almost any storage area.	Dust can be emptied into the trash.
Vacuum Cleaner	Sucks dust out of PC.	Almost any storage area.	Dust can be emptied into the trash.

SPECIAL CLEANING COMPOUNDS AND DEVICES

There are a variety of antistatic cleaning compounds and cleaning kits sold. See Figure 4–2. They contain detergents and antistatic compounds in a water or volatile chemical solution. Some are sprayed on while others are wiped on. Antistatic cleaning compounds coat the surface of a component with chemicals that drain off the static charge. They leave an oily conductive residue that sometimes clouds monitor screens and makes other components feel sticky.

Figure 4–2 *Special cleaning compounds and devices*

Dust sprays just blow the dust from specific areas within the PC. They are good at getting into tight spots. They are bad in that they do not remove any dust, they just adjust the distribution of the dust. Nonetheless, this is often helpful in making fans spin freely again and removing heavy dust from areas that restrict airflow. A risk with compressed air dust removers is that the cans cannot be heated or they might explode (as is the potential with any compressed gas cleaner) and they can potentially increase the static charge of electronic components.

A better approach to removing dust is to vacuum it away. Sometimes dust adheres tightly to electronic components and cannot be lifted by vacuuming. In this instance, blowing the dust sometimes dislodges it. However, using a small brush to mechanically loosen the dust is a better approach. Caution must be exercised to ensure that static discharge does not damage any sensitive components. Once the dust is loosened, it is then removed by vacuuming.

When vacuuming, the chance of static damage to components is increased. There is no chance that components can be sucked off a board (although in one PC troubleshooting seminar a student swore that they did just that). However, the flow of dry air through a vacuum can increase static potential, so care should be exercised.

WATER-BASED CLEANING COMPOUNDS

Water and water-based compounds (including spit, and my bet is that we have all used it at one time or another) can be used to clean a PC. Water-based detergents that are not biodegradable should not be purchased and used to clean PCs.

The hazard with water-based cleaners is contact with high voltage components like the monitor and the power supply. High voltages and water do not mix and electrical shock or worse could result. Given enough time, water can dissolve almost anything. However, we are rushed and do not have the time for water to work on most occasions. It is possible to wash some electronic components and cards in water and have them survive. In one of my first PC classes in 1981, a student swore that they washed the boards of their computer in Woolite to remove accumulated metallic foundry dust. Sometimes dust (especially that with metallic content) and humidity can short out PC boards. There were no sparks generated here, only PC logic failures and resultant program crashes.

There are times when you certainly would wash PC boards off in water or in a water-and-detergent solution. The only time to use water directly is when the PC has been in a flood or a fire. The PC electronics are already wet anyway. The trick is making sure that the boards are completely dry before using them. We have wet memory SIMMs and immediately used them in a PC, as well as some other boards, on our first TV appearance. In both cases, they worked without incident. In another attempt a VGA video card was wet and placed in a PC to operate. There was no video, but the PC did boot. It required several hours of drying before the video board resumed working. The key here is ensuring that any components are thoroughly dry before applying power to them.

Water and water-based compounds are good for cleaning PC surfaces. Water-based compounds contain water and some detergent additives—for instance, glass cleaner. See Figure 4–3. The recommended procedure is to spray them on a cloth and then use the wet cloth to clean the component's surface. Spraying the compound on the component directly can have it dribble into cracks and crevices, reaching and potentially damaging sensitive electronics.

Water and water-based compounds are good for cleaning stains caused by accidental spillage on PC components or by grease and oil from handling PC components. They break down and dissolve the compounds in these stains.

Figure 4–3 *Water-based compounds*

Water cannot be used in every situation. Recall the example in Chapter 3 where coffee was spilled on the keyboard of a PC and we ran it under a water faucet to dissolve and remove all the last stubborn coffee stains. The running water cleaned all the stains, but caused some keys not to work. necessitating the purchase of a new keyboard.

ABRASIVE COMPOUNDS

Sometimes to remove stubborn stains on plastic and metal PC surfaces, chlorine abrasive compounds are used to augment water-based compounds. See Figure 4–4. They scrub out ground-in dirt and stains on both plastic and painted surfaces. Lightly abrasive compounds should be used on painted surfaces so as not to damage the paint. They remove some paint regardless, but not so much as to severely damage the surface. Stronger abrasives are sometimes needed on plastic surfaces when they have been scraped or heavily soiled.

Figure 4–4
Chlorine abrasive compounds.

ALCOHOL AND VOLATILE COMPOUNDS

Alcohol has been used to clean disk, tape, and diskette drive read/write heads. It dissolves the magnetic dust and grit that accumulates on those components coming in contact with the read/write heads. There are two important things to remember about using alcohol: first, it is flammable. There was a case of a service engineer being severely burned when using alcohol to clean a CRT screen and a static discharge ignited it. Since alcohol burns with a colorless flame, it is extremely dangerous and should not be used for casual cleaning. Second, when cleaning PC disk and tape drive components with alcohol, a compound solution with a small percentage of water should be used. See Figure 4–5.

CD cleaners use alcohol to clean the surface of CDs. They provide special tools for wiping the CD surface without scratching it. See Figure 4–6. The cleaning compound is primarily alcohol. CDs should not be cleaned with other compounds because they can damage the plastic CD surface. Once we tried acetone (nail polish remover) to remove a particularly stubborn smudge from the surface of a CD. This only made the smudge larger, rendering the CD unreadable.

CDs get dirty quickly when handled frequently. Surface scratches and dirt can make them easily unreadable. Oftentimes it is not readily obvious that a CD has become damaged. Only when the specific area having the scratch or dirt is read does the CD fail. When having difficulty reading a CD, the first thing is to examine the surface closely for scratches and dirt and then to try cleaning the CD.

Since frequent handling damages CDs, it is a good policy to handle them as little as possible. Although they only cost pennies to manufacture, CDs contain software worth hundreds of dollars. Proper storage in jewel cases or special CD traveling cases preserves CDs.

Figure 4–5
Alcohol compound

Figure 4–6 *CD cleaning kit*

Storing data CDs is more critical than music CDs because the impact of dirt or a scratch on a data CD is to make some data unreadable, thus effectively destroying the CD. Scratches on music CDs result in skips or misses in some music, but largely the CD is still useable.

Other volatile chemical cleaners and degreasers are designed to specifically clean electronic components. They do not harm sensitive electronics. Because they are volatile chemicals and often toxic in very large quantities, they must be handled and used with care, as shown in Figure 4–7.

When there are electrical connection problems, volatile chemical cleaners can make sure that the electrical contacts are grease and dirt free. They work best for cleaning the specific types of dirt found that are a result of PC card manufacturing.

Figure 4–7 *Volatile compounds*

They also work best cleaning hard to reach or hard to clean electrical connections. Volatile cleaners are not general-purpose cleaners so they do not dissolve all kinds of dirt and grime. They should be used sparingly because of their toxicity and their limited cleaning capabilities.

Some electrical contacts are best cleaned mechanically. Rubbing an eraser across them buffs them, removing residue that reduces electrical connectivity. Plastic erasers used by draftsmen are the best for this abrasive cleaning. The normal pencil erasers have an acid chemical content which tends to etch pits into electrical contacts. These pits can make the electrical contacts addicted to periodic erasure.

Most PCs do not require chemical cleaning, they only require periodic dust removal. There are from time to time situations that arise requiring the use of special cleaning tools. In these cases cleaning compounds beyond those used in cleaning dust from PCs are employed.

The PC Cleaning Process

To thoroughly clean a PC requires an organized approach, follow these steps:

1. **Setup**—Pick a cleaning area and collect all of your cleaning supplies. The most common supplies used in thorough cleaning are water-based detergent compound, abrasive scrubbing compound for plastic surfaces, brushes, vacuum cleaner, special disk and CD-ROM drive cleaners, lint-free cloths, plastic contact eraser, and possible volatile contact cleaners for special contact cleaning problems. See Figure 4–8. The cleaning area should have a working area of about the size of a folding table (30 inches by 72 inches). Be sure appropriate static discharge precautions are in place.

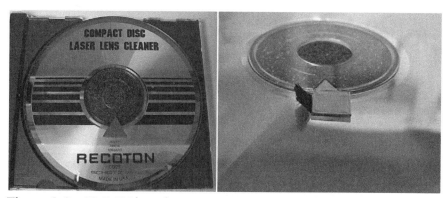

Figure 4–8 *CD-ROM lens cleaner*

Since thorough cleaning requires disassembling and cleaning out the insides, paper to take notes, markers to document the configuration, and strips of masking tape or a bolt holder are needed. Use paper to diagram exactly where all the cards and cables are connected so the PC can be reassembled exactly as it was disassembled. Markers are used to write on components critical configuration and assembly information. Masking tape strips hold the bolts for the PC components. Alternatively, a bolt holder can be fashioned from egg-carton foam. This conveniently holds the bolts in an organized fashion. See Figure 4–9. Each time a group of bolts is removed, stick them with tape to the component they are used to fasten into the PC or place them in one area of egg-carton bolt holder and label exactly where they were used. It is also a good idea to back up the PC before cleaning and document the IRQs and system configurations. For an NT system, you might also want to create a repair disk. These are all good preventive measures that serve as an "insurance policy" in case something unexpected occurs during the dis- and reassembly of the PC during the cleaning process.

2. **Disassembly**—Completely disassemble the PC. Remove all cards, the main logic board, the power supply and disk drives. In this manner we start from the inside and work our way out. Diagram where everything connects and is installed. Place the cards and motherboard to the side in a static-safe location.

Figure 4–9 *Egg-carton foam bolt holder*

3. **Clean the chassis**—First clean the empty chassis. Vacuum out all dust and use water-based detergent cleaners to remove stains. Wipe down all surfaces with a lint free cloth.

4. **Clean the power supply**—The first component to clean is the power supply. It is usually the dustiest. Be sure it is unplugged. If it is really dirty, you will need to open it and brush it and vacuum it out. Blow the remaining dust out with compressed air when it cannot be dislodged with a brush. Examine the fan. If the bearings are bad or it does not rotate freely, consider replacing it with a new one exactly the same size using equivalent DC power. Once the power supply is thoroughly cleaned, reinstall it into the chassis.

5. **Clean the disk drives**—This means the fixed disk drives, CD-ROM drive, and the floppy disk drives. Vacuum them, taking the necessary static discharge precautions. When the dust is caked on, use a soft brush to dislodge it. The front panel and CD-ROM enclosure surfaces can be wiped with water-based detergent cleaner if there are stains. Blow out the slot in the floppy drive and the CD-ROM drive. If the drives are extremely dirty, consider cleaning the inside with a floppy disk and a CD-ROM lens cleaner once the PC is completely reassembled. After they are cleaned, reassemble them back into the chassis.

6. **Clean the boards**—Vacuum all cards and the main logic board while observing static discharge precautions. Resocket all socketed chips by placing the board on a flat static-free surface and pushing the chips back into their sockets. Remove SIMMs and DIMMs from the main logic board. Wipe them with a lint-free cloth, again observing static discharge precautions, and reseat them into their sockets. You also should verify that jumpers on the board are firmly in place. This is especially important for older boards.

   Reinstall the main logic board, then the option cards. Wipe all edge connectors with a lint-free cloth. When there is heavy dirt that is not removed from an edge connector by wiping with a lint free cloth, consider using an abrasive plastic eraser to remove it. Check all of the contacts and connectors to be sure they are clean.

7. **Complete reassembly**—Connect all cables. Inspect each cable connector for dirt and broken contacts. Replace bad and marginal cables as needed. Examine all push-pin connectors for broken and bent pins. Install cables without straightening pins when possible. Straightening pins can over stress the point of contact between the pin and the circuit card, causing the pin to break off. Minimizing mechanical movement by leaving pins bent somewhat reduces the chance of breaking off a pin.

8. **Clean the keyboard and mouse**—Detach both the mouse and the keyboard from the system before beginning the cleaning. Brush off the keyboard and vacuum. Use lint-free cloth or cotton swabs dipped in water-based detergent to wipe down the keys and to swab between the keys as needed. Remove the mouse ball from the under side and clean the ball and the rollers with cotton swabs. Making sure to get all extra lint buildup off the rollers. Blow out any dust with compressed air. A brush can be used to clean the lenses for the optical sensors. Do not use lubricants or antistatic wipes in the mouse because any oily residue can coat the optical sensor lenses, causing the mouse to malfunction. The ball itself can be cleaned with water to remove dirt and grime buildup. Dry thoroughly before reassembling.

9. **Power up**—Without replacing the outside cover, plug the machine back in and power up. Ensure that the PC boots as before and that the power supply fan is operating properly, creating airflow within the PC.

10. **Reinstall the chassis cover**—Now power down and replace the final chassis cover. If you have not already done so, wipe it down with a lint-free cloth. Use water-based detergent to remove any stubborn stains. Remember to spray the water-based detergent on the cloth first before wiping off the chassis cover stain.

11. **Clean the cable connections**—Prior to powering up the computer, clean and check the cables and their connection points using a damp cloth. Be careful as you do this as some of the connectors, especially RJ-45 connectors commonly used with networks, can be easily damaged over time.

12. **Power up and clean the diskette and CD-ROM drives**—Test the floppy and CD-ROM drive to see if they can read diskettes and CDs OK. Use a cleaning disk to remove any stubborn dirt from floppy drive read/write heads or from the CD-ROM drive lens.

13. **Clean the monitor**—Vacuum out the rear and top of the monitor to ensure that there is clear airflow through the vent slots in the monitor case. Use a water-based detergent compound sprayed on a lint-free cloth to wipe down and clean all surfaces. Scratches and stubborn stains on the plastic surfaces can be cleaned with a mild chlorine abrasive compound. The abrasive should be applied to a lint-free cloth and then wiped on the scratch or scuff mark. The monitor screen should be cleaned using a water-based glass cleaner sprayed on a lint-free cloth.

14. **Clean Speakers and Other External Devices**—Power off each external device that needs cleaning. Remove dust by vacuuming the device's vents. As with cleaning a monitor, a water-based detergent compound

sprayed on a lint-free cloth is used to wipe down and clean all surfaces. Scratches and stubborn stains on the plastic surfaces may be cleaned with a mild chlorine abrasive compound. Apply the abrasive to a lint-free cloth and then wipe it on the scratch or scuff mark.

Once complete, the PC is cleaned and ready to return to service.

CONTACT AND CONNECTOR CLEANING

Sometimes special cleaning must be performed on electrical connectors and contacts. This was especially true in early PCs. Connectors can be cleaned be using volatile cleaning compounds specifically designed to clean electronic components and electrical contacts. These compounds dissolve greasy residues and wash them away. They then dry quickly without leaving a greasy residue themselves. Sometimes In rare instances, contact-enhancing compounds can be used to make better electrical connections. See Figure 4–10. We cannot definitively say that contact enhancers have solved a specific PC cleaning problem. We have tried using them to improve SIMM electrical connections. They did no harm, but their beneficial effect could not be decidedly documented either. This makes their use a last desperation measure.

Electrical contacts should not normally need cleaning. Only in especially dirty and humid environments is there a need to clean electrical contacts. Another time electrical contacts may need cleaning is if they have not been cleaned for several years. Over a long time, they can build up resistive residue that can necessitate cleaning.

Figure 4–10
*Contact
enhancer*

REMOVING DUST—CHASSIS, POWER SUPPLIES, FANS

Dust inside the PC retains heat in the chips because it acts like an insulating blanket blocking conductive airflow, thus keeping heat generated inside the chip inside the chip. Hot chips draw more current and consequently create more heat. That heat is retained in the chip, causing it to draw more power. This vicious cycle eventually either stabilizes or the chip fails. Cleaning a PC periodically reduces the impact of dirt and dust accumulation. The frequency of cleaning varies depending upon how dirty and dusty the PC's environment. PCs in coal mines need frequent and regular cleaning because coal dust invades and adheres to everything. To complicate matters, coal dust is conductive because it is composed largely of carbon. In offices with smokers, there are very fine dust particles from the smoke. This dust can shorten the life of disk drives and other PC components.

A rule of thumb is that a PC should have an annual inspection and clean up. Our servers run 24 hours a day seven days a week (24x7) for months and months without cleaning. They are cleaned about once a year or when upgrades are performed, but anytime the computer is opened up—such as for installation of a new component—is a good time for a brief hose-out with a vacuum.

For PCs that require industrial-strength operation, some power supplies provide superior power output and cooling for the PC. These can be installed in place of the standard power supplies. Most desktop PCs do not need industrial-strength power supplies. However, if a PC is being used as a network server, a power supply upgrade may be in order to support the added disk drive power requirements. Generally, servers operate with more than two disk drives. Several of ours have seven drives.

Brushes are used to loosen dust adhering to PC components. The dust adheres because the PC components are electrically charged, attracting the oppositely charged dust particles. Once loosened by a brush, it can be vacuumed out of the PC. See Figure 4–11. When using brushes, care must be taken not to build up static charges that can harm PC components.

Keeping dust out of a PC is impossible because the principal cooling mechanism for PC components is the air flowing across the surface of the components. Each PC is designed with a specific airflow pathway through it.

Disruption of that airflow pathway causes the PC to overheat. Recall the case where a second fan was installed in a PC to improve airflow. However, it blew air out of the PC rather than sucking the air into the PC. This disrupted the airflow and caused the PC to overheat. Another factor that can

Figure 4–11 *Brushes*

affect airflow is uncovered expansion card slots. Make sure that each expansion slot has a cover so there are no empty open slots that change the air flow.

The best cleaning mechanism is to keep the PC's environment free and clear of dust. When the PC is in a dirty and dusty environment, components have a shortened life. We have worked on PCs in an office where there were dogs. The dog hairs and associated dirt shortened the life of several PC components, especially disk drives. Moving the PCs from the floor to a desktop improved the reliability, but did not totally solve the problem.

Study Break

Cleaning Your PC

Open your PC to see how dirty it is inside.

1. Remove the cover from your PC and examine the interior for dust and dirt. Look at the power supply fan to determine the build-up of dust and other contaminents. Clean the PC interior as required.

2. Examine the monitor and other peripheral components for dust accumulation. Are there any areas with extraordinary dust accumulation? Make note of them. Clean the monitor and peripheral components as required.

A+ 4.2 PC Power and Other PC Operating Environment Hazards

A primary cause of PC and PC component failure is bad power. Power spikes and surges tend to shorten component and PC life dramatically. At a minimum, a surge suppressor should protect all PCs. A more detailed discussion of PC power follows.

Power Problems and How to Spot Them

Electrical power is one of the most important things influencing the health of a PC. PCs like a nice stable electrical environment with no power surprises. When there are electrical surges and spikes, they can potentially harm the chips in the PC. Typical power problems are:

- **Power spikes**, which are short duration, very high voltages. Lightning hitting the electrical power grid at some point often causes them. Turning off an electrical appliance may also cause spikes. Voltage spikes might get through the power supply and into the PC's chips. Such a high voltage spike may burn out a chip. You would not see fire and smoke (in rare cases that is possible), but the high voltage would burn out some part of a chip just the same. The result again would be some type of PC failure.

- **Surges**, which are like a spike, but of longer duration. A surge is a higher than normal voltage for a noticeable period of time. It can, if high enough, cause the DC voltages inside the PC to increase beyond specifications. This stresses the chips just as a 20-volt bulb would be stressed if it were plugged into a 120-volt line. In the case of the bulb, we would see it burn brightly for an instant before blackening out. In the case of our PC, we do not see it glow or anything, but we may have a memory chip failure just when the PC was cranking away on the month-end spread sheet.

- **Voltage sags**, which are the opposite of surges. They are low voltage for a significant period of time. They are caused by equipment that uses lots of electrical power being on the same power line as your PC. A simple radiant foot heater plugged into the wall outlet along with the PC can cause some terrible voltage sags (and surges) as it turns on and then later goes off again. The damage to the PC can be twofold here. If the sag is severe enough and long enough, it could cause the PC's power supply to not give the proper voltage level to the PC logic and memory, immediately causing an error. If it does not cause an immediate failure, it may cause the PC to draw more current through its components. This is like trying to cram a size nine foot into a size four shoe. When the foot gets into the shoe, the shoe never returns to its original shape. In a similar fashion, chips can be destroyed by the high current load they experience in a voltage sag.

- **Brownout**, which is a long-term sag caused by the inability of the local power company to provide sufficient power for the demands of all users. The voltage in a brownout can drop below 90 volts. Brownouts occur from 7 to 9 AM and 6 to 8 PM, the peak power demand periods.
- **Blackout**, which is a total loss of power caused by damaged power distribution systems or power generating equipment or downed power lines.

Surge suppressors, uninterruptible power supplies, or stand-by power supplies solve power problems. All PCs must, at a minimum, have a surge suppressor in their power line. Voltage sags can be avoided by giving each PC its own power line to the power distribution box. When nothing else (like coffee makers, heaters, etc.) is on the same line, your PC should be relatively protected from voltage sags. If there is a severe thunderstorm overhead, that is the time you could experience a lightning strike. The surge from lightning strikes can go right past the surge suppressor and into the PC's logic destroying it. In that case, it may be best if your PC is really valuable, to unplug the PC and disconnect every electrical connection into the PC. Turning off the wall switch offers some protection, but not complete protection because a high voltage lightning spike can jump across the contacts in the wall switch.

Surge Suppression

Surge suppressors reroute voltage spikes and surges back into the power line or to the ground. This stops these spikes and surges from reaching the PC and causing damage.

SURGE SUPPRESSOR SPECIFICATIONS AND TERMINOLOGY

The electrical rating describes the power handling ability of the surge suppressor. Typical specification is: 120 VAC; 15A; 60 Hz; 1,800 Watts. This unit operates on a standard North American 115-120 volt Alternating Current line—a standard wall outlet. The 15A states that it can draw up to 15 Amps of current before overloading the internal fuse or circuit breaker. The Watts defines the maximum power (Volts times Amps or 120 X 15 = 1,800 Watts.) Here are some terms you should know:

- **MOV—Metal Oxide Varistor** is the principal protector against surge and spike damage. Most surge suppressors use a single MOV between the hot and the return line. Better surge suppressors use three MOVs. This is referred to as three-mode protection.
- The **clamping voltage** is the minimum voltage that activates the MOV. Any voltage above this level crosses the MOV and returns to the source, bypassing the PC. The lowest clamping voltage measured by Underwriters Laboratories is 330 volts. Lower levels are better. Clamping voltages 50% higher than the electrical rating of 120 volts (around 180 volts) are typical.
- The **clamping time** is the time delay before the MOV activates. A lower time means better protection because quick reaction to the surge lowers the time that high voltage can damage the PC. MOVs react typically in nanoseconds.
- **Maximum surge voltage** describes the maximum voltage the MOV can absorb without damage. The higher the voltage, the better the MOV can absorb the surge without damaging itself.
- **Maximum surge current** specifies the maximum current the MOV can pass without damage. The higher the current passed, the better.
- **Maximum energy dissipation** describes the amount of energy that a MOV can pass before the MOV is worn out. More joules means that the MOV will last longer.
- **Voice rejection and/or noise attenuation** describes the amount of noise or electrical interference that can be removed from the input power by Electromagnetic Interference (EMI) and Radio Frequency Interference (RFI) filters in the surge suppressor. See Figure 4–12.

Surge suppressors are the first defense for power problems. Surge suppressors require periodic replacement because their MOVs degrade as they absorb power hits. The more hits they absorb, the more they need to be replaced. Better overall protection is provided by stand-by power supplies and uninterruptible power supplies.

Personal Computer

Wall Socket Connection

Figure 4–12   *Surge suppressor components*

Uninterruptible Power Supplies (UPS)

An alternative to a surge suppressor or protector are devices such as uninterruptible power supplies or similar stand-by power supplies.

These can be uninterruptible power supplies (UPS) or stand-by power supplies (SPS). See Figure 4-13. Both SPS and UPS devices basically perform the same function. An uninterruptible power supply performs better than a stand-by power supply. A UPS is similar to a bathtub with water running into it. When the water stops running into the bathtub, it keeps running out the drain until the bathtub is empty. No tub stopper must be removed to empty the bathtub into the drain. UPS power continues direct from the battery. Just as would the water continue running out of a bathtub when the input spigot is turned off.

With a stand-by power supply, the tub fills somewhat more slowly and the drain has a stopper. The stopper must be removed to have the bathtub water continue down the drain. Similarly with an SPS, the battery must be

Figure 4–13 *SPS versus UPS operation*

switched into providing electrical power for the PC. With a UPS, no switching is required. Most PC power systems are SPSs.

The cost of an SPS or UPS is about $.50 to $1.00 per Watt. A PC requires a 200 to 650 Watt SPS or UPS depending upon the options installed. The greater the wattage of the UPS or SPS unit, the longer the PC operates without power being supplied. A 200-Watt unit may run for as long as 10 minutes while a 650-Watt unit may run for 30 minutes or longer.

Both SPS and UPS units require periodic battery replacement. Their batteries degrade over a period of several years until they do not hold a charge. Furthermore, SPS and UPS surge suppression capabilities diminish as their MOVs and other components age. The major benefit of using an SPS or UPS over an ordinary surge suppressor is that when power fails and you are working on a PC, the SPS and UPS provide the opportunity to save your work in progress. They also permit a graceful PC shutdown, which can avert some Windows problems from occurring.

Radio Frequency Interference (RFI)

RFI noise is everywhere. It is radiated in the air as well as being noise caused by other electrical equipment on the same power line. Electric motors and fluorescent lights produce lots of RF noise. The risk here is that the noise can enter the PCs logic and cause it to make errors.

RFI noise visibly effects monitors. Once a PC's monochrome monitor started breathing (making a shimmering display) on me. The image on the monitor moves in and out as though the monitor is taking shallow breaths. It looked like the monitor was defective. So it was returned as defective. Through a lot of convincing, IBM gave me a new monitor.

It was installed immediately upon returning to the office. After a short time, the new monitor also began breathing. So PC components were powered off to determine when the power drain on the circuit would stop and the breathing would cease. As the PC was about to be turned off, the breathing stopped. So the PC components were turned on one at a time, only to discover that the breathing started when a high intensity lamp next to the monitor was turned on. When the lamp was moved around the outside of the monitor, the breathing followed it. Oops! It looked like a new monitor was not needed after all.

A simple test for the presence of RF signals and noise can be performed using a cheap AM radio. Tuning the radio into the lowest or highest AM frequency normally produces no sound output because there are no stations broadcasting at those frequencies. However, when that same radio is moved close to a PC, static noise comes from the radio due to the RF generated by the PC. Moving the radio two feet from the PC eliminates most of the noise. Physical separation of RF source from the PC is the most effective way of eliminating RFI problems.

There is a desktop fan used to cool my office by circulating air during the warm summer months. This fan is located 2 to 3 feet from the PC's 21-inch monitor. Even with this separation, the fan causes the monitor to breathe or jiggle.

Storing Electronic Components

Electronic components have both an operating physical environment and a storage physical environment. The temperature ranges and humidity for an operating PC is a narrower range than is the storage environment, as shown in Table 4.2.

Table 4.2 *Operating versus Storage Environment*

Parameter	Operating Range	Storage Range
Temperature	10 to 35 degrees Centigrade or 50 to 95 degrees Fahrenheit	−20 to 60 degrees Centigrade or −4 to 140 degrees Fahrenheit
Humidity	15% to 80% relative humidity with no condensation	10% to 90% Relative humidity with no condensation

Electronic components should be stored in containers or bags designed to prevent damage from static discharge. This is particularly true of RAM memory SIMMs and DIMMs, and CPUs. Furthermore, since CPU chips can be very expensive and are small enough to be hidden in a pocket, they should be stored in a locked access-controlled area.

The storage area can be exposed to sunlight and does not need to be heated. However, when removing and installing disk drives from a cold environment, they should be given sufficient time to warm up prior to use. Rapid temperature changes are not good for the internal mechanical components of fixed disk drives, where tolerances are very tight. Minimizing temperature shock on a disk fixed drive is best to assure reliable operation.

Study Break

Radio Frequency Interference Sources

Check out the sources of RFI using a battery-powered AM radio.

1. Get a small battery-powered AM radio with good batteries. Tune it to the top or bottom of the AM dial where there are no stations. Hold it up in the middle of the room. It should be perfectly silent.

2. Next move it over the top of the PC monitor. What happens? Move it slowly away from the monitor. How far away must it be to become quiet again?

3. Test the power cord going into the PC in a similar fashion.

4. Test the desk lamp on a desk.

5. Try testing an electric pencil sharpener.

The goal here is to develop a feeling for the presence of and impact of Radio Frequency Emissions.

A+ 4.3 Safety Procedures for High Voltage and Laser Equipment

Some safety precautions are required when servicing and working on PC components. Generally, a malfunctioning component is replaced in its entirety and not repaired—for instance, a bad CD-ROM drive is replaced by a newer faster CD-ROM drive for less than the original CD-ROM drive cost. There is no replacing components in the CD-ROM drive and thus no reason for opening it up and being exposed to the laser inside the drive.

Being aware of potential dangers is the first step in preventing serious injury. For example, neckwear can become caught in fans and other moving components. While the motors here are not so powerful as to represent a potential death threat, they can easily strain sensitive neck muscles. Furthermore, they represent a static discharge danger to the PC components. Consequently, it is prudent to ensure that any neckwear does not hang into the components being worked upon. Lasers and high voltages are the primary cause of more serious injury when working on PCs. Other causes of injury are baggy sleeves, long hair, and neckties.

Laser Safety

A laser (Light Amplification by Stimulated Emission of Radiation) is a device producing a monochromatic light beam in which all the waves are in phase or are coherent. All lasers contain four primary components, regardless of use.

- **An active medium**—This can be solid crystals such as ruby or Nd:YAG, liquid dyes, gases like CO_2 or helium/neon, or semiconductors such as GaAs. The active medium atoms have electrons that can be energized to a meta-stable level by an energy source.
- **An excitation mechanism**—This pumps energy into the active medium by optical, electrical, or chemical stimulation.
- **A high reflectance mirror**—This reflects 100% of the laser light.
- **A partially reflective/transmissive mirror**—This mirror reflects less than 100% of the laser light and passes/transmits the remainder on to the desired destination.

Most laser injuries are eye injuries. They represent about 70% of the injuries from exposed lasers. The potential for laser-induced injury varies for different parts of the eye. Laser radiation can injure the eye's cornea, lens, or retina. This depends upon the type of laser (that is, the wavelength of the light emitted by the laser), the intensity of the light beam, and how the different parts of the eye absorb the laser energy.

Laser light beams between 400 nanometers (nm) and 1400 nm can be focused by the cornea and lens on the retina. When the beam forms a point of light on the retina, it focuses the power and increases the potential for damage. Diffused laser light beams have a large angle. They are labeled an extended source and produce a large image on the retina. With a large image, energy is not concentrated in a small area.

Nonetheless, both point source and diffuse laser light can injure the eye. Potential laser injuries to the eye include temporary welder's flash of the cornea, formation of cataracts, and burning of the retina from light absorption and conversion to heat.

Lasers may also injure the skin, but are of much less concern unless they are high power infrared lasers. Lasers creating ultraviolet light can cause sunburn, skin cancer, and accelerated aging. High power and prolonged exposure are required to produce skin injuries.

Warning labels identify the manufacturer's classification of the lasers used in the PC component they manufacture. Laser classification is based upon the following:

- **Emitted light wavelength**—When a laser emits multiple wavelengths, the most hazardous wavelength determines the classification.

- **Average power and limiting exposure time**—Continuous wave (CW) or repetitively pulsed lasers are classified using the average power output wattage and the limiting exposure time designed into the laser component.

- **Total energy in Joules per pulse, pulse duration, pulse frequency, and beam exposure**—Pulsed lasers are classified using the total energy per pulse output, the duration of the pulse, the repetition rate of the pulses and radiant energy of the pulse beam.

Laser classifications are:

- **Class 1 lasers**—are not hazardous for continuous viewing or are designed to prevent human access to laser radiation. These can be low-power lasers or higher-power embedded lasers in laser printers. CD-ROM, CD-RW, and DVD drives use Class 1 lasers.

- **Class 2 visible lasers**—emit 400 to 700 nm visible light. Because of normal human aversion responses, this class does not normally present a hazard unless viewed directly for an extended time period.

- **Class 2A visible lasers**—emit 400 to 700 nm visible light that is not intended for direct viewing. During normal operation, they do not produce eye injury if accidentally viewed directly for less than 1,000 seconds. Bar code scanners use Class 2A lasers.

- **Class 3A lasers**—do not normally cause eye injury when viewed momentarily. However, they present a hazard when viewed using lenses like a loupe or a telescope.

- **Class 3B lasers**—present both eye and skin hazards when viewed directly. Class 3B lasers are not hazardous when diffusely reflected unless viewed at close proximity.

- **Class 4 lasers**—are eye and skin hazards. Eye injury can result from both direct and reflected beam exposures. They are capable of producing skin burns and also starting fires.

Lasers are used in CD-ROMs, DVDs, and printers. See Figure 4–14. They can potentially blind a person when pointed directly into their eye. Even when not permanently blinded, a person can suffer some retinal damage from exposure to laser light.

Figure 4–14
CD-ROM Laser Label

Laser safety measures include keeping the laser in its protective covering, power interlocks to prevent inadvertent exposure, disconnecting power, covering the laser with shrouds to prevent exposure, and wearing eye protection. As a fundamental safety measure, access to the work area where lasers are exposed should be restricted so that someone does not walk into the service area and become accidentally injured by a laser beam.

Whenever working on laser equipment, safety dictates that the laser should be covered so that if it is inadvertently powered on, people are not exposed to damaging laser light. This means that CD-ROMs and DVDs should not be opened where the laser can be exposed. Interlocks that prevent an exposed laser from powering-on should not be bypassed during service. Laser protective eyewear is available and can be worn to protect from inadvertent laser exposure. Protective eyewear is designed to be used with Class 3B and Class 4 lasers.

High Voltage Components and Safety Procedures

The second safety area is protection from exposure to high voltages. PCs convert 120 AC 60 Hz or 240 AC 50 Hz power into 5-volts and 12-volts DC power. The 5-volt and 12-volt power is low voltage and not generally hazardous to humans, while 240-volt power is potentially lethal for humans.

The basic safety principal for handling high voltages is to have a ground that bypasses the person servicing the high voltage component. The ground must route the high voltage directly to earth ground for the facility. Each facility and work area should have an earth ground that is directly wired to a metal stake driven into the earth outside the building. The earth ground for the PC (the green lead) should be connected to the earth ground for the work area and the facility.

All tools should provide adequate insulation to prevent shock from AC power. Power tools should be grounded, insulated, or battery-powered for optimal safety. When working on or around electrically charged equipment, conductors, or circuits, OSHA's "Safety Related Work Practices" require using insulated tools. The sidebar provides excerpts from the OSHA regulations pertaining to working on electrically charged equipment.

> *CFR 1910.269, APPENDIX B*
> *NOTE: .. When any object is said to be insulated, it is understood to be insulated for the conditions to which it is normally subjected...*
> *... Installations energized at 50 to 300 volts: the hazards posed by installations energized at 50 to 300 volts are the same as those found in many other work places ... the employee must avoid contact with the exposed parts, and the protective equipment used (such as rubber insulating gloves) must provide insulation for the voltages involved.*
> *CFR 1910.335, Safeguards for Personnel Protection*
> *... When working near exposed energized conductors or circuit parts, each employee shall use insulated tools or handling equipment if the tools or handling equipment might make contact with such conductors or parts. If the insulated tools or handling equipment are subject to damage, the insulated material shall be protected ...*
> *... Protective equipment shall be maintained in a safe, reliable condition and shall be periodically inspected or tested, as required by 1910.137 ...*
> *CFR 1910.137*
> *... Insulating equipment shall be inspected for damage before each day's use and immediately following any incident that can reasonably be suspected of having caused damage ... Insulating equipment with any of the following defects may not be used: a hole, tear, puncture or cut ... Repaired insulating equipment shall be retested before it may be used by employees ...*

High voltages are in the power supply, the power supply switch, the power cord, and the monitor. The high voltage from the wall outlet enters the PC from the rear and is commonly routed to an AC power switch on the PC's front panel. Newer PCs have the high voltage controlled by relays inside the power supply so that no dangerous voltages are exposed to humans. Generally, hazardous voltages are kept inside the power supply.

Since power switches on PC front panels have potential high-voltage power running to them, all leads must be covered by electrical insulation that insulates both 120-volt and 240-volt power. When the switch is being worked upon, the PC should be unplugged from its AC power source.

When working on other PC components that are not high-powered, the PC should be grounded via the power cord or a separate ground connection from the chassis to the facility earth ground. Optimal safety would employ both the power cord and the separate earth ground.

All power circuits should be on circuit breakers. For servicing, 15 ampere circuits are sufficient. Operating circuits may have higher amperage.

Low-voltage power can be hazardous when it is shorted to ground and produces high current flow and high heat in the shorted circuit. Working around a powered-on PC with tools or even jewelry could cause this type of situation, so always unplug the PC before beginning to work on or with it.

The heat from a low-voltage short can easily and seriously burn a person. To be absolutely safe and prevent being burned, service personnel should remove metal objects like rings and bracelets from their hands and wrists. Metallic neckwear also presents a potential safety hazard if it shorts a low-voltage circuit.

PC Power Supply Safety

When work is done inside a PC power supply, such as replacing a failed fan, the power supply should be unplugged from its AC power source. Special attention must be paid to the high-voltage connections inside the supply to ensure that they do not become shorted during any repairs performed inside the power supply.

Some PC power supplies have safety circuits built in that shut them down in the event of a DC short. Older power supplies incorporated such a crowbar circuit, but some of the newer, cheaper supplies do not. Supplies without such protection just keep supplying DC power to the shorted connection, causing heat and potential fire damage. If a PC powers up and fails to boot, carefully check all power connections, especially those into 3.5-inch floppy drives. Feel the power lines to determine if any are warm or hot. This is a certain indication of a power short.

Liquids are hazardous inside power supplies. Water causes high-voltage shorts, and volatile compounds can catch fire, resulting in serious burns. Power supplies should not be cleaned using liquid cleaners. In a seminar, we tried replacing a burnt-out fuse in a power supply that was in a PC that had

had water sprayed into it during a fire. The PC was fine, but the power supply fuse was burned out. We replaced the fuse and went to demonstrate that the power supply had been returned to service by powering it on. When we did, blue flames shot out the rear through the fan. Liquids should never be used in a power supply.

Monitor Voltages and Safety

Monitors use a high-voltage transformer to provide voltage to the picture tube screen, making electrons emitted at the rear of the picture tube fly into it. The voltage levels generated are in the 10,000s of volts. When a monitor is powered down, this high-voltage is still retained by the picture tube. It can eventually drain off, but this can require days or weeks. Such high voltage is potentially lethal to humans. Also, AC power flows directly into the monitor, exposing that high-voltage any time the monitor is worked on.

Since monitors are typically not serviceable in the field, there is little need to open them up and expose these high voltages. However, in the rare instance when monitor adjustments or repairs are performed, the monitor should be disconnected from AC power, have its chassis grounded to the facility earth ground (not the power cord ground) and the picture tube high-voltage drained to ground. A screwdriver attached to the facility earth ground and inserted into the picture tube feed from the high-voltage transformer dissipates the high-voltage charge, reducing the potential shock hazard.

All tools used to adjust and work on a monitor must be insulated. They should be able to insulate the service person from a 100,000-volt electrical charge. And, only trained technicians should undertake this type of work.

Study Break

CD-Cleaning and Maintenance

Clean a CD-ROM drive using cleaning supplies obtained at a local audio or electronics department store.

1. Get a CD-ROM lens cleaning kit from a local audio store or an electronics department store.

2. Use the lens cleaner to clean the lens of a CD-ROM drive by inserting the cleaning disk and performing the DIR command several times.

3. Find a CD-ROM drive that is behaving badly. Clean the lens of this drive. Does it improve its behavior? If not, examine the CD-ROMs that are being read by the drive. Are they dirty or badly scratched?

4. Try an XCOPY command to see if the CD-ROM drive can read the CD-ROM after cleaning. Remember to remove all data from the target drive using a DELTREE after you are finished testing the CD-ROM drive.

A+ 4.4 Hazardous Waste Disposal

The PC contains some items that use hazardous materials. The most common are batteries used in the PC and in the PC's SPS or UPS. Other items requiring hazardous waste or recycled waste disposal include the monitor, laser toner cartridges, chemical cleaning compounds and solvents, and paper.

Batteries

Lithium batteries were used at one time to power the CMOS memory in PCs. Lead Acid batteries are used to provide backup power in SPS and UPS units. NiMH and Li-Ion batteries are used in laptop PCs for mobile power. These batteries all contain toxic materials and compounds such as lead and mercury. *If a battery is leaking make sure you are wearing gloves before you touch it, and make sure you thoroughly clean the area around where you used and removed the battery to ensure there are no residual chemicals present.* The batteries do wear out over time, requiring replacement with new batteries. When the old batteries are disposed of, they should be set aside and sent to the special battery disposal section of the local municipalities' waste disposal facility. These battery disposal sections recycle some battery components for raw materials (like the lead) and dispose of others in an environmentally safe fashion.

CRTs

Cathode Ray Tubes (CRTs) are a potential hazard because of the picture tube. They also have transformers that may contain toxic chemicals. The picture tube contains lots of glass and a high vacuum inside. If it is cracked or broken, it could implode (the opposite of explode) and spray glass shards in its immediate vicinity. As a result, old CRTs should be sent to an appropriate office equipment recycling facility where their picture tube and other internal components are safely recycled.

Laser Toner Cartridges

Laser toner cartridges contain plastic parts and some toxic materials so they should not just be thrown away. It is a good idea to wear gloves when you change the cartridges, and occasionally you should vacuum the particles out of the printer. Toner cartridge manufacturers provide recycling mailers with the toner cartridges when they are sold. These should be saved in a safe place along with the toner cartridge box. Once the cartridge is expended and can no longer be used, it should be shipped back to the manufacturer's recycling facility.

Recycled cartridges often are sold with the provision that the expended cartridge be returned to reduce the price of the replacement cartridge. Cartridge recyclers provide mailing labels that can be attached to the recycled cartridge box to send it back to the cartridge recycling facility.

In both instances, the boxes and packing materials should be saved to facilitate shipment of the expended laser cartridge to a laser cartridge recycling facility.

Solvents

Alcohol and volatile solvents are sometimes used in small quantities to clean PC components. They are quickly vaporized in the atmosphere. When large quantities are used, they must be applied in a room that vents their fumes through an air scrubber to the outside. The best approach for disposing of volatile solvents is to minimize their use.

Other

Water-based detergents and other cleaning supplies should be biodegradable or they should not be purchased and used. Biodegradable supplies can be disposed of by pouring into a building drain that runs into a sewage treatment facility. Pouring these chemicals down a storm drain or any other untreated drain is not an acceptable disposal procedure. Only drains running into sewage treatment facilities provide acceptable disposal for these biodegradable chemicals.

Checking Batteries

Use a multimeter to check the voltage levels of batteries used in any PC equipment such as speakers, MP3 players, and dictation devices.

1. Get a multimeter and test the voltages in PC devices using batteries. The batteries should be at or above their specified voltage. Any batteries below their designated voltage level are suspect and should be replaced.

2. Power off the PC and unplug the UPS. Open the battery compartment and test the battery voltage level. If it is below the specified voltage level, consider replacing the battery.

A+ 4.5 Electrostatic Discharge (ESD) Procedures

Static electricity is an electrical charge at rest. Friction and separation most commonly create static electricity. Friction causes heat which excites the molecular particles in a material. When two materials are later separated, electrons transfer from one material to the other. This electron transfer creates an absence or surplus of electrons in the materials. This absence or surplus produces an electrical field known as static electricity.

Simply separating materials always generates static electrical fields. The intensity of the static electricity generated depends upon the materials separated, the amount of friction between the materials, and the relative humidity at the time of separation. Common plastic typically creates an intense static charge. Low humidity such as present when air is heated during the winter also promotes generation of intense static electrical charges.

A material like copper that easily transfers electrons between atoms is called a conductor. Copper has "free" electrons. Other conductors are metals, carbon, and human sweat. Insulators are materials that do not readily transfer electrons. Well known insulators are common plastics, glass, and air. Conductors and insulators may become charged with static electricity. Because of their free electrons, charged conductors discharge rapidly when they come close to another conductor with a different potential.

Typical electrostatic voltages generated by common daily activities are shown in Table 4.3.

Table 4.3 *Activities and ESD*

Activity	Static Electricity Produced 10% Relative Humidity	Static Electricity Produced 55% Relative Humidity
Walking across carpet	35,000 volts	7,500 volts
Walking across untreated vinyl floor	12,000 volts	3,000 volts
Working at a bench	6,000 volts	400 volts
Opening a plastic envelope	26,000 volts	7,000 volts
Picking up a plastic bag	20,000 volts	1,200 volts
Removing chips from plastic tube	2,000 volts	400 volts

Electrostatic discharge or static discharge is a very high voltage spark with almost no current. ESD can last from a few nanoseconds to microseconds.

Static discharge can give you and a PC a very nasty shock. Remember to try this for fun: Carry your PC on a rubber wheeled cart across wool hotel carpet on a cold dry winter day, then touch the door handle to a hotel room. Zappo, static discharge shoots several inches. The PC should be fine because the cart and the human carry the static charge to ground.

The real danger with static discharge is to the PC's chips. Particularly the newer high density CPU, logic and memory chips. When the chips receive a more or less direct static discharge in one pin, that can damage or destroy the chip. A charge that can destroy chips may not be noticed or felt by a human.

ESD Damage

Static electricity or electrostatic discharge can cause circuits in chips to have breakdowns in the gate oxide, shorting the circuit, spiking junctions, or latching the logic to a fixed state, often rendering the chips unuseable. This shorting by static electricity is possible because circuit components in chips are only a few atoms wide. Even the small current produced in a static discharge looms large to such circuit components. ESD at relatively low voltage levels of between 200 to 2,000 volts is dangerous to the most densely packed chips. These chips are CPUs, Application Specific Integrated Circuits (ASICs), and RAM chips.

As chips get smaller and more powerful, the risk and cost of ESD damage increases. ESD damage cannot show up for days, weeks, or months after the ESD shock occurs. ESD is as short as one billionth of a second. Its most visible and dangerous form is lightning in thunderstorms. Voltages as low as

200 volts can damage devices. ESD is felt at around 3,000 volts and heard at around 6,000 volts. Visible sparks occur at levels of about 8,000 volts or more. At low voltage levels, ESD is not harmful to human beings, and cannot be felt, heard, or seen. Yet it still damages or destroys electronic components.

Because high-voltage ESD tends to travel over the surface of the PC or component when neutralizing the charge, assembled PCs are less susceptible to damage than are disassembled PCs. Our portable PCs have withstood without incident many ESD events because they were fully assembled so that the chassis provided a pathway for the discharge to follow. Some keyboards and other devices are designed to absorb and conduct a static discharge of as high as 17 KVA to ground.

Protecting from ESD

Eliminating static charge generation and transfer is primarily accomplished by grounding service personnel and PCs. Some prevention techniques are as follows:

- **Service personnel grounding**—Static wrist straps drain off a service person's static charge. The wrist strap or ESD cuff must stay in constant contact with bare skin. It has a cable connecting it to a ground. Wrist straps have a current-limiting resistor for personnel safety. Wrist straps are tested frequently to ensure that they operate correctly. If attaching a wrist strap is impractical, special heel straps or shoes can be used to ground service personnel. Heel straps and shoes must be used in conjunction with a dissipating floor to be effective.
- **Protective ESD clothing/smocks**—Even though a wrist strap is used, clothing must not come in close contact with components or computer boards because the material in clothing generates high static charges. Protective ESD coveralls or smocks serve as a barrier/shield between an electrostatic field on clothing and the sensitive components.
- **Antistatic or static dissipating mats**—Mats provide a controlled discharge of static voltages when grounded. Surface resistance is designed to generate no more than 100 volts when sliding computer boards across the mat's surface.
- **Antistatic or static dissipating chairs**—Physical movement of the chair and your feet on the floor charge chairs. An antistatic chair is conductive with conductive wheels, and/or the frame grounded by a drag chain to the floor.
- **Antistatic or static dissipating floor or floormat**—Floormats dissipate static charges from personnel moving in a room. Conductive tile

or floor treatments are used to dissipate static charges if mats are not practical or cause a safety hazard. Floormats prevent accumulation of static electricity by quickly draining it from workers. They protect potentially volatile areas from dangerous sparks. Floormats should be made of resilient sponge base material designed to reduce standing worker fatigue. Mats must have a grounding strap. Maximum effectiveness requires grounding the mat using the strap and keeping its surface clean. Industry specifications for smooth surface mats have a surface-to-surface resistance $4x10^4$ ohms and a surface-to-ground resistance $4x10^4$ ohms. Specifications for diamond plate surface mats have a surface-to-surface resistance 10^5 ohms and a surface-to-ground resistance 10^5 ohms.

- **Air ionizers**—Air ionizers provide some protection when all static electricity generators cannot be removed from an area. An air ionizer creates a stream of ionized air that neutralizes static charges for a short period of time.

- **Electrostatic field meters**—These meters measure the electrostatic voltage in a given area.

- **Charge plate analyzer**—These analyzers evaluate ionization systems by how quickly applied charges are neutralized.

- **Static awareness labels**—ESD-sensitive PC components and cards must be labeled to warn that they must be opened only in ESD-controlled environments. ESD damage to PC cards or components occurs most often when they are disassembled and are improperly handled. Damage is manifested in complete or intermittent failures. The following procedures prevent ESD damage:

  - Use an ESD-preventive wrist or ankle strap to ground you to the component being worked upon. Ensure that the wrist or ankle strap has good skin contact.

  - When handling PC components or touching any internal PC components, always use a wrist strap connected to one of the following:

    - Installation screws on the installed module or power supply,
    - Special ESD wrist strap connectors built into the PC (if present), or
    - Any unpainted chassis surface to make good electrical contact with the chassis.

- Handle PC cards by their edges only.

- Avoid contact between the PC cards, components, and clothing. A wrist strap protects only the card from ESD voltages on the body. ESD voltages on clothing may still cause damage.

- After removing any PC card or component, place it on an anti-static surface or in a static-shielding bag. PC cards or components that are being shipped should be immediately placed in a static-shielding bag.
- Periodically check the resistance value of antistatic straps to ensure they are between 1 and 10 million ohms (megaohms).
- Humidity reduces the potential for static discharge. During cold dry winter months, increasing the humidity in a facility reduces the incidence of ESD. Aquariums throughout the office provide added humidity and a pleasant and soothing view. Alternately, humidifiers can also provide the required humidity without the aesthetic view. Both are excellent mechanisms for increasing humidity and reducing the potential for ESD. Fabric softener in a water solution can be sprayed around a room to temporarily reduce the potential for ESD.

Common ESD Environments

Virtually all environments have static charges develop when materials are separated. The amount of static build up depends upon the materials, the humidity and the duration of the separation process, for instance, opening a bag versus sliding or rolling a PC across a desktop. Environments that have lots of plastic compounds tend to have a greater propensity to build static charges than environments that do not.

Environments with insulators like plastics having a surface resistance ranging from 10^{12} to 10^{20} ohms build large static charges, hold them for several hours, and attract conductive dirt. This produces conductive paths dangerous to electronic semiconductor components.

Conductive materials having surface resistances ranging from 10^2 to 10^4 ohms do not hold static charges unless they are isolated (insulated) from a grounding path. Once connected to a grounding path, they discharge their static charges in nanoseconds.

Ideally, static-free environments should be based on dissipative materials. Dissipative materials have a surface resistance ranging from 10^4 to 10^{12} ohms. Dissipative materials permit lessening of static charges at controlled rates, not in sudden damaging discharges.

Common ESD environments where PCs and components are susceptible to ESD damage exist while PCs are disassembled and during transportation or movement of components and circuit boards. This includes shipments to a facility and movement of components within a facility.

This is particularly true in cold dry environments. Table coverings, flooring, and carpets can contribute significantly to the buildup of static charges.

Nonconductive plastic and vinyl flooring create unwanted static charges. Conductive, static dissipative flooring minimizes static charge build up.

ESD Inventory

Make an inventory of the measures in place in your facility to prevent or reduce ESD.

1. Are there specific times each year when there is low humidity? Are special static discharge precautions taken at those times?

2. What measures are generally in place to reduce ESD in the general office environment? Are antistatic carpets and mats used? Are PCs, desks, and carpets grounded so static charges can drain away? Is the air humidified?

3. What measures are used in PC service areas? Are there antistatic mats and straps available and used when equipment is disassembled? This is especially important when working on CPUs and memory. Are there standard ESD practices and procedures for your organization?.

■ Summary

This chapter covered PC maintenance, cleaning, and safety procedures. These are an important part of everyday PC operation but oftentimes ignored. The first section involved proactive measures to be taken around regular preventive maintenance of the PC overall and its individual components. This was followed by a detailed discussion of power-related issues and the types of hazards that can affect the PC's operating environment such as power surges and brownouts along with some safeguards against these hazards.

The next section covered safety procedures specific to high- and low-voltage power components and laser equipment that is commonly found in CD-ROMS. The types of technologies used in these products can cause damage or injury if not used wisely, and the PC technician is at risk without sufficient knowledge of potential dangers and diligent practice of safeguards.

The section on hazardous waste focused on the types of waste material generated by common PC components such as batteries, toner cartridges, video displays, and even the products used to clean the systems. For each of these topics, proper handling and disposal procedures were covered.

The last section of this chapter detailed the issue of electrostatic discharge (ESD). It covered the causes of this hazard and effects of it on PCs and their components, and the methods for preventing it from occurring.

Following proper safety, cleaning, and ESD procedures and precautions prolong the useful life of PCs and PC components. More importantly, they help avert unanticipated hardware failures causing serious work delays and disruptions.

▲ CHAPTER REVIEW QUESTIONS

▲ Multiple Choice

1. *SPS means?*

    A. Stand-by Power Source

    B. Stand-by Power Supply

    C. Static Power Supply

    D. Static Power Source

    Answer: B. Stand-by Power Supply

2. *A principal enemy of most PCs is _____.*

    A. grease

    B. soot

    C. dust

    D. sand

    Answer: C.dust

3. *Water must never be used directly to clean PCs.*

    A. True

    B. False

    Answer: B. False

4. *Special cleaning compounds are used to clean _____.*

    A. the outside of the PC chassis

    B. electrical contacts and connectors

    C. the PC case

    D. the monitor

E. the keyboard

Answer: B. electrical contacts and connectors

5. *What PC component collects the most dust?*

A. the display controller

B. RAM

C. the keyboard

D. the power supply

Answer: D. the power supply

6. *Dust causes _____.*

A. fixed disk motor failures

B. heat to build up in PC components

C. monitor flickering

D. sticky keyboard keys

Answer: B.heat to build up in PC components

7. *Water based cleaners are dangerous _____.*

A. when cleaning monitors

B. around high-voltage components

C. on RAM

D. near option cards

Answer: B.around high-voltage components

8. *All PCs should have _____.*

A. a 20-amphere circuit supplying power

B. a surge suppressor in the input power line

C. an Uninterruptible Power Supply

D. a Stand-by Power Supply

E. all of the above

Answer: B.a surge suppressor in the input power line

9. *A surge is _____*

A. a loss of power

B. a change in power

C. an instantaneous increase in voltage

D. a short duration increase in voltage

E. a static discharge

Answer: D.a short duration increase in voltage

10. *MOV means ....* .
    A. Metal On Varistor
    B. Metallic Oxygen Variable Resistor
    C. Metal Oxide Resistor
    D. Metal On Resistor
    Answer: C. Metal Oxide Resistor

11. *A power line spike is commonly caused by ....*
    A. coffee makers on the PC power line
    B. the power company transformers
    C. lightning hitting a phone line
    D. thunderstorms
    Answer: D. thunderstorms

12. *To absolutely ensure that lightning does not damage a PC you must _____.*
    A. turn off the power to the PC
    B. install a surge suppressor
    C. disconnect all cables from the PC
    D. unplug the PC
    Answer: C.disconnect all cables from the PC

13. *ESD stands for _____.*
    A. Electro Sensitive Device
    B. Electrostatic Device
    C. Static Electricity
    D. Electrostatic Discharge
    E. Electronic Sensitive Discharge
    Answer: D. Electrostatic Discharge

14. *What materials generate static charges?*
    A. Steel
    B. Plastics
    C. Water
    D. Carbon
    Answer: B. Plastics

15. *Abrasive compounds are helpful in cleaning _____.*

A. plastic surfaces

B. semiconductor chip surfaces

C. SIMM sockets

D. rubber cable stains

Answer: A. plastic surfaces

16. *To prevent damage from static discharge* _____.

A. wear a wrist strap touching your skin and grounded to a common earth ground

B. increase humidity in dry environments

C. wear antistatic smocks or coveralls

D. install static dissipative floor mats

E. test and inspect static dissipative components regularly

F. none of A through E above

G. all of A through E above

Answer: G. all of A through E above

17. *PC CD-ROM drives, DVD drives and CD-RW drives use* _____.

A. Class 3 lasers

B. Class 4 lasers

C. Class 2A lasers

D. Class 1 lasers

Answer: D. Class 1 lasers

18. *When working with lasers, the greatest danger is* _____.

A. blown CPU chip

B. skin burn

C. erased nonvolatile RAM

D. hair loss

E. none of the above

Answer: E. none of the above

CPUs, RAM, and Main Logic Boards

▲ **Chapter Syllabus**

A+ **5.1** **CPU Chips and Their Operating Characteristics**

A+ **5.2** **Random Access Memory**

A+ **5.3** **Main Logic Boards**

A+ **5.4** **PC Bus Architectures**

A+ **5.5** **CMOS Setup**

This chapter covers the specific terminology and specifications describing main logic boards, CPU chips, and random access memory. A detailed understanding of these parts will help in determining which PC core components can be replaced and upgraded.

The key components of a PC system lie in the PC chassis. These components, Central Processing Unit (CPU), Random Access Memory (RAM), and Main Logic Board (MLB) form the heart of any PC system. They are the primary determinants of PC performance and provide the ability to add the ancillary components that tailor each PC system to the tasks that it is to perform—for example, run games, prepare documents, and surf the Web.

The CPU is the component that performs all the work. We think of it as the hands of the PC. No brains in the CPU, but very fast hands. The CPU swaps data with the RAM across a CPU bus. The RAM provides the work space for the software

243

running in the PC. It is volatile, which means that it loses its contents when electrical power is turned off. The main logic board provides the mechanical mounting for the CPU, RAM, and option boards. It is designed with a hierarchical structure of buses to support option cards with different bus interfaces—Industry Standard Architecture (ISA), Peripheral Component Interconnect (PCI), and Advanced Graphics Port (AGP) interfaces.

This chapter examines these components in detail.

A+ 5.1 CPU Chips and Their Operating Characteristics

Intel is the largest manufacturer of PC Central Processing Unit (CPU) chips. Some CPU chips that compete with the Intel CPU chip functionality are manufactured by American Micro Devices (AMD) and Cyrix. These chips provide performance equivalent to some Intel chips at substantially lower prices. Apple computers use chips manufactured by Motorola and some servers use Alpha chips manufactured originally by Digital Equipment Corporation that are not exact functional duplicates of the Intel chips. These chips run other operating systems like Apple's OS or Unix or they run Intel chip emulation programs permitting Windows to run on them at lower performance levels. Windows NT has been adapted to run directly on Alpha chip computers. Regardless of the CPU chip features, the main difference between chips boils down to better performance. What really matters is how the CPU chip design delivers faster software execution. Chip features are nice, but the bottom line is execution speed. Let's examine these chips in greater detail.

The core or heart of a PC is the CPU (Central Processing Unit) chip. It is a complete computer on a single chip. By "complete computer," we mean that this chip has everything needed to execute program instructions performing data manipulation: a control unit, an Arithmetic Logic Unit (ALU), data registers, cache memory, and more. These microprocessor CPU chip internal units are driven by a raw PC clock signal external to the CPU itself. How effectively and efficiently the CPU runs software depends on its design or architecture. The CPU's architecture describes the internal way it processes data, which is one of the most important factors in determining overall PC performance. Another significant performance factor is raw external clock signal speed or the megahertz (MHz) speed at which the CPU processes data. The CPU's external interfaces describe how it transfers data to and from the memory, the supporting chip set, and other devices in the PC.

Intel CPU Chips

Intel was, among others, a pioneer in developing a microprocessor CPU chip. As mentioned above, microprocessor CPU chips have a complete computer on a single chip. CPU chip or microprocessor CPU chip capabilities have increased at an exponential rate in the 30 years since they were originally developed. This increase in capability is largely due to the ability to fabricate and produce more powerful semiconductor CPU chips in larger quantities. Intel produces the largest number of microprocessor CPU chips used in PCs today. The Intel microprocessor CPU chip architecture evolved from the design of Intel's 8088 CPU chip introduced in April 1979. This CPU chip was used in the original IBM PC marketed in 1981. See Table 5–1.

CPU chips perform three basic functions within the PC: data input/output (I/O), CPU control functions, and arithmetic logical operations. Separate components in the CPU chip perform these functions. The CPU passes software commands and data to other parts of the PC requesting them, and back to the CPU through the I/O unit. Data from the I/O unit is translated into a useable form for the ALU by the control unit. ALU performs arithmetic and logical operations on the data, as directed by the control unit. Arithmetic operations are addition, subtraction, multiplication and division. Logical operations are "and," "or," "not," and "exclusive or." The ALU hands the results of its arithmetic and logical operations back to the I/O unit, which in turn transfers the results to CPU registers, PC RAM, or elsewhere. These functions are identified in how the CPU chip interfaces to the other components in the PC. See Figure 5–1.

INSTRUCTION SETS

CPUs are designed as Complex Instruction Set Computers (CISC) or as Reduced Instruction Set Computers (RISC). A single CISC instruction can be designed to perform a complex operation, while in a RISC CPU, there is a smaller set of basic instructions that can be combined to create complex instructions. Consequently, a CISC instruction needs a long time to finish because the electrical signals used to perform the work must flow through many logic gates. RISC instructions finish quickly compared to CISC instructions because they use few logic gates. A RISC instruction completes in about one fifth the time required to complete a CISC instruction. However, generally four RISC instructions are needed to perform the work of a single CISC instruction making a RISC CPU faster than a CISC CPU. In reality the equation is more complex but the end result is generally true. An offsetting factor is that if the software is optimized for a CISC CPU, the RISC

Table 5.1 *Intel CPU chip summary*

CPU Chip	Internal Word Size	Data Bus	Addressable RAM	Clock Speed	Internal Cache	Math Co-CPU chip	Operating Systems
8088	16 bit	8 bit	1 Mb	4.77 MHz to 10 MHz	None	External	DOS
8086	16 bit	16 bit	1 Mb	4.77 MHz to 10 MHz	None	External	DOS
80286	16 bit	16 bit	16 Mb	6 MHz to 20 MHz	None	External	DOS
80386 DX	32 bit	32 bit	4,096 Mb	16 MHz, 20 MHz, 25 MHz, 33 MHz, and 40 MHz	None	External	Windows
80386 SX	32 bit	16 bit	16 Mb	16 MHz, 20 MHz, and 25 MHz	None	External	Windows
80486 DX	32 bit	32 bit	4,096 Mb	25 MHz, 33 MHz, and 50 MHz	8 Kb	Internal	Windows 3.x
80486 SX	32 bit	32 bit	4,096 Mb	16 MHz, 20 MHz, and 25 MHz	8 Kb	Disabled External	Windows 3.x
80486 DX	32 bit	32 bit	4,096 Mb	20/40 MHz, 25/50 MHz and 33/66 MHz	8 Kb	Internal	Windows 3.x
Pentium 80586 DX	32 bit	64 bit	4,096 Mb or More	60 MHz, 90 MHz, 120 MHz, 133 MHz, 166 MHz, 200 MHz and higher	8 Kb instruction 8 Kb data	Internal	Windows & Windows NT
Pentium Pro	32 bit	64 bit	4 GB	166 MHz, 200 MHz and higher	8 Kb instruction 8 Kb data and 256/512Kb and 1 Mb L2 cache	Internal	Windows NT

Table 5.1 *Intel CPU chip summary*

Pentium MMX	32 bit	4 GB	166 MHz, 200 MHz and higher	16 Kb instruction 16 Kb data	Internal	Windows
Pentium II	32 bit	4 GB	200 MHz, 233 MHz, 266 MHz, 300 MHz, 400 MHz, and 450 MHz	16 Kb instruction 16 Kb data and 256Kb L2 cache	Internal	Windows
Celeron	32 bit	4 GB	333, 350, 400 MHz and higher	16 Kb instruction 16 Kb data and 128 Kb L2 cache on 300a and 333 MHz and higher Celerons		Windows
Pentium III	32 bit	4 GB	400, 500 and 600 MHz and higher	16 Kb Instruction 16 Kb data and 512 Kb L2 cache	Internal	Windows & Windows NT
Xeon	32 bit	64 GB	400, 500 and 550 MHz and higher	16 Kb Instruction 16 Kb data and 512 KB, 1 MB or 2 MB L2 cache	Internal	Windows NT Unix

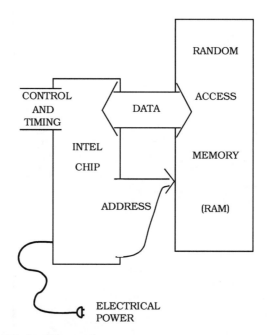

Figure 5–1 *CPU chip PC interfaces*

CPU may need to complete more instructions to run the software, equalizing the CISC and RISC performance.

Intel CPUs are CISC CPUs. Manufacturers such as Motorola and Compaq produce the RISC CPU chips found in Macintosh computers and high-end PC servers. They comprise a very small percentage of the CPU chip market. AMD and Cyrix Intel-compatible CPU chips are CISC CPU chips like Intel's CPU chips. Intel, AMD, and Cyrix chips use the x86 instruction set, which gets its name from the Intel CPU chips with 86 in their product name. This set of CPU chip instructions has evolved with the introduction of the 80386 CPU chips, the MMX extensions, and the Pentium III 3D instructions. The 8088/8086 and 80286 CPU chips had fewer instructions and operating modes. This means that programs written for 80386, 80486, and Pentium CPU chips cannot run on 8086/8088 and 80286 CPU chips. Since 8088/8086 and 80286 CPU chips are obsolete, programs that do not run on them is not much of an issue. The 8086/8088 and 80286 CPU chips worked on 16 bits internally, while 80386, 80486, and Pentium CPU chips work on 32 bits.

The 32-bit 80386 class CPU chip instruction sets are all compatible. Intel had to introduce the 80486 CPU chip without changing the instruction set because so many programs ran on the 80386 CPU chips. More compatible programs were written, increasing the importance of keeping the core instruction set compatible in future CPU chips.

MMX defined 57 new instructions. It was the first significant instruction set change since the introduction of the 80386 a decade ago. The newest CPU chips from Intel, AMD, and Cyrix support MMX or Multimedia Extensions. The MMX instructions provide a performance increase for multimedia programming. MMX instructions process large amounts of similar data at the same time with a single instruction. MMX instructions are especially useful in processing graphics, video and audio data. MMX is an extension of the x86 instruction set. CPU chips supporting MMX instructions run all software that ran on non-MMX CPU chips. However, programs designed for MMX CPU chips are not backward compatible unless the program determines a non-MMX CPU chip and different coding is used where MMX instructions are employed as a result. The new Pentium III CPU chip adds yet another instruction set extension aimed at improving 3-dimensional graphics performance. This is above and beyond the MMX instruction set extension.

The extensions to the x86 architecture are going to be abandoned in favor of a new CPU chip architecture designed from scratch. Intel and Hewlett Packard are designing a new CPU chip architecture, IA-64. These CPU chips will be 65-bit CPU chips using a new instruction set specifically designed to raise CPU chip performance to a new level. The new Intel CPU chip is code-named Merced. It is also designated as the "P7" because it is the seventh generation of PC CPU chips. The new CPU chip must perform the x86 instructions because backward compatibility remains a dominant factor in PC hardware and software products.

CPU MOUNTING

CPU chip packaging has evolved dramatically over the last 18 or more years. The early CPU chips used a Dual In-line Pin (DIP) package. This evolved within about four years to a Pin Grid Arrays (PGA) package. PGAs (which we think of as the golfing package) come in several different sizes. Intel's Pentium II CPU chips come on a Single-Edge Contact (SEC) cartridge. The SEC cartridge contains more than just the CPU chip. See Figure 5–2.

The socket mating the CPU to the main logic board has evolved along with the chip packaging. The first socket for PGA chips was Socket 0. Socket 0 had fewer pins, a different mechanical CPU chip insertion and a different pin layout from the Socket 7 or Socket 8 used in newer PCs.

Socket 7 and Socket 8 are the most common sockets used today. Socket 7 mates Intel Pentium CPU chips and AMD K5 and K6 Pentium CPU chip

Figure 5–2 *Old CPU chip packages*

clones to main logic boards. Socket 8 only mates Pentium Pro chips to main logic boards at this time.

When installing any PGA CPU chip in a socket, the pin one rule applies—"Always connect pin one to pin one." Some PGA chips are designed so that it is impossible not to connect pin one to pin one in the socket, but in other cases it is possible. When pin one is not connected to pin one, our experience is that the CPU chip is rendered inoperative when power is applied to the main logic board. Pin one on the CPU chip is generally identified by a square solder pad around the pin, a notch on the chip, a white dot on the chip's surface, or in some position relative to the label of the chip. See Figure 5–3.

Figure 5–3 *Intel Pentium PRO CPU PGA chip top and bottom*

Intel Pentium Pro and Pentium CPU chips cannot be inserted incorrectly into the socket. The arrangement of the pins on the CPU chip forms a specific pattern that fits into a socket in only one position. Some Intel 386 and 486 CPU chips could be inserted incorrectly into sockets, resulting in PC malfunction and often CPU chip destruction.

SEC cartridges use a connector slot rather than a socket. SEC cartridges insert into a Slot 1 connector or a Slot 2 connector, similarly to other PC cards. SEC cartridges are also keyed so that they cannot be inserted incorrectly. See Figure 5–4.

CPU MODES

The CPU operating mode controls how the CPU chip views memory and manages the programs using memory. Intel CPU chips operate in real, protected, and virtual real or virtual 8086 modes.

REAL MODE • The original 8088 CPU chip PC only addressed 1 MB of memory. DOS ran programs that worked within this memory limitation. DOS was a single-task-at-a-time operating system. It only permitted one program to run at any given time. This type of DOS operation has been carried forward with each new CPU chip. DOS one-task-at-a-time operation is still especially important for PC diagnostic programs that directly manipulate the PC hardware. One good example is programs that flash the BIOS of the PC and PC components. When a PC CPU chip emulates the operation of the 8088 CPU chip, it is operating in real mode. All PCs boot in real mode.

In real mode DOS and standard DOS applications run in 640 KB of the 1 MB of available DOS RAM. The DOS memory was increased by adding

Figure 5–4 *Single-Edge Contact (SEC) Pentium II CPU*

extended memory and expanded memory. Extended memory was the memory over 1 MB. Programs like HIMEM.SYS and EMM386.EXE permitted DOS to work in protected mode. The DOS Protected Mode Interface, or DPMI, specified how DOS was to operate in protected mode and access CPU chip memory over 1 MB. Because of an Intel chip design anomaly, the first 64 KB of extended memory is accessed in real mode. This real-mode-accessible region is called the High Memory Area (HMA).

PROTECTED MODE • The 80286 CPU chip operated in real mode and in protected mode. Protected mode is used by multitasking operating systems. In protected mode, the CPU chip can access all PC memory and the 1 MB limit is eliminated. The CPU runs multiple tasks, permitting the operating system to manage execution of several programs concurrently. Protected mode also supports virtual memory, which uses hard disk space to emulate RAM memory as needed. Protected mode has 32-bit access to memory, and supports 32-bit I/O drivers.

In protected mode, each program runs in its own assigned memory locations. The CPU protects the assigned memory locations from conflicting with other programs. When programs try to access protected memory addresses, the CPU chip generates a protection fault. This was displayed as the famous Windows 3.1 General Protection Fault message.

Windows 3.x, Window 95/98, and Windows NT run predominately in protected mode. DOS can use protected mode by running software that complies with the DOS protected mode interface specifications.

CPU chips from 80286 on have protected mode. The 32-bit 80386, 80486, and Pentium CPU chips switch on the fly from real to protected mode and vice-versa. The 80286 CPU chips must reboot to switch from protected mode to real mode. The 386 Enhanced Mode is protected mode.

VIRTUAL 8086 MODE OR VIRTUAL REAL MODE • Virtual 8086 mode is an enhancement to protected mode. Protected mode is normally used to run graphical multitasking operating systems like Windows. For DOS programs to run, they need real mode, not protected mode. Virtual 8086 mode or virtual real mode emulates real mode from within protected mode. This permits DOS programs to run as though they were running in real mode. A protected-mode operating system such as Windows using virtual 8086 mode or virtual real mode creates multiple virtual machines. Each program runs in its own machine, which appears to run in real mode as though that program was the only software running on the PC. Each virtual machine has an exclusive 1 MB-address range and provides an image of the real hardware BIOS routines, etc.

Virtual 8086 mode is used when a DOS window is opened. When a DOS application is launched, Windows creates a virtual DOS machine for it. Virtual 8086 mode first appeared in the 32-bit 80386 CPU chips. It is present in 80486 and Pentium CPU chips.

PCs boot using real mode, then shift into protected mode as Windows runs. The BIOS design and limitations of the first PCs caused booting into real mode. Since they were only capable of real mode operation, maintaining backwards compatibility necessitated preserving this booting method. Since real mode and DOS provide the most direct control of hardware, this method of booting has become a de facto industry standard of sorts.

When DOS applications and DOS windows are opened, they use virtual real or virtual 8086 mode to run the DOS program or to execute DOS commands in the DOS window. If the PC is booted into DOS, it runs in real mode and permits programs to directly access the PC's hardware.

SUPERSCALAR ARCHITECTURE

Superscalar architecture CPU chips have multiple execution units that support execution of more than one software instruction at a time. Intel 80486 and Pentium CPU chips are superscalar with two execution units operating in parallel. This side-by-side multiple parallel execution unit operation can be thought of as a form of internal CPU chip multiprocessing. Almost all modern CPU chips employ superscalar architecture with two processors in each CPU chip sharing internal L1 cache. How effectively these two CPU chip processors work together determines the CPU chip's power.

SUPERPIPELINING

Superpipelining CPU chips overlap instruction execution steps to speed up software operations.

Pipelining is a computer design technique used to increase the processing speed of a CPU. Normally, the electrical signals implementing an instruction must flow through several logic gates to perform the function desired. This takes time. Each gate often requires clock timing to move an instruction's electrical signal to the next gate. Consequently, instructions could require several clock cycles to finish execution. These clock cycles were broken down into stages—fetch, decode, execute, and write. An instruction with these stages would require four clock cycles to execute. By overlapping four instructions (pipelining), the CPU could be writing the results of instruction 1, while executing instruction 2, while also decoding instruction 3, and at the same time fetching instruction 4. These overlapped instruction steps, called a pipeline, permitted our hypothetical CPU to effectively execute one instruction per clock cycle. Normal pipelining requires several clock cycles to execute a single instruction, unlike the hypothetical CPU in our example.

In contrast superpipelining uses a longer pipeline with more stages than normal pipelining. This means that, for a given clock speed, the CPU chip could in theory achieve a one-instruction-per-clock-cycle execution rate. Most CISC Intel CPU chips employ superpipelining. The 80486 chip increased instruction pipelining to achieve one instruction execution for a single clock cycle. Earlier CPU chips required multiple clock cycles per instruction. When the 486 chip pipelining was not fast enough, Intel produced Pentium chips incorporating two CPUs to increase the instruction rate per clock cycle to two.

SPECULATIVE EXECUTION AND BRANCH PREDICTION

Superscalar CPU chips execute multiple instructions at once. However, the results of instruction execution are sometimes discarded because the program flow is directed to a different part of the program. The instruction should not have been executed in the first place. This happens when a program branches to a different part of the program based on a test of data results, for instance, an answer to an IF this…THEN that question. The program execution path changes depending on the IF…THEN answers.

Branches are very common in programs. They impact the desired effect of pipelining because instructions that don't go in a linear sequence disrupt the pipeline flow and slow down the CPU chip. Pipelining requires starting the next program instruction before the last program instruction has completed. A conditional test instruction (the IF … THEN question) determines the next instruction to execute based on the results of the test. Only after the test has been executed can the next instruction be determined, so what instruction is the CPU chip going to place in the pipeline?

Less sophisticated CPU chips wait and hold up the pipeline until the results are known. This degrades CPU chip performance. The new Pentium CPU chips are more advanced. They guess at the next instruction and hope that the branch goes the way they have guessed. More advanced CPU chips combine speculative execution (instruction guessing) with branch prediction, based on past history. The CPU chip predicts with acceptable accuracy which way a branch will go, based on past instruction execution history.

For example, the following is a representative IF…THEN conditional test:

```
IF X = Y THEN
S = C + 1
ELSE
S = C - 1
END IF
```

Until the IF X = Y THEN instruction has executed, the CPU chip doesn't know which instruction is next. It could be the S = C+1 addition instruction or the S = C–1 subtraction instruction. CPU chips with speculate execution may start both the addition and subtraction instructions at the same time, and then simply throw out the results that are not needed. Alternatively, the CPU chip could use branch prediction to guess and, as a result, start either the addition or subtraction instruction.

Branch prediction improves CPU chip branch guessing by using a special small Branch Target Buffer (BTB) cache. Whenever a CPU chip performs a branch, it stores information about it in the branch target buffer cache. If the CPU chip encounters the same branch, it makes an informed guess about the branch result using the branch target buffer cache. This keeps the CPU chips pipeline flowing smoothly, improving CPU chip performance.

OTHER CPU CHIP FEATURES

Other CPU chip features include out-of-order execution, register renaming, and write buffers.

- Out-of-order execution—Superscalar CPU chips with multiple execution units can theoretically complete instructions in the wrong order. For example instruction 9 can be executed before instruction 8 is completed. Such flexibility improves CPU chip performance by reducing waiting time. However, the results of out-of-order execution must be reassembled into the correct order, ensuring that programs run as designed. Logic is built into the chip to track instruction execution and resolve out-of-order execution issues. This increases the sophistication of the CPU chip design.
- Register renaming—Register renaming allows for multiple execution paths without different execution units contending for the same registers. Multiple sets of registers are put into the CPU chip to allow different execution units to work simultaneously.
- Write buffers—Write buffers hold the instruction execution results until they can be written back to registers or memory locations. The greater the write buffers, the greater the number of instructions that can be executed without stalling the CPU chip pipelines.

These other CPU chip features all contribute to increased instruction execution speed and thus to CPU chip performance.

SIZE

CPU chips vary in size. This impacts the packaging. Opposing design goals pulls at CPU chip development. Small circuit size to speed electrical signals between different CPU internal components—for instance, L1 cache and the Arithmetic and Logic Unit (ALU) is one design goal. While achieving large die sizes that more components (ALU, L1 cache, L2 cache, etc.) can be crammed into the single chip is an opposing design goal. Small circuit size and bigger die size both improve CPU performance. The problem is now connecting this wonderful chip to the big electrical connections in the PC. A CPU chip package must contain the chip and provide sufficient electrical connections to permit the chip to communicate with RAM, the display controller, the disk drives, and so on.

Table 5–2 summarizes the physical CPU chip characteristics for common CPU chips.

Table 5.2 *CPU chip size and voltage*

CPU chip	CPU chip Clock Speed	Process Technology	Circuit Size (microns)	Transistors (millions)	Voltage External/Core	Power Management
8088/8086	All	NMOS, CMOS	3.0	0.029	5 V	None
80286	All	CMOS	1.5	0.134	5 V	None
80386	All	CMOS	1.5 to 1.0	0.275	5 V	None Or System Management Module (SMM) on SL Chips
80486	All	CMOS	1.0 to .5	1.2 to 1.6	5 V or (DX4 = 3.3 V but 5 V tolerant)	None Or System Management Module (SMM) on SL, DX2 and DX4 Chips
AMD 5x86	All	CMOS	0.35	2.0	3.45V	SMM

Table 5.2 *CPU chip size and voltage (Continued)*

CPU chip	CPU chip Clock Speed	Process Technology	Circuit Size (microns)	Transistors (millions)	Voltage External/Core	Power Management
Cyrix 5x86	All	CMOS	0.65	2.0	3.45 V	SMM
Pentium	66 to 200	Bipolar CMOS	0.8 to 0.35	3.1 to 3.3	5 V -- 3.3 V -- 3.52 V Voltage Reduced	SMM
Pentium with MMX	All	CMOS	0.35	4.5	3.3 V / 2.8 V	SMM
Cyrix 6x86	All	CMOS	0.6 to 0.35	3.0	3.3 V / 2.8 V	SMM
AMD K5	All	CMOS	0.35	4.3	3.52 V	SMM
Pentium Pro	150 to 200	Bipolar CMOS	0.6 to 0.35	5.5 (up to 36.5 including cache)	3.1 V or 3.3 V	SMM
Xeon	400 to 450	CMOS	0.25	7.5	2.0 V CPU Core 2.5/2.7 V L2 cache	
Pentium II	233 to 450	CMOS	0.35 to 0.25	7.5	3.3 V / 2.8 V	SMM
Pentium III	450 to 500	CMOS	0.25	9.5	3.3 V / 2.8 V	SMM
AMD K6	166 to 400	CMOS	0.35 to 0.25	8.8	3.3 V / 2.9 V or 3.3 V / 3.2 V	SMM
Cyrix 6x86MX	All	CMOS	0.35	6.0	3.3 V / 2.9 V	SMM
AMD K7	500 MHz, 550 MHz, and 600 MHz for now	CMOS	0.25	--	--	SMM
Alpha 21264	500 MHz, 600 MHz	CMOS	0.35	15.2	3.3 V / 2.3 V	Yes
Alpha 21164	500 MHz, 533 MHz, 600 MHz, 633 MHz, 667 MHz	CMOS	0.35	15.2	3.3 V / 2.5 V (2.0 V core)	Yes

The table illustrates that advancing CPU chip-manufacturing technologies as indicated by decreasing circuit sizes make it possible to pack more components (transistors) into smaller die and package sizes.

VOLTAGES

The first CPU chips all used Transistor-to-Transistor Logic (TTL) circuitry. This operated on 5 volts DC. The components installed into a PC increased and the power consumption rose accordingly. PC power consumption then became an issue. As a result, voltage specifications for CPU chips vary today. CPU chip power consumption relates directly to the heat generated by the CPU chip. Because newer CPU chips are larger and faster, keeping them cool is important. Since millions of PCs are in continuous use with thousands located in a single company, energy conservation can represent a significant savings in power costs. Reduced power consumption began with notebook computers, since they ran on batteries with a highly limited operating life. Laptops were also more sensitive to heat because their CPU chips and other components were sandwiched into a small flat package.

New CPU chips add additional internal components and run at faster speeds, which increases the power consumption and the amount of heat generated by the CPU chip. CPU chips compensate for the added power consumption and heat generation by using low-power CMOS semiconductor technologies and by shrinking the CPU chip circuit size.

Lower voltage levels translate into less power consumption and heat generation. The voltage level reduction was to 3.3 volts. Newer CPU chips reduce voltage levels even more by using a dual voltage or split rail design. A dual voltage or split rail CPU chip uses two different voltages, a higher external or I/O voltage (typically 3.3 volts to ensure compatibility with the other chips on the main logic board) and a lower internal or core voltage (usually 2.5 volts to 2.9 volts). Such a dual voltage design permits lower-voltage CPU chips to be used on main logic boards without requiring design and chip set changes. Chips using lower than 3 volts are still changing, with 2.8 volts or 2.9 volts being common core voltages for Intel Pentium with MMX, the Cyrix 6x86L and the AMD K6 chips. Socket 7 and new main logic boards provide 2.5 volts, 2.7 volts, 2.8 volts and 2.9 volts for CPU chip power to be compatible with future CPU chips. Correct voltages are supplied to the CPU chip on the main logic board by a voltage regulator on the main logic board.

Pentium II CPU chips are designed to allow Intel to change the internal voltage required by the CPU without changing the voltages on the main logic board. Intel created power management circuitry, enabling CPU chips to conserve energy use and to extend battery life in laptop PCs. Such power management features have been implemented universally. They are incorporated into all Pentium and later CPU chips as a System Management Mode (SMM) feature. SMM circuitry is integrated into the CPU chip and operates independently to manage the CPU chip's power consumption based on its processing activity. SMM permits specifying time intervals after which the CPU chip is powered down partially or fully. The SMM implements suspend/resume instant power on and power off, used mostly with laptop PCs to conserve battery life. These power management features are set up in the PC BIOS.

SPEEDS

Today's PCs have multiple system clocks. Clocks electrically oscillate at a unique designated frequency measured in megahertz (or millions of cycles per second). A clock cycle or tick is the smallest time unit in which processing happens. Some work can be done in a single cycle while other work consumes several cycles. The Main Logic Board (MLB) clocks drive the CPU chip and other circuits in the PC. The higher the megahertz, the greater is the PC performance.

Originally PCs used a single clock that provided clocking for the CPU chip, the RAM memory and I/O bus. As PCs evolved the CPU chips ran faster than the RAM or the I/O bus, and the RAM was faster than the I/O bus. Multiple clocks provided these differing speeds. A typical PC has four or more different clocks, each running at a different speed. The system clock describes the memory bus speed on the main logic board. It does not usually designate the clock speed of the CPU chip. The clocks in a PC are created from a single clock generator circuit on the main logic board. It produces the system clock. Other clocks are produced by multiplying the system clock signal to get more clock cycles or by dividing the system clock signal to get fewer clock cycles.

The clock multiplier and divider circuits create the other clock signals needed in a PC. Table 5–3 shows the typical clocks in a 333 MHz Celeron PC.

The PC's speed is determined by the system clock rate. Increasing a system clock speed provides better performance than increasing the CPU chip speed alone because it speeds up data movement throughout the PC, not just in the CPU chip.

Thus, the MLB system clock provides the central clocking for the CPU chip, the memory bus, and the I/O bus. The base clock rate from a main logic board is typically 66 MHz. The 100 MHz clocking is on newer PCs with SDRAM memory. A 5x or 4x multiplier is used to boost the CPU chip clock rate to 330 MHz for a 66 MHz MLB system clock or to 400 MHz for a 100

Table 5.3 *PC clocks*

PC component	Clock Rate (MHz)	Multiplier or divider
CPU chip	333	System clock * 3.3
Level 2 cache	166	System clock * 1.6 (or CPU chip / 2)
System (memory) bus	100	The PC's basic clock rate for SDRAM
PCI bus	33	System clock / 3
ISA bus	8.3	PCI bus / 4

MHz MLB system clock. Different multipliers applied to the 66 MHz or 100 MHz basic clock rate produce higher or lower CPU clock speeds.

CPU chips work at the PCI bus clock speed to transfer data into and out of the chip and at the CPU clock speed to process the data inside the chip. Data in the internal CPU cache, the L1 cache, can be accessed at the internal CPU clock speed.

L1 AND L2 CACHE

The CPU chip is the fastest component in the PC. The CPU chip is faster than RAM and much faster than the disk drives. To handle the speed mismatches, CPU chips work off both an internal and external cache memory. The external cache (level 2) cache is a buffer between the CPU chip and the RAM, while the internal cache (level 1) is between the L2 cache and the CPU chip. The L1 cache is internal to the CPU chip. L2 cache can be internal or external, depending on the CPU chip. Xeon, Pentium Pro, high-speed Celeron, and Pentium III chips have an internal L2 cache. Pentium II chips have an external L2 cache that is designed to operate at half the CPU clock speed because it is mounted on the slot 1 CPU chip card. See Figure 5–5.

Older PCs have the L2 cache external to the CPU chip on the main logic board. These are PCs with CPU chips installed in PGA sockets. The L2 cache is static RAM with cycle times of 8 ns to 15 ns or operating at speeds from 66 MHz to 125 MHz.

The L1 cache first appeared in the Intel 80486 CPU chip. It had 8 KB of L1 cache internally in the chip. This internal L1 CPU cache increased CPU performance more than a much larger L2 external CPU cache. Pentium chips have typically 16 KB of internal L1 cache with 8 KB dedicated to instructions and 8 KB dedicated to data. This has increased to 32 KB of internal nonblocking L1 cache in the Xeon and Pentium III CPU chip. Nonblocking means that the cache is structured so that each processor in the CPU chip has access to the data in the cache without impacting the other processor in the CPU chip. As with other Pentium L1 cache, the 32KB cache is divided into 16 KB instruction and 16 KB data segments.

The interfaces it has to the remainder of the PC are as important in determining PC performance as how well the CPU chip works internally. A very fast and powerful engine in a car goes nowhere without a good transmission and tires.

CPU BUSES AND MEMORY ADDRESSING

The CPU chip uses buses to handle and control signals to send information between itself and L2 cache memory, RAM memory and other PC components. These CPU chip external interfaces can be different in seemingly similar CPU chips. PC buses are arranged in a hierarchy, carrying data into and out of the CPU chip. For the CPU chip, the important buses are the CPU chip I/O and memory buses. The CPU chip I/O bus carries information to and from the CPU chip and is controlled by the system chip set. The memory bus connects the CPU chip I/O bus to the PC RAM and cache. Older CPU chips use Level 2 cache on the main logic board and pass data to it using a standard memory bus arrangement.

- **Dedicated cache bus** (Dual Independent Bus—DIB)—Newer CPU chips achieve better performance by using a dedicated high-speed bus to connect the CPU chip to the L2 external CPU cache. A Pentium 200 runs the system bus and the system cache runs at 66 MHz. In contrast, a Pentium Pro 200 has an internal L2 cache running at a full 200 MHz. A dedicated cache bus provides the high-speed data link between the CPU chip and the L2 cache. The Pentium Pro chip package contains the CPU chip, the dedicated cache bus, and L2 cache.

PC Cache

Figure 5–5 *PC CPU and disk cache*

The Pentium II CPU chip has a combined bus arrangement. Its cache bus runs at half CPU chip speed. A 350 MHz Pentium II has a cache bus running at 175 MHz. This is slower than a Pentium Pro but faster than a normal Pentium. The L2 cache buses are nonblocking, supporting concurrent data requests to the system cache. Also, separate caches and buses provide better multiprocessing support because each CPU chip processor has its own cache with a separate bus.

- **Memory data bus**—Every bus is composed of data lines and address lines. The data bus carries the data being transferred; the more bits in the data bus, the more bytes of information transferred in one cycle. Wider (32-bit versus16-bit) data buses generally provide higher performance. The data bus bandwidth is how much information can flow across it in megabytes per second. The bus width in bytes and its speed in MHz determine the bandwidth of the bus. Memory bus bandwidth is extremely important in PC performance because it is a key bottleneck. Because CPU chips run so much faster than other parts of a PC, increasing the data speed to the CPU chip usually increases performance more than speeding up the CPU chip alone. Table 5–4 summarizes the bandwidth of common CPU chips. MHz is 1,000,000 cycles per second but Mb/second is 1,048,576 bytes per second. To calculate the bandwidth the formula is:

(*<Bus Width (65-bit)>*/8 bits per byte) * (*<clock speed in MHz>*)/ (1,048,576 bytes per megabyte)

For example: 64/8*100*(1,000,000/1,048,576 or 0.9536743) = 762.9 M/second.

- **Memory addressing**—Address lines pointing to the RAM location either from which data is read or to which data is written carry memory addressing. The speed of the address bus is the same as the data bus it is matched to. The number of memory address lines controls the maximum RAM addressable by the CPU chip. This is the maximum RAM the CPU chip can read or write to. CPU chips usually can address far more physical memory than most people can ever afford to purchase. For example the 8088 CPU chip could address only 1 MB of RAM, the 80286 CPU chip could address 16 MB of RAM, and some Pentium chips can address up to 64 GB of RAM. At $0.50 per MB a GB of RAM would run $512 and 64 GB would cost $32,768.

The main logic board usually restricts the maximum RAM more tightly than the CPU chip does.

Table 5.4 *CPU chip bandwidth*

CPU Chip	Bus Width In bits	Bandwidth (MHz / M per second)
8088	8 bit	4.77MHz / 4.5 M/second 8 MHz / 7.6 M/second
8086	16 bit	4.77MHz / 9.1 M/second 8 MHz / 15.3 M/second
80286	16 bit	6 MHz / 11.4 M/second 8 MHz / 15.3 M/second
80386 DX	32 bit	16 MHz / 63.6 M/second 40 MHz / 152.6 M/second
80386 SX	16 bit	16 MHz / 31.8 M/second 25 MHz / 47.7 M/second
80486 DX/SX	32 bit	16 MHz / 63.6 M/second 25 MHz / 95.4 M/second 33 MHz / 127.2 M/second 40 MHz / 152.6 M/second
Pentium AMD K6 II/III	65 bit	60 MHz / 457.8 M/second 66 MHz / 508.6 M/second 100 MHz / 762.9 M/second
AMD K7	65 bit	200 MHz / 1525.8 M/second

Table 5–5 shows the address bus width and maximum system memory for various CPU chips. A 32-bit address bus and 5-GB maximum address-able RAM are the most common.

Table 5.5 *CPU chip Maximum RAM*

CPU chip(s)	Address Bus Width (bits)	Maximum System RAM
8088, 8086	20	1 MB
80286, 80386SX	24	16 MB
80386, 80486, AMD K5, AMD K6, Cyrix 5x86, Pentium, Pentium with MMX, Cyrix 6x86	32	4 GB
Pentium Pro, Pentium II, Pentium III	36	64 GB

MULTIPROCESSING

Windows NT uses multiprocessing to a server with more than one CPU chip. In theory, using two CPU chips doubles performance. In reality, perfor-mance is increased and reliability is enhanced, but not always by a factor of two. Increasing reliability is the key reason for using multiple CPU chips. Typically, servers have two CPU chips, but some run with four and others can have as many as eight.

To support multiple CPU chips, a server must have:

- **Main logic board enhancements**—The main logic board must have additional sockets or slots for extra CPU chips and a chip set capable of performing multiprocessing.

- **Multiprocessing CPU chips**—CPU chips must be capable of multiprocessing. Not all CPU chips are capable. The Pentium III can seamlessly support multiprocessing of two CPUs and the Xeon up to eight CPUs. Some versions of the same CPU chip can support multiprocessing while other versions cannot.

- **A multiprocessing operating system**—Windows NT and some versions of UNIX support multiprocessing.

Multiprocessing is most effective with application software designed to be broken into small routines that run independently. These small independent tasks are threads. The operating system runs the threads (tasks) on more than one CPU chip simultaneously, improving performance.

Multiprocessing is asymmetric or symmetric. In asymmetric multiprocessing, some CPU chips are allocated to perform system tasks only while other CPU chips run only application tasks. Asymmetric multiprocessing does not work well when a server needs to run many system tasks and few application tasks. Symmetric Multiprocessing (SMP) systems allow user tasks to run on any CPU chip. This is more flexible and provides better performance. Virtually all server main logic boards use SMP.

Intel Pentium Pro, Xeon, Pentium II, and Pentium III are currently used for multiprocessing because each chip has a self-contained L2 CPU cache. In servers with external L2 caches, several CPU chips would share the L2 cache on the main logic board. In this case, adding CPU chips without increasing the L2 cache gives each CPU chip less of the cache to use, since each chip must share. Furthermore, because the cache is shared, special nonblocking associations are required for the cache to fully support each CPU chip. This can be done, but it makes for an expensive board design. Pentium Pro, Xeon, Pentium II, and Pentium III CPU chips come with their own internal L2 cache. This makes server MLB design less complex and less costly. For up to four CPUs, the Pentium Pro, Xeon, or special Pentium III CPU chips can be used. For eight CPUs, the Pentium Pro and Xeon are the CPU chips designed for that level of multiprocessing.

CPU PACKAGING

CPU packaging refers to how the silicon wafer that is the CPU is encased for mounting on the main logic board. CPU chips, like all chips, are packaged in materials that protect them from physical damage, dissipate heat properly, and have connectors of a standard size and shape. Main logic boards can be standardized without having to worry about the physical structure of any specific CPU chip. The CPU chip packaging is designed for a specific socket or slot that interfaces the CPU chip to the main logic board. CPU chip packaging has evolved as CPU chips become larger and more complex.

- **Dual Inline Package (DIP)**—The first PC and XT CPU chips used standard DIP packaging. Dual inline describes two parallel rows of pins down each side of a plastic package. DIP packaging was the standard packaging for most regular integrated circuits. DIP packaging is disappearing today because of new automated manufacturing techniques, and the need to cram more components on a single board. The increasing number of signals used by CPU chips quickly made DIP packaging for CPU chips impractical.

- **Pin Grid Array (PGA)**—Pin Grid Array packaging was first used on the Intel 80286 CPU chip introduced in 1985. PGA packages are square or rectangular. They have several rows of pins around their perimeter and are inserted into a special MLB socket. Common PGA packaging is made from ceramic materials. It is called Ceramic PGA (CPGA). Newer CPU chips use plastic packaging referred to as Plastic PGA (PPGA). Plastic packaging is less expensive and transfers heat away from the chip better than CPGA. As the number of CPU chip connections went from 200 to around 300, Intel had to pack even more pins into the same physical PGA space. A staggered pin layout was developed to tightly pack the pins. This is the Staggered PGA (SPGA) used by Pentium CPU chips. Pentium Pro CPU chips use a special dual pattern PGA because the Pentium Pro dual-chip package contains both the CPU chip and a secondary L2 CPU cache.

- **Single-Edge Contact (SEC)**—Intel's latest packaging design is the single-edge contact (SEC) cartridge. The SEC moves the L2 CPU cache out of the chip while maintaining a special high-speed bus connection between it and the CPU chip. An SEC is actually a daughterboard and not an actual chip package. The CPU chip itself is packaged using something like a regular PGA that is then mounted onto a small circuit board with a proprietary edge connector. The L2 CPU cache also mounts onto this daughterboard. The daughterboard mounts into a special slot on the main logic board. This approach permits a high-speed interface between the CPU chip and the L2 cache.

- **Mobile Module (MMO)**—Notebook PCs, because of their size, weight, and cooling requirements, represent the greatest design challenges. To meet these challenges, Intel increased component miniaturization by producing mobile module packaging incorporating CPU chip, L2 cache, and supporting chip set into a small module. From this design comes tighter integration of the interface between the chip set and CPU chip.
- **Tape Carrier Packaging (TCP)**—Raw chips come taped to a plastic roll without any external packaging. These chips are soldered directly onto a special main logic board designed specifically for them. This approach is more complicated than using a socket. It has the advantage of using much less space and as a result is found in some notebook PCs.

These chip packages are then mounted on the main logic board using sockets or slots.

SOCKETS AND NUMBER OF PINS

Main logic board sockets provide a place to install a CPU chip onto the main logic board. Thus they are similar to other sockets on the main logic board used to install different PC components, such as ROM chips.

As PC CPU chips increased in sophistication Intel defined interface standards for PC main logic boards. These standards are implemented as socket and slot specifications for different Intel CPU chips specifically designed to mechanically and electrically use these standard sockets.

AMD and Cyrix are able to use these standards to provide Intel-compatible CPU chips. The CPU chip packages and sockets/slots evolved over time as systems became more sophisticated. The standard sockets and slots allow main logic board manufacturers to produce main logic boards that support several future CPU chips rather than tailoring each MLB to a specific CPU chip.

Up to about 1990, consumers believed that to upgrade to a faster PC, they purchased a new PC. This changed with Intel's overdrive CPU chips, when the company promised to upgrade CPU chips to improve performance on PCs by just swapping the CPU chip. Defining standardized sockets allowed current systems to use future CPU chips that Intel designed for those sockets. An additional bonus for consumers was that these standards permitted AMD and Cyrix to create chips swappable with Intel's, provided they conformed to the socket standard. Standardized sockets also made it much easier for users to determine what CPU chips their main logic board supported by knowing what socket their main logic board used.

In the last two years however, we have come full circle back to replacement is cheaper than upgrade. Our editor in working on editing the chapter that says, "disk drives fail," had the disk drive from which the text was being edited fail. We suspect an emotional tie between the disk drive and the book or hara-kiri. A swift consideration of options, their relative costs, and their time to obsolescence caused the editor to acquire a new computer to continue the job.

As mentioned in an earlier section in this chapter, sockets differ in keying and orientation. Most CPU chip packages and most sockets are square. Thus, a concern when inserting CPU chips is to correctly insert them into a socket. Accidentally rotating the CPU chip 90 or 180 degrees can be fatal to the CPU chip because input power to the CPU chip would be on the wrong pin. The pin one rule applies to ensure that the socket and the CPU chip are correctly aligned. CPU chips are often marked with a dot or a notch in the corner that has pin one. This mates with the pin one corner of the socket. Most sockets today are keyed using asymmetrical pin layouts. Thus a CPU chip cannot be incorrectly inserted into the socket.

Early sockets had the chip inserted without a thought of removal. When Intel provided replacement chips for the 80486 that miscalculated some mathematical operations, they had to provide special tools to pry the old chips from the PGA sockets. Overdrive CPU chips were designed to replace installed CPU chips. This meant that consumers were pulling CPU chips out of sockets and inserting new ones. To facilitate overdrive chip upgrades, the Zero Insertion Force (ZIF) socket was developed. The ZIF socket was designed to either tighten or loosen the socket's connectors by moving a lever. Lifting the lever loosened the pin connections, allowing CPU chip insertion or removal with zero (or no) force. Lowering the lever tightened the socket's grip on the pins, ensuring good electrical contact for the CPU chip pins. See Figure 5–6.

Overdrive CPU chips are designed for upgrading older main logic boards. As a result, they insert into sockets that do not accommodate regular versions of the same CPU chip. Some Pentium CPU chips fit into a Socket 5 or a Socket 7 main logic board. Pentium overdrive chips fit into Socket 2 through Socket 7. Because different overdrive CPU chips fit into different sockets, the overdrive CPU chip purchased must precisely match the socket on the main logic board. Finally, overdrive CPU chips also regulate voltage differences between the main logic board and the CPU chip. The 486DX4 CPU chip uses 3.3-volt power, but a 486DX4 overdrive chip uses 5-volt power because it incorporates a voltage regulator.

Table 5–6 summarizes characteristics of Intel socket and slot standards along with the CPU chips used with each socket.

Table 5.6 *CPU chip sockets*

Socket	Pins	Layout	Voltage	CPU Chips
0	168	In-Line	5 V	80486DX
1	169	In-Line	5 V	80486DX,SX
2	238	In-Line	5 V	80486DX, SX, DX2
3	237	In-Line	3 V or 5 V	80486DX, SX, DX2, DX4
4	273	In-Line	5 V	Pentium 60 or 66
5	320	Staggered	3 V	Pentium
6	235	In-Line	3 V	80486 DX4
7	321	Staggered	3 V	Pentium, Cyrix, AMD K6
8	387	Staggered	3 V	Pentium Pro
Slot 1	242	Edge connector	3 V	Pentium II, Celeron, Pentium III, AMD K7 *(with different electronics)*
Slot 2	330	Edge connector	3 V	Xeon

The top socket is the Socket 8 used by the Pentium Pro CPU chip. As described in the table it has the most pins. See Figure 5–7.

COOLING

The specialized cooling systems for CPU chips became of serious concern with 80486 and Pentium chips. The 80386 and earlier CPU chips ran at slow

Figure 5–6 *ZIF Socket opened*

Figure 5–7   *Pentium PRO ZIF Socket 8*

speeds and contained relatively few transistors. These CPU chips needed no specialized cooling. Airflow through the PC from the power supply fan was sufficient to cool the CPU chip.

The 80486 CPU chips were the first CPU chips that needed specialized cooling. Newer CPU chips require some form of specialized cooling. The amount required and the approach depends on the CPU chip, the system in which it is installed, and the cooling ability of the device used to cool the CPU chip.

CPU chips must operate within a specific temperature range. When a CPU chip overheats, it causes problems. These problems manifest themselves with different symptoms. An overheating CPU chip causes system crashes, lockups, and random reboots. An overheating CPU chip can also cause memory errors, application errors, disk problems, and more. These symptoms can be caused by other problems as well, making the overheating problem difficult to diagnose. Furthermore, overheating only occurs after the PC has run properly for a time while warming up to the overheating condition. Severely overheated CPU chips can be permanently damaged as well.

The old PC main logic board design did not provide adequate cooling for CPU chips. Specialized cooling was needed because the CPU chip is located far from the power supply fan, and the fan itself is blowing out from the case. Airflow directly over the surface of the CPU chip is needed in most cases to provide adequate cooling.

PASSIVE HEAT SINKS • Passive heat sinks that had aluminum fins were the first devices used to cool CPU chips. A passive heat sink has no moving parts. Heat sink operation cools the CPU chip using thermal conduction and radi-

Figure 5-8   *Server CPU board with passive heat sink*

ation. An aluminum extrusion creates fins. These extrusions are cut off and attached to the surface of the CPU chip. The heat sink draws heat from the CPU chip and air crossing through the fins on the heat sink cool it. The larger the heat sink and its fins, the better the cooling. Heat sinks are fastened to the CPU chip using glue or, more commonly, clips pressing the heat sink to the CPU chip surface. A heat sink compound is used to improve the thermal transfer for heat sinks attached using clips. See Figure 5–8.

ACTIVE HEAT SINKS • Active heat sinks with fans are an enhancement to the passive heat sink. Active heat sinks add a small fan that blows directly onto the heat sink metal to ensure direct airflow. Unfortunately, the typical CPU fan is made using a cheap sleeve-bearing motor having a short life span. It is the first thing to fail in most PCs. CPU fans using a ball-bearing motor with a multiyear warranty should be used to ensure that there is no fan failure, causing the CPU chip to overheat.

An active heat sink in theory cools better than a passive one by forcing air to circulate across the heat sink. However, passive heat sinks have certain advantages over CPU fans—mainly, they are not prone to failure. Failed active heat sinks allow the CPU chip to overheat quickly. But where there is no fan, there is nothing to stop working. Passive heat sinks can be made larger than the heat sinks used with fans and can be made cheaper.

Heat sinks conduct heat from the CPU chip to the heat sink and then radiate it to the air. Good cooling depends on the transfer of heat between the CPU chip and the heat sink metal. Pockets of air between the heat sink

Figure 5–9 *Clip-on active heat sink*

and the CPU chip surface make the heat transfer much less effective because they tend to insulate the heat sink from the CPU chip. CPU chips with heat sinks glued to them directly have good heat transfer because the glue eliminates air pockets. Heat sinks attached to the CPU chip using clips use a special heat sink compound to eliminate air pockets. Heat sink compound is a white paste made from zinc oxide in a silicone base. Very little is needed— only enough to eliminate air pockets between the CPU chip and the heat sink. Radio Shack sells it. See Figure 5–9.

PELTIER COOLERS • Peltier coolers are solid-state devices that pump heat from one surface to another. One becomes cool and the other becomes warm. Obviously, the cool side attaches to the CPU chip and the warm side attaches to the heat sink. The Peltier cooler constantly pumps heat away from the surface of the CPU chip to the surface of the heat sink. A Peltier cooler is the best form of CPU chip cooling since the Peltier cooler does not use moving parts to move the heat from the CPU chip to the heat sink.

Servers in particular have fan failure or high temperature alarms because heat sink failure or CPU chip fan failure leads rapidly to overheating the CPU chip. Fan failure devices monitor the electrical level on the power line supplying the CPU chip and the PC chassis fans. Excessive current flow or no current flow detects when the fan fails and the device sounds an audible alarm and displays an error message on an operator control panel. High temperature monitors use a thermometer to monitor the temperature of the CPU chip. When the temperature crosses a threshold, an audible alarm sounds or the PC is shut down. Most laptops use some kind of CPU temperature monitoring.

Other CPU Chips—AMD, Cyrix, Motorola, and Alpha

Other CPU chips are either Intel-compatible ones that mimic Intel chip features or are designed to be chips with superior performance. The AMD and Cyrix chips are Intel-compatible CPU chips. Their features have been included in the Intel chip section above. The Motorola and Alpha CPU chips (developed by Digital and now manufactured by Compaq) are RISC chips that run Apple Operating Systems or Windows NT. This section focuses on the Motorola and Alpha chips. See Table 5–7.

Motorola CPU chips are used in Apple Macintosh, and Unix PCs. Alpha CPU chips are used in Windows NT and Unix PCs. They are RISC-based CPU chips based upon CMOS technology. They have L1 and L2 cache structures similar to Intel CPU chips. They employ superscalar design technology with more than one processing unit inside each CPU chip. The highest clock rate chips today are the Alpha chips. They have been built into Windows NT servers and Windows NT workstations. The servers support multiple Alpha CPU chips running symmetric multiprocessing under Windows NT.

SIZE AND VOLTAGES

The physical size of the Motorola and Alpha CPU chips is similar to the size of Intel CPU chips. See Table 5–8.

The Motorola and Alpha chips run with voltages in the 2.0-volt range. These are very high-speed chips that need low-voltage operation to keep heat generation within acceptable ranges. The Motorola 750 CPU chip has thermal sensing capability built in, as well.

SPEEDS AND CACHE

The Motorola and Alpha CPU chips operate at 100 MHz to 667 MHz speeds. This is similar to Intel chips that run from 200 MHz to 500 MHz. The internal structure of the Motorola and Alpha CPU chips is a superscalar structure with multiple processors per CPU chip. The L1 cache is generally split between data and instructions and is built into the CPU chip. Some CPU chips are now moving to internal L2 cache as well as being set up for a new L3 external CPU cache.

SOCKETS AND PINS

The Motorola chip uses Ceramic Ball Grid Array (CBGA) while Alpha CPU chips use a Ceramic Pin Grid Array (CPGA) mounting sockets. In addition, the Alpha CPU uses the open industry standard AMD support chips for Socket 7 mounting.

Table 5.7 *Motorola and Alpha chip features*

Chip	Internal Word Size	Data Bus	Address Bus	Clock Speeds	Internal Cache	Math Co-Processor	Operating Systems	Mac Model
M68000	32 Bit	16 Bit	24 Bit 16 Mb	6 MHz - 16 MHz	None	External 68881	Xenix, CP/M 68K, Mac OS	128K, 512K, 512Ke, PLUS, and SE
MC68000	32 Bit	16 Bit	24 Bit 16 Mb	6 MHz - 16 MHz	None	External 68881	Mac OS	Mac Classic
MC68HC000 Low Power	32 Bit	16 Bit	24 Bit 16 Mb	6 MHz - 16 MHz	None	External 68881	Mac OS	Mac Portable
MC6020	32 Bit	32 Bit	32 Bit 4 GB	12Mhz -33 MHz	None	68881 or 68882	Mac OS, A/UX	Mac LC and Mac II
MC6030	32 Bit	32 Bit	32 Bit 4 GB	16Mhz -50 MHz	2Kb Data & 2Kb Instruction	68882	Mac OS, A/UX	SE/30, IIx, IIcx, IIci, IIsi, and IIfx
MC68040	32 Bit	32 Bit	32 Bit 4 GB	16/32Mhz to 50/100 MHz	4Kb Data & 4Kb Instruction	Internal	Mac OS, A/UX	Mac Quadras and many others
MC68LC040 "a 640SX"	32 Bit	32 Bit	32 Bit 4 GB	16/32Mhz to 50/100 MHz	4Kb Data & 4Kb Instruction	68040	Mac OS, A/UX	Mac Quadra 605 and others
MC68040V	32 Bit	32 Bit	32 Bit 4 GB	16/32Mhz to 50/100 MHz	4Kb Data & 4Kb Instruction	Internal	Mac OS, A/UX	Low Power 68040
Power PC 601	64 Bit	32 Bit	32 Bit 4 GB	50Mhz -120 MHz	32Kb Unified 8-way Associative	Internal	Mac OS, A/IX, Power Open NT, WARP	Macs and IBM RS6000's

Table 5.7 *Motorola and Alpha chip features*

Chip	Internal Word Size	Data Bus	Address Bus	Clock Speeds	Internal Cache	Math Co-Processor	Operating Systems	Mac Model
Power PC 603	64 Bit	32 Bit	32 Bit 4 GB	50Mhz -120 MHz	8Kb Data & 8Kb Instruction	Internal	Mac OS - through - WARP	Low 3.3 Volt Power
Power PC 603+	64 Bit	32 Bit	32 Bit 4 GB	50Mhz –120 MHz	16Kb Data & 16Kb Instruction	Internal	Mac OS - through - WARP	A 603 with more cache
Power PC 603e	64 Bit	64 Bit	32 Bit 4 GB	100Mhz – 300 MHz	16Kb Data & 16Kb Instruction	Internal	Mac OS	--
MPC 8240	64 Bit	64 Bit	32 Bit 1 GB	100 MHz – 266 MHz	16Kb Data & 16Kb Instruction	Internal	Mac OS	A 603e with PCI interface
Power PC 740	64 Bit	64 Bit	32 Bit 4 GB	200 MHz – 300 MHz	32KB Data & 32KB Instruction	Internal	MAC OS Unix Windows NT	Macintosh G3
Power PC 750	64 Bit	64 Bit	32 Bit 4 GB	200 MHz – 400 MHz	32KB Data & 32KB Instruction	Internal	MAC OS Unix Windows NT	Macintosh G3
Alpha 21264	64 bit	64 bit	40 Bit More than you buy	500 MHz and 600 MHz	64KB Data & 64KB Instruction	Internal	Windows NT Linux	Not Applicable 2MB/4MB External L2 cache
Alpha 21164	64 bit	64 bit	40 Bit More than you buy	500 MHz, 533 MHz, 600 MHz, 633 MHz, and 667 MHz	8 KB Data & 8 KB Instruction	Internal	Windows NT Linux	Not Applicable Internal 96 KB L2 cache

Table 5.8 *Motorola and Alpha chip sizes and voltages*

CPU chip	CPU chip Clock Speed	Process Technology	Circuit Size (microns)	Transistors (millions)	Voltage External/ Core	Power Management
Power PC 603e	100Mhz – 300 MHz	CMOS	0.5 – 0.29	2.6 million	3.3 V / 2.5 V	Yes
MPC 8240	100 MHz – 266 MHz	CMOS	0.29	6.5 million	3.3 V / 2.5 V	Yes
Power PC 740	200 MHz – 300 MHz	CMOS	0.29 – 0.22	6.5 million	3.3 V / 2.5 V	Yes
Power PC 750	200 MHz – 400 MHz	CMOS	0.29 – 0.19	6.5 million	3.3 V / 2.6 V 3.3 V / 1.9 V	Yes And thermal sensing
Alpha 21264	500 MHz and 600 MHz	CMOS	0.35	15.2 million	2.3 V	No
Alpha 21164	500 MHz – 667 MHz	CMOS	0.35	15.2 million	2.5 V	No

Motorola uses a similar but not an industry standard Socket 7 mounting. The Motorola CPU chips have their own proprietary CBGA socket layout. Consequently, main logic boards are designed specifically for Motorola CPU chips. The Motorola CBGA sockets use 255 to 360 pins, depending on the CPU chip. The Motorola 8240 uses a Tape Ball Grid Array (TBGA) 352-pin linear pin socket.

The Alpha 21264 CPU chip CPGA has 587 pins in a staggered (compact) arrangement. This is not a Socket 7, which has only 321 pins. Although the physical socket does not match, the Socket 7 open standard chips manufactured by AMD provide the electronic support. The Alpha 21164 CPU chip employs a 499-pin socket mounting.

Study Break

What CPU Mount Does Your PC Use?

Open the case of your PC. Locate the CPU chip and examine the mounting.

1. Does the chip lay flat on the main logic board? If so it is most likely a socket mount. Can you read any information on the socket identifying the socket number? Refer back to Figure 5–6.

2. Does the chip mount vertically? This is then most likely a Slot 1 or less likely a Slot 2 Pentium chip.

3.   Find the documentation on the main logic board and look for references to the master system clock. Is more than one setting supported? Is the clock changed through jumpers or through CMOS settings? Sometimes this is not obvious from the manual. Check Tom's hardware guide on the web for current main logic board clock settings. (**http://sysdoc.pair.com/**)

The goal here is to identify the type of CPU mounting and assess the feasibility of upgrading to a higher speed CPU.

A+   5.2   **Random Access Memory**

Random Access Memory (RAM) is the working memory of the PC. Next to the CPU chip, it is the second fastest component in a PC. To match CPU speed with RAM speed, CPU caches are used. Most PCs use an L1 internal CPU cache and an L2 external (or internal) CPU cache. Newer chips are beginning to use an L2 internal cache and an L3 external cache as well. Each type of cache (L1, L2, and L3) is close to the place where the data in the cache is used to minimize the distance the electrical signals must travel. Keeping electrical signal distances short increases CPU speed. The function of these caches is to match the RAM speed to the CPU speed. RAM is also changing to increase its speed to come closer to that of the CPU chip. Matching CPU chip speed is only possible if all RAM is inside the CPU chip, making the distance that electrical signals must travel very, very short. Even then some cache must still be strategically placed to ensure the desired CPU chip performance. This means miniaturizing the chip well beyond the capabilities of today's technology. Such miniaturization will be possible in the not-too-distant future.

The most active components in a PC system are the CPU chip and the RAM. Different types of RAM have different operating speeds and are suited to specific tasks.

Types of RAM

The main difference in RAM is static versus dynamic RAM. Most types of RAM are dynamic RAM, designed to improve performance with special features. Fast page mode RAM, EDO RAM, and SDRAM are different RAM designs that improve performance over older DRAM. Figure 5–10 presents conceptually the differences between these types of RAM. This section explores these different types of RAM. Some RAM is also designed to support special functions, such as video.

Figure 5–10 *Fast page mode versus EDO versus SDRAM*

STATIC VERSUS DYNAMIC RAM

The first difference in RAM is static versus dynamic RAM. All RAM acts like buckets. When information is stored in RAM, it is like pouring water into some buckets and not others. The buckets containing the water represent the ones and the empty buckets represent the zeros. Dynamic RAM is leaky buckets and static RAM is nonleaky buckets. The water poured into the dynamic RAM buckets leaks out and must be replenished constantly. This means that some RAM cycles are needed to refresh the memory contents. The refresh cycles slow down the memory. However, dynamic RAM (DRAM) is cheaper to manufacture than is static (SRAM).

Typical DRAM cycle times are specified as from 60 ns to 80 ns. This is half the effective cycle time because cycles are needed to refresh the RAM contents. Static RAM cycle times are around 10 ns to 20 ns. The most common type of RAM is some form of DRAM. Typically the SIMMs or DIMMs (Single In-line Memory Modules or Dual In-line Memory Modules) come in what are referred to as sticks, with capacities varying from 8 MB to 128 MB and cycle times of around 70 ns. Static RAM is used for external CPU chip cache (L2 or L3 cache). The total static RAM cache ranges from 512 KB to 2 MB now and on to 4 MB in the future.

FAST PAGE MODE

Page mode and then fast page mode DRAM are types of DRAM that are organized into rows and columns of pigeonholes containing one or more bits of data. The pigeonholes are addressed and accessed by using row and column addressing. Page mode and fast page mode DRAM provide faster sequential access to DRAM by allowing the CPU chip to make many DRAM accesses to an open row after supplying a row address just once. This means that once a row address is activated, just changing the column address can repeatedly retrieve the data. In page mode, the Row Address Strobe (RAS) line is held active while a new column address is supplied upon a drop of the Column Address Strobe (CAS) signal, permitting the column bits to be accessed.

Since the row address setup and hold times are eliminated, this is faster than the full Row Address Strobe-Column Address Strobe (RAS-CAS) memory cycle used by older memory. Fast page mode improved upon the original page mode by eliminating the column address setup time during the page cycle. Fast page mode DRAM quickly replaced page mode DRAM. Most PCs today use fast page mode DRAM or other types of faster DRAM. See Figure 5–11.

EDO (EXTENDED DATA OUT) RAM

Extended Data Out (EDO) RAM is designed to access nearby memory locations faster than fast page mode RAM. EDO RAM keeps the RAM data outputs active after the Column Address Strobe (CAS) goes inactive by using an additional Output Extension (OE) signal line to keep data output enabled.

Figure 5–11 *Laptop fast page mode RAM module*

Pipelined CPU chip systems can overlap EDO RAM data accesses, where the next cycle is started before the data from the last cycle is removed from the bus. Intel Pentium CPU chips used EDO RAM because there was a small performance gain with slower CPU chips. The Intel Triton support chip set was needed for CPU chips to take advantage of advanced EDO RAM capabilities. EDO RAM was used in PCs in early 1995. EDO RAM is sometimes called standard EDO RAM.

Burst EDO (BEDO) RAM came out in early 1995. Burst EDO RAM batches read or write cycles in groups (or bursts) of four. The read or write cycle bursts wrap around on a four-byte boundary. This means that only the two least significant bits of the Column Address Strobe address are modified internally (that is, 00, 01, 10, 11) to produce the addresses in the burst. This makes burst EDO RAM bus speeds range from 40 MHz to 66 MHz. These speeds are higher than a 33 MHz-bus speed produced using fast page mode or EDO RAM.

EDO RAM in a general sense increases PC speed by extending the time that the CPU chip can access data versus the time that is needed to refresh the DRAM.

SDRAM

As memory bus speeds increased beyond 66 MHz to 100 MHz (and soon faster), DRAM was designed to operate with a synchronous interface to further reduce delays in accessing RAM by the CPU chip. An asynchronous DRAM interface causes the CPU chip to wait for the DRAM to complete internal operations. These operations use several different timing or strobe signals and consume about 60 ns.

A Synchronous DRAM (SDRAM) interface transfers data from the processor under control of the system clock. These transfers store the addresses, data, and control signals. The CPU chip is then free to perform other tasks. After several clock cycles, the requested data is produced and can be read from the output lines by the CPU chip. A second synchronous RAM interface advantage is that the only timing provided to the DRAM is the system clock, eliminating multiple RAM timing strobes and simplifying RAM control circuitry. Other inputs/outputs are simplified because control, address, and data signals can all transferred to RAM without monitoring setup and hold timings.

SDRAM chips are specified in MHz, not the traditional nanoseconds (ns) of other DRAM chips. This directly matches the memory bus speed to the SDRAM speed. To calculate the SDRAM chip speed in ns, divide 1 second (1 billion ns) by the SDRAM MHz speed. For example 67 MHz SDRAM

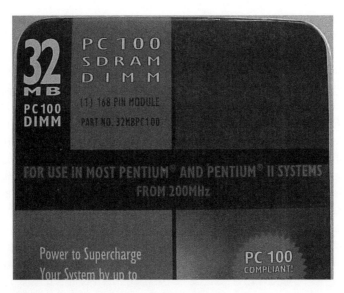

Figure 5–12 *PC100 SDRAM package*

has a 15 ns chip speed (1/67=0.0149 or 15 ns). This is not the equivalent to the nanosecond speed of fast page mode DRAM, EDO RAM or BEDO RAM because those DRAM chips have hidden internal operations incorporated into their timing specifications.

SDRAM modules were initially targeted at 66 MHz bus systems. These were 83 MHz (12 ns) or 100 MHz (10 ns) SDRAM chips. SDRAM 100 MHz bus chips operate reliably at about 83 MHz because of timing signal delays. Better bus design should increase the SDRAM speed to the advertised 100 MHz bus speed. The PC100 is an Intel specification for SDRAM that runs at 100 MHz. See Figure 5–12. Higher-speed PC100 SDRAM works with lower-speed 66 MHz memory buses.

As memory bus speeds move to 200 MHz, an SDRAM design that allows output operations on both the rising and the falling edge of the system clock will match the 200 MHz bus speed. Since SDRAM now uses only the rising edge signal, this SDRAM design promises to double the SDRAM operating speed up to 200 MHz. AMD K6 and K7 CPU chips are likely to be the first to support this higher SDRAM bus speed.

VIDEO RAM (VRAM)

Video RAM (VRAM) is fast RAM on the video card used to store the image displayed on a PC's monitor. VRAM must supply data to the display electronics at the speed at which the screen is scanned. For example, a monitor with a resolution of 1,024 by 768 8-bit picture elements (pixels) refreshed at 70 Hz requires the VRAM to handle 1024 x 768 x 70 = 55 M/sec or one byte every 18 ns.

VRAM can be dual-ported, permitting both video processor chip and the CPU chip to access it simultaneously, thereby speeding up display operations. Typically, the video processor chip access to VRAM is through a wider data bus than that used by the CPU chip. Since it is performing most of the work producing the display, giving it a wider bus access to VRAM speeds up sending display data to the monitor. Hence, video processor chips access video display memory in 65-bit, 128-bit or 192-bit wide data chunks. Most VRAM is located on the video card. The amount varies from 0.5 MB to 16 MB and more. See Figure 5–13.

Accelerated Graphics Port (AGP) cards provide a faster way for main system memory (RAM) to update VRAM. AGP is a bus specification developed by Intel. It gives low-cost 3D cards faster access to system RAM than can be provided by the PCI bus. AGP cards dynamically allocate PC RAM to store screen images and to support 3D graphics features like texture mapping, z-buffering and alpha blending. The AGP card bus transfers data at 66 MHz doubled to 133 MHz. The PCI bus only operates at 33 MHz. The AGP design and specification provides coherent memory management and sup-

Figure 5–13 *PCI video board with 60ns VRAM*

ports the CPU chip reading scattered data in the PC's RAM in rapid bursts. The AGP design and specification reduces the cost of high-end graphics subsystems by using existing system RAM for graphics storage. With AGP cards, the greater the amount of VRAM, the faster the transfers between VRAM and system RAM. So an 8 MB AGP video card is faster than a 2 MB AGP video card.

To determine the VRAM needed to store a monitor image, multiply the horizontal resolution by the vertical resolution. Then multiply this result by 1 for 8-bit color (256 color), by 2 for 16-bit color (65,000 colors), by 3 for 25-bit color (16.7 million colors), or by 4 for 32-bit color (4 billion colors). For example, a 640-by-480 pixel resolution display with 8-bit color (256 colors) requires 640 * 480 * 1 = 307.2 KB VRAM on the board. Increasing the color depth to 16.7 million colors (25-bit color) requires 921.6 KB VRAM, or about 1 MB VRAM. Most PCs use a 800-by-600 (SVGA) or a 1,025-by-768 (XGA) resolution on a 15-inch or a 17-inch monitor. Thus 1024 * 768 * 2 = 1.6 MB. A graphics board would need at least 2 MB of VRAM to provide 16-bit color at 1,025-by-768 resolution. AGP 3D graphics boards deliver 1,600-by-1,200 32-bit color images requiring about 8 MB of VRAM or more for fast display operation.

WRAM (WINDOWS RAM)

WRAM (Windows RAM) is a special type of dual-ported VRAM that is used on Matrox video cards. WRAM is fast, dual-ported video RAM that has special features, such as dual-color block-write mode for fast text and color fill acceleration in Windows applications. These features and the dual ports provide high-speed video performance at all resolutions and color depths. The performance of dual-ported WRAM compared to single-ported memories increases with higher resolutions, color depths, and refresh rates.

RAM Operating Characteristics and Parameters

RAM has different operating characteristics and parameters. We have already discussed some of these. This section looks at some additional RAM parameters.

MEMORY BANKS AND INTERLEAVING

DRAM memory chips are slower than CPUs. They require charging time equivalent to their access time. See Table 5–9. The table illustrates the concept of interleaving. The RAM Speed in the table must be faster than the 1 or 2 wait states determined by the computer clock rate. Today's CPU chip clock

Table 5.9 *RAM vs. CPU clock speeds*

Clock Speed/ Duration		Computer Clock Cycle Time in Nanoseconds			--------- Minimum RAM Speed ----------- in Nanoseconds		
Clock Speed MHz	Clock Tick Duration in Nano- seconds	0 Wait State 2 Clock Cycles	1 Wait State 3 Clock Cycles	2 Wait States 4 Clock Cycles	0 Wait States 2 Clock Cycles	1 Wait State 3 Clock Cycles	2 Wait States 4 Clock Cycles
6	166.667	333.333	500	668	150	200	300
8	125	250	375	500	120	150	200
12	83.333	166.667	250	332	80	120	150
16	62.5	125	187.5	252	80 (Interleave)	100	120
20	50	100	150	200	80 (Interleave)	80	100
25	40	80	120	160	80 (Interleave)	80	80
33	30.303	60.606	90.909	120	70 (Interleave & Cache)	70	70
50	20	40	60	80	70 (Interleave & Cache)	70	70
100	10	20	30	40	60 (Interleave & Cache)	60	60
400	2.5	5	7.5	10	PC66 SDRAM	15	15
500	2	4	6	8	PC100 SDRAM	10	10

speeds of 400 MHz and 500 MHz easily outstrip memory speeds. As a result, memory must interface through an L2 and an L1 cache to the CPU chip. SDRAM is not interleaved but is still slower than the CPU chip. SDRAM speeds are presented in the table for comparison purposes.

Matching CPU chip speed or CPU L2 cache speed to memory chip speed is accomplished by interleaving memory banks. When CPU chip speed is roughly twice as fast as the memory chip speed, the PC charges (prepares) a location in one bank for use, while during the same clock cycle it retrieves the contents of another location in a twin sister (or brother) bank. It then switches banks. It retrieves from the second bank and charges the first. It then retrieves from the first while again charging the second. This is called memory interleaving. See Figure 5–14.

Memory interleaving was evident in older 386 and 486 PCs. Memory expansion was performed using specific SIMM (Single In-line Memory Module) configurations because of the memory bank interleaving. For example some typical allowable memory sizes were:

- Four banks of 256-KB chips for 1 MB total RAM,
- Two banks of 1-Mb chips for 2 MB total RAM,

Figure 5–14 *Memory bank interleaving*

- Four banks of 1-MB chips for 4 MB total RAM,
- Two banks of 5-MB chips for 8 MB total RAM,
- Two banks of 5-MB chips and two banks of 1 MB chips for 10 MB total RAM, and finally
- Four banks of 5-MB chips for 16 MB total RAM.

Figure 5–15 shows SIMM banks.

With dual in-line memory modules (DIMMs), a single DIMM could provide two memory banks for interleaving by 486 CPU chips. Since Pentium CPU chips had 65-bit data paths, two DIMMs were required to permit memory bank interleaving. Since SDRAM did not require bank interleaving, as PCs moved to the faster SDRAM, single DIMMs provided the RAM required without bank interleaving.

Figure 5–15 *SIMM memory banks*

MEMORY BUS (8-BIT, 16-BIT, 32-BIT, AND 65-BIT)

The pathway between the PC's system RAM and the CPU chip has changed significantly since the introduction of the PC in 1981. Early PCs were so slow that memory was accessed through the normal ISA bus. In these PCs, memory expansion was accomplished by installing memory expansion cards in Industry Standard Architecture (ISA) bus slots. The first memory transfers to the CPU chip were over an 8-bit bus. The 8088 chip was a 16-bit chip with an 8-bit data pathway into and out of the CPU chip. The 80286 chip moved to a 16-bit bus. Memory and CPU chips were still so slow that installing memory expansion cards into the ISA 16-bit bus provided RAM expansion. In this case the transfers between RAM and the CPU chip were 16-bit transfers.

The emergence of 32-bit 80386 and 80486 chips began to change the system RAM bus connection to the CPU chip. These changes were necessitated by higher CPU chip speeds and faster memory speeds that both exceeded the capabilities of the ISA bus. A special memory bus was required because the ISA bus couldn't meet the transfer speed requirements of the CPU chips. The bus data width changed to a 32-bit width and then on to a 64-bit width with the introduction of Intel Pentium chips around 1990. Today, system RAM and Video RAM both operate with high-speed 65-bit buses connected to the CPU chip.

PARITY VERSUS NONPARITY

Parity is an error-checking mechanism employed in memory design to detect hardware memory errors. Parity provides an extra parity bit (memory test bit) for every 8-bit memory byte. Single In-line Memory Modules (SIMMs) are specified as 8 by 32 for nonparity memory and as 9 by 36 for parity-protected memory. This means that 8 by 32 memory stored 8 bits per byte for a total of 8 x 4 = 32 bits. It had no parity checking. In contrast, parity memory stored 9 bits per byte or 9 x 4 = 36 bits. This provided 4 extra parity bits on each SIMM.

Parity would be set as odd or, more likely, even depending on the number of 1s stored in each byte. Even parity added an extra 1 bit when the 8 bits in a byte contained an odd number of 1s. If a single bit changes from 1 to 0 or from 0 to 1, the parity would not match when it was recomputed as the byte was retrieved from memory.

Parity is best described as like a dryer. When you put in an even number of socks to dry (the socks being equivalent to our ones), the dryer always returns an odd number of socks (ones). The data is stored in bytes and the parity computed and stored with each byte. Upon retrieval it must match or there is a memory error.

Parity is only mathematically about 95% effective in detecting errors. If an even number of bits change, parity fails to detect the error. While missing even the smallest error is intolerable in PCs, parity is highly effective because double-bit memory errors are extremely rare (one stands a better chance of hitting a $100 million lottery jackpot than getting a double-bit memory error).

Most PCs do not use memory parity as a memory error checking mechanism because all SIMMs are tested quite thoroughly for errors. If a memory error happens, the PC behaves very badly and crashes almost immediately after it is started. Servers are a different story. They must operate reliably without memory errors. This means that they use 9 by 36 SIMMs or DIMMs and error-correction circuitry to correct single-bit errors and detect double-bit errors. This will be discussed in more detail soon.

SINGLE IN-LINE MEMORY MODULES (SIMMS)

A SIMM is a single in-line memory module. It has from six to nine RAM chips mounted on one side or both sides of a small circuit board. SIMMs come in 30-pin and 72-pin sizes. SIMM (or DIMM) only specifies the RAM packaging and not the type of RAM. Any RAM type—fast page mode, EDO, or SDRAM—can be found in each module configuration. Normally, two SIMMs are required to expand Pentium memory due to bank interleaving. In Figure 5–16, the bottom 3-chip SIMM actually has chips mounted on both sides of the SIMM module.

Both 30-pin and 72-pin SIMMs are notched on one side so that they cannot be incorrectly installed. The 72-pin SIMMs are also notched in the middle. They are placed in the SIMM socket and rolled or rocked back into place. See Figure 5–17.

Figure 5–17 *SIMM sockets*

Figure 5–16 *30-pin and 72-pin SIMMs*

Clips on either side of the SIMM socket mounts hold the SIMM firmly in place. SIMM removal is accomplished by moving the metal (or plastic) tabs in the SIMM socket to the side, releasing the SIMM from the socket.

DUAL IN-LINE MEMORY MODULES (DIMMS)

Dual in-line memory modules (DIMMs) are primarily used for SDRAM. DIMMs provide a 65-bit (72-bit with parity) wide data path. As a result, they can be used one at a time on Pentium boards. DIMMs of different capacities can be mixed unless there is associative memory interleaving. Such interleaving makes memory expansion in some PCs and servers much more structured than in any old desktop PC. Figure 5–18 shows a typical DIMM.

DIMMs are inserted by pushing them straight down into the DIMM socket. When inserted properly, plastic retainer clips at each end of the socket snap into place, securing the DIMM. Most new PCs use Synchronous DRAM in DIMMs.

ECC RAM

Error-correcting codes are used to correct single and multiple bit errors in server disk and memory operations. Error-correcting codes employ multiple bits to detect and correct errors.

In network servers and some PCs, RAM uses the 4 extra parity bits found in 9 by 36 bit SIMMs or DIMMs, combined with more sophisticated Error-Cor-

Figure 5–18   *168-pin DIMM*

recting Circuitry (ECC), to detect and correct single bit memory errors. The next study break exercise illustrates how error correcting codes work.

In one of my 80286 PCs, we installed an Orchid Technology memory board that used three extra bits of RAM to detect and correct memory errors. ECC memory is used routinely in network servers, but it is rarely found in PCs. similar error-correcting codes (or circuitry) are used to detect and correct errors on data stored on disk drives. In this case, several extra bytes of information are stored on the disk to perform error correction.

Study Break

ECC Operation

The operation of error-correcting codes is illustrated using a simple example. By adding three extra bits, single-bit errors in four bits can be detected and corrected.

1. Using Figure 5–19, write down any four bits in positions one through four.

2. Next write these bits down in the circle areas number one through four.

3. Then using even parity to always have an even number of ones, create the bits encompassed by circle 5, circle 6, and circle 7. Write these bit values in positions 5, 6, and 7.

4. Now alter a bit position. Any bit position will do. Using the altered bit value, recalculate bits 5, 6, and 7.

5. Determine bits do not match the originally created bits. The circled area **unique only to** those mismatched bits is the bit that is in error.

This is the simplest illustration of the operation of error-correcting codes.

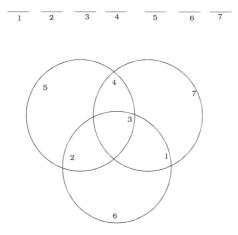

Figure 5–19   *ECC operation*

A+   5.3 **Main Logic Boards**

The primary function of the main logic board is to provide a mechanism for interfacing ROM, RAM, cache RAM, and PC cards to the CPU chip. MLBs generally provide mounting for RAM SIMMs, ROMs, PC card bus connections, L2 cache memory, and power supply connections. The newer MLBs have serial, parallel, IDE, and floppy controllers and more integrated into their design. They come in different form factors and layouts that are all based on the original IBM PC AT form factor.

System boards fall into two general categories, either integrated or non-integrated. An integrated system board has most of its components, such as video and mass storage interfaces, physically mounted on the circuit board. You typically find integrated system boards today in lower-end bundled systems (from such manufacturers as Compaq, IBM, and HP just to name a few) because they are cheaper to manufacture. The drawback to integrated system boards is that if an integrated component fails, the entire system board may need to be replaced. Some components on the system may not be easily upgraded. This can make upgrading a PC expensive because the upgrade requires purchasing a new system board.

The other category is a nonintegrated system board. This system board is unique because most of its components, such as video and storage, are not mounted physically on the system board. Video and storage in this case physically sit in the expansion slots. Today nonintegrated system boards have the disadvantage of bus transfer limitations impacting system speed. Servers use special nonintegrated system boards to facilitate easy CPU chip replacement in the event of failure and to provide the ability to have multiple CPU chips in the same server.

Types of Main Logic Boards

Main logic boards are further classified by their form factor. The form factor is determined by the board's mechanical size, how the integrated controllers attach to external devices, and the mounting hole layout.

The first clone MLBs duplicated the mechanical layout of the original PC and PC XT MLBs. They then moved to a PC AT form factor when the PC AT came out in 1985. Today's main logic boards are derived from the AT form factor. They evolved to baby AT form factors and finally to ATX form factors. Table 5–10 summarizes form factor features for different MLB styles.

The key element driving the design of main logic boards is the bus structure feeding the CPU chip. This structure is arranged in a hierarchical fashion, depending on the supporting chip set. The CPU chip connects to the host bus. This connects to the L2 (or L3) CPU cache and the host bus bridge chip. Next the PC's main SDRAM and the VRAM connect to the host bus through the host bus bridge chip. A bridge chip translates the electrical signals and timing from one bus to another. It may contain some data buffering to support speed-matching functions.

The VRAM connection flows across AGP bus connections for most MLBs produced today. The host bus bridge also connects to the much slower (33 MHz) PCI bus. Moving down the hierarchy, the next bridge chip bridges the ISA 16-bit bus to the PCI bus. Connected into the bridge are IDE and USB ports. Supporting chips may also connect in the slower serial and parallel port connections as well. Data flows from the slower devices and buses at the bottom of the hierarchy to the higher speed PCI bus in the middle of the hierarchy to finally the fastest devices and the CPU chip at the top of the hierarchy. See Figure 5–20.

Buses are used to connect in PC peripheral components and devices. The host bus is at the top end of the bus hierarchy. It operates directly with the CPU chip, the RAM, and the AGP port through a bridge Integrated Circuit (IC). The bridge integrated circuit matches the speed, electrical load, and voltage levels of the host bus to the other buses it services. Similarly, the

Table 5.10 *MLB form factor features*

MLB Form Factor	CPU Chip Mounting	RAM Mounting	Power Connector	Keyboard Mouse Connectors	Other Component Connectors
PC XT Style	DIP Socket	DRAM sockets	P8 and P9	Keyboard DIN	ISA 8-bit Bus
AT Style	PGA Socket	DRAM sockets	P8 and P9	Keyboard DIN	ISA 16-bit Bus
Baby AT Style	Typically ZIF PGA Socket 5 Or ZIF PGA Socket 7	DRAM Sockets And/or SIMM sockets	P8 and P9	Keyboard DIN	ISA 16-bit Bus VESA Bus PCI Bus Dual IDE Floppy Serial Parallel
New AT Style	ZIF PGA Socket 7	SIMM sockets And /or DIMM sockets	P8 and P9 Or ATX style	Keyboard and Mouse Mini-DIN	ISA 16-bit Bus AGP Bus PCI Bus Dual IDE Floppy Serial Parallel
ATX Style	ZIF PGA Socket 7 or Slot 1	SIMM sockets And/or DIMM sockets	ATX style	Keyboard and Mouse Mini-DIN	ISA 16-bit Bus AGP Bus PCI Bus Dual IDE SCSI (a few) Floppy Serial Parallel

main PCI bus is limited in terms of the devices that can connect to it. PCI-bus-to-ISA-bus and PCI-bus-to-PCI-bus bridge Integrated Circuits (ICs) support expansion of the primary PCI system bus into other ISA and PCI buses into which PC cards connect. The connection to the host bus for these other buses is a bridged connection, not a direct connection. Bridged connections have added delays or latencies in their data transfers. As a result, bridged buses are slower than direct buses when it comes to transferring data to the CPU chip. Because some buses have electrical load limits, they are bridged into a primary PCI bus that then passes their data via a host bus bridge to the host bus and RAM. PC main logic boards with more than 4 PCI slots are likely to be bridged in this fashion.

Some brand name manufacturers such as Compaq built their own MLB designs that did not conform to the standardized MLB styles discussed here. These proprietary boards used Intel and competing chip sets to provide

Figure 5–20 *CPU board general structure*

the bus and data hierarchy feeding into the CPU chip. Their ability to accept upgraded components or to be replaced by standardized MLBs was limited.

Now that we have examined MLBs in general let's discuss the standardized MLB styles in more detail.

PC/XT STYLE

PC/XT style is the simplest MLB design. The ISA 8-bit bus connected directly to the CPU chip. Memory and all I/O flowed across the bus. This was possible because of the slow CPU chip speeds. RAM was installed in DRAM sockets for individual chips. The power connectors were the old P8 and P9 style connectors. There was a single DIN connector at the rear of the MLB to connect in the keyboard. All display, disk drive, serial port and parallel port connections were made with ISA bus PC cards. This board may be found at PC antique shows today. Just think, the Antique Road Show program in 2031 will feature such boards as great treasures!

AT STYLE

The AT-style board form factor started in 1985 with the IBM PC AT. It laid the foundation for almost all MLBs for the next 15 years. The original AT

MLB was not that much different from the XT-style MLB. Basically, the ISA bus connected directly to the CPU chip. The difference here was that the ISA bus was now a 16-bit bus. Memory and all I/O flowed through this 16-bit ISA bus. Slow 80286 CPU chip speeds made this possible. With the AT, the ISA bus approached its top clock rate of 8 MHz. RAM was installed in DRAM sockets for individual chips or in DRAM add-on PC cards. The old P8- and P9-style power connectors attached the power supply. The P8 and P9 designations came from the original IBM PC; the power connectors on it were labeled P8 and P9. Power supply manufacturers adopted these designations as a de facto industry standard. They are now being replaced with industry standard ATX-style connectors.

A single DIN connector at the rear of the MLB connected in the keyboard. All display, disk drive, serial port, and parallel port connections were made using 8-bit or now 16-bit ISA bus PC cards. One added feature was that the PC setup was now performed using a CMOS setup and diagnostic program on floppy disk. This was the first PC that permitted changing setup parameters without opening the PC.

As the 80386 and 80486 CPU chips appeared, the AT style of main logic board changed to meet new PC hardware and configuration needs. The 80386 chip PC had external L2 CPU cache and the 80486 chip PCs had both internal L1 and external L2 CPU cache. This necessitated a host bus structure that connected the L2 cache, the system RAM and the CPU, separate from the 16-bit ISA bus structure. The VESA local bus that speeded data transfers to the display controller card VRAM provided faster graphics. Soon other faster devices like fixed disk drives were connected to the PC using the VESA bus. See Figure 5–21.

Around 1990, the Extended Industry Standard Architecture (EISA) bus was introduced to compete with IBM's Micro Channel Architecture (MCA) bus. The EISA is fading out of existence because the boards were expensive to purchase and the added performance was not more than Intel's PCI bus performance. In the 90s Intel's PCI bus and plug-and-play PC cards arrived. Each of these steps changed the architecture of the AT-style MLB.

As Pentium CPU chip PCs began to dominate the market, the AT-style MLB evolved to its present configuration. The hierarchical structure with host bus connecting CPU chip to L2 cache and bridging to memory, AGP buses, and PCI buses was implemented. The physical connections supported the standard keyboard DIN connector, P8 and P9 power connectors, 16-bit ISA bus card slots, and PCI bus card slots. Recently, AGP graphics card bus slots have emerged to again speed up graphics data transfers.

Figure 5–21 *AT-style 80486 main logic board*

BABY AT STYLE

The baby AT-style boards had all the same features as the AT-style boards except that they were smaller. Chassis mounting for baby AT-style boards and AT-style boards varied slightly. Virtually all PC chassis accommodated these variations. As chip sets required less MLB space, the baby AT-style board form factor became more prevalent. In Figure 5–22, the board has a Socket 7 CPU chip mount and both P8 /P9 and an ATX-style power connectors. The baby AT board pictured has two ISA 16-bit bus connectors, three PCI bus connectors, and one shared (PCI or ISA) connector slot.

ATX STYLE

The current Pentium PC systems use an ATX-style MLB. This board differs from the AT and baby AT styles in that it has more PC subsystems built onto the board. ATX-style boards provide a home for the CPU chip, L2 CPU cache, system RAM, BIOS ROM, ISA bus card slots, and PCI bus card slots. In addition, they incorporate serial port, parallel port, mini-DIN keyboard, mini-DIN mouse connections, Universal Serial Bus (USB), and IDE controller connections. The device connectors for the serial, parallel, mini-DIN, and USB ports are routed to a special connector bracket on the rear of the ATX-style MLBs. Power supply connections also differ from the P8 and P9 connectors on the older AT-style and baby AT-style MLBs. See Figure 5–23. The big difference between ATX-style and AT-style boards is that the ATX-style boards have either Slot 1 or Socket 7 CPU connections while baby AT-style

ATX Style
Power
Connector

Serial and
Parallel Port
Connectors

IDE Controller
Connectors

168-pin Dual In-line
Memory Module
Sockets

Keyboard
Connector

Supporting
Chipset

P8 & P8
Power
Connectors

Advanced
Graphics
Port
Card Bus Slot

Peripheral
Component
Interconnect
(PCI) 32-bit
Expansion
Card Bus
Slots

CMOSBattery

Zero Insertion
Force CPU
Chip Socket

Keyboard
ROM

Dual
ISA or PCI
Card Slot

Industry Standard
Architecture (ISA)
16-bit
Expansion Card
Bus Slots

Figure 5–22   *Baby AT-style MLB*

boards are mostly Socket 7 boards. The ATX Socket 7 MLB in Figure 5–23 has on the right an ISA 16-bit bus connector, a combined ISA 16-bit/PCI bus connector, and four PCI bus connectors. The Socket 7 CPU chip is on the left side along with the serial, parallel, USB, mouse and keyboard connections below the CPU chip on the bottom. Above the CPU chip are sockets for three (3) DIMMs. Directly above the DIMM sockets are the floppy disk connector, the IDE interface connectors and the ATX power supply connector. The ROM BIOS chip is mounted just below the middle PCI bus connector.

Figure 5–23   *ATX Socket 7 style MLB*

Figure 5–24 *ATX-style Slot 1 MLB*

The ATX-style Slot 1 main logic board is shown in Figure 5–24. It differs from the Socket 7 MLB in the number of PCI and ISA bus connectors. An additional ISA bus connector is provided. As with the Socket 7 ATX-style board, one connector is a combined 16-bit ISA/PCI bus connector. The serial, parallel, USB, mouse, and keyboard connections are at the left side bottom of the board. Above them is the ATX-style power connector and the Slot 1 connector for the CPU daughterboard. As we move upward, we encounter the DIMM sockets and finally at the top the floppy disk and IDE connectors. Directly in the middle of the board is the AGP connector for the video card. The ROM BIOS chip is mounted just below the rightmost PCI bus connectors.

Now that we have toured each style MLB, we should briefly examine each component. In determining MLB suitability for a PC, several factors are important. These factors are CPU chip socket or slot, board style, number of ISA slots, and number of PCI slots. Differences in CPU chip mounting and numbers of slots are the greatest areas of variability in board design.

MLB Components

The components installed on MLBs are serial communications ports, a parallel port, IDE or EIDE disk controllers, RAM, CPU chip, ROM BIOS, and external L2 CPU cache. Newer boards also incorporate USB ports. Some of these components are replaceable or upgradable while others are not. These integral MLB components reduce the need for expansion cards in the PC. Expansion cards are still used for modems, local area network (LAN), sound cards, and video controller cards. Additionally, other peripheral devices may require other controllers (for instance, SCSI controller cards).

Figure 5-25 *AT MLB serial connectors*

COMMUNICATION PORTS

Most main logic boards come with two serial ports built into the board. These are COM1 and COM2 serial ports. They can be configured through the CMOS setup program to COM3 or COM4 settings or can be entirely disabled. ATX boards route these serial ports to 9-pin "D"-shaped connectors on the rear of the ATX board. The AT-style (AT style and baby AT style) boards have 10-pin connector blocks that run through ribbon cables to 9-pin "D"-shaped connectors that fit into card slot mounting brackets or mounting holes in the rear of the chassis. The 10-pin connector blocks have the pins arranged in either one of two configurations. See Figure 5-25.

The headers are wired with two distinct types of pin outs. See Figure 5-26. One type of header connects the pins down one side to the ten-pin connector while the other has them crisscross the connector.

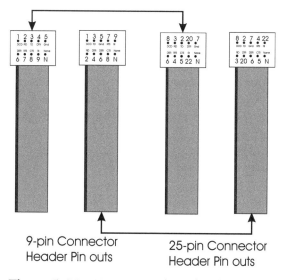

9-pin Connector
Header Pin outs

25-pin Connector
Header Pin outs

Figure 5-26 *AT MLB serial port header pin outs*

Pin outs for both 9-pin serial connectors and 25-pin serial connectors are shown in Figure 5–26.

ATX MLBs route serial port connections to 9-pin "D"-shaped male connectors on the rear of the chassis. The serial ports are used to connect a mouse or a palmtop PC to the MLB.

PARALLEL PORT

MLBs generally provide a single parallel port connection. This port can be set as compatible, bi-directional, EPP, or ECP. The configuration is set using the CMOS setup program. The parallel port connection is made using a 25-pin "D"-shaped female connector. ATX-style MLBs have this connector routed to the rear of the chassis. The parallel port connector is located over both serial port connectors in an ATX-style main logic board.

UNIVERSAL SERIAL BUS (USB) PORTS

Newer main logic boards provide Universal Serial Bus (USB connections). USB provides an easy way to expand the peripheral devices attached to the PC. It configures itself automatically (provided the correct drivers are loaded) and transfers data between the peripheral device and the PC at high speeds. A USB bus in theory can support 128 devices but practically our guess is that 10 devices is a more realistic upper limit. USB connections run out the rear of ATX-style chassis. The USB is a 1.5 MBPS or 12 MBPS serial port for connecting a variety of peripherals to the PC. USB devices include scanners, printers, mice, keyboards, CCD cameras, palmtop PCs, and more. The USB devices either run into hubs or are daisy-chained to permit several devices to use the same USB port. Windows 98 has software support for USB devices built in, but this must often be augmented by driver software provided by the USB device manufacturer. USB devices are plug-and-play devices. There may be differences between each USB port on the rear of the PC. We have installed a USB scanner that did not work on one USB port but worked on the other USB port.

IDE/EIDE AND FLOPPY CONTROLLERS

The connectors for cabling to IDE or EIDE fixed disk drives are built into the main logic board. These component connectors on ATX-style boards do not route to the outside because the fixed and floppy drives are installed internally. The IDE/EIDE controllers on newer main logic boards are Ultra Direct Memory Access (UDMA) controllers, capable of transferring data between the disk drive and the main logic board in bursts of 33 M per second. Each

IDE controller is capable of supporting two IDE devices. So the main logic board can support four IDE devices total. This permits installation of two fixed disk drives, a CD-ROM drive, and a high capacity Zip or Super Disk drive in a single PC. When there are more IDE devices to install, an additional IDE controller board must be installed in a PCI bus slot. Windows 95/98 must be configured to use the main logic board UDMA capabilities because its default configuration is not to use DMA disk access. The IDE/EIDE headers on the main logic board are 40-pin headers, and the floppy disk drive header is a 34-pin header.

SIMM AND DIMM SOCKETS

SIMMs and DIMMs were mentioned earlier in this chapter, but this section provides more detail about their functionality and usage.

Main logic boards have provided many different combinations of SIMM and DIMM sockets to accommodate changing RAM configurations. The earliest main logic boards had sockets for DRAM chips. This gave way to the first 30-pin SIMMs. These were the mainstay of memory chips for many 80386 CPU chip and 80486 CPU chip PCs. As PCs moved to Pentium CPU chips, the MLB RAM sockets moved to 72-pin SIMMs. Many main logic boards provided combinations of 30-pin and 72-pin SIMM sockets. As Pentium CPU chip speeds increased and SDRAM became the predominate type of system memory, DIMM 168-pin sockets were installed on main logic boards. At first there were combination SIMM and DIMM socket boards. Today most MLBs use SDRAM and DIMMs. With SDRAM and DIMMs there is no need for memory–bank interleaving. The RAM capacity is determined by the total capacity of the DIMMs installed in the main logic board sockets. In our MLB pictures there are three DIMM sockets on both the Baby AT-style the ATX-style main logic boards.

CPU SOCKETS

CPU chips are attached to main logic boards using PGA sockets or Slot 1 CPU daughterboards. Main logic boards support either PGA CPU chip mounting or Slot 1 CPU daughterboard installation. The PGA CPU chip mounting is most often on newer main logic boards a Socket 7 mount. This is used to install Intel Pentium, AMD, and Cyrix chips. Older main logic boards used Socket 5 mounts for Pentium CPU chips. The Slot 1 mount is used for new Pentium II, Celeron, and Pentium III CPU chip systems. The CPU daughterboard and active heat sink fan assembly mount directly on the main logic board as a unit.

Figure 5–27 *L2 main logic board CPU cache*

EXTERNAL CPU CACHE—L2 CACHE

The L2 CPU cache for Socket 7 CPU chips was installed on the main logic board. Several static RAM chips comprised L2 CPU cache. It was possible in this case to upgrade or, if needed, repair the L2 CPU cache because the static RAM chips were installed in DIP sockets on the main logic board. Today L2 CPU cache is usually a single chip on the main logic board or, in the case of Slot 1 Pentium CPU chips, installed on the CPU chip daughterboard. The L2 cache is no longer repairable or upgradable. Upgrades or repairs are performed by replacing the main logic board or the CPU chip daughterboard. Figure 5–27 shows 20 ns static RAM chips on an 80486 main logic board.

Study Break

Motherboard Style

Go to the rear of the PC and examine the serial port, the parallel port, and the keyboard and mouse ports. This indicates the style of motherboard used in the PC.

1. ATX-style and proprietary MLBs have the serial, parallel, keyboard, and mouse connectors clustered together on the left side of the main logic board. AT-style may have the serial and parallel port connectors mounted in the metal card slot covers.

2. Open the PC case and find the power connections to the MLB. Are there two separate connectors labeled P8 and P9, or is there a single unified connector? The separate connectors are used on AT-style motherboards. Replace the power connector.

3. Do ribbon cables run from the serial port connectors to the MLB? AT-style MLBs connect to these ports with ribbon cables.

Brand name systems have some ATX-like features but also employ proprietary mounting features to make MLB replacement require a MLB from that manufacturer. Of course, in most cases it is cheaper to replace both the MLB and the chassis rather than pay for a proprietary MLB from a brand name manufacturer.

A+ 5.4   PC Bus Architectures

The rows for the connectors into which circuit cards are plugged are called expansion slots. These cards are expansion cards because they often expand the basic PC capabilities. Daughterboards are also plugged into the main logic board. A daughterboard typically contains a CPU chip and is the core of the system, as opposed to expanding the PC's capabilities. Main logic boards contain two general-purpose buses today and some special purpose buses. The general-purpose buses are the ISA 16-bit bus to maintain backward compatibility with older PC expansion cards and the PCI bus for newer expansion cards. Specialized buses are the AGP bus and the VESA bus, providing high-speed data transfer between the CPU chip and graphics memory. See Figure 5–28. The Universal Serial Bus (USB) interfaces devices to the PC main logic board. It is a specialized bus not targeted at PC expansion cards.

These buses transferred one, two or four bytes at different clock speeds. Table 5–11 summarizes the data transfer rates and clock speeds of different buses.

The main logic board buses have evolved from the 1981 PC's Industry Standard Architecture (ISA) 8-bit bus to meet the increased performance demands placed on PCs while preserving compatibility with PC expansion cards sold in the market.

Buses are targeted at either general purpose or specialized applications. Specialized buses focus mainly on speeding up video operations. Most buses transfer all bits of a byte in parallel. The USB and IEEE 1394 buses are serial

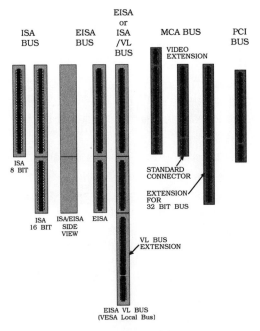

Figure 5–28 *Bus connectors*

Table 5.11 *Bus clock speeds*

Bus Type	Speed—Bits Transferred
ISA – 8 Bit	8 MHz – 8 bits
ISA – 16 Bit	8 MHz – 16 bits
MCA – 16 bit	24 MHz – 16 bits
MCA – 32 bit	24 MHz – 32 bits
EISA	33 MHz – 32 bits
PCI Peripheral Controller Interconnect Bus (Intel)	33 MHz – 32 Bits 66 MHz – 64 bits
Local Bus – 32 bit (VESA Standard)	System Clock Speed – 32 Bits (about 50 MHz)
Advanced Graphics Port (AGP)	133 MHz – 32 bits
PCMCIA (Personal Computer Memory Card International Association) *Laptop PCs*	8 MHz – 16 bits (asynchronous)
Card Bus *Laptop PCs*	33 MHz – 32 bits (synchronous and asynchronous)

buses. Bus mastering permits peripheral controllers to take control of the bus and transfer data faster than if the CPU chip exclusively controlled the bus. Buses can connect directly to the CPU Chip/Memory bus or they can be bridged into that bus through a PCI bus. Hot swappable buses permit changing expansion cards after bus I/O activity quiets down. Data transfers can be asynchronous, transferring one, two or four bytes at irregular intervals, or isochronous, transferring bursts of data at irregular intervals. Finally, precise internal PC clocks control some buses while others operate independently of internal PC clocks. These buses play a major role in PC peripheral component expansion and configuration.

Table 5–12 summarizes bus features.

Table 5.12 *Main logic board buses*

Bus Type	General Purpose vs. Specialized	Parallel vs. Serial	Bus Master	CPU/Memory Bus Connection *Bridged via PCI bus vs. Direct Connection*	Hot Swap	Data Transfers *Asynchronous vs. Isochronous*	Control Clock
ISA	General Purpose	Parallel	No	Bridged	No	No	Yes
EISA	General Purpose	Parallel	Yes	Bridged	No	Yes	Yes
VESA LB	Specialized	Parallel	Yes	Bridged	No	NA	System Clock
PCI	General Purpose	Parallel	Yes	Direct	No	Yes	Yes
SPCI	General Purpose	Parallel	Yes	Direct	No	Yes	Yes
Hot-pluggable PCI	General Purpose	Parallel	Yes	Direct	Yes	Yes	Yes
AGP	Specialized	Parallel	Yes	Direct	No	NA	Yes
CardBus	General Purpose	Parallel	Yes	Bridged	Yes	Yes	Yes
Zoomed Video	Specialized	Parallel	Yes	Bridged	Yes	NA	No
USB	General Purpose	Serial	No	Bridged	Yes	Yes	No
IEEE 1394	General Purpose	Serial	Yes	Bridged	Yes	Yes	No

ISA

The Industry Standard Architecture (ISA) bus began as an 8-bit expansion bus in 1981 that permitted the PC to address 8 MB of RAM. This one-byte-wide 4.77 MHz IBM PC bus had a theoretical bandwidth of about 4.5 megabytes per second. Increasing the bus clock speed to 8 MHz increased the theoretical bandwidth to 7.5 megabytes per second. Eight (8) data lines were added, changing it to a 16-bit bus with the introduction of the PC AT in 1985. This 8-bit expansion increased the theoretical throughput to 15 megabytes per second and permitted the PC to address 16 MB of RAM. However, memory access operations above the first megabyte required two steps, limiting the effective data rate to about 8 megabytes per second. This speed is adequate for mouse controllers, modems, and similar low-speed devices. Disk drives and LAN boards need higher transfer rates to provide acceptable PC performance.

As CPU chips used faster and wider data paths, the basic ISA bus design did not keep pace. Many ISA expansion cards remain 8-bit wide bus cards. The few cards with 16-bit data paths, such as older SCSI fixed disk controllers, graphics adapters, and LAN network cards, remain constricted by the low bandwidth of the ISA bus. Newer buses provide the bandwidth required by higher-speed PC expansion cards. See Figure 5–29.

The 16-bit AT bus is implemented on most main logic boards to provide compatibility with thousands of ISA bus cards sold and installed in PCs. These cards are low-end performance cards. Most main logic boards have some type of ISA bus expansion card slots. However, ISA expansion slots may be coming to an end. The low-speed parallel and serial ports that resided on ISA cards are now integrated into most main logic boards. Both Intel and Microsoft are calling for an end to ISA slots in the PC 99 System Design Guide, a specification for PC hardware design and configuration.

Figure 5–29 *ISA PC card edge connector*

EISA

As mentioned earlier in this chapter, the ISA main logic board buses evolved to the Extended Industry Standard Architecture (EISA) bus around 1990, in response to IBM's introduction of the PS/2 and the Micro-Channel Architecture (MCA) Bus. The EISA bus was compatible with all ISA 8-bit and 16-bit PC expansion cards. It also supported newer 32-bit EISA cards. The EISA bus was cleverly conceived. To accommodate all card types, the connector slots were made to permit deeper insertion of EISA cards while supporting the standard insertion depth of the ISA 8-bit and 16-bit cards. See Figure 5–30. Furthermore, EISA was an early step toward plug-and-play PC expansion card configuration. This was to answer IBM's MCA bus software configuration and PC card setup. The EISA bus used a special configuration program and parameter files set for each software configurable PC card. The main logic board BIOS had to support the EISA bus software configuration. The EISA bus accomplished the goal of having PC buyers think of an alternative PC design from IBM's PS/2 featuring the MCA bus. The EISA bus failed as a major bus alternative because it was used mostly with ISA cards and the expensive EISA cards did not increase performance that much over cards in an ISA bus. The ISA bus met most PC card expansion needs. There were EISA 32-bit SCSI controller cards and LAN cards manufactured that were expensive so they did not sell well.

The EISA bus laid the foundation for Intel to produce chip sets that made PC design and manufacturing easier. The PCI bus supports such chip sets.

Before the PCI bus replaced the EISA bus, the Video Electronics Standards Association standardized a separate video bus that sped up video operations. It was the VESA local bus.

Figure 5–30   *EISA bus card edge connector*

VESA Local Bus or VL-Bus

The VESA local bus was used on 80486 systems to improve both display and disk drive performance. The VESA bus operated at system clock speed. Since most 80486 systems operated at speeds that were less than 33 MHz (the 80486 chips became clock-doubling chips—for instance, 80486 33/66 MHz chips), matching the VESA local bus to system clock speed was not a problem. The VESA bus speed increased the display refresh performance and was also used to increase disk drive performance. This is similar to the data transfer speed enhancement provided by AGP port systems operating at a speed of 133 MHz. See Figure 5–31.

The VESA bus extended the capabilities of ordinary ISA bus slots by adding an extra extension connector to the main logic board. This connector extension carried the VESA bus data at system clock speed.

Sometimes the VESA bus was called the VL-bus (VESA local bus). In this case it was used for both video and disk I/O data transfers.

Micro-Channel Architecture Bus

IBM developed the micro-channel architecture bus. The MCA first appeared on the IBM PS/2 PCs in the 1987. It supported 8-bit, 16-bit, and 32-bit data transfers at 24 MHz. The MCA bus competed with the EISA bus but it had one serious marketing failure—it was not backwards compatible with the ISA bus cards on the market. To expand a PS/2 system, a PC owner had to purchase new and expensive MCA bus PC cards. The MCA bus has all but disappeared today. It is difficult to find any information on it even at IBM's website.

Figure 5–31 *VESA bus card edge connector*

PCI

The Peripheral Component Interconnect (PCI) has become the main bus used in PCs today. It started by performing 32-bit transfers at 33 MHz but is moving to support 66 MHz 65-bit data transfers. The PCI bus supports PC plug-and-play configuration capabilities.

Pentium processors with higher MHz speeds made the slow and narrow ISA bus a bottleneck between the processor and PC card expansion components. Intel created the Peripheral Component Interconnect (PCI) bus to alleviate this bottleneck. See Figure 5–32.

The PCI bus runs at its own clock speed, separate from the system clock speed. The original 32-bit-wide bus running at 33 MHz with a maximum speed of 132 M/second is widely implemented in PC systems. PCI has simplified PC hardware configuration by supporting plug-and-play and by supporting shared IRQ assignments.

The PCI bus supports 125-pins per card slot. Added 65-bit extension connectors similar to the 16-bit extension connector to the ISA bus somewhat doubles the bus bandwidth. A further increase to a 66 MHz clock speed increases the maximum potential bandwidth to 264 Megabytes per second. PCI cards run on either 5 volts or 3.3 volts. A notch cut into the edge connector toward the computer chassis's front which mates with a corresponding

Figure 5–32 *PCI bus card edge connector*

key in a 5-volt connector slot designates the 5-volt cards. The 3.3-volt cards have their designating notch cut toward the rear of the PC chassis. This 3.3-volt card notch corresponds with a key in a 3.3-volt connector slot. Universal cards fit either slot and run on either 5-volts or 3.3-volts.

The PCI bus is limited to ten electrical loads. Since most cards are more than one load, a practical limit to expansion cards inserted into a PCI bus is three or four cards. Using more than one PCI bus in a system mitigates this card limitation. In most PCs, bridge chips connect multiple PCI buses. The bridge chips install between one PCI bus and another.

Small Form-Factor PCI

Small form-factor PCI (SPCI) is a miniaturized PCI card format designed for space-constrained applications like laptop PCs. SPCI is designed to be a compact and inexpensive means to install add-in peripherals, such as LAN adapters, permanently or semipermanently into a PC. Similar to full-size PCI cards, SPCI cards connect directly to a PCI bus. Direct attachment reduces card cost and complexity as compared to cards using bridges. SPCI cards cannot be hot-plugged (inserted into a running PC). SPCI cards are installed by removing chassis covers and not by plugging into a conveniently accessible slot.

Hot-Pluggable PCI

Hot-pluggable PCI enhances standard PCI with hot-plug capability, permitting the PCI bus to be used in nonstop applications. The hot-plug capability lets the PCI bus compete with other hot-pluggable buses in applications, like telephone switching, that cannot tolerate brief lapses of operation. Similar to SPCI, hot-pluggable PCI connects to a PCI bus without bridging. Isolation buffers on the card are needed to keep card-generated signals from corrupting traffic on an operating bus during card insertion and removal, increasing the cost of hot-pluggable PCI cards.

Advanced Graphics Port Bus

The graphics display consumes more bandwidth than a PCI bus delivers. An XGA 1,204 by 768 pixel image with 16-bit color depth uses about 1.5 MB of data. Refreshing this at 75 Hz requires a bandwidth of 75 times 1.5 MB or over 100 megabytes per second. In contrast, the ancient Color Graphics Array (CGA) cards with four colors or two (2) bits of data at 320 by 200 pixel resolution per image required 128,000 bits of data refreshed at 60 Hz or over

900 kilobytes per second. New 3-D graphics make possible modeling texture mapping and object hiding. These features used in creating detailed 3-D images require enormous amounts of data. Further 3-D graphics adapters need fast access to the data.

The Accelerated Graphics Port (AGP) bus solves this problem. AGP ports appeared with Pentium II motherboards. They are less like a bus and more like a point-to-point connection, dedicated to connecting graphics adapters directly to main logic board RAM memory. The AGP port's focused work streamlines its design to achieve maximum speed. Such speed gives AGP graphics adapters fast access to texture and buffer data. AGP cards access data directly from the PC's RAM system memory without using the CPU chip, reducing the need to store the data in special graphics card memory.

AGP is much faster than PCI. A 33-MHz 32-bit PCI bus provides roughly 132 megabytes per second bandwidth. The AGP 32-bit width runs at clock speeds up to 133 MHz, producing a maximum bandwidth of roughly 532 megabytes per second. AGP graphics cards do not have to share this bandwidth with other devices, making the maximum bandwidth available to them at any time.

An AGP drawback is only one AGP device can be installed in a PC. In the event that a system has two displays as supported by Windows 98, a second PCI bus graphics adapter is needed for the second monitor. Similar to the PCI bus, there are two different voltage designs for the AGP bus. The most common is a 3.3-volt design and the other is a 1.5-volt design. As demand for increased bandwidth will certainly continue, higher AGP bus clock speeds and wider data paths are likely to meet such demands.

PC Card or PC-MCIA Bus

Around 1990, rapid growth in sales of laptop PCs inspired development of smaller, lighter, and more portable PC devices. PC card versatility and power made these portable devices common equipment on almost all laptop PCs. PC card technology has been standardized by the Personal Computer Memory Card International Association (PCMCIA). New PC card applications include smart cards, TV set-top boxes, automobile electronics, and more. PC card compact size and ruggedness make them an ideal solution in such applications.

The PC card standard specifies three physical types of PC cards; each use the same length and width and 68-pin connector. The single difference between Type I, Type II, and Type III cards is heights of 3.3 mm, 5.0 mm, and 10.5 mm respectively. This means that thinner cards can be used in thicker slots, but thicker cards cannot be inserted into thinner slots.

Type I PC cards are typically memory devices such as RAM, flash, OTP, and SRAM cards. Type II PC cards are often I/O devices, such as data/fax modems, and LAN cards. Type III PC cards are mini disk drives. There are extended cards for components that must remain outside the laptop PC, such as wireless communication antennas.

PCMCIA Standard Release 1.0/JEIDA 4.0 of June 1990 defined a 68-pin interface, Type I and Type II PC card form factors, electrical requirements for memory cards alone, and the Card Information Structure (CIS) critical to interoperability and PC card plug-and-play capabilities. PCMCIA Standard Releases 2.0, 2.01 and 2.1 from 1991 to 1994 defined an I/O interface, added to the 1990 standard. Release 2.0 included dual-voltage memory cards and card environmental requirements. Release 2.1 added the ATA specification, the Type III card, and the Auto-Indexing Mass Storage (AIMS) specification. Also included was the initial Card Services Specification. Release 2.1 enhanced the Card and Socket Services Specification, and improved the Card Information Structure. In February 1995, the PC Card Standard was again revised to improve compatibility and add 3.3-volt cards, DMA, and 32-bit CardBus bus mastering.

The latest CardBus implementations increase the speed and performance of the PC cards from something resembling that of an ISA bus adapter card to that of a PCI bus adapter card. This makes implementation of high-speed LAN and SCSI I/O PC cards effective.

Zoomed Video

Zoomed Video (ZV) is either 16-bit or 32-bit CardBus PC card technology to connect video data streams from a PC card source directly to a PC's video adapter. Zoomed video uses a dedicated data path from a PC card socket to the video adapter's feature port. This path either skirts the CardBus bridge in connecting from the card socket to the video controller; or connects through the controller with the card video data traversing the CardBus bridge en route to the video controller. Zoomed video cards have bus mastering capability that permit them to perform data transfers without using the laptop CPU chip or DMA and thus avoiding transfer of high-bandwidth video data over the PC's PCI bus. This leaves the PCI bus available for CPU traffic to and from system memory, etc. Zoomed video uses a standard PC card form factor and eliminates the need for a second dedicated PCI bus supporting video data. Zoomed video and audio data travel directly from the PC card socket to the video controller and audio coder/decoder (or codec), respectively. Consequently, this data cannot be modified by the laptop's CPU chip in real time. Zoomed video is a special-purpose interconnection providing a fixed video/audio pipe into a laptop PC.

USB

The Universal Serial Bus (USB) is being rapidly and broadly implemented in both desktop and mobile computers. USB operates at a top speed of 12 MBPS (effectively 8 MBPS). This speed adequately services mice, pointing devices, keyboards, some monitors, and cameras. USB devices are connected to ports on a hub device linked in a tree-wiring topology. Each device tree connects to a PC USB root-hub port through which the PC communicates with the tree's USB devices. USB devices attach to all ports with standard 5-conductor cables.

Most main logic boards include USB ports, while IEEE 1394 FireWire bus connections are provided using add-on PC adapter cards. The rapid increase in Universal Serial Bus (USB) and in IEEE 1394 serial bus is happening because:

- They have simpler and more user-friendly connectors and cables for these serial busses.
- They connect multiple devices to a bus using hubs or chaining to form a tree structure.
- They have bandwidths that match or exceed parallel busses.
- They operate with low power consumption.
- They provide plug-and-play self-configuration for connected devices.
- They provide the capability to hot swap devices.
- They employ protocols supporting a broad range of transport services, including isochronous (guaranteed transmission bandwidth) service to multimedia applications.

These are compelling reasons for serial busses to replace the ISA and potentially the PCI parallel busses. USB root-hub ports provide some 5-volt power for low-power devices. The root-hub ports support high-powered device attachment when they provide their own power from an AC source or from batteries. USB permits easy attachment and detachment of devices through plug-and-play software that finds devices, assign addresses to them, and sets them up. USB software communication sends data packets from a source to a destination using logical pipes designed to perform specific functions. There are separate packet types for data and for control information. USB supports asynchronous communication for simple devices like mice and keyboards and isochronous communication guaranteeing a set portion of the available bus bandwidth for more demanding multimedia applications that have stringent latency limits.

USB devices may control their power consumption rather than being controlled by the PC. USB devices can automatically enter a suspended low-power consumption state if the bus to which they connect becomes inactive. The suspended devices can resume operation at their presuspend consumption level when they awaken.

These features make USB a cost-effective and user-friendly general-purpose attachment mechanism for many PC peripherals.

IEEE 1394 or FireWire

Apple Computer's FireWire bus has evolved into the IEEE 1394 high-speed serial bus. The IEEE 1394 specification covers several busses ranging in performance from about 25 MBPS to 400 MBPS. This will likely be increased to 1.2 GBPS and higher speeds.

IEEE 1394 is a general-purpose serial bus for connecting high-speed peripherals to PCs. IEEE 1394 bus connections include connections between consumer AV electronics made possible by the peer-to-peer communication supported by IEEE 1394 bus-mastering features. Similar to the USB bus, the IEEE 1394 bus attaches multiple devices to a PC, as well as supporting peer-to-peer device connection like directly connecting a scanner to a printer. The IEEE 1394 buses can connect multiple devices through a hub or can connect a hierarchy of serial buses, each supporting up to 63 device attachments. Bridges transfer data between buses in the hierarchical IEEE 1394 bus configuration.

Like USB, IEEE 1394 bus communication uses packet transmission between devices. IEEE 1394 transaction software services present application software with read, write, and lock services. Each service translates into packet sequences in a link software layer that are transmitted over copper wires or fiber-optic cable. The IEEE 1394 provides both asynchronous and isochronous communication.

The IEEE 1394 bus has plug-and-play capability. When IEEE 1394 devices are added or removed from a bus, all devices connected to the IEEE 1394 bus reset and then perform a self-identification and enumeration process. Unique addresses are then assigned to all devices and normal bus operation resumes. A single device functions as bus manager. It performs bus power management, optimizes performance, maintains bus-connection information, and manages isochronous bandwidth allocation.

IEEE 1394 costs more than USB. IEEE 1394 bus power management depends on the power consumption of the IEEE 1394 Physical (PHY) layer.

The IEEE 1394 standard specifies a device's physical layer be powered on whenever the device is connected to the IEEE 1394 bus. Devices that are not powered on can split an IEEE 1394 bus into two separate segments. IEEE 1394 devices can draw up to 1 Watt of power when attached to an IEEE 1394 bus. These present problems in lower power consumption applications, such as those of laptop PCs. Both bus-powered and self-powered devices can attach to an IEEE 1394 bus. The bus manager reads the power source for each node and each node's power requirements. Using that information, the bus manager node sends power enabling or disabling packets to individual nodes to budget IEEE 1394 bus power.

Study Break

PC Buses

1. Examine your PC to determine what bus connections it supports. Examine the outside of the chassis of a PC. Are there any ports labeled USB or IEEE 1394? If so the PC supports both buses. None labeled? Are there any small rectangular ports? USB ports are usually placed together with one over the top of the other. Some Compaq PCs have both USB and IEEE 1394 ports in the front, hidden by a sliding panel.

2. Open the chassis. Examine the card slots. Are they ISA, PCI, AGP or something else? Use Figures 5–22 and 5–28 to help identify the different bus connectors. What colors are the different connectors in the PC?

The goal here is to determine for a specific PC what option card expandability is supported.

A+ 5.5 CMOS Setup

Complementary Metal Oxide Silicon (CMOS) refers to a semiconductor fabrication technology that produces low-power chips. In PCs, CMOS chips were first used in the PC AT to store configuration and date information. The setup memory based upon Complementary Metal Oxide Silicon (CMOS) technology became known as CMOS setup memory. The more proper and accurate terminology is nonvolatile memory or nonvolatile RAM (NVRAM). In PCs, NVRAM stores basic configuration information and today the system Basic Input/Output System (BIOS). The BIOS comprises programs that perform power on self test (POST), CMOS setup functions, and real mode input/output data operations. Setup information is changed by BIOS rou-

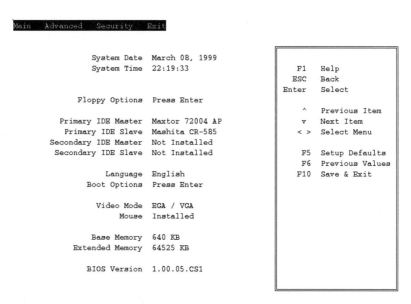

Figure 5–33 *CMOS setup initial menu*

tines (the CMOS setup) entered as the PC boots or by diagnostic programs. This section examines the PC setup and control parameters that are changed by the BIOS CMOS setup program.

Depending upon the PC BIOS, usually striking a specific key enters the BIOS setup program. Some commonly used keys were DEL, F1, or F2. Once the key is struck during system boot, the CMOS setup program in BIOS is started; the menu that controls the basic system settings is shown in Figure 5–33.

Basic Settings

Basic CMOS system settings generally establish the following:
- The system date and time
- The type of floppy disk
- The main logic board IDE controller connections
- The language for the setup program menus
- How the system boots
- The initial video operating mode
- Whether a mouse is detected
- The RAM detected
- The Revision Version of the BIOS

The basic settings vary from PC to PC, depending upon the main logic board, CPU chip, and RAM. Some options are simple, while the importance of others is much less evident. Some settings are for informational purposes and are not configurable. Many new PCs automatically determine the optimal CMOS settings and do not permit operator changes to those settings. These are displayed differently from the settings that can be changed. For example, a new Dell Inspiron laptop does not permit disabling L2 cache. Some older PC BIOSs support enabling/disabling L2 cache.

DATE/TIME SETTINGS

This simply sets the date and time used by the PC to date- and time-stamp all events. The critical factor here is compliance with the year 2000 (Y2K) date change. Simple test programs verify Y2K compliance (readiness). The time settings use a 24-hour clock. Other software, like the date and time commands in DOS, changes these settings.

FLOPPY DRIVE TYPES

These settings control the floppy disk drives. They work with the two drives A and B, supported by the single floppy disk interface on the main logic board. Each floppy drive can be set to:

- **Disabled**—Prohibits access to the floppy drive. This acts as a security measure, thwarting use of floppy drives for booting the PC and bypassing the operating system security.

- **360 KB**—This sets the designated floppy drive to support the original XT 5.25-inch double sided nine sector per track floppy drive.

- **1.2 MB**—Drive A or drive B is set to support the AT 5.25-inch double-sided fifteen sector-per-track floppy drive.

- **720 KB**—This sets a floppy drive to support the original PS/2 3.5-inch double density nine sector-per-track and 80-track floppy drive.

- **1.44/1.25 MB**—This is the most common drive setting. It is for 3.5-inch 80-track floppy drives with 18 sectors per track.

- **2.88 MB**—This sets the designated floppy drive to support 160 track 3.5-inch floppy drives with 18 sectors per track.

Floppy drives must match the CMOS settings. Mismatches cause the floppy to malfunction by being unreadable, but can also trash a diskette's contents.

IDE CONTROLLER SETTINGS

The IDE controller settings match the IDE disk or CD-ROM to the system. IDE fixed disks must have the system recognize the correct drive geometry— cylinders, heads, and sectors per track—to read and write data to the fixed disk drive. IDE device configuration options are:

- **Auto Configured**—In this setting, the main logic board reads the configuration settings from the IDE drive itself. It uses the settings read to determine the read/write addressing it uses to access data on the fixed disk drive.
- **User Definable**—This setting permits manual control of the configuration. When the IDE drive does not contain the setup information (a real rarity today) or does not perform best with the automatic information, then using manual settings configures the main logic board to work with the fixed disk drive. The manual settings require entering the number of cylinders, the number of heads, and the number of sectors per track and then the setup program computes and displays the maximum capacity available on the IDE disk drive.
- **Disabled**—This setting is for unused IDE ports, permitting reassignment of their resources to other peripheral devices.

With large (over 2 GB capacity) IDE drives, there is a problem working with a BIOS that was originally targeted at disk drives under 100 MB. The limitation is not manifested so much in terms of total capacity, but rather in terms of the maximum number of cylinders addressable by the IDE controller and how they are translated into sector addressing that the operating system can use. The IDE translation mode determines how this is accomplished. Translation mode options are:

- **Auto detected**—Let the disk drive tell if translation is required and how the translation is to be accomplished.
- **Extended cylinders-heads-sectors**—In this case the number of cylinders is greater than 1024 cylinders and translation must be performed.
- **Standard cylinders-heads-sectors**—In this case the number of cylinders is less than 1024 cylinders and translation is not required. This translation is sometimes identified as Cylinders-Heads-Sectors (CHS) translation.
- **Logical block**—This is the Logical Block Addressing (LBA) supported by some IDE disk drives.

In cases where LBA translation mode or an extended translation mode is required and cannot be provided, the disk drive capacity is limited to the maximum capacity realized using 1024 cylinders alone. On an old main logic board we got only 512 MB out of a 1.2 GB disk drive when the BIOS did not support LBA translation.

A Multiple Sector Setting permits the main logic board to transfer data from the disk drive to the RAM, transferring several sectors with single interrupt. The settings are:

- **Auto Detected**—Lets the main logic board detect the optimal setting.
- **8 Sectors/Block**—This setting manually sets the number of sectors at eight sectors per block for each interrupt.
- **4 Sectors/Block**—This setting manually sets the number of sectors at four sectors per block for each interrupt.
- **Disabled**—This uses whatever setting the software comes up with, most likely one sector per interrupt.

This setting is like the sector-interleave setting in reverse. It is saying how fast is your CPU and how much buffering is available? Can the CPU chip run off and do lots of work before needing to service the fixed disk or must it constantly watch it? The faster the CPU chip and the more buffering, the more sectors per interrupt.

The fast programmed I/O mode determines how the main logic board behaves with disk I/O operations. Typically disk I/O is performed using program steps to transfer the data to RAM. There are different protocols used by different IDE drives to accomplish these transfers. The main logic board queries the IDE drive and uses fastest programmed I/O protocol to transfer data to and from RAM. The settings are Auto Detected and Disabled.

BOOT SETTINGS

The boot settings determine the device from which to boot as well as initial operating states of the main logic board and CPU chip.

Most newer PCs permit booting from several devices. This is sometimes specified as first boot device, second boot device, third boot device, and fourth boot device. These boot devices are selected in sequence from first to fourth. If a device is not found or does not work, then the next device is selected. The boot device settings are:

- **Disabled**—This inhibits booting from this boot device setting.
- **Floppy**—The boot device is specified as floppy drive A.
- **Hard Disk**—The PC boots from the active partition drive typically assigned designated by drive letter C.
- **CD-ROM**—The boot device is the CD-ROM drive. Special bootable diagnostic and installation CD-ROMs are required. As the old flop-

pies fade into the sunset, this will become the primary system-software installation device. At that time, booting from the CD-ROM will be critical.

- **Network**—This is for corporate environments where tight control of PC configurations is necessary. In this case the OS boot programs are loaded from a special network server.

The System Cache setting enables or disables the L2 cache on the main logic board.

The Boot Speed selects the system speed. In the old dual-speed CPU chips, the CPU chip speed could be set to main logic board clock speed (nonturbo) or maximum CPU chip clock speed (turbo). The word turbo crept into PC jargon based upon its use in the Battle Star Galactica television program. Their rockets had a turbo setting that was no doubt inspired by turbo-supercharged cars in manufacture at that time.

The Num Lock setting just puts the keyboard into numeric Lock State upon boot.

The Speaker setting permits the speaker to beep and emit the audio diagnostic sounds. Disabling it just makes booting quieter.

Setup Prompt causes the message identifying the key (in my case here F1) that enters the CMOS setup BIOS program.

A Hard Disk Pre-delay setting is used to permit a hard disk to initialize itself fully before being accessed by the main logic board and the operating system. It can be set to disabled or individual times ranging from 3 to 30 Seconds.

The typematic programming settings determine the keyboard auto-repeat behavior. Setting Typematic Rate Programming enables typematic operation. The Typematic Rate Delay is the amount of time before the keyboard automatically repeats an individual keystroke. The Typematic Rate is how many keystrokes per second is the typematic repetition rate. The smallest delay is a quarter (0.25) second and the fastest repetition rate is 30 keystrokes per second. Most people can adapt easily to these rates.

Advanced Settings

The advanced system settings cover:

- Peripheral Configuration
- Advanced Chip Set Configuration
- Power Management Configuration
- Plug and Play Configuration
- Event Logging Configuration

Event-logging configurations are specific in some newer BIOSs or a network server BIOS. Event logging would likely be supported by the BIOS for a Pentium Pro CPU chip PC because these chips were designed specifically for network servers demanding reliability. It is much less likely that this would be a feature in a desktop PC.

PERIPHERAL CONFIGURATION

The peripheral configuration sets up the peripheral components built into the main logic board. These peripheral components are serial and parallel ports.

The IDE and floppy interfaces are also enabled or disabled here permitting their IRQ and I/O address resources to be used by other peripherals in the event they are not needed. The settings are:

IDE INTERFACES • This setting controls the main logic board built-in IDE interfaces. The settings are:

- **Auto**—Automatically detect the interface.
- **Disabled**—Disable the interface, freeing its resources.

FLOPPY INTERFACES • This setting controls the main logic board built-in floppy disk controller. The settings are:

- **Auto**—Automatically detect the presence of a floppy drive.
- **Enabled**—Enable permanently the floppy drive interface.
- **Disabled**—Disable the interface, freeing the resources. This setting can also be used as a security setting. If the interface is disabled, any floppy drives in the system will not work. Combine this with the security features and it removes the ability to put information into a PC or to boot a PC from a floppy disk drive. Disabling is more secure than making sure that the system is only bootable from the fixed disk. By disabling the floppy drives, you can prevent any viruses from entering a system through a floppy diskette. Because the PC cannot read floppy disk drives, viruses have one less pathway to enter your PC.

SERIAL PORTS • Serial port configurations are set here. Each main logic board has two built-in serial ports. These ports can be set up as COM1, COM2, COM3, COM4, or disabled. The basic setting is Auto or Disabled that either disables the port, freeing the resources for other peripheral components, or automatically assigns them to COM1 or COM2.

The serial ports can be manually set to the COM1, COM2, COM3, or COM4 I/O address and IRQ settings. Standard PC settings for COM1-4 are:

COM Port	I/O Address	IRQ
COM1	3F8	IRQ4
COM2	2F8	IRQ3
COM3	3E8	IRQ4
COM4	2E8	IRQ3

When choosing these settings it is best to not disable a COM port on the main logic board, but rather assign it to an unused COM port setting. For example, if a mouse uses COM1 and COM2 is used by an internal modem, then set the main logic board second COM port to COM3. This sometimes works better than disabling the COM port. Other COM port settings are:

COM Port	I/O Address	IRQ
COM1	3F8	IRQ3
COM2	2F8	IRQ4
COM3	3E8	IRQ3
COM4	2E8	IRQ4

These settings flip the IRQ lines but retain the same COM port I/O addresses.

PRINTER PORT • Printer ports can be set to Auto or Disabled. The Auto setting has the main logic board use default settings for the built-in parallel port. Otherwise, manual settings for the parallel port can be selected from the following:

LPT Port	I/O Address	IRQ
LPT1	378	IRQ7
LPT2	278	IRQ7
LPT1	378	IRQ5
LPT2	278	IRQ5

The original PC/XT used IRQ 7 for the parallel Line PrinTer (LPT) port. The AT assigned IRQ 5 to a second parallel port. The main logic board has only a single parallel port built into it. However, that built-in parallel port can have either LPT1 or LPT2 settings.

The Port Mode setting is most critical for proper device operation. The compatible mode provides output only. It operates like an old PC AT parallel port. Bi-directional mode is an AT port that, using the control lines, permits both output and input operation. This is a two-way interface, but a very slow two-way interface because input data is received a half-byte (nibble) at a time. The Enhanced Parallel Port (EPP) mode is a high-speed bi-directional port. There are revisions to this parallel port operation specification. This BIOS supports Revision 1.7. The Extended Capabilities Port (ECP) conforms to the IEEE 1284 parallel port specification. Specific peripheral devices attached to the parallel port require a matching setting. Sometimes what appears to be a better setting for a device is not really better. Worst case scenario is that all four settings must be tested to determine for a specific peripheral what is the correct or optimal setting.

ADVANCED CHIP SET CONFIGURATION

On older PCs, this configuration option controlled a variety of detailed main logic board operating parameters dealing with RAM, video, and CPU chip functions. These option configuration selections have been reduced today to a very few because the BIOS is designed to self-configure most options based on the installed components. For example, on older systems there were several configuration settings for CPU chip clock ticks per memory cycle. Today the BIOS determines the type of RAM—for instance, fast page mode or EDO RAM—and automatically adjusts to the optimal timing for that type of RAM.

The one rule to remember here is that when a PC does not work, always choose the default settings. Several times we have tried choosing settings that make a PC run faster by tweaking up the CPU-chip-to-RAM interface, only to discover that the PC performed much more poorly than before. In virtually every instance, choosing the BIOS defaults not only made a nonoperational system operate, but improved the performance overall.

BASE MEMORY SIZE • This sets the real memory in the PC to 512 KB or 640 KB. Most systems have sufficient RAM today so setting it to the traditional 640 KB is best. Some diagnostics and games that require more conventional RAM to run may not operate if 512 KB is chosen.

ISA LFB SIZE • This is an ISA bus parameter that sets a buffer size. In most new PC systems, this setting would be disabled. Otherwise the setting is 1 M. ISA bus parameters are largely ignored or disabled in most new PCs. This is because the ISA bus is playing an increasingly minor role in peripheral component connection to the PC.

VIDEO PALETTE SNOOP • The video palette snoop feature permits sharing a common palette between ISA add-on cards and a built-in graphics controller. This feature is most often not required in new PCs, so it can be disabled.

LATENCY TIMER (PCI CLOCKS) • This is the maximum number of clock ticks that a PCI card must wait before it can access the PCI bus. The access in a Pentium Pro chip PC might be guaranteed to PCI bus cards after 66 clock ticks. Sometimes there are no menu options to select for this configuration option. Whenever there are no menu selections, it is best to not change the number. Changes are more likely to degrade than improve performance.

SIMM DETECTED • This option was automatically determined by the BIOS upon memory installation and power up operation. The PC CMOS setup displayed:

Bank 0 SIMM Detected   EDO mode
Bank 1 SIMM Detected   None Installed

POWER MANAGEMENT CONFIGURATION

Power management is a real anathema to Windows 95/98 because they have power management functionality built in that often conflicts with the BIOS power management features. In the case of Windows PCs, it is best to disable the power management features in CMOS setup and let Windows control the power-saving features. The BIOS power management features are:

- **Enabled—Disabled**—This turns on or off the power management functions.
- **IDE Power Down—Enabled**—When power management is enabled, this functions controls power to the fixed disk drive. Power is removed after a designated interval.
- **VESA Video Power Down—Sleep**—This feature controls power to the monitor. It shuts off display output after a specific interval.
- **Inactivity Timer—10 minutes**—This sets the interval duration before the power down state for the monitor and disk drive are entered.

Laptop PCs a have much more extensive power management setup because they are designed to squeeze as much capacity out of internal battery power as possible.

Power control saves energy. It is not a factor in extending the life of PC components because most components are designed to operate without failure for 5 or more years. With PCs becoming cheaper, they become obsolete well before any components are likely to wear out from being powered on 24 hours a day 7 days a week.

PLUG AND PLAY CONFIGURATION

These configuration settings are required to effectively work with the plug-and-play features of Windows. The Internal Configuration Utility (ICU) works with Windows to perform plug-and-play PC card configuration. The options are to use ICU which installs the BIOS plug-and-play software and then relies on booting with a plug-and-play OS, namely Windows 95/98 or perhaps the new Windows NT 5.0. Otherwise a setup utility assigns system resources to bus slots and peripheral components. The IRQs that can be assigned in this case are IRQ 5, 9, 10, 11, and 15. IRQ 5 is typically the LPT2 IRQ. IRQ 9 is linked to IRQ 2 that also cascades IRQs 8 through 15, but can be assigned to a peripheral component. Typically LAN cards have used this interrupt. IRQs 10 and 11 are generally unassigned in most systems, and the secondary IDE controller or SCSI controller cards use IRQ 15.

EVENT LOGGING CONFIGURATION

Event logging is not a typical BIOS configuration option. In some PCs, it is predominately used to track memory errors. It logs single- and multiple-bit ECC Errors. This would give an idea of memory problems. In network servers it may be used to track other failures (e.g. cooling fan failures) as well.

Memory parity may be set using advanced setup options. This setting is not under the logging area but rather in the Advanced Chip Set Configuration settings typically. Because memory is mentioned here, we will discuss it now. Memory parity settings can be parity or no parity. This means that an extra bit must be provided for each 8-bit byte to maintain an even (or an odd) number of ones in each byte stored. Nonparity SIMMs or DIMMs have 32 bits while parity SIMMs or DIMMs use 36 bits or one extra bit per each memory byte on the SIMM or DIMM. The Error-Correcting Code (ECC) uses these four extra parity bits to perform single-bit error correction and double-bit error detection.

Passwords and Security

The CMOS setup permits assignment of administrative and user passwords to provide system security. This prevents anyone from starting and using the PC without knowing the user password. Further BIOS settings cannot be altered without using the administrative password. These security settings cannot be bypassed easily by software. They can make a Windows 95/98 system quite secure. However, these CMOS passwords do not protect a system that is powered-on in Windows. They only protect the system when it is first powered on. Leaving a running PC to eat lunch makes that PC nonsecure.

Exit

The Exit setting exits the setup with an option to Exit Save or Exit Discard the configuration changes made.

The CMOS setup options presented here were for a specific system. They are typical of the settings found on most PCs today. However, when there is any doubt about CMOS setup parameters, it is always best to choose and install the default settings.

Study Break

CMOS Setup

Shut down a PC and restart. Enter the CMOS setup program to determine what options can be set.

1. Shut down your PC and then reboot. Watch the screen to determine when and how the CMOS setup program is entered. Strike the key that starts the CMOS setup program (F1, F2, or Delete).

2. Check the main menu selections. Are the date and time correct?   Reset them as needed.

3. Look at the floppy and fixed disk specifications. Make a note of the fixed disk type and geometry. Is LBA mode used to access the drive?

4. Find the chip set and integrated peripherals (the built-in serial, parallel, and IDE controllers) options. What settings can be changed?

5. Find if you can an option that enables/disables the L2 cache. This is likely not supported on newer PCs.

The goal here is to familiarize the reader with the different setup options and features controlled by the CMOS setup program.

Summary

This chapter has covered the main logic board in extensive detail. The many types of PC CPU chips, characteristics such as size, speed, and their relative performance metrics were covered in the first section. Section two went into further detail about RAM and its evolution, covering topics such as types, operating characteristics, and parameters.

The primary purpose for the Main Logic Board (MLB) is to provide a mechanism for interfacing ROM, RAM, cache RAM, and PC cards to the CPU chip. Section three, on main logic boards, provided a review of material presented in an earlier chapter, as well as new details on the types of MLBs and their functionality.

The next section, on PC bus architectures, provided details about the various types of buses and connectors used. Separate comments on well-known architectures such as ISA, EISA, PCMCIA were presented. Additionally, some of the lesser-known buses such as VESA were covered as well, providing a well-rounded view of the types of buses the reader might encounter.

The final section, CMOS setup, provided information on the purpose and functionality of the Complementary Metal Oxide Silicon (CMOS) semiconductor. CMOS settings and setup options were discussed, as well as the relationship between this chip and the PC BIOS.

▲ CHAPTER REVIEW QUESTIONS

1. *PCI means?*

    A. Peripheral CPU Interconnect

    B. PC Component Interconnect

    C. Peripheral Component Interconnect

    D. Peripheral Component Interconnection

    Answer: C. Peripheral Component Interconnect

2. *The fastest Pentium CPU chip is?*

    A. Pentium MMX.

    B. Celeron.

    C. Pentium III.

    D. Pentium II MMX.

    Answer: C. Pentium III.

3. *Pentium is a _____ microprocessor?*

    A. CMOS technology

    B. CISC

    C. superscalar

    D. 80386 32-bit based

    E. All of the above

    Answer: E. All of the above

4. *Which CPU chips do Macintosh computers use?*

   A. AMD

   B. Cyrix

   C. Intel

   D. Motorola

   Answer: D. Motorola

5. *Which CPU chips contain internal L2 cache?*

   A. Pentium Pro

   B. Xeon

   C. Celeron

   D. Pentium III

   E. None of the above

   F. All of the above

   Answer: F. All of the above

6. *What buses are most commonly found on main logic boards today?*

   A. ISA, PCI, FireWire, USB

   B. ISA, PCI, AGP, USB

   C. ISA, PCI, VESA, USB

   D. EISA, PCI, AGP, USB

   Answer: B. ISA, PCI, AGP, USB

7. *A PCI bus does not have a fixed clock speed.*

   A. TRUE

   B. FALSE

   Answer: B. FALSE

8. *A VESA bus does not have a fixed clock speed.*

   A. TRUE

   B. FALSE

   Answer: A.—It runs at the speed of the main logic board core clock.

9. *Main logic boards have built in:*

   A. IDE controllers, a floppy controller, serial ports, parallel ports

   B. IDE controllers, a floppy controller, serial ports, a SCSI controller

C. IDE controllers, a floppy controller, serial ports, mouse ports

D. IDE controllers, a floppy controller, serial ports, a parallel port

Answer: D. IDE controllers, a floppy controller, serial ports, a parallel port

10. *EISA buses accept _____.*

    A. ISA cards

    B. EISA cards only

    C. PCI cards and EISA Cards

    D. VESA and EISA cards

    Answer: A. ISA cards

11. *The ISA bus is bridged into the _____ on main logic boards.*

    A. EISA

    B. ESA

    C. USB

    D. PCI

    Answer D. PCI

12. *CMOS setup determines*

    A. Floppy drive speed

    B. Keyboard typematic speed

    C. Disk drive capacity

    D. Floppy drive B booting

    Answer: B. Keyboard typematic speed

13. *The first 16-bit bus was?*

    A. The PCI bus

    B. The EISA bus

    C. The MCA bus

    D. The ISA bus

    E. The AGP bus

    Answer: D. The ISA bus

14. *L2 cache is*
    A. Secondary disk cache
    B. External CPU cache
    C. Faster than L3 and L1 cache
    D. Level 2 memory

    Answer: B. External CPU cache

15. *CMOS sets PCs to boot from?*
    A. The fixed disk
    B. The floppy disk
    C. The CD-ROM
    D. A network
    E. All of the above

    Answer: E. All of the above

16. *Pentium II and Pentium III CPUs install in main logic boards using*
    A. Socket 7
    B. PGA
    C. Slot 1
    D. Slot 2
    E. None of the above

    Answer: C. Slot 1

Printers

This chapter describes the operation of the major types of printers, their components, description and resolution of common printing problems, and preventative maintenance.

▲ Chapter Syllabus

A+ 6.1   **Printing Concepts, Components, and Operation**

A+ 6.2   **Printer Connections and Configurations**

A+ 6.3   **Resolving Common Printer Problems**

A+ 6.4   **Printer Servicing and Preventative Maintenance**

A+ 6.1 Printing Concepts, Components, and Operation

A big PC problem area is printing. Most printer problems are caused by mismatches in printer driver programs and fonts used by application programs. When a program like Microsoft Word formats a document, it formats it for a specific type of printer. If the printer at the other end of the parallel port is not the printer specified in the application that does the formatting, bad things happen.

Resolving printer problems requires determining what controls the printer, whether it's DOS, the application, or Windows. In the old DOS world, the application program was responsible for the printer and print formatting. It was a simpler world back then as well. There were few fonts with which to contend. Sharing data between PCs was limited because it all had to be transferred using floppy diskettes.

Things have changed dramatically since then. LANs make file sharing, printer sharing and font sharing between PCs an every-minute occurrence. Users have access to several different printers. It's a real jungle out there. Printers are controlled by Windows and the network server and are not controlled by the applications. Applications now format and display a document according to the printer on which they expect it to print. Change the printer specification, and the document display changes as well. DOS only transfers data to a designated printer port.

Windows prints in a multiple-step process. The application program stores a document in a special storage format that is editable. Microsoft Word uses a DOC format. Universal storage formats used by Windows desktop publishing programs are Rich Text Format (RTF), Hypertext Mark Up Language (HTML or HTM) format, and, less commonly, Standard Generalized Markup Language (SGML) or eXtended Markup Language (XML). The desktop publishing application opens these files and processes them to produce a display output that we view. Windows has helped install an appropriate printer driver that controls the printer.

When a user requests a printout of a document through the application program, the program prepares the print data stream according to the printer and printer driver being used, as specified on the PC. When printing to a laser printer, the format used is typically Hewlett Packard Page Composition Language (PCL). The formatted file is transmitted through the printer cable or a network connection to the printer. The printer processes the PCL commands to format the data for printing. In a laser printer, the document is printed a page at a time.

For an inkjet printer or dot matrix printer, the document is printed a line at a time. The printer driver sets up printing pages and lines. The actual formatting is done by the laser printer or, for inkjet or dot matrix printers, by the PC.

Generally, there are several reasons for a printout to be different than expected:

- Talking to the wrong printer—Your application is set for printing on an IBM Graphics Printer when you are attached to an HP Laser printer. Check the application carefully to determine what it expects for a printer. Some older applications assigned a printer to each document. This means that even though one document printed okay, another might not because it was assigned by an application to a different printer.

- Fonts change—The document was set in CG Times font and you have only fixed spacing Courier font. This makes a big difference in the printout.

- Page setup—The document was set for a page with 0.5-inch margins on each side and 0.75-inch margins at the top and bottom. Your PC has the margins set at 0.75-inch on each side and at 1-inch on top and bottom. Lots of fun here. You have more pages with less per page. Printers can control margins independent of the PC. Document settings in PCs today generally override or reset the printer internal settings to those used by desktop publishing software. At one time this was not necessarily the case.

- Slow printing—Printers print slower under Windows applications than under DOS applications because Windows prints graphically instead of using fonts built into the printer. Thus, Windows applications can print fancy TrueType characters. On inkjet and dot matrix printers, graphics must be printed in unidirectional mode for proper print head alignment. However, some printers can print with their internal scalable fonts under Windows using a scalable font driver. Such a driver uses the printer's internal printer fonts for draft mode printing and for faster bi-directional printing. Many things cause slow printing, such as:

  —The printer CPU is slow—16 MHz versus 35 MHz versus 166 MHz.

  —The printer has a slow print engine (that is, a slower paper feeding and imaging system).

  —Your printer has only 2 MB RAM. If you print graphics, pictures, images, or many different special fonts, the PC must prepare the data for printing and cannot offload any work to the printer.

—You are using a slow PC. Someone once told me that to create the Bitstream fonts on their XT required a mere 17 hours of continuous processing. Today PCs mostly use True Type scalable fonts. Nonetheless, the PC preprocesses a document to prepare it for the printer. A slow PC means slow printing.

—Your PC has only 8 MB RAM and only 40 MB of free disk space. This may not be enough working space for printout preparation.

—Your serial port connected to the printer is running at 9,600 BPS and not 19,200 BPS expected by the settings specified for the printer. For data to be received properly across a serial port connection, both devices have to use the same speed (data clocking). Otherwise they cannot clock in the bits accurately. The PC's serial port settings must exactly match the settings expected by the printer (that is, baud rate or speed, data bits, parity type, and stop bits). For example, HP laser printers commonly use 9600 BPS, 8 data bits, none or no parity, and 1 stop bit. Any mismatch and there is no communications.

The quickest way to solve printer problems is to check everything from the PC to the printer to assure that they are all set up consistently.

Laser Printers (Page Printers)

Laser printers are page printers. They must receive an entire page of data before they print anything. Partial pages are printed only when there is a form-feed character at the end of the data sent to the printer.

Laser printers process data received in Hewlett Packard Page Composition Language (HP-PCL or PCL) format or in Adobe PostScript (PS) format. There are several versions of each format. The latest PCL format is HP-PCL-6. A printer that is capable of HP-PCL-6 can also print HP-PCL-5 and earlier versions. The latest HP-PCL version has more capabilities than earlier versions. So printing HP-PCL-5 on an HP-PCL-6 capable printer just means that the document being printed does not take full advantage of the printer's capabilities.

Translating this into simpler terms, it means that an HP LaserJet 8000 printer supporting HP-PCL-6 can print output destined for an HP LaserJet-4 printer supporting HP-PCL-5. This has specific advantages when it comes to producing specific quality printout as we will discuss soon.

Most laser printers support PCL. The latest printers can process both PostScript and PCL output. Inkjet and other printers have other output formats that are aimed at line printing and not page printing. For example, ESC/P and ESC/P2 are printer control languages used to control the printer fonts and other printer functions like line spacing, bold, etc., on Epson inkjet and dot matrix printers. The newer 24-pin and inkjet printers use the ESC/P2 control codes. A major difference between these printer control languages is that the ESC/P2 models have the capability of printing internal fonts programmed into the printer in scalable sizes, from 8 point up to 72 point, and the ESC/P models could print limited font sizes. A second difference is, under Windows, the ESC/P2 printers, using a special scalable font driver, can print using the printer's internal scalable fonts and print draft mode fonts. Printing with these fonts is much faster than with the fonts generated by Windows. The ESC/P printers only print using Windows graphical fonts, which is much slower.

Early printing used fixed-size fonts. These were precise bit maps (dot configurations and spacing) for each size character. They were wasteful of PC disk drive space and very inflexible. Scalable fonts reign today. These fonts are constructed using vectors (drawn by lines and curves). The drawing can be scaled to any size making one font specification fit any printing requirement. Scalable fonts are Microsoft's True Type fonts and PostScript fonts. The True Type scalable fonts are the ones most generally used today, although PostScript dominates the publishing industry. See Figure 6–1.

Laser printers have a CPU and RAM to process the PC output and transform it into a page print image for printing. Fonts require some processing. They can be processed once and then stored in the printer's RAM while the entire document is printed. Graphics and images require more processing. This is where a printer with a faster CPU outperforms one with a slower CPU.

The large majority of laser printers produce black-and-white images. However, lower-cost color printers are emerging. They use dye sublimation, thermal dot, thermal wax, and thermal resin technologies to produce color images. Cyan, magenta, yellow, and black colored toners are fused to paper using a heat-driven printing process. Color printers several techniques to produce color images including:

- **Thermal dye transfer or dye sublimation printers**—these printers heat dye containing ribbons and transfer the dyes to specially coated paper or transparencies. Thermal dye transfer or dye sublimation printers are expensive and slow. They can produce continuous-tone photographic quality images. These printers require special costly paper and cannot be used with cheap xerographic paper.
- **Thermal wax transfer printers**—these printers melt wax-based inks and print them as dots on regular paper or transparencies. Images printed as dots must be dithered to produce a full range of colors. As

Figure 6-1 *Windows 98 Fonts*

a result images comprised of dots are not photographic quality but they can be very good. The big advantage of thermal wax transfer printers is that they do not need special paper, They also print faster than dye sublimation printers.

- **Wax jet, solid ink jet or phase change printers**—these printers melt dyed wax and spray it on paper similar to ink-jet printers spraying ink on paper. The sprayed wax produces bright colors on virtually any type of paper. Wax jet, solid ink-jet or phase change printers are slow and somewhat expensive to operate.

Black-and-white laser printers are heat process printers that fuse the ink to the paper using a heated roller fuser unit. Color lasers are similar to black and white laser printers but they use from three to four different colored toners to produce the image.

Laser printers are the fastest style of printer. Their speed ranges from about 4 pages per minute to 32 pages per minute, depending on the printing engine, the CPU processing speed and the amount of RAM in the printer. Laser printing CPUs now range in speed from 24 MHz Reduced Instruction Set Computers (RISC) to 166 MHz RISC microprocessors. Printing graphics slows down the page per minute printing speed.

Laser printers feed from paper trays that hold from 100 sheets to a full ream of paper, as shown in Figure 6–2. Some have single bin feeders while others have dual bins. They also perform duplex printing, printing both sides of a piece of paper without the operator's having to remove the paper from the printer and refeeding it. The sheet feeders can handle envelopes, but the printer must often reorient the printing to have the address print properly on the envelope. They also print on overhead transparencies. A special transparency film designed to handle the heat fusing process must be used.

Laser printers print using a six-step process:

1. **Cleaning the printer drum**—A soft plastic cleaning blade scrapes loose toner from the drum to prepare it for the next image.

Figure 6–2 *Laser printer paper trays*

New laser printer engines eliminate the transfer corona assembly. By eliminating the high-voltage corona wires used for preconditioning exposure, ozone gas (O3) emissions are eliminated. The reduction of colorless and odorless ozone gas improves workplace environmental quality and lengthens printer life. A charging roller in the toner cartridge and a charging transfer roller in the printer replace the high-voltage corona wires. Unlike the transfer corona assembly of the past, the black foam-like charging transfer roller is designed to be replaced as part of normal printer periodic maintenance procedures.

2. **Charging or conditioning the printer drum**—A high-voltage negative charge placed on the corona wire is transferred to the drum by rotating the drum under the wire. This may be called *preconditioning exposure.*

3. **Writing or forming the image**—The previously charged drum is exposed to a scanning laser beam to form an uncharged image on the surface of the drum. This is sometimes referred to as scanning exposure.

4. **Development**—Charged toner sticks to the uncharged image area on the drum and is repelled by the charged nonimage area of the drum. This develops the invisible noncharged area into a visible image.

5. **Transferring the image to paper**—The drum rotates permitting the paper and the drum to move together. As the paper and the drum contact each other the toner is attracted off the drum and onto the paper. This is possible because a second corona wire charges the paper. This may also be called transfer and separation.

6. **Fusing or fixing the image onto the paper**—The paper with its charged toner image is passed through heated rollers that apply both heat and pressure to fuse the toner onto the paper.

Understanding the steps in this printing process is important for the A+ certification test. This printing technology uses electrostatic charges to form the image on the drum and transfer it to the paper; and a heat-fusing process to fuse the ink to the paper. See Figure 6–3.

Inkjet Printers

The most inexpensive color printers are inkjet printers. They print both black-and-white and color images by using two ink cartridges, a black cartridge and a color cartridge with three heads, one each for cyan, magenta, and yellow. The cartridge contains the ink and the electronics to control how it is deposited on the paper. Inkjet printers spit the ink at the paper to form an image on the paper from ink dots.

Fuser   Corona   Drum
Unit   Wire   Unit

Figure 6–3 *Laser Printer Components*

The resolution varies from 360 by 180 dots to 1440 by 720 dots. The images formed are of very crisp quality even though they are printed a line at a time. Paper feeding and movement are critical to producing a high-quality inkjet image. Any shifting during the printing process tends to blur the image. A second key factor is the paper itself. Paper that absorbs too much ink tends to produce a washed-out image. Higher density paper produces a better printout.

Inkjet printers use sheet-fed paper. A hopper holds the paper or envelopes that is fed through a sheet at a time. Printing orientation is changed electronically to print envelopes.

Their printing speed is okay for home use and as an auxiliary office color printer. They print slower in color than when printing black-and-white images alone. Color printing speed starts at about two pages per minute and goes up to seven pages per minute.

Inkjet printers print on paper and transparency film. However, they must use special inkjet transparencies to assure that the ink is held in place and does not smear before it dries.

Dot Matrix Printers

The oldest PC printing technology is dot matrix printing. This is impact printing with print head pins hitting an inked ribbon to produce an image on paper. Dot matrix printers are useful in situations where multipart forms need to be produced. The print head pins impacting the ribbon produce an image on the top form. The impact also produces images on the remaining forms.

Color ribbons are used to print color images. The colors are in bands on the ribbon. The print head moves between bands to print each color. Multiple passes are required to produce the color image. Inkjet printers are more efficient because they can print multiple colors in one pass. This reduces the number of passes needed to create the color image, making the inkjet printer faster.

The ink in the dot matrix printer ribbon lubricates the pins in the print head. Poor lubrication causes the pins to freeze in the print head. This often overloads the printer's electronics, causing expensive repairs or printer replacement. Frequent ribbon replacement with certified ribbons is important for long printer life.

Dot matrix printers can use sheet-fed paper, but more often they use pin-fed paper. Multipart forms are typically designed to be pin fed. This means that the paper has strips on each side extending beyond the common 8.5-inch width. These strips have pin-feed holes punched in them. They are fed into pin rollers on each side of the printer. When a dot matrix printer uses sheet-fed paper, pressure sensitive rollers permit feeding the printer a sheet of paper much like inserting it into an ancient typewriter. Dot matrix printers can be adjusted for form thickness, paper type (sheet or pin-fed), and paper width.

Paper Feeders

The paper feeding mechanisms are built into most printers. Sheet feeding is the most common type of paper feeding mechanism. Single sheets are fed from a paper tray built into the printer. Inkjet printers have a hopper that holds upwards to 50 sheets of paper. Laser printers have trays that hold from 100 sheets to a ream of paper.

Envelopes can be fed into printers from the paper trays or hoppers. They feed in lengthwise. Printing is reoriented electronically so that it appears normally on each envelope. Both inkjet and laser printers can print envelopes directly, or they can print envelope labels when a larger mailing is performed. Dot matrix printers required attachment of special sheet feeding mechanisms to feed in sheet paper stock or envelopes. These never worked with any exceptional reliability.

Laser and inkjet printers do not print on multipart forms. Because they print faster than dot matrix printers, they print multiple copies of the same form in cases where more than a single copy is required. Multipart forms require a pin feed paper handling mechanism to precisely position the form for printing.

Both laser and inkjet printers print transparency film. Transparency film is fed through the normal sheet feeding mechanism on both printers.

Laser printers often have a side feed tray that can be used for special printing, as shown in Figure 6–4. The tray is opened and several sheets of transparency film are placed into it for printing. Once printing is complete, the extra transparency film is removed and the tray closed up. Printing then resumes using the normal paper trays.

Transparency film must be designed for use with laser printers because of the heat fusing process. Using the wrong transparency film can have disastrous consequences for a laser printer. For example, using the wrong transparency film on an old Panasonic laser printer caused the film to disappear into the printer. The printer ate the transparency. It was nowhere to be found inside the printer when the printer was opened. So a second sheet was fed into the printer with the same result. Finally, when a third sheet was also eaten entirely by the printer, a much more detailed examination revealed that the three sheets of transparency film had wrapped tightly around the fuser's idle roller. Similarly, using the wrong transparency film in an HP

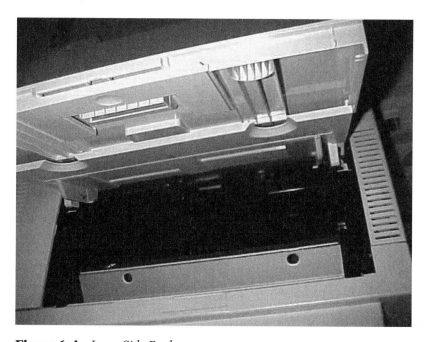

Figure 6–4 *Laser Side Feed*

LaserJet 4 printer caused the film to melt inside the printer. It gummed up the fuser unit, necessitating an expensive replacement.

Study Break

Laser Printer Operation

Find a Laser Printer and identify the different components.

1. Locate a laser printer. Determine the paper path through the printer.
2. Open the printer and remove the printing cartridge. Can you see the components that scrape the cartridge? They may not be visible because they can be inside the cartridge.
3. Are any corona wires visible? Similarly to the scrapers, these could also be located inside the drum/toner cartridge today.
4. Can you locate the fuser unit? It should be very warm to the touch.

The goal here is to visualize the laser printing process and steps required to form an image and fuse it to paper.

A+ 6.2 Printer Connections and Configurations

Several printer connections are used to connect printers to PCs. These connections have different operating characteristics and speeds. They include wired media as well as infrared wireless links, as shown in Figure 6–5.

Figure 6–5 *Windows 98 printers*

Parallel Port

The parallel printer port is the most common connection. It transmits data to the printer from the PC a byte at a time. The fastest printer data transfers use the parallel port, although serial and infrared ports are sufficient to drive printers at their maximum printing speed. Parallel ports operate over 26-conductor cables that have a 26-pin male connector at one end and a 34-conductor Centronics connector at the opposite end. Newer printers use a high-density connector in place of the bulky Centronics connector (Figure 6–6). These cables typically vary from 6 to 15 feet in length. Special cables can extend the distance a parallel interface can cover to some 30 or 40 feet. Overall, though, parallel cables run short distances at higher speeds.

The PC's parallel interface can be set up to operate in several different modes. These include a compatible mode that emulates the old PC–printer interface providing output only mode, a bidirectional mode providing input and output capabilities, an Enhanced Parallel Port (EPP), and an Enhanced Capabilities Port (ECP) conforming to IEEE-1284 specifications. The ECP and EPP modes sometimes do not work with older printers. In these instances, downgrading to bidirectional or compatible mode may resolve the printing problem. Bidirectional, EPP, and ECP modes may require IRQ and DMA channel resource assignments in addition to the standard LPT1 port I/O address resource assignment.

Figure 6–6 *Laser parallel port connection*

Serial Port

Serial ports are used to send data to printers as well. They need a special printer cable because they are not talking to a modem but rather talking to a printer. Modems are Data Circuit Terminating Equipment while printers and PCs are Data Terminal Equipment. This means that, for the 26-pin serial cable, transmit-data leaves the PC and printer on pin 2 and receive-data enters on pin 3. If a standard serial cable were used to connect the printer to the PC, then the parallel connections in the cable would connect pin 2 on the printer to pin 2 on the PC. Pin 2 to pin 2 would have transmit-data from the PC and the printer colliding in the cable. In this instance, pin 2 transmit data on the PC must be connected to pin 3 receive-data on the printer and vice versa. See Figure 6–7.

Serial communications to the printer operates at 9,600 bits per second or 19,200 bits per second. The speed the printer is using must match the speed that the PC is using exactly. At 9,600 bits per second, the character-per-second rate is about 960 characters per second. Similarly, 19,200 BPS is about 1,920 characters per second. A printed page of characters alone is about 1,500 characters. Because text is printed as graphics, that number is much larger today. Each page is described using PCL or PostScript commands that are processed by the printer to create the image. However, if it took 15,000 characters to describe a page, this would at 19,200 BPS require about 8 seconds to transmit the page to the printer. This is around an 8 page per minute printing rate. This means that a serial connection can probably outpace any inkjet or dot matrix printer, but it may not be fast enough for the latest 32 page-per-minute laser printer. The benefit of a serial port for printer connections is that they can connect over a longer cable than a paral-

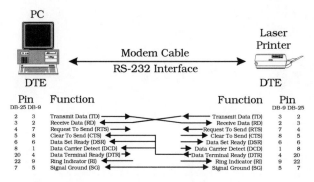

Figure 6–7 *Serial printer cable configuration*

lel port. However, serial printer connections operate at slower speeds than do parallel port connections.

Serial communications requires defining the character setup. Each character is transmitted across the serial port beginning with a start bit and ending with a stop bit. This means each character is 10 bits long. The data inside the ten bits (start–8 data bits–stop) is 8 data bits. These bits are sent in ASCII code. As a standard, ASCII code has seven information bits. The eighth bit can be used to signal parity. However, since most data contains images and other binary information, it would require translation to an ASCII form and then translation back to a binary form for final printing. Transmitting 8 bits with parity requires unnecessary translations. Consequently, printer serial ports are set to 8-data bits with no parity and one stop bit.

LAN

Local area network connections for printers are very common. Printers can be directly attached to a server through its parallel port or they may be directly attached to the local area network using their own internal network interface card (NIC). Data is routed to them directly or via a printer queue on a server in the network. When a printer is set up, it is configured for local print processing with the necessary drivers. The data is then routed to a printing queue on the network, as shown in Figure 6–8.

Figure 6–8 *Network printers*

Figure 6–9   *Printer properties*

Browsing the network servers under Windows locates network printers. Then they are added as ports in the properties setup for the printer. Network printers are referred to using a network universal naming convention with the server being identified first and the printer second. Figure 6–9 identifies the server \\MOULTON2 and the port \HP4NTRAID.

Adding a printer port permits browsing the network to find other active printer ports.

Windows uses a universal printer driver that works with several page composition languages and minidrivers that work directly with the printer hardware. The PC client universal driver communicates across the network to the printer server and the minidrivers in it directly controlling the printer. Typical network printer errors are failing to find the printer on the network (because it is powered off or has been changed in some fashion) or a mismatch between the PC printer definition and the network printer. Lost printers are easy to see and resolve. Misconfigured printers can result in printing junk and wasting paper on a remote network printer.

Infrared Link

An easy means to link PCs to printers is across an infrared connection. In this case, there is no physical connection between the printer and the PC. Both PC and printer must have infrared ports that are in direct line of sight. The distance between them must be short, several feet maximum. The PC must have the infrared software link installed, as shown in Figure 6–10.

Infrared links are great for connecting printers to palmtop and laptop PCs for printing. Printing without cables makes the printing process very easy as long as there is a direct line of sight between the laptop IR port and the printer IR port (Figure 6–11).

The IR port can be assigned to either a virtual serial or a virtual parallel port. See Figure 6–12. Regardless of its assignment, it acts much like a serial port.

Data is sent in bit-serial fashion over the IR link to the printer. IR speed varies from 9,600 BPS to 15,200 BPS. Faster IR speeds will be available soon, boosting the transfer rate up to 4 million bits per second. These high-speed IR ports are emerging on some laptop and palmtop PCs as well as newer printers.

Ports not being in range and bad driver software cause problems with IR ports. In some cases, there is no way to connect devices using the IR ports because the driver software does not match. Troubleshooting indications

Figure 6–10 *Infrared software setup*

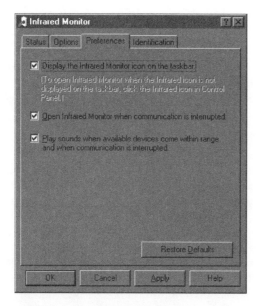

Figure 6–11 *IR port options*

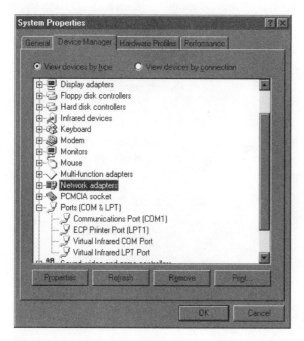

Figure 6–12 *IR virtual ports*

point to no physical or IR link connection. As a result, it is easy to mistake this for a hardware problem when it is really the driver programs. If the IR port spots another IR device, it signals that a device is in range. When this happens, generally the IR hardware is operating properly. If communications still do not work, then adjust the IR port speed downward until the speeds match and communications works. Otherwise search for better driver programs.

Study Break

Setting Up A Printer

Let's define a new printer for Windows 95 or 98.

1. Open My Computer and then printers.
2. Click on Add Printer to start the add printer wizard.
3. Click on next and then select local printer and click next again. Windows builds a driver data base to facilitate adding the new printer.
4. From the list of printers, select HP by hitting H twice or three times. Next hit tab to change panes in the Add Printer Wizard box. Scroll down until you can select HP LaserJet 4. Then click next. Keep the existing printer driver, and move on to the next wizard box to select the printer port.
5. Pick the LPT1 port. Click next and then select a name like HP LJ4 Test. Click next.
6. Skip printing the test page unless there is a real printer attached to the port. Click finish to have the new printer appear with your printers. To clean up, just delete the printer you created.

The objective is to walk through the process of adding a printer. Not all printers are set up using the Add Printer Wizard. Some printers come with a setup program that performs all the necessary steps to install the printer and its drivers into Windows 95/98/NT.

A+ 6.3   Resolving Common Printer Problems

Laser printer service typically requires examining print quality and checking a printer's display panel for error codes, determining a probable source of the problem, and swapping the part that will solve the problem. The repair process requires printer disassembly to make the repair, and then reassembly and testing to determine whether the problem was solved. Unfortunately, laser printers are advanced electromechanical devices where any single problem may have several possible causes. As laser printers have become more complex, trial-and-error troubleshooting has become less efficient.

To exactly determine the correct cause of a laser printer problem, it is necessary to test sensors, switches, and voltage levels while the printer is running, as well as observing relevant mechanical operations. Since printers are generally not designed to operate with the covers open or any parts removed, such tests are almost impossible.

Laser printer troubleshooting decisions can be based on print quality and general error codes. Using these criteria alone, it is difficult to rapidly and correctly identify a single printer problem cause.

Laser printers come in a wide variety of sizes and shapes. Their repair is limited to parts that are easily replaceable. In most cases, this is the printer toner cartridge and drum unit. Some printers may have replaceable fuser units and other small components. We have had laser units that have had drums, fuser units, fuser heating elements, cooling fans, ozone filters, and memory replaced.

Table 6–1 provides a summary of simple laser printer problems and possible solutions.

Simple laser printer problems have required replacement of fusing units, paper rollers, and fans. These were all modular components that were easy to identify and replace.

Paper Feed and Output

Printers handle paper today very well. The most that may need to be done in high static-charge situations is to fluff the paper to reduce the charge by holding the sheets together.

Fluffing is separating the paper by running your thumb across each end of the ream of paper.

Paper should be loaded with one specific side up in the laser printer. This is because during manufacturing the paper tends to curl slightly in one direction. The paper manufacturer usually indicates on the paper ream cover which side should be up with a message like "Image This Side First." Often this is the side that is considered the bottom of the ream because little advertising or descriptive material is printed on that side.

High humidity can also impact paper feeding adversely. It makes sheets stick together and become limp. In this event, it may be necessary to replace the paper with new, dry paper for printing to resume normally.

Table 6.1 *Laser printer problem resolution summary*

Laser Symptom	Probable Cause	Repair	Approximate Cost	Failure Rate
Pages run together	Need form-feed between pages	Add form-feed characters or page breaks to document	$0	Frequently
Memory overrun errors	Not enough RAM	Add RAM	$50 or more	Once
Prints bad pages	Wrong print driver or	Replace Windows print driver	$0	Occasionally
	Corrupted soft fonts	Reconfigure Windows Application Reset printer, then download fonts to printer		
Print pages are not the same or print wrong fonts	Wrong fonts	Install fonts on PC Reset printer, then download fonts to printer Add RAM to printer to hold soft fonts	$50 and up	Occasionally
Lines in printout	Old drum Dirty printer	Replace drum init Vacuum printer	$50 to $200	About every one to six months
Faded printout	Old drum unit Low on toner	Replace drum Refill toner	$50 to $200	About every one to three months
Frequent jams	Dirty printer	Clean printer or reduce printing volume	$0	About every 2 to 4 years
	Bad paper	Replace paper	$20	
	Bad transparency film	Replace transparency film	$25 per box	
Failure to print	No power Bad or disconnected cable	Power on–check lights Replace cable	$0 $15	Rarely
Slow printing	Slow Printer CPU Fast RISC CPU 16 MHz or more needed for high speed printing today	Upgrade printer Add after-market CPU cartridge	$500 to $3,000	All the time

Paper Jams

A main reason for paper jams is old or low-quality paper. This frequently results in paper that sticks together from retained static charges or that is too wet, due to high humidity in the environment. Replacing the paper with fresh paper is the best cure for this problem.

Other paper jam problems are caused by the paper feeding and control rollers in the printer. When these get worn or dusty they do not feed the paper properly. We had an HP LaserJet 4 printer that was exposed to dust from a construction project. The dust killed the paper feeding rollers to the point that every few pages there was a paper jam. Replacing the rollers with new ones cured the problem.

The same printer had some problems printing from an add-on 500-sheet paper tray. This was caused by improper tension adjustment in the tray. Adjusting the paper tray tension cured this problem.

On an older Canon printer, the ozone inside the printer corroded all the rubber rollers, causing constant paper jams. In this instance, as well, replacement of the rubber rollers solved the paper jam problem. Because new printers do not create ozone, this is not likely to happen with them.

When paper jams occur, it is important to be sure you get all the paper out, as little bits of paper left in the printer can cause additional paper jams.

Error Indications

Printers have warning lights and self-test diagnostics. When errors occur, the lights may flash and a diagnostic message can appear. These messages are helpful in finding most common errors. Sometimes problems can be obvious, like a printer power supply failure. In that event, a printer replacement is most likely in order.

In other cases, bad printing signifies a failure. We had a dot matrix printer that started printing erratically. In this case, the printer's self-test diagnostics ran fine. The problem was a failure of the printer's PC parallel interface. Fortunately for us, the printer had a serial interface that worked. This corrected the problem for about a year, then the printer quit altogether, necessitating replacement.

PRINTING TO THE WRONG PRINTER

A common printing failure with laser printers is misprinting, where the printer prints a page with several characters, then ejects the page, only to print another page with several characters and then eject that page, and so on until the paper supply is exhausted or the printer is reset.

Sending graphics to the printer and resetting the printer midstream causes this problem. Since the printer lost its downloaded fonts and graphics setup, it does not know how to handle the subsequent data stream sent by the PC. This causes the print–eject cycle as the printer interprets the graphics characters as text data for printing. Resetting the printer and dumping the print job from the PC or network printing queue solves this problem.

CORRUPTED PRINT FILES

Some print files are corrupted. When these are printed, they cause a printer error message. The message is caused by the printer acting on the data to be printed as though it were control commands to the printer. The problem is resolved by sometimes restarting both the PC and the printer from a power-off state or by fixing the offending data file. A file can be fixed by opening a new data file window in the program that was used to create the original file and cutting and then pasting the contents of the old file into the new file.

PRINTER TIMEOUT

Another common PC printer error message is the Windows timeout message. In this instance, the printer has not responded to a Windows printing request in the time expected by Windows, so Windows displays the error message. Timeout messages could be lessened if a printer had additional RAM installed to provide increased data buffering. Since Windows automatically retries the printout, typically printing is resumed without incident.

NETWORK PRINTER OFFLINE

When a printer or network server is offline, printing to the network printer results in network error messages. Network software is designed to send error indications to network administrators in the event of paper outages and similar malfunctions at network printers.

FAILED PRINTER ELECTRONIC COMPONENTS

More difficult laser printer problems may have different indications. Fortunately, problems with printer electronics are rare. Nonetheless, some older laser printers, for example, would have horizontal black lines on printouts. This has several causes, including defective laser assembly, improperly seated fiber optic cable, or Direct Current (DC) controller problems. Inspecting the laser assembly and laser diode, the fiber optic cable, the DC controller, and other parts for damage identifies these problems. When no damage is apparent, an Original Equipment Manufacturer (OEM) repair manual is consulted to determine the most likely cause for the problem.

On those older printers, another problem is a black page with white bars. The likeliest cause for this problem is a bad scanner assembly. But is the scanner assembly really bad or did the laser contrast go out of calibration? The laser assembly is mounted in the scanner and the laser's job is to expose the drum. A look at a test print verifies that the drum was exposed because the entire page is black. Next the scanner assembly sweeps the laser beam across the page, using the scanner motor. This function must also have occurred because the page is black from left to right.

This print error occurs when a laser printer cannot detect the laser beam. When a laser beam cannot be detected, the printer turns the laser on full and then turns it off several times, attempting to detect a change in the output level. The white bars are printed when the laser is turned off. With time, a variable resistor found on the laser printer's main logic board can fall out of calibration. This causes the intensity of the laser to be too low for the DC controller to detect it.

On those printers sometimes a laser-beam-detect malfunction error message occurs whenever the laser beam is not detected for about 2 seconds or more. There are several electrical causes and solutions to this error message. The DC power supply could have malfunctioned. A multimeter check for 6-volt DC output verifies a failed DC power supply. When 6-volts DC is not present, the DC power supply is replaced and the laser printer retested. The laser scanner unit might also be defective. Exchanging the scanning unit with a known good one, and retesting solves this problem. Finally, the problem could be a defective DC controller board. Exchanging with a known good DC controller board, then retesting corrects this.

This error message could be caused by mechanical problems including:

- **Malfunctioning laser shutter**—To prevent a user or technician from becoming exposed to the laser beam, a laser shutter is built into the scanner unit. The shutter is opened when the printer cover is closed with a toner cartridge in place. On the rear of the toner cartridge is a tab that opens the shutter. When this tab is missing on the toner cartridge, the shutter cannot be opened.

- **Loose fiber optic cable**—A fiber-optic cable often runs from the scanner unit to the DC controller. This fiber-optic cable can become loosened or damaged, not permitting the laser to travel to the DC controller to register. This problem commonly occurs due to mishandling.

- **Bad scanner cables**—Cable assembly connectors and crimps develop open and shorted connections from vibration and use or from mishandling, like disconnecting cables by pulling on the cable, not the connector. Most laser printer cables use IDC (Insulation Displacement Contact) connectors. IDC connectors act like a knife to the wire with which they make contact. Over time such contacts can cut the wire in half, with only the insulation holding the wire in the connector. When this is suspected, tugging lightly on an individual wire will cause the wire to break free from the connector.

PRINTER FUSER PROBLEMS

Other laser printer problem symptoms like ghosting print, fuser assembly wear, toner buildup on the fuser roller, and void printing occur when the fuser assembly is not running at the correct temperature. Over time, a thermal resistor (thermistor) controlling the fuser assembly collects dirt, dust, and toner. This causes the fuser's heat roller to wear out more quickly than it normally should. More significant is that it causes the fuser assembly to run both hotter and colder than designed.

Buildup of dust, dirt, and toner on the thermistor insulates it and retains heat in the heat roller. When a laser printer with dust, dirt, and toner buildup is first turned on, extra heat is needed to get past the dust, dirt, and toner on the thermistor. Such extra heat causes toner to build up even more on the heat roller, exacerbating the problem. As the printer is used, this dust, dirt and toner becomes nice and hot, retaining heat as the fuser assembly cools. This hot material makes the printer think that the fuser is at the proper temperature.

These are representative of the types of problem symptoms found with printers.

Print Quality

Since human eyes can only distinguish up to a resolution quality of 600 dots per inch (DPI), it is difficult to observe that a higher DPI resolution constitutes better print quality.

Each printer has a built-in self-test function that prints a test pattern. This test pattern tests alignment of the dots that compose images from the printer. Poor dot alignment means a blurry image and poor print quality.

A reason for poor print quality on inkjet printers is the electrical contacts for the ink cartridge become covered with dirt or ink. When the contacts are not clean, the ink doesn't print correctly from all nozzles. Also, a damaged interface between the printer an the PC can cause blurred or corrupted printing as well.

Higher-resolution printing from laser printers does not reproduce on copying machines correctly. The graphics images tend to fade out. Areas that have gray scale fill copy unevenly. This is because the copying machines cannot focus on the image. They get false readings of gray scale intensity from high resolution (600 DPI or higher) graphics images. In this instance, lower resolution (300 DPI) and coarse graphics reproduce better on copying machines. Setting the printout for 300 DPI and coarse graphics causes the laser printer to print the image as dots, which a copying machine can focus on and accurately copy. On new printers, there may be no driver setting that directly controls the resolution and graphics printing. In this instance, using a different printer driver may be required to achieve the desired results. For example, on our HP LaserJet 8000 printer, we set the printer driver to be that of a LaserJet 4 printer, providing the requisite resolution and graphics printing settings. Since the HP LaserJet 8000 is compatible with the LaserJet 4 printer, everything prints as expected.

Sometimes memory overruns happen on laser printers. Other incompatibilities may occur. In this case, setting a printer as LaserJet II-compatible may resolve the problems. The LaserJet II became a de facto industry standard. Its PCL printer language was implemented in printers made by many different manufacturers. Most new printers also emulate the HP LaserJet II printer today. Since it had relatively simple features, most documents print just fine on any printer supporting that de facto printer standard.

Safety Considerations

There are several safety considerations when working with printers. The first is the most obvious and the most neglected with laser printers. That is the size and weight. Lifting a heavy laser printer can cause serious back injury. High-end laser printers are both bulky and heavy. They really require more than one person to lift them.

The next safety area is the laser itself. There is a potential for eye damage if the laser is activated and shines into an eye. Laser printers have interlocks to prevent this. Safety precautions outlined in the Original Equipment Manufacturers (OEM) maintenance manual should be followed to prevent eye injury from the printer's laser.

In laser printers, the fuser unit is heated. It is possible to be seriously burned by coming in contact with a heated fuser unit. Just as there are safety precautions recommended by the Original Equipment Manufacturer that should be followed for the laser, there are other recommendations for handling the fuser unit. These should be followed.

The final area is electrical power. Most printers operate their logic with low-voltage circuits. However, there are high-power areas in laser printers. In older printers, the corona charging wires carried high voltages while the printer was operating. The OEM recommendations for power protection should be followed when servicing any printer. Most simple maintenance functions like toner cartridge replacement may only require powering down the printer. Others, like adding paper can be done at any time. However, care should be exercised when clearing paper jams on some printers to assure that the power is off. Generally, these printers have a power interlock switch that kills the power to the printer when the printer is opened. To be safe, this switch should not be bypassed.

Study Break

Laser Printer Page Printing

Laser printers print a page at a time. Until the laser printer buffer is full, it does not print.

1. With a laser printer directly attached to LPT1 port on your PC, open a DOS Window.

2. Enter the command in the root directory DIR>LPT. This routes the directory display to the printer and not to the screen. It performs a very simple and effective test of the printer's operational status.

3. The printer may not print or may print some but not all of the directory information. A difference in the page size of the data may cause some to be left in the printer's buffers and not printed.

4. On the printer control panel, press the form-feed button. The last printer data should print and the final page should eject.

5. Perform the DIR>LPT1 command again and again. Notice that the second directory printout begins in the middle of a page and not at the top of its own page. Clean up the printer by form-feed on the control panel.

This exercise illustrates the page printing operation of laser printers.

A+ 6.4 Printer Servicing and Preventative Maintenance

Most printer preventive maintenance involves cleaning and ribbon, inkjet cartridge, or toner cartridge replacement. When replacing ribbons, ink cartridges, or toner cartridges, the printer should be cleaned, removing the accumulated paper dust. Furthermore, it is good policy to, depending on use, periodically vacuum out the paper and other dust from within the accessible areas of the printer. Fans should be checked for noise indicating bearing wear. They should be cleaned as well because they tend to accumulate significant amounts of dirt.

Dusty environments are hard on printers. The dust puts an added burden on sensitive mechanical components, especially those that handle the paper moving through the printer. Sometimes cleaning the components to remove the dust may not be enough to ensure the printer operates as expected.

Replacing cartridges is a constant maintenance task (Figure 6–13). This is replacing toner cartridges in laser printers and ink cartridges in inkjet printers. Using certified or recycled toner cartridges has been debated as a good cost-saving or a bad life-shortening approach for printers. With the first laser printers, there was no choice—replacement toner cartridges were purchased from the OEM. This was great for the laser printer manufacturer because they could make lots of money on the cartridges. These cartridges delivered excellent print quality and high-speed printing. Whatever price the OEM supplies sell for, you pay.

Is a new toner cartridge really new? They are not totally new any more. Parts of new toner cartridges have been used before. On the side of new Hewlett Packard toner cartridge boxes the phrase, *"May contain material collected in the HP Toner Cartridge Recycling Program."* is found. The plastic a toner cartridge is made of must be recycled. Billions of toner cartridges are

Figure 6–13 *Laser cartridge bay*

used each year. Without some recycling program, we would be inundated with old toner cartridges.

The quality of an Original Equipment Manufacturer (OEM) toner cartridge is consistent. Yet they are more expensive. Remanufactured cartridges start with an empty toner cartridge. It is disassembled and cleaned and charged with new toner. This produces a toner cartridge refilled for about half the price of a new toner cartridge.

While this sounds great, quality control problems, scam artists, misconceptions, and new toner cartridge designs have greatly impacted toner cartridge remanufacturing.

A recharged toner cartridge is as good as the company performing the cartridge recharging. Cost is the main reason for using recharged toner cartridges. The savings can be upwards of 50%. Inconsistency is the greatest pitfall of using recharged cartridges. Recharging a toner cartridge requires skill. It is not a cut-and-dried process. Further contributing to this problem is the inconsistency of the manufacturer who produces the toner and other materials for this industry. If these obstacles were not enough to overcome, laser printer manufacturers have started designing toner cartridges that are very difficult, if not impossible, to recharge. The biggest risk of using a recharged cartridge is that it may mechanically jam and thus destroy the gears in the laser printer. This could result in a costly printer repair or replacement.

Inkjet cartridges can be refilled as well. There are kits that provide color and black-and-white ink for refilling inkjet cartridges. The problem here is getting ink with the correct flow properties. If the ink flows improperly, the image produced by the refilled cartridge will be poor. Unlike replacement laser toner cartridges, refilled inkjet cartridges cannot damage the printer.

Study Break

Removing Laser Printer Toner Cartridges

Remove and reinsert laser printer toner cartridges.

1. Use several different laser printers. For each printer remove the toner cartridge. Note that each manufacturer and model of printer is somewhat different.

2. Do some printers use the same cartridges? They may because the actual print engine may be manufactured by Canon. Our Canon and HP Laser printers share many of the same components.

3. Once the laser cartridge is removed, note the paper dust and dirt buildup in the printer. This should be vacuumed or wiped out of the printer

4. Replace the cartridge to return the printer to its former operating state.

This exercise illustrates the most common maintenance procedures performed on printers.

Summary

This chapter has presented information on troubleshooting and maintaining printers. It has described how printers work, the source and resolution of common printer problems, servicing and preventive maintenance procedures, and printer-to-PC connections and configurations.

In the first section, basic printer concepts were presented along with common reasons for printer problems, such as inconsistency in fonts specifications, printer versus port speed and similar issues. This led directly into the next section on how to resolve these types of problems. The next section focused on avoiding problems by performing regular service and maintenance functions on printer components.

The final section in the chapter discussed the types and configurations for printer port connections and how they operate.

▲ CHAPTER REVIEW QUESTIONS

1. Non-impact printers are the same as laser printers?

A. TRUE

B. FALSE

Answer: B. False—both inkjet and laser are nonimpact

2. Negative charges attract toner during:

A. inkjet printing

B. laser printing

C. dot matrix printing

Answer: B. laser printing

3. *The IRQ of a printer port can be set at different levels.*

    A. TRUE

    B. FALSE

    Answer: A. TRUE

4. *Which is the correct sequence for the laser printing process?*

    A. cleaning, conditioning, writing, developing, transferring, fusing

    B. conditioning, cleaning, writing, developing, fusing, transferring

    C. conditioning, cleaning, writing, developing, transferring, fusing

    D. cleaning, conditioning, writing, developing, fusing, transferring

    Answer: A. cleaning, conditioning, writing, developing, transferring, fusing

5. *During printing an error message is displayed. The PC has printed recently and no changes have been made to the PC software or hardware. You check to see that the printer is turned on. Where do you look next?*

    A. to see if the correct printer driver is installed

    B. to see if the printer will print attached to a different PC

    C. to see if the printer is online

    D. to see if the printer is selected as default

    Answer: C. to see if the printer is online

6. *Discharging the negative charge on the drum that represents the printed image is which step of the laser printing process?*

    A. transferring

    B. conditioning

    C. fusing

    D. writing

    Answer: D. writing

7. *Positively charging the paper to pull the toner from the drum is performed during which phase of the laser printing process?*

    A. writing

    B. transferring

C. conditioning

D. fusing

Answer: B. transferring

8. *When attempting to print to a laser printer, the printer hangs with "warming up" on its display panel. What should be checked first?*

   A. that the PC is setup to print to the correct port

   B. the cable is plugged in

   C. the correct driver is installed

   D. the printer is powered on

   Answer: A. that the PC is setup to print to the correct port. (Answer focuses on trying the easiest thing first, then the more difficult things.)

9. *In what laser-printing step is a large negative charge placed on the drum?*

   A. fusing

   B. transferring

   C. conditioning

   D. cleaning

   Answer: C. conditioning

10. *Toner is deposited onto the drum surface in which laser-printing step?*

    A. writing

    B. conditioning

    C. developing

    D. transferring

    Answer: C. developing

11. *Toner is bonded to the paper during the _____ step of the laser-printing process.*

    A. writing

    B. transferring

    C. conditioning

    D. fusing

    Answer: D. fusing

12. *The six (xerographic printing) steps in laser printing are?*

   A. charge drum—expose image—form image—copy image—fix image—clean drum

   B. charge drum—expose image—develop image—copy image—fix image—clean drum

   C. charge drum-form image—develop image—transfer image—fix image—clean drum

   D. charge drum—expose image—form image—transfer image—fix image—clean drum

   E. charge drum—expose image—copy image—transfer image—fix image—clean drum

   Answer: charge drum—form image—develop image—transfer image—fix image—clean drum

13. *What adjustments can be made to dot-matrix impact printers?*

   A. paper thickness, paper type

   B. ink color, paper type

   C. paper thickness, ink color

   D. ink speed (impact strength), ink color

   Answer: A. paper thickness, paper type (pin or sheet feed)

14. *What isn't important to consider when storing in laser printer paper?*

   A. ream size

   B. humidity

   C. temperature

   D. storage location

   Answer: A. ream size

15. *Which part of a printer cannot cause a paper jam?*

   A. fuser unit

   B. scanning or registration guide

   C. scanner assembly

   D. developer unit

   Answer: B. scanning or registration guide

16. *If a laser printer does not feed paper what is the first thing you do?*

    A. remove options

    B. remove accessories

    C. examine paper trays

    D. examine toner cartridge

    Answer: C. examine paper trays

Laptop PCs

▲ Chapter Syllabus

A+ 7.1 Laptop
Configurations and
Components

A+ 7.2 Common Laptop
Problems

Laptop computers have special problems due to their integrated design and portability. This chapter examines the unique components of laptop computers, the problems associated with them, and some solutions to those problems.

A+ 7.1 Laptop Configurations and Components

Laptop computers come in a variety of forms. Some are small hand-held—palm-size—pocket organizer replacements, others are highly portable—minilaptops that are cut down versions of laptop PCs, aimed at e-mail and writing, and others are high-end laptop systems that can rival the performance of low-end desktop PCs. (See Figure 7–1.) Each has built-in and replaceable components.

Figure 7–1 *Palmtop and desktop replacement laptop PCs.*

The hand-held pocket organizer PCs are mostly fixed in configuration and function. The memory is the single component that can be enhanced. Hand-held PC CPUs are fixed as well as the input/output options. Similarly, on the minilaptop PCs, the options are limited. Their input/output capabilities are greater than the palm-size PCs, but more limited than the high-end laptops. The highly portable laptop PCs may have different memory and disk drive options, and the capability to use some PC bus (formerly the Personal Computer Memory Card International Association—PCMCIA Bus) cards.

Laptop PCs have more capabilities and features. Some are built in, like the sound card. Others are options that are configured and may be upgraded at a later time, like memory or disk drive. These laptops plug into docking bays or port replicators making it easy to use them as both a portable and a desktop PC. Figure 7–2 shows some removable components including battery, floppy disk drive, and CD-ROM drive.

Figure 7–2 *Laptop components*

The CPU chip is also exposed in the figure. Table 7–1 lists a general comparison of features.

Laptop expandability comes from adding in components that are compatible with the main logic board and the chassis design. For example, some laptop main logic boards accept Pentium CPUs that range from 200 MHz to 300 MHz while others are designed to work with a variety of AMD K6 CPU chips set at varying speeds. As a result, upgrading the CPU chip in a laptop is possible, but not a recommended field upgrade. Although CPU chips are socketed, you must get the precise low-power CPU chip and fan that will fit the mechanical form factor and main logic board CPU-supporting chip set to upgrade laptop CPUs. See Figure 7–3. Note the foam rubber spacer that directs airflow into the fan from outside. This foam rubber spacer caught the

Figure 7–3 *Laptop CPU and fan*

Table 7.1 *Portable PC Components*

Type	Size/Weight & Batteries	Technical Features	Comments
Palmtop or Hand-held (Gryphon-class systems, such as 3Com Palm Pilot devices and Mercury-class systems, such as HP 600, 300 and 200 series hand-held PCs)	Palm Size 0.6 to 1.1 by 3.1 to 7.8 by 2.1 to 4.7 inches and 1.5 to 20 oz. Two AAA Type, AA Type, NiMH or Li-Ion batteries	Display – Gray scale 160 by 160 to —256 color half VGA (640 by 240) —4 to 6 inch diagonal Pen Input – Big time Keyboard – None or minisized VGA Port – None CPU – RISC from 16MHz to 75 MHz ROM – 1 to 8 MB Contains Windows CE RAM – 1 to 16 MB Disk Drives – None Flash Memory Card – One Compact Flash Type II PC Card Slots – None or one PC type II CD-ROM Drive – None Sound – Single speaker Serial Port – One Infrared Port – Yes and Fast IR (4Mbps) Parallel Port – None USB – None Wireless Communications Cards – Modem and LAN	Windows CE (an HP palmtop still supports DOS)
Minilaptop (Jupiter-class systems, such as HP Jornada 820 hand-held PC and the Sharp Mobilon Pro PV-5000)	Lap Size to File Folder Size 1.1 to 1.3 by 6.8 to 1.4 by 3.7 to 8.9 inches and 2 to 3 lbs. One NiMH or Li-Ion battery	Display – 256 color VGA 640 by 480 —256 color SVGA 800 by 600 —6.3 to 9.4 inch diagonal Pen Input – Yes Keyboard – Good size VGA Port – None to one CPU – RISC from 100 MHz to 190 MHz ROM – 16 MB – Contains Windows CE RAM – 16 MB to 32 MB Disk Drives – None Flash Memory Card –One Compact Flash Type II	Windows CE Windows 98

Table 7.1 *Portable PC Components (Continued)*

	PC Card Slots – None or one PC type II CD-ROM Drive – None Sound – Single speaker Serial Port – One Infrared Port – Yes and Fast IR (4Mbps) Parallel Port – None USB – None (coming soon) Wireless Communications Cards – Modem and LAN		Windows 98 Windows NT
Full Size Laptop	Lap Size 1.6 to 2.3 by 12.5 to 14.1 by 8.8 to 10.8 inches and from 6 to 10 lbs. One, two, or three NiMH or Li-Ion batteries	Display – 256 color VGA 640 by 480 – 12.1 inch —32–bit color XGA 1024 by 768 – 15 inch —AGP VGA with 4 MB Video RAM Pen Input – No Keyboard – 87 Key To W95 Key Near Full-Size VGA Port – One with up to 1600 by 1200 resolution CPU – Pentium II 300 MHz – AMD-K7-2 333 MHz ROM – 64 KB to 128 KB – Boot and BIOS RAM – 32 MB to 128 MB –EDO or SDRAM Disk Drives – Floppy, ZIP, and up to 8 GB IDE Flash Memory Card –PC Card Type II PC Card Slots – One to Three PC type II or Type III CD-ROM Drive – 24x or DVD and Smart Bay Sound – Stereo with Multimedia Sound Line-in, Microphone-in and Headphone-out Jacks Serial Ports – Two Infrared Port – Yes and Fast IR (FIR) 4Mbps Parallel Port – One USB – One or Two Wireless Communications Cards – Modem and LAN (PC Bus cards) Game Port – None or One Expansion Chassis Port – One PS2 Keyboard/Mouse Port – None or One		

fan blades because it was crushed by the housing and stopped the fan. Repositioning the foam rubber spacer solved the problem. The fan sucks air in from the bottom of the PC and blows it across the CPU heat sink, then out the side channel.

Typical laptop CPU and supporting chip set combinations are shown in Table 7–2.

Each chip set varies in L2 CPU cache and RAM types supported (EDO versus SDRAM). Video, disk drive, and other components are added by the laptop manufacturer as their board design and form factor permits.

Table 7.2 *Laptops and common supporting chip sets*

Laptop CPU	Supporting MLB Chip sets
Pentium MMX 200 – 266 MHz – Tillamook	Intel 430TX Mobile
Pentium II 200 - 233 MHz – Deschutes	Intel 430TX Mobile
Pentium II 266 - 300 MHz – 333 MHz - 366 MHz Deschutes	Intel 440BX Mobile
AMD K7-2 350 MHz—366 MHz - 380 MHz	Super 7 Mobile

LCD—Liquid Crystal Display

The most prominent LCD display feature is size. They vary from 12.1-inch display to 15-inch diagonal display. (See Figure 7–4.) This is up from 11-inch and smaller LCD sizes used in earlier models. Displays support varying resolution and colors on the LCD and higher resolutions with more colors on the external monitor port. The resolution varies from VGA (640 by 480 resolution) to XGA (1024 by 768 resolution) for the LCD panel and upwards to 1600 by 1200 for the external display port. Colors range from 256 color displays to 32-bit true color display. Some laptop LCD panels do not display the high-color images as well as external monitors display them. This is because of the way those LCDs produce the colors.

Although they are all labeled liquid crystal displays because of the base technology used in their design, there are variations that can make the display more visible from an angle and in brighter lighting conditions. In bright sunlight, virtually all LCD displays are not visible. Today, most portables use the Thin Film Transistor (TFT) LCD flat-panel display active-matrix display.

A TFT screen has each pixel (dot or illuminated spot) controlled by from one to four transistors. TFT technology provides the best resolution of all the current flat-panel display technologies and is the most widely used. TFT screens are often referred to as active-matrix LCD displays.

Figure 7–4 *Laptop with 15.1-inch display*

DSTN, or Double-Layer Super-Twist Nematic, is a passive-matrix LCD technology using two display layers to counteract color shifting that is produced by other super-twist LCD displays. DSTN displays are labeled dual-scan LCD displays.

CSTN, or Color Super-Twist Nematic, is an LCD technology developed by Sharp Electronics Corporation. Unlike TFT, CSTN is based on a passive matrix and consequently is less expensive to produce. Original CSTN displays produced in the early 90s suffered from slow response times and image ghosting. Image ghosting is having the image remnants remain in one spot on the screen when the image moves to another spot on the screen. In Windows, setting mouse tails on helps track the mouse position on screens that have slow responses to image movement and image ghosting. Advances in the technology are making CSTN a viable alternative to active-matrix displays. CSTN displays can provide 100ms response times, a 140-degree viewing angle, and high-quality color rivaling TFT displays at about half the cost.

Both DSTN and CSTN displays must be backlit (having a light source behind the display) for optimal viewing. TFT displays produce their own light at each pixel and do not require behind-the-screen lighting. See Figure 7–5.

High Performance Addressing (HPA) is a passive-matrix display technology providing better image response rates and contrast than conventional

Figure 7–5 *TFT laptop display.*

LCD displays. HPA displays do not produce as crisp an image and are not as fast as active-matrix (TFT) displays; however, they are considerably less expensive to manufacture. Some computer manufacturers use HPA LCD displays in low-cost notebook computers.

All LCD displays are sensitive to heat. High heat and direct sunlight darken them, making them unable to display any image. The high heat and direct sunlight can destroy the display if the exposure is of sufficient duration. No matter what technology is used, the displays do not provide good image visibility in direct sunlight. Some shade or reduced lighting is needed for best visibility. The recommendation here is to never use a laptop in direct sunlight like Sandra Bullock did in the movie "The Net" in the beach scene. Hollywood knows little about laptop PCs.

The surface of the displays is made of soft nonreflective plastic. This can become scratched by the smallest amount of abrasive material. Laptop LCD screens require periodic cleaning and dust removal. This should be performed using a nonabrasive lint-free cloth. Gunk on the screen should be removed using a wet lint-free cloth. The water dissolves the gunk while the lint-free cloth does not scratch the LCD surface. It is possible to use cleaning chemicals on the LCD screen. However, a cloth dampened with plain water should remove all but the most stubborn gunk from the LCD screen.

Similarly to Cathode Ray Tube (CRT) displays, LCD displays can etch an image if the same image is left displayed for a long time. This happened on one of our laptops that had the same image displayed for about three days straight. The image light areas remained bright after the image was moved. The good news is that over time (about a week or more) the display returned to normal operation and was not damaged. To avoid such problems, a Windows screen saver or the power management function that turns off the monitor should be activated. On back-lit displays, the LCD should be powered down during periods of inactivity to prevent burning out the back-light lamp.

Sometimes a bad LCD display pops up. These bad displays have lines running through them. The colors in those lines generally are not visible leaving a blank line in the display. In these instances, the source of the problem is the connection between the LCD and the PC. Changing the angle of the LCD panel or moving it down towards the keyboard and then immediately back into operating position often fixes the electrical connection between the laptop PC and its LCD, correcting the problem.

The visibility of an LCD depends on the viewing angle. They are most visible when viewed straight-on. Viewing at an angle causes them to darken. This is great on airplanes when one desires privacy for playing strip poker on their laptop, but not good when viewing results with the boss or a group is important. Viewing many LCD displays from the far right side to far left side greatly degrades LCD display visibility. TFT displays provide the widest viewing angle.

Battery

Nickel-cadmium or NiCad batteries powered early laptop computers. These had a short operating duty cycle and quickly developed a charging memory effect, preventing them from being fully recharged after several uses. This was especially true when the batteries were not fully discharged with each use.

My first laptop was a 386 DX 20 MHz system with 4 MB RAM and a 500 MB disk drive. The NiCad batteries were not removable but rather an integral part of the PC. I purchased it because I was scheduled to travel to Australia and New Zealand and I wanted to play solitaire electronically while on the 20+ hour flight. I did fire up the laptop on the plane after we were about an hour out of San Francisco only to discover that the batteries lasted 20 minutes (386 DX 20 MHz, 4 MB RAM, and 500 MB disk drive ate copious amounts of power). I only had about 18.5 hours of flying time left where I could no longer play solitaire.

Today laptops use Nickel Metal Hydride (NiMH) or Lithium Ion (Li-Ion) batteries. Both provide superior performance to NiCad batteries, with the best performer being the Li-Ion batteries. All batteries develop a charging memory, preventing full recharge of the battery over time. With NiMH bat-

Figure 7–6 *Laptop Li-Ion battery*

teries, this can be from 6 months to a year of proper use. Proper use means full discharge before recharge. With Li-Ion batteries this is about a year. Li-Ion batteries last longer than NiMh batteries under use. They can have about a 20% or greater operating cycle. Most laptops today use power management functions and Li-Ion batteries to produce operating times of up to 8 hours or more. See Figure 7–6.

Smart batteries change the charging cycle so that they are discharged before charging, thus reducing the effect of charging memory. Batteries are also removable and used in combinations of two batteries or sometimes three batteries to extend the operating cycle life.

Laptops that are not active for some time or that sense battery failure, enter suspend mode where almost all activity is stopped. The display is inactive, the disk drive ceases rotating, peripherals are not powered, and the CPU enters a lower operating speed state, looking only for power switch or keyboard activity. This keeps battery power drain to a minimum. The operating state of the laptop prior to entering suspend mode is stored in a special partition on the disk of the laptop so that it can be restored when the power switch is activated.

Batteries are recharged in the laptop. Some laptop PCs recharge the battery while that are operating, and others require that the battery be in the laptop with the laptop powered off for them to recharge the laptop. Generally, on each laptop there is a small monochrome LCD display that shows the battery charging status. External battery chargers are also available. Figure 7–7 shows a laptop status panel illustrating AC power present, PC card slots A

Figure 7–7 *Laptop status panel*

and B occupied, and battery charged. The power switch and the display panel power-off switch are on the right. When the display panel is closed, the display panel power switch cuts power to the panel, blanking the display.

Laptops can be run without their batteries when plugged-in to an external AC power source. Generally, hitting the power-off switch on the laptop removes power to the computer only under normal operation power-off scenarios. Because of suspend mode operation and Windows power management, it is possible for a laptop to enter an operating state where the power off/on switch is ignored totally. In this case removing both the AC power and the battery resets the laptop. By removing the battery and the AC power, all electrical energy is removed from the laptop computer, resetting it to a power-off state.

AC Adapter

Laptop AC adapters are "ball and chain" adapters. They contain a transformer that converts AC power to DC power for either 120-volt 60-cycle or 240-volt 50-cycle AC power. The power adapters automatically sense the 120-volt or 240-volt input power and produce the required DC output. The typical output voltage and current varies for different laptops. Clone laptops use AC power adapters that produce a 19-volt DC output with the amperage varying from 2 to 3 amps. The adapter plug into the laptop is a female connector where the center post is positive and the outside conductor is negative, as shown in Figure 7–8.

Palmtop and other laptop PCs require different voltage and amperage output levels. The critical output parameter here is less voltage and more amperage (Figure 7–9).

Mixing AC adapters on laptops is not recommended, but we have used different adapters between different laptop PCs. When the adapter did not provide sufficient amperage, the PC ran but did not maintain its internal battery. If anything caused the battery to discharge, the PC would not run. In other cases, we have run laptops with the 13-volt DC output from an automobile cigarette lighter jack. It ran fine on the lower voltage. We used it to

Figure 7–8 *Laptop AC adapter*

Figure 7–9 *Palmtop AC adapter*

power the laptop while performing GPS navigation in the car. This is the best use for an automobile cigarette lighter of which we can think.

PC Card Bus—Type I, II, and III Cards

Add-in components for laptop PCs use the PC card bus connectors. Most laptops provide both Type II and Type III slots for PC cards. The PC card (PCMCIA card) adapters are 17-bit adapters with 68 pins in two rows.

Type I, Type II, and Type III cards have the same electrical interface, but their thickness is different. All PC cards are 85.6 mm long by 54 mm wide. Type I cards are 3.3 mm thick, Type II cards are 5 mm thick, and Type III cards are 10.5 mm thick. The Type III PC bus cards take up the mechanical space of two Type II cards. This means that the PC card bus connections on a typical laptop PC can handle one PC card bus Type III card or two PC card bus Type I or II cards. A single Type III and a single Type II card configuration is generally not supported unless a special extension adapter is used to unblock access to the second Type II card slot. Figure 7–10 shows one Type II and one Type III card slot in the same laptop PC.

Add-in components for laptops that come in PC card bus form are LAN adapters, modems (both wired and wireless), SCSI adapters for external SCSI devices like JAZ drives, video input devices, some hard drives, and multifunction adapters that are both LAN and modem.

These PC card bus adapters use plug-and-play installation under Windows 95 and 98. Windows 98 works best with PC card bus adapters, although there can still be problems. One of our laptops has both a multifunction and a SCSI Type II PC card bus adapter installed. The SCSI adapter must be installed after the multifunction adapter for the plug-and-play installation to work properly. Furthermore, the laptop must have the proper BIOS to sup-

Figure 7–10 *Laptop PC card slots*

port Windows 98 installation and the PC card bus plug-and-play function. One of our laptop PCs would not function under Windows 98. It could not find the PC card bus plug-and-play devices until the laptop BIOS was flash upgraded to the latest release.

The PC cards use socket service drivers to detect insertion and removal of PC card devices. This permits warm removal and insertion of the PC card. A second level of card services drivers understands the function of the card—LAN, modem, or combo—and provides the drivers enabling it to work with Windows. Under DOS, several specialized drivers had to be loaded to enable socket services. Oftentimes these were specific to the laptop and the PCM-CIA cards being used. Making PC cards work under DOS and Windows 3.1 was a daunting task. Windows 95 improved this and Windows 98 improved this more. When installing PC cards in a Windows PC, they should be installed last, after the PC is completely configured and operating without them. Once the PC is running, the PC cards can be installed by inserting them into the PC card bus socket. Socket services recognizes that the PC card is installed and initiates the software driver installation process. As stated earlier, the sequence of insertion is important, with certain cards needing to be installed prior to inserting other cards.

The most common problems with PC cards, aside from plug-and-play installation problems, are problems with the pigtail connections to LANs, phone lines, etc.

These pigtail connections tend to break or the connector pins become bent, rendering them nonfunctional. Connecting and disconnecting the pigtail connectors is done constantly, providing countless opportunities to break the wiring in them or to bend one of their connector pins (Figure 7–11).

When a specific PC card adapter malfunctions, it is easy to spot a software problem by examining the PC card icon in the Systray. Systray is a Microsoft Windows term. See Figure 7–12.

To remove a PC card, just double-click on the Systray icon and double-click on the card to remove when it displays the stop card panel. Figure 7–13 illustrates the socket services sequence of removing a PC card. The laptop PC

Figure 7–11 *PC card pigtail connectors*

Figure 7–12 *PC card Systray icon*

then replies that it is okay to remove this card. After acknowledging removal, the card is no longer shown as an active PC card.

Right-clicking on the Systray icon provides the adjust PC card properties and disable PC card tray icon display. When adjusting PC card properties, the control panel PC card function is activated.

Expanding the Systray icon and adjusting PC card properties selection by double-clicking it identifies the operating PC cards and the card services settings. Cards not identified have software driver problems. Cards identified and nonfunctional usually have pigtail connector problems. See Figure 7–14.

The last PC card problem area is heat. Airflow across the cards drawn by the laptop CPU cooling fan is the principal cooling mechanism for these cards. Any blockage of airflow and both the CPU and the PC cards can easily overheat. The laptop should always be set on something providing sufficient airflow.

Figure 7–13 *Socket services PC card removal*

Figure 7–14 *PC card Systray icon expanded*

CD-ROM Drives

CD-ROM drives are a key laptop component. They are used to install software and to hold data for some laptop applications like GPS mapping programs. The CD-ROMs are removable units fitting in a bay that can hold either a CD-ROM or a battery. The extra battery extends the laptop operating time when not on AC power.

New CD-ROM units have both the CD-ROM and floppy disk drive in the same unit. Others have a combination DVD drive and floppy. This conserves space and increases the functionality of the laptop. DVD drives can hold lots of data, making mapping programs and other graphics programs useful on the road away from the office. See Figure 7–15.

Figure 7–15 *Laptop DVD/CD-ROM drive*

CD-ROM units are 5.25-inch IDE drives mated to special carriers and docking connectors. Similar to laptop fixed disk drives, they can be removed from and reinserted into the laptop as needed. They should not be removed or inserted while the laptop is powered up and in operation. If this is done, the laptop can lock up Windows, requiring a power-off and reboot to restore it to normal operation.

Docking Stations

Docking stations provide an added convenience for laptop PCs that are used both as a mobile unit and as an office PC. The laptop can be connected to the docking station through its expansion port, as shown in Figure 7–16. This single connection then makes connections to the other peripherals used by the laptop PC, including the monitor, speakers, keyboard, mouse, printer, floppy disk, and more. Typically a lever assists in disconnecting the docking station from the laptop PC. Also, guides help align the expansion port connectors in the docking station and the laptop.

Some docking stations are more than port repudiators, permitting installation of ISA bus and PCI bus option cards and added disk drives. Most

Figure 7–16 *Docking station front and rear.*

laptops do not require such expansion because they get the added disk drive space from network server drives.

Fixed Disk Drive

Most laptop fixed disk drives are removable units. They are 2.5-inch IDE drives mounted in a carrier specific to each style of laptop. Laptop drives range in capacity from 0.5 GB to 8 GB. Figure 7–17 shows a laptop IDE drive removed from its mounting slot. A special IDE connector mates to the laptop PC, making the drive removable.

Figure 7–18 shows an empty laptop mounting bracket on the left, a 2.5-inch IDE drive used on a laptop prepared for mounting in a 3.5-inch drive bay, and a 2.5-inch drive in a laptop drive carrier. The push-pin connector on the 2.5-inch IDE drive connects to a small ribbon cable that runs to the mating connector on the 2.5-inch laptop drive carrier. The laptop 2.5-inch drive is connected to the ribbon cable and bolted into the carrier. Mounting the drive in a 3.5-inch drive bay requires attaching mounting brackets to the drive and a special 2.5-inch to 40-pin IDE cable connector.

Note in the figure that power is provided the 2.5-inch drive through a power connector connected to the rightmost connector pins. Power is supplied to the 2.5-inch drive through the single connector on the end of the drive. Drive failures are easily fixed by replacing the faulty drive with a known good drive. The problem with this approach is that all data on the old disk drive is typically lost, thrilling all involved with the replacement.

Figure 7–17 *Laptop IDE drive*

Figure 7–18 *2.5-inch drives*

Networking Cards

Laptops are generally connected to a network when in the office. This is essential to back up critical data on servers and to exchange files and e-mail with other PCs. The PC cards connecting to a LAN are generally Type II PC cards with a pigtail connection supporting either twisted-pair wiring or coaxial cable wiring or both types of wiring. The pigtail connection to the network is through a standard Mod-8 (RJ-45) unshielded twisted-pair connector or through a coaxial cable BNC (push and turn) connector.

Laptop networking PC cards support mostly Ethernet although some token ring cards are produced. Figure 7–19 shows both a single Ethernet adapter and a combination modem/Ethernet PC card. The combo card supports only unshielded twisted-pair Ethernet while the Ethernet-only card provides both Mod-8 and BNC connectors.

These LAN PC cards are plug-and-play in laptop PC card slots under Windows 95 and Windows 98. They support Ethernet at 10 MBPS speeds. Newer cards provide Ethernet support for both 10 MBPS and 100 MBPS Ethernet. Combo cards are installed as multifunction parent devices under socket services. Card services then installs the Ethernet network and modem drivers. Failed LAN cards are not repairable and are replaced. Pigtails can be replaced unless the connector in the PC card is broken. If the modem component of a combo card fails, then the card could be used as a LAN-only card. The modem part is not repairable.

Figure 7–19 *Laptop LAN PC cards*

RAM

RAM can be upgraded or replaced in laptop PCs. Access to RAM is through the laptop keyboard. Typically the RAM is installed as SIMMs or DIMMs in sockets under the laptop keyboard. The trick is determining how to remove the keyboard. In clone laptops, the plastic cover over the LCD status panel and the stereo speakers is removed first. It is usually pried open on the LCD panel side exposing the speakers and the status panel. See Figure 7–20.

Lifting the keyboard reveals the RAM SIMMs or DIMMs. Laptop keyboards are attached to the chassis electronics by one or two ribbon cables. These cables permit moving the keyboard aside to replace the RAM SIMMs or DIMMs.

RAM expandability is determined by the main logic board and supporting chip set. The RAM sockets fit specific RAM chips. RAM for laptop PCs is sold in specific chip configurations for a specific laptop manufacturer and model computer. The RAM is typically EDO or SDRAM in a SIMM or DIMM configuration. Figure 7–21 shows RAM installed in a laptop PC.

Laptop memory is often memory without parity. This works fine until there is a memory error. In that case, the software just dies when it hits the memory location that is bad. In one case, this meant that Windows final installation quit in exactly the same procedure each time during installation. Good memory was used up to the point where the Windows product code

Figure 7–20   *Status panel plastic cover removed*

Figure 7–21   *Two 144-pin DIMMs in laptop sockets*

was entered, then the laptop died. It appeared to be a software problem or a configuration problem, but it was not either. Bad memory caused the failure. A simple replacement fixed the problem. Most laptops are burned in for 24 to 48 hours before being delivered to the customer. When this burn-in is performed properly, bad components are caught and replaced before the laptop leaves the factory.

Study Break

Study Break: Laptop Components

Let's find a hapless laptop and examine its components.

1. Get hold of a laptop computer. Examine its underside and locate the bays for the RAM, fixed disk and CPU. They should be identified by some simple printed icon.

2. Examine the bays to determine if they are secured by a locking bolt. This is usually located near the bay release slider.

3. Remove the locking bolt for the fixed disk drive. Release the locking slider tab and remove the fixed disk. Examine the mechanical mounting bracket to determine how to remove the fixed disk from it. Replace the fixed disk, the fixed disk bay cover, and the locking bolt.

4. Similarly, remove the locking bolt for the RAM bay. On some laptops, unlocking and lifting the keyboard accesses the RAM bay. Examine the RAM. Are there any free slots for adding additional RAM? Replace the RAM bay cover and locking bolt.

5. Now in a similar fashion remove the locking bolt and cover for access to the CPU. Is the CPU fan readily accessible and removable? Can it be cleaned of dust easily? Replace the CPU cover and locking bolt.

These procedures would be used to replace or clean the key components of a laptop PC.

A+ 7.2   Common Laptop Problems

There are many laptop problems. The simplest come from plain physical abuse, while more complex problems are caused by the interaction of PCM-CIA cards with other laptop components. Many problems are solved simply, while a few require more hardware and software configuration work.

Dropping the Computer

The most common and preventable of the many types of problems seen with laptops comes from dropping the computer itself. Laptop cases should have a Velcro strap that secures the laptop inside the case. It is easy to remember to fasten the strap. Often if only the case's zipper secures the laptop, the zipper is left unzipped. This results in the laptop falling out of the case the second it is picked up for travel. Most laptops can survive a fall, but battery interlocks and other plastic components can be broken. The most critical part subject to breakage is the LCD panel. In this case data can be removed from the laptop using an external monitor or just swapping removable fixed disk drives with a replacement laptop.

All laptop-carrying cases should have an internal Velcro strap that holds the computer in place. This prevents the laptop from falling out of an unzipped case. Significant physical damage to the laptop case and LCD screen necessitate factory repair. We have repaired plasma panels on some early Toshiba portable computers, and it was ugly. When repairing laptops, there is always the moment of truth or point of no return where some plastic case components must be pried apart. It is easiest to have factory repair personnel with plenty of spare chassis parts on hand perform these repairs.

Temperature Extremes

Another common problem area specific to laptop PCs is temperature shock. When traveling with a laptop PC you should never leave it in the cold for an extended time period. The laptop should be kept as warm as a human. This means that those laptops left overnight in the car during the dead of winter or in the summer heat are candidates for potential disk failures.

The cold causes condensation inside the disk drive. The smallest amount of moisture inside a drive makes them fail. One of our early Toshiba laptop computers was left overnight in a car in early November. When it was powered on the next day it failed. If a laptop is left outside in freezing temperatures overnight or for an extended period of time, warm it up slowly over several days before attempting to power it up. The long warm up period gives any condensation inside the computer an opportunity to return to water vapor without causing damage to the laptop when it is powered on.

Heat is also a great enemy of laptops and PC cards. There needs to be adequate air circulation around the laptop to ensure that everything inside stays cool. Do not run a laptop on carpet because the laptop can sink into the carpet, preventing air from flowing into the CPU cooling fan intake. At least once or twice we have had laptops quit because they had inadequate airflow.

Fortunately no damage was done because the internal heat sensor powered off the laptop when it detected overheating. The CPU cooling fan should be checked and cleaned of debris when overheating is suspected.

Laptop overheating is avoided by providing adequate space around the laptop for air circulation. Cleaning the laptop fan exhaust should be performed periodically to ensure adequate airflow through the laptop chassis.

Exposure to X-rays

One question many laptop travelers have is "can I pass my laptop through the X-ray machine at airports without harm?" We used to always pass them around the X-ray machines at airports until one of our students (a West Point graduate in the military) told us that he always ran his disk drives through the X-ray machines without incident. Since then, for over ten years and hundreds of flights, our laptops have always passed right through the X-ray machines without a problem.

Unexpected Configuration Problems

The PCMCIA bus and DOS laptops were very tricky machines to configure. Socket services had to be run under DOS. Laptop and PC card manufacturers failed to uniformly implement PCMCIA bus standards. This resulted in laptop manufacturers having to certify specific PC cards for their machines. With Windows 95 and Windows 98 this changed. Today PC cards fulfill the plug-and-play promise.

A common problem is "losing" the laptop CD-ROM drive, meaning that the CD ROM becomes unexpectedly "invisible" to the computer when looking for files, directories or devices—it's there at one time only to be lost later. Reinstalling the CD-ROM drivers or installing DOS 17-bit CD-ROM drivers in CONFIG.SYS and AUTOEXEC.BAT can correct the problem. Sometimes on older laptops Windows must be reinstalled for it to pick up the CD-ROM drive correctly. In one laptop it required specific IDE disk drivers for the CD-ROM drive to be found. Once they were installed, the CD-ROM reappeared.

Keeping the driver programs and the BIOS of the laptop up to the latest release levels is a good way to prevent unexpected configuration problems. The manufacturer's website should be checked for software driver and laptop BIOS updates about every 6 months. Migrating a laptop to Windows 98 (if it has the resources) with a fresh software install is a means of resolving some laptop plug-and-play problems.

Windows Configuration Problems

Often installing Windows on a laptop is a daunting task. This is especially true when network and other types of PC cards are required. USB bus connections can also cause installation problems. The best installation strategy with a laptop is to install Windows on a clean system with no PC cards inserted or USB devices connected. Once this clean Windows installation is complete, then the PC card devices can be inserted one at a time. LAN cards and modems are good first. SCSI and strange devices last. Finally, USB devices are connected. Typically there are two USB ports. When a USB device is not working in one port try the other port. Sometimes IRQ steering adjustments are required to make PC cards work. IRQ steering reroutes hardware IRQs for the PCI bus. IRQ steering loads the interrupt vector table. Interrupt vectors are software pointers to small programs called interrupt routines that perform the functions needed to satisfy the interrupt. On PCs the interrupt vector table is 256 4-byte pointers residing in the first 1,024 bytes of RAM. Each interrupt number is assigned to a specific task. The 16 IRQ lines are assigned to 16 of the interrupt vectors or pointers. See Figure 7–22.

The IRQ steering settings are in the Control Panel – System – Device Manager – System Devices – PCI Bus menu selection. In laptops, PC card bus components and other laptop components are tied together using the PCI bus. The PC card socket services must be tied to the PCI bus to function properly. This can require steering PCI bus IRQs to the PC cards.

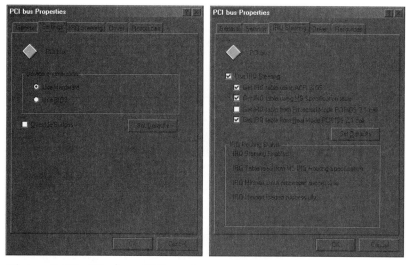

Figure 7–22 *Windows IRQ steering*

Power Management Problems

Laptops have hardware power management functions. These can often interfere with Windows power management software. Suspend-to-disk features automatically activate when low power is detected. This often confuses laptop users into believing that their laptop has malfunctioned when it is merely in power-saving hibernation. Proper configuration of power management options in Windows and in laptop hardware is essential for trouble-free operation.

Damage to Connectors

Plugging and unplugging pigtail connectors from PC cards can cause the connector pins to become bent. When this happens, the cards fail to operate properly. Pigtail connectors from other PC cards will not necessarily work with a specific card because each card manufacturer has their own pigtail connector design.

Pigtail connectors should be periodically checked for bent or damaged pins to prevent them from causing problems. Having spare pigtail connectors can resolve some problems. However, if the pins in the PCMCIA card get damaged, then replacing the card is the repair option of necessity.

Display Problems

When operating a laptop with an external video display, the display resolution is often increased beyond the XGA 1024 by 768 resolution of the laptop LCD panel. This works fine until the laptop is returned to LCD panel operation, which cannot provide the high resolution of the external monitor. Two things can happen. The LCD can fail to display anything at all (either black or diagonal lines) or it can display a portion of the high-resolution display. This problem is easily fixed by returning the display to the VGA or XGA resolution supported by the LCD panel.

Laptop LCD displays can have an image burned into them by leaving the image on the screen for several days. Screen savers or power management functions prevent this problem. On an LCD that did retain an image, over several days it gradually returned to normal operation erasing the image. Since most laptops have a top panel switch that turns off the LCD panel when it is folded down, the better solution to is to fold the laptop display down, thus turning off the display.

A more common LCD problem is bad pixels. LCD panels in clone PCs can have up to 10 bad pixels—ones that remain lighted all the time. Manufacturers are reluctant to replace them with good LCDs. This is one draw-back to purchasing low-priced nonbrand name computers.

Clocking Problems

It is possible to overclock PC CPUs. Overclocking is running the CPU at a MHz clock rate that exceeds the manufacturer's specified clock rate. For example, 200MHz Pentium Pro CPU chips run fine at 233 MHz. However, CPU overclocking in laptop PCs is dangerous because an overclocked CPU produces more heat than one running at the specified clock speed. It is possible to damage the CPU in a laptop with overclocking. Other components could potentially be damaged.

Study Break

PCMCIA Card Installation

Installing PCMCIA cards in a laptop is a common procedure, performed most often by laptop owners. Generally, they install a modem card or a LAN card or both.

1. Get a Laptop that has no PCMCIA cards installed.
2. Find a modem card with the driver software from the manufacturer. If there is no modem card, a LAN card will work as well. Be sure to have the latest driver software from the manufacturer on floppy diskette
3. Also make sure you have a Windows CD or that the Windows CAB files are located in the laptop fixed disk in a Windows\options\cabs directory.
4. Power up the PC and be sure Windows is completely booted. Now insert the PCMCIA card in a PCMCIA socket on the laptop. Windows should beep and announce that new hardware has been found. Windows should now proceed to load the software for the PCMCIA bus and the driver programs for the PCMCIA adapter card.
5. If requested, use the diskette of driver programs for the card to complete the installation.
6. Restart the laptop as Windows requests.

Go to Control Panel, click on modems, click on the diagnostics tab, highlight the port that has the modem icon, and click on more info. Does the modem return some diagnostic messages? If so, it is installed correctly. With a LAN board click on system, then click on device manager, and expand the network adapters icon. If the LAN board is listed and there are no red or yellow icons, it is installed correctly.

Summary

This chapter has described common laptop PC components. It has illustrated which components are field replaceable and which require factory repair. The first section was dedicated to a detailed discussion on portable system components and their configuration. Components covered included:

- CPUs and their associated chip sets
- LCD displays
- Batteries
- Power adapters
- PC and networking cards
- CD ROMs and fixed disks
- Docking Stations
- RAM

The next section covered common problems associated with portable computers and suggested solutions and/or preventive measures. The types of problems discussed included concerns about environmental factors such as damage from impact, temperature extremes, and X-ray machines; display problems; difficulties with the operating system; and device drivers. The solutions suggested were as simple as using cases with an extra Velcro strap to fasten the laptop into the case and keeping the laptop warm to keeping laptop driver programs and BIOS revisions current.

▲ CHAPTER REVIEW QUESTIONS

1. *Laptops use _____ batteries.*

    A. alkaline

    B. nickel

    C. lithium

    D. NiMH

    Answer: D. NiMH

2. *Which LCD is typically backlit?*

    A. None are.

    B. TFT

C. DSTN

D. Super-Twist

Answer: C. DSTN

3. *Pentium CPUs are the only CPUs used in laptops.*

   A. TRUE

   B. FALSE

   Answer: B. FALSE

4. *What are standard components on all laptops?*

   A. RAM, CPU, CD-ROM, floppy, modem

   B. CD-ROM, ZIP, floppy, SCSI drive

   C. LCD, CPU, RAM, floppy, PCMCIA bus

   D. LCD, CPU, LAN, floppy, fixed disk

   Answer: C. LCD, CPU, RAM, floppy, PCMCIA bus

5. *What is the greatest danger to laptop LCD displays?*

   A. dust

   B. driver programs

   C. etching

   D. direct sunlight

   Answer: D. direct sunlight

6. *What is the difference between Type I, Type II, and Type III PC cards?*

   A. the number of pins in the connector

   B. the length and width

   C. color

   D. thickness

   E. data transfer speed

   Answer: D. thickness

7. *A laptop CD-ROM drive and the fixed disk drive are _____ drives.*

   A. SCSI

   B. IDE

C. PCMCIA

D. MFM

Answer: B. IDE

8. *Laptop computers cannot use SCSI.*

A. TRUE

B. FALSE

Answer: B. FALSE

9. *Laptop field replaceable units include?*

A. fixed disk drive

B. floppy disk drive

C. CD-ROM drive

D. LAN card

E. modem card

F. all of the above

G. none of the above

Answer: F. all of the above

10. *Modems use pigtail connections to connect to* ....

A. the telephone line

B. the serial port and the telephone line

C. the PC card bus and the phone line

D. none of the above

Answer: A. the telephone line

11. *Laptop disk drives are* ....

A. IDE 1-inch drives

B. SCSI 2.5 inch drives

C. removable 3.5-inch disk drives

D. IDE 2.5-inch drives

Answer: D. IDE 2.5-inch drives

12. *Most laptop PC cards are* _____

A. Type I

B. Type II

C. Type III

D. none of the above

Answer: B. Type II

13. *Laptop computers have no USB ports.*

    A. TRUE

    B. FALSE

    Answer: B. FALSE

14. *Which laptop battery lasts longest?*

    A. alkaline

    B. NiCad

    C. NiMH

    D. Lithium

    E. Li-Ion

    Answer: E. Lithium is an element not a battery—Li-Ion is the battery.

15. *A big source of laptop destruction is?*

    A. heat

    B. dust

    C. water

    D. dropping

    Answer: D. Dropping. Water also destroys laptops but who uses them under water?

16. *The most visible display used with a laptop computer is?*

    A. TFT

    B. CRT

    C. DSTN

    D. CSTN

    E. none of the above

    Answer: B. Since laptops can be connected to an external CRT monitor, that is the most visible.

LANs and Communications

▲ **Chapter Syllabus**

A+ 8.1   **LAN Concepts**

A+ 8.2   **Internet Access**

A+ 8.3   **Installing and Configuring Network Interface Cards**

A+ 8.4   **Network Problem Manifestations**

Most computers are networked today. This has implications for identifying and resolving PC problems. This chapter describes basic networking concepts and terminology. It covers LAN and Internet communications. Once a PC is network-connected, maintenance and troubleshooting take on new and more complex dimensions because when network connections fail, the entire PC often freezes.

A+	8.1

LAN Concepts

The original concept of networking was dumb terminals and mainframe systems. Today most networks consist of personal computers and specialized PC servers. These are called Local Area Networks (LANs) because they connect the PC and servers in a single building and facility. Specialized PC servers are based on the technologies implemented in the PCs found on every desktop. They enhance and augment these technologies, focusing them on the LAN server function to create specialized PCs to act as network servers. However, it is easiest to think of servers as PCs on steroids.

An understanding of networking concepts is necessary in troubleshooting and fixing PC problems because almost all business PCs are—and soon many home PCs will be—networked. In this section we look at the basics of networking PCs.

The most fundamental networking concept is that networks are implemented in hardware, software, and channels. The hardware is the PC networking components needed to implement a network, mostly network interface cards (NICs) added to a PC. Software is the programs that operate the LAN and transfer data from PC to PC. Channels are the wiring, hubs, bridges, routers, etc., that interconnect PCs to form a network. These hardware, software, and channel components are conceptually combined together in a layered model to perform the functions necessary to transfer data between PCs.

The next fundamental concept is that network functions and the PC hardware, software and channel components that perform them can be divided into seven logical layers. This is called the ISO seven-layer model. This seven-layer model is described in detail in networking specifications that every manufacturer of network components follows. Each manufacturer implements the layers in a standardized fashion, but not perfectly according to the specification. However, since Windows software dominates the PC marketplace, most manufacturers of PC products follow the Windows seven-layer model implementation.

The ISO seven-layer model is a networking functionality yardstick that explains networking hardware, software, and channel functions. See Figure 8–1.

Before walking through the ISO reference model, we need to examine what is required to establish compatible communications between a PC and a server. There are two sides to compatibility: data format compatibility and networking compatibility, as shown in Figure 8–2.

```
┌─────────────────────────────────────┐
│         Layer 7 Application          │
│                                      │
│   Application Program Data Formats    │
│        User Network Dialog           │
├─────────────────────────────────────┤
│        Layer 6 Presentation          │
│                                      │
│         Feature Mapping              │
│         Code Translations            │
├─────────────────────────────────────┤
│          Layer 5 Session             │
│  Establish, Maintain and Terminate   │
│           Logical Links              │
├─────────────────────────────────────┤
│         Layer 4 Transport            │
│                                      │
│       Maintains End-to-End           │
│         Message Integrity            │
│        Reassembles Messages          │
├─────────────────────────────────────┤
│          Layer 3 Network             │
│                                      │
│             Routing                  │
├─────────────────────────────────────┤
│         Layer 2 Data Link            │
│                                      │
│       Data Communications            │
│            Protocol                  │
├─────────────────────────────────────┤
│         Layer 1 Physical             │
│                                      │
│       Electrical - Mechanical        │
│            Interface                 │
└─────────────────────────────────────┘
```

Figure 8–1 *ISO seven-layer networking model*

Data Format Compatibility

Data format compatibility begins with simple data transmission speed compatibility. Both the PC and the server (which might be another PC or could be a mainframe computer, often referred to as a "host") must communicate at the same speed or bits per-second transmission rate. The modems and the LAN boards (Network Interface Cards) used determine speed compatibility.

CODE COMPATIBILITY

Code compatibility is simple to solve because almost all computers today use either the underlying ASCII code or extended binary coded decimal interchange code (EBCDIC). IBM mainframe computers use primarily EBCDIC code while all the remaining computers in the world use ASCII. What is the

Compatibility

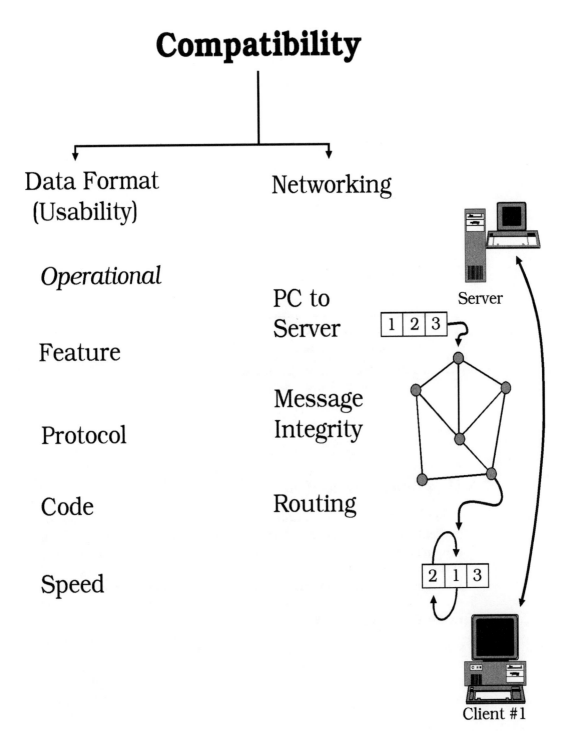

Data Format
(Usability)

Operational

Feature

Protocol

Code

Speed

Networking

PC to
Server

Message
Integrity

Routing

Server

Client #1

Figure 8–2 *Compatibility*

maximum number of characters or bit combinations that must be handled with code compatibility? There are 256 possible combinations of eight bits.

PROTOCOL COMPATIBILITY

Protocol compatibility is more difficult than code compatibility because we must account for every protocol handshaking scenario. Protocols are similar to a language in that there are specific handshake messages that coordinate information exchange between sending and receiving devices. Visualize, if you can, the equivalent English handshake messages for a local phone call.

> *Caller*—Dials number
> *Answerer*—Hears call; *Hello?*
> *Caller*—Hello
> *Answerer*—This is Pete, can I help you?
> *Caller*—Is Jeremy there?
> *Answerer*—No he is teaching today.

Each phone call scenario must be covered to achieve protocol compatibility.

FEATURE COMPATIBILITY

Feature compatibility is the next level. This requires matching the keyboard keys and the display size to what the communicating software expects. How many of you have worked with a PC as a VTxxx terminal on a VAX or used a PC as a 3270 terminal on an IBM host? How well did you like the keyboard mapping and display layout? What happened when it came time to display 132 characters on the PC's 80-character-wide screen?

OPERATIONAL COMPATIBILITY

Operational compatibility is the final requirement to get useable data from a server into a client computer. Operational compatibility is determined by the data formats used by the application program. Lotus spreadsheets use WKS or WK1, etc., files while Excel Spreadsheets use XLS files. What are some different images file formats? We have JPG, TIF, PCX, BMP, RLE, AVI, CDR, and more.

Terminal emulation requires speed-code-protocol-and-feature compatibility. PCs running programs caused us to be concerned with operational compatibility.

Networking Compatibility

Networking compatibility is concerned with sending data across complex networks. A network is comprised of nodes and links. They usually form a mesh- or weblike arrangement. The goal with a complex network is to have data stuffed in at the source end and then have it pop out at the destination end of the network. The network transfer of data from source to destination across a complex network requires performing three functions, described here:

- The first function is that the data must be routed between source and destination. Which way does it travel through a network? Does it go down the right hand pathway, the left-hand pathway or the straight through pathway?

- Next data must be sent through the network in small chunks rather than in larger blocks. The opportunity for having an error in a large block of data is very good. When an error occurs, the entire block must be retransmitted. With smaller chunks, the chance of error is much less and only the small chunk must be retransmitted. The problem of message integrity arises with the small chunks. If we chop up a message into chunk 1, 2, and 3, when it is received it must be reassembled as 1, 2, and 3. We have to be sure that chunk 2 belongs to us and does not belong to someone else.

- We must make sure that we establish and maintain a one-to-one or end-to-end connection between the client and the server. This **logical link** must be maintained for the duration of the communications activity. In LANs, this end-to-end connection is visible on the PC client as extra disk drives.

Understanding how to make a terminal compatible with a host computer lays the foundation for understanding the seven-layer ISO networking model. Now we are ready to understand the seven-layer model layers and their functions.

THE ISO SEVEN-LAYER MODEL

The ISO (International Standards Organization) was the focal point for development of the Open System Interconnection-networking model. This model divides up the functions needed for communication between a client and a server into seven-layers. (Yes, you might think of this as the ISO/OSI networking model. Confused? Keep in mind that the "S" is always in the correct spot.)

This seven-layer networking model divides up the communications in an arbitrary (but logical) fashion amongst the layers. In the real world, hardware and software communications products must work reliably first, then perform the ISO layer functions. Consequently, these products did not precisely follow the hierarchical structure defined by the ISO model.

Let us match compatibility to the seven-layers. First the seven-layers and their associated compatibility functions are:

- Application (Layer 7)— Operational Compatibility
- Presentation (Layer 6)— Feature Compatibility
- Session (Layer 5)—End-to-End or Logical Link Compatibility
- Transport (Layer 4)—Message Integrity Compatibility
- Network (Layer 3)—Routing Compatibility
- Data Link (Layer 2)—Protocol Compatibility
- Physical (Layer 1)—Speed Compatibility

Most communications and LAN products today are described and discussed using the International Standards Organization's (ISO) seven-layer networking model. This model is a set of general specifications for describing how communications products should be constructed so that they can communicate with each other (be interconnected). Figure 8–3 shows how the layers are implemented in PC products.

ISO (International Standards Organization)
or
OSI (Open Systems Interconnection Model)

ISO Layer	Compatibility	PC Component
7 - Application	- Operational	Application
6 - Presentation	- Feature/Code	Windows
5 - Session	- PC to Server	TCP
4 - Transport	- Message Integrity	TCP
3 - Network	- Routing	IP
2 - Data Link	- Protocol	LAN Board
1 - Physical	- Speed	LAN Board
		Wiring

Figure 8–3 *ISO Layers versus compatibility versus PC*

Which layer does speed compatibility fall into? Layer 1 covers speed compatibility. The physical layer wiring and electrical transmission can be summarized into two simple data communications parameters: speed and distance. The LAN card in the PC and the network wiring components implement this.

Protocol compatibility is handled by Layer 2, the data link layer. The function of a data link protocol is to get information from point A to point B error free. It uses message handshakes to perform its function. The LAN card in the PC implements the protocols. The protocols distinguish Ethernet networks from token ring networks.

The network layer performs routing compatibility, sending data from source to destination. This is implemented by the IP portion of the Windows TCP/IP protocol software.

The transport layer provides end-to-end message integrity compatibility. It assures that entire messages are moved through a network from source to destination. This is implemented by the TCP portion of the Windows TCP/IP protocol software.

The session layer provides a logical one-to-one or end-to-end connection. This layer, Layer 5, provides the entry point to the network. This is also implemented by TCP portion of the Windows TCP/IP protocol software.

The presentation layer provides feature compatibility. This is performed by the PC's operating system that is, in most cases, by Windows (95/98 or NT).

The application layer covers operational compatibility. It is largely the function of the application program to solve operational compatibility. Almost all programs accept data files in different operational formats.

ISO seven-layer model Layers 1 and 2 are implemented by the PC's Network Interface Card (NIC) and the network wiring. ISO Layers 3,4, and 5 are implemented by Window's TCP/IP protocol software. Finally, Windows and the application software implement Layers 6 and 7. All networking hardware, software, and channels can be fit into this seven-layer networking model.

Types of Local Area Networks

A local area network (LAN) is having the PCs in a facility communicating with central servers or each other. To communicate, the PCs must be connected together by a communication channel that is most often copper wiring. The most favored type of wiring is telephone wire, or unshielded twisted-pair (UTP) wiring. This wiring comes in different categories or grades. The most popular type of telephone wire is category-5, rated at speeds up to 100 MBPS. Category-6 wire is now being implemented. It is rated at speeds over 155 MBPS. Other types of wiring have been used in LANs but they are found less frequently than UTP wiring. Fiber-optic cable is also used in LANs. It is used to provide high-speed connections between network components and to provide electrical isolation between different parts of a network.

For a PC to be connected to a LAN, it must contain a LAN card (a Network Interface Card—NIC) and LAN card driver software that integrates the LAN card into the operating system in each computer. Furthermore, the operating system LAN components must be installed as well. Chapter 16 contains more information on this as well.

The servers run a network operating system (NOS). This is usually a Windows NT Server or Novell NetWare program. Servers are typically NetWare-based, Windows NT-based, or Unix-based. Clients connect to each different type of server using different communications software. See Figure 8–4.

Users view the LAN as an extension of their PCs. To them, it appears as though there are now extra disk drives and printers attached to their PC. To transfer data from their system to the server, the user merely copies the file from a local disk drive C: to a server disk drive F. See Figure 8–5.

Most people think that the type of network means Ethernet or token ring. Others believe that it is a Novell NetWare or Windows NT Server net-

Figure 8–4 *Typical LAN*

Figure 8–5 *Local area network from client PC viewpoint*

work or they may say they have a twisted-pair network. These are all characteristics of their network, but it does not define the network type. What defines a network type is how people actually use the network.

Actually, LANs share PC resources among multiple PCs connected to the LAN. Disk drives and printers are shared among all LAN-connected PCs, but how they are shared, controlled, and managed is what determines the type of network. Network types are either client-server or peer-to-peer. Client-server LANs are centrally managed. Typically large LANs or combinations of LANs with wide area network (WAN) or Internet communications serve big organizations. In contrast peer-to-peer LANs are small LANs serving fewer than 10 PCs, where management of access to resources is decentralized. Each PC controls access to its disk drives and printers. In reality, virtually all LANs today have a combination of client-server and peer-to-peer operations. See Figure 8–6.

Either type of network can be implemented with Ethernet or token ring technologies, different wiring, and Windows NT and Novell NetWare. Ethernet and token ring are the types of Network Interface Cards (NICs) used to communicate between PCs on a LAN, the wiring physically connects the devices on the LAN, and Windows NT and Novell NetWare are the software platforms for implementing client-server networks. Any combination of these LAN components can be used to implement peer-to-peer or client-server networks.

The key issues in determining the type of local area network is the number of PCs to be attached to the network, and how the resources are going to be managed. Other considerations involve what the key networking

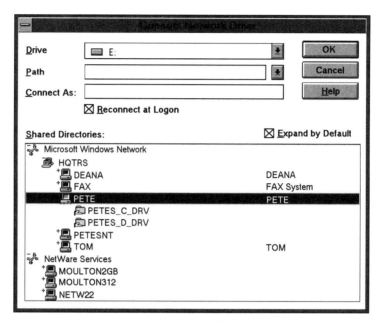

Figure 8–6 *Windows NT peer-to-peer and Novell client-server connections*

applications for the organization are, what software products are used to implement these applications, and the location of each to another.

Network Interface Cards

Different types of networks are implemented using specialized Network Interface Cards (NICs). There are NICs for Ethernet, the token ring, Asynchronous Transfer Mode (ATM) networks, and more. Most LANs focus around two popular Network Interface Cards, Ethernet and token ring.

Ethernet is the most widely installed LAN technology today. Ethernet is a standard specified by IEEE (Institute for Electrical and Electronic Engineers) 802.3. The original architecture for it was developed by Xerox and then marketed by Xerox, DEC, and Intel. Ethernet uses the Carrier Sense Multiple Access/Collision Detection (CSMA/CD) communications protocol, operating at speeds of 10 MBPS, 100 MBPS, and 1 GBPS. This protocol is discussed further in the section "Ethernet CSMA/CD," later in this chapter.

The Ethernet standard allows for the use of coaxial cable, fiber, and specific categories futuristic-pair cable. Ethernet networks are wired using hubs that act as wiring hubs, network bridges, or high-performance switches.

A token ring network is another type of LAN. All the workstations in a token ring network are connected in a ring or star topology. Information cir-

culates around this ring using a token-passing scheme to prevent workstation signals from colliding when they try to send a message at the same time.
The standard for the token ring protocol is IEEE 802.5. The most widely recognized implementation of token ring networking would be the IBM token
ring network. Although not as popular as Ethernet, it is an effective and reliable networking scheme.

ARCnet is an older LAN technology. In an ARCnet LAN, information
flow is controlled using a token bus scheme. ARCnet can use coaxial cable or
fiber lines. Because of this, ARCnet also could have longer transmission distances as compared to the other LAN technologies. In addition to this, its
overall cost was at one point less than the other LAN technologies, thus giving it some popularity in the market. Lacking equivalent data speeds, ARC-
net has faded as a major player in LAN technologies.

Table 8–1 summarizes differences between Ethernet and token ring
networks.

Table 8.1 *LAN Technology Comparison*

	Ethernet	Token Ring
Number of nodes	1,024 per segment	255 per ring
Speeds	10MBPS, 100MBPS, and 1GBPS	4MBPS, 16MBPS, 100MBPS, and 155MBPS
Cable	Unshielded twisted-pair (UTP) Category 3, 5 and up. Coaxial cable – RG58 Fiber-optic cable – multimode and single mode	IBM Type 1 and Type 2 shielded twisted-pair. Unshielded twisted-pair (UTP) Category-3, 5 and up. Fiber-optic cable – multimode and single mode
Protocol	Carrier Sense Multiple Access with Collision Detection (CSMA/CD)	Token Passingpassing
Networking components	Active wiring hubs Bridges Switches Routers	Active wiring hubs Bridges Switches (rare) Routers
Transport protocols Supported ISO Layers 3, 4, and 5	TCP/IP SPX/IPX NetBEUI	TCP/IP SPX/IPX NetBEUI
Transmission	Half duplex or full duplex	Half duplex
Data Encoding	Digital transmission using Manchester encoding	Digital transmission using differential Manchester encoding

An emerging LAN technology is Asynchronous Transfer Mode (ATM). It uses a cell relay protocol at transmission speeds of 25 MBPS, 155 MBPS, and 622 MBPS. An ATM NIC connects to ATM switching hubs to perform both LAN functions and multimedia telephony. Windows 98 software supports LAN functions and Internet communications using ATM NICs. ATM is a technology that can implement both LAN communications and wide area network communications, in contrast to Ethernet, which is a LAN technology alone. Furthermore, ATM's cell relay protocol can easily allocate communications channel capacity among voice, video, and data traffic, as demanded. Ethernet performs this traffic balancing less effectively. ATM was developed in anticipation of providing desktop PCs the ability to perform a variety of communications tasks, including acting like a TV, a video telephone, and an Internet access terminal, simultaneously.

Network Protocols

Protocols are the languages of data communications. The primary objective of a protocol is error-free transfer of data from one end of an electrical communications channel to another.

There are protocols at different levels in a network. The lower-layer protocols we are focusing on here are implemented in the NIC hardware. Higher-layer protocols are implemented in software. The principal software protocols that permit PCs to exchange data across a LAN are TCP/IP, SPX/IPX, and NetBEUI. TCP/IP is the software protocols used for Internet communications, SPI/IPX are the software protocols supporting Novell NetWare client-server networks, and NetBEUI is the Windows protocol used for simple PC LANs.

In general, all protocols are thought of as the rules of communication. For example, think about how people communicate in a classroom. While the instructor is talking, everyone is quiet. They are quiet because they know that if they all talk at the same time, they disrupt what the instructor is trying to communicate to everyone.

If someone needs to speak, they raise their hand so that the instructor stops speaking and allows them to communicate their thoughts. When they are done speaking, the instructor waits an appropriate amount of time before responding. If the instructor did not wait, then the instructor would talk over the student and make their communication misunderstood. This is nothing more than a set of rules instructors and students follow to communicate effectively. Data communications protocols work in the same fashion.

Understanding hardware protocols is important for network troubleshooting and design. These protocols are less visible to us because they are embedded in the products and services we purchase. Furthermore, for products from one vendor to talk with the products of another vendor, these protocols must interoperate. They must work exactly the same way in both vendors' equipment. Let's take a look at two of these protocols.

ETHERNET CSMA/CD

Ethernet uses the hardware communications protocol CSMA/CD (Carrier Sense Multiple Access/Collision Detection) to facilitate the communications from point A to point B. This makes Ethernet, regardless of how it is constructed, operate as a bus network. See Figure 8–7. The Carrier Sense Multiple Access with Collision Detection (CSMA/CD) is a simple protocol and is statistical in nature. It responds well to bursts of activity.

CSMA/CD protocol operation is similar to Citizens Band radios. Each station bids for access. Sometimes collisions happen.

When that occurs, the stations back off and retry at a later time, determined by the "automobile theory of insurance" algorithm. In the "automobile theory of insurance," a person having a collision is prevented from getting back on the road again right away because the automobile repair, as determined by the insurance company, varies unpredictably from a short to a long time. Furthermore, people with a second automobile collision must wait even longer before being able to get their insurance reinstated, enabling them to drive again.

In the CSMA/CD protocol, the back-off algorithm is called binary exponential back off. Each station determines a random interval of time that must elapse before it can again attempt communication. Those stations with one collision must multiply their delay time by a factor of, say, two before attempting to communicate again. This means that stations with one collision must wait even longer before attempting to communicate on an Ethernet.

The benefit of CSMA/CD protocol is that devices can be added to or removed from the network at any time without disrupting the network. However, some network servers and PCs constantly send diagnostic frames to assure that connections across an Ethernet are still valid. When the server dies or that connection is lost, this can easily cause these PCs to crash.

The component that sets all of these parameters is the Network Interface Card (NIC). That is to say, buying an Ethernet card means you will be using CSMA/CD, and the connectors on the card determine the cabling used and the speed of data transfer.

Figure 8–7 *CSMA/CD protocol bus network*

TOKEN-PASSING RING

The token-passing ring protocol is a sophisticated protocol. It is deterministic, that is each and every station gets its turn on the ring. It operates like a train running around a track with one boxcar carrying all the packets from PC to PC. The train runs at either 4 MBPS(20 miles an hour) or 16 MBPS(80 miles an hour). It never stops. The token is a flag on the engine of the train. The token ring's greater sophistication (demanded by the requirement to keep the ring operating regardless of hardware failures) causes more operating overhead. Diagnostic messages constantly flow on the ring. See Figure 8–8.

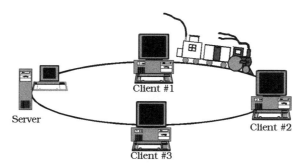

Figure 8–8 *Token-ring token passing*

Similar to Ethernet networks, token ring networks are hub-wired. This is absolutely necessary to assure reliable operation. If the ring were to break at any point, the entire network of stations would be inoperative and unable to communicate.

The token ring employs wiring hubs called Multistation Access Units (MAU). Although the token ring is a ring of wire, on the surface the wiring topology does not seem to be a ring but rather a star, each point wired from the MAU. See Figure 8–9. Wiring topology for LANs today is star wiring from network hubs. This star wiring prevents common Ethernet and token ring PC wiring glitches from disabling the entire network. A single break in the token ring wire would halt all traffic from circulating around the ring. Similarly, no electrical signals can traverse a broken Ethernet bus. Hubs prevent breaks in both token ring and Ethernet wiring from shutting them down.

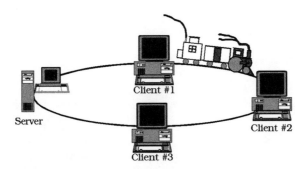

Figure 8–9 *Token-ring wiring topology*

To run at 16 MBPS over unshielded twisted-pair wire, active hubs that perform signal retiming are required. IBM's active hubs have two components: a Controlled Access Unit (CAU), which is the intelligent part of the hub, and a Lobe Access Module (LAM). In token ring wiring with CAUs and LAMs, each LAM connects up to 20 devices (PC clients or servers), and each CAU supports up to four LAMs. You must use a CAU/LAM combination for the token ring to work. A single CAU with fully populated LAMs supports 80 devices. Maximum token ring size is 255 devices. The 255-device maximum is a token ring design limitation as specified by IEEE and IBM. It is determined by the maximum length of the wire in any token ring network and the electrical signal propagation delay (the time it takes the token to electrically travel around the ring).

NETWORK TYPES AND COLLISIONS

In the token ring network, devices speak to each other by taking turns. Devices using Ethernet can speak at the same time. Where two devices transmit at the same time there is a collision. Most LAN technologies can only have a single transmission down a cable at any given time.

Full versus Half Duplex

Full-duplex data transmission means that data can be transmitted in both directions on a signal carrier at the same time. For example, on your local area network, if you had full-duplex transmission, one workstation can be sending data and at the same time be receiving data from another machine. Full-duplex transmission implies a bidirectional line (one that can move data in both directions simultaneously).

Half-duplex data transmission means that data can be transmitted in both directions on a signal carrier, but not at the same time. So if your local area network uses a technology that has half-duplex transmission, one workstation can send data on the line and, when the transmission is done, receive data on the same line. Like full-duplex transmission, half-duplex transmission implies a bidirectional line (one that can carry data in both directions, but not at the same time).

Ethernet was designed to work on a single line with half-duplex transmission and collisions. Newer Ethernet networks support point-to-point full-duplex transmission.

CSMA/CD protocol is the basic Ethernet protocol used by 10 MBPS, 100 MBPS, and gigabit Ethernet. However, with higher-speed Ethernet implementations, the protocol has an additional full duplex (two-way simultaneous transmission) version. This eliminates any collisions on the full duplex links. When upgrading from 10 MBPS to 100 MBPS to full GBPS operation, system architectures remain the same. Both CSMA/CD mode for shared media applications and full-duplex mode for interswitch and high-performance server connections are retained. To support these various modes, a new gigabit NIC architecture using existing fiber channel components to perform low-level optical and data encoding functions are married to the CSMA/CD or Medium Access Control (MAC) data link control level. By combining Ethernet Medium Access Control (MAC) with selected fiber channel physical layer components that are familiar to users, all existing operational modes and system architectures can be retained while using fiber channels for gigabit data transmission. See Figure 8–10.

Understanding the protocols that LANs use helps in understanding how devices on a network communicate. Now let's take a look at the different types of cabling that we can use to link the devices together.

Network Cabling

The network cable is what binds the LAN in your office physically. How this cable connects all the devices in your office together is referred to as the

Figure 8–10 *Ethernet switch*

physical topology of your network. There are two types of topologies, however, that refer to your network, the logical topology and the physical topology.

A good example of the difference is the token ring network. The network operates by circulating a token around a ring that all devices attach to. This can be illustrated by drawing a circle and then drawing each device attached to that circle. This is logically how the token ring network is designed, but it is not exactly how it is physically wired together. Token ring networks are wired together in what we call a star topology. This means that there is a wiring hub or some other wire-concentrating device centrally located, and that device on a separate piece of twisted pair wire connect to this hub. If you were to illustrate this you would draw a box representing the hub, and from the box you would draw lines to each of the devices representing each device's independent connection to the hub. Even though the physical topology is a starlike design, token ring networks still operate logically as a ring. See Figure 8–11.

Token Ring Operating Topology

Token Ring Wiring Topology

Figure 8–11   *Ring vs. star topologies*

There are three main types of topologies you may encounter, star (the most common of the three), bus, and ring.

- **Star topology** is the most common type of wiring topology today. Although not as expensive as a bus topology, it is not very costly to set up and it is designed to be fairly fault tolerant. In a star topology, each device in the network is branched off a central hub unit. The hub performs a signal regeneration (or repeater) function. It takes an attenuated (soaked up) digital pulse and recreates it back into its original form. The star topology design is very simple to set up and adding new devices to the network is easy if you have a free connector

Figure 8-12 *Ethernet wiring hub*

on the hub. If a wire gets damaged, then the machine connected to that wire is the only one affected because the electronics performing the repeater function (signal regeneration) electrically isolate the machine from the other machines attached to the same hub. If the hub goes down, then all machines are affected. This makes it very easy to troubleshoot problems on a star topology. Both token ring and Ethernet networks use star topologies. Star topologies also can use all cable types—coaxial, twisted pair, and fiber. See Figure 8–12.

• **Bus topology** is the easiest to set up and the one that uses the least amount of cable. It consists of a single cable that is simply strung from one device to the next. This is usually done with coaxial cable. At either end of this cable is a terminating resistor that makes the wire become a closed electrical circuit. All devices share this communication path by taking turns sending and receiving information on the single wire. This means all devices hear all transmission being sent, but they ignore all transmissions not addressed to them. The simplicity of this design makes it ideal for use in small LAN environments, as well as being a cost-effective solution. The disadvantage of this however is in the lack of fault tolerance in the design. If there is a break anywhere along the wire, the whole network goes down. If this wire runs through the walls, it can be rather frustrating to find the break and repair it. Additionally, if terminating resistors go bad or one is removed, again the whole network is shut down. Originally, early PC LANs were wired with 50-ohm coaxial cable using this topology. The Ethernet design permits a maximum of 1,024 machines per Ethernet, comprising five segments and four repeaters. A more practical limit is about 20 to 50 per Ethernet. With bridged or switched Ethernet networks, hundreds to thousands of PCs can be interconnected

- **Ring topology** is designed exactly as it is named. In a physical ring topology, all devices are connected to one another by tapping into or by facilitating a wire ring connection. Information in this topology then flows around the ring in a single direction. This design is like the bus topology, in that it is also not very fault tolerant. If the ring is broken at any point or if a device linking the segments of the ring together is removed, the ring goes down completely. In practice, the LANs that use this topology have devices attached to them that compensate for this occurrence. Additionally most ring topologies use redundant ring paths to keep the network up in the event a single ring goes down. Fiber Distributed Data Interface (FDDI) is an example of a network using ring topology.

There is also what some people refer to as mesh topology, but you are very unlikely to encounter this type in local area networks because the added reliability provided by a mesh network links is offset by added wiring costs. An example of mesh network is the Internet. In the Internet, redundant links and alternate paths provide increased network reliability and capacity.

Now that you understand the different topology types, let's look at the cables that makes up the physical connection of the networks.

COAXIAL

The first widely accepted commercial uses of LANs were as broadband (analog transmission method) networks built in the early '80s. These networks used 75-ohm coaxial cable, the cable used in cable TV today. In 1982, the first Ethernet products were developed by an alliance of Xerox, Intel, and Digital; these products were eventually marketed by Digital. These early Ethernet LANs used a 50-ohm coaxial cable as opposed to the previous broadband use of 75-Ohm coaxial cable. In this design, all devices communicated and were attached across a single strand of coaxial cable (bus topology). The primary drawback of this LAN wire design is that if the cable breaks at any single spot, the entire LAN fails to operate. Coaxial can also be used in a star topology, but today this is very uncommon.

Coaxial cable is composed of one physical channel that carries the signal. Surrounding this physical channel is a layer of insulation followed by another concentric physical channel. This outer channel serves as a ground. Many of these cables or pairs of coaxial tubes can be placed in a single outer sheathing and, with repeaters, can carry information for a great distance. Depending on the technology used and other factors, twisted pair and optical fiber are alternatives to coaxial cable. See Figure 8–13. Early PC LANs using the thin coaxial cable could be configured for a standard segment of 185 meters or an extended segment of 300 meters. Five short or standard segments could be connected using repeaters, with each active segment containing 30 PCs. PCs could not communicate with PCs that were separated by more than two repeaters. When configured as an extended segment, the coaxial cable Ethernet could not be extended using repeaters. There were electrical limitations on the number of devices connected so that the extended segment Ethernet could only support 100 PCs.

Coaxial Cable Anatomy

Copper Wire
Core

Insulation

Wire Mesh

Outer Insulation

Figure 8–13   *Coaxial cable*

TWISTED PAIR

To overcome the problems associated with coaxial cabling, twisted-pair cable and wiring hubs were used. All clients and servers are wired to hubs using unshielded twisted-pair wire. In this case, if one cable broke, only that link to the hub was impacted. The demand for higher LAN transmission speeds required reduced signal crosstalk (signal crossover interference) from the cable. A cable grading scheme or category level was developed. The highest level will soon be category-6, rated to support transmission at speeds up to about 155 MBPS. The original telephone wire is category-3, rated at speeds up to 10 MBPS. Category-5 wire is rated at speeds up to 100 MBPS. and is the most widely used cable for telephony and LAN wiring today. The distance between the PC and the wiring hub is similar for all cable types. It is about 100 meters or 330 feet maximum.

Twisted pair is a set of ordinary copper wires that connects home and many business computers to the telephone company, or to a LAN. Electrical signaling is sent back and forth across this pair of wires. Since electrical signals travel across both wires, electromagnetic induction between pairs of wires may occur (This is known as crosstalk and can interfere with transmissions). To reduce crosstalk between pairs of wires, the two insulated copper wires are twisted around each other (thus becoming a twisted pair). Each signal on twisted pair requires both wires. Most twisted-pair cable contains multiple pairs. In some cases, the twisted pairs are enclosed in a foil shielding that functions as a ground. This is known as shielded twisted pair (STP). More commonly, the pairs are simply wrapped in a vinyl insulator. This is known as unshielded twisted pair (UTP). Token ring networks use shielded twisted pair primarily. It operated at speeds up to 16 MBPS over IBM's Type-1 shielded cable and runs today at 100 MBPS over STP Type 1a cable and UTP category-5 cable. Ethernet uses UTP. It began operating at 10 MBPS over category-3 cable but has evolved to fast Ethernet at 100 MBPS over category-5 UTP cable.

Twisted pair is now frequently installed with two pairs to the home, with the extra pair making it possible for you to add another line (perhaps for modem use) when you need it.

Twisted pair comes with each pair uniquely color coded (that is, blue/blue white, green/green white, brown/brown white, and orange/orange white color-coded pairs) when it is packaged in multiple pairs. Different uses such as analog, digital, and LAN Ethernet require different pair multiples.

Although twisted pair is often associated with home use, a higher grade of twisted pair is often used for horizontal wiring in LAN installations because it is less expensive than coaxial cable.

The wire you buy at a local hardware store for extensions from your phone or computer modem to a wall jack is not twisted pair. It is a side-by-side wire known as silver satin. The wall jack can have several configurations (for instance, RJ-1, RJ-45, Mod-8 offset) and pinouts (for instance, 2-wire, 4-wire, or 8-wire), depending on the kinds of wire the installation expects will be plugged in (for example, digital, analog, or LAN). (That's why you may sometimes find when you carry your notebook computer to another location that the wall jack connections won't match your plug.) See Figure 8–14.

FIBER

Fiber-optic cable refers to the technology of transmitting information as light impulses along a glass or plastic fiber. See Figure 8–15. The fiber-optic

Unshielded Twisted Pair Anatomy

Twisted Pairs

Outer Insulation

Figure 8–14 *Twisted-pair*

cable used in LANs is usually multimode with a graded index of refraction. Refraction bends the light so much as it travels though the glass fiber that the light cannot escape the fiber during its journey.

Multimode cable has a core diameter of 62.5 microns and a cladding diameter of 125 microns. The amount that light is bent increases as the light moves to the outside of the core, near the cladding. In the center of the cladding, the bending ratio is 1 to 1; at the outside, it is 1 to 1000. In this manner, light traveling down the core is bent back inward toward the center of the core until it emerges at the opposite end of the fiber cable.

The single mode fiber cable is used in telecommunications for telephony transmission. It works on reflection. The core size is so small (8.3 microns) that the boundary between the core and the cladding forms a mirrorlike surface, similar to the reflection that creates mirages in the desert. The light traveling through the core is reflected off this surface until it emerges at the other end of the fiber cable. Single mode cable is capable of longer runs and higher transmission speeds than is multimode cable. Multimode cable can run up to 6,000 feet before requiring a repeater. It operates at speeds up to 1 GBPS. In contrast, single mode cable can run about 20 miles before requiring a repeater and operate at speeds up to 40 GBPS. As LANs move to higher speeds, more single mode cable will be employed to interconnect LAN components.

Fiber-optic cable carries much more information than conventional copper wire and is far less subject to electromagnetic interference. Most telephone company long-distance lines are now fiber optic. Transmission on fiber-optic cable requires repeating (signal regeneration), like digital transmission over copper wire does, but the distance between repeaters is significantly longer.

The glass fiber requires more protection within an outer cable than copper. This helps protect it from impact and other possible destructive occurrences.

Fiber-optic transmission passes an optical signal (flash of light) over an optical link using an *electrical data signal* and a *modulated light signal*.

The electrical data signal enters a driver which turns on and off (modulates) a source of light to produce a modulated light signal. The modulated light signal then travels through the fiber-optic cable until it reaches a light sensor (photoreceptor diode) at the far end. This sensor, sometimes called a *detector*, converts (demodulates) the light signal into a small electrical signal. This signal passes through an amplifier that transforms it into a detectable electrical signal. The driver and the light source together are the transmitter. The detector and amplifier make up the receiver. The principle benefits of fiber-optic transmission are that:

- Fiber is capable of very high speeds—there is no electrical interaction at higher speeds as there is in twisted-pair wiring.
- Fiber is good for harsh physical environments—strong electrical fields or water does not disrupt transmission.
- Fiber isolates electrically on site from another—this eliminates problems caused by ground loops and electrical storms.

In spite of the benefits of fiber-optic cabling, we are not likely to be running fiber-optic cable to each desktop. Wiring from wiring closets and the repeaters therein to the desktop remains unshielded twisted pair. To support the high transmission speeds required (more than 10 or 16 MBPS) for video, the unshielded twisted-pair wiring needs to be UL Level V (or Electronic Industries Association/Telecommunications Industries Association category-5) wiring.

For these reasons and because the installation of any new wiring is labor-intensive, few communities yet have fiber-optic wires or cables from the phone company's branch office to local customers.

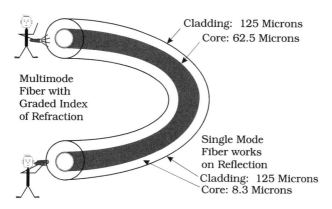

Figure 8–15 *Fiber cable operation*

Peer-to-Peer versus Client-Server Networks

Now it is time to examine the software used to bind the network together. The software chosen for a network determines how a network communicates and how we administer users and nodes.

The two main types of network software operation, as identified earlier, are peer-to-peer and client-server. Most software today offers the ability to choose either type or a combination of both types of networking. As an example, a Windows 95-based PC can be a peer in a peer-to-peer solution as well as be a client in a client-server network on a single network or on an extended network. Before we look into the various software options, perhaps we should define peer-to-peer and client-server.

A peer-to-peer network is one in which all the devices on the network are considered equals. This means that each machine is responsible for maintaining its own users, resources, and how others can access those resources on the network. This is a network that is easy to set up and maintain since logging on to a server is not required.

Client-server describes the relationship between two computers in which one acts like a client, making a service request to the other, the server, which responds to the request. The client-server model has become one of the central ideas of network computing. Most applications written today use the client-server model. In this model, the application runs on two systems, with the client portion focusing most commonly on the resource-minimal tasks like data presentation and lighter processing, allowing the server to focus on the resource-intensive tasks it is geared for, such as data storage and retrieval. Using this scenario, the clients—usually PCs—can be smaller, less powerful, and therefore, less expensive systems which share the resources of a server for the big work.

In the past, the term has been used to distinguish distributed computing by smaller dispersed computers from the centralized computing of mainframe computers. But this distinction has for the most part disappeared, since mainframes and their applications function now using the client-server model.

In the usual client-server model, at least one computer is always active and awaiting requests from the clients. This computer runs a special operating system software called the NOS (Network Operating System). This software allows the server to create and administer users, monitor and control security, and provide shared resources to clients. Examples of NOSs would be Windows NT Server and Novell NetWare. The other computers attached to the network then act as clients, making requests of the server. These requests may be for shared information on the server, to log on and secure access to the network, or for the use of shared peripherals, like printers. In order for the client to be able to make these requests, the client must be running special software called the client software. This software allows the client to communicate with the server in a fashion that the server understands. TCP/IP is an example of this software. If the server uses TCP/IP to communicate with clients, then the client must also load TCP/IP. Today, Windows 95/98 comes with the client's software as part of the complete operating system. Earlier systems like Windows 3.x need separate software drivers provided by the NOS manufacturer.

Table 8–2 summarizes the conditions that influence the choice between peer-to-peer and client-server approaches.

Table 8.2 *Peer-to-peer versus client-server*

Peer-to-peer	Client-server
Very few machines to connect together	There are a large number of computers and users to setup and administer
Lower cost, NOS purchase unnecessary	Centralized control over shared resources is needed
Setup is easier, complex user and groups are not required	You have support for distributed applications that require a client-server NOS
Network security is not a concern	Security is a concern

Windows 3.11

Windows 3.11, also known as "Windows for Workgroups," was not Microsoft's first attempt at networking software. Microsoft had been in the networking arena for many years, selling a client-server product called LAN Manager. The trouble with LAN Manager was that it had to compete with a market-dominant Novell NetWare. However, most networks using this LAN Manager software were relatively large PC networks.

There were a large number of computers that were not networked because the cost of networking them using client-server software was prohibitive. Also client-server software required trained staff to administer it. Most nonnetworked users, however, could see the benefit of having network capabilities. What they needed was a software package that allow them to do a lot of the things that client-server software did that was inexpensive and required no specialized staff. This was the reason for the explosion of peer-to-peer packages in the very early 90's. The two dominant products were LANtastic by Artisoft and Microsoft Windows for Workgroups 3.11.

The biggest advantage to Windows for Workgroups over LANtastic was the fact the networking software was built into the operating system itself. In other words there were very few things you had to load in the CONFIG.SYS or the AUTOEXEC.BAT in order to get the network running. Second, these drivers were included with the disks that came with the Windows for Workgroups product.

The following is the only driver that had to be loaded in the CONFIG.SYS file for Windows 3.11 to provide network capabilities.

```
DEVICE=C:\WINDOWS\IFSHLP.SYS
```

The IFSHLP.SYS file is used to provide real-mode support for the IFS Manager. The IFS Manager is a software component for Windows 3.11 responsible for passing information to the appropriate device, including networked devices.

The following is the only line required by Windows 3.11 for the AUTOEXEC.BAT file.

```
C:\WINDOWS\NET START
```

This line is used to initialize the programs used by Windows 3.11 and bind them to the network adapter.

When a Windows for Workgroups computer is not seeing the network, these two files are a good place to start troubleshooting. If there is a problem with either, error messages indicating that the network adapter is not functioning or that a server cannot be found are flashed on the screen. These screens scroll by quickly, so be sure to use the F8 key to see a line-by-line execution of both the CONFIG.SYS and AUTOEXEC.BAT file.

PROTOCOL.INI FILE • When Windows for Workgroups is installed, the setup program creates a file called PROTOCOL.INI. This file is used to define network parameters used by Windows for Workgroups networking. There is little need to examine and modify this file. Using the network icon under the control panel changes all the settings in it. The only exception is if more than one network card is used in the machine. In this case, settings such as the IRQ and the I/O address must be set on the boards to not conflict with each other. Generally, setting IRQ and I/O addresses is a function of setting up the LAN hardware. The best way to view and edit the PROTOCOL.INI file is to use the program SYSEDIT. Below is an example of a PROTOCOL.INI file.

```
[network.setup]
version=0x3110
netcard=ms$ne2clone,1,MS$NE2CLONE,4
```

```
transport=tcpip-32n,MSTCP32
transport=ms$netbeui,NETBEUI
lana0=ms$ne2clone,1,tcpip-32n
lana1=ms$ne2clone,1,ms$netbeui
[net.cfg]
PATH=C:\NET\NET.CFG
[MS$NE2CLONE]
[Link Driver NE2000]
[MSTCP32]
BINDINGS=NE2000
LANABASE=0
[NETBEUI]
BINDINGS=NE2000
LANABASE=1
SESSIONS=10
NCBS=12
```

NETWORK SETUP • To change and configure the network setting under Windows 3.11, you use two different programs. The first is the Window's setup, found in the MAIN window group under the program manager. The second item is the network control panel, which we examine after going through the network setup program.

When entering the MAIN group, locate and double-click on the WINDOWS SETUP icon. When this icon is double-clicked, it opens a window that allows configuring many areas of Windows networking. Point to the word OPTIONS on the Windows menu bar, then click and select CHANGE NETWORK SETTINGS. The Window in Figure 8–16 appears.

From here, many PROTOCOL.INI file settings can be modified The first option, Networks, permits choosing the networks in which this machine participates. The Microsoft Windows Network is the peer-to-peer choice. If this machine is also going to work on a client-server network, then select an additional network from those listed in the drop-down box. If another network is chosen, add the programs for that network to the computer as well as any configuration parameters that may be required in the CONFIG.SYS and AUTOEXEC.BAT files. In Figure 8–17, a Novell NetWare network has been chosen along with the Microsoft Windows Network

Sharing allows setup for sharing devices across the network. Selecting this option here allows others to access and use disks and printers attached to this PC. Enabling this does not mean, however, that existing disks and printers are shared automatically. In order to share a disk and files on the disk, a share must be set up, by using the File Manager once sharing is enabled. Likewise, to share printers, the Print Manager is used to set up the share. See Figure 8–18.

Figure 8–16   *Windows 3.1 network setup*

Figure 8–17   *Windows 3.1 networks*

The network drivers menu selection allows selection and configuration of the network communication software. Specifically, this is referring to the driver used by Windows 3.11 to communicate to the PC's network adapter and the transport protocol. Both items must be selected correctly or the PC cannot talk with or be able to see the network. See Figure 8–19.

Figure 8–18 *Windows 3.1 sharing*

The PROTOCOL.INI file sets the network adapter driver to be used. This allows Windows to bind the transport protocol to the adapter board when the transport protocol is selected. The PC uses a command in the AUTOEXEC.BAT file to load the actual driver file. The references here specify the type of NIC and the specific setting for the card like the IRQ and the I/O address. These would then be displayed in the [netcard] section of the PROTOCOL.INI file. The word NETCARD in the brackets would be replaced with the name of the actual card type displayed in the netcard= line. So, in the example of this file displayed earlier in this section, the [netcard] section is the [MS$NE2CLONE]. This section then has several lines of text reflecting the parameters set for the card. With the example displayed earlier, since the card is using all automatic settings, the section is left

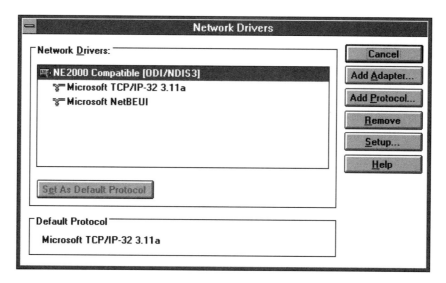

Figure 8–19 *Windows 3.1 network drivers*

Figure 8–20   *NE2000 compatible card software setup*

empty. If they were not, then a list of the parameters displayed would be seen. See Figure 8–20.

A transport protocol must be selected for a network. Transport protocols perform the functions assigned to Layer 3, Layer 4, and Layer 5 of the ISO seven-layer model. The same transport protocol must be used on all machines for the network. If needed, multiple protocols can be used in a network. However, life is simpler and networks tend to be more reliable if only a single transport protocol is used. In this example, the client is using both NetBEUI and TCP/IP. Once these are set, Windows then loads this during the Windows start-up sequence. If a network other than a Windows network like NetWare is selected, then additional transport protocol drivers may need to be loaded in the AUTOEXEC.BAT file.

Like choosing an adapter, choosing a transport protocol requires setting certain parameters for each protocol selected. These parameters are different for each protocol. As an example, below is a picture of TCP/IP settings for Windows for Workgroups. There are a number of settings that must be supplied to Windows in order for it to use TCP/IP. These settings would be available through a network administrator. If an NT server using DHCP (Dynamic Host Configuration Protocol) is available, then just select it and the Windows NT server configures these settings automatically for you during the log on. More detail is provided in Chapter 16. See Figure 8–21.

As with the adapter, choosing the protocol and the settings for that protocol writes that information to the PROTOCOL.INI file. This information is written into the [protocol] section. Multiple [protocol] sections are created when more than one protocol is used under Windows. The section name is based on the names found in the *transport=* line of the [net-

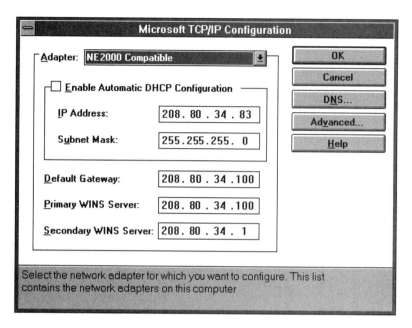

Figure 8–21 *Windows 3.1 TCP/IP configuration*

work.setup] section. So in the earlier example of the PROTOCOL.INI file, there is a section [MSTCP32] for TCP/IP and a section [NETBEUI] for NetBEUI.

THE NETWORK CONTROL PANEL • The network control panel is used to configure the connection of the computer and user to the network. The network control panel is entered through the Windows 3.1 control panel. Connecting to the network implies the log-on process of supplying a password and a user name. Depending on what type of network the PC is connecting to, there can be individual settings that need to be configured. The key setting is the workgroup identification. If it is not set to the correct workgroup name, it becomes more difficult to find other peer-to-peer networked PCs on the LAN because only your workgroup is easily visible. Double-click on the network control panel to see the window in Figure 8–22.

This window controls the peer-to-peer network settings used by Windows for Workgroups. The network is organized as workgroups. Each machine belongs to a workgroup, and the workgroups that the machine belongs to can be switched. Additionally, from here passwords can be changed as needed.

Figure 8–22   *Windows 3.1 Microsoft Windows Network*

WINDOWS 95/98

Windows 95/98, like Windows 3.11 for Workgroups, can provide peer-to-peer connectivity. Unlike Windows for Workgroup, it also comes with client software to allow it to behave as a client on multiple kinds of networks. This makes Windows 95/98 very flexible, whatever network it is integrated into. To configure Windows 95/98 for networking, open the network control panel. The easiest way to do this is to point to the network neighborhood and click the right mouse button. Next, select properties for the adjacent pop-up menu, as shown in Figure 8–23.

This window controls all aspects of networking with a Windows 95 client. Notice the tabs across the top of the window. Each tab controls a different aspect of networking.

The first tab, Configuration, sets the client type, adapter cards, protocols used, and services loaded. An example of these would be Client for Microsoft Network, NE2000 adapter, TCP/IP, and File and Print sharing.

These choices can be added or removed from this screen, or if they have any defining properties, those can be set from here as well. An example of that would be the necessary TCP/IP settings required for this computer to talk across the network. Another example of this would be the properties for the client type. Client for Microsoft Networks has within its properties the ability to have this machine behave in a peer-to-peer fashion, or as a Win-

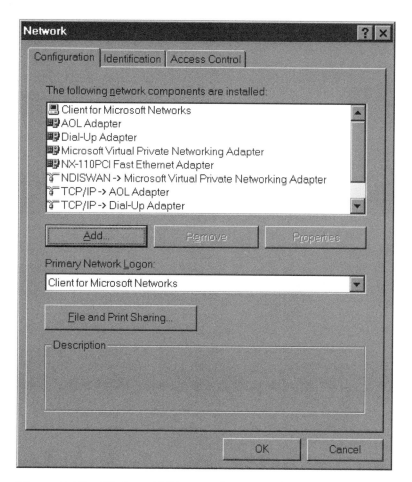

Figure 8–23 *Windows 95/98 networking control window*

dows 95 client on an NT client-server network. To set up a peer-to-peer network under Windows 95/98, the service file and print sharing for Microsoft networks must be loaded.

One of each of these items must be selected for the PC to communicate across the network. Not all of these things are set automatically when the plug-and-play system picks up the network interface card. The Identification tab is shown in Figure 8–24.

The Identification tab sets the identification and the name of the peer-to-peer workgroup. The name used is the name that appears to other users that are using the network neighborhood. This name is also the name that is used by other users creating shares on this machine.

Figure 8–24 *Workgroup identification*

The Access tab sets the access level for this computer. See Figure 8–25. The two choices offered reflect the different types of networks in which this client participates. User level security indicates that security is based on a user's name and the password. In order for this to work, there has to be a centralized security provider like an NT server or a NetWare server.

Share-level security is security that is set for each resource share the machine has. A share represents a resource that the user of the machine designates as useable by other users. The user creating the share then chooses what level of use the other users have with this share. For example, a user may set one of his shared disk drives as read only and the other as full access.

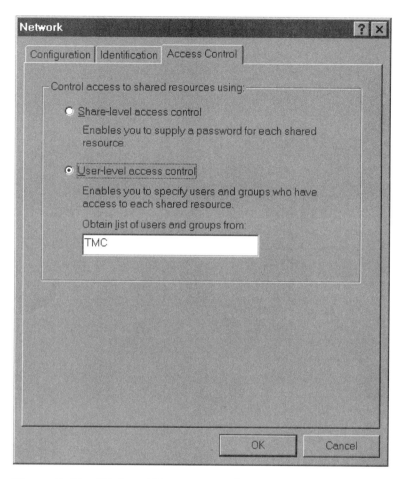

Figure 8–25 *Windows 95 access control*

Any user on the network then has that assigned level of access when using the share. The level of access has nothing to do with the user logging into the network with a specific name and password. Thus, share level access is designed for a peer-to-peer network

WINDOWS NT

Windows NT differs from the other systems in that it can be configured to use a server operating system and it can be a client operating system. These are known as Windows NT server and as Windows NT workstation respectively. When installing NT, make sure to install the server version for client-server networking.

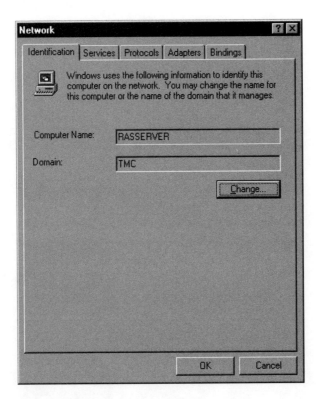

Figure 8–26 *NT networking panel*

If you install Windows NT workstation, you can participate in Windows peer-to-peer networks. This permits supporting up to ten active connections into your PC. Servers in contrast can support hundreds of active connections. The advantage of using Windows NT is that the settings that are used to set up and configure the machines are almost identical. Let's look at the configuration screens for NT.

After installing NT, view the control panel for the networking by pointing at the network neighborhood and clicking the right mouse button, then choosing properties from the pop-up menu. Figure 8–26 appears. Much like Windows 95/98, the different tabs control different aspects of networking. Each has specific settings that must be there in order for your network to work.

The Identification section is used to define this machine on the network. When using a peer-to-peer network, this is used to define the workstation name and workgroup in which they participate. On a client-server network, this is used to select a domain.

Figure 8–27 *Windows NT services configuration*

Windows NT uses domains as a way of creating a single administrative unit. All machines that are part of the domain are subject to domain control and rights. The machine that controls the domain is known as the Primary Domain Controller (PDC). Each domain has a single PDC. A domain may also have Backup Domain Controllers (BDC). A domain can have more than one BDC. If a PDC or a BDC cannot be found during the log-on process to verify a name and password, the user is not able to access the domain and log on.

The Services section controls the services running on the NT computer. Both servers and workstations use services. Services are used by the machine to provide certain functions to users that connect to it, or for users using it. An example of this would be Remote Access Service (RAS). RAS allows the machine to act as a dial-in or a dial-out computer, thus providing remote access to another network or to the network to which this machine is currently attached. See Figure 8–27.

To add a service, click on the "add" button to get a list of services not already installed. It is important to note that services take vital memory resources, so the more services loaded the slower and less efficiently the Windows NT machine runs. It is a good habit to always remove services that are not being used. Additionally, each service may have properties that must be set in order for it to perform as expected. Some services have no properties to set.

Some basic NT services are:

Computer browser—finds shared PCs and servers on a Windows network.

DHCP relay agent—permits forwarding of Dynamic Host Configuration Protocol broadcasts across a router to a remote DHCP server to assign IP addresses to the broadcasting PC.

RIP for Internet Protocol—enables IP routers to exchange routing information.

RPC Service—permits programs with Remote Procedure Calls (RPC) to run procedures on other PCs.

Server— sets up the server side of client-server networking; this is the server message block protocol.

Simple TCP/IP services—provides simple client-side TCP/IP network functions like Daytime and Quote of the Day.

Workstation—this is the client service for the server message block client-server network.

The Protocol section is used to install and configure any of the protocols NT can use. Like Windows 95/98, NT can use multiple protocols. This allows NT to participate on almost all networks types. If a machine cannot see other machines on the network, come here to make sure the right protocol is being used and that it is configured properly. See Figure 8–28.

As with services, it is best to limit the number of protocols used with Windows NT. Not only do protocols require precious memory resources, but they may also slow down the performance of Windows NT machines on the network. Common protocols that may be implemented on NT machines are:

DLC (Data Link Control) protocol—used to access IBM mainframe computers.

NetBEUI protocol—the original Windows peer-to-peer networking protocol.

NWLink IPX/SPX compatible transport protocol—used to communicate with Novell NetWare servers.

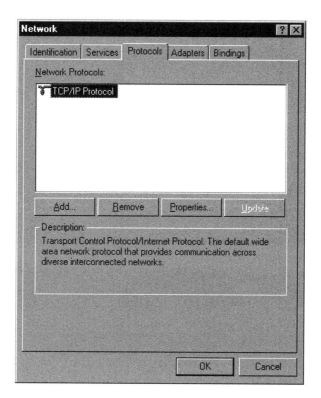

Figure 8–28 *Windows NT Protocol section*

Point-to-Point Tunneling Protocol (PPTP)—used to tunnel through TCP/IP networks and securely access resources on remote servers. The Remote Access Server software uses this protocol. PPTP encapsulates NetBEUI protocol and other communications and transmits them securely to a remote server over an IP network.

Streams environment—a client server protocol used in Windows and NetWare environments to support continuous data streams (for instance, MPEG video) between multimedia devices.

TCP/IP Protocol—the most commonly used suite of protocols today. TCP/IP supports both LAN and Internet communications.

When installing a protocol, make sure you know all the settings that are required for configuring it. As an example, with TCP/IP know the IP address, DNS server, and routers. Without these, loading the protocol is not enough to make the network function. Select protocol and then use the properties button to configure.

The Adapters section, like protocols, is used to add, remove, and configure any hardware network adapter in the machine. NT can have multiple adapters installed in it. This means an Ethernet network card and a Ring token ring network card could be installed in the machine at the same time. Doing this allows this machine to route network traffic from one side of the network to another. See Figure 8–29.

During the installation of Windows NT, the setup program was given information about the network card(s) that are installed in it. It needs to know this because it has to load the correct drivers for each NIC. Additionally, the operating system needs to know certain hardware parameters that are specific to each card. From this screen, parameters for any of the installed adapters can be added, removed, or changed.

The Bindings section is used to show how the various service, protocols, and adapters are bound together as well as the order within which each is bound. See Figure 8–30. This means that not all services and protocols have to be bound to every adapter in the machine. Oftentimes, network performance can be improved by changing the binding order. For example,

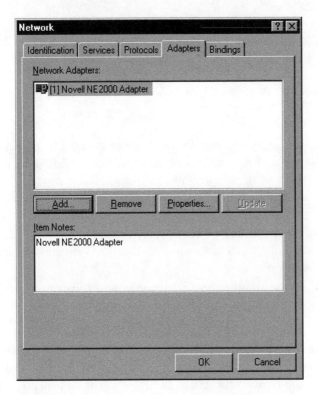

Figure 8–29 *Windows NT adapters section*

Figure 8–30 *Windows NT binding section*

TCP/IP and NetBEUI run on a Windows NT machine. If NetBEUI is used to communicate to all the machines on the network and TCP/IP is used to communicate on the Internet only, binding NetBEUI higher in the binding order means that the Windows NT machine uses NetBEUI first when any network request is sent. Since users communicate more often across their network to one another instead of across the Internet, placing TCP/IP higher than NetBEUI would enhance performance.

The bindings are displayed graphically so the order is easily visible. By clicking on the plus sign next to a service, protocol, or adapter, the orders of bindings can be viewed. These graphical binding displays can be used with the move up or move down buttons to change the bindings order. Notice also that bindings can be enabled or disabled, as well.

NETWARE

NetWare is client-server network software. It is provided with a server NOS and client software for both Windows and DOS. See Figure 8–31.

The NetWare client programs for DOS and Windows 3.11 were originally IPX.COM and NETX.EXE. The IPX.COM program was tailored during installation to a specific LAN board. This tailoring involved setting IRQ and I/O port settings into the IPX.COM file. NetWare client software became more generalized with the Open Data link Interface (ODI) software. This employed a base driver program LSL.COM which permitted up to four protocol stacks (like SPX/IPX and TCP/IP) to use the same LAN board. The board driver program, TOKEN for IBM token ring cards, used a general NET.CFG file to get the board IRQ and I/O address parameters. The NET.CFG file was a text file easily edited using any text editor. This made adapting to different board configurations relatively easy.

Novell's transport protocol stack, the Sequenced Packet Exchange / Internet Packet Exchange (SPX/IPX), was loaded using IPXODI.COM and the NETX.EXE programs. This software was provided with NetWare version 3.xx. Version 4.xx of NetWare replaced the NETX.EXE program with Virtual Loadable Modules (VLMs) that were loaded using the VLM manager program VLM.EXE.

Figure 8–31 *NetWare DOS client programs*

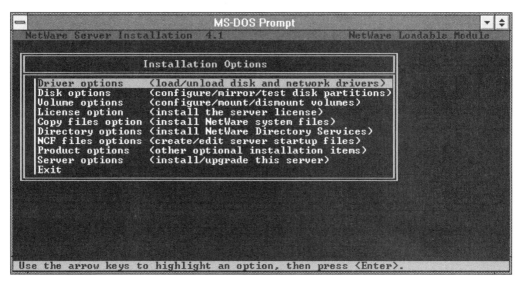

Figure 8–32 *NetWare server installation menu*

Today the Novell NetWare client is built into Windows 95/98 and Windows NT. Novell provides special client software that enhances the security and performance of the basic Windows NetWare clients as well. Accessing Novell NetWare servers is done with TCP/IP for NetWare 5.xx or by SPX/IPX for Novell 3.xx and 4.xx servers.

NetWare servers make a good diagnostic tool because they are easily accessible using NetWare drivers on a bootable DOS diskette. Installing NetWare server software requires setting up a small DOS partition on the fixed disk drive, then running the NetWare installation disk to copy the software and configure the server's fixed disk drives and LAN boards for network operation. See Figure 8–32.

Server software installation and configuration starts with installing and configuring the LAN board drivers. Then the disk drives have volumes installed and formatted for use. The format is a Novell NetWare format and not a DOS or Windows format. Then software is copied to the disk drives and the server is set to administer. In the final steps, an administrator must log on to the NetWare server and configure users, file access permissions, disk compression, printer sharing, and the other common tasks associated with configuring a network server.

Windows 98 Network Options

Let's set up Windows 98 peer-to-peer networking. Find a PC with a network adapter installed. It can be a working PC on an existing LAN as long as you remember to cancel the changes to the network setup we are making.

1. Get to a PC that has Windows 98 networking software installed. Open the networking configuration window. It is entered using the control panel and clicking on the network icon or by highlighting the network neighborhood on the desktop, clicking the right mouse button and selecting properties. The window that appears should look like Figure 8–23. Remove all existing network setup by highlighting each item and selecting remove. Be careful here to not click on the access control tab because it changes the existing network configuration. We do not want to do that. So follow the steps below carefully to avoid changing the existing configuration.

2. Click on the add button, select service, and click on the new add button.

3. Select File and printer sharing for Microsoft Networks and click OK.

4. In the panel should appear Client for Microsoft Networks, Dial-up Adapter, TCP/IP (or Net-BEUI), and File and printer sharing for Microsoft networks.

5. Select Add, pick Protocol, Microsoft, NetBEUI (or TCP/IP), and click OK. The NetBEUI protocol should appear in our list.

6. Select Add, pick Adapter, Novell/Anthem, NE2000 Compatible, and click OK. The NE2000 should be linked to the NetBEUI (and TCP/IP) protocols. The Dial-Up adapter is linked to these protocols as well.

7. Click on Client for Microsoft Networks and then click properties. Verify the Quick logon menu selection is checked. Click OK.

8. Click on file and print sharing and verify both file and printer sharing options are checked.

9. Click on the Identification tab, enter a computer name, workgroup name (for example, our favorite HQTRS), and enter a computer description—Pentium III 500 MHz screamer.

10. Click on the Access control tab and select share level access control.

11. This completes the peer-to-peer network setup. Clicking OK will cause the computer to reboot and implement the changes we specified. So if the computer is on an existing network, *click on cancel* to avoid changing the existing network settings.

Internet Access

Almost all PCs are configured to access the Internet. It is probably the most common use of home PCs today. Typically, Internet access is performed using cable modems, using dial-up networking into a local Internet Service Provider (ISP), or using subscription-based software such as America On-Line (AOL) or similar services provided by Internet Service Providers (ISPs). AOL software can also be used with LAN connections and high-speed cable modems.

Internet communications use Transmission Control Protocol/Internet Protocol (TCP/IP) software. This software is built in to Windows 95/98, Windows NT, and it can be added to Windows 3.11. As an example, AOL software supports TCP/IP communication to AOL via the Internet. Web browser software and AOL software are the applications that are used to surf the Internet. See Figure 8–33.

Dial-up and AOL connections require no special IP address assignment for access to the Internet. When logging on to AOL or an ISP, they automatically assign an IP address to your connection. This is similar to DHCP in Windows networking in that the IP addresses are assigned dynamically as users require them, but it is not Windows DHCP.

Cable modems are set up like any local area network configuration. They often require a fixed IP address assignment for the PC to precisely identify their subscribers. This fixed IP address is unique to the cable modem system. The cable modem connection functions like a gigantic LAN and the IP address assigned is not a direct Internet IP address. In the cable modem, network routers reassign this internal cable modem IP address to an official working Internet IP address. Cable modem access is high speed and available 24 by 7—24 hours a day and 7 days a week. It is simple to operate because it is as though your PC had a direct LAN connection to the Internet.

In Figure 8–33, the PC is set up to access the Internet using a local area network. As long as the LAN TCP/IP is set properly, the PC can use it to access the Internet. Setting the LAN connections properly requires that domain name servers, routers, and high-speed links into ISPs must all be configured to pass TCP/IP packets from the PC to the Internet and vice versa.

Figure 8–33 *Internet Explorer network setup*

Similarly, AOL software can be configured for access to AOL using a LAN and the Internet. See Figure 8–34.

With AOL, the LAN and modem configurations are setup using the setup button on the sign-on screen shown in the middle of the figure. Expert add menu selection displays both the LAN and dial-up connections defined for this AOL installation. The LAN connection figures out the TCP/IP details automatically. It can also be manually configured.

The modem configuration for AOL is setup automatically by selecting menu options using the AOL software. Windows dial-up connections to the Internet are similarly set up automatically with a Windows Internet connection Wizard.

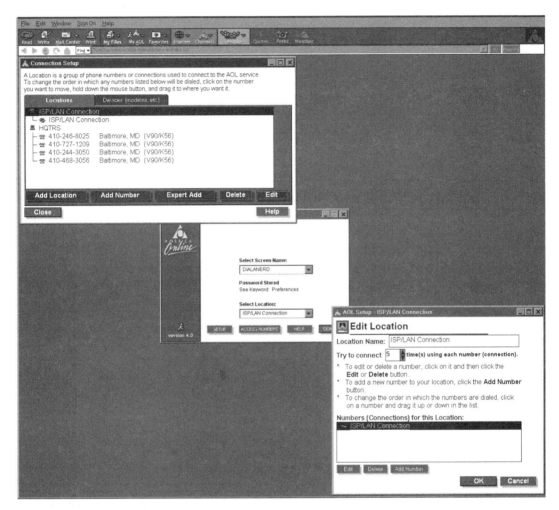

Figure 8–34   *AOL TCP/IP LAN configuration*

There is more discussion on Windows dial-up networking in Chapter 16. If these connections are not configured properly or if there are problems on the Internet when accessing web sites, the PC can easily lock up or crash. PCs are highly sensitive to communications problems. When troubleshooting any PC performance or lock up problems one of the first questions should be "Were you connected to a LAN or the Internet?"

Testing an Internet Connection

This exercise sets up an AOL connection and tests access to the Internet via AOL.

1. Get a PC with installed modem and AOL software. We are going to use this to set up and verify connection to AOL.

2. Open the Control Panel and select modems. Test the modem installation by selecting Diagnostics, the COM port with the modem board icon next to it and the modem description beside it. Click more information to display the modem commands, responses and the highest modem transmission speed (it should be 115,200 bps). When this response is received, the modem is working properly. If not, then there is likely to be either bad driver software or hardware configuration conflicts that must be resolved for the modem to operate properly. Write down the COM port number to which the modem is assigned.

3. Install the AOL software using its installation Wizard. AOL software does not use Windows dial-up networking to operate. It contains its own modem control software. The AOL installation process guides you through modem selection and assigns phone numbers for accessing AOL. Let AOL complete the automatic installation process.

4. If the AOL software cannot detect a modem during installation, the modem may not be responding appropriately. Select a Hayes compatible modem and use the COM port setting of our working modem. (alternatively, if the modem manufacturer and description matches any of those on the list, pick it or one that is close to it).

5. Try to connect. If the AOL software cannot talk to the modem (that is, cannot initialize the modem) we have not reached first base. Go to the AOL setup menu, pick expert setup (it is not for experts but just quicker), select Devices (modems, etc.), pick the modem and select edit. The modem should appear highlighted in a panel. Verify the correct COM port is selected, the speed is set for 115,200 bps, and the speaker volume is loud.

6. Edit commands and enter in the modem setup string line: AT &F s9=1 ^M These commands loosely translate to: AT means Attention modem, s9=1 means modem detect carrier signal in one millisecond, ^M sends a carriage return character to the modem. Hit OK and Close. Try reconnecting. If the modem does not initialize, we have a hardware or driver configuration error in the PC or a bad modem. If the modem dials the line, and connects, we are fine. If the modem tries to dial the line and there is a phone problem it is likely to return a message of "no dial tone." The worst case is where the modem dials the number and nothing.

7. If the modem dials the number and nothing happens, pick up the phone and call the AOL access number to verify that a computer is answering that phone and not the telephone recording stating that it is a long distance call.

The goal of this study break was to setup and troubleshoot a dial-up connection into AOL. Similar steps would be followed to test any dial-up connection.

A+ 8.3 Installing and Configuring Network Interface Cards

The network interface card (NIC) is the interface between the PC and the network cabling. The job of the NIC is to prepare, send, receive, and control the flow of data from the machine. So far the software side of the network has been examined, but without NICs the network does not work. There are many different types of NICs. Only NICs of a particular type can communicate with one another. This is because they use different languages, called data communications protocols, as mentioned earlier. So an Ethernet card using CSMA/CD cannot talk directly to a token ring card using token-passing ring protocol.

Installing a NIC is like installing any other adapter into a PC. Basically, the PC case is opened and the NIC card is installed in an open bus slot for the type of bus it uses, that is, ISA bus slot or PCI bus slot. It is then bolted into place and the case is closed. Now the fun part begins. Like all adapters, LAN adapters must have a unique IRQ, I/O, DMA, and shared memory areas. Setting these parameters varies from NIC manufacturer to NIC manufacturer. Older cards used jumpers to set the parameters, others used an EPROM that can be configured using special configuration programs. Most of today's cards are Windows 95/98 plug-and-play cards.

Jumpers

Some NICs have special jumpers in addition to those that set IRQ and I/O port address. These jumpers indicate to the NIC the cable type to use and how to configure its driver circuits to operate on that cable. For example, early Ethernet NICs used coaxial cable. They could be configured for a standard cable segment length of 185 meters or an extended cable segment of 300 meters. The 185 meter configuration permitted repeaters while the 300 meter configuration did not. Jumpers on the Ethernet NIC determined the cable configuration.

Some NICs have more than one port that they use to connect to different cable types. As an example, Ethernet cards use three different cable types. Each of these cable types has a different type of connector. In some NICs, jumpers set which cable connector is active. This also can be done using the configuration software that may come with your card. Newer cards are self-sensing and automatically adjust to the cable type connected.

Software Setup

Most LAN NICs today are configured using the Windows plug-and-play configuration software and driver programs that come with Windows 95/98 or Windows NT. Some boards were configured using special configuration software to change IRQ settings and I/O port address settings. These boards were manufactured around the time that the IBM MCA bus was sold in PS-/2 systems. Western Digital manufactured several Ethernet boards that were configured in this manner.

Software setup enables the PC's operating system to communicate and control access to the NIC. For the operating system to do this it must recognize and install driver software that communicates with the NIC. Similarly to other installed adapters, a software driver program makes the operating system recognize and work with the NIC. Software driver programs must precisely match the NIC installed. The only exceptions being NE1000 and NE2000 NICs. These NICs became the standard to which clone NIC cards were designed and manufactured. These clone boards use generic Novell / Anthem-compatible drivers. See Figure 8–35.

WINDOWS 3.X SETUP

With Windows 3.X Setup for the NICs, the file that is key is the AUTOEXEC.BAT. In this file we load the DOS real mode driver that allows DOS to interface with the NIC. A typical statement would be the following:

```
LH C:\NET\NE2000.COM
```

This statement only loads the board driver, not any of the supporting drivers. As an example with NetWare, you must load supporting software as well as the board driver. Additionally, this software must be loaded in a specific order if it is to interface properly.

```
LH C:\NET\LSL
LH C:\NET\NE2000.COM
LH C:\NET\IPXODI.COM
LH C:\NET\VLM.EXE
```

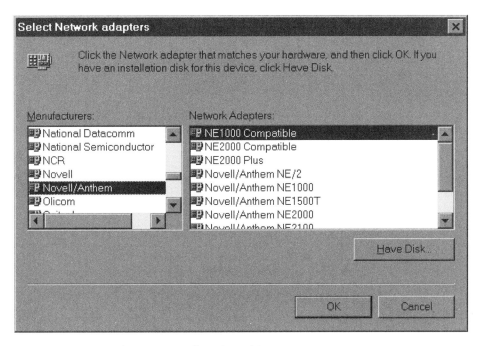

Figure 8–35 *Windows 98 Novell/Anthem drivers.*

The commands above are used to load the LAN software for Novell Net-Ware in a DOS or Windows 3.1x client PC. The software loaded is the link support layer—(LSL.COM), the Novell NE2000 NIC driver—(NE2000.COM), the Internet Packet Exchange open data link interface protocol software—(IPXODI.COM), and the Virtual Loadable Module—(VLM.EXE DOS) client software control program.

A very easy and common mistake made when networking with Windows 3.x and DOS is mixing up the loading order of the above. When these drivers load they display a message that can help you determine what may be wrong. The only trouble is that these messages display quickly and then are gone. To aid in troubleshooting, put a pause line between each.

```
LH C:\NET\LSL
pause
LH C:\NET\NE2000.COM
pause
LH C:\NET\IPXODI.COM
pause
LH C:\NET\VLM.EXE
pause
```

When each command is successful the following messages are displayed:

LSL.COM:

NetWare Link Support Layer v2.14 (941011)

(C) Copyright 1990-1994 Novell, Inc. All Rights Reserved.

The configuration file used was "C:\NET\NET.CFG".

Max Boards 4, Max Stacks 4

NE2000.COM

Novell NE2000 Ethernet MLID v2.02 (941014)

(C) Copyright 1991 - 1994 Novell, Inc. All Rights Reserved.

IRQ 11, Port 240, Node Address C07C0017CB L

Max Frame 1514 bytes, Line Speed 10 Mbps, Bus ID 0

Board 1, Frame ETHERNET_802.3, LSB Mode

Board 2, Frame ETHERNET_802.2, LSB Mode

Board 3, Frame ETHERNET_II, LSB Mode

Board 4, Frame ETHERNET_SNAP, LSB Mode

IPXODI.COM

NetWare IPX/SPX Protocol v3.01 (941031)

(C) Copyright 1990-1993 Novell, Inc. All Rights Reserved.

SPX CONNECTIONS 60

IPX PACKET SIZE LIMIT 1500

Bound to logical board 1 (NE2000) : Protocol ID 0

VLM.EXE

VLM.EXE - NetWare virtual loadable module manager v1.20 (941108)

(C) Copyright 1994 Novell, Inc. All Rights Reserved.

Patent pending.

The VLM.EXE file is preinitializing the VLMs..............

The VLM.EXE file is using extended memory (XMS).

You are attached to server MOULTON3

These messages indicate that the networking software loaded into DOS and set the PC up as a NetWare client successfully.

WINDOWS 95/98 INSTALLATION

Installing adapters under Windows 95/98 is somewhat easier because it is all done within the operating system, not in configuration files. There are three ways to add an adapter under Windows 95/98. First, it can be added during installation or by being recognized by the plug-and-play configuration feature. That is a good reason for using new plug-and-play compatible cards. Second, the add new hardware Wizard can be used. This approach uses the plug-and-play technology to recognize the card and install it. Information can still be entered manually, but if it is plug-and-play compatible, then it reduces the information that must be provided. Third, open the network control panel and use the "add adapter" function. See Figure 8–36.

In all these examples, be sure to have the driver file from the manufacturer. The driver file may not actually be a driver. In fact many times it is nothing more than an INF file. This information file is used by Windows 95/98 to determine how to configure the existing drivers to work with the card.

WINDOWS NT INSTALLATION

Windows NT is much like Windows 95/98. NICs can be installed during installation of Windows NT, or installed using the network control panel and selecting the adapter tab, followed by the add button. Also, like 95/98, a driver file and an INF file are needed to complete the installation. Some adapters have software drivers that come with NT. A good thing to note is that a Windows 95/98 driver rarely can replace an NT driver. It is critical to have the correct driver for the operating system.

Figure 8–37 is the Add Adapter screen for Windows NT 4.0. Again, be sure to have all the correct settings as well as drivers.

Board versus IP Address

In PC networks using TCP/IP, there are two addresses that impact the network. One is the board address and the other is the IP address. The board address is the six character 48-bit universal address encoded on the board by a manufacturer. IEEE issues this Medium Access Control (MAC) address to PC card manufacturers in blocks. The manufacturers encode ROM chips (Programmable Array Logic—PAL chips) installed on the network interface card. The MAC Address (Medium Access Control) allows each board from a manufacturer to have a unique address at the data link layer (Layer 2) of the OSI model.

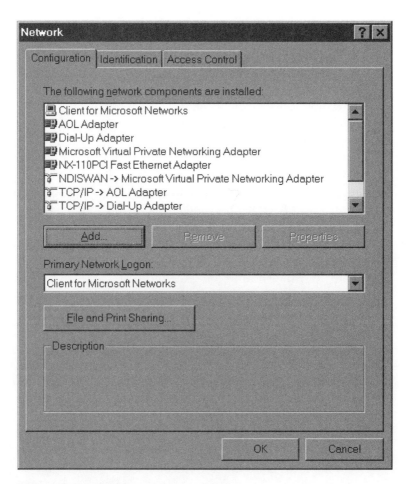

Figure 8–36   *Windows 98 network setup*

Network addressing refers to the way the network identifies the node (workstation, server, etc....) as a unique entity. This is the Internet Protocol (IP) address assigned by software as part of configuring the network. For example, the IP address given a PC by an ISP when it accesses the Internet. A typical IP address would be 208.80.68.70. This IP address is married to the MAC address by TCP/IP software modules. The IP address is assigned at the network layer (Layer 3) of the ISO seven-layer model.

IP addresses are like street addresses. Think of an IP address as comprised of "state id. city id. street id. house number." The four numbers are a similar means to specifically identify each PC attached to the Internet. An IP address identifies something like "a corporate or regional network. a sub-network. a server host network. a PC."

Whenever there are duplicate MAC or IP addresses, the cards with those duplicate addressees have problems using a network. MAC addresses only work on narrow segments broken up by bridges or switches. Bridges work only in Layers 1 and 2 of the ISO model. IP addresses work in sections of a network divided by routers. A router functions in ISO model Layers 1, 2, and 3. Each address plays a specific role in networking. The potential problem with networking and both MAC and IP addresses is again conflicting addresses. MAC address conflicts are more serious than IP address conflicts because the MAC address is burnt into the LAN card hardware and as a consequence cannot be easily changed. On each segment of a network the MAC address must be unique to the node. It is possible to get two cards from a manufacturer having the same MAC address. In this case, neither card works properly on the network. Since the MAC address is designed into a physical component, the solution usually is to swap out one of the conflicting boards.

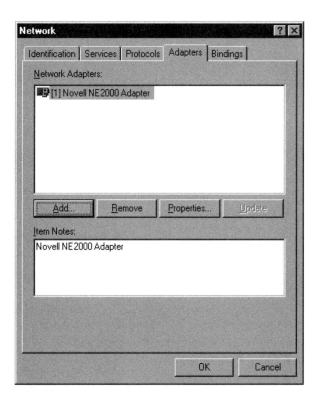

Figure 8–37 *Windows NT adapter setup*

Token ring cards could use the universally administered address (the hard-wired MAC address) or a software-assigned address (a MAC address loaded by configuration software into the token ring board). With such software-assigned addresses, the board would be reconfigured by software. In the early days of the token ring (1987) delivery of token ring adapters stopped for about a month or so because it was said that IBM had manufactured an entire semitrailer load of token ring boards with the same MAC address.

Network or IP addresses can also conflict. Only one machine is allowed to have a specific IP address. If two machines have the same IP address, they both have troubles communicating. Getting a new address from a network administrator easily solves this. Dynamic Host Configuration Protocol resolves this problem by leasing IP addresses to active PCs on a network. This is similar to the IP address assignment performed when accessing the Internet.

Network address conflicts are easier to diagnose, since Windows usually displays a message indicating the conflict. MAC address conflicts are not so forthcoming.

Study Break

Viewing Windows 98 Network Configuration

Examine the Windows network configuration to determine the assigned IP address on a Windows 98 TCP/IP networked PC.

1. Find a TCP/IP networked Windows 98 PC. Open the control panel and then open networks.

2. Select the TCP/IP linked to the LAN adapter card. Select properties and record the following:
   Fixed IP address or Obtained Automatically
   DNS Configuration—server IP Address
   WINS Configuration—WINS server IP addresses
   Gateway configuration—Gateway IP address.

3. Exit the network setup. Go to the START button and select RUN. Enter WINIPCFG and hit Enter. Use the list arrow to the right or the adapter display entry to select the LAN adapter from the drop-down list. Does the IP address and Default Gateway match what you found?

4. Click on More Info>>>. Does the WINS server match?

5. IF DHCP is functioning properly and there are free addresses, you should be able to renew all IP address leases. Click on Renew All to see if the lease start time is reset to the current date and time.

This exercise illustrates Windows TCP/IP networking setup and the WINIPCFG simple diagnostic and reporting tool.

A+   8.4   Network Problem Manifestations

Networks cause many types of problems. Although PC technical support personnel are not usually expected to solve all these problems, it is helpful to understand what networking problems could arise and how such networking problems might be solved. This helps to enhance relationships with clients by providing a broader perspective from which to troubleshoot PC problems. Oftentimes what appears to be a PC hardware problem is really caused by difficulties in the network the PC is attached to. Users have no idea why their machine is saving files slowly when saving them to N: drive. Understanding that it is a slow network may help explain to them what the source of the problem may be.

Reduced Capacity—Bandwidth Loss

The maximum amount of data that can be sent across a network cabling per second is referred to as "bandwidth." This is an indication of the total capacity of the wire and network. Imagine the network as a pipe. The pipe at its best can pass 10 million gallons of water per second. This means that the sources of water all combined cannot send in total any more than 10 million gallons in one second. Networks allow all nodes access to this capacity, but just like the pipe, all of the devices share the total capacity and cannot exceed its total capacity. In effect, this total capacity is divided or shared among all devices attached to the network.

When a loss of capacity on the network occurs, then PCs usually experience a slowdown in all operations, especially disk drive operations. Disk operations usually have some software looking at the network all the time. Whenever that software looks at a network connection and there is a heavy network load, it experiences long delays. This manifests itself in the software freezing. In the example above, if one of the sources of water uses 5 million gallons a second of the total capacity of 10 million gallons a second, then all the other sources now only have a total of 5 million gallons per second to divide up. This causes a loss of performance for them and all operations requiring water experience a long delay. This capacity tapping can occur on a network, for example, when a bad NIC continuously transmits diagnostic messages or error signals on a network.

Most networks have a network analyzer or some software that can be used to identify where a loss of capacity is occurring. Windows NT has the System Management Server Software that, when installed and properly configured, can display utilization of the network links connected to the SMS server and other reporting servers. This reports a percent utilization of the LAN. When the utilization of an Ethernet is constantly above 40% or a token ring above 70%, there are likely congestion problems. Protocol analyzers used by network service personnel also record similar utilization statistics and more. To resolve load problems, bridges or switches are used. These isolate loads to specific segments of a LAN and thus can reduce overall network load.

Data Loss

Another networking problem can be data loss. Since capacity has been limited, it is possible to have your communication time out. This results in a full to partial data loss with the transmission. It is vital that the offending source be removed from the network, or many of the users you support could suffer the same fate.

Another cause of potential data loss is from the collision of signals. On a digital network, there can be only a single carrier signal. If two signals exist, they cause a collision, resulting in potential data loss. An occasional collision is not to worry about, but consistent collisions can result in a more serious problem.

Ethernet uses repeaters to extend network distances. Most active hubs perform the repeater function. Repeaters, while boosting the electrical signal cause a small delay in the signal propagation across the network. Ethernet nodes must see collisions to know that data has been corrupted. To ensure the Ethernet NICs see collisions, there are minimum and maximum Ethernet packet sizes. When the repeater delays cascade, it is possible with both the minimum and maximum Ethernet frame sizes to have collisions go undetected. It is not easy to configure an Ethernet so that it has undetected collisions, but it happens. Only a few most distant nodes in such a misconfigured Ethernet network have the problem of undetected collisions. PC users would see these undetected collisions as data loss.

On wiring hubs, there is usually a collision light that indicates collision occurrences. Generally, a red or amber light indicates collisions. If the collision light is on continuously, a problem is indicated. Most times when the collision light is on nearly continuously, it indicates a cable fault. Sometimes it could indicate a network misconfiguration resulting in excessive collisions. A network analyzer can be used to find the potential problem machine. Cable faults are resolved by replacing bad cable with good cable. Other excessive collision problems are resolved by installing bridges or switches in the network. The bridges and switches in essence create multiple networks, isolating collisions to each network on opposing sides of the bridge or switch. When bridges or switches break a network down into sufficiently small network chunks, collisions problems should subside.

Reduced Performance—Slow Networks

Reduced network capacity results in loss of performance. This is, however, not the only reason for loss of performance. Additionally, the servers used and how often they are accessed can result in a slow network response and performance loss. As an example, if a company had one server and that server provided file sharing, email, faxing, and administrative functions, it would be a very busy (heavily loaded) server. When it was busiest, the greatest performance loss would be experienced and the longest network delays would be encountered. To solve these problems, distribute these functions over several servers, thus better distributing traffic.

A PC using Windows 95/98 Explorer that is connected to a network and that has a network drive opened, grinds to an inexplicable halt whenever there are significant network delays. Explorer accessing the network link and waiting for a response from that link before continuing a requested operation causes this. Furthermore, Explorer or other application software in the PC may have open network connections and may be sending idle or data messages across the network. Network delays caused by performance loss, slows down these applications, which in turn cause all of Windows to operate more slowly.

Windows NT servers provide a performance monitor function that records CPU utilization and other performance parameters in a graphical display form. There is similar performance monitoring software for Windows 95/98. With Windows NT, simply activating the NT task manager and selecting Task Manager provides a graphic display of the NT PCs CPU utilization and memory usage. Both of these can help in identifying an overworked server or client PC.

Additionally, servers need to be the highest performance machines in the office. Slower performance machines can be used, but then expect to experience performance loss. By giving the server the most RAM, the fastest CPU, and the Redundant Array of Independent Disks (RAID) fixed disk hardware technology, the server's ability to service network requests is significantly increased.

■ Summary

This chapter has described PC networking concepts and some networking software. The key to troubleshooting and understanding PC networking is that all networks are comprised of hardware, wiring, and software components. Once a PC is network connected, the network connection can make it seem like other PC components have failed when in fact the problem may reside in the network and not in the PC at all. PC problems in this case must be isolated to the PC hardware, the PC software, or the network.

▲ CHAPTER REVIEW QUESTIONS

Multiple Choice

1. *OSI means*
    A. Open System Interconnect
    B. Open System Interconnection
    C. Operating System Interconnection
    D. Open Service Interconnection
    Answer: B. Open System Interconnection

2. *The OSI model has _____ layers.*
    A. three
    B. five
    C. seven
    D. six
    Answer: C. seven

3. *A LAN is*
    A. limited area network
    B. PCs and servers
    C. a network operating system
    D. PCs wired together

E. a local area network

F. all of the above

Answer: E. a local area network

4. *What are two types of LANs?*

A. Ethernet and token ring

B. local and wide area

C. Novell and Microsoft

D. peer-to-peer and client-server

Answer: D. peer-to-peer and client-server

5. *What type of wiring is found in LANs?*

A. twisted pair

B. coaxial cable

C. fiber optic cable

D. unshielded twisted pair cable

E. none of the above

F. all of the above

Answer: F. all of the above

6. *Ethernet operates like a*

A. star

B. bus

C. ring

D. train with one boxcar

Answer: B. bus

7. *Ethernet is faster than the token ring.*

A. TRUE

B. FALSE

Answer: A. TRUE

8. *ATM is a new LAN and networking technology used with PCs.*

A. TRUE

B. FALSE

Answer: A.TRUE

9. *Windows provides _____ for NICs.*
   A. TCP/IP software
   B. SPX/IPX software
   C. NetBEUI software
   D. driver software

   Answer: D. driver software

10. *IBM developed Ethernet.*
    A. TRUE
    B. FALSE

    Answer: B.FALSE

11. *All NICs _____.*
    A. are PCI plug-and-play cards
    B. Ethernet or token ring cards
    C. connect to twisted-pair network wiring
    D. work with TCP/IP software
    E. all of the above

    Answer: D. work with TCP/IP software because there are ISA NICs, ATM NICs, and fiber cabling in LANs.

12. *NIC stands for*
    A. Network InterConnection
    B. Network Interface Card
    C. Network Interconnection Card
    D. Network Interface Connection

    Answer: B. Network Interface Card

13. *Windows network protocol software covers ISO Layers?*
    A. Layer 6, Layer 5, and Layer 4
    B. Layer 5, Layer 4, and Layer 3
    C. Layer 1, Layer 2, and Layer 3
    D. Layer 2, Layer 3, and Layer 4

E. Layer 3, Layer 4, and Layer 6

Answer: B. Layer 5, Layer 4, And Layer 3

14. *TCP/IP stands for*

A. Transmission Control Protocol/Interconnection Protocol

B. Transmission Control Protocol/Internet Packet

C. Transmission Control Protocol/Internet Protocol

D. Transmission Control Packet/Internet Protocol

Answer: C.Transmission Control Protocol/Internet Protocol

15. *The most popular type of LAN wiring is*

A. radio frequency connections

B. coaxial cable

C. fiber-optic cable

D. twisted-pair cable

E. all of the above

Answer: D. twisted-pair cable

16. *Network performance degrades because*

A. servers are under-powered

B. excessive or peak traffic on the network

C. unusually high collisions

D. large file transfers

E. all of the above

Answer: E. all of the above

DOS Architecture

▲ Chapter Syllabus

A+ 9.1 DOS Functions

A+ 9.2 DOS Components

A+ 9.3 Key System Files

DOS (Disk Operating System) has been the core operating system on personal computers for many years. The original version of DOS used about 14 KB of RAM in a 1981 PC. Tim Patterson originally wrote it in the late '70s. It was adapted from CPM (Control Program for Microcomputers) and called QDOS, the quick and dirty operating system. To Microsoft and IBM, it became PC DOS 1.0. The most visible difference between the two operating systems was the floppy diskette drive was A: in PC DOS and C: in CPM. Microsoft bought QDOS from Seattle Computer Products for whatever use they wanted for fifty thousand dollars and then licensed it to IBM and the world for up to fifty dollars per PC. PC DOS was released in August of 1981. The three key programs were COMMAND.COM (3,231 bytes), IBMBIO.COM (1,920 bytes), and IBM-DOS.COM (6,400 bytes), for a total size of 11,551 bytes. With buffering, it consumed about 14,000 bytes of RAM. DOS 2.0 arrived in March of 1983.

Its size had increased to 39,552 bytes. DOS 3.0 followed this in August of 1984, just prior to the launch of the 80286 PC AT. DOS had now become bloated at 58,926 bytes. With the AT in 1985 arrived PC DOS 3.1 coming in at 60,534 bytes. Other ignominious versions of DOS including DOS 4.0 (not noteworthy), DOS 5.0 with good memory management, and DOS 6.0, the last MS DOS. DOS 6.22—the last official DOS release in May of 1994—was 133,557 bytes. In contrast, the Windows 98 DOS of today is 317,957 bytes. The size of DOS has increased about as fast as has Microsoft's sales.

DOS is very simple, yet capable of running diagnostic and hardware configuration programs on today's Pentium-based PCs. It provides not only a platform with which a user can access hardware, manage disk space, and launch applications, but it is also very useful as a quick, simple operating system for a technician to load to help in troubleshooting a system. You cannot run a full version of Windows 95 from a single floppy disk, but you can run DOS and several diagnostics utilities from a single floppy.

DOS has internal commands and functions built into COMMAND.COM, IO.SYS, and MSDOS.SYS and external commands and functions like FDISK and FORMAT. The external commands are separate programs accompanying DOS and installed in a DOS directory on the fixed disk. Windows builds upon this base by providing a Graphical User Interface (GUI) with point-and-click menus and programs. In contrast, DOS is operated by entering commands typed on a command entry line.

A+ 9.1 DOS Functions

DOS has evolved over the years until the current Windows 98 version. The significant and good versions are:

PC DOS 1.0 is the original PC DOS released in 1981. A classic comprised of COMMAND.COM, IBMBIO.COM and IBMDOS.COM. It supported single-sided floppy diskette drives of 160KB capacity.

PC DOS 1.1 was the first revision, issued in 1982, of PC DOS. It supported the much needed double-sided 320KB floppies. We ran four floppy diskette drives on a single PC with this DOS for a grand storage total of 1.44MB. Awesome!

PC DOS 2.0 is the PC DOS for the PC XT released in 1983 that supported the first 10MB fixed disk and 360KB floppy diskettes. We really began to cook then.

PC DOS 2.11 released in 1984, was a revised and cleaned up PC DOS 2.0. We created our first LAN using DOS 2.11.

PC DOS 3.0 in 1984 supported the first 1.2 MB floppy drives.

PC DOS 3.1 is the PC AT DOS released in 1985 supporting CMI boat anchor 30 MB fixed disk drives in the PC AT. Most CMI drives were defective and failed just after the warranty period of one year expired. They made really good boat anchors.

PC DOS 3.2 and PC DOS 3.3 were basically improvements on PC DOS 3.1. They did begin providing more real mode memory for use by applications by incorporating HIMEM.SYS. HIMEM.SYS probably first came with DOS 3.0 or 3.1, but we really did not begin to use it until DOS 3.2 and 3.3. It was used with disk drive cache and RAMDRIVE. DOS 3.3 was the first DOS sold separately from a PC.

DOS 4.0 was released in 1988. It started the 1.44MB floppy diskette drive support. We think of it as the Joan Rivers (a very yucki yucky DOS.) version of DOS. Microsoft really began seriously selling DOS separate from PCs in earnest with the release of DOS 4.0. In this case, the COMMAND.COM was retained, but IO.SYS and MSDOS.SYS replaced IBM-BIO.SOM and IBMDOS.COM, respectively.

DOS 4.01 in 1989 is the PS-/2 (Pretty Stupid Computer #2 Oops, sorry IBM.) DOS.

DOS 5.0 saved us in 1991 and began the serious DOS support of Windows 3.xx. Memory management was a key feature here.

DOS 5.01a and DOS 5.02 improved upon a good product and improved memory management features for Windows.

DOS 6.0 and DOS 6.1 is the last great DOS that can be purchased separately from Windows. It provided improved memory management and good disk compression, both of which were sorely needed at the time. DOS 6.0 was released in 1993.

DOS 6.22 is Microsoft's last independent DOS product. After DOS 6.22, all DOS was incorporated into or paired with Windows 95/98.

Windows 95 DOS is incorporated into Windows to perform part of the boot up process for Windows. It also supports a DOS command prompt operation with the external DOS commands stored in the \windows\command directory. Sometimes this DOS is referred to as DOS 7.0. It retains COMMAND.COM and IO.SYS but MSDOS.COM becomes a text file helpful in the booting process. IO.SYS incorporates many DOS features including

HIMEM.SYS functions, SMARTDRV functions and more. Windows 98 DOS came out in 1995 with Windows 95.

Windows 98 DOS is the current version of DOS. It is the DOS that is placed on the Windows emergency recovery diskette.

The DOS operating environment handles one program at a time.

> DOS performs one function at a time. Its applications can multitask–print and continue working data simultaneously. The multi-tasking is built into the application program, not DOS. Windows is a multitasking operating system (or environment). Windows 3.xx performed cooperative multitasking, requiring the operational control of the multitasking to be controlled by both Windows and the Windows applications. Windows 95/98 and Windows NT perform preemptive multitasking. They control exclusively the multitasking environment. In Windows, printing and other work can continue, all at the same time. While writing this book, we would upload files to the Internet while at the same time continue writing with **MS Word**.

It DOS is a very simple operating environment that requires the application software to perform all special data formatting and input/output operations. This means that the application programs must provide any special drivers or other software enhancements to use the components attached to the PC. The applications become responsible for a large part of the operating environment of the PC under DOS.

Because DOS works on one task or program at a time, it provides an excellent troubleshooting environment for PCs.

DOS can directly manipulate the PC hardware. In contrast, Windows program's direct hardware manipulation is much more restricted and in some cases prohibited entirely. Direct hardware manipulation is limited by the capabilities of the DOS release. For example, DOS 6.2x can only work with FAT-16 disk drives. In order to work with FAT-32 disk drives, Windows 95/98 DOS must be used.

FAT stands for File Allocation Table. It is the physical structure that DOS uses to access the data stored on the fixed and floppy disk drives. The entire data access structure is comprised of the directory of files on the fixed disk and the FAT. The FAT points at the allocation units containing the actual data and chains them together to form a series of allocation units (containers) for a file's data.

DOS provides the user and the computer with several key functions. These functions include managing the PC system, managing the disk drive, managing files stored on the disk drive, and launching applications.

PC System Management

DOS is a key tool for managing your system. It comes with a host of small programs, the external DOS commands, that control important system functions.

For example, MEM is a DOS command that displays a PC's current memory configuration. This is crucial when trying to maximize a PC's memory resources so application programs run more efficiently or to optimize DOS for running Windows 3.x. Another important DOS utility is the Microsoft Diagnostics Program (MSD). This is very helpful in displaying a PC's current system configuration.

A major benefit of having such utilities included with DOS and DOS requiring little disk storage space, is that most DOS diagnostics tools and DOS itself can be saved on a single bootable floppy disk. This bootable floppy disk then becomes an important PC troubleshooting tool.

Disk Management

Not only does DOS manage your system resources, but it also has utilities to manage your PC's fixed disk drive. One of the more important and useful utilities is FDISK. FDISK is a utility that you use to create and remove partitions on your fixed disk. The different versions of DOS provide different FDISK capabilities and functionality. Partitioning is only one of the disk management operations that DOS has to handle; there is also formatting, compressing, and backing up and restoring files as well.

The central function of disk management is to subdivide the disk's capacity into manageable chunks that can store the data placed on the disk drive. All disk drives are basically formatted into *sectors*. Each sector holds 512 characters (or bytes) of data. This sector size is used almost universally on all disks regardless of their total capacity. Sectors are not, however, the basic unit of storage capacity used by DOS and Windows. The disk drive sectors are used in chunks called clusters or allocation units. Allocation units may be comprised of 4, 8, 16, or more sectors.

Allocation units are managed using a file allocation table or FAT. Originally DOS used FAT with 16,000 entries, which is referred to as FAT-16.

The diagram below illustrates how the DOS directory and the File Allocation Table (FAT) work together. When files of data are stored on a disk drive, a directory entry and a FAT chain are created. See Figure 9-1. The directory entry contains the number of the beginning allocation unit (or cluster) of the chain of allocation units containing the data comprising the file. The FAT is just a table of numbers in sequence. So location, say, 0025 contains a number pointing to the next allocation unit in the chain. In Figure 9-1, the file entry points to FAT entry number 102 for beginning cluster (or allocation unit) 102. The 102nd entry in the FAT table contains the number 103 pointing to the next FAT entry and identifying the next allocation unit in the chain of allocation units containing the data on the disk drive. The 103rd entry points to FAT entry 125, FAT entry 125 points to 126, FAT entry 126 points to entry 127 and 127 contains all ones, signaling the end of the FAT chain. The file is comprised of Allocation units 101, 102, 103, 125, 126, and 127.

Actual directory and FAT displays from an old version of Norton utilities are shown in Figure 9-2. The directory entry for IO.SYS points to the FAT table entry of 002, and the directory entry for MSDOS.SYS points to the FAT entry of 019. Following the IO.SYS chain links us from allocation unit 002, to 003, 004, 005, 006, 007, 008, 009, 010, 011, 012, 013, 014, 015, 016, 017, and finally 018. The EOF mark is in FAT location 18 in the FAT table. The next location is location 19, the start point for the MSDOS.SYS file.

Data is stored on the fixed disk in chains that are one allocation unit right after another. However, as files are modified they grow or shrink. To save them away, DOS needs additional clusters. It cannot get them exactly following the original clusters so it just grabs the next available allocation unit to place at the end of the chain. This means that the chains become broken into chunks called blocks. Noncontiguous blocks mean that DOS has the file stored in clusters (or allocation units) that are not next to each other on the disk.

The 16-bit FAT permitted DOS to store data on fixed disks that had a maximum capacity of around 30MB. To increase the useable disk size, DOS permitted varying the sectors per allocation unit. By varying sectors per allocation unit, FAT-16 was able to expand the maximum addressable drive capacity to 2 GB. Thus with FAT-16, DOS and Windows could divide a large disk up into 2 GB partitions and then store data in those partitions. In the case of 2 GB partitions, 64 sectors of data (32 KB) were assigned to each allocation unit. Such a breakdown was efficient for storing large files, but not small ones. A small file of a few characters (or bytes) would use a single 32-KB allocation unit. Most of the 32-KB allocation unit was wasted space.

The FAT-16 structure is now being replaced by a FAT-32 structure, which more efficiently stores data on the fixed disk. Similar to FAT-16, FAT-32 also varies the sectors per allocation unit. However, because it subdivides the disk into a different overall structure, the sectors per allocation unit increase more slowly than they do with FAT-16. With small improvements, the allocation in unit size can be one sector, or 512 bytes. With larger drives,

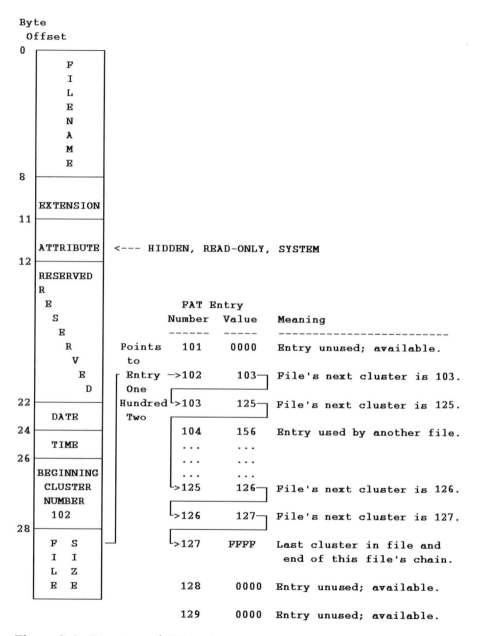

Figure 9–1 *Directory and FAT entries*

Boot sector and master boot record use allocation units 0 and 1.

Name	.Ext	Size	Date	Time	Cluster	Arc	R/O	Sys	Hid	Dir	Vol
IO	SYS	33430	4-09-91	5:00 am	*2*	Arc	R/O	Sys	Hid		
MSDOS	SYS	37394	4-09-91	5:00 am	*19*	Arc	R/O	Sys	Hid		
PETE486P	1	0	9-12-91	11:28 pm	0	Arc					Vol
BAT		0	9-12-91	11:38 pm	62					Dir	
DISKFIX		0	11-23-91	7:05 am	1583					Dir	
DOS50		0	9-12-91	11:38 pm	63					Dir	
NOVELL		0	9-12-91	11:38 pm	73					Dir	
PCKWIK		0	9-12-91	11:38 pm	1585					Dir	
PDOX35		0	9-12-91	11:38 pm	70					Dir	
PE		0	9-12-91	11:38 pm	71					Dir	
QEMM		0	11-27-91	3:21 pm	72					Dir	
TEMP		0	11-27-91	3:17 pm	74					Dir	
UTIL		0	9-12-91	11:39 pm	75					Dir	
WINDOWS		0	12-09-91	9:02 pm	988					Dir	
124	BAT	51	12-16-91	4:40 pm	356	Arc					
386SPART	PAR	12288000	1-20-92	2:39 am	8145	Arc		Sys	Hid		
Sector 130											
64	BAT	48	12-12-91	7:18 am	561	Arc					
80		48	12-12-91	5:55 pm	562	Arc					

FIXED DISK DIRECTORY (*OLD* NORTON UTILITIES)

Object	Edit	Link	View	Info	Tools	Quit		F1=Help
Sector 1								
--	--	*3*	4	5	6	7	8	
9	10	11	12	13	14	15	16	
17	18	<EOF>	*20*	21	22	23	24	
25	26	27	28	29	30	31	32	
33	34	35	36	37	<EOF>	39	40	
41	42	43	44	45	46	47	48	
49	50	51	52	53	54	55	56	
57	58	59	60	61	<EOF>	<EOF>	64	
<EOF>	0	0	0	0	0	<EOF>	<EOF>	
<EOF>	<EOF>	<EOF>	76	<EOF>	<EOF>	<EOF>	80	
81	82	83	84	85	86	87	88	
89	90	91	92	93	94	95	96	
97	98	99	100	101	102	103	104	
105	106	107	108	109	110	111	112	
113	114	115	116	117	118	119	120	
121	122	123	124	125	126	127	128	
129	130	131	132	133	134	135	136	
137	138	139	140	141	142	143	144	
145	146	147	148	149	150	151	152	
153	154	<EOF>	156	157	158	159	160	
FAT (1st Copy)							Sector 1	

FIXED DISK FILE ALLOCATION TABLE (*OLD* NORTON UTILITIES)

Figure 9–2 *Norton Utility Directory and FAT display*

it increases to four sectors per allocation unit. This is much more efficient use of the disk drive space than with FAT-16.

File Management

File management and disk management may seem like the same category, however, they are very different. DOS provides you with a host of commands and utilities that you can use to manipulate and manage the files on your drive. These commands are discussed later on in this chapter.

The objective of file management is to be able to read and write files in an organized and efficient fashion to and from the disk. To fulfill this objective, there must be a management structure allowing those files to be tracked. This can be a daunting task when thousands of files are stored on a disk drive. DOS organizes your files by creating a hierarchy of directories (or folders). Files are stored in these directories which consist of a list of logical locations mapped to a set of physical locations. This mapping allows DOS to locate, delete, rename, and fix problems with stored files. This hierarchical structure has not changed significantly even in Windows 95/98, which uses an almost identical file storage structure.

This same hierarchical file management structure is employed with Windows NT's NT File System (NTFS). The major difference between the NT File System (NTFS) and the DOS/Windows file management is that NTFS provides additional management attributes for the directories and files so that they can be shared across networks. However, the hierarchical file structure remains basically the same.

As with any good organizational structure, there are rules as to how those files are stored. For example, the number of characters in a file name and what characters can be used in file names are part of such rules.

For DOS, files are named using the following standard format:

<NNNNNNNN>.<XXX>

Where the first "NNN" pattern is any combination of up to eight letters and numbers, and the "XXX" designates a file extension of up to three letters. The extension frequently is used to indicate what type of file this is. For example, in the case of AUTOEXEC.BAT, the file name is "AUTOEXEC" and the ".BAT" extension is a standard DOS designation for a batch file.

Besides BAT files, some other common extensions found in DOS and their file types are:

- EXE: executable files, typically programs
- COM: command files
- SYS: system files
- DAT: data files

Managing Applications

The DOS applications architecture is shown in Figure 9-3. Applications communicate with DOS directly through the DOS Applications Program Interface (API). DOS comprises programs that perform system configuration and data management functions. Applications are programs that produce useful information for PC users. For example, XCOPY is a DOS program for copying files, while MSWord is an application for writing books and seminar notes.

This API interfaces to the COMMAND.COM for internal DOS commands and to the external DOS command programs like FDISK, MEM, MSD, etc.

The application is responsible for the details of using the video card, printer, and other PC hardware and peripherals.

Game programs come with extensive driver software to maximize their use of the PC's display.

DOS does provide rudimentary memory management functions (for instance, the ability to load programs into different memory areas to maximize conventional memory) and limited multitasking for terminate-and-stay resident (TSR) programs such as DOSKEY.

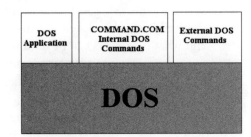

Circa 1981-1995

Figure 9–3 *DOS applications architecture*

DOS facilitates installing and launching applications on PC systems. DOS is designed to load and execute programs in conventional memory (the lower 640 KB) from a PC disk drive. PC RAM under DOS can be classified as real mode memory and extended memory. Real mode memory is the first megabyte (plus 64 KB of HIMEM) of RAM addressable when the CPU chip is operating in real mode emulating an old 8088 CPU chip. Extended memory is addressed in protected and other modes. It is all the memory available above 1 MB in the PC. DOS real mode memory is conventional memory (the first 640KB), HIMEM (the first 64KB over the 1 MB boundary that is real-mode-addressable due to a design flaw in Intel CPU chips—Oops, it's not a flaw but rather a feature), and finally the upper memory area. The upper memory area (UMA) maps BIOS, VGA BIOS ROM, video paging RAM segments, expanded memory paging RAM segments, I/O card RAM swap areas, and more.

A typical DOS program loads the entire application program into the computer's conventional memory as well as all or some of the data it uses. Depending on the type of program, it may need to access several different memory areas, like extended memory or conventional memory (the lower 640 KB). PC memory management under DOS and the PC memory areas are discussed in more detail in Chapter 13.

Additionally, DOS is the common interface that most of the application programs use to interact with your computer's hardware. For example, a computer game that uses a CD-ROM drive does not communicate directly with the CD-ROM drive whenever it needs to access the data stored on the CD. The game actually passes a request to DOS. DOS then schedules the processes that have to occur in order to access the CD-ROM drive and transfer data to the application.

Study Break

DOS CHKDSK

Run the CHKDSK command, from DOS on a PC with a **16-bit FAT** partition to see what messages you get.

1. Run **CHKDSK *.* /V** to check the directory and FAT structure of a 16-bit FAT disk drive. It should run through a listing of the files on the drive and finish with a display similar to the following:
   C:\USER.NEW
   C:\SYSTEM.NEW
   C:\DETLOG.TXT
   C:\NETLOG.TXT
   C:\NOVLOG.TXT

2,146,631,680	bytes total disk space
56,852,480	bytes in 3 hidden files
6,914,048	bytes in 211 directories
568,950,784	bytes in 7,074 user files
1,513,914,368	bytes available on disk

32,768 bytes in each allocation unit
65,510 total allocation units on disk
46,201 available allocation units on disk

655,360 total bytes memory
505,424 bytes free

Examine the messages displayed.

2. Did you see 655,360 total bytes memory? This is the first 640KB used by DOS. If the number is lower, the PC possibly has a virus infection.

3. What is the total disk capacity and allocation unit size? For 2GB drives and FAT-16, the allocation unit size is 32KB or 64 sectors.

4. Were any error messages displayed?
   Errors found, F parameter not specified.
   Corrections will not be written to disk.

This message indicates that there are conflicts between the directory and the FAT. Since we have not as yet used the /F parameter, DOS does not resolve those conflicts. DOS only displays where they are on this fixed disk. After we recover as many files as we choose, we can then run CHKDSK with the /F parameter. It corrects the discrepancies between the FAT and the directory. When this is done, some data on the fixed disk is lost.

5. Did you see a message like:
   A:\FASTCOPY.ARC
   Allocation error, size adjusted.
   No chain for this entry, size will be set to 0?
   This message says that the directory entry size did not match with the FAT size so the size will be set to zero. Helpful, isn't it?

6. Was a message similar to this message displayed?
```
29 lost clusters found in 7 chains.
Convert lost chains to files (Y/N)? n
  29696 bytes disk space
     would be freed.
```

This message means that several chains of clusters discovered in the FAT have no corresponding directory entry. These chains are converted to files when CHKDSK /F is run. The files are placed in the root directory with the name FILE0000.CHK, FILE0001.CHK, etc. The FILE00xx.CHK files may contain salvageable data.

7. Did a message similar to this appear?

```
A:\FASTCOPY.ARC
    Is cross linked on cluster 255
A:\HDAT.ARC
    Is cross linked on cluster 255
A:\MIPS.ARC
    Is cross linked on cluster 255
```

This message shows three files all sharing the same cluster. Files are not sharing or caring things. Can this be true? No! What is true here? Two files are bad and one file might be good.

8. Our last potential CHKDSK message is:

```
A:\FASTCOPY.ARC
    Contains 2 non-contiguous blocks.
A:\HDAT.ARC
    Contains 2 non-contiguous blocks.
```

This message is innocuous. It shows that files are stored in noncontiguous allocation units. It might mean that we are having reduced performance from our fixed disk drive. This problem pales in comparison to the problems indicated by the proceeding error messages.

9. Find a diskette that has been corrupted by a magnet like our Mr. Bill or Super Dave labeled diskette. Run CHKDSK /V against it to see some real error messages. Can it recover the errors?

Whenever a DOS or Windows program is exited abruptly, allocation unit (or cluster) chains with no corresponding directory entry may be left on your fixed disk. These chains with no directory entry can eventually congest the disk, reducing space for additional files. It is a good policy to once a week or more often perform a CHKDSK /F test for DOS or a SCANDISK for Windows of each fixed disk drive or partition on your PCs. When any lost chains are found, they should be converted to files and then erased from the fixed disk.

A+ 9.2 DOS Components

The architecture of DOS is best or easiest understood by examining its key software components. DOS is a software package comprising of several programs. These programs provide services to the user, hardware, and applications.

The user interacts with DOS using the command prompt. The default command prompt is the C:\> with the blinking cursor that appears when you first boot your computer using DOS. Note that you can change the command prompt, but the standard prompt is as described above.

We call this the command prompt because it is here where the user can enter DOS commands like MEM or DIR. The command prompt is created by the COMMAND.COM DOS component. COMMAND.COM is loaded as part of the DOS boot sequence, and can be found in the root directory of any bootable disk.

The commands that you type in at the command prompt are interpreted by COMMAND.COM and then passed on to the core files of the DOS operating system.

With Windows 95/98, you can open a DOS command prompt in Windows. Similarly, in Windows NT, a DOS prompt window can be opened. These windows are not DOS but rather an emulation of DOS using a COMMAND.COM program. Windows NT does not come with any DOS at all. If problems develop with Windows NT, Windows NT has a special recovery diskette that permits booting and repairing an NT installation. Windows 95 and 98 do come with a Windows DOS. Exiting Windows 95/98 and restarting in MS DOS mode enters this DOS.

COMMAND.COM is generally found in the root directory of a bootable disk. This means floppy disks as well as fixed disks. Additionally, COMMAND.COM can often be found in the C:\DOS directory found on a hard disk that has the full DOS operating system installed on it. More recent versions of DOS (6.0 and above are a kinder and gentler DOS) permit booting without COMMAND.COM being in the root directory.

The core system files provide the application and hardware interaction of DOS. They are also found in the root directory of your disk drive if it is bootable. Microsoft DOS core system files are MSDOS.SYS, COMMAND.COM, and IO.SYS.

IBM DOS core system files are IBMDOS.COM and IBMBIO.COM. These files receive the commands from either the user or the application and translate them into requests for the computer's ROM BIOS (read only memory basic input/output system) interface. So when a user types in DIR at the command prompt, the following occurs:

1. The command is interpreted by COMMAND.COM and translated into a form that is useable by the DOS core system files.
2. The core system files in turn translate the request into more detailed BIOS commands.
3. BIOS then executes these detailed commands, activating the various hardware components needed to fulfill the user's DIR request.

4. The hardware, upon completing the requested task, produces the data desired or generates an error message code that is returned to BIOS. BIOS returns the data or error message code to DOS.

5. DOS hands the output results or error message code to COMMAND.COM for it to display for the user.

6. COMMAND.COM then determines what to display for the user and hands the request back to DOS, which passes it to BIOS, which creates the actual video image displayed on the PC's monitor.

Figure 9-4 shows conceptually the interaction between the DOS system components. Applications follow a nearly identical procedure except that application requests bypass *COMMAND.COM* and communicates directly with the DOS core system files. DOS then hands the results produced to the applications program which creates a display for the user that it hands back to DOS and then to BIOS for it to create and display the actual image. In some rare cases applications may talk directly to hardware bypassing DOS altogether. This is not common.

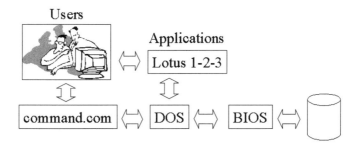

Figure 9–4 *DOS Components and architecture*

Study Break

Changing COMMAND.COM Locations

This exercise creates a bootable diskette with COMMAND.COM on it, then boots from the diskette and switches the location of COMMAND.COM.

1. Use FORMAT /S to create a bootable floppy diskette. Copy the EDIT.COM program to the diskette. EDIT.COM can be found in the \windows\command directory.

2. Shut down Windows and reboot into DOS by using the diskette. Run EDIT from the diskette. Now remove the diskette from the disk drive and exit EDIT using ALT-F-X keys. An error message "Not ready reading drive A:" should appear when DOS tries to read COMMAND.COM from the diskette. Select the option "Fail" and Windows DOS (the kinder and gentler DOS) should respond "Current drive is no longer valid>". This permits you to specify c: as a valid drive, which should return you to the c:> prompt.

3. Run a DIR command. The directory should display.

4. Run a DIR COMMAND.COM /S command to see where DOS is locating COMAND.COM. It should be found in the root directory and in \windows\command directory.

5. Enter the command SET to display the environment space. This should display the COMSPEC=A:\COMMAND.COM from where DOS tried to reload COMMAND.COM.

This exercise illustrates how DOS searches for COMMAND.COM when an application program throws it out of memory and then, upon exiting, reloads COMMAND.COM.

A+   9.3   Key System Files

To better understand the DOS operating structure, let's examine the key files that make up DOS as well as the files used to configure DOS on a personal computer. This goes beyond the three key DOS files COMMAND.COM, IO.SYS, and MSDOS.SYS and covers the function of other key files like HIMEM.SYS and SMARTDRV.EXE. Additionally, we examine the DOS boot process and how these files work together to create the working environment for DOS application programs. It examines those key system files loaded in CONFIG.SYS and in AUTOEXEC.BAT. The commands and examples here generally represent DOS operations. However, different versions of DOS respond differently to these commands. This means the examples represented here may not work precisely as explained depending upon the DOS version being used, for instance, DOS 5.0, DOS 6.22 or Windows 95/98 DOS. More details on DOS commands and memory management are covered in Chapter 13.

IO.SYS

IO.SYS (originally IBMBIO.COM) is one of the three files that make up the core system files of DOS. "IO" here stands for input/output. It is a read-only hidden system file, and is located in the root directory of a bootable disk.

During the PC boot process, the cold boot loader program in the fixed disk master boot record or in the floppy boot record loads IO.SYS. It then proceeds to load the remainder of DOS.

After DOS has been loaded, the primary job of the IO.SYS is to handle the input/output functions for the PC. It handles the communications needed between the various devices in the PC to perform functions, such as moving data between a PC's fixed disk drive and video card.

MSDOS.SYS

MSDOS.SYS (originally IBMSYS.COM) is the second of the core system files. Like the IO.SYS, it is a read-only hidden system file. Its main job is to break the DOS user and application commands into smaller tasks and schedule them for completion by IO.SYS and a PC's BIOS. For example, a DIR command may be broken down into components that find the directory on the designated disk drive, read the directory information, format the information it read so humans can understand it, and send the output to the video display card and monitor. In this manner, it performs application and file management functions for the PC.

MSDOS.SYS provides the application program interface (API) for PC applications and for COMMAND.COM.

COMMAND.COM

COMMAND.COM functions primarily as the command interpreter for user commands. Unlike the first two DOS components, COMMAND.COM interacts directly with user inputs, breaking them down into system commands that are then passed down to MSDOS.SYS and finally IO.SYS. COMMAND.COM also is responsible for the display of the command prompt when the computer is booted under DOS. COMMAND.COM also incorporates many of the DOS commands we use. These commands are what we term "internal commands," since they are part of COMMAND.COM. Below is a list of some of the internal DOS commands that reside in COMMAND.COM. Table 9-1 identifies internal DOS commands.

This is not an exhaustive list of internal DOS commands, just the most frequently used and helpful commands. In addition to internal commands, COMMAND.COM runs external commands. External commands differ from internal commands in that they are separate program files while internal commands are part of COMMAND.COM. For example, the FORMAT command is a program file called FORMAT.COM. These programs are typically found in the DOS directory of a PC's C: drive. If you are using Windows

95, external DOS commands are found in the C:\WINDOWS\COMMAND subdirectory. Table 9-2 lists some of the DOS external commands. This list is not an exhaustive list, but rather describes some of the most useful external DOS commands.

Table 9.1 *Some internal DOS commands*

CALL	CD (Change Directory)	CLS (Clear Screen)
COPY	DEL (Delete)	DIR (Directory)
ECHO	LH (Load High)	MD (Make Directory)
PATH	PAUSE	PROMPT
REM (Remark)	REN (Rename)	RMDIR (Remove Directory)
SET	TYPE	VER (Version)

Table 9.2 *Some external DOS commands*

ATTRIB (Attribute)	CHKDSK (Check Disk)	DELTREE (Delete Tree)
EDIT	FDISK (Fixed Disk)	FORMAT
MODE	MEM (Memory)	MSCDEX (Microsoft CD ROM Extension)
SCANDISK	SMARTDRIVE	XCOPY

CONFIG.SYS

The CONFIG.SYS file is a system file. It's main purpose is to load drivers used by other devices or applications.

It differs from other system files because it is not a program itself, but rather, a list of commands that are executed when DOS is loaded during the PC boot process. CONFIG.SYS does not automatically have read-only, hidden, or system attributes like IO.SYS and MSDOS.SYS do. However, it is possible to assign a read-only attribute to prevent accidental damage to it.

In fact this file was designed as a control structure intended to be altered or customized to suit a particular computer configuration. This file can be easily edited using the edit command, the notepad utility, or any other text editor.

Although it can be edited or even deleted, this does not make CONFIG.SYS unimportant. This file may be the most important file under DOS.

DOS uses the CONFIG.SYS to load hardware driver programs and to configure parameters used by applications that run on the computer. A driver program talks directly to the PC hardware. It forms a bridge between

DOS (or Windows) and the hardware component. Driver programs know how much buffering a card has, its I/O port address, which IRQs it can use, and more.

The CONFIG.SYS file is only important on disks that are bootable. So on floppies and additional fixed disk partitions, you are not likely to find this file.

These parameters used by CONFIG.SYS include memory management, environment variables, and special system drivers for services like disk compression under DOS. The CONFIG.SYS should be found in the root directory of the floppy or bootable portion of the fixed disk you are currently using.

If you are curious about the CONFIG.SYS, now is a good time to look at it. Do this by typing at the C:\> prompt: EDIT CONFIG.SYS.

The DOS Editor should open and display a file that looks something like the one below. Alternatively, enter TYPE CONFIG.SYS.

```
Device c:\dos\himem.sys
REM Loads HIMEM from C:\dos
Device c:\dos\emm386.exe NOEMS x=a000-c7ff
REM Loads EMM386.EXE from C:\dos
REM Sets type of memory requested to XMS only
REM Excludes UMA Video display area from use
DOS  = HIGH,UMB
Device = oakcdrom.sys /D:mscd001
REM Loads a CD-ROM device driver and identifies it as
MSCD001
Devicehigh  = c:\dos50\smartdrv.sys 2048 2048
REM Loads SMARTDRV and allocates 2MB for disk cache
Device = c:\dos50\ANSI.SYS
FILES  = 30
BUFFERS = 10
Stacks = 9,256
Lastdrive = e
REM Sets last DOS drive to E--- not networked
```

Okay, this is more organized than most CONFIG.SYS files you find. When performing PC service, it is a good idea to create CONFIG.SYS files that are well-organized and that contain documentation on the commands appearing in the file.

In this manner then other service personnel examining the CONFIG.SYS file understand exactly how it has been configured for this specific

PC system. Furthermore, they need not search for some long-lost DOS manual to be able to modify properly the CONFIG.SYS file. This makes CONFIG.SYS much easier to troubleshoot and read. Neat or sloppy CONFIG.SYS files work just fine with DOS because DOS is not picky about their appearance, only about the structure of the commands within the file.

The job of this file is to load before COMMAND.COM and to configure memory, environment variables, and to load any special device drivers. Let's break this file down into its various parameters.

FILES, BUFFERS, STACKS, AND LASTDRIVE

Files, buffers, stacks, and lastdrive are parameters that configure some fairly important areas of your computer. None of these parameters are necessary in a CONFIG.SYS file because there are default values for each if they are missing. Assigning these, however, can have a profound effect on whether certain components may can function under DOS.

```
FILES = 30
```

The files parameter indicates to DOS how many file handles it is to keep track of simultaneously. A file handle is nothing more than a pointer to an open file.

This affects the system when you are using applications and you attempt to open more files than DOS is set to keep track of. In such a case, DOS would respond with an error indicating you have too many files open. The files setting can range from 0-255. The default value for files is 8, but a recommended value is 60 for Windows. Each file handle uses about 64 characters of RAM.

Logically, you may think that it is best to set this to 255 and avoid such an error. This is, however, a bad practice as the higher you set this, the more conventional memory is used to track them. That is a problem when you need as much conventional memory as possible free to run a particular application. The approximate 15KB reduction in conventional memory may be sorely needed. A good range for the files parameter is between 30 and 90.

```
BUFFERS = 10
```

The "buffers" parameter, like files, indicates the number of disk buffers to set.

Buffers act as a temporary holding place for data as opposed to placing it on the disk. Using buffers accelerates accessing information, since it is being found now in RAM instead of on the disk. These buffers are similar to a disk cache program like SMARTDRV, only with far less sophistication and efficiency. For that reason, if you are running a disk cache, your buffers should be set to a number between 10 and 48 because the SMARTDRV and the buffers then all fit into the HIMEM area. If a higher value is set, then the buffers load into conventional memory. Each buffer uses about 532 bytes of RAM. When you are not running a disk cache, set buffers higher, towards 50. Buffers permit setting a secondary buffer cache that can speed up disk I/O for 8086 (antique) CPU chip computers. The syntax for specifying secondary buffer cache is BUFFERS = 30,6. The number 6 specifies the secondary buffer cache. Windows 95/98 PCs automatically load the SMARTDRV disk cache, so a secondary buffer cache setting is rarely used.

```
STACKS = 9,256
```

Stacks are designed to handle hardware interrupts while an application program is active. Think of them as bookmarks. If you are reading a book and your dog whines at the back door, you get a bookmark and mark your page so that when you return to your reading after letting the dog out, you can pick up where you left off. Programs work the same way, when a hardware interrupt is issued. Once answered, the application must pick up where it left off. The stack is used in this case as the bookmark. Most software does not require the stacks, they have their own stack set designed into them. If, however, you get an "Exception Error 12", or a "Stack Overflow" error, you can compensate for this by increasing the stacks variable.

The first variable in the stacks line is for the number of stacks. This can be a number from 0 through 64. Setting it to 0 means no stacks are to be used. The second number sets the size of the stacks. Valid ranges for that are 0 through 512 bytes. Again, 0 here would indicate no stacks are being used. As with files and buffers, more and larger stacks use more conventional memory, which may cause problems for programs that require large amounts of conventional memory.

```
LASTDRIVE = E
```

"Lastdrive" specifies to DOS what the last valid drive letter is. This saves memory so that the "lastdrive" letter is not by default set to Z. On standalone older DOS PCs, the "lastdrive" letter defaulted typically to E. However if you have this computer connected to a network you may have to set this to a higher letter. As an example, if you are on a NetWare Network using the VLM shell or on a Microsoft Windows Network, the last drive parameter must be set to Z. Valid settings for this range from A to Z. Windows DOS automatically sets the "lastdrive" letter to Z.

"DEVICE =" AND "DEVICEHIGH=" PARAMETERS

You should may have noticed there are several of these types of parameters in the sample CONFIG.SYS file. The device line indicates that there is a device driver or service-specific driver that needs to be loaded during the boot process. Let's examine more closely the device lines of this CONFIG.SYS file.

The basic DEVICE parameter syntax is:

DEVICE[HIGH]=[Drive Letter - C:][Directory Path]driver-file-name [Parameters for that driver]. This is illustrated below by pointing to HIMEM.SYS in the C:\DOS\ directory.

```
DEVICE = C:\DOS\HIMEM.SYS
```

This statement is designed to load the memory manager HIMEM.SYS. There is a more detailed discussion of HIMEM.SYS later in this chapter.

If you use extended memory (XMS) for applications, this HIMEM.SYS must be loaded. Windows 3.x always uses extended memory and consequently, requires loading this driver. In order to load DOS into upper memory, HIMEM.SYS must first be loaded to activate extended memory (XMS) operation in the PC, then DOS=HIGH must unlock access to the HIMEM area.

```
DEVICE = C:\DOS\EMM386.EXE AUTO RAM X=A000-C7ff M9
```

This statement loads the second DOS memory manger, EMM386. This memory manager is required if you need to have expanded memory (EMS) for an application or if you wish to make the upper memory area available to device drivers and some terminate-and-stay-resident applications. The parameters that follow the loading of the memory manager specify how it is to configure the memory of the computer. We examine these parameters in more detail later.

```
DEVICEHIGH = C:\DOS50\SMARTDRV.SYS 2048 2048
```

This statement loads the disk-caching driver for SMARTDRV. This is actually the device driver for DOS version 5.0.

In DOS 6.0 and later, the device driver for SMARTDRV was only loaded from the CONFIG.SYS file to use double buffering for SCSI drives. Caching was initiated by loading SMARTDRV from the AUTOEXEC.BAT file.

You may have also noticed that this statement starts with DEVICEHIGH instead of just DEVICE. This designation is used simply to load the driver into the upper memory blocks as opposed to the conventional memory DEVICE uses. If there is no space in the upper memory blocks for the driver, then it loads in to is loaded into conventional memory.

```
DEVICE = C:\DOS50\ANSI.SYS
```

This statement loads the ANSI enhancement driver. This driver can be used to define functions that change display graphics, control cursor movement, and reassign keys. The ANSI.SYS device driver supports ANSI terminal emulation of escape sequences to control your system's screen and keyboard. This device driver is little used except in a few cases when some applications required it. This driver can be loaded into the upper memory as well by using DEVICEHIGH.

DOS=HIGH,UMB

This line plays two roles in the CONFIG.SYS file. First, it tells DOS when the HIMEM.SYS driver is loaded to load a portion of DOS into the HIMEM area of memory. This can help a lot in freeing up conventional memory for your DOS applications. Second, when using the EMM386 memory manager, it opens the upper memory blocks for usage by device drivers.

This statement can be written in another fashion in the CONFIG.SYS file. In the later versions of DOS the line would look like this:

```
DOS = HIGH

DOS = UMB
```

Either way is equally effective. We prefer to have fewer lines in our CONFIG.SYS file, so we use the first style of DOS statement. It is possible to force DOS to remain in conventional memory with the DOS=LOW. The DOS=NOUMB parameter can also unlink conventional memory and the upper memory area. However, there are few benefits to DOS users for doing this so these commands are rarely used.

More detail on DOS commands and memory management under DOS are covered in Chapter 13.

SHARE

Share supports file sharing and locking on the PC's disk drives. This is required by some applications that can open many files (and possibly the same file twice) and for network operation. The installation parameter is:

```
INSTALL=C:\DOS\SHARE.EXE /L:25
```

In this example, the /L parameter sets the number of locked files at 25.

AUTOEXEC.BAT

The AUTOEXEC.BAT is a batch file. Batch files contain a list of user commands that are executed when the user types in the name of that batch file. In essence, it is an executable file like a program. The commands contained in it are executed in a line-by-line order, starting with the first noncomment line at the top of the file and moving to the line displayed at the bottom of the display file.

This type of execution can make the running of many DOS commands much easier. What makes the AUTOEXEC.BAT different is that, by virtue of its name, it runs automatically at the end of the boot process. This can be very helpful, since there are many DOS commands you may need to run in order to set up your machine correctly. Just imagine how cumbersome it would be to have to type each DOS command with its accompanying switches and parameters.

To better understand the AUTOEXEC.BAT file let's dissect one. This is a good example of an AUTOEXEC.BAT file.

```
PATH C:\DOS;C:\WIN;C:\;C:\PE;C:\UTIL;C:\NET
REM Sets path
set TEMP=d:\temp
REM Sets Temporary storage directory to D: drive
prompt $p $g
REM creates my type of prompt
LH C:\DOS\MSCDEX.EXE /D:CD01 /M:10
REM loads the CD-ROM extension program with 10 buffers
C:\DOS\SMARTDRV.EXE
REM loads disk cache with default values
LH C:\DOS\doskey
REM loads everybody's favorite memory resident program
DOSKEY
```

This AUTOEXEC.BAT may look simple, but it contains most of the key commands needed in an average AUTOEXEC.BAT file. If a typical AUTOEXEC.BAT is a bit messier it may be because this file was dressed up for publication in this book. Whenever you install new software, that software may alter a line, add a line, or remove a line from the AUTOEXEC.BAT file. Like the CONFIG.SYS, you should organize it so it makes more sense and is easier to troubleshoot. The other thing to keep in mind is that each of these lines is just a written DOS command. That means you could type each line in at the DOS prompt as you see them here and they would do the same thing. Let's examine the lines of this file.

PATH C:\DOS;C:\WIN;C:\;C:\PE;C:\UTIL;C:\NET

The PATH statement is common in most AUTOEXEC.BAT files. It sets the search path that is used to locate a COM, EXE, or BAT file when it is typed in at the command line. So let's say you wanted to run a small batch file called TEST.BAT; you type that file name in at the DOS prompt and immediately DOS would begin looking for the file. First DOS looks for the file in the directory you happen to be in when you typed in the command. If it is not found there, then DOS begins to systematically look for the file in the directories that are specified by the PATH statement. Many times when stymied by an application not running, an investigation will reveal that the application would not run from the DOS prompt because the PATH statement did not specify the directory where the program resided. This being the case, putting every directory in the PATH statement seems like a good idea. One can certainly try, but the number of characters in a PATH statement is limited to 127 characters.

You may see in an AUTOEXEC.BAT file a line that looks like this:

```
PATH=%PATH%;C:\DOOM
```

This is a way to add to your existing PATH statement without rewriting it. The %PATH% is a special batch file variable that represents the entire first PATH statement plus any additional directories that need to be added. The C:\DOOM is the addition to the line. Most installation programs create AUTOEXEC.BAT lines using the %PATH% variable. Virus scanning programs in Windows create an AUTOEXEC.BAT command line that uses the %PATH% variable so they only add to the existing path and do not alter it.

Normal batch file variables are %1, %2, %3, etc. These are used to enter variable data into batch files. For example, copying data from drive C: to drive D:, or E:, could be done by a batch file statement COPY C:\path\filename %1\path\filename. The %1 would be the placeholder for either D: or E:, depending on the designated target drive.

Another way to extend the path would be to use an APPEND command in this file. The APPEND command permits programs to open data files in directories that are different from the directory containing program files. An example of the APPEND command is:

```
APPEND C:\MYDATA;C:\WKSDATA;
```

SET TEMP=D:\TEMP

The SET command is used to place text string variables in the PC's environment space. The environment space is an area in the conventional memory that is used to store common and often used text string variables. It is convenient and fast for applications to access these variables. Think of it as the 7-11 of PC memory. By typing set and a parameter, you place that parameter into the environment space. Let's take a look at the DOS prompt. Type in "set" and hit the enter key. You should see a display similar to Figure 9-5.

Figure 9–5 *DOS SET command display*

The list that appeared appears contains the user-settable environment variables. Notice that PATH is in there. Okay, let's set another variable. At the DOS prompt, type SET PCID = <YOUR NAME>. When this is complete, type in SET again at the DOS prompt and see what happens. You should see the change illustrated in Figure 9-6.

So a variable was added to the environment space; in this case the variable is PCID and its value is Jeremy. The SET TEMP=C:\TEMP specifies to DOS that the directory where it should store its temporary files is C:\TEMP.

PROMPT $P $G

This command is used to set the prompt as it appears on the screen. By default that prompt is set to the PG parameters. The $P is so that the

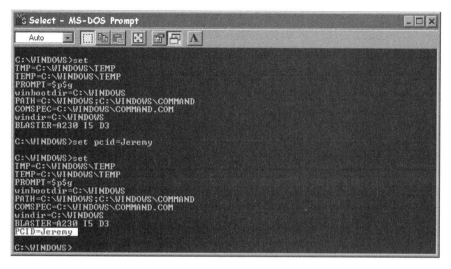

Figure 9–6   *Environment space modification from SET command*

PATH of what directory you are in is displayed in the prompt and the $G is to put a greater than symbol after the path so it does not run into the cursor. There are a number of different prompt parameters you can set, as shown in Table 9-3.

Table 9.3 *Prompt command special characters*

$Character	Output
A	The & Character
B	The | Character
C	The (Character
D	Date
E	The ESC Key (For invoking ANSI.SYS)
F	The) Character
G	The > Character
H	Back Space, Deletes Character Left of Cursor
L	The < Character
N	Designates Current Drive
P	Designates Path

Table 9.3 *Prompt command special characters*

Q	The = Character
S	Space
T	Time
V	DOS Version
_	(Underscore) Move Cursor to The Next Line

Additionally you can type in PROMPT followed by anything and it will display that as the prompt. Try it out; type "prompt Turn the page please." In order to create fancier prompts, the ANSI.SYS device driver must be loaded and its special escape sequences used to change the prompt.

LH C:\DOS\MSCDEX.EXE /D:MSCD001 /M:10

This line loads the CD-ROM interface service MSCDEX (Microsoft CD-ROM extension). Your CONFIG.SYS file must have a DEVICE or DEVICE-HIGH command that loads a CDROM device driver.

This driver should come with the CD-ROM or you can usually get it off the Internet from the CD-ROM drive manufacturer's web site. In the DEVICE line, there should also be a /D:drivername parameter. This parameter is referenced in the MSCDEX line of the AUTOEXEC.BAT. Until this line is executed, the CD-ROM does not function.

The LH at the beginning of the line is an internal DOS command, "which stands for load high." This command tells DOS to load MSCDEX driver into the upper memory area if there is enough space for it. If there is not, then DOS automatically loads MSCDEX into conventional memory.

Some flags and switches used by the MSCDEX.EXE are:

/D:MSCD001—Identifies the CD-ROM device driver. The driver flag MSCD001 must match the parameter specified by the /D switch in the CONFIG.SYS file.

/M:10—Sets the number of sector buffers to be used by MSCDEX. This may increase CD-ROM performance.

/L:letter—Assigns a drive letter to the first CD-ROM drive. If there is more than one CD-ROM drive, DOS assigns additional CD-ROM drive letters from available drive letters.

/S—Shares the CD-ROM drives on a Windows for Workgroups LAN.

> The AUTOEXEC.BAT executes each line in order. This means that if you wish your disk caching program to work with your CD-ROM, you must make sure that the line that loads the disk cache program is after the line with MSCDEX.

C:\DOS\SMARTDRV.EXE

This runs the DOS disk-caching program SMARTDRV. This program when loaded uses a portion of your extended memory for a disk cache. This can increase both the write and read performance of your fixed disk drives and CD-ROM drives. This line does not have the LH in front of it. The reason for this is that SMARTDRV does not require the LH command to load itself in the upper memory areas because SMARTDRV is designed to load itself there by default. Like using the LH command, SMARTDRV loads into conventional memory if the upper memory area is already full. SMARTDRV disk performance is dependent upon the amount of RAM installed in the PC. Figure 9-7 illustrates that optimal performance is achieved with 2 Mb of RAM assigned to SMARTDRV.

SMARTDRV can be loaded in both CONFIG.SYS and AUTOEXEC.BAT. When it is loaded in CONFIG.SYS, it enables the double buffering operation required for compatibility with some fixed disk controllers. This compatibility ensures proper addressing of sector data on the drive. No real caching is performed in this case. When SMARTDRV is run from AUTOEXEC.BAT, it sets up the disk cache. SMARTDRV can be run from AUTOEXEC.BAT alone without the double_buffering enabled. However, if your PC's disk controller requires double_buffering, and it is not enabled, you run the risk of trashing data stored on the fixed disk drive.

LH C:\DOS\DOSKEY

This last command line in the AUTOEXEC.BAT file is one that is not essential. DOSKEY is a DOS TSR (Terminate-and-Stay-Resident) program (external DOS command) that adds additional functionality to your keyboard. Like MSCDEX, you can load this external DOS command into the upper memory blocks by using the LH command before it.

MODE

Mode is a DOS command that sometimes appears in the AUTOEXEC.BAT file. It is used to speed up the keyboard typematic repetition rate, and to set

Figure 9–7   *SMARTDRV Windows launch time in seconds vs. RAM size*

up printing on serial ports rather than on parallel ports. The command for speeding up the keyboard the most is:

```
MODE CON: Rate=30 Delay=1
```

This sets the typematic rate at 30 characters per second and the start delay to 1 second.

ANSI.SYS

ANSI.SYS is device driver software that adds additional keyboard and screen control features to DOS. These features match the specifications created by the American National Standards Institute (ANSI). A few old DOS programs required these extended features. They generally are not required by software today. Some of the screen display features are identified in the prompt command above.

HIMEM.SYS

HIMEM.SYS is one of the two programs used by DOS to manage PC memory. Of the two programs, it is the essential memory manager. Although loading DOS on your PC does not require HIMEM.SYS, using Windows and other DOS applications needing extended memory requires that HIMEM.SYS be loaded.

The function of HIMEM.SYS is to control the memory above 1,024KB in your computer. This memory manager provides access to two areas of memory in your computer. The first area is the extended memory (XMS) and the second is the HIMEM area, which is the first 64 KB of memory above

1,024 KB. As we discuss later in Chapter 13, HIMEM is a key memory management program because all memory above 1,024 KB is basically managed by HIMEM.SYS.

The HIMEM area and expanded memory (EMS) are created from XMS. When the following statement in the CONFIG.SYS file accompanies HIMEM, DOS loads a large portion of itself into the HIMEM area.

```
DOS=HIGH
```

HIMEM.SYS also manages the rest of your memory from 1,088KB to your maximum amount of extended memory (XMS). Windows 3.x can run on systems that use only extended memory and the HIMEM area.

EMM386.EXE

EMM386.EXE is the second of the DOS memory managers. Its job is to provide access to upper memory areas, which are divided into upper memory blocks (UMBs), and to emulate expanded memory (EMS) in extended memory (XMS). Expanded memory is required for older DOS and Windows 3.x programs that use expanded memory. If you do not need expanded memory, the EMM386.EXE memory manager also provides access to the upper memory blocks when using the following line in the CONFIG.SYS.

```
DOS=UMB
```

Upper memory blocks (UMBs) permit DOS to load device drivers and other software into the upper memory area. This can provide more conventional memory for use by DOS programs. The DOS programs that use the largest amounts of conventional memory are typically game programs.

Note
It is possible to configure EMM386 to function without creating any expanded memory in extended memory. This is done using the switch setting NOEMS when you put the DEVICE line in the CONFIG.SYS file for EMM386.EXE.

Study Break

Examining CONFIG.SYS and AUTOEXEC.BAT

Examine the CONFIG.SYS and AUTOEXEC.BAT file on your PC.

1. Open a DOS Window on your PC. Enter DIR CONFIG.* /S at the C:\ root directory. This should list any old and current copies of CONFIG.SYS. If there is no CONFIG.SYS, try using CONFIG.DOS or another CONFIG file.

2. EDIT the CONFIG file by entering EDIT CONFIG.SYS. This should launch the DOS editor and load CONFIG.SYS into it.

3. Open a second DOS window. Now identify the commands used in CONFIG.SYS and, in the second DOS window, enter HELP followed by the command name. For example, HELP LAST-DRIVE. Follow the help menu to understand the options set for the command.

4. Perform the same procedure using AUTOEXEC.BAT in place of CONFIG.SYS.

5. Are there any commands that have options that look helpful? Try this one. In a DOS Window enter PROMPT $p $g. Does the prompt change? Try PROMPT $D $p $g. What happens? Try also PROMPT $D $T $p $g. What happens?

This exercise illustrates some of the CONFIG.SYS and AUTOEXEC.BAT file command options.

■ Summary

This chapter has covered the DOS operating system fundamentals. The three main sections in this chapter focused on functions, components, and key system files used in this operating system. The first section, on DOS functions, provided a detailed view of file, disk, and PC system and application management topics. The next section provided a brief introduction into DOS components, which led directly to the final section that covered important DOS system files and their purpose and use. Separate discussions on each significant file provided detail on the function of the file and its characteristics.

▲ Chapter Review Questions

1. *How is CONFIG.SYS used?*

   Answer: It matches PC hardware to DOS.

2. *How is AUTOEXEC.BAT used?*

   Answer: It starts TSR and other programs frequently used by PC operators.

3. *What commands are not in CONFIG.SYS?*

   Answer: CONFIG.SYS contains Device= or Devicehigh= parameters, but no DOS prompt commands.

4. *When a command is entered at the DOS prompt, what program starts processing it?*

   Answer: COMMAND.COM

5. *What command formats a disk drive and makes it bootable?*

   Answer: FORMAT /S

6. *How is DRIVER.SYS used in a CONFIG.SYS file?*

   A. to install more than two (2) floppy drives

   B. to permit more drivers to follow

   Answer: neitheration—DRIVER.SYS was used to modify floppy diskette configuration parameters.

7. *What is the drive letter of the second DOS partition?*

   A. C

   B. D

   C. E

   D. F

   Answer: First DOS partition is assigned the drive letter C; the next partition is assigned the drive letter D.

8. *CONFIG.SYS is used for?*

   Answer: Loads hardware drivers and memory management programs. Configures DOS to the PC hardware.

9. *AUTOEXEC.BAT is used for?*

   Answer: Loads added software e.g. DOSKEY to custom configure DOS operation.

10. *What commands are not found in CONFIG.SYS?*
    A. DEVICE=, DEVICEHIGH=, SMARTDRV.EXE
    B. SHARE.EXE, LASTDRIVE=, HIMEM.SYS
    C. MODE, DOSKEY, MSCDEX
    D. EMM386.EXE, SHARE.EXE, BUFFERS=
    Answer: C. MODE, DOSKEY, MSCDEX

11. *Commands typed at the DOS prompt are acted on by* _____.
    Answer: COMMAND.COM

12. *What command formats a drive and installs DOS?*
    Answer: FORMAT /S

13. *MSDOS boots in which sequence?*
    A. IO.SYS, MSDOS.SYS, COMMAND.COM, CONFIG.SYS, AUTOEXEC.BAT
    B. MSDOS.SYS, IO.SYS, COMMAND.COM, CONFIG.SYS, AUTOEXEC.BAT
    C. COMMAND.COM, IO.SYS, MSDOS.SYS, CONFIG.SYS, AUTOEXEC.BAT
    D. IO.SYS, MSDOS.SYS, CONFIG.SYS, COMMAND.COM, AUTOEXEC.BAT
    Answer: D. IO.SYS, MSDOS.SYS, CONFIG.SYS, COMMAND.COM, AUTOEXEC.BAT

14. *Each FAT entry uses one:*
    A. cluster
    B. sector
    C. byte
    D. track
    E. allocation unit
    Answer: A. cluster or E. allocation unit

15. *Which command removes a directory and all of its contents?*
    A. RMDIR

B. RD

C. DEL

D. DELTREE

Answer: D. DELTREE

16. *What is the size limit of a DOS primary or extended partition logical drive?*

A. 4 GB

B. 1GB

C. 504 MB

D. 2 GB

Answer: D. 2GB

17. *Which files are placed on a fixed disk drive by running the FORMAT /S command in DOS 6.22?*

A. IO.SYS, MSDOS.SYS, and COMMAND.COM

B. IO.DOS, MSDOS.DOS, and COMMAND.COM

C. COMMAND.COM, AUTOEXEC.BAT, and CONFIG.SYS

D. MSDOS.SYS, CONFIG.SYS, and COMMAND.COM

Answer: A. IO.SYS, MSDOS.SYS, and COMMAND.COM

18. *Memory above 1 megabyte is _____.*

A. high memory

B. expanded memory

C. upper memory

D. base memory

E. extended memory

Answer: E.extended memory (XMS) is best, but B. is also correct

19. *The clusters that make up a single file on a fixed disk drive are called?*

A. a chain

B. a fragment

C. a sector

D. a track

Answer: A. a chain

Windows 3.x Architecture

▲ Chapter Syllabus

A+ 10.1   **Windows 3.x Functions**

A+ 10.2   **Windows 3.x Components**

A+ 10.3   **Windows 3.x Key System Files**

Windows 3.x is an operating system that utilizes many of the DOS components. Windows augments DOS by adding an easy-to-use graphical user interface (GUI) and a multitasking kernel (KRNL) that provides the ability to use more than one application at the same time and supports virtual memory operation. This chapter examines the functions, components, and key system files of Windows 3.x. To understand how Windows and DOS work together, you first need to examine a typical PC that has both Windows 3.x and DOS installed. Windows 3.x modifies DOS to provide:

- A graphical user interface
- Access to extended memory (XMS) and expanded memory (EMS) for applications
- Virtual memory for applications machines
- Cooperative multitasking—permitting to a limited extent multiple functions running on the same PC at the same time

The popularity of Windows lies in its ability to make a graceful transition from the DOS command line to the Windows graphical environment. Furthermore, Windows standardizes to some extent the interface for all users. Consequently, once you have used one Windows application, it is easy to learn another.

The basic structure of Windows is:

- The graphical user interface (GUI) supporting the display, keyboard, and mouse
- The Window's application programming interface (API) and its Windows extensions
- The dynamic link libraries (DLLs)
- The kernel that modifies DOS
- The memory managers

Windows 3.x rests on a foundation created by DOS. The key to successful Windows 3.x operation is to configure DOS optimally. Optimally here stands for reliable operation with Windows, not maximizing the amount of conventional PC memory (more on this later).

One last note—the DOS configuration commands go hand-in-hand with Windows 3.x because Windows relies on DOS components to perform some functions. Thus, understanding the functions, components, and key files of DOS is also essential for Windows 3.x troubleshooting.

A+ 10.1 Windows 3.x Functions

Since Windows 3.x is an operating system, using DOS components, that provides a GUI, DOS is not used to manage the same functions examined in the previous chapter. Windows can perform, for example, disk caching, when 32-bit disk access and file access are activated.

Windows-specific applications perform file, application, and print management. For example, the Windows file manager (WINFILE) performs file management tasks, while the program manager (PROGMAN) manages applications.

These applications then communicate with the appropriate DOS component or, in some cases, with the hardware, after being passed through Windows components. Just like DOS, Windows does not understand the word FORMAT but the Windows 3.x file manager talks with BIOS to perform the FORMAT function or, in a DOS window, FORMAT communicates with BIOS via Windows. Windows 3.x also has multiple components performing similar translations for Windows. For example, Windows WRITE

Figure 10–1   *Windows 3.x architecture*

must send data to a printer. In this case, just as the file manager talks with BIOS, WRITE communicates with BIOS to send data to the printer.

Figure 10–1 illustrates this GUI/operating system breakdown. The diagram illustrates the interaction of DOS and Windows components.

Windows manages the system resources for application programs. The graphical user interface comprises USER.EXE and GDI.EXE. They in turn use driver programs for the display (VGA.DRV), the keyboard (KEY-BOARD.DRV), and the mouse (MOUSE.DRV). The graphical interface uses a data area that is 64 K (referred to technically as a heap, like a heap of data, or a heap of garbage—oftentimes with Windows one seems exactly like the other). When you measure your available resources (click on help and then click on "about program manager"), this is one of the parameters measured.

Below the GUI are the applications with their dynamic link libraries (DLLs) tailoring them to the Windows environment and thus to the PC hardware components.

DOS and the Windows kernel coordinate activities in the system. They use special programs to manage RAM (HIMEM and EMM386), disk access (SMARTDRV), printers (HPPCL.DRV for HP LaserJet and compatibles), and the network (VNETWARE.386). IPX and NETx are still required, along with Windows VNETWARE.386, to have the workstation access the network through Windows.

To make Windows work effectively with your PC, you need to know the key program players. Those players are the DOS memory management programs, the disk cache programs, and the network programs. Novell's programs are IPX, NETx, VNETWARE.386, and VIPX.386. The remaining programs are important for understanding Windows, but they are less directly involved in making it work. Making Windows perform reliably requires a knowledge of Windows operating structure and, in particular, its memory management structure.

DOS driver programs are used by Windows to control the hardware directly, just as they do for DOS. The Windows kernel (KRNL) provides the scheduling and cooperative multitasking capabilities. Other Windows components provide the graphical user interface (GDI.EXE and USER.EXE) and implement Windows 3.x applications (the application dynamic link libraries—DLL and EXE program components). They run through the kernel and the DOS drivers to provide the fancy VGA displays for the PC user.

Let's examine the Windows applications that provide the management functions.

Managing Applications

Windows 3.x is designed to handle 16-bit applications. Under Windows 3.0, applications were designed to run in a 16MB address space. This was to provide the capability to run on 80286 CPU chip systems. The 80286 and many of the 80386 SX CPU chips could only address a maximum of 16MB. There was little need for Windows to be capable of working with more RAM.

This address space is implemented using virtual memory. In Windows 3.1, this address space was increased to the 4 GB address space used by both Windows 95/98 and Windows NT today. Most Pentium CPU chips are capable of addressing 4 GB of RAM, maximum. Hence, just as Windows 3.xx is limited to 16 MB, Windows 95/98 and NT address 4 GB of memory.

Any unused virtual memory is a combination of XMS and swapfile storage on the PC's fixed disk drive. Windows supports and manages virtual memory access for all applications.

This is a necessity, not simply a nicety, because many systems running Windows 3.x had small amounts of RAM (2 or 4 M). Just starting Windows

Figure 10–2 *Windows 3.x memory usage*

on a PC requires about 1.5 MB disk space for swapping even if it is a 16 MB RAM system.

Windows substitutes disk space for RAM for both programs and data. See Figure 10–2.

The 1.5 MB disk space used when Windows started was for program swapping to the disk drive and not for data. There may be lots of space used for temporary data swapping, depending upon the software you are running. There are TIFF (*.TIF) files that contain high resolution scanned graphic images which can easily be about 1 MB alone. Try placing a few of those images on a single desktop publishing page and see how Windows 3.x slows to a crawl on that page.

When Windows 3.x runs out of space in any of the disk areas it uses, bad things happen. Consequently, picking a good strategy for providing Windows 3.x with ample disk swapping space is important to reliable and effective operation.

The options for Windows disk space files are a temporary swapfile, a permanent swapfile, or no swapfile. Running with 64 MBRAM or more? Try the no swapfile option for fun. It could speed up Windows because there is less of a need for Windows to swap data to disk. Selecting the Windows 3.1x control panel, then 386 enhanced mode, then virtual memory and change sets this up. The drop-down panel permits changing the swapfile type and specifying its size.

TEMPORARY SWAPFILE

The temporary swapfile that grows and shrinks as determined by available disk space is WIN386.SWP. It appears when you start Windows and is removed by Windows upon exiting. To see it, open a Windows DOS box and perform DIR on C:\WINDOWS. A better way of handling program swapping for Windows 3.x is with a permanent swapfile.

PERMANENT SWAPFILES

Windows 3.x can use a permanent swapfile for program storage. This file is named:

 386SPART PAR 12288000 1-21-92 5:48p HSA

The 386SPART.PAR file is located in the root directory of the drive you specify when it is created. The drive must be one of the physical disk drives on your system. Network and RAM disk drives cannot be used for 386SPART.PAR. This file must be placed in contiguous locations on the disk drive. When you create a permanent swapfile, defragment your disk drive with DOS 6.0-6.2 DEFRAG, Norton's SPEEDISK, or PCTOOLS compress.

To create a permanent swapfile in Windows 3.0:

1. Click on the Windows file menu selection.
2. Run SWAPFILE. This only works when Windows is in real operating mode. To start Windows in real mode, type WIN /R.

To create a Windows 3.1 swapfile:

1. Use the control panel 386 enhanced menu selection.
2. Select Change Virtual Machine Settings.

3. Create a permanent swapfile that is about 4 Mb to 8 Mb when possible.

It was once rumored that only a small permanent swapfile is required for Windows. We tried operating with a 1MB swapfile, but discovered that this degraded Windows performance. Heavy Windows users may require a larger swapfile.

DATA SWAPPING

The data swapping area is specified in the SET C:\TEMP statement in the AUTOEXEC.BAT file. It should point at a disk drive (volume) that has plenty of free space. Windows applications that run out of data space usually give the unrecoverable application error or general protection fault messages or other equally bad responses to the user.

As an exercise, go into the 386 enhanced section of the control panel. From the 386 enhanced section, click on the Virtual Memory button and review the different virtual memory settings.

APPLICATIONS ARCHITECTURE

DOS applications, in contrast to Windows applications, are designed to operate in conventional memory (the lower 640 KB). As a result, the Windows 3.x application architecture created both a Windows system virtual machine (which we refer to as a Windows virtual machine) and DOS virtual machines.

Figure 10–3 shows the Windows 3.x application architecture with the Windows virtual machine (Windows system virtual machine). The Windows system virtual machine (or Windows virtual machine) ran all the Windows 16-bit applications, performing cooperative multitasking between them. The problem here is that when one Windows application crashed, this typically crashed the Windows system virtual machine as well. DOS applications run

Figure 10–3 *Windows application architecture*

in separate DOS virtual machines, not in a single virtual machine. So when a DOS application crashed, it was less likely to crash all of Windows because it was more isolated from the other Windows applications.

With the release of Windows 3.1x, the operation of the Windows system virtual machine (or Windows virtual machine) was altered to make it more resilient. This alteration had Windows watch the applications more carefully to spot potential memory conflicts. When they were spotted, Windows issued a general protection fault, hopefully permitting the PC user to shut down the offending application without killing the entire Windows system virtual machine. While not foolproof, this did improve Windows reliability.

The main user interface for Windows is the desktop. The desktop is the area that encompasses the entire screen. Applications icons reside in this area.

The default interface for the desktop is the program manager; it provides a standard interface for all applications by assigning each application executable (EXE file) a graphical icon. These icons are then organized into program groups. Figure 10–4 shows the program manager with program groups and application icons.

The program manager is not the heart of the GUI but rather the user interface into the GUI. It is specified by the shell= statement in the [boot] section of the SYSTEM.INI file.

You can substitute other programs in this line and have them start as the user interface to Windows. For example, try using WINFILE.EXE, the

Figure 10–4   *Program manager Groups and Icons*

Figure 10–5 *File manager icon properties*

executable file for the file manager under windows. In this case when you start Windows, the file manager becomes your user interface.

Just as the program manager is not the heart of Windows, icons used to represent programs are only pointers to the actual executable programs. When you double-click on an icon, it indicates to Windows that it must load and run the executable file, much like DOS does when you type the name of the executable at the command prompt. This is illustrated in Figure 10–5, showing the icon properties. To see how this works, go to the icon for the file manager and select it by doing a single click on the icon. Now simply hit the Alt+Enter keys to view the icon properties. Alternatively, after clicking on the icon, you can go to the file menu and select properties.

You should see a window that pops up that allows you to edit information about the program.

The file properties can be changed to point at a different location for the program using the browse button and to change the icon representing the program by selecting the change icon button. Other properties are available to specify a working directory for the program, run the program minimized, and specify a shortcut key for the program. Running a program minimized makes it appear as a small icon on the Windows 3.1 desktop; when it is launched, it does not jump up in a Window or full screen. Assigning a shortcut key provides a means to launch the program without using the mouse. In this instance, a key combination can be used to run the program.

Managing Disks and PC Components

Disk management under Windows 3.x is done using the DOS FDISK program. FORMAT is incorporated into the Windows file manager, but it is largely DOS dependent. Similarly, other PC components are managed using the driver programs that were run under DOS and that used the PC's ROM BIOS.

Windows began to move away from such DOS dependency with the implementation of 32-bit disk access and 32-bit file access with Windows 3.1x versions.

These drivers were some of the first to bypass the DOS BIOS structure.

It is important to understand the evolution of disk management software under both DOS and Windows because they lay the foundation for the disk configuration, management, and diagnostic software used by Windows 95/98 and Windows NT PC's today. Knowing what role DOS plays and how Windows has changed that role gives us a good understanding of which disk configuration, management, and diagnostics tools to employ.

For example, most disks are configured using DOS because it provides direct access to the physical hardware. Some SCSI disks may be low-level formatted and tested using ROM software on the SCSI controller card. DOS has limitations in the functions and capacities with which it can work. For large disks, it can be used to set up the initial partitions, but may not be used to build very large partitions or SCSI RAID sets. Using BIOS or special disk driver software helps us understand the role SCSI adapter card ROM software plays in configuring and accessing attached fixed disks and the appearance of that disk drive to the Windows software running on the PC.

WINDOWS 32-BIT DISK ACCESS FUNCTIONS

Thirty-two bit disk access is provided by Windows 3.1x for non-SCSI disk drives and specially designed SCSI disk controllers (one old DTC SCSI controller supported 32-bit disk access).

Thirty-two bit disk and file access is initiated through the control panel 386 enhanced selection. Change to virtual machine settings to see the 32-bit disk and file access options as shown in Figure 10–6.

There are two 32-bit functions:

1. 32-bit disk access available in Windows 3.1 and Windows for Workgroups 3.10 and 3.11
2. 32-bit file access available in Windows for Workgroups 3.11
   Let's look at 32-bit disk access first.

32-BIT DISK ACCESS (FAST DISK)

Thirty-two bit disk access was developed to speed up disk access over that provided by the PC BIOS. Some PC BIOSs perform fixed disk I/O better than others. Windows uses 32-bit disk access, also known as fast disk, to offset lackluster BIOS performance.

Figure 10–6   *Thirty-two bit disk and file access selection*

Fast disk loads into memory a set of virtual device drivers that enhance PC BIOS by intercepting the interrupt 13H calls to the hard disk controller and redirecting them to either the 32-bit interface with the hard disk controller or the system BIOS, whichever is most efficient. Even though Windows runs in protected mode, it still switches back to real mode for DOS programs or to communicate to DOS and the system BIOS. This switching is time consuming and, when bypassed, potentially speeds up our PC. This is great for tech-heads but most people do not even sense the increase in speed provided by 32-bit disk and file access. For example, if a DOS program running in real mode needs to read from a file, under Windows it must first issue an interrupt 21H in real mode. This gets trapped and switched to protected mode so that the 386 enhanced virtual devices can interpret it. If none of the devices claim the interrupt 21H call, then it is sent on to DOS in real mode. DOS processes the call and eventually issues an interrupt 13H that in turn is trapped and switched to protected mode to have the virtual devices evaluate it. If this second interrupt is not claimed, then it is passed to the BIOS and then to the fixed disk controller. As you can see, there is unnecessary switching performed. In Figure 10–7, fixed disk interrupt processing without 32-bit disk access is illustrated.

Figure 10–7 *Fixed disk access using PC BIOS*

The virtual devices that are used by Windows to enable 32-bit disk access are listed in the SYSTEM.INI file's [386 Enhanced] section. The Western Digital Controller Statement was required for 32-bit disk access to work. The SYSTEM.INI [ENH] section statement was:

device=*wdctrl

This set up Windows communication with WD 1003-compatible fixed disk controllers and was required in most cases for 32-bit disk and file access to work. Note that the asterisk in front of wdctrl denotes that it is an internal component of Windows and not an external device driver. Other related SYSTEM.INI file statements and their descriptions are:

; 32BitDiskAccess=OFF <= original win31
32BitDiskAccess=ON
; OverlappedIO=off <= original win31
OverlappedIO=ON

PageBuffers=16

**;Specifies the number of 4 Kb page buffers Windows
;uses to store asynchronous read write pages
;when 32BitDiskAccess is activated. Default=4**

Also, SCSI disk controllers do not support 32-bit disk access without special drivers. We have used an AMI SCSI disk controller that supported 32-bit disk access.

WINDOWS WITH 32-BIT DISK ACCESS SWITCHED ON

When fast disk (32-bit disk access) is turned on, things work differently, as shown in Figure 10–8. Windows now processes the interrupt 13H in protected mode instead of sending it back to real mode and the BIOS. Fast disk is then communicating with the controller without a switch, saving the time wasted every time a switch was made. Additionally, fast disk supports overlapped I/O. This means multiple requests can be made to the disk. All requests get queued so that when one request finishes, the next one is serviced immediately. Paging to and from the Window's swapfile also occurs in the background with overlapped I/O.

To activate Windows 32-bit functions, you change the virtual memory settings through the control panel. Changing virtual memory settings opens a control window shown in Figure 10–9. At the bottom of the virtual memory control window is a box that activates 32-bit disk and file access.

The 32-bit disk access feature appeared first. It minimized the PC's CPU chip switching between real mode and protected mode operation and thus speeded up disk input/output operations. The 32-bit disk access was based on compatibility with Western Digital fixed disk controllers. It used several Windows internal drivers including *Int13 (trapped interrupt 13), *PageFile (performed virtual memory paging), *BlockDev (the core 32-bit disk management component creating and managing fixed disk drive service requests), and *wdctrl (the component talking to standard Western Digital disk drive controllers).

The 32-bit file access, similarly to 32-bit disk access, reduces switching between real and protected mode. Thirty-two bit file access performs these functions for interrupt 21 calls. This is implemented by the VFAT.386 and IFSMGR.386 device drivers that, similarly to BIOS routines, control reading and writing data to the fixed disk drive. VFAT.386 and IFSMGR.386 operate in protected mode, while the BIOS routines are relegated to real mode. Thirty-two bit file access is more than just intercepting interrupt 21 calls. It also performs disk caching. The VCACHE.386 component performs fixed cache functions equivalent to SMARTDRV.EXE while running in protected mode.

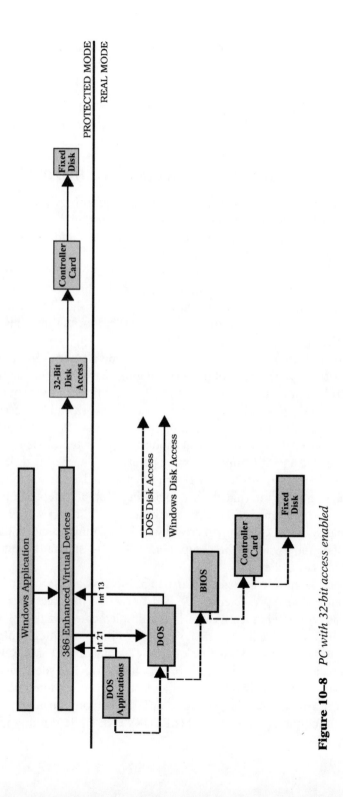

Figure 10–8 *PC with 32-bit access enabled*

BLOCKING 32-BIT DISK ACCESS

Sometimes Windows does not enable 32-bit disk access as illustrated in Figure 10–9. This happens when the disk controller is incompatible with fast disk. The Window's virtual device that lets fast disk communicate with your controller is *wdctrl. This virtual device works with any controller that is Western Digital 1003 compatible (IBM AT used this type of controller). As long as Windows senses during installation that there is a WD 1003-compatible controller, it adds the needed virtual devices for fast disk. Does that mean that if your controller is not WD 1003 compatible that you cannot have 32-bit disk access? The answer is no, if Microsoft limited fast disk to those controllers that are WD 1003 compatible, that would limit their market. As we said, Windows comes with just one virtual device for talking to disk controller cards, but manufacturers of disk controllers may provide a virtual device driver for their specific controller that supports fast disk. In general, most IDE drives work with the Windows virtual device for the WD 1003.

If you have checked to see if you have the ability to use fast disk, you may notice that the ability is there but it is still disabled by Windows. This is because Windows cannot assume that you are working on a desktop PC

Figure 10–9 *Thirty-two bit disk access disabled*

instead of a laptop PC. Some laptop PCs come with power saving features that will shut down a disk (stop it from spinning) to conserve the batteries. Sometimes this power-saving feature may not recognize that 32-bit disk access is actually using the interrupt 13H to access the disk (they only look for it to come from the BIOS). If this happens, the disk may stop spinning in the middle of a disk write, thus causing the loss of data or its corruption. The best recommendation is not to use fast disk on laptop and notebook PCs, or at least if possible turn off the power-saving features.

32-BIT FILE ACCESS

Window's 3.1x 32-bit disk access improves disk performance under Windows, but Windows for Workgroups 3.11 provides the added capability of 32-bit file access. These features are both implemented in Windows 95/98, as well as in NT.

Viewing Figure 10–10 enables you to surmise how 32-bit file access improves upon 32-bit disk access. Let's review how 32-bit disk access improved performance.

Thirty-two bit disk access improves performance by processing the interrupt 13H in protected mode instead of switching it to real mode to be handled by the BIOS. It also allows overlapped I/O. Although it stops the switching of the interrupt 13H, it still sends the interrupt 21H to DOS. This involves switching from protected mode to real mode. This wastes time. When 32-bit file access is turned on, the virtual device VFAT.386 now handles interrupt 21H in protected mode directly. When loaded, VFAT.386 inventories the physical hard drives of your system and assigns itself to those supporting 32-bit disk access, or those that have a real mode mapper for the drive.

Some disk drives do not support protected mode 32-bit disk access. They can still use 32-bit file access when 32-disk access is disabled because Windows provides a 32-bit protected-mode-compatible interface via the real mode mapper component. This Windows component is RMM.D32. It is not loaded directly but is loaded by the VXLDR.386 Windows component as required to provide a compatible 32-bit protected mode disk access interface for VFAT.386.

That means when 32-bit disk access is not used, then 32-bit file access does not activate. Drive controllers not supported by the Windows *wdctrl device driver may be supported by one from the controller manufacturer.

When you cannot use 32-bit disk access, you can use 32-bit file access, but you do not get peak performance. See Figure 10–11. Thirty-two-bit file access still works because Windows for Workgroups comes with a real mode

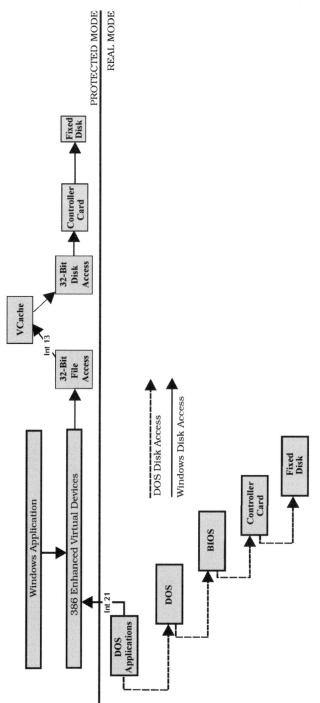

Figure 10–10 *Windows 3.1x 32-bit file and disk access operation enabled*

mapper that services protected mode I/O's from the VFAT.386. The file that does this is RMM.D32, found in your system subdirectory. This file is not specifically loaded from any of the.INI files, rather it is used if you have the following device lines in your SYSTEM.INI [386] Enhanced section:

```
device=ios.386

device=vxdldr.386
```

These lines are not added until 32-bit file access is turned on for the first time and the system either detects that 32-bit disk access is disabled, or there is a compressed disk. Compressed disks cannot use 32-bit disk access.

Managing Files

Windows provides file management capabilities that improve on those offered by DOS. The improvements are to make managing files easier for users. They utilize the GUI interface and an object model to view, copy, delete, and launch programs manipulating the files. The Windows file manager implements these file management capabilities. Of course, files could still be manipulated using the old DOS commands. However, Windows file

Figure 10–11 *Thirty-two bit file access enabled and 32-bit disk access disabled*

Figure 10–12 *Windows 3.x file manager*

manager gives less sophisticated users a mechanism to work with their files easily.

The file manager opened separate windows within the file manager program for each disk drive it was working on. This is shown in Figure 10–12 with separate windows being open for drive C, a local drive, and drive N, a network drive.

Object-oriented file management means the user can select a file and, holding down the right mouse button, drag the file to the desired location and drop it in its new location.

This would then cause Windows to copy or move the file. The file drag and drop can be more precisely controlled using the SHIFT and CTRL keys to move and copy the file respectively.

```
SHIFT = move the file

CTRL = copy the file
```

Furthermore, Windows allows data files to be associated with particular applications. The Windows file manager can launch programs associated with specific file types. This association is performed using the file name extension. Hence, TXT extensions are associated with the Windows 3.x notepad application. Double-clicking on those files would launch notepad and load the file contents into it for editing. Similarly, other common application programs have file associations built into Windows 3.x. Users can also create new file extension types and associate those with specific applications.

Printing

Windows also manages printers and printing. It provided the driver programs for printers so that any application could use any printer installed under Windows. This removed most hardware dependencies from Windows application programs; the applications focused on the application functions and not on the hardware installed in the PC. Since it is impossible for Windows to include drivers for every piece of hardware as part of the standard operating system, manufacturers of special hardware began to provide drivers for the Windows environment.

However, they did not need to provide separate drivers for each application program. This simplified application development and made Windows operation more reliable. Figure 10–13 illustrates Windows' printer setup.

As part of Windows 3.x, print spooling was implemented. Unlike DOS applications, Windows applications did not print directly to the printer, but rather printed to the Windows print spooling program.

Printing under Windows 3.1x is different from printing under DOS. Windows 3.1x prints all images and text in a document as graphics images. Most printers implement either HPPCL (HP Page Composition Language) or PostScript page description language to print graphical printouts from text or other files. Graphical printout permits font scaling as opposed to printing fonts as specific bit patterns. The Windows printer drivers get data from the application in a specific printer command format. They in turn translate that into HPPCL or PostScript commands recognized by the printer and then pass the translated information (the graphics printout) to the printer for printing. However, if Windows were to wait during this translation process while the printer printed chunks of data and then requested more data, printing any document would occupy Windows and bore the user for inordinate periods of time. Consequently, Windows translates the printing into the graphical command language output and stores it on disk in a print spooling queue. The print manager then sends the graphical image from the print queue on disk to the printer as controlled by the printer. Passing the graphical image to the printer uses fewer PC resources (CPU cycles) than translating and passing at the same time. Consequently, the print manager can send the data to the printer as a background task while the PC user continues their work.

One of the most troublesome areas with Windows 3.x is printers. They seldom print what we expect, and can be insanely slow.

In Windows, printer drivers and some DLL programs control printers. The printer driver programs for HP LaserJet 4 printers are:

```
HPPCL   DRV  152,192 11-01-93 3:11a

HPPCL5A DRV  428,672 03-10-92 3:10a

HPPCL5E DRV  399,888 11-01-93 3:11a

HPPCL5E1 DLL  75,468 11-01-93 3:11a

HPPCL5E2 DLL  58,672 11-01-93 3:11a

HPPCL5E3 DLL 100,001 11-01-93 3:11a

HPPCL5E4 DLL  24,576 11-01-93 3:11a
```

Figure 10–13 *Windows 3.x printer setup*

Windows interfaces to printers through driver programs. This means that any application running on Windows can access the printer attached to the PC and use its full functionality (more or less). Problems often arise because the printer is not set up in the same fashion on every PC, different printers are on different PCs, and PCs have different fonts installed. When Windows translates the text and images into a printer graphics language for printing, it makes the translation based on the graphical font definitions installed with Windows on the PC. When a document is created on a PC that has different graphical font definitions than the PC printing a document, the PC printing the document must use the graphical font definitions it has to print the document. Since these are not exactly the same as those on the original PC where the document was created, the printout looks different— for instance, the page breaks and paragraph layouts hit at different points than expected. This difficulty is avoided by imbedding the font definitions in the document created so that Windows can use them to perform the printing. Desktop application programs would provide the option to embed the fonts when saving or when printing a document.

CONFIGURING PRINTERS IN WINDOWS 3.X

Printer installation and configuration is performed using the Windows control panel. See Figure 10–14.

Bit-mapped and TrueType Fonts are both installed using the fonts selection in the control panel, as shown in Figure 10–15. With Windows 3.1x, Adobe Type Manager fonts were installed and managed by a separate Adobe Type Manager program. TrueType fonts that appeared in earnest in Windows 3.11 have effectively replaced all these for most PC-based desktop-publishing applications use. Since many of the early fonts were bit-mapped

Figure 10–14 *Control panel printer configuration*

images of the characters, and the bitmap files differed from font vendor to font vendor, special software—for instance, the Adobe Type Manager—was needed to transfer the fonts into any document using them. The special program would assist Windows in creating a graphical image while printing a document.

One basic printer problem that impacts HP LaserJet 4 printers is the memory specification. It is very easy to get memory overflow errors with a LaserJet 4 printer. When documents were translated into graphical images, they were much larger than the memory in the printer could hold. A single print page requires about 1.5 MB of RAM in the printer to print. Furthermore, the printers did not talk back to Windows, informing Windows of the memory they had available to store the printing image. Consequently, when Windows printed, it had to estimate the amount of data to transmit before stopping to permit the printer to print the image. The amount of data to send appeared to be a guess on Windows part that was determined by the printer memory entered in the Windows 3.1x control panel printer configuration box as shown in Figure 10–15. If the memory installed in the printer was incorrectly specified or other things happened to make the printer miss the graphical commands, a memory overflow message ensued and the printout turned to junk. Such an event was painfully evident by an error message on the printer's operator control display panel or by the pile of paper containing garbage characters in the printer's output paper bin.

When printing high-resolution graphics and pictures, the Windows 3.1x printers required as much memory as you can afford to install. HP recommended 6 MB, but 10 MB or more was better. In spite of the Windows

Figure 10–15 *Windows 3.x control panel printer configuration menu*

settings for the LaserJet 4, we still had memory overruns with less than 6 MB of memory.

One solution to memory-overrun situations was to install the printer as a LaserJet II printer with 2 MB of RAM. This older printer driver seemed to manage printing and memory very well.

HP LASERJET 4 SETUP OPTIONS

The HP LaserJet 4 menu permits selecting the amount of memory installed in the printer, the printing resolution (300 or 600 dots per inch), and the page protection mode. The best resolution we as humans can differentiate without magnifying glasses is 600 DPI. We can tell that shading in an image is not uniform, but we cannot pick out the dots. When printing a document to be copied by a xerographic copier, it is best to print the image at 300 DPI and have the graphics as coarse images. This produces printed images that have dots that the copier can focus in on and produce a consistent printed image. Refer to Chapter 6 for more information.

The page protection feature reserves printer memory for printing complex text or graphics. With page protection, a printer can create an entire page image in its memory before printing it. Setting page protection helps prevent printer memory overrun errors.

Sometimes regardless of how the resolution and page protection features are set memory overflows. This happened to us with 6 MB or less of printer memory. One solution to this problem was to set up the HP LaserJet 4 printer as an HP LaserJet Series II printer.

HOW WINDOWS USES PRINTERS

Windows uses printers in a different manner from DOS. When printing in DOS, text characters are sent to the printer for printing. In order to print graphics, DOS employs a graphics program (GRAPHICS.COM) to produce bit-mapped output for the printer.

Windows treats printers as graphics devices and sends output to them in graphics mode. The print driver for the printer under Windows converts the application program's printer output into a graphics image for printing, similar to what GRAPHICS.COM does for DOS.

It may shift to text mode for some printing, but to Windows, all printers are graphics devices and in general it tries to print to them in the highest graphics resolution permitted. One printer setup option is to print TrueType fonts as graphics. When we set this option, Windows printed a test page in 24 to 26 seconds as opposed to 30 to 31 seconds when it was not set. The implication is that switching Windows to text mode for printing slows Windows down.

PRINTER DRIVERS

A printer driver is a program that controls a printer. Whenever a document is printed, the printer driver assumes control and feeds data with the correct printing control commands to the printer. Windows comes with a variety of printer drivers for the common printers. They must be installed before a printer can be used. Updated drivers can usually be downloaded from a printer manufacturer's website.

To take maximum advantage of all a printer's features, the printer drivers for that printer should be installed under Windows. If these drivers are not available, or if they cause serious printing problems, most Windows PCs have HP LaserJet printer drivers that can be used as a general driver for most printers. Because many printers implement HP graphics language, they in effect emulate HP LaserJet printers. The text or generic printer driver is useful for sending text data quickly to any printer.

Fax drivers are used to create data for transmission by fax modems. Postscript drivers are used to generate output for text-to-slide production. Because PostScript is used to produce high quality printed documents, installing PostScript drivers permits PC users to view documents as though they were printed on a PostScript printer. Using the print preview function in any application makes Windows display the page as it would appear if printed on a PostScript printer.

Both of these drivers produce files that are then transmitted to other devices that print the desired copy.

FONTS AND FONT MANAGERS

One troublesome aspect of printing is fonts. Frequently, font reproduction can vary from printer to printer, in ways that are not always predictable. There are also both display and printer fonts.

Display fonts were used by Windows to produce screen images and menus. With Windows 3.0, a limited number of screen fonts were provided. These were fonts comprised of bit maps for different display resolutions like EGA and VGA displays. Printers used printer fonts for printing. The trick with Windows was to match the display fonts to the printer fonts so that the documents represented on the display screen matched the printout. This became simpler with Windows 3.1 because TrueType fonts were introduced.

When applications use TrueType fonts, the same font could be used for both the display and the printer.

Fonts can also be classified as bit-mapped or scalable.

Bit-mapped fonts use specific bit images of the characters to create the display or printout. Scalable fonts describe to the display or printer how to construct the character and then what size to make it. This meant that a document using TrueType scalable fonts could be enlarged or shrunk to any size and the fonts would scale up-and-down smoothly with a document on the display screen. With Windows 3.1; bit-mapped fonts have all but disappeared.

The bit-mapped fonts remaining are the standard Windows menu display fonts including Courier, Fixedsys, Modem, MS Serif, MS-DOS CP 437, Small Fonts, Symbol, System, and Terminal. Some of these fonts come with bitmaps for 8514, VGA, and CGA displays. When viewing fonts in the control panel under fonts, the display icons show TT for TrueType and A for bit-mapped fonts. These standard Windows menu display fonts are retained for backwards compatibility with previous versions of Windows.

Scalable printer fonts are TrueType and Adobe Type Manager (ATM) fonts. TrueType font processing is built directly into Windows. ATM font processing requires that the ATM driver program be added to Windows. Both font management programs have their merits and more fonts than any Windows user could ever hope to employ in a document. Since the support for TrueType fonts was built into Windows and thus did not require special driver software, TrueType fonts are used by most Windows systems today.

Installing too many fonts can consume lots of disk space and can reduce your GUI data heap capacity. Under Windows 3.x, TrueType fonts are installed in the WINDOWS\SYSTEM directory. ATM fonts are installed wherever specified.

All fonts display and print depending upon the printer's capability and display resolution. Smaller fonts cannot be accurately displayed on a VGA resolution (640 by 480) display. Larger fonts can also appear to have jagged edges. "Hinting" is the name of the technique employed to improve the typeface display as a type font by your PC. A typeface character does not match perfectly with the dots on your display or printer. Hinting determines which are activated to produce the typeface or font on your display or printer.

The most common problem encountered with fonts is that users install far too many fonts, more than they could ever possibly need. For example, on our systems there are over 400 fonts installed and we use about 50 of them, tops. Windows 3.1 systems with lots of fonts installed ran the risk of reducing the system resource heaps to low levels that would crash Windows when many different fonts were used in preparing documents. These fonts had to be loaded into the graphical resource heaps for Windows 3.1 when they were used. We found that many times when printing the graphical resource heaps under Windows 3.1 would drop to zero much to our surprise. We were able to observe this because we were monitoring the resource heaps as we printed. This sometimes causes our PC to crash. A normal PC user would just see the PC crashing and have no idea why. The simple solution would be to just install the fonts that were required.

USING THE CONTROL PANEL

The Windows 3.x Control Panel provides access to several setup and tuning capabilities. Significant among these is access to the 386 Enhanced Mode operation for altering the multitasking and virtual memory options of Windows 3.x.

The features in the Windows Control panel vary depending upon the version of Windows. Windows for Workgroups has more and slightly different features than does normal Windows. The Control Panel in Figure 10–16 is from a Windows for Workgroups PC.

Color changes the screen colors, and fonts installs different fonts. True-Type fonts are the easiest to install. The mouse, desktop and keyboard options alter the look and feel of Windows to suit the PC user's preferences. The Control Panel options are used to add printer driver programs, add printer fonts, configure printers, and share and attach to network printers (Windows for Workgroups). Date and time settings modify the date and time, quite obviously, while international changes the display representation of the date and time. The network selection permits configuring network boards and protocols. Open Data Base Connectivity (ODBC) provides Windows SQL database access to Dbase, FoxPro, MS Access and Paradox database applications. The 386 enhanced selection controls time slicing, the swapfiles, and disk access. It is one means of tuning Windows. Multimedia

Figure 10–16
Windows for Workgroups control panel

and sound card driver programs are installed using the drivers selection. If a speaker driver is installed, the sound selection can assign sounds to different operator actions, such as starting and closing Windows. With Windows for Workgroups, you have a fax option for your electronic mail that is installed and managed using the FAX control panel selection.

Study Break

Fonts

Let's examine the fonts installed on your system. This exercise works similarly for Windows 3.1 as well as Windows 95 and Windows 98.

1. Start up Windows and open the control panel.

2. Find the fonts icon and click on it. The fonts installed in Windows should appear. They will most likely be displayed as icons.

3. Go to the menu and select view and then list fonts by similarity. The fonts should be listed with a notation of whether they are similar or not similar to other fonts.

4. Under view, be sure the status bar is checked. It should be displayed at the bottom of the fonts window. In the status bar the total number of fonts installed should be displayed. How many fonts are installed on the PC?

5. When viewing the fonts, display how many of the fonts are not similar or Windows just doesn't know whether they are similar or not similar.

The goal of this exercise is to give you a better understanding of the fonts typically installed on a user PC.

A+   10.2   **Windows 3.x Components**

Windows components are:

- Driver programs, interfacing PC hardware to Windows software
- Dynamic link libraries (DLLs), implementing application programs
- The kernel, providing all the system control and scheduling functions
- Graphical user interface, consisting of GDI.EXE and USER.EXE
- The resource heaps, storing graphics information for GUI
- INI files, controlling starting Windows and applications programs.

Some of these components are configured and manipulated using the control panel icons, while other components are the core components of Windows and not directly manipulated by the control panel icons. Let's look at these briefly.

Driver Programs

Driver programs are required to interface Windows 3.x to the PC hardware. Windows 3.x or the hardware component manufacturer can provide them. Driver programs know intrinsically how to transfer data between the PC's RAM and the specific hardware component. They are written to work with specific interrupt requests (IRQs), input/output ports, and memory ranges. They buffer requests, queue them for processing and perform other detailed tasks that support the PC hardware. Standard driver programs are provided for the mouse, the keyboard, and the display.

MEMORY MANAGEMENT AND DISK CACHING

The HIMEM and EMM386.EXE programs perform Windows 3.x memory management. The HIMEM program enables the use of Extended Memory (XMS) and creates the HIMEM area from it. EMM386.EXE creates Expanded Memory (EMS) and turns other extended memory into the Upper Memory Area (UMA) dividing it into Upper Memory Blocks (UMBs). The DOS SMARTDRV provides the disk cache driver for Windows 3.x. Only with Windows 3.11 are there 32-bit disk and file access drivers that largely replace the SMARTDRV disk cache.

LOCAL AREA NETWORK DRIVERS

LAN driver programs are required for network interface cards produced by hardware manufacturers. Under Windows 3.x, the hardware manufacturer typically provided the LAN card driver programs. They were not provided as standard drivers with Windows 3.x. This has changed with Windows 95/98. Many LAN NIC card drivers are provided with Windows 95/98. Once installed, the NIC card drivers must be bound (linked to) to the protocols that communicate between PCs across the LAN.

Generally, the hardware manufacturers provide the software for Windows 3.x, Windows NT, and Novell NetWare, as well as other operating systems. The NetWare software for a 3Com Ethernet board is LSL.COM, 3C509.EXE, IPXODI.COM and then the Windows 3.x or NetWare VLM programs. These drivers are loaded and configured in DOS prior to running Windows 3.x.

Novell NetWare dominated the DOS LAN marketplace. Because of this domination, most DOS and Windows PCs used the Novell software for LAN communications. With Windows 95/98 networks, the LAN environment has changed. They are more widely populated with TCP/IP protocols and Microsoft's software than Novell's.

Dynamic Link Libraries

Dynamic link libraries are either DLL or EXE file types. They implement specific functions or tasks for applications. For example, a spell-checking function in a desktop publishing program is performed by a single DLL.

The EXE programs that run under DOS and produce the error message "This program requires Windows to execute" are dynamic link library programs relying on the Windows GUI for many of their display and operator interface functions. They are not to be confused with the EXE programs commonly used in DOS. This means that dynamic link libraries have both a DLL and an EXE extension.

"Dynamic" means something that happens on the fly while Windows is running, link points to the address or start point of another program, and "library" means that there are many of them to accomplish specific tasks under Windows. The EXE programs are DLLs that usually launch an application program. They rely on other DLLs that are loaded and unloaded in Windows memory as required to perform the application program's functions. Windows itself and applications that run under Windows rely on many DLLs. Most DLLs are common to many programs and Windows. They are stored in the \windows and \windows\system folders. Application programs store common DLLs in those folders as well. They also store other DLLs in the folder into which they install.

The Kernel

The kernel performs the most important core functions of an operating system. The kernel schedules and coordinates execution of applications and of input/output operations. Windows NT, OS/2, and other operating systems have kernels. Windows 3.x also comes with its own kernels, as shown in Table 10–1.The standard mode kernel was provided with Windows 3.0 to permit it to run on 286 CPU chip PCs.

Table 10.1 *Windows 3.x kernels and operating modes*

Kernel Program	Size	Date Time	Windows Mode
KRNL286.EXE (Windows 3.0)	71,730	03-10-92 3:10a	Standard mode
KRNL386.EXE (Windows 3.1, 3.11)	75,490	03-10-92 3:10a	386 enhanced mode and real mode

The 386 kernel operated in both real and 386 enhanced mode. Real mode was required to provide compatibility for older driver programs that would only operate with the PCs BIOS. With Windows 3.1x, the applications migrated to operating and 386 enhanced mode to take advantage of the virtual memory space and the faster 386 enhanced mode display and disk driver programs.

Windows kernels interface between DOS and DOS memory managers to provide access to the PC's extended memory (XMS) for Windows 3.x.

GDI.EXE and USER.EXE

Windows graphical user interface is created at system startup. The actual interface is a combination of two programs, GDI.EXE and USER.EXE. GDI.EXE is the Windows graphical display interface manager and USER.EXE is the Windows input manager. These programs together are responsible for managing all the Windows created systemwide and the drawing of items on your screen. To display the system resources, select Help and then About from the program manager. This produces Figure 10–17, which shows free graphical resources in the Windows 3.x display. Both of these programs use data areas called the graphical resource heaps to manage these items. The graphical resource heaps are approximately 64 KB in size and operate in real mode, regardless of what operating mode was selected at startup. Why so small a size for such a large task? Windows does this because calling objects from a known area 64 KB in size is faster than doing the same across large regions of memory.

When you start Windows, your graphical resource area is about 80 to 85% free. It never gets much higher because some graphical resources are used by the Windows 3.x desktop and the program manager. Each additional window you create in your shell or in an application takes approximately 2% or more of the available resources. View the resources used by choosing Help followed by About in program manager. This displays the free resource percentage down at the bottom of the screen. When your resources get down below the 15% mark, you are not able to open additional windows, regardless of the total amount of RAM your machine has installed. Additionally, a

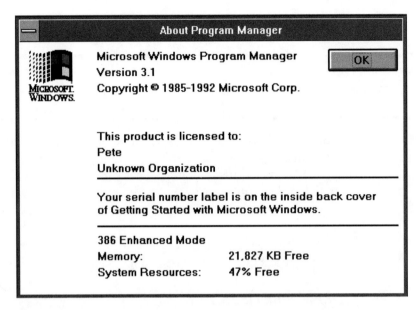

Figure 10–17 *Program manager showing free graphical resources in Windows 3.x*

program like print manager, when loaded, may only need 2% of your resources, when it comes time to print, requires 20% to perhaps 50% of your resources. Running out of resources is a surefire way to make Windows slow way down.

When you display Help and About in program manager, Windows shows the resources available in the graphical heap with the least resources. Typically the USER.EXE heap runs out of resources first.

Resource Heaps

To view the Windows 3.x resource heaps go to Help and then About in the program manager. HA.EXE is a program that continually monitors your heaps while you open and close Windows applications. See Figure 10–18. It provides more detail on the use of the resource heaps than does the Windows 3.x control panel display. When you run out of space in your resource heaps, there is not much to do but shut down Windows and restart to correct the problem. This means that detailed information about the resource heaps is interesting but not that helpful in solving problems. Because they do tell you when your resources are exhausted or near exhaustion, which puts Windows at risk of crashing, a PC user is able to avert a crash by shutting down Windows.

Figure 10–18   *Heap Alert detailed display*

Windows Graphical Resources

This exercise examines the Windows graphical resources and how to monitor them.

1. Get a Windows 95 or Windows 98 PC. Open the control panel and click on System.

2. Click on the performance tab and look for system resources. What percentages are free? This represents the heap with the fewest resources. When the number is low, the PC is in danger of crashing.

3. Use the Windows Explorer and open the Windows directory. Find the program RSRCMTR.EXE. Double-click on it to launch it. What resources does it display as available? Do they match with what you saw under the control panel display?

The resource monitor program, RSRCMTR.EXE, permits us to continuously view the available graphical resources. By placing it in the Windows\start menu\programs\startup folder, the resource meter can be launched when Windows starts. Its icon then appears in the SYSTRAY, providing a continuous monitoring of all available graphical resources.

A+   10.3   Key Windows 3.x System Files

Installing Windows is as simple as running the setup program. However, making it run reliably and speedily is not so simple. Let's examine key Windows 3.x components in a PC to see precisely how they impact performance and operation. Later we examine these files in detail to discover the results produced by different parameter values.

Several files play a key role in Windows operation. These files are:

INI files—These are the program initialization files. They tell Windows and Windows applications how to configure themselves for operation under Windows. There are two key files for Windows alone. These are the WIN.INI, equivalent to the DOS AUTOEXEC.BAT file, and the SYSTEM.INI file, equivalent to the DOS CONFIG.SYS file. Generally, the SYSTEM.INI file configures Windows with the PC's hardware, while WIN.INI sets up the desktop display and applications under Windows. INI files are most often text files that can be edited with any editor program. Once edited and Windows is restarted with the new files, its operation is altered. See Figure 10-19.

```
 Volume in drive C is EISA50MHZ_2
  Volume Serial Number is 1B3B-08D1
  Directory of C:\WIN
123W          INI    4454       02-08-93 11:51a
ALDUS         INI     671       02-08-93 11:05a
AMIDLGIC      INI      77       09-23-91  1:48p
AMIDRAW       INI     246       01-30-93  4:23a
AMIDW         INI    8283       06-18-92 10:56a
AMIEQN        INI     898       06-03-92  2:47p
AMIFONT       INI     301       01-30-93  4:18a
AMIIMAGE      INI     447       04-09-91  8:26a
AMILABEL      INI   10014       06-19-92  9:52a
AMIOW         INI   23822       12-17-91 12:05p
AMIPRO        INI    6463       02-09-93  3:40p
AMIVISD       INI    4958       02-08-93 11:37a
ATM           INI    6455       02-09-93  3:22p <= sets up Adobe Type Manager
CONTROL       INI    4253       02-09-93  7:19p <= sets up Windows Desktop
CORELCHT      INI    1797       02-08-93 11:45a
DOSAPP        INI    1144       02-09-93  7:00p <= sets up DOS Applications
EXCEL         INI      52       02-08-93 11:38a
PROGMAN       INI     217       02-08-93 10:46a<= sets up Program Manager
SYSTEM        INI    3914       02-09-93  6:36p <= sets up hardware
WIN           INI   14669       02-09-93  7:22p <= sets up Windows programs
WINFILE       INI     150       02-08-93 10:43a
WPM           INI     184       02-09-93  7:10p
SOL           INI      33       02-09-93  6:46p <= sets up Solitaire Game
     28 file(s)   95326 bytes
        11606016 bytes free
```

Figure 10–19 *Some Windows 3.1x INI files*

• GRP files—Group files describe the program groups displayed by Windows.

- DLL files—These files are the application program designed to work specifically in the Windows graphical environment. DLL files are found in application subdirectories and in the Windows\system directory.
- SCR files—SCR files are the screen saver displays used by Windows. They reside in the Windows directory.
- DRV and SYS files—These are the hardware driver programs used by Windows to communicate with the PC's hardware. They reside in the Windows\system directory.
- Windows fonts are described by FON, FOT and TTF files. Each font has its associated files. These files reside in the Windows\system directory.
- INF files—INF files are used by setup to configure Windows. Altering them changes the setup process.
- EXE files—Windows programs are implemented as executable (EXE) files. These are not the same as DOS executable files because they need the Windows GUI environment operating to be executed. All Windows programs are EXE files save one, which is a COM file. The WIN.COM program is the key Windows COM file.
- WAV files—These files are the sound files for Windows. They can be used by the speaker driver program (available from the Microsoft forum on Compuserve) to produce various sounds on your PC's speaker.
- BMP files—BMP files are large bit-mapped graphics used for various displays. Because of their large size, it is not good to use those graphics.
- PIF files—These files are used to start DOS applications under Windows. It is not necessary to start all DOS applications using PIF files, but when special control of the DOS application is needed, the PIF files provide that control. PIF files are not used to start Windows applications.
- ICO and LIB files—Windows icons are described in these files. The icons are either individual icons or libraries of icons. Once an icon is chosen for an application under program manager, the ICO and LIB file are no longer needed. However any change to the relationship between the Windows icon under program manager and the program usually causes you to reinstall the icon.
- COM files—There are very few COM files in Windows today. The most important file, and the one that we're all familiar with, is the one that launches Windows, WIN.COM.

- FON and TTF files—FON and TTF files are files that describe Windows fonts. The FON files are for bit-mapped fonts and the TTF files describe TrueType fonts. Both files are typically found in the Windows\fonts folder.
- HLP files—HLP files provide the help menu displays for Windows. They are the electronic instruction manual that comes with Windows.
- 386 files—The 386 files are drivers and Windows components that are not built into Windows. They support network connectivity, 32-bit disk and file access, and other Windows features.

Windows uses other file types for specialized functions. Most play a minor role compared to the INI files. If the INI files are not set up properly or if another file (for instance, a font file) specified in an INI file is not found by Windows 3.x at startup, bad things happen. Understanding the INI files is important for fixing Windows problems without needlessly rerunning SETUP.

INI Files

Much like DOS uses certain files to configure itself (CONFIG.SYS and AUTOEXEC.BAT), Windows uses several specific files to configure itself during startup. The two files are the SYSTEM.INI and WIN.INI. The SYSTEM.INI file determines how the PC hardware interacts with Windows. It is also a key file for making Windows operate properly in 386 enhanced mode.

Both SYSTEM.INI and WIN.INI are used by Windows 95/98 to preserve compatibility with Windows 16-bit (Windows 3.x) applications. For example, Corel Draw 5.0 is one application program that uses settings in the WIN.INI file under Windows 95/98.

We are going to look at WIN.INI first.

WIN.INI

The WIN.INI file controls how your Windows applications operate with Windows. One function of the WIN and other INI files is to provide the mechanism for Windows to remember where you last retrieved a text file versus an AmiPro file, etc. INI files are altered constantly by Windows. When Windows 3.0 was first introduced, all application INI statements went into the WIN.INI file. Today many applications maintain their own set of INI files in the Windows subdirectory and elsewhere. These two INI files are the precursors to the registry file used in Win95.

The one problem with the WIN.INI file is that statements always get placed there but none ever seem to be removed. Cleaning up a WIN.INI file can be a chore. The easiest way to accomplish this is to start with a simple WIN.INI file, then add back the program statements from the "dirty" WIN.INI file for each Windows application installed. If statements are missed, the applications typically do not start and give a brief error message.

There are many sections to the WIN.INI file. Some standard Windows sections are identified below. They include:

[**Windows**]—contains Windows look-and-feel information and is changed using the control panel.

[**Desktop**]—describes desktop look and is changed using the control panel.

[**Extensions**]—associates files with applications.

[**intl**]—sets Windows up for international operation.

[**ports**]—identifies the ports available to Windows, for example, COM and printer ports.

[**FontSubstitutes**]—identifies fonts that can be substituted for other fonts.

[**TrueType**]—tells Windows whether TrueType fonts are turned on for all applications.

[**Sounds**]—causes sounds to be made for certain Windows events.

[**mci extensions**]—identifies multimedia file types.

[**Compatibility**]—ensures applications display properly.

[**winsetup**]—identifies the path to which Windows was installed.

[**fonts**]—identifies installed fonts for Windows.

[**embedding**]—describes how applications interact with Windows.

[**colors**]—sets up the Windows colors. This is controlled through the control panel.

[**Windows Help**]—tells Windows where to display the help screen.

[**MRU_Files**]—tells Windows where to find specific files. This is similar to the path statement.

[**spooler**]—records print spooler setup information.

[**PrinterPorts**]—tells Windows the printer port configurations.

[**devices**]—associates printer descriptions with printer ports for Windows.

Each section is identified in the file by being placed inside brackets. Within the sections are the commands that Windows and application programs use to configure themselves to operate on this particular Windows PC. Some sections are changed using the Windows control panel. The application program may change others or they just may be references that the application program uses.

> [**Panasonic KX-P4420,LPT2**]
> [**Network**]
> [**HPPCL,LPT2**]
> [**WINFAX**]
> [**AnyFax**]
> [**WfxPbLinks**]
> [**PSPLUS**]

Other sections like the ones above may also be included in the file. These depend upon the options installed in Windows and the applications installed upon PC.

UNDERSTANDING WIN.INI

Let's examine a WIN.INI file. This first statement loads the programs that you want to run every time Windows is started. The NWPOPUP.EXE program is for Novell Networks. Other commonly used programs can be loaded with the load statement as well.

```
[windows]
load=nwpopup.exe resgauge.exe d:\aftrdark\ad.exe redbtn.exe
```

If you want to jump into an application when Windows starts, place the file name after the RUN= line.

```
run=
```

These are standard WIN.INI file statements. They permit Windows to beep in specific circumstances. The NullPort statement identifies to Windows that all ports are assigned to physical devices.

```
Beep=yes
NullPort=None
```

The statements that follow identify the driver program for printer port 1. The first line is a comment, as indicated by the semicolon (;) preceding the text. Normal device and other WIN.INI commands are statements that appear on a single line with an equal sign following them. They are disabled by placing a semicolon (;) at the beginning of the line.

```
;default printer specification from Control Panel is below.
Spooler=no
device=Panasonic KX-P4420,HPPCL,LPT1:
```

The next statements set up some of the graphical user interface parameters. Typically these parameters are changed using programs found in the

Windows control panel. For example the colors and the desktop configuration can be changed using control panel applets.

```
BorderWidth=3
KeyboardSpeed=31
CursorBlinkRate=200
DoubleClickSpeed=820
MouseThreshold1=4
MouseThreshold2=6
MouseSpeed=2
```

This statement specifies the program extensions that are executable.
```
Programs=com exe bat pif
```

These statements control programs.

```
Documents=
DeviceNotSelectedTimeout=15
TransmissionRetryTimeout=45
```

This statement specifies a swap disk if different from the Windows default drive.
```
swapdisk=
```

ADDED PARAMETERS FOR WINDOWS 3.1 VERSUS WINDOWS 3.0. • The CoolSwitch determines whether you can Alt-Esc or Ctrl-Esc from applications. The control panel programs control the other parameters.

```
CoolSwitch=1
ScreenSaveActive=0
ScreenSaveTimeOut=120
KeyboardDelay=0
DosPrint=no
NetWarn=0
```

Slower displays (like LCD displays on laptops) use this mouse trails setting. The mouse trail setting delays removal of the mouse pointer image as the mouse is moved around the screen. This gives the mouse the appearance of leaving a trail. On displays with slow refresh rates the mouse trail helps the user to locate the mouse when it is moved rapidly.

```
                        MouseTrails=7
```

This sets up our desktop display parameters. These settings can also be modified using the "Display" dialog found in the control panel program group. The grid granularity sets up a spacing grid that Windows uses to create the desktop.

```
[Desktop]
```

```
Pattern=0 68 166 29 168 68 34 17
Wallpaper=(None)
TileWallpaper=1
GridGranularity=0
IconSpacing=60
```

This section goes on and on, identifying file extensions associated with any application we have launched from Windows. It covers both DOS and Windows applications.

```
[Extensions]
smm=C:\AMIPRO\amipro.exe ^.smm
sam=C:\AMIPRO\amipro.exe ^.sam
doc=winword.exe ^.doc
cal=calendar.exe ^.cal
crd=cardfile.exe ^.crd
trm=terminal.exe ^.trm
txt=C:\PE\GOPEB.BAT ^.TXT
pcx=pbrush.exe ^.pcx
bmp=pbrush.exe ^.bmp
rec=recorder.exe ^.rec
LZH=LH.BAT ^.LZH
.  .  .  .  .  .  .  .  .  .  .  .  .  .  .  .
cdr=D:\WINAPPS\COREL\CORELDRW\coreldrw.exe ^.cdr
```

The country settings for the PC are specified here. The country setting also controls the default settings for time and date, along with other standard defaults specific to the country, such as typical currency symbols. This section just grows and grows with seemingly no end as well.

```
[intl]
sCountry=United States
iCountry=1
iDate=0
iTime=0
iTLZero=0
iCurrency=0
iCurrDigits=2
iNegCurr=0
iLzero=1
iDigits=2
iMeasure=1
s1159=AM
s2359=PM
sCurrency=$
sThousand=,
sDecimal=.
```

```
sDate=/
sTime=:
sList=,
sShortDate=M/d/yy
sLongDate=dddd, MMMM dd, yyyy
```

This specifies the display colors that we have chosen. Changing these numbers can have some wild results. Try PUNK for a unique color combination. These settings can be changed once Windows is active using the display dialog in the control panel program group.

```
[colors]
Background=105 128 0
AppWorkspace=255 255 128
Window=255 255 255
WindowText=0 0 0
Menu=255 255 255
MenuText=0 0 0
ActiveTitle=64 128 128
InactiveTitle=128 255 255
TitleText=255 255 255
ActiveBorder=255 128 64
InactiveBorder=255 128 128
WindowFrame=0 0 0
Scrollbar=129 129 129
```

Here the PC's physical ports are identified—that is, assigned a number. The LPT port lines assigned printer port number 1 to LPT1 and printer port number two to LPT2. Nothing follows the LPT port assignments because there are no setup parameters that Windows controls for them. In contrast, when Windows assigns a number to a COM port, it also specifies the speed and character layout. The EPT designation stands for enhanced parallel port.

```
[ports]
; A line with [filename].PRN followed by an equal sign
causes
; [filename] to appear in the Control Panel's Printer
Configuration dialog
; box. A printer connected to [filename] directs its output
into this file.
LPT1:=
LPT2:=
LPT3:=
COM1:=9600,n,8,1
COM2:=9600,n,8,1
COM3:=9600,n,8,1
```

```
COM4:=9600,n,8,1
EPT:=

FILE:=
LPT1.OS2=
LPT2.OS2=
```

This specifies where Windows Help box appears. Move yours around and then exit saving changes to see what range of movement is permitted here.

```
[Windows Help]
Xl=609
Yu=163
Xr=945
Yd=579
Maximized=1
```

This section begins the display and printer font identification to Windows. These are standard Windows display and printing fonts.

```
[fonts]
Modern (Plotter)=MODERN.FON
Roman (Plotter)=ROMAN.FON
Script (Plotter)=SCRIPT.FON
MS Sans Serif 8,10,12,14,18,24 (8514/a res)=SSERIFF.FON
MS Serif 8,10,12,14,18,24 (8514/a res)=SERIFF.FON
Small Fonts (8514/a res)=SMALLF.FON
```

Use Windows TrueType fonts as identified below. These are the fonts loaded by the Windows graphical user interface and used to produce documents and screen displays.

```
Arial (TrueType)=ARIAL.FOT
Arial Italic (TrueType)=ARIALI.FOT
Courier New (TrueType)=COUR.FOT
Courier New Italic (TrueType)=COURI.FOT
WingDings (TrueType)=WINGDING.FOT
Motor (True Type)=C:\WIN\SYSTEM\motorn.fot
................
Timpani Bold Italic (True Type)=C:\WIN\SYSTEM\timpanit.fot
TimpaniHeavy Italic (True Type)=C:\WIN\SYSTEM\timpnihi.fot
ZurichCalligraphic Italic (True
Type)=C:\WIN\SYSTEM\zurichi.fot
Lincoln (True Type)=C:\WIN\SYSTEM\lincolnn.fot
```

The TrueType section specifies whether TrueType fonts should be used only in applications or whether Windows can use both TrueType and bit-mapped fonts.

```
[TrueType]
TTEnable=1
TTOnly=0
```

Now WIN.INI specifies font descriptions that are assigned to the printer ports. These make it possible for all Windows applications to print with the same fonts.

Below is the weird [wt4gpi8s56bz] Windows 3.1 specification for printer fonts. This is sometimes found on Windows PCs with desktop publishing applications installed. It helps Windows match the screen display to the printed output.

```
[wt4gpi8s56bz]
```

The operating parameters for the printers and printing programs installed on our PC are described next.

```
[HP LaserJet Series II,LPT1:,LPT2:,LPT3]
Memory=4491
Number of Cartridges=1
Cartridge 1=30
[HPPCL,LPT1]
duplex=0
prtcaps=32896
paperind=5
winver=310
sfdlstyle=16
numcart=1
cartindex1=
[HPPCL5A,LPT1]
prtcaps2=3
```

Printer specifications are often required for special programs such as send/receive fax modem programs. The font specifications for the WINFAX program are below.

```
[WINFAX]
Fax Path=d:\appsw\winfax\data\
Fax Device=Class1
modem=*F2
Paper Format=Letter (8.5 x 11 inches)
Orientation=Portrait
Dial Prefix=
Resolution=Standard
```

```
Retries=0
Call Progress=Yes
CSID=MCO—Remote
Sender=Pete Moulton
Header Left=The Moulton Company
Header Center=Building User Knowledge, Since 1980
Header Right=FAX # 410 988-9861
Max Tx Rate=9600
Retry Time=60
Dial Control=Busy
Volume=Med
Speaker Mode=Connect
Dial Mode=Tone
```

Network printer assignments are specified in the WIN.INI file as shown below.

```
[Network]
LPT2:=MOULTON676/PANASONIC
LPT2-OPTIONS=8,1,8,30,0,,PETE
```

Other printer assignments are also specified in the WIN.INI file as shown below.

```
[PrinterPorts]
PCL / HP LaserJet=HPPCL,LPT1:,15,45,LPT2:,15,45
Canon LBP-8II=LBP8II,None,15,45
Epson 9 pin=EPSON9,None,15,45
IBM Graphics=IBMGRX,None,15,45
IBM Proprinters=PROPRINT,None,15,45
PostScript Printer=PSCRIPT,FILE:,15,45
```

This covers the major printer specifications. Next come setup and operating parameter specifications for the XTALK communications program.

```
[XTALK]
ModemCom1Name=Hayes V9600
ModemCom1Prefix=ATDT
ModemCom1Suffix=^M
ModemCom1Setup=ATS0=1^M
ModemCom1Init=^M~ATV1E0X4^M~AT&M4&B1&Y2&C1&D2^M
ModemCom1Hangup=~~+++~~ATH0^M
ModemCom1Ok=OK^M^J
ModemCom1Error=ERROR^M^J
ModemCom1Connect=CONNECT^M^J
ModemCom1Speed=CONNECT %^M^J
ModemCom1Dial=TONE^M^J
```

```
ModemCom1Ring=RING^M^J
ModemCom1NoDial=NO DIAL^M^J
ModemCom1Busy=BUSY^M^J
ModemCom1Carrier=NO CARRIER^M^J
Maximized=0
DirXwp=D:\WINAPPS\XTKWIN\PHONE
DirXws=D:\WINAPPS\XTKWIN\SCRIPTS
DirFil=D:\
Editor=c:\pe\PE2.exe
Startup=e
Backups=1
Secret=0
Paste=1
OutNumber=
WatchDial=1
CustomPrefix=ATX0DT
CustomSuffix=^M
CustomSetup=ATS0=1^M
CustomInit=^M~ATV1E0X0^M
CustomHangup=~~+++~~ATH0^M
CustomOk=OK^M^J
CustomError=ERROR^M^J
CustomConnect=CONNECT^M^J
CustomSpeed=CONNECT %^M^J
CustomDial=TONE^M^J
CustomRing=RING^M^J
CustomNoDial=NO DIAL^M^J
CustomBusy=BUSY^M^J
CustomCarrier=NO CARRIER^M^J
CustomChange=0
ModemCom1Change=1
Comm=16384
LdNumber=1 619 755-2019
ModemCom1ARQ=CONNECT %/REL^M^J
```

Now several applications are setup in the WIN.INI file. For example the following WIN.INI statement sets up the clock display format. The clock display is in analog or digital format.

```
[Clock]
iFormat=0
```

The following lines specify the solitaire game parameters.

```
[Solitaire]
Back=11
Options=67
```

Windows comes with a simple terminal program. It is pointed at COM1 with the following WIN.INI statement.

```
[Terminal]
Port=COM1
```

The Windows calculator can be set to a normal or to a scientific calculator. The scientific calculator can be set up to do different types of scientific calculations. This statement determines how the scientific calculator is setup.

```
[SciCalc]
layout=0
[Paintbrush]
width=552
height=144
clear=COLOR
```

The above entries are associated with the Windows utilities and games we use.

There were about five pages of other program parameter specifications that we just removed to reduce the amount of redundant data we examine. We stopped here because it looks like Corel Draw wins the award for the shortest program specification. It uses only two lines.

```
[CorelDraw]
Dir=D:\WINAPPS\COREL\CORELDRW
```

This finishes off our quick tour of the WIN.INI file. Next let's see what can be done with it.

As an exercise, use Windows WRITE to open the WININI.WRI found in the C:\WINDOWS subdirectory. This gives the Windows documentation of special WIN.INI file parameters. The best way to understand the Windows 3.1x INI files is to work with them on a Windows 3.1 PC. If that is not available, you might be able to find information in the Microsoft knowledge base at the Microsoft web site, although searching the Microsoft knowledge base for specific information is like searching for a needle lost on the moon, which is of course more difficult than searching for the same needle in a haystack.

SYSTEM.INI

In this next section we examine SYSTEM.INI. This section also presents some of the changes we can make in it and their impact on Windows.

The SYSTEM.INI loads and configures Windows for your hardware and software. Every time you add something new to your PC that is used through Windows, this file is updated. This, like any text file, can be edited and viewed though most text editors. A word of caution before you make changes—some lines can have a drastic effect on Windows. Some lines can stop Windows from running. For the most part you do not edit this file through a text editor, instead you rely on the Windows control panel or the Windows setup program to make the modifications. In this section, we examine in greater detail the important sections of the SYSTEM.INI file as well as provide you with additional hints that may improve Windows performance. The parameter settings (lines) you see here are some of the more common settings. However, your PC may contain different ones because it has a different configuration. Some of the entries you see are ones that must be added and are rarely used.

To begin viewing, select the RUN command from the file menu and execute SYSEDIT. SYSEDIT is probably the best way to view the SYSTEM.INI file. It only views and edits the seven most important files for Windows. These files are:

AUTOEXEC.BAT
CONFIG.SYS
SYSTEM.INI
WIN.INI
PROTOCOL.INI
MSMAIL.INI
SCHDPLUS.INI

These files establish the operating environment for Windows as it boots up. They establish the memory configuration, the desktop interface, the local area network operation, and the operation of key Windows programs such as Microsoft Mail and the scheduler program.

SYSTEM.INI FILE SECTIONS

Sections in the SYSTEM.INI file like the [boot] section, [386enhanced] section (containing device= lines), and the [keyboard] section have parameter settings assigned automatically, based on choices that were made at the time Windows was installed.

These settings are not cast in stone, but changing some of them could cause Windows to function incorrectly. The key SYSTEM.INI sections are:

- [boot]—This section of the SYSTEM.INI file lists all the Windows modules and drivers needed for Windows to configure itself every time Windows starts. These files are typically found in the \windows\system folder or directory. Unless otherwise noted all the following lines are essential. Changing or disabling any of them could cause windows not to start. If windows does not boot, try using the /b parameter to create BOOTLOG.TXT.

- Remember also to be careful about changes you make. If by accident you hit a key and make a change you cannot find, then close the file and answer "no" when prompted to save.
- [boot description]—provides the descriptions displayed by the SETUP.EXE program for display, keyboard, network, etc. These are the current choices for the basic hardware configuration options.
- [drivers]—other names for drivers are included here.
- [keyboard]—provides special keyboard settings for different PC keyboards, for instance, 84-key versus 101-key versus 104-key. The entries in this section are required. Unlike other sections in the SYSTEM.INI file, these lines have no defaults.
- [mci]—lists multimedia drivers installed.
- [386ENH]—the 386 enhanced mode operation section; sets up operating parameters for the operation of Windows in the 386 enhanced mode. It controls multitasking operation, swapfiles, networking operation, and the virtual machine device drivers that are loaded to activate the Windows virtual machine.
- [standard]—This section controls Windows in standard mode operation. It is little used because the real power of Windows 3.x comes from operating in 386 enhanced mode.
- [NonWindowsApp]—controls the DOS virtual machines. The DOS virtual machine behavior can be changed here. However, this is typically left empty so that the default values are used.
- [NETWARE]—When NetWare LAN software is used with Windows, this section configures that software.

Not all sections appear in every SYSTEM.INI file. Some sections are always present in every SYSTEM.INI file like the [386ENH], the [boot] and the [boot description] sections.

SELECTED SYSTEM.INI FILE PARAMETERS

There are many SYSTEM.INI file parameters. The file we examine contains the typical parameters placed in the system INI file by SETUP. Some additional parameters may be there as well. However, there are many more SYSTEM.INI parameters that can be used in the file. These other parameters are seldom used.

Let's now tour the SYSTEM.INI file, looking at some of the parameters in turn from top to bottom. The file used in these notes is not in the identical sequence as other SYSTEM.INI files encountered because it was set up by hand to demonstrate the SYSTEM.INI file parameters. The parameters shown in this file cover the parameters in most other SYSTEM.INI files. Follow along by opening your SYSTEM.INI file on your machine using the Windows Notepad.

The SYSTEM.INI file parameters are as follows:

```
[boot]
```

The [boot] section parameters are:

```
shell=progman.exe
```

shell=filename—This line tells windows what shell it is going to use. Setup assumes the program manager shell PROGMAN.EXE. The program manager that displays the Windows Icon menus is run by this SYSTEM.INI file command. The shell could also be set to the Windows file manager, WINFILE.EXE.

```
network.drv=netware.drv
```

network.drv=filename—This line names what type of Windows network (Winnet) driver you are going to be using. The Windows for Workgroups default is wfwnet.drv, and Novell is netware.drv. These were the principal drivers used in Windows 3.1, although some PCs were configured to work with Banyan Vines networks.

The netware.drv statement is required for using Windows on NetWare. Different drivers are required for other network software such as IBM's OS/2 LAN server software that uses NETBIOS.

```
language.dll=
```

language.dll=filename—This line tells Windows which language DLL (dynamic link library) to use for language-specific functions. This enables Windows to appear in French, Italian, German, etc. This line is changed using the international control panel icon or by rerunning setup. The default is blank (none), in which case Windows uses the built-in English (US.) library.

```
sound.drv=mmsound.drv
```

sound.drv=filename—Indicates the name of the system sound driver you are using. You can change this yourself by editing the SYSTEM.INI. These statements control the PC's speaker and communications ports. Under Windows 3.11, the sound driver is a multimedia sound driver. The original Windows 3.1 sound driver specification line was:

```
sound.drv=sound.drv)
comm.drv=comm.drv
```

This is the communications driver specification for your serial communications port.

```
;386grabber=vgadib.3gr
;286grabber=vgacolor.2gr
;display.drv=svga256.drv
```

The lines above specify SVGA display drivers. The semicolon (;) at the beginning of the line is the comment character, so it disables the SVGA drivers.

The grabber and display driver statements controlled the Windows 3.x displays. To change display types, change those statements.

386grabber=filename—This setting assigns the grabber for Windows. Grabbers make a DOS application visible when you run it in Windows 386 enhanced mode. This item is changed when you change display driver settings.

286grabber=filename—This is the same as above only it is used when Windows runs in standard mode as opposed to 386 enhanced.

display.drv=filename—This is your windows display driver. It determines what resolution and how many colors Windows uses. Make sure your monitor and card support this driver. This is changed through setup in the main group or from DOS setup. The default is blank (none). The most common is VGA.DRV, the windows standard 640x480 VGA display driver.

```
386grabber=vga.3gr
286grabber=vgacolor.2gr
display.drv=vga.drv
```

The above statements set up the standard VGA display drivers for the Windows standard VGA. Other special display driver programs for a specific manufacturer's VGA board being used in a PC are installed by changing the 386grabber, 286grabber, and display.drv lines. There is a fourth line in the 386 enhanced section that must also be changed for specific manufacturer's VGA boards.

```
fonts.fon=vgasys.fon
fixedfon.fon=vgafix.fon
oemfonts.fon=vgaoem.fon
```

These three statements set up the PC's menu fonts.

oemfonts.fon=filename—This font specification defines the font for your display settings. The OEM character set is changed running setup under

DOS. The default is blank (none). For higher resolutions or larger display fonts, use the 8514 series of fonts.

fixedfont.fon=filename—This is the fixed font used by Windows 2.x applications. This is changed when you change your display settings.

fonts.fon=filename—This font is used as the proportionally spaced system font. This item is also changed through the display settings in setup. The default is blank (none).

Substituting different font statements here can make the display characters larger or smaller because these are bit-mapped fonts. When 8514 fonts are used on a VGA screen, the letters contain more dots so they appear larger on the VGA display. If the CGA fonts are used, then the display characters would appear smaller.

The character size varies because for a given display there are only a fixed number of dots, more dots for an 8514 than for a CGA. The 8514 fonts have more dots in each character to keep the same relative physical readable size for the character, when it appears on the 8514 display with 1,024 by 768 dots. When the 8514 fonts are used with a VGA display, they produce larger visible characters, since each character has more dots than the VGA fonts. VGA fonts have fewer dots because the total VGA dots are only 640 by 480 dots.

```
mouse.drv=filename
```

This statement specifies which mouse driver you are going to be using. This setting is changed through the Windows setup. The Microsoft mouse driver is specified by the command:

```
mouse.drv=mouse.drv
```

Other mouse drivers are listed below. They include the Mouse Systems mouse drivers for the PS/2 mouse port as well as those for the serial ports COM1 AND COM2.

```
; mouse.drv=msmouse1.drv
: mouse.drv=mscmouse.drv
; Mouse Systems driver for COM1
; mouse.drv=msmouse2.drv
; mouse.drv=mscbc3.drv
; Mouse Systems driver for COM2
keyboard.drv=keyboard.drv
```

This is your keyboard driver, as selected during setup. To change this parameter, use setup in the main group.

```
[keyboard]
subtype=
```

```
subtype=#—This helps the keyboard driver discern special
features of a particular keyboard. To change this setting
go through the Windows setup.
;type=3
;Type 3 is for 84 key AT keyboard.
type=4
;Type 4 is for 101 key AT keyboard.
```

These statements specify the type of keyboard used by Windows. A 101-key keyboard is specified as Type 4 and an 84-key keyboard is specified as Type 3. If a 101-key keyboard is identified as a Type 3 keyboard, some keys fail to operate.

type=#—This section uses a value to specify the keyboard type. In the absence of a type, the keyboard driver (KEYBOARD.DRV) selects the type. Below is a chart showing the different keyboard types. Changes are made through the Windows setup in the main group.

Number	Type
1	83 Key IBM PC XT Compatible
2	Olivetti 102 Key
3	84-86 Key IBM PC AT Compatible
4	101-102 Key IBM Compatible

```
oemansi.bin=
```

oemansi.bin=filename—For PCs using other than code page 437, the code page translations for US OEM/ANSI. Changes are made in the DOS setup under Code Page.

```
keyboard.dll=
```

Keyboard.dll=filename—This DLL defines keyboard layouts for non-US keyboards. If you use any keyboard other than IBM PC, XT, AT, AT&T 301/302, or Olivetti 83-key, then you have an entry on this line. Changes are made through the Windows setup in the Main group.

```
;Required for Adobe Type Manager SEE also line AFTER fonts
system.drv=atmsys.drv
;Required for Adobe Type Manager SEE also line BEFORE fonts
atm.system.drv=system.drv
```

In this example the Adobe Type Manager is being used. It requires substituting ATMSYS.DRV for the SYSTEM.DRV. ATM fonts and Windows True-Type fonts can be used at the same time without difficulties.

To remove ATM, just revert to the original line:

```
;system.drv=system.drv
```

The system.drv=filename tells Windows what your system hardware driver is going to be. To change this, run the Windows setup from DOS and select a new system.

```
taskman.exe=filename
```

The taskman.exe=filename describes which task-switching application you will use when you use CTRL + ESC. To change this you must edit the SYSTEM.INI file itself. The default is Taskman.exe. This statement only appears when a different task manager is used.

```
drivers=filename
```

Describes installable drivers or aliases of installable drivers that load when Windows starts. Installable drivers are DLL files. The drivers also may have parameters that are defined with their alias in the [drivers] section of the SYSTEM.INI file. You will probably not change this setting. The installation program of the specific software you install usually does changes.

```
CachedFileHandles=#
```

Sets the number of EXE and DLLs that stay open. Like disk cache, Windows keeps the recently used EXE and DLL files in memory instead of closing them. When they are used again, Windows performance is increased because it accesses them from memory rather than from the fixed disk. The parameter can be 2 to 12 file handles. The default is 12.

CacheFilesHandles can cause a problem when running Windows off a server if the network setup limits the number of concurrent open files on the server. When the server setting is less than 12, lower Windows' CacheFile-Handles. Changes are made using SYSEDIT.

```
SCRNSAVE.EXE=(None)
```

Windows 3.1 incorporates screen savers. These are disabled by default as specified by the SCRNSAVE.EXE= (None) line.

```
[boot.description]

nework.drv=NetWare Device Driver for Windows v1.03

language.dll=English (American)

;keyboard.typ=All AT type keyboards (84–86 keys)
keyboard.typ=Enhanced 101 or 102 key US and Non US
```

```
keyboards

; mouse.drv=Microsoft, or IBM PS/2
mouse.drv=Mouse Systems (or VisiOn) connected to COM2
display.drv=Super VGA (1024x768, 256 colors, small fonts)
;aspect=100,96,96
;display.drv=VGA

system.drv=MS-DOS or PC-DOS System
```

When you run setup, the boot description display gets its information from the statements above. Note the old network driver statement and the new statement.

[386ENH]

The 386 enhanced section of the SYSTEM.INI file contains special hardware setup parameters that make the PC operate or not operate with Windows. These parameters and their influence on the PC are shown below. This section contains 386 enhanced mode operating parameters and virtual device driver program specifications. The section has the settings for 32-bit disk access, virtual memory, Windows scheduling priorities, and the Windows virtual device drivers. The virtual drivers in this section are loaded from the many device statements. They can be actual files like "device=vpmtd.386," or as an "*" with a name like "device=*vpd." The files that end with the ".386" extension are actual files found in the \windows\system folder or directory, whereas the names with the "*" are built in virtual devices to the WIN386.EXE kernel.

If you find this confusing, think of it as the difference between internal and external commands in DOS. There are approximately 144 possible entries in this section, not to mention the numerous "device=" entries. The average SYSTEM.INI file will contain from 30 to 40 of these lines. In this section, we look at a good portion of the possible lines found here, but not all lines appear in every SYSTEM.INI file.

Probably the most confusing section in the SYSTEM.INI file is the [386ENH] section because every time new software or hardware is added to a Windows 3.x PC, lines are also added to the [386ENH] section. To discover what happened, copies of the SYSTEM.INI file before and after the hardware/software changes were compared.

When problems occurred after installing something, the changes causing the problem were often located in this section. As an example, when installing a new fax/modem and WinfaxPro from Delrina, we were warned about speed mismatches between different class fax machines. Furthermore, we were offered an opportunity to have the setup compensate for this. After installation, we could not send a fax. All faxes sent were garbled. Several days later, after trying everything short of reinstallation, we noticed a line in the [386ENH] section: COM2FIFO=1. This added line caused a speed mismatch. By changing the line value to 0 (disabling value), we overcame the fax problem. The solution took several days because we did not notice the change in the [386ENH] section.

To solve these problems and understand the [386ENH] section, we applied the philosophy of line-by-line organization to the [386ENH] section. This approach separates the "device=" statements and groups them together alphabetically. It then groups the remaining lines alphabetically. Now any time a line is added to the [386ENH] section, it is easily found because it is either in a wrong group or out of alphabetical order. Even without organizing the file, a before-and-after comparison is effective in determining what has been changed in the file.

Organization is a good tool to help troubleshoot problems. To organize, you must know what you are organizing. In the fax example, part of the problem was we did not know the impact of any of the lines. In that case, how were we to be sure which line caused a specific problem without knowing what each line did?

```
AllEMSLocked=on/off
```

Turning this on keeps all EMS contents from being swapped to the swapfile, even the DOS applications. This setting supersedes any PIF settings. This setting should be used if you are using a disk cache in expanded memory. This entry must be in the SYSTEM.INI file. The default value is off.

```
AllXMSLocked=on/off
```

This entry probably is not used. It is better set to off. It keeps Windows from swapping information from the XMS to the swapfile, overriding PIF settings. This parameter must be manually added.

```
AllVMsExclusive=on/off
```

This entry forces all programs to run exclusively in full screen mode. Again it overrides PIF settings. Try using this if you have any TSR or old network software that is incompatible with Windows. This line is manually added and is defaulted to off.

```
AutoRestoreScreen=on/off
```

Tells Windows who restores DOS applications screens when multitasking, the application or Windows. If the setting is on, then Windows is responsible. It stores the applications screen information in memory until it is restored. The advantage to this is that Windows restores the screen faster than the application. The disadvantage is that the screen is stored in extended memory (XMS), reducing the XMS available for other applications. If the entry is off, the application is responsible for the screen, which reduces performance but does not use additional RAM. The default is on. You must add this line to the SYSTEM.INI file.

```
MaxBPs=1024
;Maximum Break Points—memory allocation for interrupts
under Windows
```

The Max Point Breaks operating reduces Windows General Protection Faults. Set this to 1,024 and randomly occurring GPFs are supposed to be reduced.

```
SystemROMBreakPoint=FALSE
```

Windows does not need the SystemROMBreakPoint=FALSE operating parameter set. QEMM and 386 MAX required setting this parameter.

It specifies whether Windows should use ROM address space between F000:0000 and 1 Mb for a break point. Windows in 386 enhanced mode normally searches this space to find a special instruction that is used as a system break point. If this address space contains something other than permanently available ROM, you should disable this setting.

```
EMMExclude=a000-afff
;x=a000-afff This is the VGA Graphics swap range.

EMMExclude=b800-bfff
;x=B800-BFFF This is the VGA Text swap range.

EMMExclude=c000-C7FF
;x=C000-C7FF This is the VGA ROM range.

EMMExclude=c800-cbff
;x=c800-cbff This is the SCSI controller ROM range.

EMMExclude=f000-ffff
;x=f000-ffff This is the system ROM range.
```

The EMMExclude parameter may cure some Windows problems. Commonly, it is not required because Windows chooses settings from a standard set and from those in the CONFIG.SYS file. In most cases, choosing the default settings for these parameters gives the best Windows performance.

EMMExclude specifies a range of memory that Windows will not scan to find unused address space. This has the side effect of turning off the RAM and ROM search code for the range. The range (two paragraph values separated by a hyphen) must be between A000 and EFFF. This scanning can interfere with some adapters that use the same memory area. The starting value is rounded down and the ending value is rounded up to a multiple of 16K. For example, you could set EMMExclude=C800-CFFF to prevent Windows from scanning the addresses C800:0000 through CFFF:000F. You can specify more than one range by including more than one EMMExclude line. The EMMExclude lines are generally not necessary for Windows' proper operation because Windows uses the memory specifications in the CONFIG.SYS file to set up the memory exclusions. The EMMExclude lines would only be used in extraordinary situations where application programs in some way corrupted Windows memory setup.

```
ebios=*ebios
```

Ebios=filename indicates the extended BIOS being used by Windows in the 386 enhanced mode. To change this, you must edit the SYSTEM.INI file. The default is whatever Windows has set up during installation. This SYSTEM.INI parameter would only be changed if its special PC hardware required it. Normally it is left at the Windows internal setting, that is, an asterisk precedes ebios.

```
keyboard=*vkd
mouse=*vmd
```

The =*vkd and =*vmd statements specify using the standard internal Windows 3.x driver programs and dynamic link libraries for keyboard and mouse.

```
network=*vnetbios, vnetware.386, vipx.386
```

The network drivers for NetWare are specified here.

```
;Set for VGA Version 3.0
;display=VDDVGA30.386
;Set for SVGA
;display=vddsvga.386
;Set For Std VGA
display=*vddvga
```

Other specifications for VGA display drivers for a Super VGA board are above. These lines must be changed along with the other VGA lines to change display types. display=filename indicates the selected display device that is going to be used by Windows. To change this, run setup in DOS.

```
device=filename
```

This specifies the virtual device drivers used by Windows in 386 enhanced mode. These commands are typically grouped in one area in the 386 enhanced section of the SYSTEM.INI file.

Other commands used in place of "device=" are:

```
transport=
```
specifies the network protocols.
```
display=
```
specifies special display drivers,
```
ebios=
```
specifies any extended BIOS that is installed.
```
secondnet=
```
specifies the second networking protocol when two networking protocols are installed.
```
mouse=
```
specifies a special mouse driver program,
```
keyboard=
```
specifies the keyboard driver. The *vkd is a standard Windows internal keyboard driver.
```
network=
```

specifies the type of network support installed. This is most often support for NetWare and the Microsoft Windows network.

The values are file names with the 386 extension on them, or a name that begins with an asterisk (*). Windows sets these lines during the initial setup or whenever you install new applications that require unique commands.

Windows adds lines based on your PC hardware. For Windows 3.1, the following is set:

```
device=vtdapi.386
device=*vpicd
device=*vtd
device=*reboot
device=*vsd
device=*v86mmgr
device=*pageswap
device=*dosmgr
device=*vmpoll
device=*wshell
device=*vhd<=set by Windows 3.0
device=*vpd
device=*parity
```

```
device=*biosxlat
device=*vcd
device=*vmcpd
device=*combuff
device=*cdpscsi
local=CON
```

The SYSTEM.INI specification local=con tells Windows that the console is the keyboard attached to the PC.

```
device=*blockdev
```

These lines described are the key SYSTEM.INI specifications for setting up 32-bit disk access and 32-bit file access. Coordinates I/O between block and 32-bit disk access devices. A disk controller card (typically IDE) that is Western digital 1003 MFM controller compatible adds the blockdev line to your [386ENH] section permitting 32-bit disk access. This line may be deleted if 32-bit file access is enabled.

```
device=*wdctrl
```

Used to communicate with WD 1003-compatible fixed disk controllers.

```
device=*INT13
```

Emulates and traps INT13h calls

```
device=*pagefile—
```

Handles the virtual memory paging

```
; 32BitDiskAccess=OFF <=original win31
32BitDiskAccess=ON
```

32bitDiskAccess=on/off—When a PC is capable of supporting 32-bit disk access, this line controls it. The default setting is off. The virtual memory settings in the 386 enhanced section of the control panel activate it. When PCs do not support this feature, the line is absent. As an exercise, go to the 32-bit disk access section and see if your PC qualifies. When set on, humans see no perceptible difference in disk performance. Generally SCSI disk controllers do not support 32-bit disk access without special drivers. We have an AMI SCSI disk controller that supports 32-bit disk access.

```
; OverlappedIO=off <=original win31
OverlappedIO=ON
```

The overlapped I/O specification permits several read and write requests to be issued to the disk before the first request is finished. This can speed up disk operations. Unfortunately but not surprisingly, most humans do not notice a speedup.

```
PageBuffers=16
```

The statement above specifies the number of 4 Kb page buffers Windows uses to store asynchronous read/write pages when 32BitDiskAccess is activated. The default value is 4. Increasing the value here could improve Windows performance, typically when a system has lots of RAM. Again, most humans would not notice a speed increase. We have increased speed and thought everything really ran faster. It probably seemed to run faster because we knew we had made the change.

```
DOSPromptExitInstruc=no
```

DOSPromptExitInstruct=on/off (or yes/no)—This turns on or off the annoying Windows 3.1x message displayed when a DOS Window is opened. Leave this unchanged for new Windows users or they may think they exited Windows. The default setting is Yes. If enabled, when you start the MS-DOS prompt, a message box appears with instructions on how to exit and switch away from the MS-DOS prompt. Disable this setting if you do not want to see the message:

```
■ Type EXIT and press ENTER to quit this MS-DOS prompt and
  return to Windows.
■ Press ALT+TAB to switch to Windows or another applicatin
■ Press ALT+ENTER to switch this MS-DOS Prompt between a
  window and full screen.
```

To change this, you must add the DOSPromptExitInstruct line to the SYSTEM.INI file. The default is on.

```
PermSwapDOSDrive=D
PermSwapSizeK=16000
```

These SYSTEM.INI controls set up the permanent swapfile. They are changed using the Windows control panel and selecting the 386 enhanced icon, then virtual memory settings.

```
LocalReboot=off
```

The default setting is On. This LocalReboot parameter specifies whether you can press Ctrl + Alt + Del to quit applications that cause an unrecoverable error in 386 enhanced mode, without restarting Windows. If this setting is enabled, you can quit the applications. If this setting is disabled, pressing Ctrl + Alt + Del normally restarts the PC.

```
COM#(1-4)AutoAssign=#/sec
```

This line sets a contention value to the available COM ports. The number controls port sharing between applications. At least one application is a DOS application. If the number is –1, you get a message asking which application is going to control the port. A 0 value means any application can use the port. The seconds value assigns a time that must expire after one application stops using the port before another can assume control. This line is set through the 386 enhanced dialog in the control panel. The default seconds is 2. It can be as high as 1000.

```
;COMBoostTime=<milliseconds>
```

Sets the amount of time in milliseconds that Windows allows a virtual machine to process a COM interrupt. This is helpful if you are seeing characters lost on your screen by communications programs. It is easy to see lost characters because text appears garbled as it is received. You must add this line yourself. The default number is 2.

```
COM#(1-4)Base=address
```

Sets the base port for the serial ports in your computer. To change these, go to the Advanced button on the ports control panel window. Check device documentation for potential conflicts.

```
COM#(1-4)Irq=#
```

This sets the IRQ for the device used at a particular serial port. Check device documentation to avoid any conflicts. If a conflict arises, try setting the value to –1 to disable input on that IRQ. The defaults for the ports are shown below. Any changes can be made from the Advanced button on the ports control panel window.

```
; device=*vhd <= set by Windows 3.0 but removed for Windows
3.1
; device=*vpd <= set by Windows 3.0 but removed for Windows
3.1
device=*PAGEFILE<=set by Windows 3.1
device=*vfd<=set by Windows 3.1
```

These statements were used by Windows 3.1

```
[NonWindowsApp]
localtsrs=dosedit,ced
CommandEnvSize=2000
```

The non-Windows application section of the SYSTEM.INI file is used to control DOS sessions. DOS applications are passed information by these statements. The local terminate-and-stay-resident line specifies the TSR programs loaded for the DOS sessions. The environment space size specifies the amount of memory to set aside for the DOS environment space.

```
MinTimeslice=20
WinTimeslice=300,100
WinExclusive=0
```

These statements specify how the CPU's time is distributed among the different Windows virtual machines or active Windows. Processors with slow clock speeds (6 MHz to 16 Mhz) should probably use the Windows default of 20 Ms as the minimum time slice. Faster CPUs, such as 50 MHz, machines could set the minimum time slice to 5 Ms. At 50 MHz, each millisecond permits the CPU to execute (conservatively) about 5,000 computer instructions (50,000,000/1,000/10 clock cycles per instruction). Five milliseconds permits each virtual machine to execute about 25,000 instructions before releasing the CPU to another virtual machine. At 500 MHz, this increases to 250,000 instructions. The best strategy here is to leave the minimum time slice set as specified by Windows. We have experimented with large and small values for the minimum time slice only to find that both large and small values made Windows operation erratic. Windows would either become very jerky or very slow, depending on whether the value is set very large or very small.

```
CGA80WOA.FON=CGA80WOA.FON
```

CGA80WOA.FON=filename—The display font used when DOS-based applications use the 80 columns and 25 or fewer screen lines. To change this, run setup and change the code page or display setting. The default is blank (none).

```
CGA40WOA.FON=CGA40WOA.FON
```

CGA40WOA.FON=filename—The same as above, however this is for the 40-column, 25-or-fewer lines screen.

```
EGA80WOA.FON=EGA80WOA.FON
```

EGA80WOA.FON=filename—The same as the CGA80WOA.FON, however this is for 80 columns with 25 or more line screens.

```
EGA40WOA.FON=EGA40WOA.FON
```

EGA40WOA.FON=filename—This is the same as the CGA40WOA.FON; however this is for 40 columns with 25 or more line screens.

```
FileSysChange=off
```

Additional NetWare parameters include the SYSTEM.INI line disabling, alerting Windows every time a file is manipulated by an application. The default value is "on" because, on a single-user PC, there are programs manipulating the files. In contrast, when a PC is networked many programs can be working with files.

```
NetHeapSize=32
```

This specifies the network heap or buffer area size. The default is 12 or 8. This is the size (in kilobytes) of the buffers that Windows in 386 enhanced mode allocates in conventional memory for transferring data over a network. All values are rounded up to the nearest 4K. Using Netware increases that value.

```
;PagingDrive=e:
```

These parameters are used to control the temporary program paging space on a fixed disk drive. The PagingDrive default value is "none." It specifies the disk drive where Windows in 386 enhanced mode allocates a temporary swapfile (WIN386.SWP). This setting is ignored if you have a permanent swapfile. If you don't have a permanent swapfile and no drive is specified or the specified drive does not exist, Windows 3.1x attempts to put your temporary swapfile on the drive containing your SYSTEM.INI file. If the specified drive is full, paging is disabled.

```
;swapdisk=c:\win386.swp
```

This sets the location of the temporary program swapfile (WIN386.SWP).

```
;MinUserDiskSpace=4096
```

This specifies disk space to leave free when creating a temporary program swapfile.

```
;MaxPagingFileSize=4096
```

This specifies disk space to leave free when creating a temporary program swapfile.

```
;TimerCriticalSection=10
;TimerCriticalSection=10000
;Typical Network Setting is 10000
;Default: 0
```

This instructs Windows how to behave in a special section of software designed to handle timer critical functions. This timer critical section of software is entered as part of all timer-interrupt code in Windows 3.1x. The parameters specify a time-out period (in milliseconds). Specifying a positive value ensures that only one virtual machine at a time receives timer interrupts. Some networks and other global memory-resident software may fail unless this setting is used. Using these parameters slows down performance and can make the system sluggish or seem to stop for short periods of time. This parameter is sometimes used for special network settings including special settings for NetWare.

```
[NETWARE]
```

The NetWare section is set up when NetWare is installed on a Windows PC. It contains the last of the special NetWare parameter settings.

```
RestoreDrives=false
```

Normally, when you exit Windows, all of your drive mappings are restored to the way they were before you started Windows, and all changes you made inside Windows are lost. If you set the RestoreDrives value to false, the mappings you made inside Windows remain when you exit Windows.

```
NWShareHandles=false
```

Normally, each virtual machine you start from Windows has its own set of drive mappings. Changes you make in one virtual machine do not affect another. If you set the NWShareHandles value to true, drive mappings become global, and changes made in one virtual machine affect all other applications. The NWShareHandles setting permits you to look at new network drives in different Windows and the nonactive Windows remain at the drive locations where you had originally left them.

Changing the SYSTEM.INI file under Windows can have disastrous results if the driver programs specified are not resident in the WINDOWS\SYSTEM subdirectory of your PC. Missing display drivers or fonts cause Windows to unceremoniously dump you out to DOS instantly. Other settings may result in strange error messages or PC lockups when Windows is running.

WINDOWS 3.1 REFERENCES TO MULTIMEDIA DRIVERS • Multimedia drivers are installed and configured using the control panel.

```
;multimedia drivers
[mci]
```

Multimedia drivers reference the MCI (media control interface) SYSTEM.INI file section.

```
CDAudio=mcicda.drv
Sequencer=mciseq.drv
```

```
WaveAudio=mciwave.drv
[drivers]
midimapper=midimap.drv
Wave1=speaker.drv
timer=timer.drv
 [speaker.drv]
CPU Speed=48
Volume=500
Version=774
Enhanced=1
Max seconds=3
Leave interrupts enabled=0
```

This is the [speaker.drv] speaker driver section for using WAV files with the PC's speaker. This matches with the Wave1=speaker.drv above line.

Altering the SYSTEM.INI file changes Windows. Before making any changes to the file, please copy it to SYSTEMIN.001. This backup copy is to ensure that you can return to the current Windows setup without reinstalling Windows.

Whenever you change the contents of any INI file, you should make a copy of the file before altering it.

We have completed our examination of WIN.INI and SYSTEM.INI files. It is now time to look at the remaining files that comprise Windows 3.1. Some of these files are programs alone while others are a combination of a program and an INI file.

USER.EXE

The USER.EXE program in Windows 3.x is one of the graphical user interface (GUI) programs. It manages Windows inputs. It keeps track of all the windows created by applications on the PC. The Windows 3.11 USER.EXE file is:

USER EXE 264,096 05-02-97 10:07a

The USER.EXE program is a DLL used by the Windows system virtual machine. To perform its Windows management function, it uses a 64KB data segment (data heap) in real mode memory. This real mode data segment is faster to access than some data segment elsewhere in memory. Such speed is needed to keep Windows actively moving for the PC user.

GDI.EXE

The Graphical Device Interface program or GDI.EXE is also a Windows system dynamic link library that manages the Windows graphic display interface. It works in conjunction with the USER.EXE program, managing the Windows by managing all the drawing objects on the screen; drawing objects are color palettes and fonts. The Windows 3.11 GDI.EXE file is:

GDI EXE 220,800 11-01-93 4:11a

It is found in the \windows\system directory along with the USER.EXE program.

WIN.COM

WIN.COM is the program that launches Windows 3.x. It is located in the C:\Windows directory. During installation, a command line reference is placed in the AUTOEXEC.BAT file which causes WIN.COM to run and launch Windows. The WIN.COM program is:

WIN COM   50,904 08-15-95 10:44a

WIN.COM has several options to modify Windows operation. The options can be viewed at any time by typing WIN.COM /? These options include:

- WIN [/B] [/N] [/D:[C][F][S][V][X]]
- /B Creates a file, BOOTLOG.TXT, that records system messages generated during system startup (boot).
- /N Causes Windows not to load network drivers.
- /D: Used in combination with one or more of the following switches for troubleshooting when Windows does not start correctly.
- C—Turns off 32-bit file access.
- F—Turns off 32-bit disk access. Equivalent to SYSTEM.INI file setting: 32BitDiskAccess=FALSE.
- S—Specifies that Windows should not use ROM address space between F000:0000 and 1 MB for a break point. Equivalent to SYSTEM.INI file setting: SystemROMBreakPoint=FALSE.
- V—Specifies that the ROM routine will handle interrupts from the hard disk controller. Equivalent to SYSTEM.INI file setting: VirtualHDIRQ=FALSE.
- X—Excludes all of the adapter area from the range of memory that Windows scans to find unused space. Equivalent to SYSTEM.INI file setting: EMMExclude=A000-FFFF.

The Windows 3.0 WIN.COM had different options for loading Windows in real mode, standard mode, or 386 enhanced mode. See the kernel section earlier in this chapter for a brief explanation of these modes.

With Windows 3.1 and 3.11, these options changed to become more troubleshooting tools as we see above.

PROGMAN.EXE and PROGMAN.INI

PROGMAN.EXE is the primary user interface or shell program under Windows 3.x. When you exit PROGMAN.EXE you exit Windows 3.x because it is the shell program. The program manager (PROGMAN.EXE) launches the application programs. They are identified as icons in several groups. These files are:

PROGMAN INI   297   05-12-99 1:38p

PROGMAN EXE   115,312   11-01-93 4:11a

In Windows 3.x, groups organize the different programs we use by containing their icons. In addition, we applied some custom settings to program manager to help us organize the groups and applications, such as automatically saving settings on exiting. To keep track of all these different settings and groups, program manager uses a file called PROGMAN.INI to record them.

Just like the WIN.INI and the SYSTEM.INI files, the PROGMAN.INI file is only a text file. Probably the easiest way to view this file is through the text editor NOTEPAD. The following is an example of a typical PROGMAN.INI and a description of what each line does:

```
[Settings]
Window=68 48 580 384 1
SaveSettings=0
AutoArrange=0
[Groups]
Group1=C:\WINDOWS\MAIN.GRP
Group2=C:\WINDOWS\ACCESSOR.GRP
Group4=C:\WINDOWS\CLOSE-UP.GRP
Group3=C:\WINDOWS\README.GRP
Group5=C:\WINDOWS\APPLICAT.GRP
Group6=C:\WINDOWS\LOTUSAPP.GRP
Group7=C:\WINDOWS\MICROSOF.GRP
Group8=C:\WINDOWS\DOSUTIL.GRP
Group9=C:\WINDOWS\WINUTIL.GRP
Group10=C:\WINDOWS\SETUP.GRP
Group11=C:\WINDOWS\WPW51US.GRP
```

The first section is [Settings], which is for controlling where program manager is located and any automatic settings that have been enabled or disabled.

The WINDOWS= parameter is for describing the location and the size of the program manager window. This parameter means:

Window=68 48 580 384 1

68 is the horizontal distance from the upper left corner of display screen.

48 is the vertical distance from the upper left corner of the display.

580 is the horizontal width of the window.

384 is the vertical height of the window.

1 specifies if the window is represented as an icon or a window.

This setting is updated every time you exit Windows with the save settings feature enabled. The measurement values are done in pixels.

```
SaveSettings=0
```

The SaveSettings= line enables or disables the Save Settings feature. A "0" is enabled while a "1" is disabled.

```
AutoArrange=0
```

The AutoArrange= line enables the Auto Arrange feature. This allows Windows to arrange the icons so they fit optimally in the program manager. A "1" indicates enabled while a "0" represents disabled.

```
[Groups]
Group1=C:\WINDOWS\MAIN.GRP
Group2=C:\WINDOWS\ACCESSOR.GRP
Group4=C:\WINDOWS\CLOSE-UP.GRP
Group3=C:\WINDOWS\README.GRP
Group5=C:\WINDOWS\APPLICAT.GRP
Group6=C:\WINDOWS\LOTUSAPP.GRP
Group7=C:\WINDOWS\MICROSOF.GRP
Group8=C:\WINDOWS\DOSUTIL.GRP
Group9=C:\WINDOWS\WINUTIL.GRP
Group10=C:\WINDOWS\SETUP.GRP
Group11=C:\WINDOWS\WPW51US.GRP
```

Finally, the [Groups] section tells program manager where it can find the GRP file for the different groups it manages. This section is updated every time you create a new item or group, or delete an item or group.

KRNLxxx.EXE

For Windows 3.11 there is only a 386 enhanced mode kernel program provided. It is:

KRNL386 EXE   76,400 11-01-93 4:11a

This program is the heart of Windows 3.x. Kernel programs are also found in Unix and Windows NT. The Windows 3.x KRNL386.EXE performs the scheduling functions for all Windows activities. It implements cooperative multitasking, based on the time slicing specified in the SYSTEM.INI file.

When initially released, Windows 3.0 provided a real mode kernel program and an enhanced mode kernel program. As Windows evolved, the real mode kernel became unnecessary and only the enhanced mode kernel was provided. In Windows 95 and 98, the enhanced mode kernel now supports preemptive multitasking. The cooperative multitasking, like real mode operation, has become unnecessary. The Windows KRNL386.EXE is loaded into memory during the boot process. It replaces the DOS MSDOS.SYS scheduling program. Hence, Windows 3.x is really an operating system itself, separate (mostly) from DOS. It only relies on DOS for memory management and disk drive input/output functions.

PIF files

Windows 3.x uses program interface files to provide backward compatibility to older DOS programs. The standard PIF files that come with Windows 3.1x are:

DOSPRMPT	**PIF**	**545**	**01-03-94 2:55a**
DEFAULT	**PIF**	**545**	**01-03-94 2:55a**

These files control the launching of the DOS program specifying the DOS virtual machine operating properties for the program. For example, multitasking of DOS and Windows applications is set at a default time slice combination or altered by using the PIF files for the DOS application. To enable multitasking, the Background box must be marked in the PIF. See Figure 10–20.

The "detect idle time" box under the advanced options should also be marked. The numbers determine processing cycle allocation between DOS and Windows tasks. This permits the DOS virtual machines to multitask under Windows 3.x.

PIF file capabilities are built into Windows 95/98 DOS program shortcuts. Altering the properties of the shortcut in Windows 95/98 changes them.

Figure 10–20 *PIF file options*

Study Break

Windows Documentation

This exercise examines the Windows 3.1 SYSTEM.INI documentation.

1. Get a Windows 3.1 PC or get a copy of the Windows 3.1.WRI files.

2. Open the SYSINI.WRI documentation found in the C:\WINDOWS directory using WRITE.EXE or WORDPAD.EXE.

3. Use your "find" feature to locate MaxBPs.

4. Browse the rest of the file.

The goal of this example was to illustrate the electronic documentation that's available with Windows on the SYSTEM.INI and WIN.INI files.

■ Summary

This chapter has examined Windows 3.1x. It has looked at the overall functions and architecture of Windows 3.1x as well as identified Windows 3.1x components. Each component was examined in some detail, and so were the key Windows 3.1x system files. The overall goal of the chapter was to provide a better understanding of Windows 3.1x and how it lays the foundation for the current Windows 95/98 operating environments. There are some underlying similarities between the Windows 3.1x operating environment and Windows 95/98 operating environments. These operating environments really are quite different in their design and implementation.

▲ CHAPTER REVIEW QUESTIONS

1. *When running Windows 3.1, how can you view the resources available?*

   Answer: Select Help, then About

2. *What is the function of WIN.INI?*

   Answer: It configures Windows for a specific user and loads programs frequently used.

3. *What is the function of SYSTEM.INI?*

   Answer: It configures Windows to PC hardware.

4. *What loads MOUSE.SYS?*

   A. AUTOEXEC.BAT
   B. CONFIG.SYS
   C. WIN.INI

D. SYSTEM.INI

Answer: Although it is possible to load it in CONFIG.SYS, it is more likely to be loaded in SYSTEM.INI.

5. *What processing mode and CPU is not supported in Windows 3.1?*

A. 286—real mode

B. 8080—real mode

C. 8086/88—standard more

D. 286—standard mode

Answer: The processor removed was the Intel 80286 chip and the mode was Windows standard mode of operation. Real mode operation is performed by the chip and used in Windows 95/98 today.

6. *Windows 3.1 displays available resources when you _____.*

Answer: Open Help/About Program Manager or Help/About Control Panel

7. *How should you save your Windows 3.1 groups before upgrading?*

Answer: Back up the .GRP files.

8. *On a DOS/Win3.x computer you start to defrag the system. Rather than running DEFRAG, the message "incorrect DOS version" is displayed. What has happened?*

A. a bootable diskette was left in the floppy drive containing a different DOS version.

B. the SYS command was accidentally run on the drive

C. both of the above

D. neither of the above

Answer: C. both of the above

9. *Which character(s) at the front of a line in an INI file make it a comment?*

A. colon

B. semicolon

C. REM

D. quotation marks surrounding the line

Answer: B. semicolon

10. *The Windows tool for viewing and manually editing INI files, AUTOEXEC.BAT, and CONFIG.SYS is:*

A. file manager

B. SYSVIEW

C. REGEDIT

D. SYSEDIT

Answer: D. SYSEDIT

11. *A new software package from a CD needs to be installed in twenty Win3.x machines. However, when installing it on any of the systems, you get a variation of the access denied error and the setup program terminates. Why won't the new software install?*

A. the CD is defective and should be replaced by the manufacturer

B. someone set EditLevel=5 in the PROGMAN.INI files for this department

C. the systems do not have enough free hard disk space

D. the new software is incompatible with your version of Windows

Answer: B. someone set EditLevel=5

12. *If Windows 3.x setup hangs during the installation, what might resolve the problem?*

A. reboot and run a:\setup /I

B. reboot, run a:\setup, and choose "safe recovery" when prompted

C. call Microsoft for a replacement diskette

D. comment out any unnecessary lines in AUTOEXEC.BAT and CONFIG.SYS

Answer: A. reboot and run a:\setup /i

13. *Windows 3.1 file associations are stored in _____.*

A. the SYSTEM.INI file

B. the OLE.INI file

C. the WIN.INI file

D. the WINASSOC.INI file

Answer: A. the SYSTEM.INI file

14. *The Windows 3.1 INI files are all?*

A. binary files edited with SYSEDIT.

B. hidden and read-only files

C. text files that can be edited with NOTEPAD

D. stored in the root directory of the disk drive

Answer: C. text files that can be edited with NOTEPAD

15.   *What is the best way for average users to modify their system settings?*

A. edit the registry and make the needed changes

B. use the control panel dialogs to make the needed changes

C. run SYSEDIT and make the needed changes to SYSTEM.INI and WIN.INI

D. a and c

Answer: B. use the control panel dialogs to make the needed changes

ELEVEN

Windows 95/98 Architecture

▲ Chapter Syllabus

A+ 11.1 Windows 3.x versus Windows 95/98

A+ 11.2 Windows 95/98 Functions

A+ 11.3 Windows 95/98 Components

A+ 11.4 Windows 95/98 Key System Files

A+ 11.1 Windows 3.x versus Windows 95/98

Windows 95/98 is significantly different from Windows 3.1x. The differences are many. A complete exploration of them is well beyond the scope of this book. A brief overview is provided here to facilitate a better understanding of the evolution of PC software and to help understand the differences in troubleshooting between Windows 95/98 and Windows 3.1x. First, Windows 98 is in general a better Windows 95. Although there are plenty of improvements, the two systems seem quite the same, barring the improvements. Windows 95/98 improved on Windows 3.1x in several general areas including:

1. Improved user interface—There are many changes and improvements made to the graphical user interface for Windows 95, making it easier for all users. These improvements included above others the task bar, Windows Explorer, and an improved desktop interface.

571

2. Plug-and-play (or plug-and-pray) installation—Plug-and-play makes it less necessary to flip switches and set jumpers. This was a major start on future PCs, which will all be configurable through the software.

3. Integrated networking software—All the networking software you could use is built into Windows 95/98. This includes TCP/IP software as well as Novell's SPX/IPX software.

4. Better operating environment—Preemptive multitasking makes Windows 95/98 more bulletproof. It also offers better handling of Windows 3.1x applications and improved Windows 95/98 32-bit applications.

While Windows 95/98 preserves some of the same overall structures as found in Windows 3.x, underneath they are really quite different operating systems. Windows 3.x relied on DOS programs for memory and disk management functions. Windows 95/98 has replaced them with 32-bit protected mode programs that are designed to better support the Windows multitasking environment. Windows 95/98 is truly a 32-bit operating system, taking full advantage of the capabilities of today's CPU chips.

Furthermore, Windows 95/98 has increased the level of network functionality incorporated into the operating system. This functionality can be seen in the TCP/IP protocol modules that make Windows easily integrate with the Internet and intranets. Support for LANs and ATM communications are now incorporated into Windows.

The design of Windows 95/98 is aimed at making technical support less necessary. We have had some Windows PCs run for months on end without being restarted. (The rule here is to keep them focused on a narrow set of tasks.)

From an A+ viewpoint, it is important to understand the commonalities and differences between DOS, Windows 3.x, and Windows 95/98. The commonalities mean that the troubleshooting procedures that are employed on Windows 3.x systems generally work the same way in Windows 95/98 systems. To recover from a general protection fault, CTRL+ALT+DEL is hit. See Figure 11–1.

In Windows 98, this key combination starts the task manager program, giving you the options of closing the offending application, other applications running under Windows, or restarting Windows. The options are similar for Windows 3.x. However, Windows 3.x is not nearly as flexible.

The differences mean that there are other areas that require new troubleshooting procedures, for example, installing hardware options with Windows 95/98 plug-and-play. Some hardware configurations require that you remove boards, then restart Windows for the plug-and-play installation features to install them properly. We had a laptop with a SCSI PCMCIA (PC

Figure 11–1
Windows 98 task manager

CARD) interface that had to be installed using the remove-then-restart-and-reinstall procedure.

New networking features mean that, in future A+ certification tests, networking questions and networking configuration will become much more prevalent. These questions were almost nonexistent in the older A+ certification tests. Furthermore, the evolution to USB peripherals that is occurring now in 1999 mitigate the need for knowledge of the RS-232 serial port details that appeared in prior tests.

More details on Windows 95/98 troubleshooting are covered in Chapter 15. Included in this chapter are:

1. Special boot options for troubleshooting—for instance, hold the left shift key or F5 key while booting,
2. The task manager; CTRL-ALT-DEL activates the task manager to remove misbehaving programs,
3. Control panel tools, for instance, the system selection,
4. Configuring and managing virtual memory and disk cache.
5. Windows 98 utilities such as the system monitor and the resource meter.

There were three versions of Windows 95, the original release of Windows 95, the OSR2 or B version of Windows 95, and the final release, the C version of Windows 95. The OSR2 or B version of Windows 95 implemented FAT 32 bit, and the C version provided software support for the universal serial bus (USB). Windows 98 has also had numerous updates. Most of these updates have had to do with improved Internet security. One major improvement is the release of the Internet Explorer 5 or IE5. Windows 98 updates and patches are available through the Internet. Windows 98 incorporates an update button which, when activated, connects to the Microsoft

Windows 98 updates site. At this site, Windows 98 patches and drivers can be downloaded to upgrade the version of Windows installed on a PC. Windows 98 also provides utilities for making backups, utilities for cleaning up fixed disk drives, and maintenance wizards. These help the PC user perform routine maintenance tasks that keep their PC operating properly. Windows 98 incorporates an active desktop feature. This feature permits receiving information directly from the Internet. The user tailors the information received from the Internet via the active desktop to suit their specific needs.

Knowing and understanding the evolution of DOS and Windows software helps troubleshoot PC problems, regardless of the operating environment being used.

Study Break

Desktop Settings

The Windows 95/98 display settings can be changed easily from the desktop. This exercise shows how the display settings are changed from the desktop. It is similar to changing the settings using the control panel, but quicker.

1. On a Windows 95/98 PC, shut down all active programs.

2. Move the mouse pointer to the desktop.

3. Click on the right mouse button. Select properties. The Windows display properties box should appear.

4. Select Cargo Net pattern and change wall paper to none. Fancy wallpaper requires more resources than simple patterns.

5. Select screen saver and change to simple flying Windows or flying through space. These screen savers require fewer CPU cycles than the Open GL screen savers. They are not things of beauty but they work just fine.

6. Select apply. The Windows display should change.

You can restore the settings to their original values. This exercise was to illustrate how easily these settings can be changed from the desktop and which settings reduced the load on the PC.

Windows 95/98 is designed to provide more reliable operation and to reduce support costs through such features as true "plug-and-play" device integration. It changes the user interface to make it easier for novice users to adapt to it easily. The famous design quote from Microsoft was that Windows 95 was designed so that your grandmother could easily use it. This was in many ways accomplished. The "plug-and-play" capabilities, however, still proved to be a support headache. Windows 95/98 provides a 32-bit operating system architecture and is no longer dependent on DOS components for its implementation.

Windows 95/98 is still launched using a Windows 95/98 DOS. This DOS performs the basic functions needed to load the Windows programs. It can also be controlled by CONFIG.SYS and AUTOEXEC.BAT for backwards compatibility to earlier DOS and Windows applications. The big step with Windows 95/98 is that networking functionality is now built into the Windows operating environment. This means that DOS driver and higher level programs are not required to network PCs with Windows NT and Novell servers.

Windows 95/98 also adds some support functions to make management and administration of multiple PCs easier. These functions are additional centralized security for network operations, the ability to edit and alter system policies (configurations), separate user hardware profiles to permit multiple users to operate a single PC, and remote administration and backup facilities. There are three versions of Windows 95: Release 950A (the original Windows 95), OEM Service Release 2 (950B adding the 32-bit FAT capability), and 950C, which incorporated Universal Serial Bus support into Windows 95. Windows 98 incorporated all these features as well as finally fixed most of the "plug-and-play" problems.

Windows releases are:

Version Designation	Description	Release Date
Win 95 Gold	Original Windows 95 (version 4.00.950)	July 11, 1995
Win 95 A	Service Pack 1 update (version 4.00.950 A)	December 31, 1995
Win 95 B	OSR 2.0 (version 4.00.950 B)	August 24, 1996
Win 95 C	OSR 2.1 (version 4.00.950 B)	August 27, 1997
Win 98	OSR 2.5 (version 4.00.950 C)	November 18, 1997
Win 98 SE	Original Windows 98 (version 4.10.1998) Windows 98 Special Edition (version 4.10.2222)	May 11, 1998 April 23, 1999
Win 9x	All versions of Windows 95 and 98	

A+ 11.3 Windows 95/98 Functions

The functions performed by Windows 95/98 are similar to those performed by Windows 3.x. However, the functions are performed by new 32-bit software components. Windows 95/98 still uses a KRNL386.EXE and USER.EXE and GDI.EXE programs, similarly to the old Windows 3.x. However, these programs have been rewritten to provide more robust and reliable operation. Furthermore, some new functional areas are added to Windows. Windows 95/98 manages disk drives and files; PC components; applications; files; networking; and printing with added functionality.

For example, Windows 95/98 uses the Explorer program in place of the Windows 3.1x file manager program. The Explorer program provides the same functions as the file manager program, but it does so through a "folders" panel that works with multiple disk drives using drop-down tree-structured navigation. In contrast, Windows 3.1x file manager opens separate panels for each disk drive. File manipulation and navigation with the Windows 95/98 Explorer is much easier for the PC user. Similarly, Windows 95/98 provides control of the PC using the control panel. Windows 3.1x also has control panel functions, but they are not nearly as comprehensive as those for Windows 95/98. Furthermore, in Windows 3.1x, the networking functions rely on DOS and add-in programs. In particular, TCP/IP networking was an additional modification to Windows 3.11. Windows 95/98 has all the networking software built in. These are just some of the examples of the added functionality provided with Windows 95/98 over the functionality originally provided with Windows 3.1x.

Managing Disks and Files

Windows 95 uses the Windows 95 DOS program FDISK to configure the fixed disk. With the first release of Windows 95 (950A), little was changed from Windows 3.x beyond the total migration to 32-bit disk and file managers that was started with Windows 3.11. There were cosmetic changes, however, that provided a new look to the system.

See Figure 11–2. Real mode drivers were included for backwards compatibility with older Windows devices. These real mode drivers are 16-bit Windows software.

With the Windows 950B release, known as OEM Service Release 2, came the long-awaited 32-bit File Allocation Table (FAT), expanding single disk partition size beyond the 2 GB limit imposed by the 16-bit FAT. Unfortunately, the 32-bit FAT feature could only be implemented by destroying all the data on the fixed disk drive when using FDISK to convert from FAT 16 to

Figure 11–2 *Windows 98 system properties*

FAT 32. Once the conversion to FAT 32 was accomplished, there was no way to return to a FAT 16 structure without again using FDISK to destroy all the data on the disk drive. With Windows 98, there is a utility program that will convert from a FAT 16 to a FAT 32 structure without destroying data on the disk drive. In this instance, a disk is not required to move from FAT 16 to FAT 32. However to revert back to FAT 16, FDISK must be used, which destroys all data on the disk drive.

Windows 95 also changed file management operations by supporting long file names.

No longer were the file names limited to the DOS 8.3 file naming convention. Longer file names means that users can give their files more meaningful, complete names. The price here is that all the older DOS and Windows programs still operate with the DOS 8.3 formats. When they encounter a long file name it is automatically truncated to fit into the 8.3 DOS file name structure. If files are referenced and not copied to different folders, the long file names remain generally intact.

Managing PC Components

The big change in managing PC components is the implementation of "plug-and-play" component installation. Thus, with special BIOS and specially designed peripheral interface cards, installation of components did not require users to set switches and jumpers on the hardware cards. Windows automatically sorted out I/O port and IRQ assignments during the installation and boot process. The most immediate impact here was on laptop installation with PCMCIA card bus controllers. Windows made installation workable with these systems. Laptop components were a nightmare to install under Windows 3.x. Windows 98 and the earlier availability of the PCI have made "plug-and-play" installation much more reliable and predictable. Changes in both Windows and PC hardware make it possible to incorporate more devices into a basic PC system.

Managing Applications

Windows application management became more reliable because Windows 32-bit applications created for Windows 98 now ran in the Windows system virtual machine, but in their separate address space. Windows 16-bit applications still run in a shared address space, making them less reliable. See Figure 11–3. This is an extension of the Windows 3.x applications architecture that makes Windows 95/98 more reliable for Windows 32-bit applications.

From an operating point of view, Windows 16-bit and Windows 32-bit applications appear similar. One major difference between Windows 16-bit

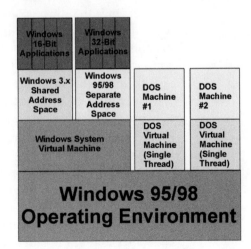

Figure 11–3 *Windows 95/98 applications architecture*

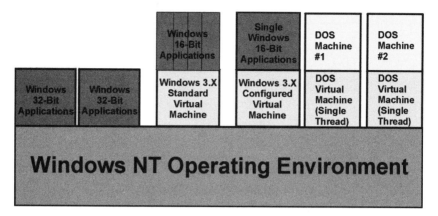

Figure 11–4 *Windows NT applications architecture*

applications and Windows 32-bit applications is that the 16-bit allocations only modify entries in the WIN.INI and the SYSTEM.INI files. In contrast Windows 95/98 modifies primarily the Registry files not the WIN.INI and SYSTEM.INI files. Also, typically the Windows 16-bit applications are much smaller in size and thus install much more quickly than do the Windows 32-bit applications. Windows 16-bit applications are less reliable than Windows 32-bit applications because they share a single Windows virtual machine. Windows 32-bit applications all run in their own separate virtual machines. Hence, a problem with one Windows 32-bit application should not impact other Windows 32-bit applications. Unfortunately, this is not always true.

The next major advance is the Windows NT operating system. Although Windows NT 4.01 was released prior to Windows 98, it is an entirely different and much more robust design than Windows 98. Windows NT was designed to be an entirely different operating environment from Windows 98. There was no concern in the design of Windows NT for backward compatibility with previous versions of Windows. Windows NT does not rely on DOS for loading and configuring disk drives. NT also changes the application architecture so that Windows 32-bit applications run in their own address space, working directly with the NT operating environment. Furthermore, Windows NT can be configured so that Windows 16-bit applications can run in a common Windows virtual machine or in their own Windows virtual machine. Figure 11–4 illustrates this. What this means is that applications run so that they do not crash NT. In Windows NT, an application itself can crash, but it is less likely. Further, if an application crashes, it is less likely to crash NT.

It is important to understand how Windows has evolved to make applications support more reliable and to perform better. This helps us understand what the next enhancements to Windows and Windows NT may incorporate. Of course, the Windows operating environments underneath the applications architecture are also more reliable as we move from Windows 3.x to Windows 95/98 on to Windows NT.

Windows NT was designed to be an entirely new operating system that supported client/server networking. It was not primarily aimed at supporting applications software that ran under DOS or Windows; such software support was an ancillary capability of Windows NT. Hence, not all DOS and Windows programs would run under NT. Windows NT server provided all the functionality required to set up a server in a client/server networking environment. Windows NT workstation was designed to provide a secure client for a client/server network.

DOS Windows NT was created from scratch in the late 80s and sold to the public in 1993 as Windows NT Advanced Server Version 3.1. As a server, it was designed to run 32-bit applications designed for Windows NT and those DOS and Windows applications that behaved well in a Windows NT environment. This means that Windows 95 is much more complex than NT because it tries to be compatible with a much wider range of DOS and Windows applications, as well as a wider range of PC hardware and software. The next step in NT evolution is likely to enhance the range of hardware components that NT works with by incorporating Windows 95/98 "plug-and-play" capabilities. As applications evolve in step with Windows 95/98 and Windows NT, these operating environments will support a greater variety of them. The biggest change area is going to be networking. Both Windows 95/98 and Windows NT have incorporated networking capabilities, but these abilities will be expanded to provide enhanced Internet and intranet features that make full use of high speed connectivity and the multimedia capabilities of future PCs.

Managing Printing

Printing is managed using two components: a universal printer driver and a minidriver. The printer driver is common to all printing.

It interprets the printing languages used by the applications programs. Some such page description languages are HP's Page Composition Language (HP PCL) and Adobe's PostScript. The minidrivers handle detailed printer-specific operations. They are the detailed printer hardware drivers and usually come from the printer manufacturer as part of the printer installation instructions and programs, or they can often be loaded from the Win 95/98/ NT installation CD.

This gives Windows 95/98 the ability to use a wide range of printers from many manufacturers.

The minidrivers are found on both Windows 98 and Windows NT systems, they are used as required and not always memory resident, they adapt specific hardware functions to Windows, and they support multiple function interfaces, such as those found in audio hardware and multifunction networking adapters in laptops.

Networking

Networking is a new capability built into Windows 95/98 and NT that was not previously found in the 3.x or earlier versions of the operating systems.

Windows provides not only the driver programs for a wide variety of network interface cards (NICs) but it also standardizes the PC's interface to Transmission Control Protocol/Internet Protocol (TCP/IP) networks, including the Internet.

This is the current Windows Sockets 2.0 application program interface (API), sometimes referred to as WINSOCK32 because 32-bit DLLs (WSOCK32.DLL and WS2_32.DLL) support the API.

This standardization has contributed to networks moving away from the dominant DOS networking protocols, NetWare Sequenced Packet Exchange/Internet Packet Exchange (SPX/IPX), and onto the more universal TCP/IP protocols. Chapter 16, "Windows Networking," provides more information on the various Windows protocols.

Windows 95/98 has several security levels aimed at supporting networking features. There is a share level of security aimed at supporting peer-to-peer networking configurations. In this case, the user specifies a password for every resource that they share on the network. User-level security is aimed at larger client-server network configurations. Here, users are validated by password on a central server. That validation determines their access to network resources—disk drives and printers. More detail on peer-to-peer versus client/server networking appears in Chapter 16. Basic LAN installation and wide area network (WAN) operations were discussed in Chapter 8, "LANs and Communications."

Windows 95/98 supports both NetWare protocols and TCP/IP protocols over a variety of network interfaces, including LAN and dial-up connections.

This is expanding with Windows 98 to include new high-speed networking technologies like Asynchronous Transfer Mode (ATM) for both local and wide area network connections.

The central thrust here is to provide high-speed connectivity locally as well as to the Internet. This will be a key area for A+ maintenance activities and troubleshooting in future PC systems.

Administrative Functions

Windows 95/98 incorporates some central management facilities that permit a single support person to centrally manage Windows PC clients. These central support mechanisms control Windows system policies (configurations). A system policy editor lets an administrator define rights and restrictions to specific resources for individual users and computers. They support establishment of default configurations for all users.

Windows can be set up from central servers (a good idea, but not necessarily recommended). Custom setup scripts control the setup process. These scripts consistently configure Windows on all PCs with a set of custom default options. Users then can modify this configuration to suit their individual needs. These individual configurations are stored in a user profile for that specific user. Is also possible with Windows NT servers to configure profiles that roam from PC to PC when the user logs on to a specific PC. While this sounds very helpful, roaming user profiles must be precisely configured to work properly.

Study Break

Windows 95/98 User Profiles

In this exercise, we set up the user profile on a Windows 95/98 PC. This will customize the PC for that specific user and permit other users to work on that PC with specific user profiles as well.

1. Open the control panel.

2. Highlight the users icon and double-click.

3. Follow the users wizard to set up a single user configuration on this PC. Either create copies of the current items and their content or create new items to save this space to set up yourself as a user on this PC.

4. Click the finish button to complete the user setup.

5. Repeat the process for a new user, but this time choose the opposite configuration of what you originally used in Step 3.

This exercise illustrates the procedure for customizing Windows 95/98 PCs for individual users.

A+   11.4   Windows 95/98 Components

The architecture components of Windows 95/98 include device drivers, a virtual machine manager, an installable file system manager, a configuration manager, the registry, the windows core operating system and a 32-bit shell. These components are implemented primarily in dynamic link libraries (DLLs) and executable (EXE) programs. There are also other types of supporting files, including driver programs (DRV, SYS, VxD, and more), registry files (DAT), initialization files (INI) for backward compatibility, and more.

Device Drivers

The Windows 3.1 device drivers were device specific and complex to develop. Windows 95 changed that by implementing a two-tiered structure. Common functions were placed in a universal driver while specific hardware interfacing was performed by minidrivers. The universal driver performed most of the functions for a specific class of device, such as a modem, a LAN network interface card (NIC), or a printer. The minidriver contains specific interfacing instructions needed to operate a single manufacturer's hardware.

The universal drivers are implemented in VxD software modules under Windows 95/98. These VxD programs are 32-bit protected-mode driver software that more than one application can use at any given time. Figure 11–5 shows some of the Windows 98 VxDs installed on a Windows 98 PC. These are typically installed in the \windows\system folder.

Minidrivers are MPD installation modules. Once installed, they become MPD modules, as shown in Figure 11–6. The figure also shows printer port drivers (PPD) and asynchronous port drivers (APD). In the figure, those modules in the \win98 folder are the installation files, and the installed files are in the \windows\system and \windows\system\iosubsys folders. These device drivers are installed when new hardware components are added to the PC. Special device drivers are provided by the hardware component manufacturer. They are stored in the WINDOWS\SYSTEM\IOSUBSYS folder and loaded by the I/O supervisor.

Figure 11–5   *Windows 98 virtual device drivers—VxDs*

Figure 11–6   *Windows 98 driver modules*

Virtual Machine Manager

The virtual machine manager provides the resources needed by each application and process running under Windows 95/98. It creates virtual machines, imaginary PC's created by software in RAM. These virtual machines run the PC applications. There are separate virtual machines for each DOS application and a system virtual machine to run the Windows applications. Windows applications share the same virtual machine, with 16-bit applications sharing the same address space and 32-bit applications using their own individual address space. To provide a migration path from Windows 3.1x to Windows 95/98, Windows 95/98 provides a single system virtual machine for the Windows 16-bit applications. Since Windows 32-bit applications do not run on Windows 3.1x, they were designed to run in their own virtual machine under Windows 95/98. Furthermore, allocating individual address space for 32-bit applications makes those applications less likely to corrupt the address space used by other applications. Because they operate in their own virtual machine and because their address space is not shared with other applications, 32-bit applications run more reliably than 16-bit applications.

The virtual machines manager performs process scheduling and memory paging functions for all applications. It also provides MS-DOS support to DOS applications requiring exclusive access to PC resources. The virtual machine manager implements preemptive multitasking operations.

Installable File System

The installable file system supports multiple file systems. In Windows 95 it supported long file names, 32-bit file allocation table (VFAT), 32-bit CD-ROM file system (VCDFS), and a redirector for network file operations. Windows 98 adds a 32-bit universal disk format (UDF) file system driver for writing to CD/RW drives. The IFSMGR.VxD arbitrates access to the different file system components. A block I/O subsystem handles the physical input/output operations. This was expanded to include support for 32-bit physical FAT in Windows 95 OEM Service Release 2 (950 B and 950 C versions of Windows 95) and in Windows 98. The 32-bit FAT (VFAT) driver provides significant improvement over Windows 3.x 32-bit disk and file access because it is reentrant and multithreaded.

Each 32-bit application running under Windows 95/98 is a process. Each process is comprised of at least a single thread of executing code. Thus a thread is a piece of executing code following a process path to produce useable results. Threads can obtain a slice of time from the operating system and they run concurrently with other threads. Reentrant programs permit multiple threads to safely execute concurrently, and also a single thread can safely reenter the program as a result of a recursive process. When an operating system can work on multiple threads concurrently, it offers better performance than an operating system that cannot.

Windows Core Operating System

The Windows core operating system is composed of USER.EXE, GDI.EXE, and the kernel, each consisting of a 16-bit and a companion 32-bit DLL. These DLLs together provide services for applications.

The 16-bit DLLs retain compatibility with earlier Windows applications and are also used where they provide equivalent functionality to 32-bit code without degrading performance while lowering memory usage. The USER.EXE program provides window and menu management services. It accepts user input. The GDI.EXE module manages graphics, deals with fonts, printing, spooling, and other graphics functions. The kernel performs the scheduling, synchronization, memory management, input/output, and console operations, among others.

Windows 95/98 32-Bit Shell

The Windows shell is based on the Windows Explorer program. The shell provides desktop tools like the start menu, the network neighborhood, my computer, the recycle bin and the briefcase. The shell provides common controls including dialog boxes, tree views, web views and list views to all Windows applications. The user profile determines the look of the Windows desktop for that specific user. The Windows Explorer program uses parameters to create the Windows desktop. For example, the Windows desktop programs are contained in the *windows\desktop* folder. Similarly, the Windows start menu programs are contained in the *\Windowsstart menu\programs* folder. The Windows Explorer program can also be run on its own to act as a general mechanism for formatting disks, copying files, and launching application programs.

DLLs

Windows 95/98 and applications are implemented using Dynamic Link Libraries (DLLs), as is Windows 3.1x.

Windows 95/98 DLLs can be 32-bit, reentrant, and multithreaded. This translates into smoother multitasking in a Windows 95/98 environment.

Windows 95/98 DLLs, similar to Windows 3.x DLLs, are separate executable programs loaded by other programs to perform specific tasks.

EXEs

Similar to Windows 3.x, EXE files are executable programs. They are a type of dynamic link library that typically is used to initiate or launch an application. Several Windows applets—small specific function programs—are EXE files alone. For example, solitaire is SOL.EXE; paintbrush is PBRUSH.EXE; and notepad is NOTEPAD.EXE.

The Registry

The registry files are the main Windows 95/98 control structures. They control Windows startup, shutdown, and the loading and execution of applications. The registries began with REG.DAT in Windows 3.1, which held the file extension associations and the OLE server applications.

Because the Windows INI files are text files of limited size, they were easily changed by users. However, because they had a linear structure, they were insufficient to provide the control mechanisms required by Windows 95/98. In contrast, the registry files are not text files and consequently require a special REGEDIT program to alter them. Furthermore, the registries are broken down into hives, each having a hierarchical structure of keys and values. Registries are not limited as to size, they provide a single source for configuring PC hardware application device drivers and more, they can be configured using standard control panel tools, they can be remotely administered, and they provide network-independent functions, permitting examination of configuration data and setting system configuration information on remote networked PCs.

The Windows 95/98 registry is now more than a single file. The Windows 95/98 Registry is comprised of the following files:

- SYSTEM.DAT. This file is used to define an individual PC configuration and the applications installed on that PC. These items include plug-and-play hardware, I/O, IRQs, and DMAs.
- USER.DAT. This file is used to define the user's preferences for the desktop and the applications.

These files are typically stored on the PC in the \windows folder. For a specific user's configuration to be present regardless of the machine they log on to, USER.DAT must be on a server. All registry files are read-only, system, hidden files. They are stored in a binary format.

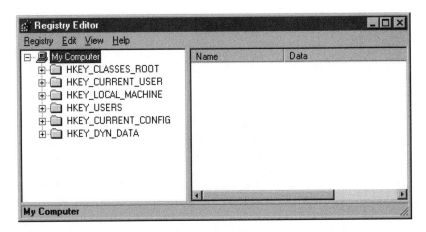

Figure 11-7   *Windows 95 REGEDIT registry view*

For the most part, these registries are inaccessible to the common user. It is possible for users to run REGEDIT. However, system administrators could block access to REGEDIT and thus block users from altering the registries.

PC support personnel can, however, view the registries using the REGEDIT program. This program is in the Windows folder or directory on the C drive. When REGEDIT is run, it loads the contents of both SYSTEM.DAT and USER.DAT into memory. Figure 11-7 shows a REGEDIT view of the combined SYSTEM.DAT and USER.DAT registries.

REGEDIT displays a hierarchical structure of the registries. In Figure 11-8, below the computer you see the root key names that start with an "HKEY" (Hive Keys) prefix which corresponds to the set of key values in the Win32 API.

An application program interface consists of programs, protocols, and tools for building software applications. An API makes it easier to develop applications by providing the building blocks that a programmer puts together to form the application. Windows, like most operating environments, provides an API for 32-bit applications—the Win 32 API. APIs are ultimately good for users because all programs using a common API have similar interfaces. This similarity and consistency helps users learn new programs.

The following list defines the "HKEY" list.

- **HKEY_CLASES_ROOT**—registers the file type name, based on its extension, of each application that uses the file. Entries are created when an application is installed. The more difficult program infor-

Figure 11–8   *Windows 95 HKEY hierarchical structure*

mation to monitor is in CLSID entries. These perform detailed application control functions like recording the installation date in a binary form to track license expirations. This is stored in the file SYSTEM.DAT.

- **HKEY_CURRENT_USER**—registers the information about the specific user currently logged into this Windows 95 PC. It contains the user's logon ID and password, as well as other information. The information is copied from the common HKEY_USER stored in USER.DAT.
- **HKEY_LOCAL_MACHINE**—registers the hardware data for the local PC. Most application program information resides here. HKEY_LOCAL_MACHINE is stored in the SYSTEM.DAT file.
- **HKEY_USERS**—registers a list of all users of this PC and their corresponding passwords. This is an accessible root key via a remote computer system. This is stored in USER.DAT.
- **HKEY_CURRENT_CONFIG**—registers the current user's desktop as well as keeps track of the most recently used documents.
- **HKEY_DYN_DATA**—registers the data used to update the system monitor display. This information is not stored in the registry files but rather is created and exists while the PC is running.

The "HKEYS" structure is shown in Figure 11–8. You expand each key by clicking on the plus sign next to the key. This is similar in structure to the Windows NT registry, but they are not identical.

The registry path to the network reveals the network drive mapping for this local computer. In the left panel under network, then Persistent, is the letter D. This is highlighted in Figure 11– 8. The right panel lists the remote path with its data value of \\Moulton1\SYS.

Registry entries can be edited. When editing registry entries, be very cautious because an incorrect value can possibly disable Windows 95. The only way to recover then may be reinstallation of Windows 95/98.

The ERU.EXE program available for Microsoft and sold as part of the Windows 95 Plus package is an excellent way to backup the registry. ERU makes copies of all key Windows files including USER.DAT and SYSTEM.DAT when the backup files are stored in a fixed disk folder. Before editing the registry and before installing new software, run ERU and store the backup, selecting the other directory option. By placing numbered subfolders under the ERU folder, you can make an audit trail of changes to the PC's registry. This audit trail permits you to return to any previous operating state with Windows 95/98. Several errors that would have normally have necessitated a reinstall of Windows were recovered by restoring the registries from audit trails.

The "Windows Protection Fault" boot message is a registry setting problem. By moving the SYSTEM.DAT registry from an identical PC, we were able to boot a PC displaying the "Windows Protection Fault" message.

Editing the registry changes the location of the Windows installation files. The registry key HKEY_LOCAL_MACHINE\Software\Microsoft\Windows\CurrentVersion\Setup contains entries for CommandLine and for SourcePath. Changing these lines can change the location from which Windows seeks the installation files. The registry key HKEY_CURRENT_USER\InstallLocationsMRU may also influence this. When Windows installation files reside on the fixed disk, it is sometimes convenient to change this registry entry to point at those installation files. Thus when the Windows configuration is altered, Windows automatically finds the files on fixed disk rather than requesting insertion of a CD in the CD-ROM drive.

Searching The Registry

In this exercise, we search the Windows registry to find a specific key value. The REGEDIT program is our primary tool for searching the Windows registry.

1. Click on the Windows start button, then select run.

2. Enter REGEDIT, then click OK. This launches the REGEDIT program and loads the registries.

3. Select edit from the menu at the top, and then select find. Alternatively, holding down the control key and tapping the F key can enter the find function.

4. In the entry panel, enter InstallLocations. Click on "find next." After awhile, InstallLocations-MRU should be highlighted under HKEY_ current_user.

5. Review the values and the MRUList order.

6. Check each value to see that it exists. Use Windows Explorer to find the appropriate folder on the disk drive identified. If the value doesn't exist, delete the value. Be sure to remove the entry from the MRUList as well.

7. Click on the registry menu item, then export registry file.

8. Export the registry file to "my documents" as TEST.REG.

9. Exit the REGEDIT program.

10. Use the Windows Explorer to locate TEST.REG under "my documents." What size is TEST.REG? If it is about 1K in size that means you have only exported the InstallLocations-MRU key. If it is much larger than 1K, then you have exported more than the single key.

11. Open WordPad. Go to C:\My Documents and drag and drop TEST.REG into WordPad. TEST.REG must be dropped on the WordPad menu bar for it to open the file as a text file. Once opened in WordPad, you should be able to view a text version of the key that was just modified. If necessary, search the text file for InstallLocationsMRU.

The goal of this exercise was to illustrate searching the registry, altering registry keys and values, and exporting registry keys.

A+ 11.5 Windows 95/98 Key System Files

In Windows 95/98 you find the same files as those used to implement Windows 3.x. While these files perform similar functions, they are not equivalent. These files and their roles are examined briefly here.

SETUP.EXE

SETUP.EXE is the file that starts Windows 95/98 installation. When a Windows PC becomes corrupted, reinstalling Windows can fix a multitude of problems. Users cause problems on Windows PCs by installing lots of software, shutting off the PC without gracefully exiting Windows, and trying unsuccessfully to recover from normal Windows errors. Running SETUP can fix these problems.

To reinitialize the registries and recover from hardware problems, Windows reinstallation can be done right over an existing Windows installation. This preserves the software settings for Windows while fixing basic registry errors. More serious software corruption problems that cannot be fixed by uninstalling and reinstalling the offending software require a clean Windows installation. This requires that you remove the existing Windows installation and reinstall Windows and all the software applications from scratch. To shorten this procedure, PC support functions often make a disk image of their standard Windows installation and use it to replace all files on the PC's fixed disk.

Remember that, prior to performing this type of uninstall/reinstall activity, it's always wise to make a full backup of your system in the case that something goes wrong during the process!

Figure 11–9 illustrates how SETUP can be run during a reinstallation process. Windows installation is discussed more in Chapter 14, "Software Installation, Configuration and Upgrade."

IO.SYS

The IO.SYS file is a hidden, read-only system file in the root directory of the bootable fixed disk drive. IO.SYS controls input/output operations for the PC. It is the first file loaded after the cold boot loader routing is loaded from the fixed disk master boot record.

Windows replaces the DOS IO.SYS with a Windows 95/98 IO.SYS file. This file has key booting parameters set into it. Hence, many CONFIG.SYS parameters are not required. The Windows 95/98 IO.SYS file automatically loads HIMEM.SYS, IFSHLP.SYS, SETVER.EXE, and the disk compression

Figure 11–9 *SETUP options*

programs (DRVSPACE and DBLSPACE) when they are present on the PC's fixed disk. Also standard CONFIG.SYS settings are applied during the booting process.

These settings with their default values shown include:

- DOS=HIGH—loads DOS into the HIMEM area.
- HIMEM.SYS—loads HIMEM to access extended memory (XMS) and load DOS into the HIMEM area.
- IFSHLP.SYS— loads the 32-bit installable file system manager.
- SETVER.EXE—provides compatibility for MS-DOS programs requiring earlier versions of DOS.
- FILES=60—not required by Windows but provided for compatibility with older software.
- LASTDRIVE=z—not required by Windows but provided for compatibility with older software.
- BUFFERS=30—not required by Windows but provided for compatibility with software using IO.SYS calls.
- STACKS=9,256—not required by Windows but provided for compatibility with older software.
- SHELL=COMMAND.COM—specifies the command interpreter with the /p switch set to indicate that it is loaded permanently and should not be unloaded.
- FCBS=4—This is only required by older programs.

Entries placed in the CONFIG.SYS file override the standard IO.SYS parameter settings. If you use applications requiring expanded memory (EMS), the EMM386.EXE must be loaded using CONFIG.SYS because it is not by default loaded by the Windows 95/98 IO.SYS. Some CONFIG.SYS guidelines for operation with Windows 95/98 are:

- Do not use the fixed disk cache provided by SMARTDRV. Windows 95/98 has built-in disk caching and double buffering.
- Remove mouse driver programs because Windows 95/98 has built-in mouse drivers.
- Remove the settings for files, buffers, stacks, and lastdrive because Windows 95/98 sets proper default values for them.

MSDOS.SYS

MSDOS.SYS performs program and file management for DOS. It is also a hidden, read-only system file in the root directory of the bootable disk drive.

Similar to IO.SYS, Windows also replaces MSDOS.SYS with a Windows 95/98 MSDOS.SYS file. This is now a text file specifying paths used to locate Windows files like the registry. See Figure 11–10.

A PC can be set up to dual boot into Windows 3.1x and Windows 95. To dual boot, Windows 3.x is installed in *c:\Windows* and Windows 95 is installed in a different directory say *c:\win95*. Then BootMulti=1 is added to the MSDOS.SYS file.

The MSDOS.SYS file can be modified using NOTEPAD to specify additional Windows boot options (see Tables 11–1 and 11–2).

Table 11.1 *[Paths] section parameters*

Parameter	Description
HostWinBootDrv=c	Boot drive root directory location.
WinBootDir=	Pointer to the Windows startup files. Typically c:\windows
WinDir=	Location of the Windows directory

Table 11.2 *[Options] section parameters*

Parameter	Description
AutoScan=1	Runs SCANDISK on restart.
BootDelay=2	Delays booting 2 seconds.
BootFailSafe=0	Enables safe mode startup.

Table 11.2 *[Options] section parameters (Continued)*

Parameter	Description
BootGUI=1	Starts the GUI. The same as Windows 3.x WIN.COM start.
BootKeys=1	Enables modifying startup using F5, F6, and F8 keys. Shift+F5 bypasses all boot files and starts Windows in Safe Mode. Shift+F6 bypasses boot files and starts Windows in Safe Mode with network support (not supported with Windows 98— it is the same as Shift+F5). Shift+F8 permits line by line examination of CONFIG.SYS and AUTOEXEC.BAT during startup, then places PC in safe mode.
BootMenu=0	Controls display of Windows 98 startup menu.
BootMenuDefault=#	Sets the menu item on the Windows startup menu. A value 3 is for standalone PC configurations and a value 4 is for networked PCs.
BootMenuDelay=30	Sets the number of seconds to display the Windows Startup menu.
BootMulti=0	A setting of 1 permits booting MS-DOS by pressing F4 or F8.
BootWarn=1	Provides safe mode start warning.
BootWin=1	Sets Windows 98 as the default operating system.
DblSpace=1	Loads DBLspace.bin.
DoubleBuffer=0	Enables double buffering required by some SCSI fixed disk controllers.
DrvSpace1	Loads DRVspace.bin
LoadTop=1	Loads COMMAND.COM and DRVSPACE.BN at the top of conventional memory.
Logo=1	Displays animated logo
Network=0	Supposed to start safe mode with networking support. No longer supported in Windows 98

COMMAND.COM and AUTOEXEC.BAT

COMMAND.COM is also installed in the root directory of the bootable fixed disk. It has normal file attributes. COMMAND.COM is used to process the DOS commands in the AUTOEXEC.BAT file.

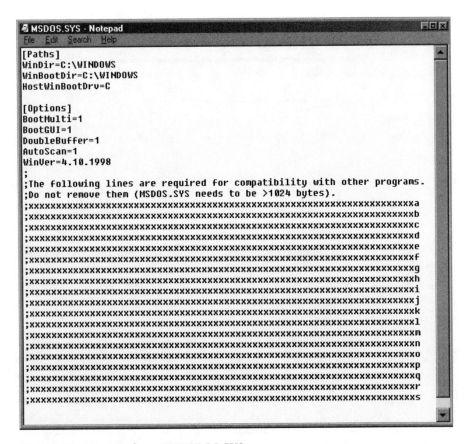

Figure 11–10 *Windows 98 MSDOS.SYS*

IO.SYS performs some AUTOEXEC.BAT commands. Consequently, including a "net start" command and a "set path" command in AUTOEXEC.BAT for COMMAND.COM execution is now unnecessary.

Windows 95/98 also sets the environment space of the PC to:

```
tmp=c:\windows\temp
temp=c:\windows\temp
prompt=$p$g
path=c:\windows;c:\windows\command
comspec=c:\windows\command\command.com
```

This makes environment space commands in AUTOEXEC.BAT unneeded as well. However, if the environment space must be set differently from the standard Windows 95/98 settings, then commands in the AUTOEXEC.BAT file are used to make the desired modifications.

When changing an AUTOEXEC.BAT file for Windows 95/98, follow these suggestions:

1. Reference only the Windows 95/98 folder in your path AUTOEXEC.BAT statement and no other versions of Windows.
2. Start paths with *c:\windows;c:\windows\command.com.*
3. Retain the previous MS-DOS directory in the path.
4. Do not run SMARTDRV or other disk cache programs—Windows provides the necessary disk caching.
5. Do not load mouse support programs—Windows provides mouse support.
6. Commands to connect to network servers can be dumped. If necessary run a batch file from the Windows startup directory to perform this task.
7. During installation unneeded statements are removed from AUTOEXEC.BAT by the Windows installation program. The only real programs run from AUTOEXEC.BAT are virus scanners and simple terminate-and-stay-resident programs like DOSKEY.

REGEDIT.EXE

REGEDIT.EXE edits the registry. As we saw earlier, REGEDIT provides the ability to examine and change registry entries directly. It loads both the SYSTEM.DAT and USER.DAT into memory for editing and displays them as a single registry. REGEDIT.EXE also permits exporting the entire registry or specific registry keys and subkeys as text files. These files are labeled with a REG extension. These REG files can then be used later to alter the registry.

REGEDIT is in the \windows folder. It can be launched by double-clicking on the icon or by going to the Windows Start, Run selection and entering REGEDIT.

SYSTEM.DAT

SYSTEM.DAT is a registry file. It is the largest registry file and controls Windows during the startup process. It contains hardware and computer-specific settings. These parameters are displayed in the hardware profiles and by the control panel device manager.

SYSTEM.DAT is stored in the \windows folder or directory. It is possible to have it reside elsewhere, but not advisable. Windows 95 makes a backup copy of the SYSTEM.DAT file as SYSTEM.DA0. Windows 98 makes several backup copies of the registry files using the SCANREG program. The

Windows 95 and Windows 98 backup copies of the registry help recover from some problems, but our experience suggests that they are largely ineffective. It is much better to use ERU registry backups stored on the fixed disk to recover from Windows registry errors.

Because the registry is reasonable complex, making it difficult for most people to understand, and because installed software typically makes multiple changes to the registry, it is easiest to keep copies of the entire registry to fix Windows problems rather than to seek the individual registry changes that would correct the Windows malfunction. Many times I have spent hours searching the registry to correct a Windows problem to no avail. In contrast, replacing the registry from a ERU backup has saved me several times.

USER.DAT

The USER.DAT registry file holds user-specific parameters that implement user profiles. Such information covers screen colors, patterns, screen savers, and the like. Similar to the SYSTEM.DAT file, the USER.DAT file resides in the \windows directory. Windows 95 also makes a backup file, USER.DA0, maintained there as well. Both files are read-only, hidden, and system files. Windows 98 makes a backup using the SCANREG program.

These Windows 98 Registry backups are stored in the \windows\sysbckup directory as rb000.cab, rb001.cab, rb002.cab, rb003.cab and rb004.cab. See Figure 11–11. They contain copies of both SYSTEM.DAT and USER.DAT.

Figure 11–11   *rb004.cab contents*

In addition they store the WIN.INI and SYSTEM.INI files. The CAB files can be opened using the Windows 98 Explorer.

WIN.COM

WIN.COM launches Windows 95/98 similarly to how it launches Windows 3.x. It can also launch Windows from the command prompt. This can be helpful when trying to isolate an error condition.

During the Windows startup, WIN.COM determines if Windows was shut down properly by examining the FAT. When it detects an improper shutdown, WIN.COM runs SCANDISK to check the drive for errors.

The WIN.COM troubleshooting options modifying Windows startup include the following:

```
WIN [/D:[F][M][S][V][X]]
```

- /D Used for troubleshooting when Windows does not start correctly.
- :F Turns off 32-bit disk access.
  Equivalent to SYSTEM.INI file setting: 32BitDiskAccess=FALSE.
- :M Enables safe mode.
  This is automatically enabled during safe start (function key F5).
- :N Enables safe mode with networking.
  This is automatically enabled during safe start (function key F6).
- :S Specifies that Windows should not use ROM address space between F000:0000 and 1 MB for a break point.
  Equivalent to SYSTEM.INI file setting: SystemROMBreak-Point=FALSE.
- :V Specifies that the ROM routine will handle interrupts from the hard disk controller.
  Equivalent to SYSTEM.INI file setting: VirtualHDIRQ=FALSE.
- :X Excludes all of the adapter area from the range of memory that Windows scans to find unused space.
  Equivalent to SYSTEM.INI file setting: EMMExclude=A000-FFFF.

WIN.COM also participates in the Windows shutdown process. It uses the FAT entry to signal that Windows shut down properly after writing the VFAT to disk successfully.

Saving Registry Files

This exercise saves copies of the SYSTEM.DAT and USER.DAT files to the root directory of the C drive as SYSTEM.00 and USER.00, SYSTEM.01, and USER.01, etc. The sequential numbering creates an audit trail of registry files, permitting the PC to be recovered to a previous operating state. This is an effective method of backing up Windows 95/98 configurations. It can be used in place of the ERU (emergency recovery utility) program to back up Windows configurations.

1. Create the following BAKREG.BAT file:
```
attrib c:\windows\system.da? -r -h -s
attrib c:\windows\user.da? -r -h -s
copy c:\windows\system.dat c:\system.%1
copy c:\windows\user.dat c:\user.%1
attrib c:\windows\system.da? +r +h +s
attrib c:\windows\user.da? +r +h +s
```

This batch file can be run in an MS-DOS window under Windows 95/98 to create backup copies of the SYSTEM.DAT and USER.DAT files.

2. Once the file is created as BAKREG.BAT, open a DOS window and run the batch file by entering:
BAKREG 00

This causes the batch file to copy the SYSTEM.DAT and USER.DAT into the root directory of the C drive as SYSTEM.00 and USER.00.

The goal of this exercise is to provide a simple technique for backing up the registry. The batch file permits you to make backup copies of the registry files and permits you to keep them in a numeric sequence starting with 00, then 01, etc.

■ Summary

This chapter started with examining the differences between Windows 3.1x and Windows 95/98. Next it examined the Windows 95/98 functions including file and disk management, networking, and more. Windows 95/98 components were identified and described and finally Windows 95/98 key system files were examined.

▲ CHAPTER REVIEW QUESTIONS

1. *The Windows 95 memory organization uses?*
   A. conventional, upper, extended memory
   B. used and free memory
   C. heaps
   D. blocks
   Answer: C. heaps

2. *Windows 95 and Windows NT Workstation support the following protocols except:*
   A. NetBEUI
   B. IPX/SPX
   C. TCP/IP
   D. DLCC
   Answer: D. DLCC

3. *The registry in Windows 95 is organized into:*
   A. keys
   B. hives
   C. values
   D. trees
   Answer: A. keys

4. *A Windows 95 and NT 4.0 utility managing the fixed disk drive is called:*
   A. file manager
   B. program manager
   C. control panel
   D. Explorer
   Answer: D. Explorer

5. *To determine if specific hardware is supported by Windows NT, check the:*
   A. HAL
   B. HCL
   C. HSL
   D. RFC
   Answer: B. HCL (Hardware Compatibility List)

6. *Assuming user level security is disabled on a PC computer, what must be done after installing file and print sharing under Windows 95 to allow users access to the computer?*

   A. no further configuration is necessary

   B. specify access permission for each individual user or group who uses the computer

   C. share a folder through Explorer or my computer

   D. reboot the computer

   Answer: C. share a folder through Explorer or my computer

7. *The Windows 3.1x REG.DAT file size exceeding 65,000 bytes can indicate:*

   A. a corrupted Windows 3.1x registry

   B. a faulty Windows installation

   C. a virus

   D. nothing, REG.DAT grows as new applications are installed

   Answer: A. a corrupted Windows 3.1x registry

8. *In Windows NT, what is used to recover from a failed boot?*

   A. DOS boot disk

   B. last known good configuration

   C. both b and c

   D. none of the above

   Answer B. last known good configuration

9. *What loads the Windows NT operating system?*

   A. NTLDR

   B. MBR

   C. NTOSKRNL.EXE

   D. MBA

   Answer: B. MBR (Master Boot Record)

10. *Windows 95 supports the following network interface cards except:*

    A. token ring

    B. Ethernet

    C. ARCnet

    D. JetDirect

    Answer: D. JetDirect

11. *Where does Win95 setup record hardware detection information?*

    A. in DETLOG.TXT

    B. in DETLOG.LOG

    C. in SETUPLOG.TXT

    D. in DETCRASH.LOG

    Answer: A. in DETLOG.TXT

12. *A new Windows application is installed and run. It works fine. However, when opening Word, which was previously installed, a general protection fault is generated, and Word terminates. After reinstalling Word, it still refuses to run. What is a probable cause?*

    A. The new application overwrote key DLL files related to Word.

    B. The Word installation files have become corrupted, and you need new installation media.

    C. Run REGEDIT to reregister Word in the registry.

    D. The new application used too much RAM and not enough is left to run Word.

    Answer: A. The new application overwrote key DLL files related to Word

13. *A Windows 95 machine generates errors while printing. A check of the resources reveals the GDI resources at 60%. After rebooting and opening just the program to print from, the GDI resources are at 75%. What steps could increase your resources?*

    A. install more RAM

    B. upgrade your video card

    C. lower your video resolution and color palette

    D. all of the above

    Answer: C. lower your video resolution and color palette

14. *The Win95 Registry is which two files?*

    A. SYSTEM.DAT and USER.DAT

    B. SYSTEM.REG and USER.RET

    C. SYSTEM.INI and WIN.INI

    D. REG.DAT and SETUP.REG

    Answer: A. SYSTEM.DAT and USER.DAT

15. *A new video card is installed and configured. When the PC is rebooted, Windows 95 hangs on the logo screen. What troubleshooting steps should resolve the problem?*

    A. Boot the computer in safe mode and change the video driver to VGA.

    B. Boot "step-by-step confirmation" and don't load anything that isn't necessary for the system to boot.

    C. Boot "Command Prompt Only" and comment any unnecessary lines from AUTOEXEC.BAT and CONFIG.SYS.

    D. Reinstall Windows.

    Answer: A. Boot the computer in safe mode and change the video driver to VGA.

16. *Windows 95 plug-and-play BIOS enables:*

    A. the devices that are not plug-and-play first

    B. the plug-and-play devices first

    C. the devices only after CONFIG.SYS is read

    D. an automatic virus scan

    Answer: A. the devices that are not plug-and-play first

17. *What is the best way for an average user to modify PC system settings?*

    A. edit the registry to make the necessary changes

    B. use control panel applets to make the necessary changes

    C. run Sysedit to make the necessary changes to SYSTEM.INI and WIN.INI

    D. a and c

    Answer: B. use control panel applets to make the necessary changes.

18. *Two primary utilities for maintaining/optimizing hard drives in DOS and Win95 are?*

    A. SCANDISK and BACKUP

    B. DEFRAG and BACKUP

    C. SCANDISK and DEFRAG

    D. SCANDISK and FDISK

    Answer: C. SCANDISK and DEFRAG

19. *A dual boot system with Win95 and Win3.11 locks up during a Windows 95 boot when it tries to load a particular device driver from CONFIG.SYS. It boots to Win3.11. To correct the problem preventing Win95 from booting, you edit c:\CONFIG.SYS but cannot find the device driver reference. Why?*

    A. Win95 automatically deleted the line that prevented the system from booting.

    B. The device file doesn't load from CONFIG.SYS; it loads from AUTOEXEC.BAT.

    C. The Win95 CONFIG.SYS is currently CONFIG.W95.

    D. The Win95 CONFIG.SYS is currently CONFIG.W40.

    Answer: D The Win95 CONFIG.SYS is currently CONFIG.W40

20. *What is the maximum number of entries in a hard disk's root directory in DOS 6.22 and Win95?*

    A. 512 entries

    B. 150 entries

    C. 1000 entries

    D. there is no limit to the number of entries in any directory.

    Answer: A. 512 entries

21. *Why won't an OS/2 application run on an NT machine?*

    A. the application accesses the hard drive directly

    B. some OS/2 applications are not compatible with NT

    C. OS/2 applications can only be run on OS/2 machines

    D. OS/2 applications must access the hardware directly

    Answer: B. some OS/2 applications are not compatible with NT

22. *Which Windows environments can use 4GB memory address space in the PC?*

    A. Windows 3.x

    B. Windows 95

    C. Windows NT

    D. B. and C.

    Answer: D. B. and C.

23. *Windows 95/98 file associations are stored in _____.*

    A. the registry

   B. the OLE.INI file

   C. the WIN.INI file

   D. the WINASSOC.INI file

   Answer: A. the registry

24. *In order to dual boot, Win3.x is installed in c:\Windows and Win95 is installed in a directory called c:\win95. What additional step must you take to enable the system to dual boot?*

   A. add BootWin=2 to the MSDOS.SYS file

   B. add BootMenu=1 to the MSDOS.SYS file

   C. add BootMulti=1 to the MSDOS.SYS file

   D. add BootDual=1 to the MSDOS.SYS file

   Answer: C. add BootMulti=1 to the MSDOS.SYS file

25. *For Windows NT to allow a remote PC to dial in, what must be installed and running?*

   A. the PPP protocol service

   B. the IPX/SPX protocol service

   C. the RAS service

   D. the Mac service

   Answer: C. the RAS (Remote Access Server) service

Disk Navigation Procedures and Management

▲Chapter Syllabus

A+ 12.1   File System Basics

A+ 12.2   DOS File Operations

A+ 12.3   Windows File Operations

A+ 12.4   Disk Management Procedures

A+ 12.5   Disk Management Utilities

All computer programs and data are in files stored on the PC's disk drives. PC users often misunderstand good data management practices and procedures. Furthermore, they do not think of using the DOS or Windows disk utilities on a periodic basis to maintain the integrity of the data stored on their fixed disk drive. Generally their first encounter with DOS and Windows fixed disk utility programs is when they are desperately attempting to recover data from a corrupted fixed disk drive. Thus, a critical skill for PC troubleshooting and maintenance is the ability to effectively use DOS and Windows disk and file maintenance utility programs. Also, an understanding of how to organize data and manage files on a PC's disk drives can be helpful in educating PC users and helping them avoid corrupting the data and programs stored on their PC's fixed disk drive. Navigating up and down the hierarchy of directories and subdirectories, as well as copying, deleting, moving, displaying, and loading files are

607

essential skills for managing data on PC fixed disk drives.

A+ 12.1 | File System Basics

Files have specific characteristics. These characteristics cover what they contain, their name, and their attributes. When we work with files, understanding the implications of these characteristics helps with the file management process. For example, understanding whether a file is a text or binary file helps us when we wish to view the contents of the file.

If it is a binary file, then we need a special filter or special software to represent the contents in a meaningful fashion to us.

Binary versus Text Files

Generally files contain text information or binary information. Text information is the 96 printable ASCII characters plus some simple control characters like Carriage Return (Cr) and Line Feed (LF). Text files in DOS and Windows end with the SUB character. The SUB character is created by striking F6 or by holding down the Ctrl key and striking the Z character (displayed as ^z).

1. To create a text file from a PC keyboard use the command:
   COPY CON filename.TXT
2. Next type the text you want in the file.
3. Finally, hit Ctrl+Z or F6.
4. The PC should display "1 file(s) copied."

ASCII—American (national) Standard Code for Information Interchange—has seven bits of information and a parity bit, which enables it to represent 128 unique alphanumeric, punctuation, and control characters. This is referred to as 7-bit ASCII. An 8-bit version of the ASCII code is used to represent international characters and symbols. The 8-bit version of ASCII does not have a parity bit. PCs use a special 8-bit version of ASCII, called IBM PC-8, to represent special graphics and foreign alphabet symbols.

Use the steps above to create a text file. Creating text files using just the keyboard is an important troubleshooting skill. There are times when you have only DOS and its ability to run batch files to perform file management miracles. Creating a series of simple batch files using the COPY CON command saves the day in those situations.

The MSDOS.SYS file created by Windows 95/98 is a text file, while the MSDOS.SYS file for DOS is a binary file containing program object code. If we try to display it, we get no meaningful output. See a notepad view of a text and binary file in Figure 12–1. The binary displays strange characters because any pattern of zeros and ones can occupy each byte of the file. Binary files use all 256 patterns of zeros and ones to represent information in the bytes contained in the file. Text files in contrast use a limited set of patterns. The set is somewhat less than the 128 patterns of zeros and ones specified by the ASCII code. This is because text files contain only a few of the 16 control characters defined by the ASCII code. The SUB character, the Cr character and the LF character are some of the ASCII code control characters.

There are few pure text files. Most files have some special formatting. HTML or HTM files are text files that incorporate descriptive markup that is recognized by web browser software. The web browser interprets the markup to translate the text file into a fancy website display. See Figure 12–2.

In Figure 12–2, the browser and the notepad program are viewing the same file. The browser is interpreting the markup in the file to produce the web page display. The source files for programs are text files. Executable programs are binary files, as are graphic images and sound files. The registries are binary files that require REGEDIT to display. Text files include special control files, such as AUTOEXEC.BAT, CONFIG.SYS, INI files (WIN.INI and SYSTEM.INI), TXT files, HTM files, and others. Email messages were largely text files until more sophisticated email programs permitted embedded images and other features. Today email is a mix of text and binary files.

File Naming Conventions

Files have names similar to our names. These file names are assigned in a standard format just like common names have. Common names use a first and last name. Files have a filename and an extension. Certain characters are permitted in filenames and extensions. Common names generally do not use punctuation characters. They are not generally used in filenames as well.

Two file naming conventions are used today: the original DOS 8.3 format and Windows 3.1 long filenames. Let's examine them in more detail.

THE 8.3 FORMAT

The DOS 8.3 filenames use up to eight characters for a filename and up to three characters for an extension, with a period as a separator. This made them 11 characters total length, not counting the separator. These characters:

"/ \ [ ] : * < > | + ; , ?

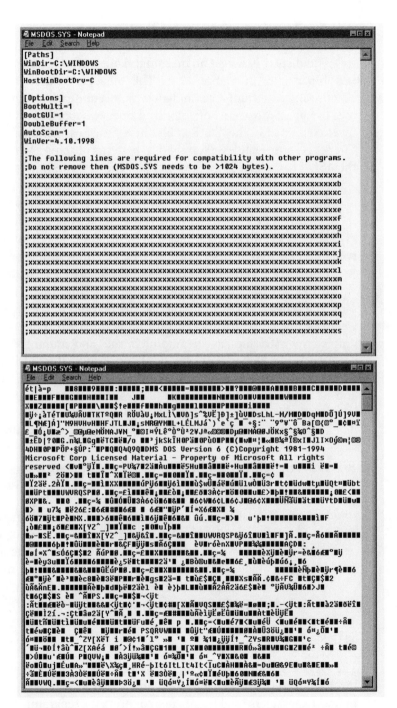

Figure 12–1 *Windows 98 MSDOS.SYS text and MS-DOS.SYS binary file*

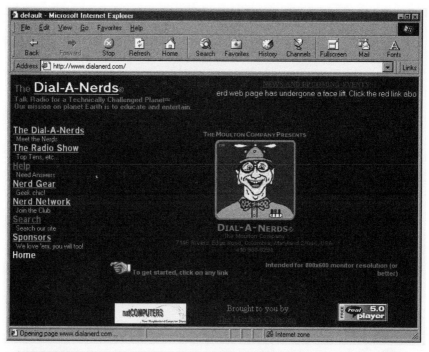

Figure 12–2 *Browser and HTML text view of web page*

cannot be used in DOS filenames. A space character cannot be used in DOS file names as well. The period is only used as a DOS file name separator character. All other characters can be used in file names. These characters include:

$ % ' - @ ~ ` ! ( ) ^ # & _

A DOS 8.3 filename example could be **filename.ext.** The name identified the contents of the file for a PC user. The extension was used to identify the file type or formatting. DOC extensions were formatted in an MS Word format, while HTM files in an HTML format used by web browsers.

LONG FILENAMES

Long filenames were implemented in Windows 95 and Windows NT. Long filenames are also used by the MAC and by OS/2 PCs. Support for both long and short filenames is available under Windows 95/98 and Windows NT, as well as translation for those applications that do not support long filenames. Windows had to supply this support because all applications initially run under Windows 95 were older Windows 3.x applications not capable of using long filenames.

The Windows 95 long file naming convention rules are:

- Long filenames can contain up to 255 characters.
- Valid characters are the same but Windows 95 can use the added characters: + , ; + [ ] .
- Spaces within names are ignored.
- Lower-case characters are preserved in long filenames.
- A complete path specification for a long filename can be 260 characters.

As you can see, this really allows you to describe the file you are using. You can even stick with file extensions, but they can be longer than 3 characters. See Figure 12–3.

When long filenames are viewed or manipulated by programs that can only work with short filenames, the long filenames are truncated at the sixth character and a ~1, etc., is substituted as a place holder for the long name characters that are missing. Sometimes the long filename is not disturbed and other times the truncated name replaces the long filename. If older DOS programs copy files with long filenames, the long filename is commonly replaced by the truncated name. If the file is not copied, the filename is not replaced.

In reality, files named very descriptively without regard to extension can be very difficult for the user to locate on a disk drive. They are difficult to

Figure 12–3 *Long filenames displayed by Explorer and DIR*

search for using the find function because it can be difficult to figure out which characters in the filename to seek. It is much easier to seek a file with only 11 characters total in the name.

Long filenames are implemented in the directory. A directory entry consists of several components. The filename field is 11 bytes in size because of the old DOS 8.3 rule. Thus the total filename length is 11 bytes. The other fields store the additional important file information, called attributes.

Microsoft discovered they could add a volume attribute in the file attribute field, which is 1 byte in size. Next, Microsoft developed a special volume-locking API. All changes to a directory entry with the volume attribute had to be processed by the special API. This now meant that no entries would change without Windows knowing about it, even when using older utilities. Additionally, this gave Windows 95 total control over all disk entries.

A long filename essentially consists of a short filename plus additional directory entries to allow for the extra characters of the long name. All directory entries in the FAT are 32 bytes in size. A long name requires a directory entry in excess of 256 bytes. Changing the directory entry size would wreak havoc on PC programs. So instead of increasing the size of the entry, what Microsoft did was assign multiple directory entries to a single long filename. Since a directory entry is only 32 characters, when several entries are used Windows must have a way to keep track of the directory entries for a single file. It does this by modifying the directory entries.

To create the long filenames, Windows modifies what is stored in the additional directory entries. The information stored there does not have to conform to the structure as seen in the preceding picture. If it did, then Windows would use far too many directory entries. Instead it uses a large portion of the directory entry for the filename itself. Windows uses some bytes to track related entries. In fact, it must have a way to associate the long filename with its short filename. If the association is lost, the file can become corrupt because all long filenames must have a short filename. Figure 12–4 shows a directory entry for a long filename and a classification entry.

A long filename directory entry starts with a sequence number used by Windows to track the entry, as well as modifications made to the entry. The attribute field lists the attributes for the file. The type defines what kind of directory entry it is, a component of the filename or a classification entry. Lastly, a checksum created from the short name entry of the file is included. This creates a directory entry with a name field of 26 bytes out of the 32 total bytes for the directory entry. This is far better than the 11-byte name field in DOS 8.3 format directory entry.

A long filename must have a short filename associated with it to be used by DOS applications. Windows generates a unique short filename for each long filename. The rules followed by Windows to create a unique short filename for a long filename are:

- As a long name is created, Windows creates the linked short name at the same time.
- If your long name is really a short name, it must be unique within the directory it resides. No other short name can be exactly like it in that directory. Filenames are not case sensitive. FILENAME.TXT and filename.txt are the same file as far as Windows and DOS are concerned.

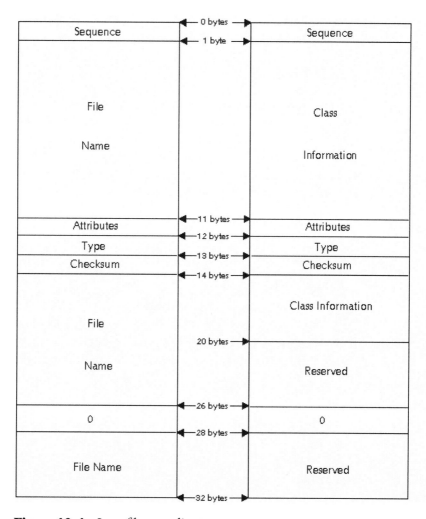

Figure 12–4 *Long filename directory entry structure*

- When creating the short filename, Windows tries several valid truncations to create the unique short name.
- If you create a short name (using the old DOS API), then the long name is the same. If the long name conflicts, then the short name cannot be created.

Using long filenames as far as DOS is concerned is no problem. Windows 95 extended the DOS INT21h interface to accommodate the use of long filenames by DOS. This software allows Windows and DOS programs to manipulate files using the short filenames.

File Attributes

File attributes control access to the file. They determine whether the file is visible and accessible to the PC users. DOS supports archive, read-only, system, hidden, directory, and volume attributes. The directory and volume attributes are not file attributes per se. They are used by the operating system and are not manipulated by the user. The attributes are stored as bits in the attribute byte for each file in the directory.

READ ONLY

Read-only files are generally programs and special parameter files that should not be moved or changed in any way. This attribute is used to prevent users from accidentally erasing or corrupting the files. Among others, the registry files are marked with read-only file attributes. The Windows system programs read from and write to this file. Hence, the read-only file attribute prevents only naive users from changing the file. DEFRAG typically does not move read-only files. The DEFRAG program is discussed later in this chapter.

SYSTEM

The system attribute denotes a file that is used by the operating system. Deleting system files could cause the system to crash.

HIDDEN

The hidden attribute makes the file invisible to the normal directory and other DOS commands as well as the Windows file manager and Explorer programs. The goal here is to keep important files from being moved or deleted from the PC's disk drives. Hiding files can also reduce directory clutter for the user. For example, many programs store data and program files in the same folder. Marking the program files as hidden would prevent them from being deleted and leave a folder displaying only the data files.

ARCHIVE

The archive attribute is to help backup programs determine if a file has been altered since the last backup. Every time a file is updated, the archive attribute is set. Backup programs reset the archive attribute when they make a backup copy of the file. Better backups are made just using the date and time stamp information available in the directory entry for the file.

CHANGING FILE ATTRIBUTES

File attributes can be viewed and changed in DOS using the ATTRIB command and in Windows using the file manager or Explorer.

The DOS external ATTRIB command options are listed in Table 12–1.

```
ATTRIB [+R | -R] [+A | -A] [+S | -S] [+H | -H]
[[drive:][path]filename] [/S]
```

Table 12.1 *ATTRIB file attributes and attribute modifiers*

Option	Description
+	Sets an attribute.
-	Clears an attribute.
R	Read-only file attribute.
A	Archive file attribute.
S	System file attribute.
H	Hidden file attribute.
/S	Processes files in all directories in the specified path.

Directory and volume attributes are not set using the ATTRIB command. Similarly, Windows Explorer can display and set file attributes. The Windows 95/98 Explorer View—Folder Option—View—Advanced settings has a box for showing file attributes in a detailed view. See Figure 12–5.

If the Explorer detailed view option is set, the file attributes are displayed in the right panel along with other file details. Selecting a file and choosing File—Properties provides a menu panel that permits selection of the read-only system, hidden, and archive file properties. See Figure 12–6.

Study Break

File Attributes

In this exercise we see the impact of file attributes by using the ATTRIB command to set them and then using the directory command or Windows Explorer to view the files.

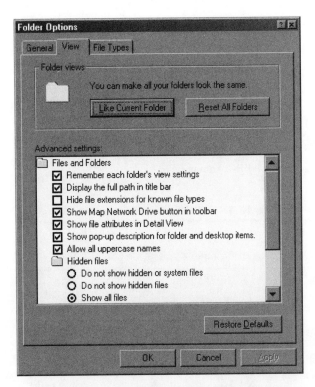

Figure 12–5
Explorer file attributes setting

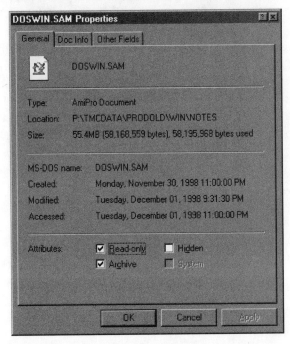

Figure 12–6
Changing file properties

1. Open a DOS window. Enter SET DIRCMD=/Ogn. This sets the directory command to sort out the files in order with subdirectories first and then alphabetically by name when it creates the directory list display.

2. Change to the root directory of the C drive. Enter the command DIR AUTO*.* to display all AUTOEXEC files that reside there. There should be several variations of the AUTOEXEC files that are the remnants of application software installations.

3. Use the ATTRIB command to set the hidden attribute on these files. The command would be:
ATTRIB AUTO*.* +H
This sets the hidden attribute on those AUTOEXEC files.

4. Again enter the command DIR AUTO*.* to display all AUTOEXEC files. Because the hidden attribute is set on the files, no files should be listed in the directory display.

5. View the root directory with Windows Explorer. Generally, the AUTOEXEC files would not display there as well because the hidden attribute is set.

6. Next enter SET DIRCMD=/Ogn /A. This sets the directory command to view all files. Similarly, in Windows Explorer select view from the top menu, then folder options. Select view again, then show all files. This sets Windows Explorer to display all the files. Apply the change by clicking OK.

7. Now view the root directory of the C drive. If the AUTOEXEC files are not visible, tap the F5 key to refresh the display.

8. Again enter the command DIR AUTO*.* to display all AUTOEXEC files. Note that this time the AUTOEXEC files are displayed because the directory command has been instructed by the /A option to display all files. To check the settings of the directory command, enter SET. This causes DOS to display the environment space. In the environment space listing should be a line DIRCMD=/Ogn /A.

9. Use the ATTRIB command to view the file attributes. The command would be:
ATTRIB AUTO*.*

10. Finally, use the ATTRIB command to return the AUTOEXEC files to their normal status. The command would be:
ATTRIB AUTO*.* -H

This exercise illustrates the use of file attributes to hide files, the ATTRIB command used under DOS to set the file attributes, and settings for both the directory command and Windows Explorer that permit listing files in the directory display regardless of their attribute settings.

DOS File Operations

DOS provides several basic functions:

- It starts programs. (This is called launching programs under Windows.) In this case, the programs are.COM, .EXE, or .BAT files stored on the disk drive.
- It provides support programs for managing files on both your floppy and fixed disk drives. This includes file maintenance functions such as copying, deleting, and renaming files.
- It provides commands that perform system functions. The DOS TIME command and the DOS DATE command display and change the PC's clock time and date respectively.

Some DOS commands are focused on file operations. COPY, DEL, MOVE, RENAME, ATTRIB and EDIT are examples of file manipulation commands. The EDIT command permits editing of text and batch files. Help with DOS commands is available at the DOS prompt by entering HELP. This causes DOS to display its on-line documentation.

Editing TXT and BAT Files

Editing text (TXT) and batch (BAT) files can be easy or tough. DOS 6.x had an EDIT command that launched the DOS text editor, as shown in Figure 12–7. This proram was originally part of the QBASIC provided with DOS 6.x. The DOS text editor makes editing text and batch files easy. It works with a mouse or with keyboard shortcuts.

Table 12-2 lists and describes the DOS text editor.

Table 12.2 *DOS editing commands*

Function	Action
Select Text	Highlight text using the mouse or by depressing the Shift key while changing the cursor position with the arrow keys
Copy Text	Press Ctrl + Ins while the text is selected
Cut Text	Press Shift + Del
Delete Text	Press Del key while text is selected
Search	Requires menu selection operation, but a search can be continued using the F3 key. Search and Replace (Change) functionality was also present.

Alternatively, text files could be created with the COPY CON command, which copies the keyboard keystrokes to a file specified by COPY

Figure 12–7 *MS-DOS text editor program*

CON. Text files could be displayed using the TYPE command. Text files could be combined using the COPY command. Files were concatenated by:

```
COPY file1.txt+file2.txt file3.txt
```

In this case, file3.txt contained the contents of file1.txt and file2.txt.

Earlier versions of DOS provided a crude text file editing capability with the EDLIN (line editor) program. This made editing files very difficult. Although EDLIN was no great editor, it was better than some of the other line editing programs that came with other operating systems.

Launching Programs

To launch a program in DOS, you type the program name in at the keyboard and strike Enter.

In starting programs, DOS looks at what was typed on the keyboard. It checks it to see if it is an internal command like DIR. If not it checks the file extension to determine if it is EXE, COM, or BAT. Since the extension is not likely to be entered, DOS searches the current diskette or fixed disk directory for the filename. Once it finds the file, DOS checks its extension. When the file cannot be found in the current directory, then DOS searches a path previously entered into the PC for the file. When the file cannot be found, DOS displays for the user:

```
C:\ >dumb
Bad command or file name
```

The path is searched for BAT, COM, and EXE files. Other files are ignored in the search.

Path Operations

This exercise illustrates how the path statement works. It requires using the Windows ATTRIB command and MODE command programs.

1. Make a directory on the C drive called test. The command is:
   MD C:\test
   Change to that directory.

2. Copy from C:\windows\command the ATTRIB.EXE and the MODE.COM commands to the C:\test directory.

3. Rename these files to A.EXE and A.COM.

4. Now create a batch file with the name A.BAT. To create the batch file enter the following commands:
   COPY CON A.BAT ENTER
   REM This is the batch file.
   Hit Ctrl Z (or F6), then Enter.

5. Now three files should reside in the test directory. These files are A.BAT, A.COM, and A.EXE. Reset the path so that it applies only to the test directory, using the following commands.
   CD C:\
   PATH>OP.BAT
   PATH=C:\TEST

6. Once the path has been reset, we are ready to begin our test of the path command. Enter A and strike the Enter key. The DOS window should display the results of the MODE.COM command since it was renamed A.COM.

7. Enter A.EXE and strike the Enter key. The DOS window should now display the results of the ATTRIB.EXE command, since it has been renamed A.EXE.

8. Finally enter A.BAT and strike the Enter key. The DOS window should now display the results of the A.BAT that was created.

9. Delete A.COM from the test directory. Enter A and strike the enter key. The DOS window should now display the results of the ATTRIB.EXE command since EXE files take precedence over BAT files and since ATTRIB.EXE was renamed A.EXE.

10. Reset the path by entering OP. This executes a batch file that stored the original path and restores the path to its original settings.

This exercise illustrates the operation of the PATH command. It shows that the PATH command searches first for COM files, then EXE files, and finally BAT files.

A+ 12.3 Windows File Operations

Windows can perform file operations using DOS commands and using the graphical user interface. The file management features of Windows changed between Windows 3.x and Windows 95/98. Windows NT 3.5x behaves like Windows 3.x and Windows NT 4.0 behaves similarly to Windows 95/98 in performing file operation functions.

All versions of Windows associate data files with applications using the file extension. Standard associations for common application programs are built into Windows. The ability to make new file associations is also provided.

Creating file associations differs with the operating system. With DOS, the application programs themselves determined file associations. DOS would merely provide a path to the data files. The path to data files was provided by the DOS APPEND command.

With Windows 3.1x, file associations were created using the file manager. Clicking on File in the file manager menu yielded a drop-down menu containing Associate. This menu item permitted associating files extensions with different specific programs. Clicking on the menu item would bring up an associate panel permitting the entry of the file extension. By typing in the extension of a standard file, the program associated with it would appear in a panel below. Those files not associated with a specific program could, using their extension and the browse function, be assigned a program association. This was a rather simplistic process.

Windows 95/98 and Windows NT manage file associations similarly. With both Windows 95/98 and Windows NT this can be accomplished using the Explorer program. Windows 95/98 provides alternative paths to the file associations panel. Using Explorer, open View on the menu bar, then Options. This brings up the view box that permits managing file types. Click on the file types tab to see a listing of the file types and the programs associated with those file types. It is more difficult to manage the file associations with Windows 95/98 and Windows NT because the file extension cannot be entered directly to identify the programs associated with it. In this case, it is necessary to scroll through the list while watching the panel to identify the file extension. This is an awkward and time-consuming process. Fortunately, most file associations are set by the applications as they are installed in Windows. Unfortunately, some applications change the file associations that you desire. In this event, you must search through these file associations to find the extension you wish to associate with a program and then reassign it.

The file associations permit Windows users to double-click on the data file to launch the associated application and to load the data file contents into the application's working memory.

Windows 3.x File Manager

Windows 3.x uses the Windows file manager (WINFILE.EXE) to perform file management operations. See Figure 12–8. The Windows 3.x file manager program represents disk drives and other storage devices, such as tape drives, as separate Windows within the file manager program. It displays all physical disk drives and all network disk drives mapped to disk drive letters in the top menu area. A path entry box permits direct selection of physical drives and mapped drives not displayed. Icons support quick changes in the disk drive file content views, for instance, sorting in alphabetical and reverse alphabetical order.

The file manager menu items include the following standard selections:

- FILE
- DISK
- TREE
- VIEW
- OPTIONS
- WINDOW
- HELP

FILE operations include selections for opening files, moving files, copying files, renaming files and setting file properties. The file selection also supports running programs, changing associations, creating directories, searching for specific files, and using wild card characters to select specific files for display, for instance, *.* (all files) or *.EXE (EXE files only).

The DISK menu selection permits copying diskettes, labeling disk volumes, formatting disks, installing the bootable system files on disks, and connecting/disconnecting network drives.

TREE operations are expanding and collapsing the hierarchical directory structure and displaying which directories (or folders) can be expanded and collapsed. Selecting the "indicate expandable branches option" causes the file manager program to place "+" symbols into those folders that have subfolders.

Figure 12–8 WINFILE program

The VIEW menu changes the display and sorting options for each disk drive Window. It also permits changing between a simultaneous directory tree and directory contents view of the disk drive or a view of the directories or contents alone. The By File Type selection permits filtering of the files displayed. This option also allows the file manager to display all hidden and system files.

A few users prefer the old Windows file manager to the newer Windows Explorer. The Windows 3.1x file manager runs in Windows 98, provided that the SCONFIG.DLL is accessible to Windows 98, so that those users preferring it can run it under Windows 95/98.

SEARCHING FOR FILES

One operation performed by the file manager is searching for files. The search option is under the File menu selection. See Figure 12–9.

Figure 12–9 *WINFILE search option*

It opens a search option box that permits specifying the type of file for which to search. The DOS DIR wild card characters are used to specify the file types. This search is equivalent to the DIR filespec /S command. Once the search is started, it displays the results in a new box. Files can be deleted from this box or dragged and dropped to move or copy them. This provides greater ease of use than with DOS commands.

DRAG-AND-DROP OPERATIONS

The Windows GUI supports drag-and-drop file operations. Using the mouse pointer and the left mouse button, files can be selected and then dragged from one file manager disk drive window and dropped into the desired directory (folder) in another disk drive window. When this drag-and-drop operation goes between two disk drives, the file is copied. If the drag-and-drop operation is on the same disk drive, the file is moved.

To more precisely control copying and moving of files, the Shift and Ctrl keys are used in conjunction with dragging and dropping file icons. Shift causes the file to be moved when dragged and dropped, and Ctrl makes the drag-and-drop operation copy the file. These keys are held while dragging and dropping the file. Alternatively, you can use the right mouse button along with the copy/cut/paste options.

EDITING TXT FILES

Windows comes with Notepad and Write applets that permit editing text files.

Notepad is strictly an ASCII text file editor that can handle files up to 64 KB in size. It provides minimal editing features and no text formatting. Notepad has the same basic features as the DOS EDIT program. It supports simple text searching, but has no replace feature. The newer version found in NT and Windows 98 has a search option and a replace feature.

Figure 12–10 *Notepad editing commands*

Cutting, copying, and pasting selections are supported with the mouse and with the DOS EDIT keyboard commands. Notepad cuts highlighted text with Ctrl+X, copies selected text with Ctrl+C, and pastes selected text with Ctrl+V or Shift+Ins. The Ctrl+Z keystroke combination undoes the last edit function. These keystroke shortcuts are used in Windows 98 editing programs as well. See Figure 12–10.

The Windows Write applet provides similar text editing capabilities. It could work with files larger than 64 KB in size. Write provides simple word processing capabilities over and above the simple text editing of notepad. With Write, images can be inserted in the documents created. The word processing capabilities of Write permit specifying fonts and font sizes, paragraph formatting, and rudimentary page layout features, including simple headers and footers. The most important feature of Write from an A+ viewpoint is the ability to work with files larger than 64 KB.

Windows Write has the ability to handle a limited number of file formats. The Windows 98 version called WordPad is the most flexible. WordPad accepts Word documents (DOC), Write files (WRI), Rich Text Format files (RTF), and text files (TXT).

LAUNCHING PROGRAMS

The philosophy with Windows 3.x for launching programs was first to start the program, then to load the data into the program. This was an extension of the DOS model of launching programs. In the case of DOS, the program had to be started first because there was no mechanism to link the data files to the application program. Windows 3.x changed that model by implementing file associations.

Windows 3.x supports launching programs in several different ways, including:

- Double-clicking on the program manager (PROGMAN) shell icons. This is the DOS model of starting the application, then loading the data.
- Running the program from the file manager (WINFILE) File—Run menu selection. This is another incarnation of the DOS model.
- Finding the data file with the file manager, then double-clicking on the desired data file. This implements the Windows file association model of launching the program. Here the program associated with the data file is launched and the data file used to launch it is loaded into the program's working memory.

Windows 3.x was the first step in implementing an object model of managing files and programs. The object model focus is away from the traditional load the program and then load the data towards using the data objects to dictate the work performed.

WINDOWS 95/98 OVERVIEW

Windows has several new features. Most important of these are the desktop, the taskbar, and Explorer. Additionally, Windows 95/98 does most of its hardware configuration using the control panel.

THE DESKTOP • When viewing Windows 95 for the first time, the desktop may appear shocking as compared to the Windows 3.x desktop. In Windows 3.x, the desktop's job was primarily to display a minimized program's icon. The Windows 95/98 desktop is similar to the Windows 3.x desktop, but it incorporates more functionality.

Because Windows 95/98 is an object-oriented system, the desktop creates a look and feel on your PC screen like the look and feel of your real desk. Just like you place items on your desk like a telephone or a bunch of papers, you can place items used on your computer on the Windows 95 desktop. Files or programs, it does not matter. To activate an object, you simply double-click on the appropriate icon. When you minimize a program, it goes to the taskbar, leaving the desktop less cluttered. See Figure 12–11.

Figure 12–11 *The Windows 95 desktop*

Windows 98 Explorer and Internet Explorer 4.0 and 5.0 combine local and web-based information sources into the Windows desktop. The desktop support makes it possible to customize the desktop, launch programs, switch between files, and keep up with changing national and international news by integrating the Internet and the World Wide Web into the desktop. The Active Desktop interface permits changing information from web pages to be placed on the desktop. For example, continually updated TV news broadcasts could be placed on the desktop. Thus, as new news is broadcast you see it immediately. Adding active content items such as news, weather, sports, or stock reports referred to regularly customizes the desktop. The desktop turns Internet information into desktop items and updates them at any time. The Active Desktop interface is automatically turned on when web style is chosen for the desktop. Otherwise, activate the Active Desktop by right-clicking on the desktop, and pointing to Active Desktop. Be sure to set View as Web Page as well. Turn off the Active Desktop interface by clicking the Start button, pointing to Settings, pointing to Active Desktop, and then clicking View as Web Page to reset the Web Page View to off.

We typically disable Active Desktop to make Windows operate more reliably. This is because problems connecting to remote resources across

Recycle Bin

Figure 12–12   *The taskbar and Start button menus*

LANs and the Internet tend to lock or stall Windows when those resources are no longer available to Windows.

Down the left side of the desktop are the standard Windows 95 objects. The taskbar and its menus are at the bottom. The desktop itself is the remainder of the screen. Data and program objects may be placed on the desktop. When this is done they are placed in a c:\windows\desktop folder. The standard objects do not appear in the folder because they are created by registry entries.

THE TASKBAR • A highlight of the new desktop is the taskbar. It provides functions similar to the Windows 3.x program manager. The taskbar is a tool that allows users to quickly start applications and switch between applications. The taskbar provides both a task list and program manager functionality. See Figure 12–12.

Two main components of the taskbar are the bar itself and the Start button. The bar is responsible for holding and displaying the minimized applications. To activate one, simply point to the item on the bar and single-click. Once clicked on, the application expands to full screen or a portion thereof. The minimized taskbar items act like buttons. An active application button on the task bar appears depressed. The task bar is always present wherever you are using Windows so when you want to switch applications, simply point to the application on the task bar and click. Program icons are no longer hidden from view. The downside to this design is cluttering the task bar with many open programs.

The start button launches applications like the Windows 3.x Program Manager. It provides a menu list of applications. Clicking the start button gives a selection menu. Pointing to one of the menu items and pausing produces additional menu lists. This continues until reaching a launch-able program that a single click launches.

On the far right side of the task bar is a box that contains a system clock and a volume control icon. Using these, the date and time can be adjusted along with the speaker volume.

The taskbar and start menu can be configured using the Settings option. The Settings option is accessed from the drop-down menu that is displayed by clicking on the start button. Clicking on settings immediately brings up the taskbar properties panel. This permits selection of all the taskbar display options including always on top, auto hide, show small icons, and show clock. The start menu programs tab permits changing the programs as they appear from the start menu. The advanced option opens up to start menu folder, showing programs listed underneath it. This folder can also be accessed using the Windows Explorer. It resides in the Windows folder. Rearranging the shortcuts and folders under the start menu\programs folder changes the way the programs appear in the start menu. Toolbars can be added to the taskbar by pointing at the taskbar with the mouse pointer and clicking on the right mouse button. A panel appears with toolbars listed at the top. In this way, different toolbars can be activated and de-activated at the user's discretion.

EXPLORING • The object model orientation found in Windows 3.x was further enhanced by the Windows 95/98 implementation of Explorer. Explorer replaces the Windows 3.x file manager. However, Explorer has more controls and operating capabilities built into it than did file manager. The Explorer model has menus to launch programs and perform system functions. In some ways the Explorer is similar to the file manager. For example, the left side of the Explorer displays a hierarchical tree of your system resources. This includes the folders (directories) present on your disk drives. These resources have been expanded to also include network connections and your desktop. The tree starts at the top with your desktop, followed by your PC disk, and the directory trees below them. The right side displays the contents of the selected item on the left side, similar to file manager displaying the directory contents in its right pane. See Figure 12–13.

Figure 12–13 *Windows 95/98 Explorer*

The primary focus of Explorer is on the data files on the disk drive; it extends the associations and object-oriented approach to managing data that Windows 3.x began. To understand the evolution from Windows 3.x to Windows 95/98, we need to examine the operation of Windows 95/98.

The Explorer covers the Windows 3.x file manager functions. Network drive mappings (connections) can be established, you can view directory lists, in different formats, and you can search for something on your drive. There are some differences, such as directories being called folders, there are a lot more icons used to identify items quicker, and you can even create shortcuts for your applications (similar to aliases with the MAC System 7).

One significant difference between the Windows 3.x file manager and Explorer is that the file manager made a separate window for each disk drive within file manager. Explorer creates a hierarchy showing all system resources and disk drives within a single Explorer window. File management is performed within this single window. It is possible to run several copies of Explorer. Each copy functions independently of the other copies. Furthermore, files can be manipulated between copies of Explorer. For example, a file can be dragged from one copy of Explorer and dropped onto a folder on another copy of Explorer, causing the file to be copied into the folder it was dropped on. The copy of Explorer that the file was dropped into performs the copy operation and the Explorer that dropped the file is now free to perform other file management tasks. In contrast, with the file manager only a single file manager copy could be run at any given time. When it was busy performing file manipulation tasks, no other file management could be performed.

Novice users adapt more easily to object-oriented operation than experienced Windows 3.x users. An advantage is that MAC users find the Windows 95 object-oriented desktop a lot like the desktop of MAC System 7.x. OS-2 is similar but the few OS-2 die hard users are in denial. Windows is a bit more politically correct because it uses a recycle bin rather than the System 7.x trash can.

SEARCHING FOR FILES

Similarly to the 3.x file manager, Explorer provides a file search capability. This is accessible from the tools menu selection of the Explorer or launched by Ctrl+F (Ctrl + Find). Similarly to Windows 3.x, dialog windows guide you through the search process. The search is performed using DOS wild card characters or using date/time or size parameters from the dialog windows.

The search results appear in a dialog window extension. This extension can be sorted by any of the file characteristics displayed, for instance, name, size, or date/time. Clicking on the file characteristic in the title bar causes the files to be sorted in ascending order for that characteristic. Clicking again causes them to be sorted in descending order. The objects found through the search function can be dragged and dropped, deleted, and otherwise manipulated using the Windows 95/98 Explorer capabilities.

DRAG-AND-DROP OPERATIONS

Similarly to Windows 3.x, Windows 95/98 supports drag-and-drop file operations. The same controls and keys apply to Windows 98 Explorer drag-and-drop operations as they do to Windows 3.x. Dragging and dropping between two drives copies files and dragging and dropping on the same drive moves the files or creates a shortcut to the file. The Ctrl and Shift keys force the drag-and-drop operation to copy the file or to move the file, respectively. Drag-and-drop operations work on folders as well as individual files.

EDITING TXT FILES

Windows 95/98 has a Notepad text editor program equivalent to the Notepad program provided with Windows 3.x. It has equivalent features to the Windows 3.x Notepad with the exception that fonts can be changed in the data being edited. Notepad is designed to edit simple BAT and other text files.

Windows 95/98 also has WordPad for word processing. Similar to Write, it can handle large files, change fonts, insert pictures, and search and replace text. Unlike Write, WordPad does not have the ability to work with simple document headers and footers separate from the main document.

LAUNCHING PROGRAMS

Similarly to Windows 3.x, programs are launched in Windows 95/98 using the Start button menus and double-clicking on the desired program icon. This is equivalent to the DOS "launch the program first, then load the data" operating model.

Double-clicking on the data associated with the program also launches the program and loads the data into the application's working memory. This is Window's object-oriented program launching.

Additionally, Windows 95/98 permits dragging the data file over to the application program icon and dropping it into the program. This is the Windows model using the data to launch the program without the data being associated with the program. Here, BMP files may be associated with the PAINT program, but they could be dragged and dropped into the Microsoft Photo Editor program, launching it and loading the BMP file into its working memory. In this case, the Microsoft Photo Editor would be used to work on the BMP image. There are some limitations here. Launching the WordPad program with a BMP file has WordPad open the BMP image as a binary file rather than inserting it as an image in some document being created. Similar results are seen with Microsoft Word.

Finally, programs can be launched from shortcut icons. Create shortcuts by pointing to a program file (an EXE file), then clicking the right mouse button. A file options menu window appears that contains a selection "Create Shortcut." Selecting this creates a shortcut file to that application (or data object). See Figure 12–14.

The shortcut object can be placed anywhere. Double-clicking on the shortcut icon launches an application. This can be a data file shortcut or a program file shortcut icon.

Open
Scan for Viruses
Quick View

Uninstaller ▶
Add to Zip
Add to Defrag.zip

Send To ▶

Cut
Copy

Create Shortcut
Delete
Rename

Properties

Figure 12–14 *Object options menu*

Study Break

Creating Shortcuts

This exercise will create shortcuts to some Windows programs on the desktop.

1. Open Windows Explorer. Select the Windows folder and sort the files by type.

2. The EXE files should appear somewhere near the top of the file panel on the right of the Explorer display. Find the WRITE.EXE file. Click on the file and drag it to the desktop. This should create a shortcut to the WRITE.EXE program.

3. Locate the "send to" folder under Windows. Drag the WRITE.EXE shortcut to the "send to" folder. This should move the new shortcut from the desktop into the "send to" folder.

4. Find a TXT file. Click on the file to highlight it, then right-click to bring up the file options menu. Highlight "send to" and then WRITE.EXE. This should cause the WRITE program to launch and open the file.

This exercise has illustrated the simplest way to create a shortcut to an EXE program. There are also other ways to create shortcuts to programs. The exercise also showed how to use such a shortcut to make convenient opening text files with the WRITE.EXE program.

A+ 12.4 Disk Management Procedures

Disk management procedures consist of preparing the disk for use and maintaining the disk once it is in operation. To prepare a disk for use, it must be partitioned, formatted, and made bootable. To maintain a disk drive, it must be checked for errors and defragmented.

Partitioning

Partitioning a disk drive is done using FDISK. FDISK is menu-driven and generally straightforward to use. The major issue is whether 16-bit or 32-bit FAT is used for the partition table.

The FAT system installed on a fixed disk is largely determined by the software release today. Older Windows 95 systems most often use the 16-bit FAT. All new Windows 98 systems employ 32-bit FAT. Windows NT systems use 16-bit FAT or NTFS partitions. There are a few exceptions. The 32-bit FAT does not work with disk drives that are less than 500 MB, for example.

The FAT system determines the partitioning strategy for the fixed disk drive. The larger the total drive capacity, the larger the allocation unit size. Large allocation units make for inefficient disk capacity utilization. This is illustrated in the exercise below.

FAT 16 VERSUS FAT 32

The major impact of using FAT 16 versus FAT 32 is in how efficiently data is stored on large fixed disks. The smaller an allocation unit size is, the more efficient the storage. It is not uncommon to increase effective disk capacity by as much as 100 MB for a 4 GB fixed disk drive by just reducing the allocation unit size from 32 KB to 8 KB.

Cluster or allocation unit sizes for various size disk drives are listed in Table 12–3.

This suggests the following partitioning strategies:

- For 16-bit FAT drives that are 2 GB in size, make two 1 GB partitions. On larger drives, use 2 GB partitions, keeping the last partition as a swap and temporary storage area.
- For 32-bit FAT drives that are up to 8 GB in size, use multiple partitions to organize your data because a smaller partition size does not improve disk utilization efficiency. For drives with greater than 8 GB capacity, create 8 GB partitions to use the drive space most efficiently.

Table 12.3 *Allocation unit sizing*

Drive Capacity	16-bit FAT Allocation Unit Size	32-bit FAT Allocation Unit Size
Less than 256 MB	4 KB or 8 sectors	Not Supported
256 MB to 511 MB	8 KB or 16 sectors	Not Supported
512 MB to 1023 MB	16 KB or 32 sectors	4 KB or 8 sectors
1024 MB to 2 GB	32 KB or 64 sectors	4 KB or 8 sectors
2 GB to 8 GB	Not Supported	4 KB or 8 sectors
8 GB to 16 GB	Not Supported	8 KB or 16 sectors
16 GB to 32 GB	Not Supported	16 KB or 32 sectors
32 GB and up	Not Supported	32 KB or 64 sectors

PRIMARY AND EXTENDED DOS PARTITIONS

FDISK breaks up a fixed disk into primary and extended DOS partitions. With 16-bit FAT, the maximum partition size is 2 GB. The primary DOS partition cannot exceed this size. Drives larger than 2 GB must have an extended DOS partition with logical drives assigned to it. Drives of 2 GB or less are also permitted to have both a primary and an extended DOS partition. With older Windows 3.x systems on smaller disk drives, it was a good strategy to set the primary partition size at 256 MB, install only Windows on it with the swap files, and make an extended partition of the remaining drive space. The extended partition would contain the program and data files.

With 32-bit FAT, large drives can be partitioned with a single primary DOS partition for Windows 98 DOS. MS-DOS does not recognize 32-bit FAT partitions, and neither does Windows NT. Hence, with MS-DOS you're limited to using 16-bit FAT partitions. With Windows NT you can also use 16-bit FAT partitions or you can use NTFS partitions. Windows 2000 should work with 32-bit FAT partitions, 16-bit FAT partitions, and NTFS partitions.

LOGICAL DRIVES

A logical drive is a subdivision of the extended DOS partition. It is limited to 2 GB in size for 16-bit FAT systems. Logical drives must be assigned using FDISK to make the extended DOS partition useable.

ACTIVE PARTITIONS

The active partition is the bootable partition. When FDISK creates a primary partition, it does not necessarily make it active. If the bootable partition is not set active, the PC will not boot. Whenever a PC does not boot from the fixed disk, one check to perform is to run FDISK and verify that the primary DOS partition has been set active.

NON-DOS PARTITIONS

FDISK can find non-DOS partitions. These can be created by other operating systems like Windows NT using the NT File System (NTFS) and NetWare. Newer versions of FDISK can remove these partitions but not create them.

FILE ALLOCATION TABLES AND THE DIRECTORY

Access to files on the disk is performed using the directory and the file allocation tables. The operation of the directory and the FAT are illustrated in Figures 12–15, 12–16, and 12–17.

Figure 12–15 illustrates a relationship between the directory and the FAT. The directory entry contains the basic information describing the file stored on a fixed disk drive. It is linked to the FAT using a beginning cluster or allocation unit number. This number points to a single entry in the file allocation table. That entry number contains the entry number of the next allocation unit in the chain of allocation units that contain the data in the file. In Figure 12–15 the directory entry points to FAT entry 102. FAT entry 102 contains a number 103 that points to the next allocation unit in the chain. That entry 103 contains a number 125. So far the file is stored in allocation units number 102, 103, and 125. FAT entry 125 points to entry 126. Entry 126 points to entry 127. Entry 127 is the final entry in the chain of allocation units storing the data in the file because it contains all ones. When DOS or Windows retrieves this file, it would first go to the directory entry, then read the data from allocation units 102, 103, 125, 126, and 127. These allocation units form a chain in the FAT. This chain of allocation units stores the data in the file. An additional illustration of this process is shown by Figures 12–16 and 12–17. These figures were taken from directory entries and FAT entries on a real disk drive using the DOS version of Norton Utilities.

When data is stored on a fixed disk, it is stored in chains that are one cluster right after another. However, as files are modified they grow and shrink. To save them, DOS needs additional clusters or allocation units. It cannot get them exactly following the original clusters so it just grabs the next available cluster to place at the end of the chain. This means that the chains become broken into chunks called blocks. "Non-contiguous blocks" means that DOS has the file stored in allocation units or clusters that are not next to each other on the disk. Such day-to-day operations lead to fragmenting files stored on the disk. To retrieve these files, Windows must move the disk read/write heads all over the disk drive slowing overall system performance. Defragmenting the drive reduces this activity and speeds up the PC. Badly fragmented disk drives exhibit excessive disk activity. The same is also true of PCs with insufficient RAM.

Figure 12–16 illustrates the contents of a DOS directory entry. Figure 12–17 displays the first sector of a 16-bit FAT.

Using these diagrams we can see how IO.SYS is stored on this fixed disk. The IO.SYS directory entry points to the first entry in the FAT that is

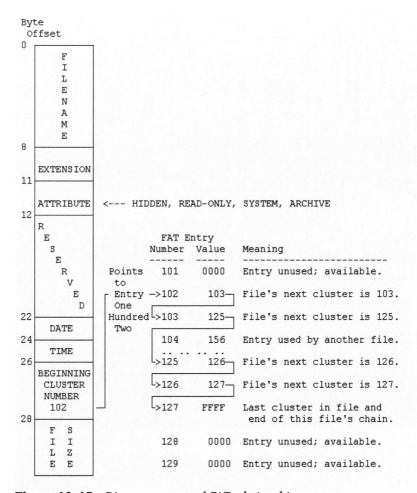

Figure 12–15 *Directory entry and FAT relationship*

Name	.Ext	Size	Date	Time	Cluster	Arc	R/O	Sys	Hid	Dir	Vol
Sector 129											
IO	SYS	33430	4-09-91	5:00 am	2	Arc	R/O	Sys	Hid		
MSDOS	SYS	37394	4-09-91	5:00 am	19	Arc	R/O	Sys	Hid		
PETE486P	1	0	9-12-91	11:28 pm	0	Arc					Vol
BAT		0	9-12-91	11:38 pm	62					Dir	
DISKFIX		0	11-23-91	7:05 am	1583					Dir	
DOS50		0	9-12-91	11:38 pm	63					Dir	
NOVELL		0	9-12-91	11:38 pm	73					Dir	
PCKWIK		0	9-12-91	11:38 pm	1585					Dir	
PDOX35		0	9-12-91	11:38 pm	70					Dir	
PE		0	9-12-91	11:38 pm	71					Dir	
QEMM		0	11-27-91	3:21 pm	72					Dir	
TEMP		0	11-27-91	3:17 pm	74					Dir	
UTIL		0	9-12-91	11:39 pm	75					Dir	
WINDOWS		0	12-09-91	9:02 pm	988					Dir	
124	BAT	51	12-16-91	4:40 pm	356	Arc					
386SPART	PAR	12288000	1-20-92	2:39 am	8145	Arc		Sys	Hid		
Sector 130											
64	BAT	48	12-12-91	7:18 am	561	Arc					
80		48	12-12-91	5:55 pm	562	Arc					

Figure 12–16 *Fixed disk directory (Norton utilities)*

address 2. FAT addresses 0 and 1 contain the boot record and partition table information. They are represented by "—" in Figure 12–17. The first address after 0 and 1 is 2. The contents of that address point to FAT entry address 3 that contains 4. We follow this chain in the diagram until it reaches address 18, which contains the End Of File (EOF) byte. The next file MSDOS.SYS begins with FAT entry 19. FAT entry 19 points to address 20, and so on.

Understanding basic directory and FAT operation is important fixed disk troubleshooting knowledge. This structure is generally carried forward into 32-bit FAT systems. Although, 32-bit FAT system details are not as simple as illustrated here.

VIRTUAL FILE ALLOCATION TABLE (VFAT)

VFAT is the Windows 95/98 file system. It is not a type of FAT, but rather software that reads and writes data to the disk drive. It uses the 32-bit protected mode or the 16-bit real mode driver programs to read and write data to the disks. VFAT is the equivalent of Windows 3.1 32-bit file access software.

VFAT is a VxD that processes read and write requests for the PC's local fixed disk. VFAT 32-bit file access operates in protected mode and supports

```
Object   Edit    Link    View    Info    Tools   Quit                    F1=Help
   Sector 1
        --       --        3       4       5       6       7       8
         9       10       11      12      13      14      15      16
        17       18    <EOF>       20      21      22      23      24
        25       26       27      28      29      30      31      32
        33       34       35      36      37    <EOF>      39      40
        41       42       43      44      45      46      47      48
        49       50       51      52      53      54      55      56
        57       58       59      60      61    <EOF>   <EOF>      64
     <EOF>        0        0       0       0       0   <EOF>   <EOF>
     <EOF>    <EOF>    <EOF>      76   <EOF>   <EOF>   <EOF>      80
        81       82       83      84      85      86      87      88
        89       90       91      92      93      94      95      96
        97       98       99     100     101     102     103     104
       105      106      107     108     109     110     111     112
       113      114      115     116     117     118     119     120
       121      122      123     124     125     126     127     128
       129      130      131     132     133     134     135     136
       137      138      139     140     141     142     143     144
       145      146      147     148     149     150     151     152
       153      154    <EOF>     156     157     158     159     160
   FAT (1st Copy)                                            Sector 1
   C:\IO.SYS                                          Cluster 2, hex 2
   Press ALT or F10 to select menus                       Disk Editor
```

Figure 12–17 *DOS 16-bit fixed disk file allocation table (Norton utilities)*

threading. This improves disk performance significantly in Windows 95/98 over Windows 3.1, which employed 16-bit real mode software to work with the FAT. VFAT was first introduced as 32-bit file access under Windows 3.11. Under Windows 95/98, VFAT handles long filenames. These names can be up to 255 characters long and may contain more than one period. Both long filenames and DOS 8.3 filenames are supported by VFAT using aliases. Every long filename has an alias entry associated with it that conforms to the DOS 8.3 filename rules. In this manner, Windows 95/98 VFAT supports older MS-DOS and Windows 3.1x programs.

Formatting

The last phase in preparing a disk drive for use is to format it and install an operating system. For most PCs, this means installing a bootable version of DOS or Windows 95/98. The FORMAT.EXE program performs these functions. Floppy disks can also be formatted from within the Window GUI, but generally fixed disk setup uses only DOS.

The FORMAT program builds the directory and the FAT depending on the partitioning performed. FORMAT /S causes the operating system on the DOS prompt drive to be installed as well. Initial formatting performs a surface verification to assure that the disk drive is useable. If it finds bad spots on the disk, it marks them as bad so they are not used to store data.

Because the disk drive hardware today performs error correction, there should be no bad spots on a new fixed disk drive. Sometimes areas of a fixed disk become corrupted. These areas are generally not restored by just formatting the drive. If, however, the surface is wiped by writing all zeros on the drive surface, and then reformatted, the bad areas may be restored to full operation.

FORMAT.EXE has the options shown below, which are further listed and explained in Table 12–4.

```
FORMAT drive: [/V[:label]] [/Q] [/F:size] [/B | /S] [/C]
FORMAT drive: [/V[:label]] [/Q] [/T:tracks /N:sectors] [/B
| /S] [/C]
FORMAT drive: [/V[:label]] [/Q] [/1] [/4] [/B | /S] [/C]
FORMAT drive: [/Q] [/1] [/4] [/8] [/B | /S] [/C]
```

Similar options are provided with the Windows GUI floppy format function.

Table 12.4 *Format command options*

Option	Description
/V[:label]	Specifies the volume label.
/Q	Performs a quick format.
/F:size	Specifies the size of the floppy disk to format (such as 160, 180, 320, 360, 720, 1.2, 1.44, 2.88).
/B	Allocates space on the formatted disk for system files.
/S	Copies system files to the formatted disk.
/T:tracks	Specifies the number of tracks per disk side.
/N:sectors	Specifies the number of sectors per track.
/1	Formats a single side of a floppy disk.
/4	Formats a 5.25-inch 360K floppy disk in a high-density drive
/8	Formats eight sectors per track.
/C	Tests clusters that are currently marked "bad."

Repairing

The SCANDISK program is the principal repair tool for disk drives. It verifies the directory and file structure. When SCANDISK is started, it presents a panel that permits selecting the physical and logical disk drives for scanning, the type of scan to perform—standard or thorough, and automatic error correction. When selecting the drives for scanning, they can be individually highlighted or highlighted together for scanning by SCANDISK. In this manner all disk drives can be scanned. When several drives are selected for scanning, the PC user manually signals the completion of scanning on each selected drive so that SCANDISK can move on to the next drive selected. For further details on SCANDISK, see the subsection in Section 12.5, later in this chapter.

Defragmenting

Defragmenting the disk drive to improve PC performance is done using the DEFRAG program. Defragmenting is the process of rearranging the clusters that contain the file data so they are accessed with minimal head movement on the fixed disk. To us, this looks like placing the clusters for a file in ascending numeric sequence. For the disk drive, this is not strictly true. Clusters in the same cylinder on a disk drive are accessed without moving the disk drive's read/write heads. Hence, clusters in the same cylinder are accessed equally fast.

More details on the DEFRAG program are covered in Section 12.5, later in this chapter.

Study Break

Disk Allocation Units

This exercise illustrates how files are stored in allocation units on the fixed disk drive.

1. Do a directory command. Record the free space on your fixed disk.

2. Create a file called T using:
COPY CON T
T Cr
Ctrl Z

3. Perform the directory command again. What is the size of the file T? It should be one or two characters.

4. How much free space is left on your disk? From the amount of free space before making the file, subtract the amount of free space after making the file to determine the allocation unit or cluster size for this specific PC system.

The result of this exercise should illustrate that a file of a single character consumes an entire allocation unit of disk space. This means that, depending upon the allocation unit size, disk space could be wasted by storing lots of small files on the fixed disk drive. Hence, fixed disk drive space is used more effectively by using ZIP to compress many small files into a single large file.

A+ 12.5   Disk Management Utilities

A key function of primarily DOS software is disk management. DOS utilities are used to partition disk drives, format them, and make them bootable. Once data and software are installed on a disk drive, other DOS and Windows utilities check the disk and file structure for errors and organize the files on the disk drive for optimal performance.

There are four basic disk management functions:

- Partitioning a disk and creating the master boot record.
- Formatting the drive to create the directory structure and install the bootable operating system.
- Checking the disk drive file structure and data files for errors and, if errors are found, examining the physical disk surface for bad areas.
- Organizing the files and data on the disk for optimal performance.

DOS and Windows utility programs perform these functions.

FDISK

FDISK is the DOS or Windows 98 DOS utility that is used to partition a fixed drive and create the master boot record. The master boot record contains a cold boot loader program and descriptive information on the capacity and layout of the fixed disk drive. It is essential for booting DOS or Windows from the fixed disk drive and for enabling DOS and Windows to read and write information from the fixed disk drive. FDISK is not used on floppy drives. FDISK is run prior to formatting a drive and making it bootable with DOS.

FDISK can also be employed as a diagnostic program to verify that a disk drive and its companion disk controller card are functioning properly. When there are malfunctions, FDISK reports that the controller is bad or that it cannot read the fixed disk.

FDISK is run from the DOS prompt. It is menu-driven, with the menu selections made in a fixed sequence controlled by FDISK. This means that a drive must have an extended partition specified before logical drives can be assigned.

When a disk is prepared with a single partition, that partition is the primary partition. Each disk drive may have a primary partition. DOS and Windows assign drive letters to the primary partitions first and then to the extended partitions. The second partition on a fixed disk drive is the extended partition. It is also possible to create an extended DOS partition on a second disk drive. The extended partition is subdivided into logical drives. These logical drives are assigned drive letters after the primary partitions have been assigned their drive letters. Only primary partitions are bootable. To be bootable they must be marked as active partitions.

The hierarchy of fixed disk partitions is:

Primary DOS partition marked active on boot drive—C
Primary DOS partition on second drive—D
Extended DOS partition on the active boot drive
Extended DOS partition on the second fixed disk drive.

The Windows 98 FDISK program supports 32-bit FAT. This means that it can view a single large drive as one partition. Earlier versions of FDISK worked with 16-bit FAT. They were practically limited to maximum partition and logical drive sizes of 2 GB. At the 2 GB size, the allocation units were assigned 64 sectors, making them highly inefficient for storing small files. At that allocation unit size, a file of one character (or byte) would use 32 KB of disk storage space. When Windows 98 FDISK is run, the message below determines whether 32-bit or 16-bit FAT is used. The differences between FAT 16 and FAT 32 were covered in Section 12.4 earlier in this chapter.

```
Do you wish to enable large disk support (Y/N)...........?
[Y]
The "Y" response implements 32-bit FAT operation.
```

This version of Windows includes improved support for large disks, resulting in more efficient use of disk space on large drives, and allowing disks over 2 GB to be formatted as a single drive.

The main FDISK menu begins with creating a primary DOS partition or logical drive. This is the first step in preparing a disk drive for use. It creates the partition table and the FAT. To be bootable, a drive must be set as active. Deleting a partition kills all the data in that partition. Once deleted, data in a partition is not recoverable unless special procedures and software

If you enable large disk support and create any new drives on this disk, you are not able to access the new drive(s) using other operating systems, including some versions of Windows 95 and Windows NT, as well as earlier versions of Windows and MS-DOS. In addition, disk utilities that were not designed explicitly for the FAT32 file system are not able to work with this disk. If you need to access this disk with other operating systems or older disk utilities, do not enable large disk support. At this time, large disk support works only with Windows 95 OSR2 and Windows 98 PCs. When these PCs are networked there are no problems transferring files across the network to other PCs without large disk support (32-bit FAT). If a PC is going to be used to support Windows 95 and Windows NT 4.0, the 32-bit FAT should not be used because it cannot be accessed by Windows NT 4.0.

are used. Displaying partition information causes FDISK to read the drive. This is the diagnostic capability of FDISK.

```
Microsoft Windows 98
            Fixed Disk Setup Program
        (C)Copyright Microsoft Corp. 1983-1998


                 FDISK Options


Current fixed disk drive: 1

Choose one of the following:

1. Create DOS partition or Logical DOS Drive
2. Set active partition
3. Delete partition or Logical DOS Drive
4. Display partition information
5. Change current fixed disk drive

Enter choice: [1]

Press Esc to exit FDISK
```

When you select option 4, Display partition information, FDISK produces a partition information display that identifies the partitions and can display the logical drive information for the selected disk drive.

```
             Display Partition Information

Current fixed disk drive: 1
```

```
    Partition Status Type Volume LabelMbytes SystemUsage
     C: 1  APRI DOS DRC 3004   FAT32    38%
  2        EXT DOS 5005  62%


Total disk space is 8009 Mbytes (1 Mbyte = 1048576 bytes)

  The Extended DOS Partition contains Logical DOS Drives.
  Do you want to display the logical drive information
(Y/N)......?[Y]


  Press Esc to return to FDISK Options
```

FDISK tries to create partitions that use the entire fixed disk drive capacity. The capacity is expressed in Kbytes or Mbytes with K = 1,024 bytes. Thus, drives appear to sometimes have a smaller capacity than advertised. Drives can be subdivided into smaller partitions as the 8 GB drive above is divided into a 3 GB and a 5 GB partition. The bootable partition has been assigned a logical drive letter C and has been set active. The Windows 95/98 FDISK performs a surface verification to assure that the fixed disk drive is readable where the system files and FAT are to be stored.

Creating an extended DOS partition is done similarly to creating the primary DOS partition. The main difference is that the menu items selected are for the extended DOS partition, and that the extended DOS partition must be subdivided into logical drives. When the extended DOS partition is created, FDISK asks whether the entire extended DOS partition should be assigned to a single logical drive. This is similar to the question that FDISK asks when creating the primary DOS partition—do you wish to use the entire disk for a primary DOS partition? If more than one logical drive is created, then disk space must be allocated to each logical drive. Once this is complete, FDISK assigns drive letters to the logical drives.

FORMAT

FORMAT sets up the allocation units and builds the disk drive directory and FAT. In spite of the FORMAT command warning that it deletes files from the disk drive, FORMAT does not really delete data from the disk drive. On a new disk drive, FORMAT establishes the allocation units. On an older disk drive, FORMAT uses the allocation units previously created. In both cases, FORMAT recreates the directory and FAT. On older disk drives, FORMAT attempts to store away the old directory and FAT in the event that the old data needs to be recovered from the fixed disk drive. When it cannot save this information, FORMAT issues a warning message stating that the data on a drive will be unrecoverable.

The new Windows 95/98 format verifies the drive in the process of laying out the allocation units, creating the FAT and creating the disk drive directory. FORMAT is run after FDISK partitions the drive.

FORMAT does not rewrite the directory and FAT tables until it has completed its disk verification. If FORMAT is stopped prior to completion, old disk information remains intact. Disk verification does not destroy the data on the disk; FORMAT leaves the data untouched and only creates a new directory and FAT.

The DOS 6.2x UNFORMAT command uses the saved directory and FAT data to restore a fixed disk to its original operating state as long as nothing has been written on the disk since the format operation.

FORMAT is used to prepare floppy diskettes for use. No partitioning of a floppy disk is performed prior to formatting it.

Floppy disk formatting can be performed from the "My Computer" object on the desktop. Open my computer and click on the diskette drive icon, then right-click for an options menu and choose Format. Floppy diskette formatting can be quick or full (which performs a surface test). Other options are to transfer the system files alone. This is equivalent to the DOS SYS command. Fixed disk formatting is done from DOS.

The FORMAT command line options are shown in Table 12–4. One option, the /C option, should be avoided because it attempts to reuse clusters. Sometimes reused clusters are really bad, and data is lost when stored in them. Because of the risk of losing data stored in those clusters, it is much better to leave any suspect clusters marked bad than it is to attempt to rejuvenate them.

SCANDISK

SCANDISK is a disk analysis and repair program for fixed disks, floppy diskettes, RAM drives and memory card drives. The Windows 98 SCANDISK works with 32-bit FAT drives. Other versions work with compressed drives. SCANDISK tests the FAT, long filenames, the file structure, the directory tree, the drive surface, and Windows Compressed drives for errors.

SCANDISK automatically repairs the errors it finds or it permits operator input to determine how errors are resolved. SCANDISK scans individual disk drives or scans all the disks.

SCANDISK uses a second copy of the FAT to fix cross-linked files and lost file fragments. A file is a chain of allocation units tied to a directory entry that contains the data in a file. Cross-linked files have the chain of allocations units, described in the FAT, pointing to different locations at some point in the chain. One FAT believes the file is comprised of allocation units that are different from the allocation units assigned to the file in the other FAT. SCANDISK resolves these cross-link references by comparing both FATs. File fragments are allocation unit chains that do not match the file size reported in the directory. Other fragments are chains of allocation units not tied to a directory entry. SCANDISK fixes these problems by adjusting the directory size information and by creating directory entries (for example, FILE0000.CHK, FILE0001.CHK) for the lost chains of allocation units.

Windows comes with SCANDISK.EXE that runs from the DOS prompt and SCANDISKW.EXE that runs under Windows. Both SCANDISK programs work with long filenames. Earlier versions of the DOS SCANDISK program did not work with long filenames.

SCANDISK has advanced scanning options illustrated in Figure 12–18. These advanced options customize SCANDISK operation to an individual user's needs. The default advanced options are all the selected options except checking files for invalid dates and times and duplicate names.

Windows and Windows applications use temporary files as scratch storage areas. These files are kept open by the application. As a result, shutting off the PC without exiting Windows gracefully creates directory errors. SCANDISK fixes these directory errors. It uses the two copies of the FAT to resolve cross-linked file errors. It also converts lost file chains with no directory entries into FILE00nn.CHK files.

SCANDISK advanced options provide for performing a nondestructive surface test of the disk drive. With the nondestructive surface test, when bad

Figure 12–18
SCANDISK advanced options

areas are encountered, SCANDISK recovers the information by rereading the bad areas and moving the recovered data to a different area on the disk. If SCANDISK recovers the data, generally it is good. The nondestructive surface test makes SCANDISK require a much longer time to complete its testing of a fixed disk drive. Large and slow fixed disks can require hours to completely test.

Windows 95/98 can be set up to perform SCANDISK maintenance automatically. By default its scheduled to run at night on a weekly basis.

There are two versions of SCANDISK, a Windows graphical utility and a DOS implementation. The Windows SCANDISK works with long filenames, while the DOS version does not. The Windows SCANDISK provides additional controls under an advanced options selection. These controls change the summary display, logging, and file correction options. The file correction options permit files cross-linked on the same allocation unit to be deleted, ignored, or preferably copied to new directory entries. Similarly, file correction options permit lost file fragments to be converted to files or to be freed, recovering the disk space for future use. SCANDISK can also be set up to check files for invalid filenames, invalid date and time stamps, and duplicate names.

The FAT System and Directories

To understand the evolution of the FAT system, we need to return to the first PC fixed disks. With the introduction of the IBM PC-XT in 1983, DOS was designed to work with fixed disks. The first XT fixed disk was 10 MB. This quickly increased to 30 MB with the release of the IBM PC-AT in 1985. DOS had built into it a fixed disk addressing capability, the File Allocation Table or FAT that limited the total disk size to 32 MB. There was a limit of 16 KB entries in the fixed disk space addressing table. Each entry could address one allocation unit or cluster consisting of four 512-character sectors. Hence, each FAT entry represented 2KB characters of disk space or a total of 2 KB by 16 K or 32 MB total disk space. DOS 4.0, 5.0, and 6.x permit the allocation unit (or cluster sizes) to be larger than 4 sectors. In this manner more than 32 MB total disk capacity can be addressed by DOS using the 16 K entry FAT (but not as efficiently as when 4 sectors are used). With Windows 95 OSR2, a 32-bit FAT was introduced which changed the effective maximum disk drive capacity that could be handled by Windows to 2 terabytes (TB).

In order for files to be placed on the fixed disk drive, they needed to be organized. DOS provided tree-structured directories. Tree-structured directories are so-named because they look like an inverted tree with branches springing out from the root of the tree. In the case of the DOS directory

Note

DOS used a 12-bit FAT to manage files on floppy drives and logical drives smaller than 16 MB. The 16-bit FAT was first introduced in DOS 3.0.

structure, the root directory is at the top and subdirectories are below it. In Windows 95/98 the directories are called folders.

Each fixed disk subdirectory or folder acts like a disk drive itself. When you move to that subdirectory by entering CD and the subdirectory name, it looks like the entire fixed disk only contains the files in that subdirectory. So then why not put all files in the root directory? The root directory has a limited number of entries. It can contain only 512 files on 16-bit FAT fixed disks, 65,535 files on 32-bit FAT fixed disks, and, on floppy diskettes, only 64 or 128 files. Subdirectories are not limited in the number of files they contain because subdirectory entries are files themselves. A comparison of file systems is given in Table 12–5.

Table 12.5 *PC file systems*

PC File System	File Allocation Table (FAT-16) DOS	File Allocation Table (FAT-32) Windows 95/98	High Performance File System (HPFS) OS/2	NT File System (NTFS) Windows NT
Maximum Size	2 GB	2 TB (TeraBytes)	4 GB	17 GB
Filename Size	8	255	254	254
Extension Size	3	3 or more	3	3
Security Features	None	None	Limited when used with LAN server software	Subdirectory and file access limitations
International Language Support	None	Unicode character encoding standard	None	Unicode character encoding standard
Crash Recovery	SCANDISK Transaction Tracking	SCANDISK Transaction Tracking	CHKDSK (OS/2 Program)	CHKDSK (NT Program) Built-in recovery features
Extended Attributes	Hidden, read-only, system and archive	Hidden, read-only, system and archive	Yes Shareable, write-protected, etc.	Yes Shareable, write-protected, etc.

FAT AND THE DIR COMMAND

Since DOS cannot address all the 512-byte sectors on a disk individually, it must group them to work with fixed disks of varying capacity. DOS can address 65,525 or 268,435,445 clusters or allocation units in its File Allocation Table. If each allocation unit were one sector in size, DOS could address 32 MB using a 16-bit FAT. Consequently, for large fixed disk drives, DOS must cluster together sectors into larger allocation units. The largest allocation unit size is 32 KB or 64 sectors.

The DIR command displays four pieces of information:

- Filename (up to eight characters)
- Extension (up to three characters)
- Size in bytes (characters)
- Date and time when created or last modified

This information is contained in the directory entry for the file along with additional information instructing DOS how to gather the sectors (which clusters it should read) off the fixed disk to form the file. The directory entry points to a beginning cluster number in the FAT. It in turn points to the next cluster number that is simply a numeric position in the FAT table. This in turn points to the next cluster number and so on until we reach a FAT entry signaling the end of the file. These FAT entries form a chain of clusters that comprise the file. This chain is associated with a directory entry through the first FAT number contained in the file's directory entry. Figure 12–15 earlier in this chapter illustrates how the DOS directory and the File Allocation Table (FAT) work together.

The boot record information is the first data stored on a fixed disk. It is stored in fixed length entries on all disks regardless of the FAT or directory structure. The boot record and the partition table are created by FDISK. FORMAT sets up the directory and FAT. It then places IO.SYS as the first DOS file on the drive and MSDOS.SYS as the second.

CHKDSK AND CHKDSK MESSAGES

The CHKDSK DOS utility program identifies and resolves conflicts between the directory and the FAT. On Windows systems, SCANDISK provides this functionality and more.

When CHKDSK *.* /V is run, a typical PC response could be:

```
Directory A:\
   A:\ARC520.COM
   A:\BWVID.ARC
   A:\CDISK.ARC
```

```
A:\CORETEST.ARC
A:\DIPSET.ARC
A:\DISKPARK.ARC
A:\DSKMON.ARC
A:\DSKWATCH.COM
A:\EQUIPCFG.COM
A:\ERRCODES.ARC
A:\FASTCOPY.ARC
```

```
Errors found, F parameter not specified.
Corrections will not be written to disk.
```

This indicates that there are conflicts between the directory and the FAT. Since we have not as yet used the /F parameter, DOS does not resolve these conflicts, only displays where they are on this fixed disk. If CHKDSK is run with the /F parameter, it corrects the discrepancies between the FAT and the directory. When this is done, some data on the fixed disk is lost.

```
A:\FASTCOPY.ARC
Allocation error, size adjusted.
No chain for this entry, size will be set to 0.
    A:\HDAT.ARC
    A:\HDTABL.ARC
    A:\HDTEST.ARC
    A:\INFO.ARC
    A:\LAND.ARC
    A:\LPT2DSK.ARC
    A:\MEMSET.COM
    A:\MEMSET.DOC
    A:\MIPS.ARC
    A:\NMI.ARC
    A:\PDIAGS.ARC
    A:\READTHIS.1ST
    A:\SPEED.ARC
    A:\TESTMEM.COM
```

```
29 lost clusters found in 7 chains.
Convert lost chains to files (Y/N)? n
  29696 bytes disk space
     would be freed.
```

This means that several chains of clusters discovered in the FAT have no corresponding directory entry. These chains are converted to files when CHKDSK /F is run. Similarly, SCANDISK converts such lost chains to files. The files are placed in the root directory with the name FILE0000.CHK, FILE0001.CHK, etc. The FILE00xx.CHK files may contain salvageable data.

Following is more bad news. Three files share the same cluster. These files are cross-linked. What can be true here? Only one file is good and the remaining two are bad. Can you tell which one is good? There is no real way to determine the good file.

```
A:\FASTCOPY.ARC
   Is cross linked on cluster 255
A:\HDAT.ARC
   Is cross linked on cluster 255
A:\MIPS.ARC
   Is cross linked on cluster 255

   362496 bytes total disk space
   319488 bytes in 25 user files
   13312 bytes available on disk

   720896 bytes total memory
   165008 bytes free

A:\FASTCOPY.ARC
   Contains 2 non-contiguous blocks.
A:\HDAT.ARC
   Contains 2 non-contiguous blocks.
```

Finally, at the end of the CHKDSK output, we see the innocuous message that our files are resident in noncontiguous clusters. This might mean that we are having reduced performance from our fixed disk drive. This problem pales in comparison to the preceding problems.

Whenever a Windows program exits due to an unrecoverable application error, cluster chains with no corresponding directory entry are often left by temporary data storage files on a fixed disk. These chains with no directory entry eventually congest the disk, leaving no space for additional files. It is a good policy to once a week or more often perform a SCANDISK test on each fixed disk drive or partition on Windows PCs. When any lost chains are found, they should be converted to files and then erased from the fixed disk.

DEFRAG

The DEFRAG program defragments files on disk drives. As described earlier in this chapter, defragmenting involves rearranging the clusters that contain the file data so they are accessed with minimal head movement on the fixed disk.

DEFRAG has few options. When DEFRAG is launched, it provides options to select the disk drive to be defragmented and a button to change the settings. The settings that can be changed are having DEFRAG optimize

Figure 12–19 *Defrag options illustrates these selections*

the program file arrangement so that applications launch more quickly and checking the disk surface for errors. These can be set to run one time or every time that DEFRAG is launched.

When the option to rearrange program files is selected, DEFRAG works with a log file to see which programs are launched most often. It then locates these programs in the order they are accessed, making them load faster. DEFRAG starts by presenting an option to select the drive to defragment. One selection is all fixed disk drives. It also provides a settings button that permits configuring DEFRAG to make the programs start faster and to check the surface for errors. Figure 12–19 illustrates these selections.

DEFRAG displays defragmentation progress in a small and in a more detailed window. The defragmentation progress identifies the clusters to be optimized as belonging at the beginning, middle, or end of the disk drive as shown in Figure 12–20. Hidden, read-only, and system files that cannot be moved are identified in the defragmentation progress detailed window.

When a drive is defragmented and other programs are actively changing data on the drive, DEFRAG restarts every time it detects a change to the data stored on the drive. This can cause defragmentation to require hours of time. Consequently, it is best to close all programs except DEFRAG when defragmenting a drive. This means disabling the screen saver and other power management features that run in the background.

As with SCANDISK, Windows 95/98 can be set up to perform DEFRAG maintenance automatically. Its default is to run at night once a week but on a different night than the night that SCANDISK runs.

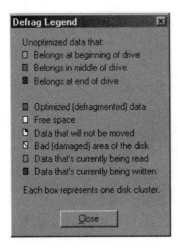

Figure 12–20 *DEFRAG detailed display legend*

SYS

SYS installs the system files on a fixed disk or on a diskette. It can be used to recover from some nonbootable disk problems. SYS can be run from a fixed disk directory while the DOS command prompt is pointing at a floppy diskette drive containing the IO.SYS and MSDOS.SYS files.

Using a DOS 6.x bootable diskette to make a Windows 95/98 fixed disk bootable is not good because the MSDOS.SYS file on the Windows fixed disk is different. The DOS MSDOS.SYS file is a binary program. The Windows 95/98 MSDOS.SYS is a text file instructing Windows how to initialize.

Study Break

CHKDSK

This exercise illustrates the CHKDSK program and functions it performs.

1. Run CHKDSK C:*.* /V. What error messages appeared?

2. Did the warning message saying that SCANDISK is better than CHKDSK appear?

3. Were there any lost clusters or allocation units not assigned to directory entries? When programs that use temporary files are exited abnormally, the temporary files are left as lost clusters or allocation units on the fixed disk drive. So this is a common CHKDSK error message.

4. Were there any cross-linked clusters or allocation units? At one time, this error was some-times found with fixed disk drives. However newer drives are much more reliable than the older drives and it is highly unusual to find this error.

5. Was the total memory size reported as 655,360 bytes? If the number was lower, scan the system immediately for viruses.

Of these error messages, the memory size message remains the most useful today because SCAN-DISK more effectively performs the functionality of CHKDSK. Under Windows NT there is no SCAN-DISK program. Windows NT uses a special CHKDSK program to verify drive integrity and fix errors.

■ Summary

This chapter has described the DOS and Windows fixed disk file and data management operations. It describes setting up fixed disk drives as well as the use of both DOS and Windows utility programs which manage data on a PC's fixed disk drives. PCs are moving to a Windows-only operating environment, which will be very focused upon PC's being attached to networks. This means that the A+ testing focus will shift to those types of PCs. DOS is not, however, any less important because it continues to be the number one tool for setting up, maintaining, and troubleshooting PC fixed disk drives. Because DOS permits direct access to the PC's hardware, it continues to be the platform that runs PC diagnostics and prepares the PC for installation of Windows 95/98 and Windows NT. The basic fixed disk drive diagnostics are typically run using DOS. This chapter has described basic DOS and Windows file system concepts, DOS file management and disk maintenance utilities, and Windows file management and disk maintenance utilities. It illustrated the most commonly used DOS and Windows disk utility programs.

▲ CHAPTER REVIEW QUESTIONS

Multiple Choice

1. *The number of boot records per hard drive is?*

    A. one boot record per drive

    B. one boot record per partition

    C. one boot record for each primary partition; no boot record for extended partitions

    D. none, the boot record is stored in the BIOS, not the hard drive

    Answer: B. one boot record per partition

2. *When installing Windows on a compressed drive, where is the swap file placed?*

    A. in the root directory of the compressed drive

    B. in the same directory into which Windows is installed

    C. on the uncompressed host drive

    D. Windows decides on the optimal place for the swap file

    Answer: C. on the uncompressed host drive

3. *Disk thrashing refers to:*

    A. a fixed disk drive has many bad sectors and has to map data around them

    B. a fixed disk drive is failing and making excessive noise

    C. the system RAM is full most of the time, resulting in excessive paging

    D. the hard drive is too fragmented to effectively manage file I/O

    Answer: C. the system RAM is full most of the time, resulting in excessive paging

4. *What does FAT stand for?*

    A. File Allotment Table

    B. File Allocation Table

    C. File Assignment Table

    D. File Allocation-unit Table

Answer: B. File Allocation Table

5. *The FAT entries are:*
   A. disk sectors
   B. numbers
   C. random
   D. allocation units

   Answer: B. numbers

6. *Which program corrects disk directory and FAT problems?*
   A. FORMAT
   B. FDISK
   C. CHKDSK
   D. XCOPY

   Answer: C. CHKDSK

7. *Which program is used to partition a Windows fixed disk drive?*
   A. FORMAT
   B. FDISK
   C. CHKDSK
   D. EXPLORER

   Answer: B.FDISK

8. *What does SCANDSK do that CHKDSK does not do?*
   A. checks the directory structure
   B. checks the FAT
   C. corrects directory and FAT problems
   D. fixes bad data files

   Answer: D. fixes bad data files

9. *What is the difference between the DOS and Windows SCANDISK program?*
   A. Windows SCANDISK only runs in a DOS window
   B. Windows SCANDISK works with long filenames
   C. Windows SCANDISK can be launched using the mouse
   D. Windows uses SDISK and DOS uses SCANDISK.

Answer: B. Windows SCANDISK works with long filenames

10. *Lost chains are commonly caused by*

 A. exiting Windows

 B. power outages

 C. abnormal termination of Windows

 D. abnormal termination of Windows applications

 Answer: D. abnormal termination of Windows applications is best but C. abnormal termination of Windows is good also

11. *VCACHE is:*

 A. an internal fixed disk manager in Windows 3.11 and Windows 95

 B. a fixed disk program in Windows 98 that manages disk cache

 C. a virtual cache manager program

 D. an EXE program

 Answer: A. an internal fixed disk manager in Windows 3.11 and Windows 95

12. *What does large disk support do?*

 A. permits MS-DOS to operate with drives over 2 GB.

 B. works with Windows NT to set up NTFS

 C. permits Windows 95 to use 4GB partitions

 D. permits Windows 98 to use disk drives over 2GB as one partition

 Answer: D. permits Windows 98 to use disk drives over 2GB as one partition

13. *Which operating system can convert to 32-bit FAT without using FDISK?*

 A. Windows NT

 B. Windows 95 OSR2

 C. Windows 98

 D. Windows 3.1x

 Answer: C. Windows 98

14. *A PC could operate with FAT-16 and FAT-32 partitions.*

 A. FALSE

 B. TRUE

 Answer: B. TRUE

15. *FAT-16 stores data more efficiently than FAT-32.*

    A. FALSE

    B. TRUE

    Answer: A. FALSE

16. *Which is the most used fixed disk utility?*

    A. FORMAT

    B. FDISK

    C. CHKDSK

    D. SCANDISK

    Answer: D. SCANDISK is best but C. CHKDSK is okay as well.

DOS and Memory Management

▲Chapter Syllabus

A+ 13.1   Types of Memory

A+ 13.2   Memory Conflicts and Their Resolution

A+ 13.3   PC DOS Memory Setup

While Windows 95/98 resolves most memory management conflicts, making memory management with them a low priority issue, still a good understanding of PC memory basics helps solve software problems. Even though Windows 95/98 Applications have the memory they need, older DOS and Windows 3.1 applications still function as though they were in a memory-limited PC. Furthermore, memory resource conflicts by hardware in the upper memory areas still pose difficult problems for Windows 95/98/NT systems. Resolving such hardware conflicts for upper memory is based on a good understanding of how DOS uses memory in PCs because that is where it all started. Windows 95/98/NT requires that there be no hardware conflicts for upper memory blocks addresses. This chapter examines DOS/Windows 3.1x memory management and Windows 95/98 memory usage.

663

This chapter is to describe the basics of memory management in the PC. This begins with how the PC chips look at memory and then how this translates into DOS, then Windows memory management. From an A+ testing viewpoint, the key information concerns the programs that permit you to configure PC memory using DOS and the memory layout. As older PC software products fade into oblivion, knowledge of the techniques for configuring PC memory using DOS will become much less important. However, the types of memory and the layout of memory will remain a foundation stone for many future PC systems.

Memory in the PC is used a variety of ways. We most often think of it as a storage place for the executable program code and the data that the program is operating on. However, memory addresses have other functions as well. For example, some memory addresses are assigned to contain ROM programs from the system BIOS and from the VGA adapter. These ROM programs perform the basic input/output operations for the PC. Other areas are assigned to heaps. Heaps are storage areas for different program parameters such as color palettes, fonts, and other graphical information used by Windows. Finally, memory is used as a buffer for swapping data between different memory areas and different hardware components. Generally pages of memory (pages vary in size depending upon the operation being performed) are swapped to the device from the page memory area and vice versa. These buffer areas are sometimes called paging areas or page frames. With these concepts in mind, let's examine the memory areas used by DOS in the PC.

A+ 13.1 Types of Memory

The CPU chips used to build the PC largely determined the types of memory in PCs. The early PCs were based upon Intel 8088 and 8086 CPU chips that could address only 1,024 K of RAM. This led to the famous Bill Gates quote stating that 640 K of RAM would be all the memory anyone would ever need in a PC. KIBM as a reserved memory area designated the remaining 384 K of RAM. In fact it had several uses. The system ROM, display text swapping, and display ROM were assigned to that memory area.

DOS memory management began to change with the introduction of the IBM PC AT using the Intel 80286 chip. This chip was capable of addressing RAM beyond the 1,024 K range. To preserve backwards compatibility with the older DOS PC systems, the original memory layout continued to be used. The 80286 chip operated in real mode and in protected mode. Real mode emulated the 8088 chip, while protected mode permitted utilizing up to 16 MB of random access memory. This 16 MB limit was imposed on DOS and Windows software until the introduction of Windows 95.

Windows 95 took advantage of the next CPU chip technology produced by Intel. This is the 80386 chip technology, which is basically used by all 80386, 80486, and Pentium CPU chips today. These chips can address 4GB of RAM. Although no PCs are built with this much RAM, the addressing capability is used with virtual memory so that applications developers can utilize a very large flat address space when building their windows 95/98/ NT programs.

The new 64-bit chip, the Intel Merced chip, will drive the next step in PC memory management. This chip will be capable of addressing terabytes of RAM.

CPU chip developments precede software developments. This statement remains largely true today, although the development of CPU capabilities requires some measure of collaboration with software developers that will utilize the CPU capabilities. As a result of CPU hardware preceding software, the CPU chips have built-in capabilities that enable software to avoid potential memory conflicts. The earliest and simplest of these capabilities was the protected mode operation of the 80286 chip. In this operating mode, the chip protected software components from using the same memory areas. It provided software with basic capabilities for detecting when programs tried to utilize the same RAM locations. Virtually all CPU chips provide similar and more sophisticated capabilities today.

As CPU chips evolved, so did other parts of the PC. The display capabilities increased and most PCs became multimedia devices incorporating CD-ROM and sound capabilities. Today's and future PCs will include video input as well. The PC system that I'm using to write this book is a multimedia PC with sound and video capabilities. I'm using these capabilities to run speech-to-text software, permitting me to dictate this material directly into the PC. Such PC component developments have also impacted memory management.

Memory management concerns have evolved from the early days of DOS where the major objective was to provide as much of the basic 640 K of RAM as possible for PC application programs. With Windows today this is less of a concern. The more important issue from a PC support perspective is ensuring that there are no hardware memory conflicts within the PC. This translates into careful configuration of the upper memory block area within the PC.

Figure 13–1 identifies the different types of PC memory.

Conventional -- (REAL Mode)

HIMEM -- (REAL Mode)

UPPER MEMORY BLOCKS (UMB) -- (Real Mode)

EXTENDED -- XMS

EXPANDED - EMS

Figure 13–1 *PC memory types*

There are five basic areas of PC memory:

- Conventional memory is the lower 640 K DOS and game users have grown to know and love.
- Extended memory is provided by any 286, 386, 486, and Pentium CPU chips in PCs having physically over 1 million characters (1,024 K) of memory installed.
- HIMEM, created by an addressing anomaly in the Intel chips, is the first 64 K of extended memory space that is above the 1 million character (1,024 K) boundary. HIMEM can be accessed in real operating mode.
- Upper memory blocks are blocks of memory in the reserved memory area not used for the display memory swapping area, ROMs, the expanded memory page swapping area, or LAN buffer areas.
- Expanded memory can be in any PC, provided the PC has hardware and software drivers that support expanded memory. Old 8088 CPU chip PCs with a special expanded memory board and driver software could access more than 640 K of memory. In 386 and above, a PC's expanded memory is created from extended memory using only special software.

Figure 13–2 illustrates the PC memory areas. On the left-hand side of the diagram, the first megabyte of memory and the HIMEM area are shown. Hexadecimal addresses for each of the significant memory areas are listed on the right-hand side of the memory areas. The equivalent K addresses are shown on the left-hand side of the diagram. Hence, the HIMEM area is from 1,024 K to 1,088 K. This corresponds to the hexadecimal addresses of 0 FF FF

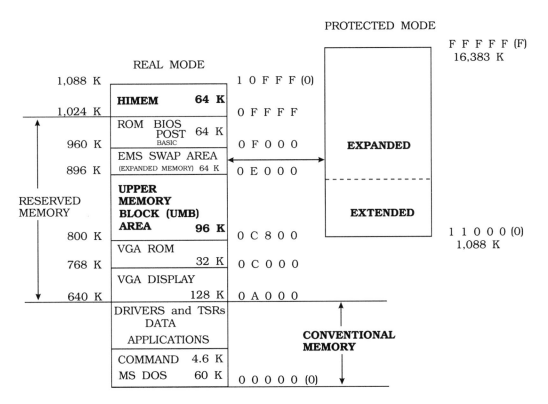

Figure 13–2 *PC memory map.*

and 1 0F FF. The left box covers conventional memory, the reserved memory area (or upper memory area), and the HIMEM area.The extended (XMS) and expanded (EMS) memory areas appear at the side of the first megabyte of memory to help illustrate EMS swapping. The diagram illustrates a maximum memory of 16 MB, which is equivalent to 16,383 K.

Conventional

Conventional memory is accessed by 8086 and 8088 chips directly and by 80286, 80386, 80486, and Pentium chips operating in real mode. In DOS-based PC systems, all the work activity was performed using conventional memory. This memory area started from address 0 K to 640 K or, in hexadecimal notation, from address 0000 to address 0A00. In real mode, Intel chips work with this memory in 64K chunks. There are 10 chunks, or memory segments, making up the 640 K of conventional memory. Almost all DOS programs operated exclusively in this area.

DOS is important as a diagnostic tool for us. Because it performs one task at a time, it is a relatively safe tool to use for resolving a variety of PC hardware problems. Furthermore, DOS diagnostic programs directly manipulate PC hardware. This capability is prohibited or greatly restricted in a Windows environment. The major drawback of using DOS and DOS-based diagnostic tools is that they operate in 640 K of RAM. This generally means limited data manipulation capabilities, especially when it comes to large fixed disks.

The lower address range in conventional memory contains the interrupt handling routines for DOS. Consequently, not all of the 640 K of conventional memory can be used to run DOS programs. The same areas are used by Windows interrupt handling routines as well.

The sidebar, "Understanding Memory Addresses," presents some detailed information on how the same memory addresses are represented in different documentation.

Study Break

Understanding Memory Addresses

Memory addresses can be difficult to follow and understand. They can be expressed in kilobytes or in hexadecimal notation.

In K or Kb notation, a kilobyte is 1024 bytes. This is different from a kilo being 1000, as we most often think. This means that 640 K of RAM is equivalent to 655,360 bytes of RAM exactly. The DOS memory management programs report available RAM in both K notation and as thousands of bytes. Generally the thousands of bytes notation is displayed inside parentheses.

Hexadecimal notation can be more difficult to understand and interpret. Hexadecimal representation of numeric values ranges from 0 to F. F represents a number 15 in decimal notation. Later in this chapter, we have some memory address calculators that use hexadecimal representation of RAM and permit you to identify readily where various hardware components occupy upper memory block addresses.

When installing hardware for DOS, upper memory block hexadecimal addresses were typically represented by 4 hexadecimal digits. This means that the starting address of conventional memory was 0000. The ending address of conventional memory was 09FF. Thus the beginning upper memory block address was 0A00 and the HIMEM beginning address was 1000.

This four-digit representation only described the upper four hexadecimal digits of the memory address. Programmers would have to deal with addresses which added a fifth hexadecimal digit to the address, such that they viewed addresses as 0A00 (0).

Extended Memory (XMS)

When PCs have over 1 MB of RAM installed, they have extended memory. Extended memory is supported by any 286, 386, 486, and Pentium CPU chips. CPU chips in protected operating mode address extended memory. Real mode operation does not access extended (XMS) memory. Real mode operation accesses only the real mode memory (the first 1MB and HIMEM).

The extended or XMS memory is the memory from which the remaining types of memory are derived. They are merely special assignments for areas of XMS memory. Furthermore, other types of memory in the PC are also implemented using XMS memory. For example, shadow RAM—a hardware memory implementation—maps ROM into XMS RAM. This is done to speed up input/output operations on older PCs. In a Windows 95/98/NT environment, shadow RAM is not required because input/output operations are implemented using 32-bit driver programs in RAM. In Windows systems, ROM is only used during the initial system setup process. Thereafter it is bypassed in favor of the 32-bit RAM resident input/ output driver programs.

In Windows systems, application programs are run in XMS memory. DOS does not a have the ability to manipulate XMS memory without running the HIMEM.SYS device driver program. As we shall see, HIMEM.SYS is the DOS and Windows 3.x program that controls XMS memory. This changes with Windows 95/98/NT. Note that Windows NT still employs HIMEM.SYS to access the HIMEM memory area.

Windows limited the useable capacity of XMS. Windows 3.x could not utilize XMS over 16 MB of RAM. This restriction was due to the amount of XMS that could be addressed by the Intel 80286 CPU chip. This restriction does not exist with Windows 95/98/NT. These Windows environments are capable of addressing the full 4 GB of memory supported by the newer Intel chip. Although most PCs have around a hundred megabytes of RAM installed today, Windows creates virtual memory which it addresses using a 4 GB flat address space model.

High Memory (HIMEM)

HIMEM was created to take advantage of an addressing anomaly in Intel chips. When CPU chips address memory and they go beyond their designed memory boundary, the memory addresses typically wrapped around to the lowest address. For example, if an upper memory address limit was 1000 and a program tried to address location 1001,the resultant address would be 001. However, in Intel chips this did not happen for the first 64,000 addresses after the million-character boundary. It meant that the first 64 K over the one-million-character boundary was addressable by the CPU chip in real mode. This 64 K is the HIMEM area.

HIMEM is a special type of extended memory. It is accessed using a driver program in real operating mode. This driver program permits placing DOS components in HIMEM, as well as managing all extended memory. Not all the HIMEM 64 K can be used because the HIMEM driver program consumes some of the memory.

Upper Memory Blocks (UMBs)

Upper memory blocks are blocks of memory in the reserved memory area not used for the display memory swapping area, ROMs, the expanded memory page swapping area, or PC expansion card or LAN card buffer areas. Upper memory blocks in the reserved memory area are accessible using DOS's EMM386 program in real operating mode. Pragmatically, there is about 96 K of RAM available into which memory-resident and hardware driver programs may fit. The remainder of the upper memory blocks (UMBs) are used by ROMs, display buffers, etc. Figure 13–3 illustrates the upper memory block address assignments for an Adaptec SCSI controller card. The challenge with DOS memory management was to place as many driver programs as possible into the upper memory block area. This was sometimes not possible because driver programs and other terminate-and-stay-resident programs required more memory to load than to run. In some cases, a 5 K program would require 32 K to load and 5 K to operate. If the 32 K were not available in the upper memory blocks, the program would be loaded into conventional memory. It is also possible to run application programs in the upper memory blocks. This is not generally practical because of the limited amount of memory available in the UMB area. Only very small DOS programs that used very little memory could operate there. Typically, programs that worked in conventional memory could not utilize UMB memory and vice versa. The DOS 6.2x SMARTDRV was the only program we saw capable of installing itself in conventional memory and then spilling over into the upper memory block area.

The upper memory block address assignments can be viewed using the Microsoft diagnostic program (MSD). It displays the memory assignments using a 4-digit hexadecimal format or the kilobyte format. Each row display represents 16 K of memory with each placeholder representing 1 K of UMB RAM. MSD displays the typical system ROM, video ROM, and video paging address ranges. It may also sense address ranges used by LAN network interface cards (NICs) and other adapter cards, provided that the driver software for these cards has been loaded. There are versions of MSD for DOS and Windows. MSD does not always query the physical hardware to determine which address ranges are in use. Sometimes it just guesses, based on what the typical standard PC hardware address assignments are. Just as in the case where your doctor says we need to open you up for open heart surgery tomorrow, the first thought that should jump into your mind when viewing output from MSD is that you need a second opinion. An MSD memory map display appears in Figure 13–4.

In the figure, we see the memory display from the 1 MB boundary down to the C000 address or the 768K boundary. MSG permits viewing all the upper memory area from the 640 K boundary to the 1,024 K boundary. The display does not permit viewing all that at one time, so the screen must be scrolled to view the portion of memory not visible. Each line represents 16 K of memory with each letter being equivalent to a 1-K block of memory. The F000 to FFFF range contains the system ROM. The D000 to EFFF range is unused and available to store programs. The other memory areas are occu-

Figure 13–3 *Windows 98 memory assignments.*

```
 File  Utilities  Help
                           ═══════ Memory ═══════
   ██ Legend:   Available  "▓"   RAM  "▒"    ROM  "░"   Possibly Available  "▓"  ↑
      EMS Page Frame "PP"   Used UMBs "UU"   Free UMBs "FF"
   1024K FC00                        FFFF  Conventional Memory
       F800                          FBFF              Total: 640K
       F400                          F7FF          Available: 600K
    960K F000                        F3FF                    614672 bytes
       EC00 UUUUUUUUUUUUUUUU         EFFF
       E800 UUUUUUUUUUUUUUUU         EBFF  Extended Memory
       E400 UUUUUUUUUUUUUUUU         E7FF              Total: 65472K
    896K E000 UUUUUUUUUUUUUUUU       E3FF
       DC00 UUUUUUUUUUUUUUUU         DFFF  MS-DOS Upper Memory Blocks
       D800 UUUUUUUUUUUUUUUU         DBFF          Total UMBs: 130K
       D400 UUUUUUUUUUUUUUUU         D7FF     Total Free UMBs: 0K
    832K D000 .UUUUUUUUUUUUUUU       D3FF   Largest Free Block: 0K
       CC00                ....      CFFF
       C800                UUUU      CBFF  XMS Information
       C400                         C7FF          XMS Version: 3.00
    768K C000                        C3FF       Driver Version: 3.5f         ↓

                            ┌─────── OK ───────┐

 Memory: Displays visual memory map and various types of memory.
```

Figure 13–4 *MSD program examining the upper memory area*

pied by ROM, are used by the VGA display, or are potentially available for storing programs. Since the other free memory areas are not contiguous, their ability to act as program storage areas is limited.

ROM ASSIGNMENTS

In the upper memory block area, standard ROM assignments are for the system ROM and the video ROM. The system ROM provides the BIOS software that controls the PC. This includes power on self-test routines (POST) used once during the boot process to determine the functioning PC hardware as well as the BIOS routines used by DOS for basic input/output activities. The highest 64 K memory segment in the UMB address range is typically where system ROM resides. This is the memory segment F000–FFFF. Some PCs required a larger system ROM area, the most notable of these was the IBM PS/2.

Video ROM occupies 32 K in the UMB C000–C7FF address range. This ROM controls operation of the PC graphics card. Other adapter cards also have ROM in the upper memory block address range. SCSI disk controller cards and LAN NIC cards typically have ROM assigned in the upper memory block address range. SCSI disk controllers often use the C800–CBFF address range for their ROM. Adaptec SCSI controllers have their SCSI-select software in ROM on the controller card. This software is used to diagnose and configure SCSI drives attached to that card. The SCSI ROM software can do low-level formatting, perform service verification, and provide adapter card setup and configuration routines. Similarly, LAN NIC cards place their ROM in the C or D UMB address segments.

In DOS-based systems, ROM address assignments were configured manually. In Windows systems, this is done more automatically, unless an adapter card requires a manual configuration to set the proper ROM address range in the upper memory blocks. Regardless of how the ROM address configuration is performed, address conflicts cause system failures.

VIDEO USAGE

Video cards also use upper memory block address ranges to page swap data between the PC's RAM and the RAM resident on the video display adapter. The display we see is produced from the RAM on the video display adapter. It contains the image viewed on the PC's monitor. To update the image, the PC must swap that RAM with the RAM the PC uses for data manipulation. This swapping is done through the video RAM address ranges in the upper memory blocks. Video adapters use the A address segment to swap graphics information between the video card memory and the working RAM in the PC. They also employ 32 K of the B address segment to perform text swapping between the display adapter card and the working RAM in the PC. The address range used was from C800–CFFF. The lower part of the C address segment (C000–C7FF) was used for video swapping by monochrome display adapters. Today this memory area is largely available to be used. With Windows 95/98/NT able to squeeze extra memory out of the upper memory block area, this area is much less important than it was with DOS and Windows 3x.

Expanded Memory (EMS)

Expanded memory was caused by accountants. In the first PCs, the major application was spreadsheets. When accountants saw the capabilities of spreadsheets to perform sophisticated financial analysis, they quickly created spreadsheets that gobbled up all available PC memory. The dominant spreadsheet program was Lotus 1-2-3. Sensing an opportunity to make more money, Lotus, Intel, and Microsoft collaborated on an expanded memory specification. As a result, any PC, provided it has special hardware and the appropriate software drivers, can support expanded memory. Old 8088 CPU chip PCs with a special expanded memory board and driver software could access more than 640 K of memory. Expanded memory support came at a cost. The cost was that pages of memory had to be swapped between the conventional RAM and the expanded memory board in 8088 PCs. This swapping required the E upper memory block address segment to act as a paging area.

In 386 and above CPU chip PCs, expanded memory is created from extended memory using only special software. Expanded memory (EMS) in 386, 486, and Pentium chip systems is created from extended memory (XMS). It requires special software. In DOS and Windows 3x, the EMM386.EXE program creates expanded memory as well as provides access to the upper memory blocks. Expanded memory is divided into pages similar to sectors on a disk drive. The pages are moved as required into the conventional memory where the chip in real mode manipulates the data. Once finished, the page is swapped back to the expanded memory. This emulates the expanded memory operation that would be performed by an 8088 CPU chip PC. Since 386, 486, and Pentium chip PCs can address XMS directly, there is no need to perform the swapping. With these systems and Windows, it is possible to emulate EMS without actually performing any swapping between the XMS and the conventional memory areas.

Sometimes DOS also needed expanded memory as a generalized scheme to manage some of the memory in 386, 486, and Pentium chip PCs. Page swapping was performed, but this page swapping provided a scheme for DOS to effectively fit all types of programs and data into its expanded memory. The expanded memory emulation is performed using protected operating mode, HIMEM to manage HIMEM and the extended memory (XMS), and EMM386 to make extended memory emulate expanded memory (EMS).

Shadow ROM

Shadow ROM is a capability that is implemented in almost all PC hardware today. It is designed to speed up overall PC input/output operations. The speedup is accomplished by copying the contents of ROM into random access memory; because ROM is 15 times slower than RAM, copying the ROM routines into RAM speeds up the PC. Furthermore, since the ROM routines are used continuously, the speed increase provided by shadow RAM can be measured. From a practical point of view, only the most geeky PC users would notice the increase in speed achieved by using shadow ROM.

Virtual Memory

Windows PCs use virtual memory. Because it is impractical and costly to install huge amounts of RAM in a PC, Windows PCs make the disk drive appear to be RAM. They create a swap file on the disk drive that then becomes part of the 4 GB CPU address space. Application program components are continually moved between this fixed disk swap area and RAM while Windows is running. The virtual memory swap files vary in size

Figure 13–5 *Windows virtual memory layout*

depending on the amount of physical RAM installed in the PC. It is possible in Windows 3x and in Windows 95/98 to set aside a permanent swap file area on the fixed disk. However, the default Windows 95/98 installation sets up a temporary swap file which works fine for almost all Windows PCs. A permanent swap file is a potential cure for an out-of-memory error message from Windows 95/98. A general virtual memory layout of Windows 95/98 is shown in Figure 13–5.

CONFIG.SYS Memory Control Statements

The DOS CONFIG.SYS file is the principal control mechanism for memory management under DOS and Windows 3x. Because Windows 95 and Windows 98 have memory management built in, they do not require a CONFIG.SYS file to perform memory management functions. If a CONFIG.SYS file is used with Windows 95/98, it is to provide backwards compatibility with older DOS and Windows 3x programs.

The CONFIG.SYS file loads the XMS and HIMEM memory management program, HIMEM.SYS. It also loads the EMS and upper memory block memory management program, EMM386.EXE. The statements that act like keys to the upper memory areas and HIMEM area are also present in the CONFIG.SYS file. The statement DOS=HIGH, UMB opens these areas for use. A typical CONFIG.SYS file basic memory control commands are shown here.

```
DEVICE = C:\WINDOWS\HIMEM.SYS
DEVICE = C:\WINDOWS\EMM386.EXE noems i=e800-efff
DOS = HIGH
DOS = UMB
SHELL = c:\dos\command.com c:\dos\ /e:2048 /p
BUFFERS = 16
FILES = 64
STACKS = 0,0
LASTDRIVE = z
```

In the CONFIG.SYS file above, the first line loads the extended memory manager HIMEM.SYS. The second line loads the EMM386.EXE program to control the upper memory area and set up expanded memory when requested. In this case, the NOEMS parameter specifies that expanded memory not be used. The I=E800-EFFF parameter specifies including the E800–EFFF range in the upper memory blocks. The DOS=HIGH and the DOS=UMB lines unlock both a HIMEM area and the upper memory blocks for use by DOS.

HIMEM.SYS and EMM386.EXE

This exercise shows the impact of Windows 98 DOS HIMEM.SYS and EMM386.EXE.

1. Create a bootable Windows 98 diskette. This is accomplished by opening a DOS window and entering the command FORMAT A: /S. From the Windows directory, copy to this diskette HIMEM.SYS and EMM386.EXE. From the Windows\command folder, copy to the diskette DOS.COM, EDIT.COM, MEM..EXE, and SMARTDRV.EXE.

2. Use the edit program to create an AUTOEXEC.BAT file with the following line: LH DOSKEY.

3. Shut down Windows 98, place the diskette in the PC's floppy disk drive, and reboot into Windows 98 DOS from the diskette. (Be sure the CMOS setup is set to boot from a diskette drive first and then from the fixed disk drive.)

4. Once the PC is booted, run the MEM program to view the memory configuration. In this case, about 202 K of conventional memory should be used to contain DOS. XMS should be available for use by Windows. If the MEM /D./P command is used, it should show that DOSKEY is loaded into the PC's conventional memory.

5. Using the edit program, create a CONFIG.SYS file that contains the statements DEVICE=HIMEM.SYS and DOS=HIGH. Now reboot the PC. This time the MEM program should show about 139 K of conventional memory used for DOS.

6. Using the edit program, add to the CONFIG.SYS file the statements DEVICE=EMM386.EXE and DOS=UMB. Now reboot the PC and rerun the MEM program. This time, only about 60 K of conventional memory is used for DOS. In all cases, the DOSKEY program still loads into conventional memory.

7. Using the edit program, change the CONFIG.SYS file by removing the statements DEVICE=HIMEM.SYS and DOS=HIGH or by turning them into remarks using REM at the beginning of each line. Now reboot the PC. What error messages do you see?

This exercise illustrates the impact of HIMEM SYS and EMM386.EXE on memory for Windows 98 DOS. This exercise could also be performed with DOS 6.22. With DOS 6.2, though, the DOSKEY program is loaded into the upper memory blocks, making the resulting available conventional memory larger. Also, the process could be repeated with SMARTDRV.EXE included in the AUTOEXEC BAT file. The last and most important point here is that the results of changes in CONFIG.SYS and AUTOEXEC.BAT vary from DOS version to DOS version. If you have lots of PCs to support with a particular version of DOS, then perform an exercise with those PCs to see what memory configurations and errors are caused by the changes you make.

A+ 13.2 Memory Conflicts and Their Resolution

Memory conflicts cause several types of problems in PCs. The most common conflict is insufficient RAM. This problem most often manifests itself on DOS PCs running games. When DOS games are run on Windows PCs, similar problems can occur. Is also possible to have Windows programs run out of memory. There are different types of memory being used with Windows. Some of it is your everyday working RAM, while other parts of memory are heaps used to store graphics information. If any of these memory areas is exhausted, typically bad things happen to Windows. So it is not enough to focus on just having sufficient RAM to run programs, but rather one must look at the entire PC system and how the memory is used to ensure that programs operate without failure.

DOS versus Windows Memory Conflicts

Windows memory conflicts are generally different from those of DOS. DOS runs one application program at a time. It does some primitive multitasking between terminate-and-stay-resident (TSR) programs and application programs. As a result, it is possible to have memory usage conflicts. But this is a rare event.

DOS memory conflicts are resolved or rather prevented by careful loading of device drivers and TSR programs. Some EMM386.EXE configurations just do not work with some PCs' BIOS. In this case, you cannot use the advanced capabilities of EMM386.EXE and the DOS memory configuration program, MEMMAKER, to maximize available conventional memory. More conservative configurations are required for the PC to operate properly.

Memory usage conflicts are much more common with Windows. In the original Windows 3.0 such memory errors produced "unrecoverable application errors" (UAEs). When Windows 3.1 was released, Microsoft vowed to eliminate UAEs. This was accomplished by renaming the unrecoverable application errors to "general protection faults" (GPFs). A general protection fault error is displayed by Windows when it detects that more than one application program is requesting the same area of RAM. Windows then displays the GPF message, permitting you to shut down the offending programs before they crash Windows. Other Windows memory errors are signaled by "illegal operation" messages. Basically, all Windows error messages are caused by some memory conflict between programs running under Windows. So regardless of what error messages are called, they are all in some way caused by memory errors and thus are memory error messages.

General Protection Faults and Illegal Operation Errors

The single most common symptom of memory conflict problems was a general protection fault between the core Windows 95 programs—the kernel, the explorer, and the control panel programs. A typical general protection fault error message is illustrated in Figure 13–6.

There are six general Windows problem sources for general protection faults and illegal operation errors. These sources are:

- Hardware failures—Misconfigured I/O cards, failed disk, overheated CPU, memory signal errors, and more.
- Resource starvation—Software needs RAM, cannot get it, and stops.
- Memory Violations—Software needs RAM, cannot have it, steals it, causes page fault, then Windows shuts it down.
- Poor error handling—Software seeks file, file not found, doesn't know what to do, and quits.
- Racing hardware—A PC waits for printer response, while printer waits for PC response.
- Infinite loops—Software runs and runs and finds nothing.

Windows can also have memory problems when the GDI.EXE and the USER.EXE data heaps are exhausted. Both USER.EXE and GDI.EXE are key Windows programs. The USR.EXE program receives input from the user and provides window and menu management functions. The GDI.EXE pro-

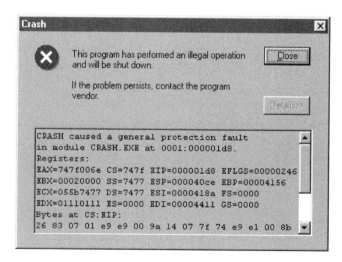

Figure 13–6 *GPF error message*

gram handles graphics, manages fonts, supports printing, and other graphics functions.

Heaps are areas of memory that get allocated to satisfy different application memory requests. Windows has both local heaps and global heaps. A local heap is contained within an applications address space, while global heaps are in the areas belonging to the system. Changes in a local heap as requested by an application require adjustments to the application's memory space. Global changes affect the shared system memory pool.

With Windows 3.x, software conflicts often caused the entire Windows environment to crash. Sixteen-bit Windows application programs sharing the same Windows virtual machine cause this. Windows virtual machines were discussed in Chapter 11. Basically, a Windows virtual machine is an imaginary PC that an application exclusively controls or shares with other applications.

In other words, all 16-bit applications ran in one single Windows virtual machine. This was changed in Windows 95/98. Similarly to Windows 3x, Windows 95/98 runs DOS applications in separate virtual machines and runs 16-bit Windows 3x applications in a single Windows 3x virtual machine. However, Windows 95/98 32-bit applications now run in separate virtual machines. Each 32-bit application has its own virtual machine, separate from the other 32-bit applications. If a single 32-bit application misbehaves, its virtual machine can be killed off. The remaining 32-bit applications would still be running in their own individual virtual machines. Because each 32-bit application works within its own virtual machine, software conflicts are reduced and Windows 95/98 reliability is increased.

Resolving Windows Problems

There are several ways to resolve Windows problems. Most often, resolving Windows problems requires reinstalling the offending software. In many cases, it can require reinstallation of Windows itself. While there may be a simple single parameter change in the software that can resolve the problem, this single change is not easy to identify. As a result, the quickest and easiest way to resolve problems with Windows software is reinstallation of the Windows software.

For example, Windows 95 would sometimes attempt to start, but instead it would freeze before the desktop was set up. Windows stopped and left you suspended with a blank desktop displaying its background pattern or wallpaper and a moving mouse pointer. However, there was nothing to select with the mouse.

In this case, restarting the PC at the command prompt and running SCANDISK to fix the directory and file structure on the disk drive solved the problem. In the process, SCANDISK (DOS) often would report directories corrupted and create several DIR000xx files. If this did not resolve the problem, then the solution was to "burn the field" and reinstall Windows 95. Reinstallation places a fresh copy of Windows 95 over the corrupted copy. The cause of this problem was a mismatch between the PC's system ROMs and the Windows 95 SCSI disk drivers.

Minor problems are evidenced by innocuous symptoms. These can be as simple as an application program locking up under Windows 95 or the warning icon displayed for installed hardware options. In most cases, reinstallation of the offending hardware or software cures the error message.

Software problems can freeze Windows 95. Because of the preemptive multitasking, the PC is most likely not totally frozen. The Ctrl-Alt-Del warm reboot keys jump you to the Windows 95/98 task manager window. The task manager window is shown in Figure 13–7. Usually, this permits you to kill off offending programs or to shut down the PC. When loading and operating too many programs with Windows 95/98 causes software conflicts, simply restarting Windows cures the problem. If a problem persists with a specific program, then uninstalling and reinstalling that software program may correct the problem. Such procedures generally work okay, but there is no guarantee.

When Windows itself has become corrupted, then a complete reinstallation is often the solution. Sometimes the registry misdirects Windows (the Windows control structure that controls loading Windows and application software components). The registry is discussed in Chapter 11.

Figure 13–7   *Task manager window*

A common example of this is a Windows general memory protection error. A faulty registry setting generates this error message. Unfortunately, the registry cannot be fixed because Windows refuses to start and displays the general memory protection error message. A reinstallation of Windows corrects this registry problem. It is also possible (but not recommended) to copy a good registry that is exactly matched to the PC's hardware and software configuration over the old corrupted registry to solve this problem. If the PC's hardware and software configuration do not match, then copying registries can potentially cause more work straightening out the configuration with the copied registry than reinstalling Windows from scratch.

With hardware problems, using the control panel to delete the hardware component before restarting Windows 95 often clears up the hardware problem. This can require some tricky footwork if the hardware malfunction locks the PC. In this case, Windows must be started in safe mode with a limited set of hardware drivers.

 You can force Windows to enter safe mode by holding down the shift key during the Windows restart process.

Figure 13–8 shows the safe mode warning display. When this happens, Windows defaults to the lowest resolution VGA display operation. The control panel functions can be used to remove or change the properties assigned to hardware components.

To change or configure the PC hardware, enter the control panel and select the system icon. Next, click on the device manager tab. This reveals a hierarchical list of devices starting with CD-ROM and ending with system devices.

Figure 13–8 *Windows safe mode notification message*

The device manager under the Windows control panel uses several different icons to indicate the status of the device. For example when a device has been disabled in a hardware profile, a red "X" appears over the device. Devices that have potential problems may display a yellow triangular warning sign with a "!" in the middle. Generally, any device displaying a warning signal has potential configuration problems.

Clicking on a device entry reveals the devices installed in the PC under that entry. For example, clicking on ports (COM & LPT) typically reveals entries for communications and printer ports. Clicking on the entry for the printer port highlights it, permitting us to then select properties from the menu below the entry window. When properties is selected, we then see a tab for resources, permitting us to manually set the port hardware parameters (IRQ, port address, and DMA channel) for the printer port as shown by Figure 13–9. In the figure the panel on the left shows a printer port that is properly installed. When Windows detects hardware conflicts, it displays a panel like the one on the right. This panel is requesting that the configuration be set manually to resolve the resource conflicts that Windows has encountered. The manual configuration panel would be displayed if the PC is booted in Windows safe mode.

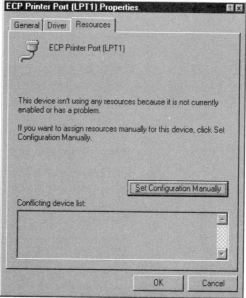

Figure 13–9   *Setting manual configuration in safe mode*

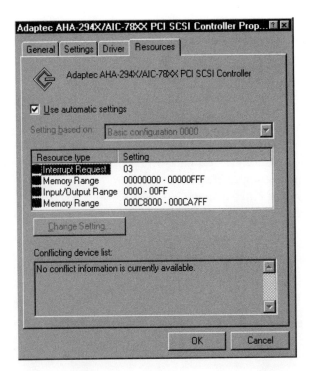

Figure 13-10 *Adaptec SCSI controller properties*

When the set configuration manually selection is clicked on, a new panel appears, permitting us to specify automatic configuration or to manually configure hardware for the card. For example, configuring a SCSI card would require setting interrupt request, input/output port range, and memory ranges for SCSI ROM. If this SCSI card was an older ISA bus card, the settings selected for Windows would need to match exactly the settings selected by the jumpers and switches on the SCSI card. Figure 13-10 shows settings for an Adaptec SCSI card.

As each resource type is selected, conflicts with resource allocations of all the devices are identified to assist in selecting a resource configuration that has no conflicts. Windows 95/98 does not necessarily identify all conflicts in this manner. There are some conflicts that are not readily apparent from the display. In this case, even though no conflicts are indicated, the device fails to work properly with the resource settings specified. To resolve such problems, one keeps selecting new resources for the device until the device begins to work because the hidden conflict is resolved. Such hidden conflicts are most often memory range conflicts, although some have been input/output port conflicts.

There are a couple of system tools that Windows provides to help improve the PC's performance and identify depleted resources. These tools are the system monitor and the system resource meter.

System Monitor

Windows 95/98 has a system monitor program that can display activity of the PC's CPU, disk, and network components. Figure 13–11 shows a typical system monitor display. While the system monitor provides an interesting display, the usefulness of this monitoring program is somewhat limited. Since Windows automatically sets many of the operating parameters for the CPU, disk, and network, there is little tuning left to the PC user. This means that even if we were to configure the system monitor program to provide information which indicated disk caching problems, we would not likely be able to modify Windows disk cache operation to improve performance. The system monitor in some circumstances can help us improve the PC's performance. When the PC is slow, we use a system monitor to identify whether it is CPU bound, has problems with disk caching, or is I/O bound. By setting up the system monitor to track CPU utilization, disk cache activity, and I/O

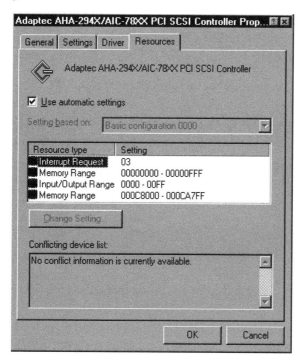

Figure 13–11 *System monitor display*

operations, we may be generally able to identify the type of performance constraint.

A more useful Windows 95/98 diagnostic tool is the system resource meter.

System Resource Meter

The system resource meter monitors consumption of the system resource heaps. It provides a taskbar icon display of resource utilization that uses green to indicate sufficient resources are available to run Windows programs. The icon changes to yellow and then to red as the system resources are exhausted. Figure 13–12 shows the more detailed system resource meter percent free display of the system, USER, and GDI memory heaps.

By double-clicking on the taskbar icon for the system resource meter, a more detailed display appears. This display shows the current utilization of each of the key windows resource heaps. The system resource meter diagnostic program has been provided with Windows 3.x as well as Windows 95/98.

Generally, to launch new Windows application programs, the resource meter should indicate that all heaps have at least 60 percent free resources available. These resources are consumed by Windows applications as they use fonts and other graphics objects. Printing also consumes huge amounts of space from the system resource heaps. Sometimes Windows programs do not return the resources to the heaps when they are closed. Consequently, when lots of programs are used and then shut down, after a period of time, Windows itself must be shut down and restarted to clean up the memory and restore the resources to the resource heaps.

MEMMAKER

MEMMAKER is the DOS program used to automatically configure the PC's RAM for Windows use. MEMMAKER was delivered with DOS 6.x. MEM-

Figure 13–12
System resource meter detailed display

```
DEVICE = C:\DOS\EMM386.EXE NOEMS x=b000-b7ff ROM=c000-c7ff x=d800-dfff ROM=f000-ffff
```

An EMM386.EXE configuration using no Expanded Memory and excluding VGA and System ROM areas.

```
DEVICE = C:\DOS\EMM386.EXE NOEMS HIGHSCAN ROM=c000-c7ff ROM=f000-ffff
```

An EMM386.EXE configuration using no Expanded Memory that scans upper memory aggressively and excludes VGA and System ROM areas.

```
DEVICE = C:\DOS\EMM386.EXE NOEMS ROM=c000-c7ff ROM=d800-dfff ROM=f000-ffff WIN=D500-D7FF WIN=D200-D4FF
```

An EMM386.EXE configuration using no Expanded Memory that excludes VGA and System ROM areas and is optimized for Windows use.

Figure 13–13 *MEMMAKER-modified CONFIG.SYS EMM386.EXE*

MAKER optimizes the PC memory by moving memory-resident programs and hardware device drivers into the upper memory blocks. The goal here is to free conventional memory for Windows 3.x use. MEMMAKER is not required for Windows 95/98/NT. Figure 13–13 illustrates CONFIG.SYS file commands modified by MEMMAKER.

Figure 13–13 focuses on the EMM386.EXE command line in CONFIG.SYS. In each case, the NOEMS parameter specifies that no expanded memory should be set aside. The X= commands are used to exclude upper memory areas. The ROM= commands identify upper memory areas occupied by ROMs. The C000–C7FF range is used by the VGA adapter ROM. The F000–FFFF memory range is used by system ROM. The HIGHSCAN command specifies releasing ROM memory areas that are used only once during the boot process and reusing them as upper memory blocks to store device driver software. The WIN= command assigns an upper memory area for Windows use exclusively. A brief explanation of each EMM386.EXE command line appears below it in the figure.

MEMMAKER automatically cycles through a series of menus to determine how to configure the PC RAM. It performs a loading process based upon the sequence in which the device drivers and programs are loaded in CONFIG.SYS and AUTOEXEC.BAT. Sometimes MEMMAKER's results can be improved by changing the sequence or order that the device drivers and the AUTOEXEC.BAT programs are loaded in.

MEMMAKER uses the space bar to change menu selections. This is not what is done typically with most other programs. After MEMMAKER is started, it permits you to select express or custom setup. In the custom setup, MEMMAKER first asks you if you have any programs that need expanded memory (EMS). Next, the advanced options permit you to specify selecting drivers and TSR programs to include in optimization, or to select them all.

We encountered some SCSI adapter drivers that could not be configured using MEMMAKER. The remaining advanced options, as shown in Figure 13–14, cover scanning upper memory aggressively, optimizing memory for use with Windows, using the monochrome display swapping area (B000–B7FF) to contain programs, keeping current memory exclusions and inclusions, and moving the extended BIOS data area from conventional to upper memory. Once these selections are complete, MEMMAKER checks to see if Windows is installed on the PC. It then optimizes the device drivers loaded by CONFIG.SYS and the programs loaded by AUTOEXEC.BAT. This process requires reboot of the PC, permitting MEMMAKER to observe how the programs are loaded and the amount of memory they require and then determine which region in the upper memory blocks can be used to load and then run the device driver or program.

Figure 13–15 shows a single memory region, Region 1, in the upper memory area.

Regions are assigned numeric values—for instance, 1, 2, 3. The resulting CONFIG.SYS and DOS statements specify the region into which the device driver or program is to be loaded. The memory configurations produced by MEMMAKER were very good. Occasionally, Windows 3.x would not run properly. This happened most often when the upper memory was scanned aggressively using the HIGHSCAN option.

In this case, it appeared as though scanning the memory aggressively by itself produced the problem. Removing the HIGHSCAN option from the EMM386.EXE command line permitted the PC to run Windows 3.x properly. This problem was readily recognized because Windows 3.1x would just

```
Microsoft MemMaker


                         Advanced Options


  Specify which drivers and TSRs to include in optimization?      No
  Scan the upper memory area aggressively?                        No
  Optimize upper memory for use with Windows?                     No
  Use monochrome region (B000-B7FF) for running programs?         No
  Keep current EMM386 memory exclusions and inclusions?           Yes
  Move Extended BIOS Data Area from conventional to upper memory? Yes



  To select a different option, press the UP ARROW or DOWN ARROW key.
  To accept all the settings and continue, press ENTER.



ENTER=Accept All  SPACEBAR=Change Selection  F1=Help  F3=Exit
```

Figure 13–14 *MEMMAKER advanced options*

```
Free Conventional Memory:
   Segment          Total
   -------     ----------------
    00B38              80     (0K)
    00BBE            1to76     (0K)
    011C6          88,992    (87K)
    02780         493,472   (482K)
  Total Free: 582,720   (569K)

Free Upper Memory:
   Region   Largest Free      Total Free        Total Size
   ------   -------------    ------------     --------------
        1   17,504  (17K)   17,600  (17K)   174,976 (171K)
```

Figure 13–15 *MEMMAKER region assignment*

lock when Windows was started. Whenever Windows locks, it is typically a memory conflict that is the source of the problem.

HIMEM.SYS

HIMEM.SYS is the device driver that controls HIMEM and EXTENDED (XMS) memory. HIMEM has some parameters that modify its operation. In almost all cases, these parameters are rarely used. The HIMEM parameters include the /M: parameter, which designates machine type. This may overcome some operating difficulties with different types of PCs. Defined machine types are shown in Figure 13–16.

Other HIMEM parameters include:

```
REM /a20control:[on|off]
```

Determines whether HIMEM.SYS controls the A20 line. The default is on. When on is specified, control is assumed only if A20 was off when loaded. The A20 line is a hardware interrupt line that activates the software for accessing the high memory area (HMA). The high memory area is the first 64 K above the 1 MB memory address boundary. With HIMEM controlling the A20 line, software operation should be more reliable and predictable.

```
REM /int15=xxx
```

Allocates extended memory for interrupt 15 interface. The default is zero bytes. Range 64 to 64 K bytes. Older DOS applications sometimes use the interrupt 15h interface to allocate extended memory instead of using the XMS (eXtended Memory Specification) method provided by HIMEM.

Number	Name	Computer type
1	AT	; IBM AT or 100% compatible.
1	JDR	; JDR 386/33
1	COMPUADD	; COMPUADD 386 systems or /m:8
2	PS-2	; IBM PS/2
2	DATAMEDIA	; Datamedia 386/486
2	UNISYS	; UNISYS PowerPort
3	PTLCascade	; Phoenix Cascade BIOS
4	HPVectra	; HP Vectra (A & A+)
5	ATT6300plus	; AT&T 6300 Plus
6	ACER1100	; Acer 1100
7	Toshiba	; Toshiba 5100, 1600 & 1200XE
8	Wyse	; Wyse 12.5 Mhz 286
8	Hitachi	; Hitachi HL500C
8	Intel	; Intel 301z or 302
8	Phoenix	; Phoenix BIOS or /m:1
12,13,14	IBM-PC	; Other IBM PC machines.
16	Bull	; Bull Micral 60

Figure 13–16 *HIMEM machine type parameters*

When such applications are encountered, manually setting the xxx value to 64 K larger than the extended memory required by the application provides enough memory for them.

REM /shadowram:[on|off]

Specifies whether HIMEM.SYS should switch off shadow RAM. When there is less than 2 Mb of RAM, the default is off; more than 2 Mb, the default is on.

REM /cpuclock:[on|off]

Determines if HIMEM changes CPU clock speed. When clock speed slows upon loading HIMEM, try on. Selecting on slows HIMEM.SYS and programs using extended memory. Default is off.

SMARTDRV

SMARTDRV.EXE is the Microsoft disk-caching program. A caching program works on the 80/20 rule of computers. There are always 80/20 rules, like the IRS 80/20 rule—they get 80 and you get 20. The 80/20 computer rule goes something like this—80% of the times you need new data, it is in the next memory location after the data you just used. So if the PC were to read a lot of data off the fixed disk into RAM, it is very likely the data the PC needs next is in RAM and not on the slower fixed disk.

SMARTDRV caches data transfers to or from the PC's fixed disk. SMARTDRV works in XMS or in the upper memory area. It is one of the few programs that will split itself between XMS and the upper memory area. SMARTDRV requires 2 MB of RAM for optimal operation. However, drive performance improvements are realized using as little as 256 K of RAM.

Depending on the amount of installed RAM in older PCs, SMART-DRV would adjust its memory size. Table 13–1 gives the SMARTDRV cache size for several different XMS memory sizes. This is a moot point today because most PCs come with more than 16 Mb of RAM. Further, cache size would vary depending upon whether Windows was being run or whether the PC was being operated with DOS alone. Typical SMARTDRV configurations are:

Table 13.1 *XMS size versus SMARTDRV cache allocation*

XMS Size	DOS Cache Size	Windows Cache Size
1 to 2 MB	1 MB	256 K
2 to 4 MB	1 MB	512 K
4 to 6 MB	2 MB	1 MB
over 6 MB	2 MB	2 MB—Optimal for SMARTDRV

The Device=c:\dos\SMARTDRV.EXE /double_buffer is entered in the CONFIG.SYS file to install double buffering for SCSI disk drives. The double_buffer SMARTDRV option is required to prevent some SCSI disk drive controllers from trashing the data they store on the fixed disk drive. It slightly diminishes (about a 4% reduction) the PC's disk performance. Double buffering ensures that the data address is correctly translated by the SCSI disk controller to the correct physical allocation unit (groups of sectors) address.

To determine whether double_buffer is required, first install double buffering with SMARTDRV, then run SMARTDRV /S at the DOS prompt. If double buffering is not required, the buffering column states no. When double buffering may be required, a "-" is displayed. A yes indicates that double buffering should be used. SMARTDRV status displays illustrating double buffering requirements are shown in Figures 13-17 and 13-18.

In Figure 13–17 the buffering status for fixed disk drives C and D as well as the CD-ROM drive E is displayed as no. This means that double buffering is not required for these drives. Figure 13-18 displays a different result.

For drives C and D, the yes status indicates that double buffering is required for these drives. The "-" status display for the E (CD-ROM) drive indicates that double buffering may be required for that drive. However, since it is a CD-ROM drive, data cannot be corrupted on the drive so for this drive, double buffering is optional.

Double buffering prevents some SCSI disk controller cards from trashing data on the fixed disk drive by helping them resolve the differences between the virtual data address provided by SMARTDRV and the actual address used on the disk drive.

```
Microsoft SMARTDrive Disk Cache version 5.0
Copyright 1991,1993 Microsoft Corp.
     Room for   2,048 elements of   8,192 bytes each
There have been   24,535 cache hits   and   2,208 cache misses
Cache size:  16,777,216 bytes
Cache size while running Windows:  16,777,216 bytes
            Disk Caching Status
drive    read cache   write cache   buffering
-------------------------------------------------
  A:        yes          no           no
  B:        yes          no           no
  C:        yes          yes          no <== Not Required
  D:        yes          yes          no <== Not Required
  E:        yes          yes          no <== Not Required
Write behind data will be committed before command prompt returns.
For help, type "SMARTDRV /?"
```

Figure 13–17 *Double buffering not required*

```
Microsoft SMARTDrive Disk Cache version 5.0
Copyright 1991,1993 Microsoft Corp.
     Room for   2,048 elements of   8,192 bytes each
There have been   24,535 cache hits   and   2,208 cache misses
```

Figure 13–18 *Double buffering required*

```
Cache size:  16,777,216 bytes
Cache size while running Windows:  16,777,216 bytes
            Disk Caching Status
drive    read cache    write cache   buffering
-------------------------------------------------
  A:        yes           no          no
  B:        yes           no          no
  C:        yes           yes         yes <== Required
  D:        yes           yes         yes <== Required
  E:        yes           yes          -  <== Possibly Required
Write behind data will be committed before command prompt returns.
For help, type "SMARTDRV /?".
```

Figure 13–18 *Double buffering required*

EMM386.EXE and Upper Memory Blocks

EMM386.EXE is the expanded memory manager program that makes extended memory look like expanded memory. EMM386 is also the program that manages access to the upper memory blocks (UMBs). There are several options for EMM386. The most commonly used parameter options are:

- AUTO—Automatically provides type of memory program requests, extended or expanded.
- RAM—Provides access to both expanded and the upper memory blocks (UMBs).
- X= 0x000-0y000—Exclude this memory range from use. Most often required when LAN boards are used.
- m9—Set the EMS page frame in the 0E000 to 0EFFF memory segment. Other choices might be

```
m1 = C000m8 = DC00
m2 = C400m9 = E000
m3 = C800m10= 8000
m4 = CC00m11= 8400
m5 = D000m12= 8800
m6 = D400m13= 8C00
m7 = D800m14= 9000
```

- NOHI—causes EMM386.EXE to load into conventional memory

- /Frame=—Sets the page frame location. /Frame=NONE runs EMS without the page frame using 64 K. Memory pages and frames are described at the beginning of this chapter.
- DOS=HIGH, UMB—This causes DOS and other programs to be loaded first into HIMEM and then into the upper memory blocks.

The memory address calculator in Figure 13–19 can be used to determine the locations of ROM and RAM buffer areas used in a PC's conventional memory, upper memory blocks, and HIMEM areas. These areas are accessed by 286, 386, 486, and Pentium chips when operating in real mode. In protected and other operating modes, the 286, 386, 486, and Pentium chips address extended, and with special software, expanded memory areas.

To locate a specific memory address, for instance, CC00, divide the address into two halves, CC and 00. Use the left half (CC) to locate first row C then column C. Next, use the right half, 00, to locate the side of the cell. The left side is 00 and the right side is FF. This approach is used in both Figure 13–19 and Figure 13–20 to locate areas in the upper memory blocks that are used for hardware ROM and hardware memory paging.

Each verticle increment is 64 Kb of memory starting from address 00000 represented by 0. The upper 640 Kb boundary 0A000 is represented by A.

Each horizontal increment or box is 4 Kb. Thus the VGA ROM that is 32 Kb in size uses addresses from 0C000 to 0C800.

Figure 13–19 *Blank memory address calculator*

Each verticle increment is 64 Kb of memory starting from address 00000 represented by 0. The upper 640 Kb boundary 0A000 is represented by A.

Each horizontal increment or box is 4 Kb. Thus the VGA ROM that is 32 Kb in size uses addresses from 0C000 to 0C800 as illustrated above.

Figure 13–20 *Memory address calculator.*

The memory address calculator in Figure 13–20 has had the conventional, VGA display, expanded memory page frame, system BIOS ROM, VGA ROM (video BIOS), and HIMEM areas identified. CMOS is located in the conventional memory area.

The page frame area is set by software, so it may be moved from the E000 memory segment to any other contiguous (unbroken stretch) of free memory. This shows about 64 + 32 or 96 K of free upper memory blocks available for holding hardware device drivers and other memory-resident programs.

Study Break

Understanding Upper Memory Blocks

This exercise uses the memory address calculators to locate areas of memory commonly used by VGA adapters, system ROM, and LAN cards.

1. Use the blank memory address calculator in Figure 13–19 to locate the address range C000–C7FF. This is a typical address range used by the VGA adapter ROM. Split C000 into

C0 and 00. Use C0 to identify the C row and the 0 column. The 00 address is on the left-hand side of the C0 block. Similarly, split the C7FF address into its C7 and FF components. Again C identifies the row and 7 identifies the column. The FF address is on the right-hand side of the C7 block. In Figure 13–20, this address range is highlighted as the VGA ROM address range. It is 32 K in size.

2. Repeat the process to locate the address range from 0000 to 90FF. This is the address range labeled conventional memory in Figure 13–20.

3. Use the same process once again to locate the address range from F000 to FFFF. In Figure 13–20 this address range is labeled the system ROM address range.

4. Run MSD and use the memory option to verify the VGA ROM address range and system ROM address range in your PC.

The purpose of this exercise was to familiarize you with the high memory area (HMA) hardware ROM address assignments typical of most PCs.

A+ 13.3   PC DOS Memory Setup

As a final look at PC memory setup under DOS, we will go step-by-step and configure PC RAM to illustrate the impact of each program in the memory configuration process.

Memory management under DOS is similar for almost all versions. DOS 6.x provides the MEMMAKER program to automatically configure a PC's RAM. It gives more precise control for loading programs into upper memory blocks. Finally, it provides an understandable MEM program. This lets you view your PC's RAM more accurately.

The bad news is that when DOS 6.x data compression and virus protection are used, you end up with significantly less memory. The DOS 6.x memory tests shown start with no memory usage and then add in driver programs to show the impact on free memory caused by changes in the CONFIG.SYS and AUTOEXEC.BAT files. We start with DOS 6.x in conventional memory. DOUBLESPACE is loaded automatically by DOS in the event that disk compression is desired. We start with no AUTOEXEC.BAT and CONFIG.SYS files, making DOS use its default values. Total conventional memory available at this time is 534 K. Figure 13–21 was created using the DOS MEM program after the PC was rebooted into DOS with no AUTOEXEC.BAT and CONFIG.SYS files.

```
Memory: _____

Modules using memory below 1 Mb:

Name            Total       =  Conventional    +   Upper Memory

--------     ---------------     ----------------     -------------

MSDOS         58397   (57K)       58397   (57K)           0   (0K)

DBLSPACE      44944   (44K)       44944   (44K)           0   (0K)

COMMAND        4992    (5K)        4992    (5K)           0   (0K)

Free         546944  (534K)      546944  (534K)           0   (0K)


Memory Summary:


Type of Memory       Total     =     Used     +    Free

---------------   --------------    --------------   --------------

Conventional      655360 (640K)    108416 (106K)   46944   (534K)

Upper                  0   (0K)         0   (0K)        0    (0K)

Adapter RAM/ROM   393216 (384K)    393216 (384K)        0    (0K)

Extended (XMS)   3145728(3072K)   3145728(3072K)        0    (0K)

--------------   --------------    --------------   --------------

Total memory     4194304(4096K)   3647360(3562K)  546944   (534K)


Total under 1Mb   655360 (640K)    108416 (106K)  546944   (534K)

Largest executable program size             546928    (534K)

Largest free upper memory block                  0    (0K)

Environment Space: _____

PATH=C:\DOS

PROMPT=$P$G

COMSPEC=C:\COMMAND.COM
```

Figure 13–21   *DOS memory configuration without CONFIG.SYS and AUTOEXEC.BAT*

The first step is to add a PATH statement and some SET statements to the AUTOEXEC.BAT file. There are no changes to CONFIG.SYS.

The DOS defaults for files and buffers are added to the CONFIG.SYS file. When the defaults are hit exactly, no reductions or increases are made to conventional memory.

```
AUTOEXEC.BAT:
prompt $p $g
path c:\;c:\dos;c:\win;
set temp=d:\temp
set tmp=d:\temp


CONFIG.SYS:
files=8
buffers=15
break=on
lastdrive=Z
stacks=9,128
fcbs=1,10


Memory:
Modules using memory below 1 Mb:
Name            Total      =   Conventional   +   Upper Memory
--------     --------------     --------------     ------------
MSDOS           58397  (57K)      58397  (57K)        0    (0K)
DBLSPACE        44944  (44K)      44944  (44K)        0    (0K)
COMMAND          4992   (5K)       4992   (5K)        0    (0K)
Free           546880 (534K)     546880 (534K)        0    (0K)
Memory Summary:
Type of Memory       Total     =     Used     +    Free
----------------  -------------    -------------  -------------
Conventional      655360 (640K)   108480 (106K) 546880  (534K)
Upper                  0   (0K)        0   (0K)      0    (0K)
Adapter RAM/ROM   393216 (384K)   393216 (384K)      0    (0K)
Extended (XMS)   3145728(3072K)  3145728(3072K)      0    (0K)
--------------   -------------    -------------  -------------
Total memory     4194304(4096K)  3647424(3562K) 546880  (534K)
Total under 1 Mb 655360 (640K)   108480 (106K) 546880  (534K)
Largest executable program size        546784   (534K)
Largest free upper memory block             0    (0K)
```

Figure 13–22 *DOS memory configuration with CONFIG.SYS and AUTOEXEC.BAT default values*

In the MEM program output above, the largest executable program size remains the same from our initial configuration. We can see that the programs using memory are MSDOS, the DBLSPACE disk cache program, and COMMAND.COM. The resulting environment space variables are:

```
Environment Space: _____
COMSPEC=C:\COMMAND.COM
PROMPT=$p $g
PATH=C:\;C:\DOS;C:\WIN;C:\QEMM;C:\NETW;
TEMP=d:\temp
TMP=d:\temp
```

The HIMEM program is run with the DOS=HIGH to unlock the HIMEM area. DOS uses HIMEM only when it is unlocked by the DOS=HIGH command. Next, we use the CONFIG.SYS file below and reboot our PC. In our new CONFIG.SYS, a REM statement stops DOS from loading into the high memory area (HMA).

```
CONFIG.SYS: _____
device=HIMEM.SYS
REM DOS=HIGH
files=8
buffers=15
break=on
Lastdrive=Z
stacks=9,128
Fcbs=1,10
```

The MEM program results also show that 64 K of XMS are being used. This 64 K is the HIMEM area. Once HIMEM is run to utilize the XMS, MEM shows the 64 K HIMEM area as being used regardless of whether it is occupied by programs or not. In our example, we lose 4 K of conventional memory because it is needed to run HIMEM. This reduces the available conventional memory to 530 K.

```
Modules using memory below 1 Mb:
  Name           Total        =   Conventional    +   Upper Memory
  --------    ----------------    ----------------    -------------
  MSDOS         58413   (57K)       58413   (57K)          0   (0K)
  HIMEM          3792    (4K)        3792    (4K)          0   (0K)
  DBLSPACE      44944   (44K)       44944   (44K)          0   (0K)
  COMMAND        4992    (5K)        4992    (5K)          0   (0K)
  Free         543088  (530K)      543088  (530K)          0   (0K)

Memory Summary:

  Type of Memory       Total      =      Used      +    Free
  ----------------  ------------      -------------   --------------
  Conventional       655360 (640K)    112272 (110K) 543088   (530K)
  Upper                   0   (0K)         0   (0K)      0     (0K)
  Adapter RAM/ROM    393216 (384K)    393216 (384K)      0     (0K)
  Extended (XMS)    3145728(3072K)     65536  (64K)3080192   (3008K)
  ----------------  ------------      -------------   --------------
  Total memory      4194304(4096K)    571024 (558K)3623280   (3538K)

  Total under 1 Mb 655360 (640K)     112272 (110K) 543088   (530K)

  Largest executable program size        542992    (530K)
  Largest free upper memory block             0     (0K)
  The high memory area is available.
```

Figure 13–23 *DOS memory configuration with CONFIG.SYS loading HIMEM.SYS*

Next, the HIMEM area is unlocked by the DOS=HIGH command. Notice that the REM preceding the device = HIMEM.SYS statement has been removed. This activates the DOS=HIGH line in the CONFIG.SYS file.

```
CONFIG.SYS: _____
device=HIMEM.SYS
DOS=HIGH
```

```
files=8
buffers=15
break=on
Lastdrive=Z
stacks=9,128
Fcbs=1,10
```

In this case, we gain conventional memory because DOS components have been moved to the high memory area (HMA) and we pick up an additional 50 K of conventional memory (increasing conventional memory to 580 K) as a result.

```
Modules using memory below 1 Mb:
  Name           Total        =   Conventional    +   Upper Memory
  --------    ----------------    ----------------     ------------

  MSDOS          13277  (13K)       13277  (13K)           0   (0K)
  HIMEM           1168   (1K)        1168   (1K)           0   (0K)
  DBLSPACE       44224  (43K)       44224  (43K)           0   (0K)
  COMMAND         2992   (3K)        2992   (3K)           0   (0K)
  Free          593568 (580K)      593568 (580K)           0   (0K)


Memory Summary:

  Type of Memory      Total     =      Used     +   Free
  ---------------  -------------    -------------  --------------

  Conventional     655360 (640K)     61792  (60K) 593568   (580K)
  Upper                 0   (0K)         0   (0K)      0     (0K)
  Adapter RAM/ROM  393216 (384K)    393216 (384K)      0     (0K)
  Extended (XMS)  3145728(3072K)     65536  (64K)3080192  (3008K)
  ---------------  -------------    -------------  --------------

  Total memory    4194304(4096K)    520544 (508K)3673760  (3588K)


  Total under 1 Mb 655360 (640K)     61792  (60K) 593568   (580K)


  Largest executable program size           593472   (580K)
  Largest free upper memory block                0     (0K)
  MS-DOS is resident in the high memory area.
```

Figure 13-24 *DOS memory configuration with DOS=HIGH activated*

Next EMM386.EXE is run to access the upper memory blocks (UMBs) and expanded memory (EMS), if required. Our CONFIG.SYS file has been modified to include be EMM386.EXE and DOS=UMB commands that configure and enable the upper memory blocks.

```
CONFIG.SYS: _____
device=HIMEM.SYS
DOS=HIGH
Device=EMM386.EXE
DOS=UMB
files=8
buffers=15
break=on
lastdrive=Z
stacks=9,128
fcbs=1,10
```

Notice we have less conventional RAM but have gained 91 K of upper memory.

```
Modules using memory below 1 Mb:
  Name          Total       =  Conventional  +  Upper Memory

  --------   ----------------   ----------------   -------------

  MSDOS        13293    (13K)     13293   (13K)        0    (0K)

  HIMEM         1168     (1K)      1168    (1K)        0    (0K)

  EMM386        3120     (3K)      3120    (3K)        0    (0K)

  DBLSPACE     44224    (43K)     44224   (43K)        0    (0K)

  COMMAND       2992     (3K)      2992    (3K)        0    (0K)

  Free        683712   (668K)    590432  (577K)    93280   (91K)


Memory Summary:


  Type of Memory      Total    =    Used     +    Free

  ---------------   -------------   -------------   --------------

  Conventional    655360 (640K)    64928  (63K) 590432   (577K)

  Upper            93280  (91K)        0   (0K)  93280    (91K)

  Adapter RAM/ROM 393216 (384K)   393216 (384K)      0     (0K)

  Extended (XMS)* 3052448 2981K)    496544485K)     25559(2496K)

  ---------------   -------------   -------------   --------------

  Total memory    4194304(4096K)   954688 (932K)3239616   (3164K)


  Total under 1 Mb 748640 (731K)    64928  (63K) 683712   (668K)


  Total Expanded (EMS)                3473408   (3392K)
  Free Expanded (EMS)*                2801664   (2736K)


  * EMM386 is using XMS memory to simulate EMS memory as needed.
    Free EMS memory may change as free XMS memory changes.


  Largest executable program size    590336    (577K)
  Largest free upper memory block      93280    (91K)
  MS-DOS is resident in the high memory area.
```

Figure 13–25 *DOS memory configuration with EMM386 and UMBs enabled*

At this point, several more steps were taken to configure the DOS memory. The SHELL command increased the DOS environment space to 2,000 characters. This reduced conventional memory by 1,744 characters (2000–256 bytes = 1744) because 256 bytes are already allocated to the environment space. The upper memory remained unchanged.

The DEVICE=ANSI.SS was added to the CONFIG.SYS file. This reduced conventional memory by about 4 K. The upper memory remained unchanged.

Next, the DEVICEHIGH= was added to the CONFIG.SYS file for both DBLSPACE and ANSI.SYS to restore the conventional memory. This resulted in about 618 K of conventional memory and 44 K remaining in upper memory.

The files were increased to 64 and the buffers to 32. The file increase reduced conventional memory to about 615 K, with 44 K remaining in upper memory.

The SMARTDRV program automatically loaded high. However, DOSKEY loaded into conventional memory. This reduced conventional memory to about 611 K, with 17 K remaining in upper memory.

Next, the DOSKEY program was loaded high using the LH command. This reduced conventional memory to about 604 K, with 24 K remaining in upper memory. Because SMARTDRV was loaded into both conventional memory and upper memory, less conventional memory is left than if DOSKEY had been loaded directly into conventional memory. However, by loading DOSKEY as the last program, conventional memory is restored to 615 K and upper memory is reduced to 13 K. The rule is to load large programs first and small programs last to provide DOS the best opportunity to fit all programs into the upper memory areas. Loading DOSKEY last increased our available conventional memory in this example.

Finally, the NOEMS command was added to the EMM386.EXE line. Conventional memory remained at 615 K, but because an expanded memory page frame is no longer needed, upper memory increased to 77 K. The final AUTOEXEC.BAT and CONFIG.SYS files in our example are shown below.

```
AUTOEXEC.BAT: _____

prompt $p $g
path c:\;c:\dos;c:\win;
set temp=d:\temp
set tmp=d:\temp
c:\dos\smartdrv.exe
Loadhigh c:\dos\doskey


CONFIG.SYS: _____
device=c:\dos\himem.sys
device=c:\dos\emm386.exe noems x=a000-c7ff
dos=high,umb
shell=c:\dos\command.com c:\dos /e:2000 /p
/f
devicehigh=c:\dos\dblspace.sys
devicehigh=c:\dos\ansi.sys
files=64
buffers=32
break=on
lastdrive=z
stacks=9,128
fcbs=1,10
```

The final memory configuration resulting from all these changes is shown in Figure 13–26. Note that DBLSPACE, ANSI.SYS, SMARTDRV, and DOSKEY are all loaded into upper memory. Only HIMEM, EMM386, and COMMAND.COM are loaded into conventional memory. The largest executable program size is 615 K.

```
Modules using memory below 1 Mb:
  Name          Total       =  Conventional   +   Upper Memory
  --------    ----------------    ----------------    --------------
  MSDOS        16749   (16K)      16749   (16K)         0    (0K)
  HIMEM         1168    (1K)       1168    (1K)         0    (0K)
  EMM386        3120    (3K)       3120    (3K)         0    (0K)
  COMMAND       4736    (5K)       4736    (5K)         0    (0K)
  DBLSPACE     44256   (43K)          0    (0K)     44256   (43K)
  ANSI          4256    (4K)          0    (0K)      4256    (4K)
  SMARTDRV     27280   (27K)          0    (0K)     27280   (27K)
  DOSKEY        4144    (4K)          0    (0K)      4144    (4K)
  Free        708352  (692K)     629440  (615K)     78912   (77K)
```

```
Memory Summary:

  Type of Memory        Total      =      Used     +     Free
  ----------------   -------------     -------------   --------------

  Conventional       655360 (640K)      25920  (25K) 629440    (615K)
  Upper              158848 (155K)      79936  (78K)  78912     (77K)
  Adapter RAM/ROM    393216 (384K)     393216 (384K)     0      (0K)
  Extended (XMS)    2986880(2917K)    1270656(1241K)1716224   (1676K)
  ----------------   -------------     -------------   --------------

  Total memory      4194304(4096K)    1769728(1728K)2424576   (2368K)


  Total under 1 Mb 814208 (795K)      105856 (103K) 708352    (692K)


  Largest executable program size         629344    (615K)
  Largest free upper memory block          78704     (77K)
  MS-DOS is resident in the high memory area.
```

Figure 13–26 *Final DOS memory configuration*

Simple CONFIG.SYS and AUTOEXEC.BAT files are shown in Listings 13–1 and 13–2. These files provide adequate conventional memory and should work for almost all DOS and Windows 3.1x configurations except those demanding the absolute maximum amount of free conventional memory.

With DOS PCs, the easiest way to configure memory is to use the MEMMAKER program. It automatically configures DOS to provide maximum conventional RAM for DOS applications. Further, its resulting configurations run reliably and predictably. However, the one rule identified above also applies to PCs using MEMMAKER to configure their conventional memory. That rule is load the bigger programs first and the smaller last. We have seen configurations where rearranging the device driver and terminate-and-stay-resident program loading order increased conventional memory significantly.

Listing 13.1 *CONFIG.SYS*

```
Device=c:\dos\HIMEM.SYS
DOS=HIGH
Device=c:\dos\EMM386.EXE NOEMS
DOS=UMB
Files=64
Buffers=10
Lastdrive=Z
shell=c:\dos\command.com /E:2048 /P
stacks=0,0
FCBS=1,0
```

Listing 13.2 *Listing 13-2 AUTOEXEC.BAT*

```
SET TEMP=C:\TEMP
SET TMP=C:\TEMP
SET DIRCMD=/Ogn /A
verify on
prompt $p $g
path c:\;c:\dos;c:\windows;......
c:\dos\mode con rate=32 delay=1
LH c:\mouse\mouse
LH c:\dos\doskey
```

These simple CONFIG.SYS and AUTOEXEC.BAT files configure PC RAM in a fashion that works on almost all PCs running DOS and Windows 3.x. If problems occur with these configurations, removing the EMM386.EXE device driver from CONFIG.SYS usually resolves the problems.

DOS Memory Layout

Use the MEM command to view the conventional and high memory configuration in your PC.

1. Open a DOS window. Enter MEM to view the memory layout summary. How much conventional memory is available?

2. Enter MEM /D /P to view the conventional memory configuration in detail. What are the very first things resident in the lowest memory locations? These are the interrupt routines or pointers (vectors) to the interrupt handling software routines (components).

3. What comes next? Device drivers for standard I/O devices.

4. The next memory locations in conventional memory should contain HIMEM, EMM386, and DBLBUFF. With Windows 98 DOS, double buffering is automatically loaded.

5. Next you should see MSDOS, some environment storage space, terminate-and-stay-resident programs, and finally the MEM program itself.

6. How many upper memory regions do you have? On our machine it is two, with the second and largest region containing system data and space reserved for buffers, FCBs, and stacks.

The purpose of this exercise was to illustrate the layout of conventional memory in a PC as viewed by the DOS MEM program.

■ Summary

This chapter has described the basics of PC memory management. This began with how the PC chips look at memory and then translated this into how DOS and Windows perform memory management.

Windows makes knowing how DOS manages memory a low-priority issue. However, a good understanding of PC memory configuration basics helps solve software problems. Memory resource conflicts by hardware in the upper memory areas continue to present difficult problems for Windows 95/98/NT systems.

Memory management for DOS is a much less critical issue than it was years ago, since most systems use Windows 95/98. However, the issue with DOS memory configuration is less one of maximizing conventional RAM and more one of configuring the memory for trouble-free DOS and Windows operation. Since most diagnostic tools rely on DOS and since Windows still must have upper memory block hardware conflicts resolved, knowing the DOS memory configurations can be helpful troubleshooting knowledge.

▲ CHAPTER REVIEW QUESTIONS

1. *What is EMM386.EXE used for?*
   Manage Upper Memory Area (Upper Memory Blocks) and Create Expanded Memory (EMS)

2. *Where does extended memory start?*
   1024 K

3. *Where is "HMA" located?*
   1024 K to 1088 K

4. *What commands are used in CONFIG.SYS?*
   A. ECHO
   B. PAUSE
   C. DEVICE
   D. DEVICEHIGH
   Answer: C. DEVICE and D. DEVICEHIGH

5. *What command in DOS do you use to enable use of expanded memory?*
   A. EMM386.EXE
   B. EXPAND.EXE
   C. EXPANDED.COM
   Answer: A. EMM386.EXE

6. *Where does the high memory area always start and how large is it?*
   A. at 1024 K for 64 K
   B. immediately after 640 K for 64 K
   C. at FFFF H (65,535) for 64 K
   Answer: A. at 1024 K for 64 K

7. *Which area of memory is most often used for BIOS programs?*

   A. conventional memory

   B. upper memory

   C. extended memory

   D. shadow memory

   Answer: B. upper memory

8. *What does MEMMAKER do?*

   A. offers you an automated way to manage upper and extended memory

   B. edits your CONFIG.SYS and AUTOEXEC.BAT files

   C. optimizes memory

   D. all of the above

   Answer: D. all of the above

9. *TSRs are usually device drivers loaded from:*

   A. the CONFIG.SYS file

   B. the AUTOEXEC.BAT file

   C. the COMMAND.COM file

   D. the Windows system directory

   Answer: A. the CONFIG.SYS file

10. *How much memory is base (conventional) memory?*

    A. 320K

    B. 640K

    C. 1024K

    D. 384 K

    Answer: B. 640K

11. *Dividing RAM into an odd and an even bank is called what?*

    A. caching

    B. interleaving

    C. DRAM

    D. memory paging

    Answer: D. memory paging

12. *Every PC with more than 1 MB of RAM does not necessarily have what type of memory?*

   A. XMS

   B. EMS

   C. conventional

   D. HMA

   Answer: B. EMS

13. *Do system ROMs ever use more than 64 K?*

   A. yes

   B. no

   Answer: B. no

14. *How much memory is used typically for VGA ROM?*

   A. 32K

   B. 64K

   C. 96K

   D. 128K

   Answer: A. 32K

Software Installation, Configuration, and Upgrade

▲ Chapter Syllabus

A+ 14.1   Operating System Installation Procedures

A+ 14.2   Software Upgrades

A+ 14.3   Booting Procedures

A+ 14.4   Loading and Adding Device Drivers

A+ 14.5   Windows Configuration

A+ 14.6   Launching Windows Applications

This chapter covers installing DOS, Windows 3.1x, and Windows 95/98. It describes the process of upgrading from DOS to Windows 3.1x and also to Windows 95. Booting the PC and launching applications is examined. When it comes to software installation, the best procedure is to install from scratch. That is, install with only the software that will be used on the PC. Trying to upgrade and preserve software configuration settings is a noble objective that can be achieved, but more practically installing from scratch gives the most reliable and best performing system. Table 14–1 presents typical installation requirements for several operating environments.

Table 14.1 *Operating system hardware requirements*

	CPU Chip	RAM	Fixed Disk
DOS	8088 to Pentium	640 KB and up	Requires about 6 MB disk space. 10 MB and up (typically 100-200 MB)
Windows 3.1x	80286 (standard mode) 80386 to Pentium	2 MB to 64 MB (Really 16 MB)	Requires 15 MB disk space. 100 MB and up (typically 500 MB to 1GB)
Windows 95	80386 DX 20 MHz but really Pentium	4 MB minimum 8 MB recommended 16 MB to 128 MB (Really 40 MB)	20 MB normal 10 MB compact installation 1 GB and up (typically 2 GB to 4GB)
Windows 98	80486 DX 66 MHz but really Pentium	16 MB minimum 32 MB and more	120 MB disk space minimum 355 MB can be used for new install 2 GB and up (typically 3 GB to 8 GB)
Windows NT	80486 DX 25 MHz but really Pentium	12 MB minimum 16 MB recom-mended 24 MB is OK 48 MB is acceptable really 64 MB and up (the more the better)	120 MB disk space minimum 2 GB and up (typically 4 GB to 16 GB)

The minimum hardware requirements for each operating system specified by Microsoft permits the operating system to run but it cannot do much more without beating the disk drive to death or having programs run out of memory. For example, we encountered a Compaq PC running Windows 95 with 8 MB RAM using a 1 GB disk drive. This was the most stressed out Compaq PC we had ever seen. It was constantly swapping data to the disk drive. Any operation required it to swap data from RAM to the disk drive. All the screen updates required disk data swapping. Consequently, even the simplest of operations took several seconds as the PC wrote and read the display data from the disk drive. It could only effectively run the Windows accessory programs and AOL software. For proper operation, more memory was required and a bigger disk drive was in order.

A+ 14.1 Operating System Installation Procedures

DOS is the starting point for installation of virtually all software operating environments. Because DOS permits direct interaction with the fixed disk drive, it is used to partition and format the disk. Generally, those partitions prepared by DOS can be translated into other formats during the operating system installation process. For example, Windows NT translates DOS FAT partitions into NTFS partitions during installation of Windows NT. Windows NT can translate DOS partitions into NTFS partitions using the Windows NT CONVERT utility program. CONVERT.EXE is an NT program that is used during NT setup to convert FAT partitions to NTFS. When NT is installed, the initial partition is always FAT, so NT installation must go through a FAT-to-NTFS conversion for all NTFS partitions. CONVERT.EXE can also be run from a DOS Window after the NT system has been installed. In most cases, Windows can be upgraded from an older version to a newer version by installing the newer version over the older version. This is fine, and sometimes it works well and preserves the configuration from the older version. However, it is wiser to work from a clean disk. Record the key configuration information and backup before doing any upgrades to the operating system. Remove the older version of Windows and the applications by reformatting the hard drive. Install the upgraded version of Windows and reinstall the necessary applications and data.

Convert FAT partition to NTFS partitions by using the convert utility provided with Windows NT. The FAT to NTFS partition conversion is performed with the command:

CONVERT x:/FS:NTFS[/V]

x:--specifies the drive to convert to NTFS.

/FS:NTFS--specifies to convert the volume to NTFS.

/V--specifies that CONVERT runs in verbose mode.

CONVERT does not currently work for FAT32.

The conversion is one way, you cannot convert back to FAT.

Although it seems like more work to reinstall all software and reconfigure a PC than simply trying to upgrade it, in most cases it is not. The smallest problems encountered in the upgrade process can require much more time to resolve than a complete installation from scratch. Furthermore, reinstalling application software onto an uncluttered Windows PC places only those DLLs that are needed by that application on that PC. Installing over an existing Windows installation can leave older unwanted and potentially system-crashing DLLs on the PC. It is better to be sure all unneeded and older DLLs are removed when upgrading from one version of Windows to another.

A fresh installation of Windows starts with prepping the disk drive using DOS, then proceeds with the Windows installation.

File Systems

A file system organizes files on a disk drive. Letters, such as "C:" or "D:", identify drives. During the boot process, these letters are assigned to drives that are formatted with a file system recognized by the operating system.

The first installation decisions are picking a fixed disk addressing scheme and a file system for the disk drives. The fixed disk hardware addressing scheme and the file system used determine the maximum partition size supported by the PC operating system.

The file system is largely determined by the operating system being used. However, there are FAT-16 versus FAT-32 choices for Windows 95B/Windows95C and Windows 98 and FAT-16, HPFS, and NTFS choices for Windows NT. These file system choices are based on the options the operating system supports, security, disk utilization efficiency, and other factors. The file system considerations are:

- **FAT-16 (16-bit File Allocation Table)** is the file system used by DOS, Windows 3.1x and Windows 95. File data is stored in allocation units (clusters or groups of 512 byte sectors). As disk capacity has increased, larger partitions are used. To accommodate large partitions, FAT-16 had to use large and therefore wasteful allocation unit sizes. On new FAT partitions, the files are sorted sequentially on the disk in large sections. Access in this case is relatively fast. However, as more files are added to the partition, and as existing files are modified and stored, file fragmentation occurs. Breaking up these files can slow down access to data on the disk drive. So FAT-16 is an inefficient and relatively slow type of disk partitioning.

- **FAT-32 (32-bit File Allocation Table)** is the latest FAT file system, developed for Windows 95 Revisions B and C and Windows 98. It is an extension of the FAT-16 file system with the ability to deal with more clusters using 32-bit allocation unit addresses. This permits larger partitions with smaller allocation unit sizes. FAT-32 develops fragmentation like FAT-16. Thus FAT-32 is a more efficient and somewhat slow type of disk partition.

- **The OS/2 HPFS (High Performance File System)** is designed to allocate contiguous space for files to prevent fragmentation that occurs with FAT partitions. HPFS assigns disk space in smaller units—as small as a single sector. This prevents wasting disk space using large

FAT allocation units. However, HPFS can be used with NT and OS/2 operating systems. Its implementation is limited.

- **NTFS (New Technology File System)** was developed for NT server to provide greater data security and better storage performance. NTFS works only with Windows NT. NTFS stores data describing directories and files on a disk in a master file table. Information on each file is held in a file record in the master file table that may be 1 to 4 KB in size. Each file is identified by a unique 48-bit identifier and described by attributes such as name, type of data, security access, and more, as required by NT. Using the master file table, files and partitions can be very large without requiring allocation units greater than 4KB.

  NTFS provides file-by-file data compression, full file access permission control and attribute settings, transaction-based operation, and more features. NTFS does not have the storage efficiency problems caused by using different allocation unit sizes or the hard disk size limitations that FAT has. Windows NT supports Redundant Array of Independent Disk drives (RAID) operation under NTFS. The only limitation of NTFS is that older software is sometimes not compatible with it.

  Only Windows NT uses the NTFS file system. DOS and Windows 95/98 cannot use NTFS. NTFS is efficient, secure, and performs well because it was designed to support Windows NT servers.

Disk drive partitioning during installation also depends on how the PC hardware addresses the sectors on the disk. This leads to a CHS (cylinders-heads-sectors) or LBA (logical block addressing) setup decision. An incorrect decision limits the ability of the PC software to access the full disk drive capacity.

The capacity of fixed disk drives has been constrained by different limiting hardware factors over the 18 years that PCs have dominated computing. The first capacity limitations were 10 MB imposed on XT PCs. They supported type 1 disk drives having a cylinder-head-sector (CHS) geometry of 312 cylinders, 4 heads, and 17 sectors per track. To calculate maximum capacity, multiply the number of cylinders X the number of heads X the number of sectors X _ K per sector (312 X 4 X 17 X _ =10MB).

Soon other drive types were supported by BIOS, so this constraint gave way to the DOS 2.0 12-bit FAT capacity limitation. The 12-bit FAT permitted 4,096 FAT entries for allocation units (called at that time clusters) of 4KB, which provided addressing for 16 MB of data on the disk drive. With the AT came DOS 3.0 and an increase of the FAT size to 16-bits and a table of 64 K possible entries. However, DOS limited the FAT table size to 16 K entries.

The allocation unit size was set at 2KB, providing a maximum addressable disk capacity of 32 MB or the size of the PC AT fixed disk. Multiple partitions permitted DOS to use disk drives greater than 32 MB in capacity. DOS 4.0 increased the FAT size to the full 16-bit addressable capacity of 64 K entries. This increased FAT size combined with 2 K allocation unit size increased the maximum addressable disk capacity to 128 MB. Allocation unit sizes were varied with DOS 5.0 to increase the maximum addressable disk capacity. By permitting allocation unit size to increase to 8 KB, the maximum addressable disk capacity reached around 512 MB.

However, hardware limitations in the number of bits assigned to the disk addressing function limited the effective maximum disk size. The BIOS interface had some bit assignment limits as well as the AT Attachment (ATA) interface specification for CHS (cylinders-heads-sectors) addressing. These hardware constraints set the upper limit to 1,024 cylinders X 16 heads X 63 sectors per track X _ K per sector or 504 MB.

Logical Block Addressing (LBA) overcame the disk capacity constraints of CHS addressing.

With LBA removing the hardware constraints, the 16-bit FAT and the sectors-per-allocation-unit assignment again limited the maximum fixed disk size. By increasing allocation unit size to 32 KB for the 64 K FAT entries, DOS and Windows 95 are able to work with drives that are 2 GB. The new 32-bit FAT removes this limitation by providing 256 M FAT entries with 4KB allocation unit sizes, easily accommodating 1 terabyte (TB) disk drives.

LBA has a hardware 24-bit address size limitation that makes the operating system capable of operating with disks that have 16 M (M=1,048,576) sectors of _ Kb, or 8 GB. This means that bootable DOS partitions are not larger than 8 GB.

Disk Preparation

Before software installation can begin, the fixed disk drive must be prepared to accept the new software. This generally involves determining a partitioning strategy, partitioning the drive with the DOS utility FDISK, and formatting the first partition with the DOS FORMAT program. The first step is determining a partitioning strategy.

As a refresher, remember that disk drive capacity is defined in megabytes. A megabyte is 1,048,576 bytes. Soon disk capacity will exceed our wildest dreams. Both FAT-32 and NTFS are capable of operating disk drives with terabyte capacities. To get the proper scaling here lets look at the definitions of size. They are:

- **One byte**—is the smallest unit of storage and information that a PC works on. A byte is the equivalent of a single character, such as "A." One byte is 2 raised to the 0th power.
- **One megabyte**—is 1,048,576 (1024 X 1024) bytes. Generally storage and data transmission capacity is measured in megabytes (2 raised to the 30th power).
- **One terabyte**—is 1,024 megabytes. This is the maximum disk drive size that can be utilized by NTFS and FAT-32 today. A terabyte is 1,099,511,627,776 bytes (2 raised to the 40th power).
- **One petabyte** —is 1,024 terabytes. Disk capacities will hit this size in about 10 years. A petabyte is 1,125,899,906,842,624 bytes (2 raised to the 50th power).
- **One exabyte** —is 1,024 petabytes. Disk capacities will hit this size in about 20 years or more. An exabyte is 1,152,921,504,606,846,976 bytes (2 raised to the 60th power).

As discussed in Chapter 12, the file allocation table (FAT) design determines partitioning restrictions. The key strategic decisions center on partitioning a disk for booting and data storage and on determining partition size. The first issue is the operating system the PC uses. The operating system installed determines the file systems that are used on the fixed disk drives. The file system selection is based on efficiency and security in protecting the data on the fixed disk drive. Most new PCs running Windows 98 use FAT-32. Windows NT PCs may use the FAT-16 or NTFS. Storage effectiveness of a file system is set by the sectors used in each allocation unit. File systems using large allocation unit sizes store data on the disk drive inefficiently. See Figure 14–1.

Files stored using file systems with smaller allocation unit sizes use disk drive space more efficiently. Small files stored in large allocation units waste disk capacity.

For convenience, a comparison of FAT-12, FAT-16, FAT-32 and NTFS is shown in Table 14–2.

The second issue is the size of the boot partition. Because PCs use the BIOS to access the disk drive, the boot partition size is limited by the maximum size that the BIOS can address. To determine how the BIOS works, the CMOS setup is used. There the disk geometry options are specified. The settings for older computers permitted disk type 46 and type 47 to have user-specified CHS (cylinders-heads-sectors) settings. Newer computers support LBA settings. The newest computers are generally set up to automatically configure the fixed disk drives attached.

File#1	File#2
File#3	

32 KB Sectors
File#1 20 KB
File#2 31 KB
File #3 8 KB

Case 1 -- Storing the three files consumes
three quarters of the disk capacity.

File#1	File#1	File#1	File#2
File#2	File#2	File#2	File#3

8 KB Sectors
File#1 20 KB
File#2 31 KB
File #3 8 KB

Case 2 -- Storing the three files consumes
one half of the disk capacity.

Figure 14–1   *Storage efficiency*

Table 14.2 *FATS and NTFS*

Partition Type	Operating System Support	Maximum Partition Size	Security	Redundant Array Of Independent Disks (RAID)	Drives Supported
FAT-12	DOS Win95/98 DOS Windows 95 a Windows 95 b Windows 98 Windows NT 3.5x Windows NT 4.0 Windows NT 5.0	16 MB with 4KB allocation unit size	None	No	Old IDE
FAT-16	DOS Win95/98 DOS Windows 95 a Windows 95 b Windows 98 Windows NT 3.5x Windows NT 4.0 Windows NT 5.0	2 GB with 32 KB allocation unit size	None	Hardware Controller	Smaller IDE SCSI
FAT-32	Win98 DOS Windows 95 b Windows 98	28-bit FAT 256 M entries 4 KB to 32 KB 1 to 8 terabytes	None	Hardware Controller	Large IDE SCSI

Table 14.2 *FATS and NTFS (Continued)*

Partition Type	Operating System Support	Maximum Partition Size	Security	Redundant Array Of Independent Disks (RAID)	Drives Supported
NTFS	Windows NT 3.5x Windows NT 4.0	Multiple Terabytes	Cannot be accessed by DOS NT Server Provides Disk and File Security Features	NT Software and Hardware Controller	Huge IDE SCSI

Once the boot process is finished, the PC is running the file system software, and the BIOS is bypassed, the partition size can be much larger. The maximum partition size for BIOS is 1,204 cylinders X 256 heads X 64 sectors per track, giving 7.8 GB maximum capacity. These limits are the maximums that a PC's BIOS can use because of hardware limitations in the number of bits assigned to the disk addressing function, as was explained at the beginning of the chapter.

Suggested partitioning strategies for different size drives are shown in Table 14–3.

These strategies are based on the file system and how the PC is used. Generally, the bigger the partition with the smaller the allocation unit, the more efficiently the disk drive space is utilized. However, Windows 95/98 must boot using a DOS partition. Windows NT can boot from either an NTFS partition or a FAT partition. If NT is booted from a FAT partition, the security for the PC is reduced because data on that drive is accessible from DOS (unless 128 sector allocation units are used).

Table 14.3 *Partitioning strategies*

Drive Size	FAT-16	FAT-32	NTFS
2 GB	C—Boot—1 GB D—Data—1 GB	C—Boot—1 GB D—Data—1 GB	C—Boot—FAT-16—1 GB (reduced security) D—Data—NTFS—1 GB
4 GB	C—Boot—2 GB D—Data—2 GB	C—Boot—1 GB D—Data –3 GB	C—Boot—FAT-16—1 GB (reduced security) D—Data—NTFS—3 GB
8 GB and up	C—Boot—2 GB D—Data—2 GB E—Data—2 GB F—Data—2 GB	C—Boot—2 to 4 GB D—Data—4 GB E—Install—2 GB	C—Boot—FAT-16—2 GB (reduced security) D—Data—NTFS—4 GB D—Install—NTFS—2 GB

A bootable partition of 1 to 4 GB should be sufficient to hold the operating system, the operating system installation files, and some applications software. The second partition should be used to store all active data. Isolating the data from the software makes for easy backup and recovery in the event of failure, permits reinstallation of the disk software installation without losing data, and easily preserves critical data when software is upgraded.

Having a third partition is useful for making backups (although it is on the same physical disk, having a separate partition backup can be extremely useful) and holding application software installation files. The third partition contains either backup of key data and program files or device drivers and other installation programs for Windows. This is not the active data but a backup copy of the active data. For example it is handy sometimes to use a program like GHOST to make a complete C boot copy on the third drive. If the boot partition ever gets corrupted, this copy can be used to quickly recover it. With disk drive capacity increasing at a dizzying rate and prices for IDE drives remaining low, a third partition backup disk is an effective insurance policy to solve software problems.

Some PCs use partition-duplicating software GHOST as described above to duplicate the data or the boot partition on a third backup partition. In the event of software failure or Windows becoming corrupted during software installation, the duplicate partition is loaded over the corrupted partition.

With Windows 95/98, the registry often becomes corrupted, causing Windows to crash, operate poorly or not boot at all (the ugly Windows protection error). Microsoft provides a simple utility ERU.EXE (the Emergency Recovery Utility) which backs up the registry and all key files that configure Windows 95/98. This utility can be found at the Microsoft web site by searching for ERU. Using ERU, the key files can be backed up to a folder on the fixed disk drive (like drive C or E or a ZIP or JAZ drive.) Backing them up on a floppy drive does not save the most important file, SYSTEM.DAT, so it is not an effective alternative. See Figure 14–2. These backup files require several MB of storage space. When the drive is accessible from DOS, the ERD.EXE program created by ERU.EXE is used to restore the snapshot backup of the PC's key configuration files. This can resurrect the registry from most corruption problems occurring with Window NT. A good strategy is to periodically perform these backups using a third partition like a drive E. In this fashion, if the primary partition is deleted or reformatted, the key Windows configuration files have not been destroyed. If an audit trail of these files is maintained in numbered folders (for example, 001,002, and

Figure 14–2 *ERU utility*

003), they can easily consume 20 to 100 MB of disk space. It is best to keep these key file ERU backups in a backup partition.

Windows NT has a built-in emergency repair disk utility called RDISK.EXE. The RDISK.EXE utility program builds a bootable emergency repair disk for Windows NT. The disk created restores the Windows NT registry and repairs corrupted Windows NT files.

Once you have prepared the disk, the next step is to partition it. The next section covers the procedure for partitioning the fixed disk.

PARTITIONING A FIXED DISK

The second step in software installation is to partition the fixed disk. Partitioning erases all data on the disk. This is not a problem with new disk drives. Partitioning an older disk with existing data erases the data from the disk and it cannot be recovered.

Several years ago, new disk drives needed to be low-level formatted before partitioning could take place. The low-level format wrote zeros or ones across the entire disk surface and tested it for flaws. Today this process has been performed at the factory for all IDE drives and SCSI drives. Furthermore, IDE drives, because they perform sector and cylinder translations, can be damaged if a low-level format is attempted.

When FDISK is run, the first screen determines the DOS and Windows files system that will be used. See Figure 14–3.

Answering "Y," the default setting, to the large disk support installs FAT-32. An "N" for no installs FAT-16. FAT-32 should work with older BIOS. In this case, the disk drive capacity may be limited because of CHS addressing due to the BIOS's inability to provide LBA-mode addressing. The next screen is used to partition the drive and examine the partitions. FDISK

Figure 14–3 *FDISK file system selection*

Figure 14-4 *FDISK main menu*

works with multiple disk drives. Selecting additional drives is performed using selection 5 on the FDISK main menu. See Figure 14-4.

The fixed disk main menu is used to:

- Create a DOS partition or logical drive.
- Set the partition as active.
- Delete partitions or logical DOS drives.
- Display partition information.
- Change to a second fixed disk drive.

Fixed disk setup proceeds by creating a DOS partition or logical drive. Option 1 permits creation of a primary DOS partition or an extended DOS partition. Logical drives are then defined in the extended DOS partition. The primary DOS partition is used as the boot partition and should be set to active. The extended DOS partition is then used to set up the remaining drive space. The logical drive designations subdivide the extended DOS partition.

Disk partitions are specified in MB. Sometimes disk vendors specify disk capacities in their absolute number of bytes, using 1,000 bytes. This can be confusing because the actual drive sizes in MB are slightly smaller, since they are defined in 1,024 byte increments. FDISK always reports partition sizes in 1,024 byte increments or true megabytes, so they may seem smaller than the advertised disk capacity.

Once a primary and extended DOS partitions have been defined and the logical drives assigned, it is time to set the bootable partition as active.

Menu selection number 2 in the FDISK main menu sets the active partition. An "A" in the status entry for that partition designates the active partition.

The delete partition or logical drive menu item is used to remove logical drives or partitions. When they are removed, all data in those partitions or logical drives is lost. It cannot be recovered. This option is used to reconfigure the partitions and thus the logical drive letter on a PC. Most PCs do not have their partitions reconfigured.

The display partition information provides a summary display of the partitions defined on the disk drive and permits viewing the logical drive assignments. See Figure 14–5.

The FDISK display partition information shows the primary drive disk letter assignment, active status, size in MB, and the file system used on the disk. The extended DOS partition and its size is also identified. When there are multiple disk drives installed in the PC, the change current fixed disk drive option permits us to partition the second, third, or fourth drive in the PC. Selecting this option also provides a convenient overview display of the disk drive capacities and partitions created for all the disk drives in the PC.

FDISK can be run at any time. Running FDISK in a DOS window under Windows 98 and striking Alt PrintScreen captured these images. This can also be done in NT or Windows 95. FDISK is also an effective disk diagnostic tool. When FDISK cannot read the disk drive, it displays an error mes-

Figure 14–5 *FDISK partition information display*

```
C:\>

C:\>format /?
Formats a disk for use with MS-DOS.

FORMAT drive: [/V[:label]] [/Q] [/F:size] [/B | /S] [/C]
FORMAT drive: [/V[:label]] [/Q] [/T:tracks /N:sectors] [/B | /S] [/C]
FORMAT drive: [/V[:label]] [/Q] [/1] [/4] [/B | /S] [/C]
FORMAT drive: [/Q] [/1] [/4] [/8] [/B | /S] [/C]

  /V[:label]    Specifies the volume label.
  /Q            Performs a quick format.
  /F:size       Specifies the size of the floppy disk to format (such
                as 160, 180, 320, 360, 720, 1.2, 1.44, 2.88).
  /B            Allocates space on the formatted disk for system files.
  /S            Copies system files to the formatted disk.
  /T:tracks     Specifies the number of tracks per disk side.
  /N:sectors    Specifies the number of sectors per track.
  /1            Formats a single side of a floppy disk.
  /4            Formats a 5.25-inch 360K floppy disk in a high-density drive.
  /8            Formats eight sectors per track.
  /C            Tests clusters that are currently marked "bad."
```

Figure 14–6 *FORMAT command options*

sage indicating that it cannot read the fixed disk. In the event of a fixed disk controller failure, FDISK displays a different message, indicating that the fixed disk controller has failed.

Once the disk has been partitioned, the next step in operating system installation is to format the fixed disk drive partitions.

FORMATTING A BOOTABLE DISK

Formatting a bootable fixed or floppy disk in DOS or Windows 95/98 is performed using the DOS utility FORMAT.COM. See Figure 14–6.

Making the formatted disk drive bootable is performed by using the FORMAT /S option. The /S option causes FORMAT to install the operating system files on both fixed disk drives and floppy diskettes. FORMAT.COM automatically installs the following files in the root directory of the formatted disk drive:

```
COMMAND COM    93,880 14-14-98 4:59p COMMAND.COM
DRVSPACE BIN   68,871 05-11-98 8:01p DRVSPACE.BIN
IO SYS        222,390 05-11-98 8:01p IO.SYS
MSDOS SYS           9 05-11-98 8:01p MSDOS.SYS
```

While the filenames are the same for both DOS and Windows 95/98 FORMAT.COM programs, the files themselves are quite different. The plain FORMAT /S command does not install memory management programs. The DRVSPACE.BIN program is used for disk compression and can usually be deleted to provide added space on floppy diskette drives. There are no CONFIG.SYS and AUTOEXEC.BAT files created.

Performing a DOS installation using a SETUP.EXE program provides a complete installation of DOS on the fixed disk.

Similarly, installing Windows 95/98 on a bootable fixed disk would provide a more complete installation by including additional files for booting into Windows 95/98.

DOS Installation

After the fixed disk has been partitioned and formatted the next step in the operating system installation process is installing DOS. DOS 6.22, the last pure DOS version before Windows 95/98 DOS, is installed using a SETUP.EXE program. This SETUP.EXE program creates an uninstall diskette as well as installing DOS 6.22. It examines your system to determine previously installed versions of DOS, the display type, and the directory in which to install the new DOS. See Figure 14–7. This setup program used standardized keys for navigation. As seen in the figure, the F1 key displays help information, the F3 key exits setup, Enter selects the menu choice, and arrow keys are used to move from menu item to menu item.

The SETUP.EXE program then proceeds to copy the DOS files to the designated subdirectory, completing the DOS installation. This installation process does not necessarily optimize memory utilization under DOS. When DOS is installed over a previous version of DOS, the AUTOEXEC.BAT and

Figure 14–7 *MS-DOS 6.22 setup*

```
Microsoft MemMaker
_____

                        Advanced Options
_____

Specify which drivers and TSRs to include in optimization?    No
Scan the upper memory area aggressively?                       No
Optimize upper memory for use with Windows?                    No
Use monochrome region (B000-B7FF) for running programs?        No
Keep current EMM386 memory exclusions and inclusions?          Yes
Move Extended BIOS Data Area from conventional to upper memory? Yes



To select a different option, press the UP ARROW or DOWN ARROW key.
To accept all the settings and continue, press ENTER.




ENTER=Accept All  SPACEBAR=Change Selection  F1=Help  F3=Exit
```

Figure 14–8 *MEMMAKER advanced options*

CONFIG.SYS file settings are preserved. Otherwise, minimal AUTOEXEC.BAT and CONFIG.SYS files are created and saved.

MEMORY CONFIGURATION

Initial DOS memory configuration is performed using MEMMAKER.EXE. After the basic DOS 6.22 installation is complete and the hardware driver and DOS TSR programs configured to run under DOS, run MEMMAKER to perform the memory configuration. This program examines the PC and observes the programs loading during the boot process to determine the optimal memory configuration. It then creates CONFIG.SYS and AUTOEXEC.BAT files that properly load the memory resident and driver programs into HIMEM and the Upper Memory Area (UMA). See Figure 14–8.

Both the DOS installation program (SETUP) and MEMMAKER are menu-driven and easy to run. DOS must be installed and the memory optimized prior to the installation of Windows 3.1x. Once these solutions steps are complete, it is time to install Windows 3.1x.

Windows 3.1x Installation

The optimal strategy for installing virtually all versions of Windows is to copy the Windows installation files to a directory on the fixed disk.

Then Windows is installed from those files copied into that installation directory on the fixed disk. In this manner, whenever the Windows files are required to upgrade or reconfigure Windows, they are readily available. If Windows is installed off a CD-ROM, then upgrades and reconfigurations to Windows would require having that CD-ROM readily available.

Windows 3.1x is installed using the SETUP.EXE program found on the first disk of the Windows 3.1x installation diskettes. This program has several command line options that are easily viewed by entering SETUP /?, as shown in Figure 14–9. These options permit customization of the Windows 3.1x installation process. Similar to the DOS SETUP.EXE program, Windows 3.1x SETUP.EXE uses the F1 key to display help information, the F3 key to exit setup, Enter to select the menu choice, and arrow keys to move from menu item to menu item.

Setup provides both express and custom installation options. The express setup option will automatically configure the mouse, keyboard, and language options. When a network is present and detected, SETUP.EXE will configure it if it can determine the NIC hardware configuration. AUTOEXEC.BAT and CONFIG.SYS files are also configured. SETUP.EXE then proceeds to install the Windows 3.1x files into a C:\WINDOWS directory. See Figure 14–10.

Other functions performed during express setup are to search all drives for available disk space when the disk space on drive C is not enough to hold the Windows installation files. Setup can also perform a partial installation of Windows if the disk space is insufficient for a full installation. When upgrading from a previous version of Windows, express setup duplicates the

Figure 14–10 *Windows 3.1x setup*

```
Sets up Windows for Workgroups 3.11 on your system.
setup  [/N]  [/I]  [/O:file]  [/S:path]  [/B]  [/T]  [/C]
[/A]
      [/H:file]  [/F]

 /N        - Sets up a shared copy of Windows for
             Workgroups from a network server.

 /I        - Ignores hardware detection. During Setup,
             the user will need to check accuracy of
             settings on the System Information screen,
             and possibly make corrections.

 /O:file   - Specifies the SETUP.INF file.

 /S:path   - Specifies a path to the setup disk(s).

 /B        - Allows use of a monochrome monitor with a
             color graphics card.

 /T        - Searches the drive for memory-resident
             (TSR) programs and notifies you about
             certain programs. For information about
             using specific programs with Setup or
             Windows for Workgroups, see SETUP.TXT.

 /C        - Turns off the search for memory-resident
             (TSR) programs.

 /A        - Administrative setup. Places Windows for
             Workgroups on a network server. Setup
             Expands and copies all files on every disk
             to a given directory, and marks them
             read-only.

 /H:file   - Batch mode setup. Sets up Windows for
             Workgroups with little or no user
             interaction. "File" is the name of the
             system settings file that contains user's
             configuration settings. If "file" is
             not in the directory from which Windows
             for Workgroups is being set up, the path
             must be included.

 /F        - Forces network card detection.
```

Figure 14–9 *SETUP command line options*

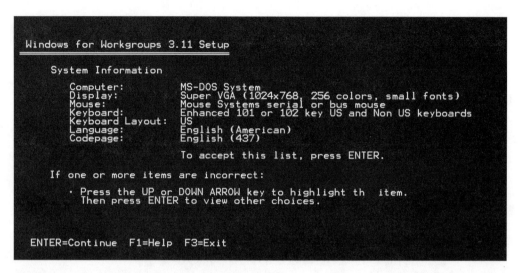

Figure 14–11   *Windows 3.1x hardware detection*

current printer installations. It also determines which applications are on the desktop and creates icons for specific standard programs.

In performing a custom setup, SETUP.EXE examines the PC's hardware configuration and reports that configuration to the person installing Windows 3.1x. Once the configuration is identified and properly detected by the installation program, SETUP.EXE proceeds to copy the Windows 3.1x program files onto the fixed disk. Once this is complete, Windows restarts. The remaining installation is performed using the Windows setup program. See Figure 14–11.

The Windows 3.1x setup program can be used at any time to change the hardware configuration. It can be run from the DOS prompt, or launched through the Windows 3.1x control panel using the Windows setup icon.

Figure 14–12   *Windows 3.1x control panel setup*

Figure 14–13 *Choosing Windows components*

When Windows setup is launched using the control panel, the display in Figure 14–12 appears. The initial panel identifies the display, keyboard, mouse, and network settings for the installed version of Windows 3.1x. Changes are made to the Windows 3.1x configuration using drop-down menus. The options menu allows you to change the system settings that control the display, keyboard, and mouse configuration; change the network settings; set up applications; and add or remove Windows 3.1x installed software components.

During installation, the Windows setup program performs three functions: setting up Windows components, setting up printers, and setting up applications already installed on the fixed disk. Setting up Windows components involves copying the system files, the accessory programs, the game programs, screen savers, and the wallpaper and sound files on the hard disk. Windows setup permits customization of the Windows installation. You can select for copying individual files, groups of files, or all the files in one area. See Figure 14–13.

For a specific set of components like accessories, Windows permits selecting individual programs such as the calculator or selecting all accessory components. See Figure 14–14.

Figure 14–14 *Selecting accessory components*

During the setup process, Windows provides the option to set the size and type of the virtual memory swap file. A permanent or temporary swap file can be selected. A permit swap file requires contiguous free disk space equal to the size of the swap file. Creating a permanent swap file creates two files, the swap file, 386SPART.PAR, and a control file, SPART.PAR. These files guarantee availability of a specific size of virtual memory. With a temporary swap file, there is no guarantee of specific available virtual memory because the contiguous free disk space needed to store the swap file may diminish as the disk drive is used and becomes fragmented. See Figure 14–15.

The best installation strategy is to set a permanent swap file, guaranteeing a specific amount of virtual memory is always the available to Windows. Windows 3.1x automatically recommends an optimal swap file size based upon the available contiguous free disk space and the PC's installed RAM, as well as specifies the maximum swap file size for the permanent swap file. Often the optimal and maximum sizes are the same. We prefer to set the swap file size at the maximum size automatically recommended by Windows 3.1x.

The selected Windows components are then copied to the fixed disk.

Figure 14–15 *Virtual memory swap file setup*

      Printers can also be installed during initial setup or after Windows 3.1x has been rebooted. The correct printer drivers should be installed for correctly attached parallel port printers and network printers that the computer uses. Installing a printer requires selecting the specific printer driver software from the list of available printers presented by Windows or using the printer drivers that are supplied by the printer manufacturer.

      See Figure 14–16.

      Once a printer is selected, the driver programs are installed. When a printer is installed, it is set to use LPT1 as the default printer port. Windows

Figure 14–16 *Windows printer setup*

automatically selects the first printer as the default printer for this PC, unless you have a network printer.

In the last parts of the Windows 3.1x installation process, Windows scans the fixed disks for applications, sets them up with icons in a program group, and gives the installer the option of installing the applications it discovers. Windows also creates the standard program groups for the control panel, accessory programs, network programs, and more. It also creates the necessary CONFIG.SYS, AUTOEXEC.BAT, SYSTEM.INI, and WIN.INI files.

DIRECTORY LAYOUT

The Windows 3.1x programs are stored on the fixed disk in a Windows directory. This directory contains EXE, INI, DLL, BMP, RLE, FON/FOT/TTF, and HLP files.

- EXE files are the Windows 3.1x applets and other programs that launch applications software under Windows.
- INI files are initialization files that hold configuration parameters for Windows programs and Windows applications programs. These parameters describe how the program will look while running under Windows.
- DLLs are the dynamic link library files implementing the application and Windows programs that run under Windows.
- BMPs are bit-mapped graphics used for icons and other Windows images.
- RLEs are compressed image files that contain the Windows start up display and other images.

- FON/FOT/TTF files are the files that describe the bit-mapped (FON) or TrueType fonts (FOT/TTF).
- HLP files contain the Windows help display information.

The accessory and game programs are EXE files residing in the Windows directory. Under the Windows directory is the system directory. This directory also stores DLL files. A good strategy with Windows 3.1x is to place all the DLL files in the system directory even if the application install programs don't put them there. This avoids duplication of DLL files and the software errors that may result from such duplication. The system directory also contains driver programs (DRV) which control the PC hardware. Standard system applications are stored in other directories under the Windows directory or elsewhere as desired. See Figure 14–17. However, most third-party applications are not installed under the Windows directory, but are usually installed in default locations specified by the application vendor.

DRIVER PROGRAMS

The Windows 3.1x driver programs include the standard display mouse and keyboard drivers as well as multimedia sound drivers, speaker drivers, communications drivers, and more. The Windows 3.1x driver programs from a typical Windows 3.1x installation are shown in Table 14–4.

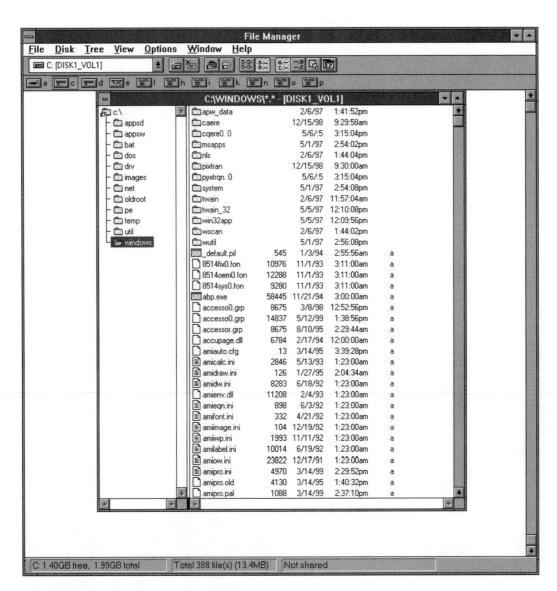

Figure 14–17 *Windows 3.1x directory layout*

Table 14.4_Windows 3.1x driver programs_

Display			
VGA	DRV	73,200 11-01-93 3:11a	
8514	DRV	92,032 11-01-93 3:11a	
SUPERVGA	DRV	73,504 11-01-93 3:11a	
SVGA256	DRV	117,440 11-01-93 4:11a	
VGAMONO	DRV	45,616 05-01-90 3:00a	
HVGA1280	DRV	82,384 04-21-92 3:13p	
HVGA960	DRV	82,384 04-21-92 2:14p	
STLTH32	DRV	157,616 03-15-94 12:42p	
STLTH32B	DRV	102,480 03-15-94 12:43p	
STLTH32H	DRV	140,096 03-15-94 12:42p	
STLTH32T	DRV	163,392 03-15-94 12:43p	

System

SPEAKER	DRV	7,088 05-28-92 4:44p
SOUND	DRV	3,440 11-01-93 3:11a
SYSTEM	DRV	2,304 11-01-93 4:11a
TIMER	DRV	4,192 11-01-93 4:11a
COMM	DRV	5,968 11-01-93 4:11a
KEYBOARD	DRV	7,568 11-01-93 4:11a
MSRLE	DRV	11,776 11-19-93 12:00a

MultiMedia Sound

MCIAVI	DRV	72,192 03-03-94 12:00a
MCICDA	DRV	13,824 11-01-93 4:11a
MCICMV50	DRV	86,816 05-26-94 12:00a
MCIMIXER	DRV	10,240 06-08-92 1:30a
MCIQTW	DRV	39,888 06-18-93 12:00a
MCISEQ	DRV	25,264 11-01-93 3:11a
MCIWAVE	DRV	28,160 11-01-93 3:11a
MIDIMAP	DRV	52,784 11-01-93 3:11a
MMSOUND	DRV	3,440 11-01-93 4:11a
ICCVID	DRV	58,880 11-19-93 12:00a

Mouse

MOUSE	DRV	10,672 11-01-93 3:11a
LMOUSE	DRV	12,928 11-01-93 3:11a
MSC3BC2	DRV	4,832 11-01-93 3:11a
MSCMOUSE	DRV	4,960 11-01-93 4:11a
MSMOUSE1	DRV	2,176 14-31-90 3:00a
MSMOUSE2	DRV	2,176 14-31-90 3:00a

Network

WFWNET	DRV	308,864 11-01-93 4:11a
NETWARE	DRV	165,632 14-24-94 2:29p

Printer

HPPCL	DRV	152,192 11-01-93 3:11a
HPPCL5A	DRV	428,672 03-14-92 3:10a
HPPCL5E	DRV	399,888 11-01-93 3:11a
PROPRINT	DRV	8,288 11-01-93 3:11a
PSCRIPT	DRV	314,576 11-01-93 4:11a

Fax Drivers

WINFAX	DRV	28,000 04-15-93 12:00a
EFAXDRV	DRV	11,776 11-01-93 3:11a
ENVOYDRV	DRV	182,352 06-24-94 12:00a
QLFXDRVR	DRV	18,741 02-16-93 1:32p
WFXCOMM	DRV	9,488 04-01-93 12:00a
WSP48024	DRV	123,920 07-14-92 4:47p
WSPDPBF	DRV	111,824 07-14-92 12:56p
WSPDPSF	DRV	109,376 07-14-92 12:55p

Shown in the table are the standard Windows 3.1x display drivers: VGA.DRV, 8514.DRV, SUPERVGA.DRV, SVGA256.DRV, and VGAMONO.DRV. The VGA card manufacturer provides the other display drivers for the specific VGA card installed in the PC if the standard drivers don't work. The standard Windows 3.1x system drivers are SPEAKER.DRV, SOUND.DRV, the SYSTEM.DRV, TIMER.DRV, KEYBOARD.DRV and MSRLE.DRV. The MSRLE.DRV is a driver program that works with run length encoded (RLE) files, which contain compressed images. The RLE files used by Windows 3.1x are wallpaper bitmaps. Windows 3.1x generally installs a single mouse driver. On this PC all Windows 3.1x mouse drivers are installed to illustrate all possible mouse driver programs because most PCs have some mouse different from an MS mouse. The most common and universal driver is the Logitech mouse driver. This is also true of Windows today. These drivers cover Microsoft mice, Logitech mice, and Mouse Systems mice. Hewlett-Packard laser printer drivers are also installed. This PC was set up with fax software so there are special fax drivers to add, as well.

These driver programs reside in the C:\WINDOWS\SYSTEM directory. GRP files describe the Windows 3.1x program groups. These files can be created and modified using the Windows 3.1x program manager. The registry concept was first used in Windows 3.1x. There is a single REG.DAT file that is the Windows 3.1x registry. It can be viewed using the command REGEDIT / V. This Registry stores information on applications running under Windows 3.1x to support dynamic data exchange between applications. It is not central to Windows itself.

Windows 3.1x installation is menu-driven. Running the Windows 3.1x SETUP.EXE program on a DOS 6.2x PC with memory configured to use XMS starts the Windows 3.1x installation process. The installation process creates a Windows directory, copies key files into that directory, and configures Windows INI flies. It can also scan for existing applications and install them automatically into program groups. At that point, the basic Windows 3.1x installation is complete.

Windows 95/98 Installation

Setup for Windows 95/98 can be performed from within Windows or from the DOS command prompt. In both cases, setup is completed using a Windows setup program and an installation wizard. A wizard is a program that leads the PC user step-by-step through a procedure, providing explanations of each step along the way. These explanations are provided in dialogue boxes with buttons indicating the next step. See Figure 14–18.

Similar to Windows 3.1 and DOS, Windows 95/98 is installed using a Windows 95/98 SETUP.EXE program.

There are several versions of Windows 95 and two versions of Windows 98. The Windows 95 versions are the original release of Windows (950 or revision A), operating system release 2 (OSR2 or revision B), and the final revision C. With Windows 98 there is the original release, and the Windows 98 SE (special edition), similar to Windows 95 OSR2. Each revision had slightly different features and capabilities. For example, Windows 95 revision A did not support the 32-bit FAT, while revisions B and C did. Further, revision C supported the USB bus.

The original version of Windows 95 could be installed using either floppy diskettes or a CD-ROM. The floppies were provided because not all PCs had a CD-ROM drive installed. There were about 19 floppy diskettes required to install Windows 95, as opposed to a single CD-ROM. However, in order to install all the CD-ROM files a working CD-ROM drive was required under DOS. The Windows 95 startup disk did not support the CD-ROM drive. The Windows 98 startup disk does support a CD-ROM drive so it makes installation off a CD-ROM very easy.

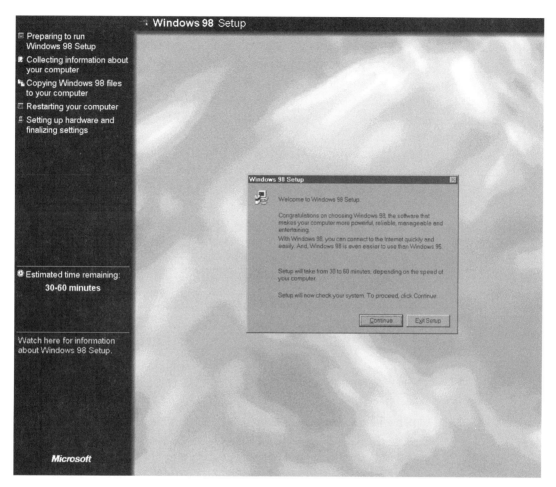

Figure 14–18 *Windows 98 setup dialog box*

Because DOS and Windows 3.1x did not automatically support a CD-ROM drive, original equipment manufacturers (OEM) generally copied the Windows 95/98 installation files to the fixed disk in a folder called \windows\options\cabs. They then installed Windows 95/98 from this fixed disk directory.

The Windows 95/98 installation files consist predominantly of CAB files, several EXE files like SETUP.EXE and SCANDISK.EXE, and other supporting TXT,BIN, and INF files. The CAB, or cabinet files, contains the Windows 95/98 software and configuration files. These CAB files are special compressed files created to contain the Windows 95/98 software. The Win-

```
Setup Options: SETUP [/C] [/iL] [batch] [/T:tmp] [/im] [/id] [/is] [/iq] [/in]
   /C          Instructs Setup not to load the SmartDrive disk cache.
   /iL         Loads the Logitech mouse driver instead of the Microsoft
               mouse driver. Use this option if you have a Logitech
               Series C mouse.
   [batch]     Specifies the name and location of the file that contains
               Setup options.
   /T:tmp      Specifies the directory where Setup will copy its temporary
               files. If the directory doesn't exist, it will be created.
               WARNING: Any existing files in this directory will be deleted.
   /im         Skips the memory check.
   /id         Skips the disk-space check.
   /is         Doesn't run ScanDisk.
   /iq         Skips the check for cross-linked files.
   /in         Runs Setup without the Network Setup module.
Note: The /a and /n options are no longer valid. Use NETSETUP.EXE instead.
```

Figure 14–19   *SETUP.EXE command display comparison*

dows 98 startup diskette has a CAB file created on it that contains diagnostic and other software needed to fix a corrupted Windows 98 installation.

RUNNING SETUP

The SETUP.EXE program for Windows 95/98 has command line options shown in Figure 14–19 similar to the command line options for Windows 3.1 x SETUP.EXE. The SETUP.EXE program for Windows 95 is slightly different from the SETUP.EXE program for Windows 98. See Figure 14–19: SETUP.EXE command display comparison. The Windows 95 setup program has /C, /iL, and /in options that are not provided by the Windows 98 setup program. The /C option causes the SMARTDRV disk cache program not to be loaded, the /iL option loads a Logitech mouse driver in place of the Microsoft mouse driver, and finally the /in option runs setup without performing the network setup. Windows 98 has three options that Windows 95 setup does not have. These options are: /ie which bypasses the emergency diskette creation, /ih which skips the registry check, and /iv which bypasses the Windows displays seen during the setup process. The Windows 95/98 SETUP.EXE program runs a Real Mode SCANDISK check, copies the files needed to run the Windows setup program, and then launches Windows setup.

Windows 95/98 installation steps are:

1. Set up and run Windows setup.
2. Gather information on the PC.
3. Copy designated files to the PC.
4. Restart the PC.
5. Perform plug-and-play hardware setup and finalize Windows software and hardware settings.

When Windows sets up and runs the Windows SETUP.EXE program, it soon displays the Windows end user license agreement (EULA) dialog box. See Figure 14–20.

It then creates a setup log file, identifies where Windows is to be installed, creates a temporary installation directory, and runs the installation wizard program.

The wizard program gathers information about your computer. Windows setup reviews the license agreement, asks the user to enter the product key code, asks the user to select or specify the directory into which to install Windows and then prepares this directory. See Figure 14–21.

Next, the Windows setup program, through the Windows setup wizard, permits the installer to select typical, portable, compact, or custom setup. These options preselect certain groups of files to install or not install, depending on the PCs available disk space. These options can be viewed as Microsoft recommendations for different types of computers. In all cases, the installer can customize the Windows 95/98 installation as though the custom setup were selected. Further Windows components can always be added after the initial installation is completed using the control panel and add/remove programs. See Figure 14–22. These installation options are used only to preselect specific Windows components as deemed best by Microsoft for that type of PC operation.

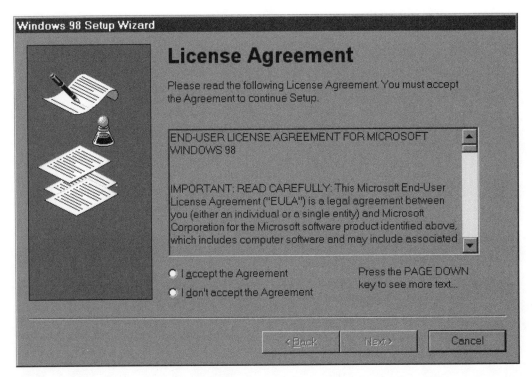

Figure 14–20 *Windows EULA dialog box*

Windows setup requests the user to enter name and company information. The user can also specify at different times in the Windows 95 and Windows 98 installation process the Windows components to install. As shown in Figure 14–23, the Windows accessories are listed, permitting them to be individually selected for installation. When selected, the amount of disk space required is displayed. The selection box also displays the amount of disk space required by setup and the amount of disk space available to install Windows.

Upon entry of the user name and company information, Windows 95 and 98 vary slightly in the installation process. Windows 95 analyzes your computer at this point. See Figure 14–24.

After the analysis is complete, Windows 95 setup moves to selecting Window's software components depending on the setup option (typical, portable, compact, or custom setup) selected. Windows 95 completes network component selection and then enters the computer identification information. Upon completion, a startup diskette is created based on user input. Then Windows 95 setup copies the requisite Windows files to the fixed

Figure 14–21 *Windows directory preparation*

disk. Once Windows setup has copied the necessary files to the fixed disk, the PC is restarted.

In contrast, Windows 98 moves directly to selecting Window's software components, depending on the setup option (typical, portable, compact, or custom setup) selected. Then Windows 98 performs the PC analysis done earlier in the sequence by Windows 95. The Windows 98 hardware analysis performed at this time is more accurate than the hardware analysis performed by Windows 95 because only Windows 98 software programs are running.

The final step, installing the plug-and-play hardware and finalizing the Windows settings, is performed during the Windows boot process. Windows displays the message "Getting ready to start Windows 98 for the first time." In this final stage, Windows setup configures the control panel, the start menu, Windows help files, MS-DOS program settings, the applications to start automatically, the date and time settings, and the final system configuration.

Figure 14–22 *Windows setup options.*

Windows installation can be performed on a new system or on an existing Windows system. When performed on an existing Windows system, the installation process does not change the application software settings. It does, however, redo the hardware installation settings. Often reinstalling Windows over an existing Windows installation is a way of fixing some hardware problems. Periodic or annual reinstallation of Windows on a clean disk drive as well as all of the applications software is also a good maintenance procedure. We often perform such installations to correct Windows problems because it takes less time than detailed troubleshooting of the problem.

DIRECTORY LAYOUT

Windows 95/98 directory layout is different from Windows 3.1x directory layout. In both cases Windows by default installs itself in a C:\Windows directory. See Figure 14–25

At the root directory level, Windows 95/98 adds some other important directories. These directories are the program files directory, the recycled

Figure 14-23 *Accessory component selection*

directory, the my documents directory and the multimedia files directory. Of these new directories the most used aside from the Windows directory and thus most important are the program files directory and the recycled directory. Application programs by default are generally installed in the program files directory. Data erased from the fixed disk is placed in the recycled directory so that it may be later retrieved if its removal was made by mistake. The recycled directory must be periodically emptied. Windows provides a menu option for emptying the recycle bin.

Under the C:\Windows directory there are some additional directories specific to Windows 95/98. As with Windows 3.1x, there is the system subdirectory or folder that holds DLL, EXE, DRV, HLP, and other files. There are also important subdirectories under the system subdirectory. One key subdirectory is the IOSYS subdirectory that contains the VxD and MPD (MIDI port driver) files.

Another key directory is the Start Menu directory. This directory establishes the structure for the start menu and the application and Windows components that are installed on the PC. The start menu structure

Figure 14–24 *Windows 95 PC analysis*

itself is in a programs subdirectory under the Start Menu subdirectory. See Figure 14–26. In the programs subdirectory is a startup folder (or subdirectory). Items placed in the startup folder are launched automatically during the Windows boot process. Not all programs that start automatically are launched using the startup folder. Some programs are launched automatically from entries in the Windows 95/98 registry. Details on the registry are provided in Chapter 11.

Changing or rearranging the folders under the programs subdirectory changes and rearranges the start menu items.

The desktop folder contains the items visible on the desktop. As things are added to or removed from the desktop, the contents of this folder (or subdirectory) change. Other folders are related to Internet software. These folders are the cookies folder, the downloaded program files folder, the history folder, MSDOWNLD.TMP folder (sometimes found on a PC when Windows has been upgraded using the Internet update option, and the temporary Internet files folder among others. The fonts used by Windows 95/98 are stored in the fonts folder in the Windows directory.

Figure 14–25 *Windows directory layout.*

Figure 14–26   *Windows Start Menu folder*

The operation and look of Windows is controlled by the contents of special file folders in the Windows directory and in the root directory. We will examine a few of the key folders here.

DRIVER PROGRAMS—DOS MODE VERSUS 32 BIT

Windows 95/98 works with both 32-bit Windows driver programs and 16-bit DOS mode compatible driver programs. Windows 32-bit driver programs provide the best PC performance because they operate correctly with the hardware and do not rely on ROM BIOS. If possible, the Windows 32-bit driver programs should always be used. This can be checked using the Win-

Figure 14–27   *Windows 32-bit driver program*

dows control panel and selecting system and then the performance tab. See Figure 14–27. This displays whether the 32-bit driver programs or the 16-bit driver programs are being used for the file system and the virtual memory. These are equivalent to the Windows 3.1x 32-bit disk and 32-bit file access drivers.

When 16-bit driver programs are installed, the performance tab displays a message stating 16-bit driver programs are used for MS-DOS compatibility. In this case, the DOS drivers in the CONFIG.SYS and AUTOEXEC.BAT file for the CD-ROM may be installed. Removing the CONFIG.SYS and AUTOEXEC.BAT drivers should normally cause Windows to install the proper 32-bit Windows drivers. The Windows 32-bit drivers are the VxD files found in the IOSYS folder.

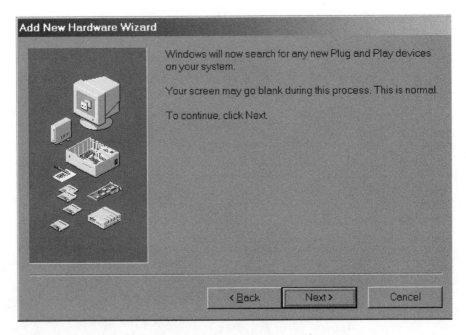

Figure 14–28   *Windows plug-and-play hardware configuration*

PLUG-AND-PLAY COMPONENTS

Windows 95/98 provides for plug-and-play hardware component installation. This plug-and-play hardware component installation is dependent on the PC's BIOS as well as the hardware component itself. Both must be designed to work with the Windows plug-and-play software. Plug-and-play software in Windows 98 works more effectively than that with Windows 95. Part of the increased effectiveness results from how the plug-and-play process is performed during Windows installation. Remember, Windows 98 performs the final plug-and-play analysis after the system is re-booted. This means that only Windows 98 software components are running while the plug-and-play installation process is being completed. As a result, Windows 98 makes fewer mistakes in configuring hardware plug-and-play components. The plug-and-play hardware installation can be run at any time by using the control panel and selecting Install New Hardware. See Figure 14–28.

Windows plug-and-play installation is a function of the Windows software and the PC's BIOS. They work together to permit Windows to identify all plug-and-play hardware components installed in the PC and to properly configure their IRQs, I/O addresses, and memory regions. Generally, all PCI bus components are plug-and-play, as are some specially designed ISA bus components. Components with hardware jumper settings are generally not plug-and-play devices.

An alternative way to make Windows 95/98 perform plug-and-play hardware installation is to actually remove the hardware driver from Windows 95/98. This is done by opening the control panel, selecting system, selecting device manager, opening the device, and removing the device from the Windows configuration. This approach works well with multimedia devices, communications ports, network adapters, modems, and some display adapters.

It is not a good idea to remove disk drives from the Windows configuration in this manner because, once the disk drive is removed, Windows cannot write the registry information to the disk drive. The registry was discussed earlier in Chapter 11. After a disk drive is removed, Windows believes it has no disk drive to which to write. This can cause Windows to lock (abruptly halt operation).

Another way to force hardware reinstallation is to set up a new hardware profile. Forcing hardware reinstallation can sometimes resolve Windows plug-and-play installation problems. This is done using the hardware profiles tab.

The current profile "original configuration" is copied to a new hardware profile name. Then Windows is restarted. During the restart process, Windows asks which profile to use to start Windows. Three choices are given: 1. Original configuration, 2. New configuration, and 3. None of the above. Selecting item "3. None of the above," causes Windows to perform the plug-and-play hardware installation for all devices. This sometimes resolves plug-and-play hardware problems, but there's no guarantee that it will.

Study Break

Hardware Profiles

This study break deals with Windows 95/98 hardware profiles, their implementation, management, and helpfulness in the troubleshooting process. Will create a new hardware profile, reboot Windows to see what this does to the Windows reboot process, and then remove the profile.

1. Using a Windows 95 or a Windows 98 PC, open the control panel, then select system and hardware profiles. This should display a panel showing the "original configuration" hardware profile.

2. Select copy and enter in the "To" box the title "current." Next click OK. Now two configurations should appear in the configuration box. One should be current and the other original configuration.

3. Click OK and then shut down and restart Windows. As Windows is restarted, you are presented with a menu option to select between current, original configuration, or none of the above as the hardware profile in which Windows is started. Select current as the hardware configuration in which to start Windows.

4. After Windows is running, open the control panel and select the system icon. Double-click to open system properties, then select device manager. Pick the ports icon and expand it by clicking on the "+." Select a communications port, preferably, COM2. Open properties and check disable in this hardware profile. Click OK. This should return you to the device manager screen where the communications port COM2 is displayed with a red X indicating it has been disabled.

5. Restart Windows and now select original configuration as the hardware profile for Windows. Once Windows is running, open the control panel and select the system icon. Double-click to open system properties then select device manager. Expand the communications port icon as before. In this case the COM2 port should not be disabled because it was disabled only in the "current" hardware profile.

6. Open hardware profiles again. Select "original configuration" and attempt to delete it. Because it is in use, Windows should prevent you from deleting this configuration. Next delete the "current" configuration. Since this configuration is not in use it can be deleted.

7. Restart Windows at this point. Now no hardware configuration profile needs to be selected because we have returned Windows to its original configuration.

The goal of this exercise was to illustrate how Windows works with different hardware profiles. If we had selected "none of the above" during our reboot process, Windows would perform a complete hardware analysis to reconfigure the plug-and-play hardware in the PC.

A+ 14.2 Software Upgrades

With DOS and Windows software products, upgrading from previous versions to newer versions is a planned migration path. Upgrade and new installation procedures are both designed into the newer versions of Windows. The goal of upgrade procedures is to preserve the existing application software installation. This saves time by not requiring all application software to be reinstalled when upgrading from one version of software to another. There are typically two drawbacks to the upgrade process. Generally when upgrading from one version of software to the next version of software, the newer software requires significantly increased hardware capabilities. These capabilities may not be installed on the existing PC. This is particularly true of free capacity on the fixed disk drive. Newer versions of software tend to require significantly increased storage capacities. For example, Windows 3.1 x could be installed on a 512MB disk drive. Upgrading to Windows 98 could require as much as 355MB of disk space. As a result, the upgrade may not be possible in this instance.

The second problem comes from the installed software itself. If the system has a bad software blend—that is, it does not run properly and crashes frequently—then installing an upgrade on top of a bad software installation can easily make things worse rather than better. The best strategy in this case is to start fresh, as a minimum by reformatting the fixed disk, then installing Windows and the application software to be used on the PC.

Upgrades preserve the existing Windows software configuration. When an existing Windows software configuration is operating reliably, then preserving that configuration is a good upgrade strategy. If, however, the existing software configuration is not reliable and solid, then a fresh configuration that removes the existing Windows installation is most likely the better strategy. In all cases, when upgrading a Windows configuration does not go smoothly for whatever reason, then a fresh installation usually resolves the problems encountered.

Users should consider upgrading to new releases of Windows whenever they become available. Generally, a new release operates more reliably and predictably than older Windows versions. For example, when Windows 95 was first released, it was more reliable than Windows 3.1x. Similarly, the first release of Windows 98 was an improvement in reliability over that of Windows 95. While features also evolved to more user-friendly levels with each release of the Windows operating system, reliability is a more important factor in the move to upgrade from one version of Windows to another. The major drawback to upgrading is that some systems are operating reliably and predictably as configured with earlier versions of Windows. The maxim "When it isn't broke, don't upgrade it" applies to those PCs reliably running earlier versions of Windows. Some of our PCs ran Windows 3.1x and Windows 95 for months without being restarted. They encountered no problems during these periods. There was no need to rush to upgrade these PCs. In contrast, several PCs that were always running newer Windows applications operated less reliably with older, earlier versions of Windows than with newer versions of Windows.

System Requirements

As a minimum to run Windows 95, an 80386 DX 20 MHz processor is required and to run Windows 98 an 80486 DX 66 MHz processor is needed. See Table 14–5. Windows NT requires resources similar to Windows 98 for a minimum system configuration. Windows 3.1x requires the fewest resources. Minimum installation requirements are a 386 SX CPU chip with 3 MB of RAM and 15 MB of disk space. Minimum hardware requirements for Windows 95/98, Windows 3.1x, and Windows NT are given in Table 14–1. Table 14–5 presents Windows 95 and Windows 98 upgrade requirements.

No need to worry today about meeting the minimum CPU chip

Table 14.5 *Windows 95/98 minimum upgrade requirements*

	CPU Chip	RAM	Fixed Disk (Free) Capacity
Windows 95	80386 DX 20 MHz	4 MB minimum 8 MB recommended	20 MB normal 10 MB compact installation
Windows 98	80486 DX 66 MHz	16 MB minimum 32 MB and more	120 MB disk space minimum 355 MB can be used for new install

requirements because 386 SX CPU chips are no longer manufactured. Actually, when it comes right down to it, the only new CPU chips you can effectively purchase today are Pentium-class CPU chips. Thus, the minimum CPU requirement is met for all Windows operating systems. Most systems are produced with 64MB of RAM so that minimum requirements are also fulfilled,

In all cases a 266 MHz or higher Pentium CPU chip or equivalent is a more realistic alternative. The recommended RAM is 8 MB for Windows 95 and 16 MB for Windows 98. About 48 MB of RAM is needed in both cases to provide effective performance. RAM size of 64 MB to 128 MB is better. The second big upgrade component is the disk drive capacity. Windows specifies the required capacity in MB of free disk space needed to install Windows. A Windows 95 upgrade from DOS may require as much as 30 MB of free disk space (equivalent to a new installation) and more typically 20 MB for an upgrade from Windows 3.1 or 10 MB from Windows for Workgroups (Windows 3.11). Realistically, a Windows 95 system should have a 2GB fixed disk with 512 MB of free capacity to run Windows 95 most effectively. Disk drive capacity for a Windows 98 upgrade varies from 120 MB to 295 MB when moving up from Windows 3.1x and Windows 95. A 32-bit FAT new installation requires less free fixed disk space. In this instance, Microsoft recommends 140 MB to 255 MB. A new 16-bit FAT installation of Windows 98 can consume as much as 355 MB of free fixed disk space. This is because the 32-bit FAT stores data more efficiently by using smaller allocation units than FAT 16 does. A client installation from across a network requires 175 MB to 225 MB of free disk space for Windows 98 because the network software as well as the installation software must run in the PC while Windows 98 is being installed.

As a practical measure, Windows 98 should be installed on systems with about a 4 GB fixed disk with 1 GB of free space.

Upgrading also requires a VGA or Super VGA adapter with sufficient memory for 16-color displays. More effective use of the PC is with a 1,024 by 768 VGA display with 256 colors. This should be on a 15-inch or 17-inch monitor. A display with 16-million (24-bit color) colors provides a better display for graphics and images. In each case, upgrading to Windows requires a mouse (using keyboard shortcuts for mouse movements really stinks) and a CD-ROM drive. It probably is possible to get Windows 98 installation diskettes, but they are rarely if ever used to install Windows 98.

Windows 98 recommends a 28.8 KBPS modem as well. The modem is needed to permit upgrades to Windows 98 from the Internet. A 28.8 KBPS modem permits upgrades across the Internet but a 33.6 KBPS works better. However, a 56 KBPS modem is best of all for Internet upgrades. However, upgrades and maintenance of Windows from the Internet at these speeds requires hours of time. The process is reduced to minutes with a higher speed cable modem. See Figure 14–29.

The Windows 98 Internet upgrade is used to upgrade Windows 98 software components and not to perform upgrades from one version of Windows to another. Windows 95 cannot be upgraded to Windows 98 via the Internet.

General Upgrade Procedure

Basically the upgrade procedure starts by running the SETUP.EXE program. This program guides you through the Windows setup process. There are different ways to run SETUP.EXE. It can be run from a DOS prompt or from within Windows. Generally starting from a DOS prompt achieves all installation objectives. However, if Windows is being installed from a CD-ROM drive, the CD-ROM drive must be configured to work under DOS by using MSCDEX.EXE loaded in AUTOEXEC.BAT and CD-ROM drivers loaded in CONFIG.SYS.

Figure 14–29 *Windows 98 Internet upgrade*

The easiest way to get a bootable DOS diskette that has drivers for most CD-ROM drives is to create a Windows 98 startup diskette using the control panel—add/remove programs—startup disk menu selection.

Use any old Windows 98 PC to create a Windows 98 startup diskette. See Figure 14–30. This diskette boots into DOS and has CD-ROM drivers for SCSI and IDE CD-ROM drives. This diskette can be used to install both

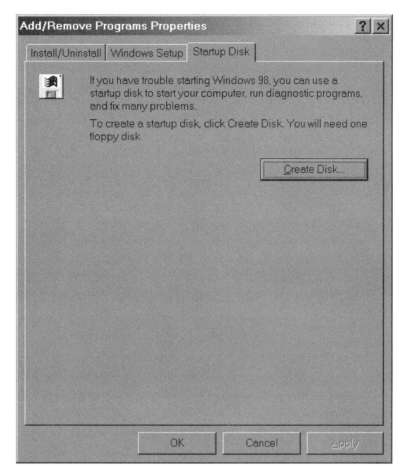

Figure 14–30 *Windows 98 startup diskette creation*

Windows 98 and Windows 95 in spite of its being a Windows 98 startup diskette.

After booting from the DOS prompt, change to the Windows 95 or Windows 98 setup directory (generally it is d:\win98, where "d" represents the drive letter of your computer's CD-ROM drive) on the CD-ROM and run SETUP.EXE. SETUP.EXE is used as an installation program for almost all software today. It began to be used as an installation program with DOS 6.22. It has been used with Windows 3.1x, Windows 95, and Windows 98. Windows NT uses WINNT.EXE or WINNT32.EXE to perform its installation.

DOS to Windows 95/98

A DOS-to-Windows upgrade can be difficult because DOS PCs have so few hardware resources. Installing DOS itself requires about six or seven megabytes of free disk space. In contrast, Windows 3.1x requires only 15 MB of disk space while Windows 98 can need 120 MB to 355 MB of free disk space. The most difficult part of upgrading from DOS to Windows is finding the required memory and free fixed disk space resources on a DOS system.

Because DOS PCs have minimal resources as compared to Windows PCs, it is best to think of an upgrade from DOS as an initial install of Windows 95/98.

The install is accomplished by booting into DOS with the proper CD-ROM drivers so that the CD-ROM drive works, then running SETUP.EXE from the Windows install directory on the CD-ROM drive. Alternatively, the install files can be copied to the fixed disk (provided there is sufficient space to hold the install files and to install the Windows upgrade) and then Windows can be installed from the files copied to the fixed disk.

Windows 3.1x to Windows 95/98

There are several scenarios for upgrading to Windows 95 and 98 from Windows 3.1x. These scenarios vary for Windows 95 and Windows 98.

UPGRADING TO WINDOWS 95

When upgrading to Windows 95 from Windows 3.1x, the preferred approach is to run SETUP.EXE from within Windows 3.1x. Windows finds the existing Windows 3.1x installation and proceeds to install Windows 95 in the same directory. During this process, the WIN.INI, SYSTEM.INI, and PROTOCOL.INI files are used to create the new Windows 95 equivalent files. Also file associations and application and network settings are transferred from the existing Windows 3.1x configuration to the upgraded Windows 95 installation. Finally, Windows 95 converts the Windows 3.1x program groups into directories used to create the Windows 95 start menu.

Because Windows 95/98 expects to be installed in a \Windows directory, upgrading Windows 3.1x installed in a \Win directory to Windows 95/98 can become difficult when Windows 95/98 is upgraded using the \Win directory of Windows 3.1x. Such an upgrade causes Windows 95/98 not to be installed in a \Windows directory. In this instance, Windows 95/98 would be installed in the \Win directory. As a result, Windows 95/98 would encounter complications when it was looking for its installed components in a \Windows directory.

Upgrading to Windows 95 and installing it into a new directory (a directory different from the existing Windows 3.1x directory) preserves the old Windows 3.1x installation. Application program settings are not moved to Windows 95 in this case. Special setup steps are needed to enable a dual-boot—that is, the ability to boot the PC into either Windows 3.1x or Windows 95. The basic steps required to set up a dual-boot Windows 3.1x and Windows 95 PC are to install Windows 95 in a separate directory from the Windows 3.1x files and to set the BootMulti=1 entry in the Windows 95 MSDOS.SYS file. Dual-boot systems are rare and only required if there is software that runs only on the older operating system, Windows 3.1x.

UPGRADING TO WINDOWS 98

Upgrading to Windows 98 from DOS or from Windows 3.1x is a significant step as compared to upgrading to Windows 98 from Windows 95 or upgrading to Windows 95 from DOS, or from Windows 3.1x. There are several different strategies.

Upgrading from DOS is like setting up a new installation. SETUP.EXE is run and the Wizard is followed to install Windows 98. The critical element here is having the needed PC hardware resources. The PC hardware resource most lacking for a Windows-95-to-Windows-98 upgrade is free space on the fixed disk drive. When upgrading from Windows 3.1x, the preferred approach is to run SETUP.EXE from within Windows 3.1x. Windows 98 copies most of the information it needs to upgrade Windows 3.1x to Windows 98 from the existing Windows 3.1x installation. The current configuration and installed programs are migrated into Windows 98 during upgrade installation. There is only one problem with this approach and that is when real-mode LAN driver and interface programs are used for Novell NetWare or Artisoft LANtastic. If SETUP.EXE is run while these programs are operating, SETUP stops and won't continue. You are also likely to get an error message that in a general sense identifies the conflicting software that prevents SETUP from completing the installation. Simply remove these programs before running SETUP.EXE, but be sure to note the network configuration information first. Windows 98 provides all the needed LAN drivers and software for peer-to-peer networking and client/server networking with Novell NetWare.

Upgrading to Windows 98 from Windows 95 is similar to upgrading to Windows 95 from Windows 3.1x. Windows 98 can be installed in the same directory as Windows 95 or it can be installed in a new directory. Running

SETUP.EXE from within Windows 95 installs Windows 98 in the existing Windows 95 directory and preserves the computer name, network settings, start menu programs, installed applications, and more. This upgrade procedure requires the least amount of user interaction. Similar to upgrading from Windows 3.1x to Windows 95, the current configuration and application settings are migrated into the Windows 98 during upgrade installation. A limitation here is that the Windows 98 directory cannot be changed to a different directory from the Windows 95 directory. To have a clean installation of Windows 98, change the directory into which Windows 98 is installed and install Windows 98 from DOS. This installation strategy option permits changing the installation directory for Windows 98, selecting setup options, entering user information, identifying the computer on the network, and changing the computer settings—for instance, the language support. Booting the PC into DOS either using a floppy, exiting Windows 95 to DOS, or using the F5 key to bypass the Windows 95 and DOS startup files can do this. (See booting discussion that follows.) Once at the DOS prompt, change to the Windows 98 setup disk directory (the directory containing the Windows 98 CAB files and the SETUP.EXE program—generally, it is d:\win98) and run the SETUP.EXE program. Installing Windows 98 into a new directory is more work because the user and network information must be respecified to Windows 98, and applications and other special driver programs may need to be installed. Installing Windows 98 into a new directory provides a more reliable Windows 98 installation overall.

When upgrading from Windows 95 to Windows 98, the Windows 95 settings and configuration are preserved to the greatest extent when Windows 98 is installed from within Windows 95. To install a clean configuration of Windows 98, the Windows 98 installation is performed from DOS as opposed to from within Windows 95.

When problems are encountered during setup of Windows 95/98, antivirus software, third-party utilities, third-party hardware driver programs, and DOS real-time programs usually cause them. During Windows 95/98 installation, the setup program may provide a general warning about conflicting software, but it is not likely to identify the specific software conflicts. As a general rule it is best to run no other software besides the Windows 95/98 SETUP.EXE program. To insure smooth installation antivirus software, third-party utilities, special hardware driver programs, and DOS real-time programs should be disabled. Returning Windows 3.1x and Windows 95 to a standard operating state (that is, VGA mode with no special Video, LAN, communications, and other drivers) using only Microsoft Windows drivers is a good strategy to follow when upgrading to Windows 98.

Special drivers and utility software designed to operate with Windows 3.1x and Windows 95 can cause problems because during Windows 98 installation older DLLs, VxDs, DRV and other Windows programs used by these special devices can be retained. Since they may not be updated to the newer Windows 98 versions, the old drivers may or may not work properly with Windows 98. For example, when installing Windows 98, if the PC enters safe mode operation there is a good likelihood that the display drivers do not work with Windows 98. To correct such problems, the most current hardware drivers and utilities should be obtained from the Internet web site of the manufacturer and installed. The latest driver and utility software is often needed for Windows 98 to run reliably. Leaving old driver and other software on a PC provides a fertile environment for a bad software mix to develop, causing Windows 98 to crash or run miserably.

Study Break

Finding Windows CAB Files

In this exercise we will look for the Windows CAB installation files on our fixed disk drive.

1. Go to a Windows 95 or Windows 98 PC.

2. Open Windows explorer, select tools from the menu bar, point to find, then click on files and folders. They should open up the search window permitting us to search for files on the fixed disk drives.

3. Under the name and location tab in the named panel enter *.CAB. Next click on find now. This causes explorer to search for the CAB files on the drive specified by the look in panel. The drive specified should be the C disk drive.

4. If no CAB files are located, then Windows 95/98 was most likely installed directly from a CD-ROM drive. When CAB files are located, note the folder where they reside. This is most often the \windows\options\cabs folder (directory).

5. Make a note of the date on the CAB files. This date can be used to determine the version of Windows installed on the PC. Check with the Windows release dates listed in Chapter 11.

The goal of this exercise was to familiarize you with where Windows installation files can be located.

A+ 14.3 Booting Procedures

Booting procedures for DOS, Windows 3.1x, and Windows 95/98 are similar. With Windows, though, the procedure involves different components. There is both a cold boot and a warm boot process. The cold boot process starts from a power off and on cycle—physically turning the computer off and then on again—or a hard PC reset. In this case, the contents of RAM are lost and the PC starts with a fresh memory configuration. To remove a virus program from memory, a cold boot is needed. A warm boot is initiated by the Ctrl-Alt-Del keystroke sequence. This does not clear memory. Virus programs can intercept the Ctrl-Alt-Del keystroke sequence before Windows processes it. This gives the virus programs an opportunity to hide themselves and survive a PC reboot. Windows 95/98 uses Ctrl-Alt-Del to perform other functions like loading the task manager program to kill off nonresponding Windows tasks.

All PC boot processes use the real mode BIOS routines. They perform the Power On Self Test (POST) of the PC's hardware. This mostly checks for the presence of several key devices, including the display controller, the keyboard, the floppy diskettes, and the fixed disk drive. On newer PCs, a CD-ROM drive is also sometimes detected (for booting), but if not present an error is not reported. The system RAM is tested to determine if it matches the RAM parameter stored in the CMOS setup parameter memory. The BIOS boot process displays on the monitor the results of its testing and any PC ROM and special device ROM messages. Generally, the last BIOS POST message displays what was discovered about the PC including CPU chip and clock speed, floppy disk drives and capacities, fixed disk drive and capacity, the presence and configuration of LPT and COM ports and the total amount of RAM detected. The process causes the PC to sometimes beep twice, indicating all is well so far. Different series of beeps without the Windows screens appearing generally indicate hardware malfunctions during the boot process. The other boot options, including the function keys, are covered later in this chapter.

Booting DOS

DOS boots using BIOS, IO.SYS, MSDOS.SYS, and COMMAND.COM. The BIOS performs the cold boot loading process in real mode. It runs a cold boot loader program that first determines the boot device. When it is a floppy diskette, the BIOS loads a cold boot loader program from the first diskette sector, the DOS boot record. If there is no floppy DOS boot record (DBR), BIOS displays "Nonsystem disk or disk error. Replace and strike any key when ready." The nonbootable floppy can be replaced by a bootable floppy and the process continued.

When the boot device is a fixed disk, the BIOS loads a cold boot loader found in the master boot record (MBR) of the fixed disk. A CD-ROM boot is similar, with a cold boot loader loading from a CD-ROM boot record. The cold boot loader program in the master boot record determines the fixed disk's partition configuration from data it stores. It locates the active bootable partition (usually drive C) and then loads IO.SYS from the active partition on the fixed disk.

If IO.SYS cannot be found, the error "Missing Operating System" is displayed. Other DOS boot errors are described in Chapter 2. The "Missing Operating System" error can sometimes be fixed by using the DOS commands FDISK /MBR and SYS C:\. FDISK /MBR rewrites the master boot record while SYS C: reinstalls the system boot files on the drive C (hopefully, the bootable) partition. This is why a bootable-diskette-troubleshooting tool should contain both the FDISK and SYS programs as described in the Chapter 3 study break exercise, "Creating a Bootable Diskette." FDISK is also discussed in Chapter 3 and Chapter 12.

Next IO.SYS is loaded to complete the boot process. IO.SYS continues to load the remaining programs. It loads MSDOS.SYS and then processes the DEVICE= commands and the FILES= and other commands in CONFIG.SYS. The DEVICE= commands load real mode hardware device drivers for special hardware installed in the PC, and the FILES= and other commands configure the PC's environment space and memory allocation for parameters and buffers. Generally IO.SYS completes the commands in CONFIG.SYS from top to bottom of the file. That is not precisely true. Some commands (for instance, DOS=HIGH and DOS=UMB) are processed first, regardless of where they appear in the file.

IO.SYS passes control to COMMAND.COM, which is installed in the root directory of the bootable partition. A SHELL= statement can redirect the loading of COMMAND.COM from another directory. When COMMAND.COM does not match the DOS IO.SYS and MSDOS.SYS files, an "Invalid Command.com" message is displayed.

Once loaded, COMMAND.COM processes the commands from AUTOEXEC.BAT. These commands load the programs that complete the DOS configuration. Some programs like SMARTDRV and DOSKEY perform special functions. Other commands like SET configure the environment space used to store DOS parameters used by application programs. A good SET command is SET DOSCMD=/Ogn /A. This causes the DIR command to display all files (/A) in alphabetical order with subdirectories first (/Ogn).

REQUIRED DOS BOOT FILES

The files needed for DOS to boot are:

- IO.SYS
- MSDOS.SYS
- COMMAND.COM.

In some cases the CONFIG.SYS file is needed to load HIMEM.SYS (DEVICE=HIMEM.SYS) and set DOS=HIGH because without them there is not enough memory to run the programs desired. When installing Windows, it is also good to have an AUTOEXEC.BAT file that loads SMARTDRV.EXE, the disk cache program. The SDMARTDRV disk cache program speeds up Windows installation by a factor of 14.

CREATING A DOS BOOTABLE DISKETTE

Using the FORMAT command creates a bootable DOS diskette. The command is:

```
FORMAT A: /S
```

or

```
FORMAT C: /S
```

to format a fixed disk drive.

The /S option causes the system files to be installed on the floppy. Other FORMAT options are described in Chapter 12. This works for DOS, Windows 3.1x, and Windows 95/98 as well. Formatting in DOS is better than in Windows because it deals more directly with the diskette drive hardware through BIOS. Windows does a fine job as well, but it has less direct hardware control.

Also installed with the current DOS and Windows versions is DRV-SPACE.BIN. DRVSPACE is only needed if there is a compressed disk that must be accessed. Often it is desirable to remove DRVSPACE from a bootable floppy to make room for other more important diagnostic and utility programs. IO.SYS, MSDOS.SYS, and DRVSPACE.BIN are all system, read-only, hidden files. To remove DRVSPACE, the system, read-only, and hidden file attributes must be removed so it can be deleted from the diskette. Changing file attributes is described in Chapter 12.

The DOS SYS command makes an empty formatted diskette into a bootable diskette. It transfers the system files from a bootable partition or diskette to the target drives. The command is:

```
SYS A:
```

or

```
SYS C:
```

This command works with DOS, Windows 3.1x in a DOS window, and Windows 95/98 in a DOS window. The interesting thing with Windows 95/98 is that the bootable floppy produced uses only IO.SYS and COMMAND.COM to perform the DOS functions. The MSDOS.SYS file is merely a placeholder. It contains the text FORMAT if the bootable diskette was produced by the FORMAT program and SYS if the bootable diskette was produced using the SYS program.

The DOS booting process is followed for DOS, Windows 3.1x, and Windows 95/98. However, for all versions of Windows, the DOS boot process is just the start of the overall boot process. There are some differences as well. The Windows 95/98 DOS uses only IO.SYS and COMMAND.COM to provide the DOS functions. MSDOS.SYS has become more a placeholder and parameter file for Windows 95/98 DOS.

BYPASSING STARTUP FILES

The DOS CONFIG.SYS and AUTOEXEC.BAT files can be bypassed during the boot process by using the F5 and F8 keys. When the PC displays the message

```
Starting MS-DOS…
```

or

```
"Starting Windows 98…
```

striking the F5 key bypasses both CONFIG.SYS and AUTOEXEC.BAT files and loads DOS. This boots the PC without any special driver programs or configuration options. During the boot DOS displays:

```
MS-DOS is bypassing your CONFIG.SYS and AUTOEXEC.BAT files.
```

or

```
Windows 98 is bypassing your CONFIG.SYS and AUTOEXEC.BAT
                        files.
```

The disk compression software DBLSPACE is still loaded into memory for Windows 98 and cannot be bypassed (not loaded). It means that about 197 KB is used to load Windows 98 DOS, in contrast to 62 KB for DOS 6.22.

The Windows 3.1x Boot Process

This section covers the Windows 3.1x boot process. Since Windows 3.1x rides on top of DOS 6.2x, the initial boot process is the same for both. The difference is that the Windows boot process starts Windows after DOS is loaded and configured. Running the WIN.COM program launches Windows. The same is also true for Windows 98, but WIN.COM launches automatically and is not launched from the AUTOEXEC.BAT file.

WIN.COM loads Windows 3.1x in 386 enhanced mode. It first loads extended memory support and the WIN386.EXE. The WIN386.EXE then loads the virtual machine manager (VMM) and all virtual device drivers (VxDs) listed in the SYSTEM.INI file. The network support virtual device driver (VNTESUP.386) starts the network VxDs including the NetBEUI protocol (VNB.386), the NETBIOS interface (VNETBIOS.386), the network redirector (VREDIR.386) and the WORKGRP.SYS device driver. The appropriate software linkages or bindings are made by VNETSUP.386. The VREDIR.386 starts the workstation service.

WIN386.EXE loads the 386 enhanced mode kernel program (KRNL386.EXE). KRNL386.EXE loads the Windows drivers (*.DRV) listed in the SYSTEM.INI file, the GDI.EXE (graphics device interface), the USER.EXE, the supporting files (like fonts files), and the network driver (the Windows for Workgroups WFWNET.DRV program).

The server service (VSERVER.386) is started and the device shares are enabled. The network device data exchange application (NETDDE.EXE) is loaded as well as the ClipBook server application (CLIPSRV.EXE). Then the WFWNET.DRV program handles the network logon and the network connections are restored. Finally, KRNLx86.EXE starts the Windows shell program (PROGMAN.EXE) or the shell identified in the Windows SYSTEM.INI file SHELL= [boot] section statement.

The Windows 95/98 Boot Process

Windows 95/98 boots similarly to DOS and Windows with some notable exceptions. The BIOS boot phase is designed to boot using a plug-and-play BIOS. A plug-and-play BIOS uses information in NVRAM (nonvolatile random access memory or CMOS RAM) to set up plug-and-play ISA bus cards. The nonvolatile random access memory enables the cards and devices built

Figure 14–31 *Hardware profile setup*

into the main logic board (MLB), maps their ROMs into memory addresses, and assigns I/O port, DMA channel, and IRQs to the cards. The BIOS then programs all cards before Power On Self Test (POST). Otherwise the cards are disabled to eliminate conflicts.

Next Windows determines the current configuration from the hardware profile. Since most PCs use only a single hardware profile, this setup does not display any visible messages. Multiple hardware profiles can be set up using the control panel. See Figure 14–31.

When more than a single profile is used, a select profile message is displayed. The message states:

```
Windows cannot determine what configuration your computer is in.
Select one of the following:
1. Original configuration
2. New configuration
3. None of the above
Enter your choice:
```

Once the choice is selected, the boot process continues. The CONFIG.SYS and AUTOEXEC.BAT files are processed next. Although not required by Windows 95/98, they provide a mechanism to ensure backward compatibility for DOS and Windows 3.1x applications. For example, they set up the DOS windows with paths and load TSR programs like DOSKEY.EXE.

Now Windows moves on to initializing the static virtual device drivers (VxDs) like Windows 3.1x does when starting in 386 enhanced mode. The Windows 95/98 virtual machine manager (VMM32.VXD) includes a real-mode loader, a virtual machine manager, and common static VxDs. There are also dynamically loaded VxDs that are supported, as well. Dynamic VxDs are loaded only when needed by Windows. The static VxDs were specified in the [386ENH] section of the SYSTEM.INI file. They are built into VMM32.VxD for Windows 95/98 or specified in the registry and the SYSTEM.INI file. Devices specified in SYSTEM.INI take precedence over devices specified in the registry.

Dynamically loaded device drivers for the network and other hardware components are loaded by a device loader (for example, *IOS. for SCSI adapter miniport drivers). When they are needed, the device loader loads and initializes these dynamic drivers in a very specific load sequence.

Upon completion of the static VxD initialization, WIN.COM has loaded and checked the core Windows 95/98 components, VMM32.VXD has created virtual machines and loaded the static VxDs, and the VxDs specified by SYSTEM.INI have been loaded. Next, the CPU chip is switched to protected-mode operation to load the KERNEL32.DLL and the KRNL386.EXE. The KRNL386.EXE loads more Windows device drivers. Then GDI.EXE and GDI32.EXE as well as USER.EXE and USER32.EXE are loaded. The fonts are then loaded, the WIN.INI values are checked and the EXPLORER.EXE shell and desktop components are loaded. Finally, Windows displays the logon screen, requesting the user name and password.

REQUIRED FILES FOR BOOTING WINDOWS 95/98

Some key parameter and program files and their role in the Windows 95/98 booting process are:

- IO.SYS—a real-mode Windows 98 operating system equivalent to DOS. IO.SYS has default drivers built into it that are loaded. They are HIMEM.SYS, IFSHLP.SYS (Installable File System help), SETVER.EXE, and DBLSPACE.BIN.
- MSDOS.SYS—a text file containing loading parameters for Windows and providing compatibility with programs requiring a MSDOS.SYS file.
- COMMAND.COM—the DOS command prompt interpreter containing the internal DOS commands, for instance, DEL and COPY.
- CONFIG.SYS and AUTOEXEC.BAT—text files used to load special 16-bit device drivers and to set up DOS window operation. These are not absolutely needed for Windows to boot.
- WIN.INI and SYSTEM.INI used to load drivers and other programs to assist with maintaining compatibility with Windows 3.1x application software. Sometimes Windows terminate and stay resident (TSR) applications are launched from WIN.INI using the LOAD= or RUN= statements in it.
- PROTOCOL.INI—a text file that sets up the network protocols and binds (links) them to the installed LAN card drivers.
- The Windows 95/98 Registry—The SYSTEM.DAT and USER.DAT provide additional loading instructions for configuring Windows and for loading Windows 95/98 TSR programs like virus scanning programs.

The Microsoft Emergency Recovery Utility (ERU) program as a way to recover from Windows failures saves these key files. When Windows 98 blew up on Bill Gates at a prerelease press conference, the ERU program and the key Windows 98 boot files created by ERU restored the PC to operating status in a minute. The ERU program was discussed in detail earlier in this chapter.

The 32-bit virtual machine manager (VMM32) program takes control from IO.SYS and continues the loading process calling the Windows programs that are needed. Windows also loads programs or program shortcuts in the C:\windows\start menu\programs\startup directory during the boot process. See Figure 14–32. Programs loaded here often appear in the Windows 95/98 SYSTRAY section of the task bar.

Windows TSR programs can be loaded are from CONFIG.SYS and AUTOEXEC.BAT, from the Windows registry, from the WIN.INI file, and from the startup directory. Of these, the registry is the most difficult to troubleshoot.

Figure 14–32 *Startup programs*

Windows 95/98 also renames some original DOS files to preserve them and to permit Windows to substitute new files it needs in their place. As a reminder, the renamed files are:

- AUTOEXEC.BAT renamed to AUTOEXEC.DOS,
- CONFIG.SYS renamed to CONFIG.DOS,
- COMMAND.COM renamed to COMMAND.DOS,
- IO.SYS renamed to IO.DOS,
- MSDOS.SYS renamed to MSDOS.DOS, and
- MODE.COM renamed to MODE_DOS.COM.

The MSDOS.SYS file contains special boot parameters for Windows. A typical MSDOS.SYS file is:

```
[Paths]
WinDir=C:\WINDOWS
WinBootDir=C:\WINDOWS
HostWinBootDrv=C

[Options]
BootMulti=1
BootGUI=1
DoubleBuffer=1
AutoScan=1
WinVer=4.14.1998
;
;The following lines are required for compatibility with other programs.
;Do not remove them (MSDOS.SYS needs to be >1024 bytes).
;xxxxxxxxxxxxxxxxxxxxxxxxxxxxxxxxxxxxxxxxxxxxxxxxxxxxxxxxxxxxxxxa
;xxxxxxxxxxxxxxxxxxxxxxxxxxxxxxxxxxxxxxxxxxxxxxxxxxxxxxxxxxxxxxxb
;xxxxxxxxxxxxxxxxxxxxxxxxxxxxxxxxxxxxxxxxxxxxxxxxxxxxxxxxxxxxxxc
;xxxxxxxxxxxxxxxxxxxxxxxxxxxxxxxxxxxxxxxxxxxxxxxxxxxxxxxxxxxxxd
;xxxxxxxxxxxxxxxxxxxxxxxxxxxxxxxxxxxxxxxxxxxxxxxxxxxxxxxxxxxxe
;xxxxxxxxxxxxxxxxxxxxxxxxxxxxxxxxxxxxxxxxxxxxxxxxxxxxxxxxxxxxf
;xxxxxxxxxxxxxxxxxxxxxxxxxxxxxxxxxxxxxxxxxxxxxxxxxxxxxxxxxxxxg
;xxxxxxxxxxxxxxxxxxxxxxxxxxxxxxxxxxxxxxxxxxxxxxxxxxxxxxxxxxxh
;xxxxxxxxxxxxxxxxxxxxxxxxxxxxxxxxxxxxxxxxxxxxxxxxxxxxxxxxxxxi
;xxxxxxxxxxxxxxxxxxxxxxxxxxxxxxxxxxxxxxxxxxxxxxxxxxxxxxxxxxxj
;xxxxxxxxxxxxxxxxxxxxxxxxxxxxxxxxxxxxxxxxxxxxxxxxxxxxxxxxxxxk
;xxxxxxxxxxxxxxxxxxxxxxxxxxxxxxxxxxxxxxxxxxxxxxxxxxxxxxxxxxl
;xxxxxxxxxxxxxxxxxxxxxxxxxxxxxxxxxxxxxxxxxxxxxxxxxxxxxxxxxm
;xxxxxxxxxxxxxxxxxxxxxxxxxxxxxxxxxxxxxxxxxxxxxxxxxxxxxxxn
;xxxxxxxxxxxxxxxxxxxxxxxxxxxxxxxxxxxxxxxxxxxxxxxxxxxxxxxo
;xxxxxxxxxxxxxxxxxxxxxxxxxxxxxxxxxxxxxxxxxxxxxxxxxxxxxxp
;xxxxxxxxxxxxxxxxxxxxxxxxxxxxxxxxxxxxxxxxxxxxxxxxxxxxq
;xxxxxxxxxxxxxxxxxxxxxxxxxxxxxxxxxxxxxxxxxxxxxxxxxxxr
;xxxxxxxxxxxxxxxxxxxxxxxxxxxxxxxxxxxxxxxxxxxxxxxxxxxs
Network=0
```

Table 14–6 shows the MSDOS.SYS file parameter options and their purpose:

Table 14.6 *MSDOS.SYS file parameters*

Parameter	Description
WinDir=C:\WINDOWS	Specifies the directory where Windows is installed and run from.
WinBootDir=C:\WINDOWS	Specifies where the Windows startup files can be found.
HostWinBootDrv=C	Specifies the Windows boot drive containing the root directory.
BootMulti=1	Enables booting two operating systems. A value of 1 permits starting MS-DOS by pressing F4 or starting with the startup menu by pressing F8.
BootGUI=1	Starts Windows automatically, like placing a WIN statement in an AUTOEXEC.BAT file.
DoubleBuffer=1	Loads the double-buffer driver needed by some SCSI disk controllers.
AutoScan=1	Runs SCANDISK automatically when the PC is abruptly restarted.
WinVer=4.14.1998	Identifies the Version of Windows installed
Bootdelay=#	Delays the boot process for # seconds.
BootFailSafe=	Starts system in safe mode. Default is 0, causing Windows to start normally.
BootKeys=	Enables (default) or disables the F5, F6 and F8 key functions during Windows startup.
BootMenu=	Displays startup menu.
BootMenuDefault=#	Picks the Windows startup menu default item. The default is 3 for Windows with no networking and 4 for Windows with networking installed.
BootMenuDelay=#	Delays startup # seconds when boot menu is used.
BootWarn=	Displays safe mode startup warning.
BootWin=	Sets Windows as the default operating system.
LoadTop=	Loads COMMAND.COM or DRVSPACE.BIN into the top of the 640 K real mode memory. Default value is 1, loading the programs into that top memory area.
Logo=	Controls display of the Windows logo while booting. Default value is 1 to display the logo.
Network=	Controls safe mode network operation. This should be disabled with Windows 98 by setting a value of 0.

Similar to the controls in MSDOS.SYS, WIN.COM also has parameters that can be used to control the Windows boot process. The WIN.COM parameters are displayed by running WIN.COM /?. WIN.COM command syntax is :

```
WIN [/D:[F][M][S][V][X]]
```

Where the parameters are:

- **/D**—Used for troubleshooting when Windows does not start correctly.
- **:F**—Turns off 32-bit disk access. Equivalent to SYSTEM.INI file setting 32BitDiskAccess=FALSE.
- **:M**—Enables safe mode. This is automatically enabled during safe start (function key F5).
- **:N**—Enables safe mode with networking. This is automatically enabled during safe start (function key F6).
- **:S**—Specifies that Windows should not use ROM address space between F000:0000 and 1 MB for a break point. Equivalent to SYSTEM.INI file setting: SystemROMBreakPoint=FALSE.
- **:V**—Specifies that the ROM routine will handle interrupts from the hard disk controller. Equivalent to SYSTEM.INI file setting VirtualHDIRQ=FALSE.
- **:X**—Excludes all of the adapter area from the range of memory that Windows scans to find unused space. Equivalent to SYSTEM.INI file setting EMMExclude=A000-FFFF.

The bootlog.txt file keeps a record of the events during the boot process. See Figure 14–33.

The status of the Windows components and drivers loaded and initialized is recorded in the bootlog.txt file. Both loading successes and failures are logged. Finding which drivers or Windows components failed to load properly during the boot process can facilitate troubleshooting a Windows installation. The event entries cover errors, failures, load success, initialization success, load failures, system initialization, device initialization, dynamic device loading and initialization, and current status.

THE WINDOWS 95/98 BOOTABLE DISKETTE DIAGNOSTIC TOOL

A bootable diskette for Windows 95/98 can be created by using the FORMAT /S command in a DOS window or by formatting a diskette using the Windows Explorer. The difference between the DOS window format and the Windows Explorer format is that the MSDOS.SYS file produced by the DOS

```
[00140A2A] Loading Device = C:\WINDOWS\HIMEM.SYS
[00140A2D] LoadSuccess  = C:\WINDOWS\HIMEM.SYS
[00140A2D] Loading Device = C:\DOS\OAKCDROM.SYS
[00140A5A] LoadSuccess  = C:\DOS\OAKCDROM.SYS
(Logo disabled)
[00140A5A] Loading Device = C:\WINDOWS\DBLBUFF.SYS
[00140A5B] LoadSuccess  = C:\WINDOWS\DBLBUFF.SYS
[00140A5B] Loading Device = C:\WINDOWS\IFSHLP.SYS
[00140A5C] LoadSuccess  = C:\WINDOWS\IFSHLP.SYS
[00140A70] C:\WINDOWS\COMMAND\DOSKEY.COM[00140A71]  starting
[00140A9A] Loading Vxd = C:\WINDOWS\system\VMM32\VMM.VXD
[00140AA1] LoadSuccess = C:\WINDOWS\system\VMM32\VMM.VXD
[00140AA1] Loading Vxd = C:\WINDOWS\SMARTDRV.EXE
[00140AA1] LoadSuccess = C:\WINDOWS\SMARTDRV.EXE
[00140AA2] Loading Vxd = vnetsup.vxd
[00140AA2] LoadSuccess = vnetsup.vxd
[00140AA2] Loading Vxd = ndis.vxd
[00140AA4] LoadSuccess = ndis.vxd
[00140AA4] Loading Vxd = ndis2sup.vxd
[00140AA5] LoadFailed = ndis2sup.vxd
[00140AA5] Loading Vxd = JAVASUP.VXD
[00140AA5] LoadSuccess = JAVASUP.VXD
[00140AA5] Loading Vxd = C:\WINDOWS\system\VMM32\CONFIGMG.VXD
[00140AA7] LoadSuccess = C:\WINDOWS\system\VMM32\CONFIGMG.VXD
[00140AA7] Loading Vxd = C:\WINDOWS\system\VMM32\NTKERN.VXD
[00140AA8] LoadSuccess = C:\WINDOWS\system\VMM32\NTKERN.VXD
[00140AA8] Loading Vxd = VWIN32
[00140AA8] LoadSuccess = VWIN32
[00140AA8] Loading Vxd = VFBACKUP
[00140AA8] LoadSuccess = VFBACKUP
[00140AA8] Loading Vxd = C:\WINDOWS\system\VMM32\VCOMM.VXD
[00140AA9] LoadSuccess = C:\WINDOWS\system\VMM32\VCOMM.VXD
[00140AA9] Loading Vxd = COMBUFF
[00140AA9] LoadSuccess = COMBUFF
[00140AA9] Loading Vxd = C:\WINDOWS\system\VMM32\IFSMGR.VXD
[00140AAA] LoadSuccess = C:\WINDOWS\system\VMM32\IFSMGR.VXD
[00140AAA] Loading Vxd = C:\WINDOWS\system\VMM32\IOS.VXD
[00140AAC] LoadSuccess = C:\WINDOWS\system\VMM32\IOS.VXD
[00140AAD] Loading Vxd = mtrr
[00140AAD] LoadSuccess = mtrr
[00140AAD] Loading Vxd = SPOOLER
[00140AAD] LoadSuccess = SPOOLER
[00140AAD] Loading Vxd = UDF
[00140AAD] LoadSuccess = UDF
[00140AAD] Loading Vxd = VFAT
[00140AAD] LoadSuccess = VFAT
```

Figure 14–33 *Bootlog.txt contents*

Figure 14–34 *Explorer FORMAT window*

format contains ";FORMAT" while the MSDOS.SYS file produced by Windows Explorer is an empty file (0 bytes).

See Figure 14–34. A bootable floppy is created when the copy system files option is checked.

A quick or full format can be performed. The full format verifies the diskette, while the quick format only rewrites the boot record, FAT, and directory areas on the diskette. See Figure 14–35. The "copy system files only" option is equivalent to the DOS SYS command installation. It can be used to make a previously formatted diskette into a bootable diskette. The procedure here is the same for both Windows 95 and Windows 98.

The DOS format program is more dependent upon the BIOS for operating with the diskettes and has more direct control. A 32-bit Windows program performs the explorer formatting. This means that sometimes the DOS formatting works better than the Windows Explorer formatting.

Figure 14–35 *Explorer FORMAT report*

Creating a Windows startup diskette also creates a bootable diskette. The startup diskette contains more than just DOS files. The Windows 98 startup diskette has CD-ROM drivers and other software installed on it that assist in troubleshooting Windows or in installing Windows.

WINDOWS 95/98 FUNCTION KEY BOOT IMPACTS OR BYPASSING STARTUP FILES

During Windows startup, the startup files can be bypassed using the following keys:

- F5. This key bypasses all startup files and enters safe mode operation directly. Booting can require quite some time because the disk cache programs are not installed during the Windows safe mode startup.
- F6. This key bypasses the startup files and enters safe mode operation with minimal network support.
- F8. This key enters the Windows startup menu, permitting startup from the following menu options:
  Normal
  Logged (\BOOTLOG.TXT)
  Safe mode
  Step-by-step confirmation

Command prompt only

Safe mode command prompt only

The default selection is 1, normal operation boot. Combining the Shift key and the F5 key (Shift+F5) causes Windows to boot to the command prompt. Entering WIN to launch the WIN.COM program then runs Windows. Combining the Shift key and the F8 key (Shift+F8) causes Windows to start in the Windows startup menu and perform step-by-step confirmation of the driver programs loaded during the boot process for the menu item selected. Some of the confirmations for booting Windows normally are:

- Load doublespace driver—disk cache and compression
- Process the system registry
- Create a startup log file (BOOTLOG.TXT)
- Process the startup device drivers (CONFIG.SYS)
- List the lines in CONFIG.SYS
- Process the startup command file (AUTOEXEC.BAT)
- List the lines in AUTOEXEC.BAT
- WIN—starts Windows
- Load all Windows drivers
- Install special drivers
- Override standard CONFIGMG—configuration manager
- Override standard NTKERN—kernel program
- Override standard VCOMM—communications
- Override standard VDD—virtual device driver
- Override standard VMCPD—virtual machine CPD
- Override standard VMM—virtual machine manager
- Override standard VMOUSE—virtual mouse driver
- Override standard VTDAPI—virtual TD application program interface
- vnetsup.vxd—virtual network support
- ndis.vxd—network device interface specification driver
- ndis2sup.vxd—network device interface specification 2 support
- JAVASUP.VXD—JAVA support
- netbios.vxd—NETBIOS interface
- ndiswan.vxd—net device interface specification wide area networks
- vredir.vxd—virtual redirector
- fs.vxd
- LMOUSE.VXD—Logitech mouse driver
- vserver.vxd—virtual server
- ASPIENUM.VXD—SCSI bus ASPI enumerator
- C:\WINDOWS\SYSTEM\vrtwd.386

- C:\WINDOWS\SYSTEM\vfixd.vxd—virtual fixed disk
- filesec.vxd—file security
- mssp.vxd
- C:\WINDOWS\SYSTEM\VSHINIT.VXD—virtual shell initialization
- vwavsyn.386—virtual wave synthesizer

This is a typical listing of the confirmations requested when booting with the Shift+F8 key. Combining the Shift key and the F5 key (Shift+F5) causes Windows to boot without loading the doublespace driver that performs both disk compression and disk cache functions. Booting using the Ctrl key alone makes Windows display the startup menu. The Shift key alone starts Windows in safe mode. The Esc key, if hit during boot up, removes the Windows animated logo screen and displays the commands being preformed during the startup process.

BOOTING TO SAFE MODE

Booting Windows into safe mode with minimal drivers is performed from the Windows Startup menu by selecting safe mode or by holding down the Ctrl key during the boot process. Booting into safe mode bypasses the real-mode configuration and loads a standard driver protected-mode configuration. The core drivers support VGA display, IDE fixed disk, mouse, and keyboard. When safe mode starts and there are other problems preventing Windows from normal startup, the conflict preventing normal startup could be in hardware settings, real-mode configuration problems, program and driver incompatibilities, or damage to the registry. Safe mode is a diagnostic tool to resolve conflicts that prevent Windows from starting normally.

BOOTING TO DOS VERSUS THE MS-DOS COMMAND PROMPT IN WINDOWS

A PC can be booted from a floppy diskette directly into Windows DOS or it can boot into Windows 95/98 and then exit to the DOS prompt. Booting from a floppy diskette into Windows DOS loads the real-mode operating system. IO.SYS starts and loads HIMEM.SYS to provide access to XMS memory and sets DOS=high. It then loads the 32-bit installable file system manager (IFSHLP.SYS). The SERVER.EXE program that provides compatibility for older DOS programs requesting a specific DOS version is loaded and the FILES=60 is set to establish a working set of file handles. Other configuration commands set are lastdrive=z, buffers=30, stacks=9,256, fcbs=4 and shell=command.com. These settings are standard settings for a Windows environment. Some settings are larger than those used in a DOS environment; for instance, DOS sets the stacks at 9,128. Placing settings into a CONFIG.SYS file can override the standard Windows IO.SYS settings.

The Windows DOS in real mode connects to the PC components using the PC's BIOS. This means that Windows DOS is important for running PC hardware diagnostics that must directly control the hardware components.

Booting into Windows 95/98 permits using a DOS Window to emulate DOS operation with Windows running in protected mode. Windows is using its 32-bit protected-mode drivers to access hardware components. The 32-bit Windows protected-mode drivers can prevent some diagnostic programs from running properly. Specifically, real-mode diagnostics often cause Windows error messages stating that the program tried to access hardware resources directly and was prevented from doing so by Windows.

Study Break

Boot Errors

The purpose of this exercise is to determine what errors occur during the boot process when specific software programs are missing from a PC.

1. Go to a Windows 95/98 PC. Make a fresh startup diskette.

2. Change to the \WINDOWS directory and rename the WIN.COM program to WINCOM.

3. Reboot the PC to see what happens. What error messages are displayed?

4. Use the startup diskette to reboot the system into Windows DOS. Change to the \WINDOWS directory and rename the WINCOM program back to WIN.COM. Next rename CONFIG.SYS to CONFIG and AUTOEXEC.BAT to AUTOEXEC.

5. Reboot the PC again and see what happens. Generally, Windows should boot normally. DOS TSR programs like DOSKEY cannot be run, but otherwise the PC should function properly.

6. Rename CONFIG to CONFIG.SYS and AUTOEXEC to AUTOEXEC.BAT. Now rename MSDOS.SYS to MSDOS. Again, reboot the PC to determine the impact of this file missing during the boot process.

7. Use the startup disk if necessary to return MSDOS to MSDOS.SYS.

The purpose of this exercise was to illustrate the impact of missing files on the Windows 95/98 boot process.

A+ 14.4 Loading and Adding Device Drivers

Device drivers are programs that interface directly with PC hardware components, such as printers, CD-ROMs, specialized boards and so forth. They are the programs that directly interact with the PC hardware. Device drivers can be loaded for DOS and Windows. Manufacturers of the devices themselves frequently provide these drivers.

DEVICE DRIVERS AND DOS

DOS device drivers are loaded using statements in the CONFIG.SYS file. The DEVICE= and DEVICEHIGH= statements load the device driver specified into lower memory or into the upper memory area. The most common device drivers loaded are the memory managers (device=HIMEM.SYS and device=EMM386.EXE) and the CD-ROM driver programs.

Device drivers are added to or modified in CONFIG.SYS manually, by special device installation programs, or by MEMMAKER.

Device Drivers and Windows 3.1x

Windows 3.1x adds device drivers on top of those loaded by DOS. It specifies added device driver programs in the SYSTEM.INI file with DEVICE= statements. Some statements load standard drivers like "device=*vfd," which specifies the standard floppy disk driver. The * denotes a standard driver. In contrast "device=vcache.386" loads an enhanced device driver for managing cache memory.

Device drivers are added to or modified in SYSTEM.INI the Windows 3.1x setup program or by special device installation programs. It is possible to manipulate the device drivers manually with a simple text-editing program like NOTEPAD.EXE. This, however, is not the recommended approach to managing device drivers for Windows 3.1x.

Device Drivers and Windows 95/98

Windows 95/98 uses CONFIG.SYS and SYSTEM.INI to install device drivers. It also has device drivers specified in the registry. The Windows 95/98 device drivers are installed during Windows setup by the plug-and-play device installation, by special device installation programs, or using the system utility in the Windows control panel. Windows 95 and Windows 98 come with device drivers for most standard PC hardware components. Windows 98 comes with the widest variety of device drivers. Still components often require added device drivers to perform to their full potential.

SPECIAL HARDWARE DEVICE DRIVERS

Many hardware components need special device drivers to activate all their features and capabilities. Windows 98 has device drivers built in for the components listed in Figure 14–36.

Figure 14–36
Windows 98 built-in device drivers

Figure 14–37 *Hardware wizard*

However, when a device needs newer or updated drivers these can be installed by entering the control panel, selecting add new hardware, letting Windows search for plug-and-play devices, then selecting the device category from the list that finally appears. Once the category is selected, a more detailed list of manufacturers appears. Each manufacturer has their components and the built-in Windows drivers listed. New special drivers can now be added by selecting the "have disk" option. See Figure 14–37.

To update drivers, the control panel's system icon can be used to select the component and open its properties. The device driver for that specific component can be updated in the properties window. This is helpful when installing new device drivers for a specific Windows component. This installation approach also provides a "have disk" option.

The "have disk" option prompts for insertion of a manufacturer's installation diskette into drive A. The files can be resident anywhere because browsing for the files is supported. See Figure 14–38.

Windows goes to the installation diskette and searches for an INF file that describes how to install the PC component. The INF files provide the Windows SETUP program with detailed information on how to install drivers for a specific hardware and software component. They specify which software files are to be copied into which specific directories. The INF files

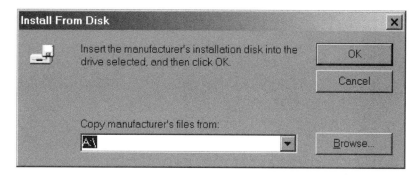

Figure 14–38 *Manufacturer installation disk window*

contain the registry updates needed to complete the installation. The component manufacturer provides INF files to guide the SETUP program during installation of the specific hardware component.

A typical INF file is listed is as follows:

```
; Setup file for Kensington Scroll Mouse minidriver
; Copyright (C) 1993-1997, All rights reserved.
[Version]
Signature="$CHICAGO$"
Class=Mouse
Provider=%Provider%
ClassGUID={4D36E96F-E325-11CE-BFC1-08002BE10318}
[DestinationDirs]
DefaultDestDir = 11     ; LDID_SYS
Serial.Copy  = 11
PS2.Copy  = 11
mouclass_CopyFiles = 12;DIRID_DRIVERS
Ser_CopyFiles = 12
PS2_CopyFiles = 12
PMouse_CopyFiles = 11
[SourceDisksNames]
91=%PMouseDisk%,,1
[SourceDisksFiles]
ksmcplx.dll=91
ksmoused.exe=91
ksmousep.vxd=91
.
.
NTuninst.EXE=91
; Manufacturer Sections
; ---------------------------------------
[Manufacturer]
%Mfg%=Mfg
[Mfg]
%PS2.Desc%=PS2_Inst,*PNP0F13,*PNP0F0E,*PNP0F12,*PNP0F0B,*PNP0F03,*PNP0F19
%Se-rial.Desc%=Ser_Inst,SERENUM\PEL0002,*PNP0F0C,*PNP0F01,*PNP0F08,*PNP0F0A,*PNP0F0F
[ClassInstall]
AddReg=MouseReg
```

```
[MouseReg]
HKR,,,0,"Mouse"
HKR,,Installer,0,SetupX.Dll, Mouse_ClassInstaller
HKR,,Icon,0,-2
; -------------------------------------
; Install sections
; -------------------------------------
;----------------- Serial Mouse Win95 -------------
[Ser_Inst]
DelReg=Prev.DelReg
Ad-dReg=Serial.AddReg,3DMouse.AddReg,3DMouse.AddUninstallReg,3DMouse.AddUninstallReg.95
CopyFiles=Serial.Copy,3DMouse.Copy
UpdateInis=Serial.Ini
[Serial.AddReg]
HKR,,DevLoader,,*vmouse
HKR,,MouseDriver,,ksmouses.vxd
HKR,,MouseType,0,Serial
HKR,,NoSetupUI,0,1
HKR,,ProviderName,,%Provider%
HKR,,DriverVersion,,%DriverVersion%
[Serial.Copy]
ksmouses.vxd
[Serial.Ini]
system.ini,boot.description,,"mouse.drv=""%Serial.Desc%
system.ini,boot,,"mouse.drv=mouse.drv"
system.ini,386Enh,,"mouse=*vmouse"
;----------------- PS2 Mouse Win95 -------------
[PS2_Inst]
  .
  .
HKLM,"Software\Microsoft\Windows\CurrentVersion\Uninstall\3DMouse\DeleteFiles",ksmousep.vxd,0,"%SYS_DIR%"
HKLM,"Software\Microsoft\Windows\CurrentVersion\Uninstall\3DMouse\DeleteFiles",ksmouses.vxd,0,"%SYS_DIR%"
HKLM,"Software\Microsoft\Windows\CurrentVersion\Uninstall\3DMouse\RestoreDriver\"%Provider%,%PS2.Desc%,0,"Standard PS/2 Mouse"
HKLM,"Software\Microsoft\Windows\CurrentVersion\Uninstall\3DMouse\RestoreDriver\"%Provider%,%Serial.Desc%,0,"Standard Serial Mouse"
HKLM,"Software\Microsoft\Windows\CurrentVersion\Uninstall\3DMouse\DeleteKey","Software\PEL\3DMouse",0,HKEY_CURRENT_USER
HKLM,"Software\Microsoft\Windows\CurrentVersion\Uninstall\3DMouse\DeleteKey","Enum\Root\PEL0002",0,""
[3DMouse.AddUninstallReg.NT]
HKLM,"Software\Microsoft\Windows\CurrentVersion\Uninstall\3DMouse\DeleteFiles",ksmi8042.sys,0,"%SYS32_DIR%"
  .
  .
ksuninst.exe,NTUninst.EXE
; -------------------------------------
; User-visible Strings
[Strings]
Provider = "Kensington"
MouseClassName = "Mouse"
DriverVersion = "1.36"
ProductName = "Kensington Scroll Mouse"
; Mfg Names
Mfg="Kensington"
; Disk Names
  .
  .
; Description of device also controlled by a shared driver
PS2_Inst.SharedDriverMsg = "Keyboard Port"
```

Figure 14–39 *Hardware list*

The INF file copies the new EXE, DRV, DLL and other software components to the system to install the special PC hardware component. It makes the needed registry changes to load these software drivers and components when Windows is restarted.

Special hardware drivers can be updated or installed using the system selection in the control panel. Opening system and selecting device manager shows a list of the hardware devices installed in the PC. See Figure 14–39.

Each item in the list has under it the devices installed in that category. As shown in Figure 14–39, this PC has an ATI 3D Rage Pro installed. By opening display adapters, you can see a list of the specific hardware installed. Then opening properties for the specific hardware component provides information on its configuration and the driver programs used by Windows.

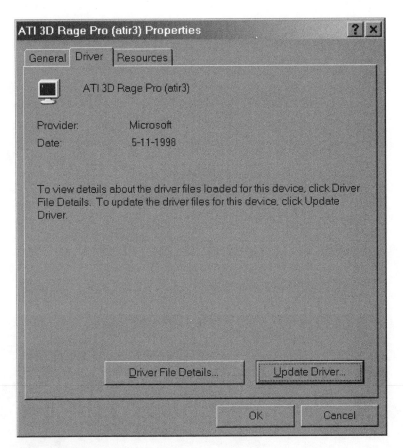

Figure 14–40 *Hardware properties*

The properties window displays general properties, the driver program, and the resources used by the hardware component. See Figure 14–40. When the driver tab is selected, the update driver button appears. This button can be used to update or to install special drivers for that specific hardware component. Similar to the "have disk" installation, Windows will search for a diskette or browse for a directory containing an INF file that installs the drivers for the selected hardware component.

Special hardware drivers are installed in both Windows 95 and 98 using these approaches. Even with standard driver support, the full features of a specific hardware component are not utilized unless special driver software for that component is installed. USB devices are a classic example. Although communication can be established with the device, often it is not integrated into the Windows installation effectively until special driver software is installed.

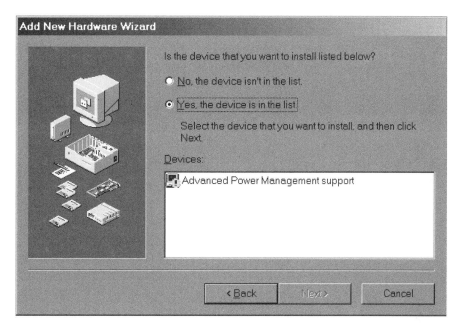

Figure 14–41 *Entering plug-and-play scan*

PLUG-AND-PLAY DRIVERS

Plug-and-play drivers can be installed by using the control panel and selecting the "add new hardware" option to cause Windows to perform its plug-and-play hardware scan in an attempt to spot new plug-and-play hardware components. See Figure 14–41. A full discussion of plug-and-play and its functionality is covered earlier in this chapter.

Study Break

INF Files

The purpose of this exercise is to illustrate the use of INF files during PC hardware component installation.

1. Go to a Windows 95/98 PC. Identify a hardware component that has special drivers like a display controller, sound board, or mouse.

2. Find the driver diskette with those special drivers. If a diskette cannot be found, locate the vendor's web site and find the latest driver files for the component.

3. Copy or set up the drivers in a \INSTALL\device_name folder.

4. Copy the (or one of the) INF file found to file_name.OLD to preserve a copy of the original file.

5. Edit the INF file using NOTEPAD or WordPad (WRITE.EXE). Locate individual sections in the file. A section is identified by [SECTION_NAME]. What sections are there? Can you find: [version], [SourceDisksNames], [SourceDisksFiles], [Manufacturer], [UninstHlp], [INF-Files], [INFOther], [SysFiles], [IniFiles], and [Strings] sections?

6. Delete the INF file and try updating the components drivers using the control panel—system—device manager to select the specific hardware component for this driver diskette, open the driver tab and use update drivers. Does it find the drivers on the diskette or in the fixed disk folder you created?

7. Use the backup copy of the INF file to restore the INF file. Repeat the process above to determine if the device drivers for the hardware component are found.

This exercise demonstrated the role that INF files play in installing and configuring Windows.

A+ 14.5 Windows Configuration

Every Windows PC has specific Windows applets, hardware components, and application programs installed that comprise the Windows configuration for that specific PC. Changing the Windows configuration is accomplished using the control panel and the "add hardware" and "add/remove programs" options. We have just examined the "add hardware" selection. Windows components and applications are changed using the "add/remove software" selection identified in Figure 14–42.

The "add/remove programs" selection permits application programs to be removed, Windows components to be added or removed, or a startup diskette to be created.

Changing Installed Options

Once "add/remove programs" is selected, the properties window appears, as shown by Figure 14–43. The first tab, install/uninstall, permits software to be

Add New Hardware   Add/Remove
Programs

Figure 14–42 *Configuration change icons*

removed from the PC. Application software installation is not typically per-formed from this menu but rather performed by a setup program provided by the software manufacturer. Uninstalling software using the "uninstall" option depends upon a DeIsL*n*.isu file specifically tailored to uninstall that application. Windows creates this file during installation. If the specific file cannot be found, then Windows cannot uninstall the application.

When this happens, the best alternative is probably to use third-party uninstall software to remove the program. Otherwise, you can reinstall and then immediately uninstall the software to remove the entries. Unfortu-nately, with Microsoft software it seems that the uninstall process still leaves some entries in the registry and some program files on the fixed disk. The only absolute way to uninstall such programs is to have the third-party unin-staller software observe the installation process to record every installation change and to assure that every registry entry and program has been removed.

Clicking on the Windows setup option displays the Windows compo-nents that have been configured for the PC. See Figure 14–44. Checking or unchecking the boxes causes Windows to install or uninstall the components.

Sometimes this is used to add or change the mix of desktop themes or to add other components like disk compression or the FAT-16 to FAT-32 conversion program. When more disk space is needed or when program interaction is causing Windows to crash, the add/remove programs selection is used to remove unneeded and potentially troublesome Windows compo-nents.

The Windows components may be installed individually or as an entire group identified in the Windows setup properties window.

Installing and Configuring Printers

Printer installation under Windows 95/98 is an easy process. It is described in the Chapter 6 study break exercise, "Setting Up A Printer," and reviewed here. Windows NT installation is a similar process to the Windows 95/98

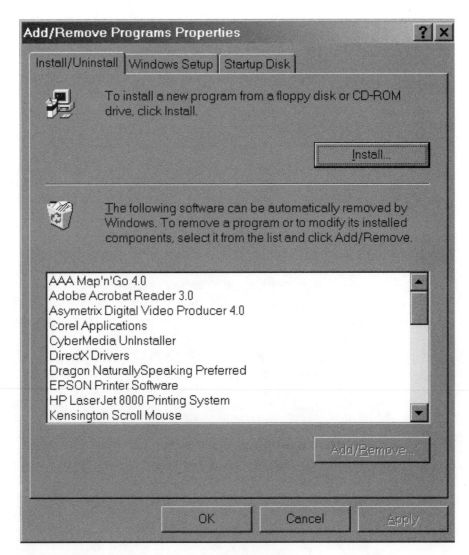

Figure 14–43 *Add/remove program properties*

installation. For DOS-based PCs, the application program was configured to operate with specific printers. For example, Lotus 1-2-3 under DOS used special SET files to configure display and printer options for the DOS-based Lotus 1-2-3 program. Windows 3.1x changed this by providing the first printer setup for all applications. Windows 95/98 and Windows NT use printer setup wizards that step you through the installation process, reducing the chance of making mistakes. Installing printers and the printer installa-

Figure 14–44 *Windows component setup*

tion wizard is activated through the control panel printers icon or through the "my Computer" printers icon. See Figure 14–45.

Clicking (double-clicking) on the icon opens up access to installed printers and the "add printers" icon. Each printer in the windows represents a printer and a queue for holding data for printout. Opening a printer displays the print queue and manages the print jobs. Opening the "add printer" icon starts the "add printer" wizard. See Figure 14–46.

Figure 14–45 *Printers icon*

Figure 14–46 *Printers window*

Once the printers wizard is started, it steps through the printer installation process. First it asks whether it is a local or network printer, then it lists built-in drivers for printers by manufacturer.

The printer to be installed is selected from this list. When a manufacturer or printer is not on the list, the "have disk" button can install the special driver software for that printer. See Figure 14–47.

After you have selected the printer from the list, then wizard queries on which port is the printer installed if you indicated it is to be a local printer.

The port options for local printers are COM1, COM2, COM3, File or LPT1. The wizard then asks for a printer name and finally offers to print a test page. This completes the printer installation and the new printer now appears as an icon in the printers window.

Sometimes printers cannot be matched exactly. Furthermore, the software controls vary from printer to printer. HP LaserJet printers are a classic

Figure 14-47 *Printer selection list*

example. When it is desired to operate a new HP LaserJet printer and the driver software is not available for it, choosing LaserJet II drivers often installs the printer and permits it to act effectively. This is because newer LaserJet printers are designed to be backward compatible with older LaserJet printers. The new printers have features that the older software cannot utilize. They can perform all the basic printing functions using the older driver software.

Network printers are as easily installed as local printers. The difference between a network installation and a local printer installation is that network is specified during the installation process and not local printer. Then the network is browsed for the specific printer queue that is appropriately shared. Once found, this is captured and assigned to the printer. Now the printing is redirected across the network to the network printer.

Sharing a printer is equally easy. A locally configured printer can be shared on any PC that is network attached by sharing the printer on the network. The printer is shared with a local password or as part of a domain with domain-administered security.

When a network-defined printer is not connected or powered on, Windows sends an error message to the user trying to print on that printer and queues the data sent for printing to that printer. Once the printer is returned to service, Windows sends the data in the queue to the printer for printing.

Study Break

Printer Operation

The purpose of this exercise is to illustrate printer operation under Windows.

1. Go to a Windows 95/98 PC that has a local printer. Open NOTEPAD and use it to edit a single page text file.

2. Print the file to the local printer. The page should print OK.

3. Now power off the printer and attempt to reprint the file. What error message does Windows display?

4. Shutdown the PC and restart. Does Windows display any startup warnings?

5. Power the printer back on. Does the page print OK?

The purpose of this exercise is to illustrate how Windows behaves when the printer is powered down or generally not available to print. The same steps can be performed using a network printer.

Launching Windows Applications

Windows applications can be launched in several different ways. This section discusses briefly the ways that Windows applications can be started, including the start menu, file associations, shortcuts, and running the program.

The most common way is to use the start menu similar to the Windows 3.1x program manager. The start menu lists the programs installed on the PC in groupings established by the C:\windows\start menu\programs directory structure. Double-clicking on the application icon or shortcut launches the application.

File associations can also start applications. Every file type is associated with an application. When the user double-clicks on the data file, Windows launches the application and loads the data into it. For example, JPG image files on our PCs are associated with the Microsoft photo editor. Double-clicking on an image file launches the Microsoft photo editor and loads the JPG image into it.

Another way to run Windows programs is to create desktop shortcuts. A shortcut is an icon that points to the EXE file launching the application. Double-clicking on the shortcut icon launches the application. These shortcuts can be placed on the desktop or in the quick launch tool bar. They are activated by a single click in the quick launch tool bar.

The final way to launch programs is to use the Windows run function. Opening the start menu and selecting run brings up the run window. See Figure 14–48.

Entering the name of the program and selecting OK launches the program. Some common program names are SOL for solitaire, CALC for the

Figure 14–48 *Run window*

calculator, COMMAND for the DOS prompt and REGEDIT for the registry editor.

Windows Run Function

This exercise demonstrates the run function.

1. Go to a Windows 95/98 PC and click on the start button. Select run and enter NOTEPAD. Click on OK to launch the NOTEPAD program.

2. Repeat the same sequence of steps to run COMMAND to open a DOS Window.

3. Repeat the same sequence of steps to run SOL, the Windows solitaire game.

4. Click on the start button and select run again. This time use the down arrow to the right of the entry panel to drop down the list of programs previously run. This should show NOTEPAD, COMMAND, and SOL in reverse chronological order (the most recently run program should be at the top of the list.)

5. Click on the Browse button and select WRITE.EXE. This should launch WordPad.

This exercise illustrated that the run function can be used to launch both Windows and DOS programs, and that it remembers the programs recently run.

■ Summary

This chapter has examined the procedures and technical aspects of installing DOS and Windows. It has listed the requirements for upgrading to newer versions of Windows. The boot procedures and startup process have been described, including special startup options for DOS and Windows. Finally, configuring device drivers and Windows software components were discussed along with procedures for launching Windows software.

▲ CHAPTER REVIEW QUESTIONS

1. 1. IFS means?

    A. Installable file system

    B. Installable fixed-disk system

        C. Inflatable file system

        D. Independent file system

        Answer: A. Installable file system

2.   *What program is used to install 32-bit FAT?*

        A. FORMAT

        B. EXPLORER

        C. FDISK

        D. SCANDISK

        Answer: C. FDISK

3.   *The Windows program used to begin Windows installation is?*

        A. FORMAT

        B. INSTALL

        C. AUTOEXEC.INF

        D. SETUP

        Answer:D. SETUP

4.   *Windows is typically installed in which directory?*

        A. WIN

        B. Windows

        C. System

        D. Windows\options\cabs

        E. Program Files

        F. WIN\SYSTEM

        Answer: B. Windows

5.   *Installing Windows 98 requires?*

        A. 8 MB RAM

        B. 486 25 MHz CPU

        C. 8 GB fixed disk

        D. 8 MB VGA card

        Answer: A.8 MB RAM minimum for Windows 95 but—16 MB is minimum for Windows 98

6.   *Windows boot problems often result from device conflicts where?*

        A. the fixed disk

        B. the registry and plug-and-play components

        C. DOS

D. SCSI devices and the registry
Answer: B. the registry and plug-and-play components

7. *Windows must be installed from a CD-ROM drive.*
    A. TRUE
    B. FALSE
    Answer: B. FALSE

8. *CD-ROM drives are not bootable.*
    A.TRUE
    B.FALSE
    Answer: B. FALSE

9. *Which files are required for DOS to boot?*
    A. MSDOS.SYS, CONFIG.SYS and COMMAND.COM
    B. IO.SYS, MSDOS.SYS, CONFIG.SYS and COMMAND.COM
    C. IO.SYS MSDOS.SYS, and COMMAND.COM
    D. MSDOS.SYS, AUTOEXEC.BAT and COMMAND.COM
    Answer: C. IO.SYS, MSDOS.SYS, and COMMAND.COM

10. *Which file is the Windows 95/98 real mode operating system?*
    A. MSDOS.SYS
    B. CONFIG.SYS
    C. COMMAND.COM
    D. WIN.COM
    E. E.none of the above
    Answer: E. none of the above

11. *Holding the F5 key during Windows boot acts like what other key?*
    A. F8
    B. Ctrl
    C. F6
    D. Shift
    Answer D. Shift

12. *Holding the Ctrl key boots Windows into*
    A. safe mode
    B. MS-DOS
    C. the Windows startup menu
    D. step-by-step confirmation

Answer: C. the Windows startup menu

13. *A cold boot is performed by*

    A. hitting Ctrl-Alt-Del

    B. powering off the PC

    C. hitting the reset button

    D. exiting Windows

    E. booting from a floppy disk in drive A:

Answer: C. hitting the reset button

14. *Application programs are launched in Windows*

    A. from the run window

    B. by double-clicking on the data

    C. by double-clicking on a desktop shortcut

    D. by clicking on a quick launch shortcut

    E. all of the above

    F. none of the above

Answer: F. none of the above

15. *PCs can boot from?*

    A. the fixed disk

    B. the floppy disk

    C. the CD-ROM

    D. a network

    E. all of the above

Answer: E. all of the above

16. *Device drivers can be installed in Windows using*

    A. the control panel–add new hardware

    B. installing the plug-and-play component in the PC

    C. the control panel–system–device manager–selecting the device and then properties and update driver

    D. running manufacturer-supplied installation software

    E. all of the above

    F. none of the above

Answer: E. all of the above

DOS and Windows Software Problem Diagnosis and Resolution

▲ **Chapter Syllabus**

A+ 15.1 Common Software Error Messages

A+ 15.2 Resolving Frequent Software Problems

A+ 15.3 DOS and Windows Utilities

A+ 15.4 Viruses and Virus Protection

This chapter covers identifying and resolving software problems in both DOS and Windows environments. Common error messages and their resolution are presented. DOS and Windows error messages vary from one version of DOS and Windows to another. Although different in content, the error messages identify common software problems. Solutions to these common software problems are examined and discussed. DOS and Windows maintenance and problem resolution utilities are identified and their use in preventing and resolving software problems is covered. Finally, there is a discussion of virus detection and virus removal. This chapter is devoted to troubleshooting and solving DOS and Windows software problems.

A+ 15.1 Common Software Error Messages

The software error messages for DOS and Windows are quite different, although they sometimes stem from common problems. Generally, both DOS and Windows errors are caused by memory conflicts, by inadequate memory, or by incorrect versions of software. The worst type of error is caused by a bad mix (or blend) of Windows software (mixing old and new virtual device drivers (VxDs), Dynamic Link Libraries (DLLs), and driver programs), causing Windows to crash with the "blue screen of death." In this instance, the quickest and most effective solution is to reinstall Windows. Reinstalling Windows is what most people dread, but it is a faster and more reliable route to solving software conflicts than trying to find the misbehaving software components. We have spent eight to ten hours seeking bad software and trying unsuccessfully to remove it from Windows in a vain attempt to solve software conflict problems, when if we had reinstalled Windows we would have been back operating reliably in about two hours.

In contrast, problems causing hardware error messages are easily corrected. Most often correcting hardware errors involves installing the latest hardware driver programs that are readily available from the Internet.

Safe Mode

Safe mode is a special Windows diagnostic mode that is used primarily to resolve hardware driver conflicts in Windows. A Windows PC is quite often thrown into safe mode during the boot process when there are problems with the basic hardware driver programs required for Windows to run. Otherwise, safe mode is entered using the F5 or F8 keys as described in Chapter 11 and Chapter 14. The basic hardware drivers are display, IDE fixed disk, SCSI disk (if a SCSI disk drive is the boot drive), and sometimes LAN card drivers (particularly if they interfere with the display drivers). See Figure 15–1. The C:\BOOTLOG.TXT file can be examined to determine which drivers are in conflict. A quick test is to remove the network adapter and reboot.

Windows sometimes thinks that it should enter safe mode when it should not. It is difficult to tell whether safe mode is needed or not. However, when Windows was just running successfully with the current PC hardware configuration and safe mode just pops up, there is a good chance it can be ignored. In this case, rebooting and selecting normal mode resolves the problem.

In safe mode, Windows does not provide detailed information for any adapter card settings because Windows has detected a hardware conflict that

Figure 15–1   *Safe mode warning message*

prevents the plug-and-play Windows components from completing the resource assignments. See Figure 15–2. The problem resolution strategy from a Windows plug-and-play software perspective is to have the user select specific settings for the conflicting hardware, such as a network card, and then reboot. The hope is that the specific selected settings resolve the Windows plug-and-play software conflict. The Windows plug-and-play software operation should properly complete configuring the PC hardware. This sometimes does not work and results in a continuous cycle of Windows rebooting into safe mode. To break out of the continuous safe mode reboot cycle, the user typically selects specific configurations for several components. These configurations can often develop new conflicts that toss the PC back into the continuous safe mode reboot cycle. The ultimate resolution may be to use different hardware components or to find better drivers for the hardware components installed.

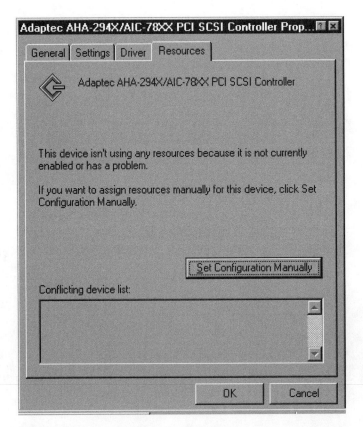

Figure 15–2 *Safe mode properties box*

The most effective hardware troubleshooting technique is to focus on the display, IDE fixed disk, and network adapter. Since the PC should boot properly without a network adapter, remove it and get the PC to boot normally. This action may require adding special display and fixed disk controller driver programs. Other components are ancillary to Windows booting normally (like sound boards and video camera inputs) and can be removed or ignored. CD and DVD drives use the IDE interface and usually do not interfere with booting any more than any IDE fixed disk drive. Zip and Jaz drives may use an SCSI interface and should likely be removed. Once the PC boots normally with the display and IDE fixed disk, then the other peripherals can be added one at a time to help the plug-and-play boot software sort out the hardware component assignments. Before adding new components, the IRQ, I/O port, and reserved RAM address settings that work for the display and the IDE fixed disk should be recorded. The settings can be documented using the Windows control panel—system—device manager selections and then selecting print.

If the PC blows up into safe mode when a new component is added, it is the culprit and needs to have its configuration set manually or requires better driver programs so Windows detects no conflicts.

In safe mode, a standard set of drivers is used for the keyboard, mouse, fixed disk and display. These standard drivers treat the display as a 640 by 480 VGA display, which causes high-resolution display desktop configurations to display at low resolution such that only part of the desktop is visible making the display less understandable. See Figure 15–3. If Windows works in safe mode, then basic drivers make it boot. Finding and changing the conflicting driver software or related hardware component configuration should permit Windows to boot in normal mode.

Driver programs are easily updated using the control panel—system— device manager. Making these selections produces a panel that lists all

Figure 15–3 *Safe mode VGA display*

devices. Nonfunctioning devices are typically identified by a red "X" or a yellow "!" warning symbol. Click on the specific device, then the driver tab, for Windows to open a wizard that updates drivers. The new driver program can be loaded from the fixed disk, a floppy diskette, or a CD.

Sometimes Windows indicates no conflicts when in fact there are. There is no outward sign that there is a problem except that the device just flat refuses to work.

In this instance, changing an I/O address or a memory address range can make all the difference in the world. Hardware conflicts in Windows are not easy to resolve. Safe mode is a tool to help resolve the most severe hardware conflicts. It is not foolproof. Changing hardware component settings and drivers one component at a time is an effective strategy for using safe mode to resolve severe hardware component conflicts.

The first component to attack when resolving such hardware conflicts is the LAN card, then the VGA card. Fixed disk hardware is the most critical for Windows to run and is generally working OK when safe mode is entered. The exception is when Windows is booted from a floppy because the fixed disk cannot boot Windows. If entering "WIN" while the DOS prompt points to the C:\windows directory is used to launch Windows, Windows may not recognize any of the fixed disks. Making the fixed disk bootable directly into Windows would correct this. Making a fixed disk bootable using a Windows bootable floppy requires that the floppy contain the SYS.COM program. This program is found in the \windows\command folder. When SYS.COM is on a bootable floppy or a readable fixed disk drive, performing the command SYS C: from the bootable floppy diskette drive A causes SYS.COM to transfer the operating system from A to C.

Other hardware component and driver conflicts are generally resolved in normal mode. Windows can boot with other conflicts and the control panel can be used to adjust and resolve hardware component IRQ, I/O port, and memory address conflicts.

Incorrect DOS Version

DOS programs are linked to a specific version of DOS. Their features and functions were designed to work with other DOS programs of that specific DOS version. For example, the DOS SHARE.EXE program for DOS 4.x had features in it that were required for using large fixed disk drives. The DOS 5.x and DOS 6.x versions of SHARE.EXE had a different set of features. Running older DOS programs with newer DOS versions could potentially cause some software compatibility problems. Microsoft set up DOS to recognize the specific DOS version with which a DOS program is to work. If the program is started with a different version of DOS, the program stops and displays the message:

```
C:\>chkdsk
Incorrect DOS version
```

This problem is prevented by placing a DEVICE=SETVER.EXE command in the CONFIG.SYS file; this command loads a version table. Windows 3.1 requires SETVER to prevent conflicts. Sometimes the version table must be modified for a specific DOS program by running SETVER to update the version table for that program.

The SETVER.EXE program to update the version table for CHKDSK above is run by:

```
C:\>setver chkdsk.exe 5.00
```

The SETVER.EXE program would enter the CHKDSK program version 5.00 information in a version table which, when queried by the DOS program, would return the DOS version information expected by the DOS program. The SETVER.EXE program function is built into Windows 95/98 IO.SYS.

The correct DOS version is only needed for DOS external commands and not for DOS application programs. For example the DOS 5.0 external commands CHKDSK, DISKCOPY, and MODE may require SETVER to run under DOS 6.22, while application programs like the old IBM Personal Editor program (PE2.EXE) or the DOS version of Lotus 1-2-3 do not require SETVER. The DOS EDIT.COM also runs with other versions of DOS without requiring SETVER because it is more like an application program than an external DOS command.

DOS programs using extended memory would not run with DOS 2.x because DOS 2.x did not support extended memory. If they were started with DOS 2.x, they would not display an incorrect DOS version message, they would display a memory error message instead.

Missing Operating System

When a DOS or Windows bootable disk has no operating system files (IO.SYS, MSDOS.SYS, and COMMAND.COM) to load, the BIOS displays a "missing operating system" or a "non-System disk or disk error" message. This error message may vary depending on the BIOS of the PC. This scenario often occurs when you have inadvertently left a data disk in the floppy drive. Typically with floppy disks the diskette is replaced or removed and the space bar hit to continue the booting process.

When this error message is displayed while attempting to boot from a fixed disk, it means that the disk is often partitioned properly, formatted properly, and viewable to the PC and DOS, but the master boot record (MBR) loader program cannot find the DOS files needed to boot. In some cases, there can be serious damage to the fixed disk as well, making it non-recoverable. When a fixed disk is damaged, this message is displayed when BIOS or the MBR loader goes to load DOS and finds a corrupted IO.SYS file.

You can tell the difference between a seriously corrupted fixed disk and a fixed disk that is OK but just does not boot by booting the PC into DOS using a bootable floppy disk containing SCANDISK.EXE and running SCANDISK.EXE. If SCANDISK.EXE runs OK, the fixed disk is good and the operating system needs to be reinstalled. When SCANDISK reports errors, your problems are more serious.

When SCANDISK runs on a damaged disk it displays error messages as it encounters errors. SCANDISK tries to recover the data and correct the errors as best it can. Severely damaged fixed disks are not recoverable. Minor damage to a fixed disk can be repaired with SCANDISK. If it is repaired, it should be replaced because there is a risk that the disk may have more serious errors in the near future.

When SCANDISK.EXE runs okay and the "no operating system found" error message is displayed, the disk and often the data on it can be recovered using FDISK and SYS. The SYS.COM DOS program installs the operating system on a formatted disk drive. When the IO.SYS and MSDOS.SYS files cannot be found, SYS C: executed from a bootable floppy in drive A reinstalls those programs and makes the drive bootable. In the event this does not succeed, FDISK /MBR rewrites the master boot record without losing any data on the fixed disk drive. Then performing SYS C: from a bootable floppy in drive A should make the drive bootable. If the boot sector of the drive is physically damaged, this procedure does not work. FDISK would then display an error message like "cannot write to fixed disk."

Error in CONFIG.SYS Line xx

When DOS or Windows 95/98 DOS boots a PC, the CONFIG.SYS file is used to match the PC hardware to DOS as discussed in Chapter 9. Sometimes there can be command errors in the CONFIG.SYS file. If CONFIG.SYS has commands it does not recognize, it displays a message:

```
Unrecognized command in CONFIG.SYS
Error in CONFIG.SYS line xx
```

Indicating that the CONFIG.SYS file has a command line error. Editing the CONFIG.SYS file and changing the specific line to a recognized command fixes the error.

In the example above, we created the erroneous command "devices=" to produce the error message. When we changed it to "device=," the PC stopped displaying the error message.

This error message is displayed when CONFIG.SYS commands are not recognized by IO.SYS. Correcting the command in CONFIG.SYS resolves the errors.

Some errors to look for in CONFIG.SYS are common typing errors like entering DEVICE= as DEVCIE=, missing "=" signs, incorrect driver specifications, and incomplete program names like DEVICE=SMARTDRV as opposed to DEVICE=SMARTDRV.EXE.

Bad or Missing COMMAND.COM

Sometimes the COMMAND.COM program as described in Chapter 9 cannot be found or it is not matched with the version of DOS being used. In this instance, DOS displays the error messages:

```
Invalid COMMAND.COM
Enter correct name of Command Interpreter
(eg, C:\COMMAND.COM)
>>
```

or a

```
Bad or Missing COMMAND.COM
```

DOS cannot find a valid COMMAND.COM or any COMMAND.COM to load into memory and permit further interaction with commands typed in by the PC user. Finding a valid COMMAND.COM that matches the DOS version being used and placing it in the root directory of the boot disk drive resolves this problem. With later versions of DOS and Windows DOS, pointing Windows to the COMMAND.COM in the Windows directory as shown below returns DOS to command line operation. Entering "c:\windows\command.com" when prompted as shown below points to COMMAND.COM.

```
Invalid COMMAND.COM
Enter correct name of Command Interpreter
(eg, C:\COMMAND.COM)
>>c:\windows\command.com
C:\WINDOWS>
```

This returns DOS 6.xx and Windows DOS to normal operation. Earlier versions of DOS would just stop running if the COMMAND.COM program was not found. Where DOS finds the command processor program is either in a default location like the root directory or c:\windows\command or in a location specified by the "SET COMSPEC = c:\dos" DOS command in the AUTOEXEC.BAT file or by a SHELL=C:\dos\command.com in the CONFIG.SYS file. The SET and SHELL commands add the COMMAND.COM location to the DOS environment space.

Bad or Missing HIMEM.SYS

When HIMEM.SYS is referenced in the CONFIG.SYS file but cannot be found during the DOS boot process, the message:

```
Starting MS-DOS...
Bad or missing C:\HIMEM.SYS
```

is displayed. If HIMEM.SYS is corrupted, the system typically locks after the "Starting MS-DOS" message is displayed, necessitating a system reboot that bypasses (using the F5 key) the CONFIG.SYS and AUTOEXEC.BAT startup files. Then simply placing the correct HIMEM.SYS file in the directory specified in CONFIG.SYS resolves the problem. HIMEM.SYS is provided with both DOS and Windows. To get a good HIMEM.SYS file, check the c:\windows folder, the C:\Windows\Options\Cabs folder, or the original Windows installation CD on a Windows 95/98 PC. Often a good copy can be found in these locations.

Missing HIMEM.SYS

Some DOS programs require access to extended memory. Windows must have extended memory available to run. HIMEM.SYS controls access to extended memory and the HIMEM area. If HIMEM.SYS is not loaded and a program requests access to extended memory, the error message below indicating that extended memory is not present and that HIMEM.SYS is not loaded is displayed.

```
C:\ >win
Missing HIMEM.SYS;
Make sure that the file is in your Windows directory and
that its location is correctly specified in your
CONFIG.SYS file.
```

Attempting to run Windows 3.1x without HIMEM.SYS loaded generated this error message. To fix this problem add to CONFIG.SYS the lines:

```
Device=c:\HIMEM.SYS
DOS=HIGH
```

With the HIMEM.SYS program residing in the root directory of the bootable drive C.

With Windows 95/98 the HIMEM.SYS function is loaded by IO.SYS and does not need to be loaded in the CONFIG.SYS file.

Windows 95/98 can also require the HIMEM.SYS program. When booted from the recovery diskette without HIMEM.SYS and the extended memory accessed by RAMDrive, Windows 98 displays these messages:

```
RAMDrive: Extended Memory Manager not present.

Warning: the high memory area (HMA) is not available.
Additional low memory (below 640K) will be used instead.
```

To fix this problem add to CONFIG.SYS the lines:

```
Device=a:\HIMEM.SYS
DOS=HIGH
```

With HIMEM.SYS program installed on the Windows bootable floppy diskette in drive A.

Swap File Error Messages

Swap files are used by Windows to store display images, program code, and other RAM contents on the disk as opposed to in RAM. The swap file creates the Windows virtual memory. In Windows 98 this is a temporary virtual memory swap file that grows and shrinks depending upon the demands placed on the PC. In Windows 3.1x, it could be a temporary or a permanent swap file. The permanent swap file was preferred with Windows 3.1x because it guaranteed a specific amount of disk space would be set aside for virtual (or paging) memory. The Windows 3.11 permanent swap file was set up using the control panel—386 enhanced mode—virtual memory selections. (Windows 3.0 used the SWAPFILE program run in real mode to create the swap file.) Windows supports changing from the default temporary swap file to a fixed permanent swap file. See Figure 15–4.

Once established, the swap file settings created SYSTEM.INI entries and SPART.PAR and 386SPART.PAR files on the fixed disk. The 386SPART.PAR file was the actual swap file. The SPART.PAR file in the Windows directory was the control file that pointed to the 386SPART.PAR file.

Sometimes the SYSTEM.INI entries would be changed or the swap file would not match the SPART.PAR and SYSTEM.INI entries. In this event, Windows 3.11 displayed the blue screen "corrupt swap file" warning message, as shown in Figure 15–5. The corrupt swap file warning is only for per-

Figure 15-4 *Windows 3.1x swap file setup*

Figure 15-5 *Swap file warning*

manent swap files because temporary swap files are created fresh whenever Windows 3.11 is launched. The corrupt swap file message, while alarming because it fills the entire PC display screen, is not a critical error message.

Deleting the corrupt swap file and setting its length to zero as instructed by Windows are the first steps in resolving the problem. Windows performs this process for you when you answer "yes" to the remove the cor-

Figure 15–6   *Setting swap file length to zero*

rupt swap file message query. See Figure 15–6. Once Windows 3.11 has created a new permanent swap file, Windows needs to be shut down and restarted for the new swap file to be used. This is not a reboot from DOS, only a Windows 3.11 shutdown and restart.

Then setting up a permanent swap file using the virtual memory settings would reestablish the permanent swap file. Windows 3.11 will recommend a swap file size automatically, but a rule of thumb is to set a swap file at about two to three times the size of the PC's installed RAM. So a 64 MB RAM PC should have a 128 MB to 192 MB swap file.

Windows 3.1x would need to be restarted to finalize the corrective procedure.

Windows 95/98 uses a dynamic swap file that Microsoft touts as a cross between a permanent and a temporary swap file. In reality using the PC's "let me specify my own virtual memory settings" menu option permits Windows 95/98 to use the equivalent of a permanent swap file. See Figure 15–7.

Setting a permanent swap file in Windows 98 in this fashion can resolve some memory problems with Windows 95/98. In any case, Windows 95/98 does not display the corrupt swap file message.

The major advantage to letting Windows set a default swap file is that it automatically sets a swap file size that lets almost all PCs deliver speedy and flawless performance for most users. Setting your own swap file can help if you are a power user experiencing memory problems with the programs that you run. In that case, a permanent swap file may make your PC run more reliably, but a human being would not notice any performance differences between Windows automatic settings and a manually set swap file. There is one swap file that Windows uses. It is possible in multiple disk systems to set this swap file on any disk drive. Normally, Windows sets it on the bootable Windows drive C. We set ours on our backup drive E.

Specifying a very large swap file is not really better than a smaller one and may in some ways degrade performance. When data is swapped to disk,

Figure 15–7   *Windows 98 permanent swap file setup*

Windows must manage that swap file. Smaller swap files have smaller data structures to process than larger swap files. Hence, a large swap file may actually degrade performance rather than improve it. The primary focus of a permanent swap file is not so much performance, but rather making Windows 95/98 perform more predictably when a large variety of programs are run.

Cannot Find a Device File Needed to Run Windows

Sometimes with Windows 3.1x and Windows 95/98, DLLs and other files referenced in the SYSTEM.INI file and in the registry are removed from the hard drive and, thereby, from the system.

When Windows is started and it does not find these files on the disk drive, Windows 3.1x displays the following message:

```
Cannot find a device file that may be needed to run
Windows.
Make sure that the PATH line in your AUTOEXEC.BAT file
points to the directory that contains the file and that it
exists on your hard disk. If the file does not exist, try
running Setup to install it or remove any references to it
from your SYSTEM.INI file.
```

```
vnetware.386
Press a key to continue
```

Or Windows 95/98 displays:

```
Cannot find a device file that may be needed to run Windows
or a Windows application.
The windows registry or SYSTEM.INI file refers to this
device file, but the device file no longer exists.
If you deleted this file on purpose, try uninstalling the
associated application using its uninstall or setup
program.
If you still want to use the application associated with
this device file, try reinstalling that application to
replace the missing file.
Dummy.386
Press a key to continue
```

The file identified in the error message is the source of the problem. With Windows 3.1x, it is referenced in the SYSTEM.INI file, while with Windows 95/98, the reference is usually found in the registry.

These error messages are resolved by adding back the missing file to the c:\Windows\System directory or by removing references to it from the SYSTEM.INI file or from the registry. To remove registry references run REGEDIT and use the search function to locate all references to the missing file. See Figure 15–8.

The registry keys are then removed to stop the error message from appearing.

Study Break

Windows 98 HIMEM

This study break exercise examines how Windows 98 DOS behaves when HIMEM.SYS is not loaded.

1. Go to a Windows 98 PC and create a startup diskette. Copy DOSKEY.EXE and MEM.EXE to the startup diskette root directory.

2. Using the DOS EDIT program or Windows Notepad edit the CONFIG.SYS file and REM out the DEVICE=HIMEM.SYS /testmem:off line in the [NOCD] section. The lines should read as follows upon completion:
   [NOCD]
   REM device=himem.sys /testmem:off

Figure 15–8 *Searching the Windows registry*

3. Shut down windows and reboot the PC using the startup diskette. When requested, boot into NOCD, start computer without CD-ROM support.

4. What error messages does Windows 98 DOS display? Do you get the RAMDrive: and Warning: messages previously identified in this chapter?

5. Run the MEM program. Does it display XMS as available? How much XMS is free? There should be none free.

6. Run LH DOSKEY. Does DOSKEY load? It should. Where does MEM show it loading? It should load into conventional memory.

7. Repeat these exercises when booting into CD, start computer with CD-ROM support. Now HIMEM.SYS is properly loaded. The results should show that XMS is available. DOSKEY still loads into conventional RAM because EMM386.EXE is needed to activate the upper memory blocks (UMBs).

This exercise illustrates that Windows 98 DOS when booted from a floppy diskette still requires HIMEM.SYS and EMM386.EXE to make XMS and UMBs available to applications.

A+ 15.2 Resolving Frequent Software Problems

There are several common Windows problems that cause Windows to request operator termination of the application program. Generally they result in Windows 3.1x and sometimes Windows 95/98 displaying a blue screen (of death) warning message. Such warning messages indicate that Windows has detected a potential conflict between programs running in Windows. If these programs continue to run it will corrupt memory or cause some other conflict which will cause Windows to crash. To prevent such a crash, Windows issues blue screen warning messages permitting the user to shut down one of the offending applications. Windows then continues (most times) to run, permitting the user to perform a normal shutdown and restart. See Figure 15–9.

Both Windows 3.1x and Windows 95/98 perform similarly here, although Windows 95/98 provides better error recovery and diagnostic tools. Blue screen messages appear because of general protection faults, illegal

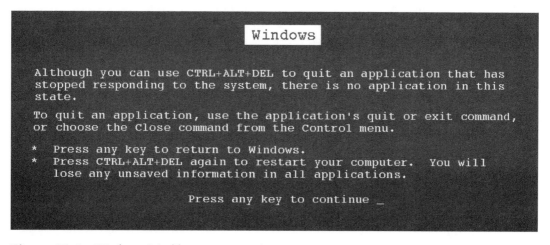

Figure 15–9 *Windows 3.1x blue screen warning*

operations, missing diskettes or CD-ROMs, and invalid directories. Applications programs running generate the blue screen messages. Windows software components themselves occasionally generate blue screen messages.

Application Program Errors

Application programs writing into RAM used by other applications cause illegal operation errors. If two programs placed code in the same memory locations, the instructions would be corrupted, making Windows unstable and causing a serious crash. Windows 3.1x and Windows 95/98 perform similarly but there are variations in response with Windows 95/98 for older 16-bit applications and newer 32-bit applications.

When a 16-bit application performs an illegal operation, Windows displays a "general protection fault" error message. See Figure 15–10.

Ignoring the error causes Windows to not execute the instruction that caused the error. Often this just leaves the program in an endless loop and forces the user to close the application. When the application is closed all data in RAM is lost. Unless the data was previously saved to disk, the user has no way to preserve the data. When the 16-bit application is executed, Windows 95/98 displays the close application box and identifies the error as a general protection fault. See Figure 15–11.

For 32-bit Windows applications, the initial application error screen is not displayed. Windows identifies the error as an invalid page fault. See Figure 15–12.

With 32-bit applications, there is no option to ignore and attempt to continue. The application must be closed and the data in RAM lost. With all memory conflict errors, it is best to immediately shut down Windows and then restart. Once memory becomes messed up, Windows does not do a particularly good job of cleaning up the memory allocations so that opening

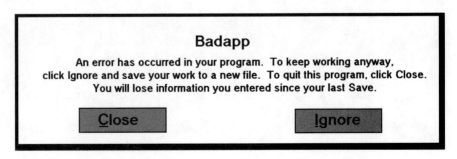

Badapp

An error has occurred in your program. To keep working anyway,
click Ignore and save your work to a new file. To quit this program, click Close.
You will lose information you entered since your last Save.

[C̲lose]   [I̲gnore]

Figure 15–10 *Windows 98 16-bit error message*

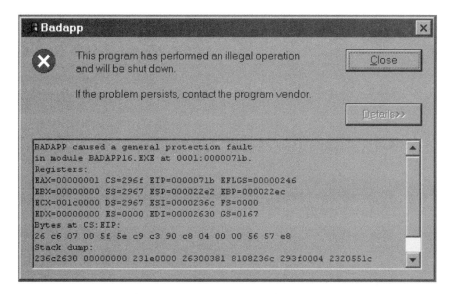

Figure 15-11 *Windows 98 general protection fault error box*

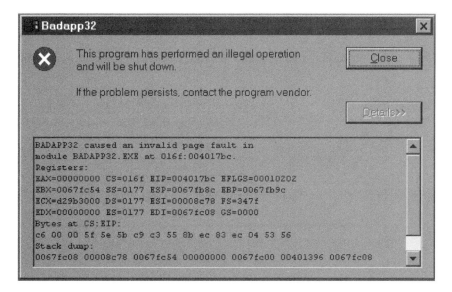

Figure 15-12 *Windows 98 invalid page fault message*

new programs are then more likely to generate additional illegal operation errors.

To troubleshoot illegal operation errors, the following steps are suggested:

1. Check the application to ensure it was not written for an earlier version of Windows. Applications written for earlier versions of Windows may have incompatibilities with Windows 95/98 that could result in operation errors.
2. Check system resources by going to the program manager help menu display and make sure they are sufficient. Windows 3.1x needs more than 60% free resources to launch new applications. Remember, the resource level reported is that of the heap with the fewest resources. This means that the other heaps have more than 60% resources available. Sometimes applications running in the background use more resources than is evident. When resources are low, close all unnecessary applications.
3. Reinstall the offending application software. Perhaps a file or a part of the program has become corrupt.
4. Run SCANDISK or CHKDSK to test the fixed disk drives. When there are lost allocation units, it could cause Windows applications to blow up or indicate a more serious fixed disk problem. Perhaps there are errors in FAT table entries causing an application to not locate some data or code. The SCANDISK automatically fixes FAT and disk errors. The CHKDSK /F command corrects or fixes those errors as well.
5. Remove the existing WIN.INI and restart Windows. Before doing this, make sure to save or rename the WIN.INI file so that it can be restored. This ensures that the error was not caused by any corrupted fonts, print drivers, or software loaded from the "Run=" or the "Load=" commands If this works, then put a (;) in front of the "Load=" and the "Run=" to prevent any software from loading. Rename the WIN.INI file to restore it.
6. In the [386ENH] section of SYSTEM.INI file, add MaxBPs=1024. This changes the memory allocation boundary for break points which can reduce illegal operation errors.
7. Call the manufacturer of the problem software to determine if there is a free fix or patch to correct the problem..

System Freezing or Application Programs Hang

Application programs that get very busy cannot respond to user input. This is a common error with communications programs. When a modem loses carrier with another modem or when a mapped drive on a local network or PC is shut down, programs using these communications links can hang. The Microsoft Internet Explorer is the program that fails to respond most often

Figure 15–13   *Hung application*

on our PCs. This happens because communications links fail and become broken.

Sometimes the timeout period expires and the PC begins responding again. Other times the hanging program never regains control from the communications software components. In this event, the hourglass pointer is displayed whenever the mouse is pointed at the application. See Figure 15–13.

Communications problems are not the only source of hung applications. Disk drive errors and problems can also cause an application to hang when data is written to the disk drive. Because Windows devotes much of its attention to waiting for the disk operation to complete before proceeding, it can appear locked. Furthermore, reading corrupted files from a disk drive causes Windows to often develop memory conflicts, producing illegal operation errors. Additional description and discussion of these errors preceded this section in this chapter.

When a program hangs, The Ctrl-Alt-Del keys are struck to bring up the task manager program. See Figure 15–14.

The task manager program labels the hung program as "not responding." Highlighting it and clicking on the end task button clears the application not responding. In this event, all data in RAM is lost. Windows does provide a second chance to continue waiting for the application to finish its I/O activities in the event that the data in RAM is critical to the user. See Figure 15–15.

The cancel button returns to Windows without closing the application, while the end task button closes the application but does not close Windows.

Low Resources

Windows user and graphics resources can run low. When resources run low, applications fail to respond and Windows can crash. Other unpleasant things

Figure 15–14 *Windows task manager*

Figure 15–15 *End task display box.*

Figure 15–16 *Windows 98 resource meter display*

can happen as well. The resource meter can monitor the resources to prevent Windows resources from running low.

The resource meter in Windows 98 is the program RSRCMTR.EXE found in the c:\windows folder (directory). Placing a shortcut to this program in the c:\windows\start menu\programs\startup causes it to be launched each time Windows boots. It then places an icon in the Systray which has a green (good), yellow (dangerous), and red (red is dead) bar display of the available Windows resources. The Systray icon appears in the upper left hand corner of Figure 15–16.

When the resources hit about 30%, the resource meter flashes a warning message. We cannot show the warning message because Windows did not see fit to permit us to recover from our low resource warning message and continue working on this chapter. However, the resulting crash message we were able to capture. See Figure 15–17. The PC is waiting for the close program dialog box to appear. It cannot be displayed because there are not enough graphic resources to create it. Consequently, the PC waits and waits and does nothing. A forced reboot is most often the only recourse.

When this message appears Windows is going down. With low resources, selecting the press any key to return to Windows and wait produces a blank screen because Windows has no resources to create or rewrite the display.

When Windows resources are low, the best resolution of the problem is to immediately close all applications and restart Windows. This cleans up Windows memory and restores the resources to their initial operating levels. Because Windows resources are automatically controlled by Windows and cannot be increased, the only solution to low resource problems is to run fewer applications simultaneously and to immediately shut down applications when resources hit critically low levels.

Missing Floppy or CD-ROM

Once an application program is started, it may require data stored on a floppy or CD-ROM. In the event that the floppy drive diskette or the CD-ROM drive's CD is removed, Windows displays the missing floppy diskette or missing CD error message.

Pointing the Windows Explorer at the floppy drive that contains no diskette causes floppy drive errors. See Figure 15–18.

The floppy drive error is easily resolved by either putting a floppy diskette in the drive or by pointing the Windows Explorer at a fixed disk drive.

Perhaps more common is the CD-ROM error message because many applications reference data on CD-ROMs. See Figure 15–19.

Again, inserting a CD easily rectifies this error. If the problem persists, the CD-ROM lens may be dirty or the CD itself may be dirty or unreadable.

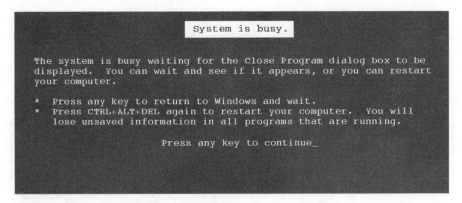

Figure 15–17 *Windows low resource crash message*

Figure 15–18
Floppy drive error message

```
                        ┌─────────────────────────────────────┐
                        │   Error Reading CD-ROM in Drive F:   │
                        └─────────────────────────────────────┘

         Please Insert CD-ROM
         With Serial Number 89D9-19EA in Drive F:

         If the CD-ROM is still in the drive, it may require cleaning.

                     Press ENTER for OK or ESC to Cancel:  OK
```

Figure 15–19   *Missing CD error message*

A lens cleaning CD will brush the lens and remove dirt that prevents it from reading CDs. Cleaning the CD can sometimes fix the problem of a nonreadable CD. Reading another CD in the CD-ROM drive easily tests this. When several CDs are unreadable, and the lens has been cleaned, then the drive itself may be bad and need replacement.

Invalid Working Directory

Programs often reference data or DLLs on the fixed or removable disks. These references can be lost or corrupted. In this event, the PC can issue error messages indicating an invalid working directory. See Figure 15–20.

   If the directory and its contents have been removed, then replacing the missing directory is required to fully correct this error. When the directory is moved to a place that Windows does not expect, then updating the directory pointer to the new directory location is all that is generally needed to fix the problem. Pointing to the correct working directory is done using the properties option for the program or its representative shortcut icon. See Figure 15–21.

```
┌─────────────────────────────────────────────────────────────────────────────┐
│ MS-DOS Prompt                                                             [x] │
├─────────────────────────────────────────────────────────────────────────────┤
│  /!\  Cannot find the working folder for this program. The program may have   │
│       difficulty locating its files and documents. Make sure that the working │
│       folder is specified correctly in the property sheets for the program    │
│       and any shortcuts to it.                                                 │
│                                                                               │
│       Do you wish to run the program anyway?                                   │
│                                                                               │
│                        ┌─────────┐      ┌─────────┐                           │
│                        │   Yes   │      │   No    │                           │
│                        └─────────┘      └─────────┘                           │
└─────────────────────────────────────────────────────────────────────────────┘
```

Figure 15–20   *Invalid working directory error message*

Figure 15–21 *Program shortcut properties*

Changing the working directory is performed by selecting the program tab and then entering the correct working directory in the Working entry section. Applying the changes immediately alters the program's working directory and permits testing to ensure that the working directory change fixed the problem. The OK selection also immediately changes the working directory, but in addition exits the properties box. If the change is not correct, the properties box would need to be reopened to again adjust the working directory.

Critical Hardware Errors or the "Option will not function" Message

Critical hardware errors prevent Windows from starting or force it to start in safe mode. Other hardware errors can cause applications to fail or functions to just not work. Soundboards and other PC peripheral components often behave in this fashion. Sometimes, the application or Windows issues error messages indicating that the option is not functioning. More often, they just stop working. In any event these errors are due to a PC peripheral hardware component and Windows mismatch. The most likely scenario is that the hardware drivers do not match Windows or they are not the latest drivers (supporting the full hardware component capabilities) required by Windows or the application. Updating the drivers and checking for hardware conflicts are the approaches used to resolve these types of errors.

To resolve these problems, the first step is to identify the malfunctioning hardware. The Windows control panel—system—device manager should display the malfunctioning devices with a red "X"" indicating that they are not functioning. The next step is to find the latest software drivers for the component on the Internet. Go to the component manufacturer's website and find technical support and software drivers. Download the drivers and place them in an install directory (folder) on the PC's fixed disk.

Next, using the Windows control panel—system—device manager, try selecting the device and the install new drivers option or just uninstall the malfunctioning device so that Windows will automatically reinstall it when it restarts. For laptop PCMCIA and card bus cards, have Windows completely running without the card plugged into the card slot. Once Windows is operating completely, plug in the PCMCIA cards one at a time for Windows to recognize them and attempt to install the driver software. Once the proper drivers are installed, the misconfiguration should be resolved. In the event this does not resolve the problem, consider using an alternative product. Hardware is relatively cheap compared to the cost of the hours of time it may take to resolve the simplest of PC misconfiguration problems.

Application Does Not Load or Start

Application programs can fail to launch. This is often caused by an application shortcut failing to point correctly to the application. When a missing application is launched, Windows immediately permits searching for the missing application to fix the problem. See Figure 15–22.

Figure 15–22 *Searching for the application*

Figure 15–23 *Missing application error message*

When the application is searched for and not found, Windows displays the missing application error message. See Figure 15–23.

Searching for the application and then pointing the shortcut to the application's location on the fixed disk drive can solve the missing application problem. This is performed using the properties selection for the shortcut to the application. The target entry area for the shortcut icon must point to the directory and the application. When this points to a valid application, the missing application error is resolved. See Figure 15–24.

The properties box permits browsing for the target application. This find target option is not an automatic search. It permits the PC user to manually view the disk directories until the application is located. A more effective approach to locating a missing application is to use the explorer search function. The explorer search function is activated through the explorer menus or by striking Ctrl-F (F equals Find). Then the missing file can be automatically located on the disk drives using wild card character searches. For example you could search for any program using the first four letters of the program name—MSINFO32.EXE could be found using MSIN*.EXE. Windows finds this file and MSINF16H.EXE when drive C is searched in this fashion. Once located, the shortcut target can be easily and accurately updated. The shortcut properties box identifies the file name of the missing or moved application.

Figure 15–24 *Shortcut target*

Cannot Log onto Network

Most PCs are connected to some type of network today. Network problems are common. They have three sources: PC hardware, PC software, or the network itself. When a PC expects to work on a network, the first activity is to have the user log onto the network servers or peer-to-peer PC sharing resources. There are two network logon options: logging on and restoring network connections, or logging on quickly to the network and only restoring network connections when they are used or accessed by the PC user. See Figure 15–25.

The quick logon option permits the PC to run faster because the network drive mappings do not require validation when the "restore network connections" option is selected. In either event, the user is logged onto the

Figure 15–25   *Network logon options*

network during the boot process unless there is a network problem that prevents logon. When the user cannot log on to the network, Windows displays
a logon error message, as shown in Figure 15–26.

Figure 15–26   *Network logon error message*

This error can be caused by not finding peer-to-peer connections while
trying to restore them or by not being able to log on to a Windows NT
domain. In both cases, the PC cannot find the logon PC or server. With peer-

to-peer networks, the network cabling could be faulty or the target peer-to-peer PC could be turned off or be (if it is a laptop) removed from the network. In a Windows NT domain, the domain controller server (the primary domain controller, or PDC) could be down. In large Windows NT domain networks, there are backup domain controllers (BDC) that take control of the network in the event that the primary domain controller (PDC) fails or is taken off the network. This means that failing to connect to the network domain controller in a large network is more likely caused by a cabling problem than by a faulty server.

"Failing to connect" error messages just indicate to the PC user that network servers and resources are not available for use. However, the user's PC can be used with the data and programs resident on its fixed disk drives. Once the network connection is repaired, the PC can be logged onto the network, normally correcting the problem.

System Resource Meter

This study break exercise examines installing and using the system resource meter to monitor system resources. It builds on the Chapter 10 study break, "Windows Graphical Resources."

1. Go to a Windows 98 PC and install a shortcut to the system resource meter in the startup folder.

2. Use explorer to open the Windows folder and find the file RSRCMTR.EXE.

3. Right click on it and select create shortcut. A shortcut is immediately created as the last file in \windows and is highlighted.

4. Right click and select cut to cut the shortcut from \Windows. Then select the \windows\program files\programs\startup folder, right click and select paste to place the shortcut in that folder

5. Restarting Windows should load the resource meter and produce a warning message. Disable the warning message, otherwise it appears each time Windows is restarted.

6. Point to the resource meter icon in the Systray. What resources are available in system, user, and GDI heaps? Double-click to see a graphic display of the available resources.

7. Open several application programs and see the resources decrease. How many programs can be opened before a low resource warning is issued?

8. If no warning is issued, use MS Word to print a complex document containing lots of graphics. Does this diminish resources to the warning point?

The purpose of this exercise was to illustrate how to make the resource meter a continuous resource monitoring tool, illustrate how system resources are consumed, and show the impact of printing on system resources.

A+ 15.3 DOS and Windows Utilities

The primary software diagnostic tools are DOS and Windows utility programs. These programs provide a variety of diagnostic and problem resolution capabilities for both hardware and software. Both DOS and Windows tools are used to resolve software problems for Windows 95/98. Each has a specific role it performs in resolving PC problems.

FDISK.EXE—Fixed Disk

The FIDSK program is the fixed disk partitioning utility. It is used to set up the PC's fixed disk drives. It also functions effectively as a fixed disk diagnostic program that detects fixed disk hardware problems. When FDISK is run, it should quickly enter its main menu, as shown in Figure 15–27.

When there are fixed disk problems. FDISK displays messages indicating that it cannot read the fixed disk drive, or that the disk drive controller is bad. These messages are displayed when there is a fixed disk hardware failure.

FDISK can also repair the master boot record (MBR). The command FDISK /MBR rewrites the master boot record on the fixed disk. This in rare instances can remove some viruses from the boot sector of the fixed disk drive. It can also help in restoring an operating system to the fixed disk.

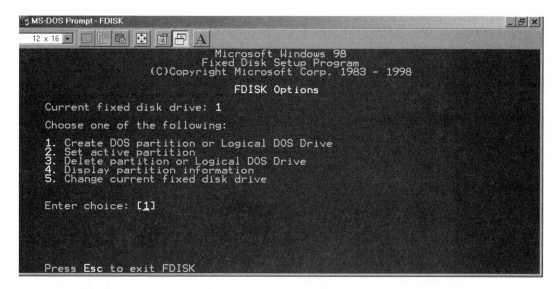

Figure 15–27 *FDISK main menu*

SCANDISK—Scan Disk Files and Directories

SCANDISK is a fixed disk FAT and directory diagnostic program primarily. It can also test the surface integrity of the fixed disk. See Figure 15–28.

Whenever Windows is shut down abruptly and not permitted to gracefully close applications and write the last registry entries to the fixed disk, Windows forces SCANDISK to run during the reboot process. This is to find and fix any corruption to the FAT and the files on the disk drive. In the hundreds of times it has run after we have shut down Windows abruptly by pulling the plug, SCANDISK has never found a problem with the FAT or the files. That may be because we have always waited for the disk activity light on the front of the PC to indicate there is no further disk drive activity.

SCANDISK can scan individual drives or all drives. The standard check option only examines the directory structure, the files stored on the fixed disk, and FAT for errors. The thorough check also tests the disk surface for

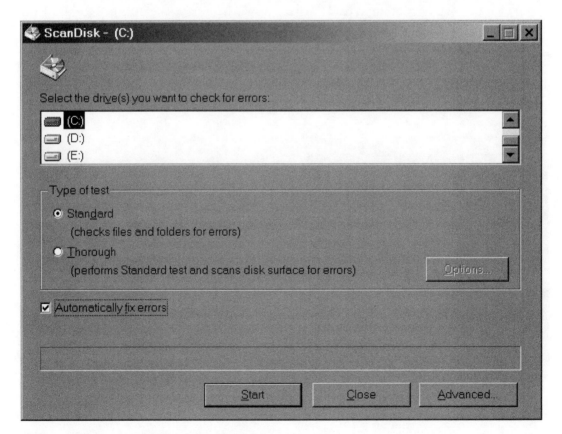

Figure 15–28 *SCANDISK menu selections*

errors. When a bad spot is found, it attempts to recover the data by reading it several times and then to move the data in that spot to a safe area of the disk. For SCANDISK to fix errors the automatically fix errors option needs to be selected.

DEFRAG.EXE—Fixed Disk Defragment

The DEFRAG program reorganizes the data on a fixed disk drive or on all fixed disk drives so that the allocation units for each file are stored next to each other. (See Figure 15–29.) This permits the fixed disk to retrieve the file data without moving the read/write heads of the fixed disk drive, thus speeding up file access.

The Windows 98 DEFRAG program moves more frequently used program files to the outside tracks of the fixed disk to further speed up access to those programs and their software components. See Figure 15–30. The goal is to minimize the fixed disk's read/write head movement, thus speeding up access to data stored on the fixed disk.

DEFRAG can also be used as a diagnostic program. While defragmenting a fixed disk, DEFRAG typically reads and writes all the files on the fixed disk. This is a test of the data integrity and the fixed disk itself. While not a thorough disk surface test like the SCANDISK advanced option performs, it

Figure 15–29 *DEFRAG drive selection*

Figure 15–30 *DEFRAG options*

is nonetheless an effective test of the disk drive with the bonus of improving performance once complete.

When DEFRAG runs, it displays progress towards completion in a compact or a detailed display. The compact progress display box is shown in Figure 15–31.

When running DEFRAG, it is best to close all other active programs except DEFRAG. Otherwise DEFRAG takes a very long time to scan the bootable drive (usually C) containing the Windows files because Windows updates the registry and other areas as DEFRAG runs. Whenever Windows performs an update, DEFRAG restarts from the beginning of the drive. Such restarts consume lots of time. Often when Windows is first installed the Windows task scheduler program is set up to run DEFRAG every night. This is fine, but sometimes DEFRAG can hang because of the programs active in the

Figure 15–31 *DEFRAG compact progress display*

Figure 15–32 *MEM summary report*

PC necessitating a forced reboot. We believe that it is best to manually run DEFRAG about once each week.

MEM.EXE—Memory Check Program

MEM displays the current memory configuration of the PC. It provides summary and detailed displays of memory contents. See Figure 15–32.

The detailed displays only cover the programs resident in real mode memory (the first megabyte of RAM). The MEM program does not display the programs resident in XMS. This program is most useful in troubleshooting DOS and Windows 3.1x memory problems. It is less helpful with Windows 95/98. MEM helps with troubleshooting by displaying those programs loaded into the upper memory blocks (UMBs) and the regions that the UMBs are broken up into. The size of each region is also displayed. This permits rearranging program loading to achieve the maximum amount of conventional RAM for DOS applications. MEMMAKER configures memory optimally for a given program loading order as determined by CONFIG.SYS and AUTOEXEC.BAT but does not change program load order so it cannot provide the maximum amount of available RAM.

```
MS-DOS Prompt                                                    _ 6 X

  12 x 16   □  □ □ □ □ □ □ □  A

C:\WINDOWS>attrib /?
Displays or changes file attributes.

ATTRIB [+R | -R] [+A | -A] [+S | -S] [+H | -H] [[drive:][path]filename] [/S]

    +    Sets an attribute.
    -    Clears an attribute.
    R    Read-only file attribute.
    A    Archive file attribute.
    S    System file attribute.
    H    Hidden file attribute.
    /S   Processes files in all directories in the specified path.

C:\WINDOWS>_
```

Figure 15–33 *ATTRIB command options*

ATTRIB.EXE—Change Attributes

ATTRIB is not a diagnostic program per se. It changes the attributes of files. The DOS and Windows file attributes that ATTRIB can change are archive (A), hidden (H), read-only (R), and system —(S). This is helpful in performing some troubleshooting and diagnostic procedures because some key system files (for instance, the registry files) are marked as hidden, read-only, and system. See Figure 15–33: ATTRIB command options.

ATTRIB is used to set files to a viewable, read/write status permitting replacement and editing of Windows control files. ATTRIB provides a /S option permitting execution in a directory and its subdirectories. This is sometimes helpful when deleting data from the fixed disk because the Windows explorer does not delete read only, hidden or system files. Further, the Windows explorer permits changing file attributes, but requires continual manual effort to complete attribute changes for subdirectories. ATTRIB with the /S option is more automatic and much faster at this task. ATTRIB also displays all the files on the fixed disk drive regardless of their attributes.

Figure 15–34 *EXTRACT command options*

EXTRACT.EXE—Cabinet File Extraction Tool

The EXTRACT program works with the Windows cabinet (CAB) installation files. This is helpful when Windows just needs a single missing DLL or DRV file to correct a problem. See Figure 15–34.

The /D option permits EXTRACT to display the contents of an individual cabinet file. When combined with the "| MORE" pipe to display 24 lines per screen, the cabinet (CAB) files can be searched to find the missing Windows driver or software component.

For example, the WD.VXD file could be located in the Windows 98 cabinet files by the following command:

```
extract base4.cab wd.vxd /a /d |more
```

Use this EXTRACT to search through all the Windows 98 CAB files starting with base4.cab and display:

```
Microsoft (R) Cabinet Extraction Tool—Version (16)
1.00.603.0 (08/14/97)
Copyright (c) Microsoft Corp 1994-1997. All rights
reserved.
 Cabinet base4.cab
 Cabinet BASE5.CAB
```

Figure 15–35 *EXPAND command options*

```
Cabinet BASE6.CAB
05-11-1998 8:01:00p A---    18,329 wd.vxd
  Cabinet NET7.CAB.
```

EXTRACT's /E command line option would extract the file from its location in BASE6.CAB.

CAB files can also be viewed and updated using the latest version of the WINZIP.EXE program. This third-party application integrates itself with Windows to handle many types of compressed library and archive files.

EXPAND.EXE—File Expansion Tool

The EXPAND program expands individual installation software component files. Software installation files for Windows 3.1x were individually compressed as opposed to being compressed as groups in cabinet (CAB) files. The individually compressed files had extensions with the last character being the underscore character; for example, EXE files were compressed as EX_ and DLL files were compressed as DL_ files. The EXPAND program expands these individually compressed files. See Figure 15–35.

The EXPAND program, similarly to the EXTRACT program, is used to replace or update Windows drivers and software components.

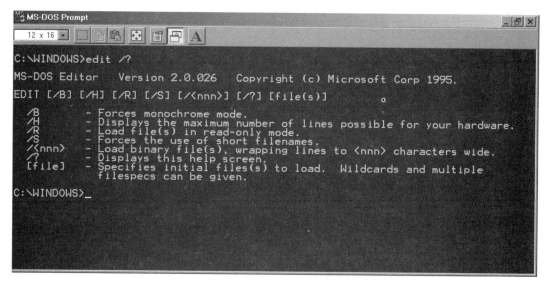

Figure 15–36 *EDIT Command options*

EDIT.COM—The Microsoft Text Editor Program

EDIT is the DOS-based text editor program. In DOS mode, it permits editing of text files like CONFIG.SYS, AUTOEXEC.BAT, SYSTEM.INI, WIN.INI and *.REG. See Figure 15–36. Windows provides an equivalent text editing capability with the Notepad program.

EDIT and Notepad are not diagnostic tools but rather programs that permit changing DOS and Windows configuration files. The text versions of the registry (*.REG) and Windows installation control files (*.INF) are text files that can be edited using EDIT or Notepad. EDIT is particularly useful, as are all the DOS diagnostics, because they operate in DOS mode, where Windows does not lock its key operating and configuration control files.

SYSEDIT.EXE—System Configuration Editor

SYSEDIT is a Windows program that opens all text Windows control files at one time. When launched, it opens PROTOCOL.INI, SYSTEM.INI, WIN.INI, CONFIG.SYS, and AUTOEXEC.BAT. See Figure 15–37. It provides the same capabilities as Notepad. SYSEDIT differs from Notepad in that it opens up all key text Windows control and configuration files at the same time.

SYSEDIT, like Notepad and EDIT, cannot edit binary files, such as the registry SYSTEM.DAT and USER.DAT files.

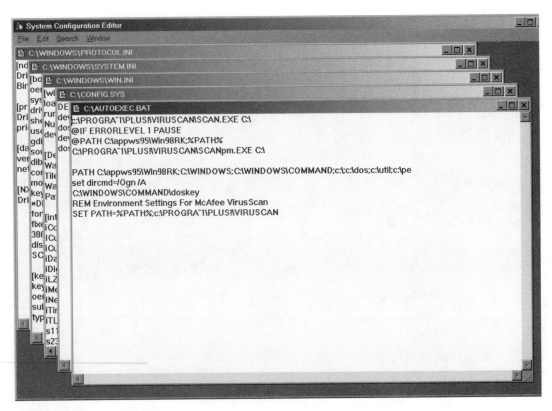

Figure 15–37 *SYSEDIT*

MSD.EXE—Microsoft Diagnostics Program

The MSD program is a diagnostic program helpful in verifying PC hardware. It displays information on the computer CPU chip and BIOS, RAM software and hardware assignments for real-mode upper memory blocks, display information, disk drives, communications, printer ports, and more. See Figure 15–38. Once a PC is booted, MSD can be run in either Windows or DOS mode.

The easiest way to run MSD is to open a DOS window and type in MSD. The PC jumps to a full screen display as MSD is launched. It can be returned to a Windows display by using Alt+Enter. Using the start menu run option launches MSD in the same fashion.

The primary use of MSD as a diagnostic tool is to report the PC hardware configuration as determined by DOS during the boot process. This can assist in troubleshooting some configuration problems such as communication port conflicts. An interesting feature is the disk drive option that reports

File   Utilities   Help

Computer...	AST/Award Unknown/80387	Disk Drives...	A: B: C: D: E: F: K: L:
Memory...	640K, 14336K Ext, 65535K XMS	LPT Ports...	1
Video...	VGA, ATI	COM Ports...	2
Network...	MS Client 4.00	Windows...	3.10 Enhanced
OS Version...	MS-DOS 7.10	IRQ Status...	
Mouse...	Not Detected 8.30	TSR Programs...	
Other Adapters...	Game Adapter	Device Drivers...	

Press ALT for menu, or press highlighted letter, or F3 to quit MSD.

Figure 15–38   *MSD menu options*

the total disk space and free disk space for each drive letter it finds. Both local and network drives are scanned and reported. Being a DOS-based program the maximum drive space is reported as 2 GB, which makes this total drive space information less useful. Free drive space is reported accurately. This can be very useful in troubleshooting application program problems. Often problems are caused by insufficient free space on fixed disk drives. PC users typically think that fixed disk space is unlimited (as indeed it seems on a new PC) when it is not. After using the PC for a year or so, the disk can become very full, causing a variety of Windows problems. The MSD disk drive report could help quickly identify which drives were very full and help resolve problems caused by insufficient fixed disk space.

The Control Panel—System—Device Manager

The device manager under the Windows 95/98 control panel controls the PC hardware installed under Windows. It identifies the hardware in device categories and then the individual devices installed in each category. See Figure 15–39. In the figure, the device manager is pointing to the general category of display adapters and showing the specific display adapter installed, a RAGE PRO TURBO AGP adapter.

The device manager can display the properties of hardware components. These properties include the IRQ setting, the I/O port address, and

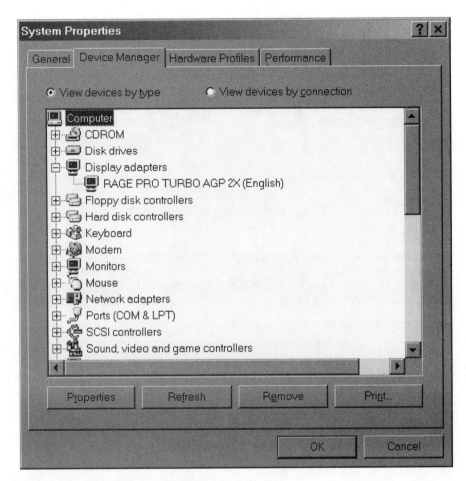

Figure 15–39 *Windows device manager*

the memory areas used. The properties can be set automatically using Windows plug-and-play capabilities or they can be set manually to bypass hardware conflicts.

When the computer entry is selected, the PC's IRQ (interrupt request), I/O (input/output) port, DMA (direct memory access) channel and memory ranges used by the PC's hardware components are displayed. This is helpful in resolving PC hardware conflicts. The control panel—system—device manager is used to uninstall software for the PC's hardware components. The process of uninstalling hardware device drivers and then reinstalling them sometimes resolves Windows hardware problems.

MSINFO32.EXE—MS System Information

The Microsoft System Information program (MSINFO32.EXE) is the Windows equivalent of the MSD program. It provides more information on the PC than does MSD. The only drawback is that it runs in Windows. The MSINFO32 program displays information on both hardware and Windows software components. See Figure 15–40.

Figure 15–40 *MSINFO32 program*

Somewhat similar to MSD, MSINFO32 displays overall system information, hardware resource assignments, and data on multimedia and network hardware components and on the Windows software environment. More importantly, under the tools menu option, it provides a set of tools to test and verify Windows hardware and software. See Figure 15–41.

Figure 15–41   *MSINFO32 tools menu*

Some of the MS system information software tools are helpful in preventing and resolving Windows problems. A short discussion of each is presented here.

DIRECTX DIAGNOSTIC TOOL

DirectX software plays an integral role in Windows 98 desktop and Internet operations. DirectX is comprised of DirectX drivers and other display, sound, music, and input driver programs. The DirectX Diagnostic tool verifies that these files are installed, that they are the correct versions, and that they are operating properly.

The easiest way to launch the DirectX Diagnostic tool is from the MSINFO32.EXE tools menu selection. Once launched, the DirectX diagnostic tool provides an introductory display with several tabs. The DirectX files and drivers tabs present the results of a DirectX diagnostic tool verification process. In most cases, no problems are found. The display, sound, and music tabs also verify the supporting DirectX software. In addition, they permit testing of the PC hardware for proper functioning with the installed DirectX software. The DirectX diagnostic tool provides mainly a verification of the DirectX software installed on the PC.

SFC.EXE—SYSTEM FILE CHECKER

The system file checker verifies the integrity of the PC's system files. It determines which files are altered and then prompts to restore the original copy of the file from its installation location (generally a CAB file). When files are known to be good, the verification information for the files can be updated from those originally recorded for the system file checker application. When Windows performs poorly this application may find Windows components that are the source of the problem,

SIGVERIF.EXE—SIGNATURE VERIFICATION TOOL

This application scans the PC's fixed disks for either files that are not signed or those that are signed. A file signature identifies:

- The version of the file—V3
- The file serial number—twenty hexadecimal digits
- The signature algorithm—md5RSA
- The issuer—generally Microsoft Windows Hardware Compatibility Publisher
- The validity dates—from 3/01/1998 3:00 AM to 2/15/00 3:00 AM
- The Public Key—RSA (2,048 bits)
- Enhanced Key usage
- Authority Key Identifier—certificate issuer is generally Microsoft corporation,
- A Thumbprint algorithm—sha1
- A Thumbprint—forty hexadecimal digits

For nonsigned files, the properties can be displayed. This may assist in verifying driver and software component compatibility with Windows. A signed file has a copyright notification in it. There are few Windows files today that are signed files. One signed file is WINIPCFG.EXE. The signature is by Microsoft Windows Hardware Compatibility Publishing. This could be used to check for legal compliance with copyright laws. When a signed program was found on a system where the software was not legally installed, that could identify a potential copyright violation.

SCANREG.EXE—REGISTRY CHECKER

The registry checker program checks the Windows registry for obvious errors and attempts to repair them. This is not a registry-cleaning program. It only detects errors and tries to correct them. Other non-Microsoft programs like Uninstaller provide a more thorough registry cleaning and verification functions. SCANREG also backs up the registry files, providing a mechanism for recovering from a corrupted registry. We prefer the ERU.EXE program for making backup copies of the key Windows startup files.

The SCANREG.EXE program that comes with Windows 98 is run automatically each time Windows 98 is started. It can also be used when installing new hardware and software components to provide registry backups in the event that the installations do not go as smoothly as expected. It would be run prior to the installation on a good working PC, and immediately after the installation to back up a successful installation.

MSCONFIG.EXE—MS SYSTEM CONFIGURATION UTILITY

The MS system configuration utility provides a menu selection control of Windows startup. It lets the user mark off the files and functions performed during the Windows boot process. In this manner, individual functions and programs can be bypassed to assist in troubleshooting the Windows booting process. See Figure 15–42. Unchecking an item bypasses it during the Windows boot process.

The Windows system configuration utility controls entries in the CONFIG.SYS, AUTOEXEC.BAT, SYSTEM.INI, and WIN.INI files as well as the Windows startup process.

VCMUI.EXE—VERSION CONFLICT MANAGER

When new software is installed or old software updated, the version conflict manager registers software components that conflict with other installed software. Such conflicting software versions are a potential source of Windows problems. Restoring original or updated versions of software components that eliminate conflicts can make Windows more reliable. On our PCs, no conflicting software versions have been identified.

ERU.EXE—Emergency Recovery Utility

The Emergency Recovery Utility (ERU.EXE) program is a powerful error recovery tool when used to make an audit trail of the key Windows files. We use ERU to create backup copies of all the key Windows files on the fixed disk in sequenced subdirectories to form such an audit trail. When copying files to a fixed disk directory, ERU backs up all the critical files. If a backup is made to a floppy diskette, the SYSTEM.DAT registry file is not backed up. When Windows startup problems occur, the SYSTEM.DAT file is the most

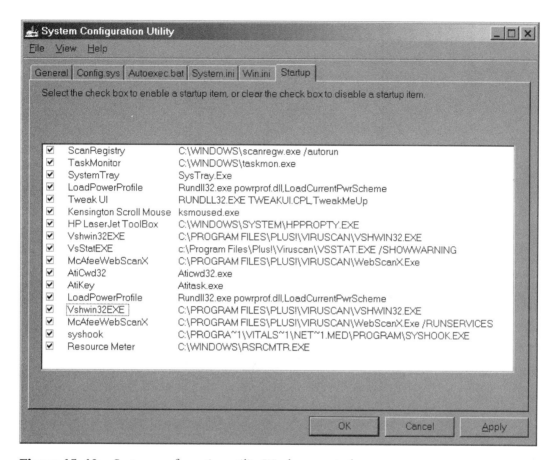

Figure 15–42 *System configuration utility Windows control*

common source. So floppy backups make ERU much less effective than the fixed disk backups. The key files copied are:

- AUTOEXEC.B_T —the AUTOEXEC.BAT file
- COMMAND.C_M —the COMMAND.COM
- CONFIG.S_S —the CONFIG.SYS file
- ERD.EXE —the DOS program that restores the files
- ERD.INF —the ERD.EXE control file
- MSDOS.S_S —the MSDOS.SYS file
- PROTOCOL.I_I —the PROTOCOL.INI file
- SYSTEM.D_T —the SYSTEM.DAT registry file
- SYSTEM.I_I —the SYSTEM.INI file
- USER.D_T —the USER.DAT registry file
- WIN.I_I —the WIN.INI file

The beauty of ERU is that it is a DOS program. When Windows doesn't start even in safe mode, booting into DOS can run the ERD.EXE program. One Windows error that prevents Windows from starting up is a Windows protection fault error. When this error occurs, Windows cannot start up. An entry in the SYSTEM.DAT file is the cause of the problem. In this case, ERD can then restore a good version of the key flies (including SYSTEM.DAT), permitting Windows to start up normally. By running ERU after each application program is installed, an audit trail of the PC's configuration is preserved. This permits returning to a previously good configuration when subsequent configurations will not start up.

Tweak User Interface—Tweak UI

The Tweak User Interface program is a control panel addition available from Microsoft. It was first offered on the Windows 95 Plus! pack CD. It can be found at the Microsoft web site by searching for Tweak UI. Tweak UI can adjust the Windows user interface by customizing the desktop, menu speed, window animation, the Internet Explorer, and more. Once installed, a Tweak UI icon appears in the control panel. Double-clicking enters the main Tweak UI menu box. See Figure 15–43.

Tweak UI provides options for automatically clearing data cached or temporarily stored on the fixed disk for the Internet Explorer and more. It also facilitates rebuilding the desktop icons while running Windows. Tweak UI is a general tool for customizing the Windows user interface.

MKCOMPAT.EXE—Make Compatible Utility

MKCOMPAT.EXE is a Windows utility targeted at resolving problems between Windows 95/98 and older Windows 3.1x application programs. It makes Windows 95/98 behave more like Windows 3.1x for those programs in an effort to prevent software errors. The MKCOMPAT is run and pointed to a specific program file on the command line. Depending upon the program referenced, MKCOMPAT returns an option selection box. See Figure 15–44.

This box provides options that make Windows behave like Windows 3.1x by not spooling print out to enhanced metafile formats, providing more stack space, misrepresenting the Windows version number and the printer device mode size, and providing Windows 3.1x style controls. These adjustments can resolve some application program compatibility problems.

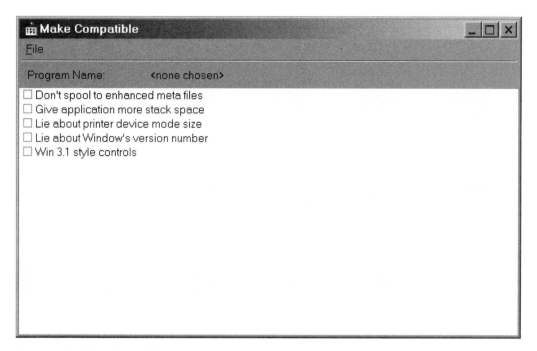

Figure 15–43 *Tweak UI box*

Study Break

Windows 98 MSINFO32.EXE

This study break exercise examines the PC using the Windows 98 MSINFO32.EXE diagnostic and configuration reporting tool.

1. Go to a Windows 98 PC, hit the start button and select run. Enter MSINFO32 and click OK.

2. Review the system information MSINFO32 reports. Are there any problem devices? This is under the components section.

3. Open the tools menu item. Run the DirectX diagnostic tool. What tests can you run? Sound and video tests probably run, but unless there is a joystick, those diagnostics won't run.

4. Run the system file checker. Does it find any out-of-date files? Are these files really corrupt? They may be, but they are not necessarily corrupted; but the verification information does not match the system file checker database.

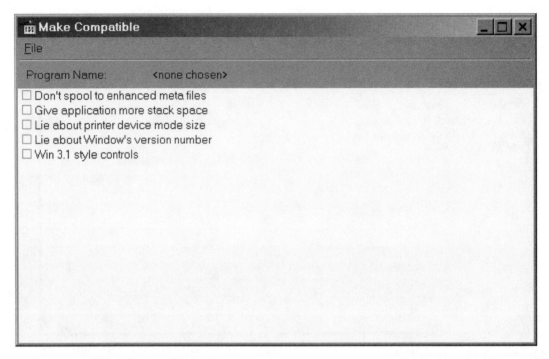

Figure 15–44 *MKCOMPAT menu box*

5. Run the automatic skip driver agent. Are any problems reported? Our PC here says that Windows had a problem getting statically allocated resource information ... hmmm ... work to do.

6. Run the system configuration utility. Are there any startup entries that are loaded twice? Disable the duplicates and restart.

7. Run the version conflict manager. Does it report problems?

The purpose of this exercise was to illustrate the Windows 98 diagnostic and configuration reporting tools.

A+ 15.4 Viruses and Virus Protection

Virus writers are prolific. What we mean here is that there are plenty of 20-to-30 year old males that slave away for hours on their PC to create a virus like the Michelangelo or the Melissa virus. Another common image is that virus writers are young pranksters to whom creating and propagating viruses is a hobby that helps them keep their coding skills fresh. Our perception here is that they are just common criminals like anyone that holds up a bank.

Some viruses have become widespread enough to gain a footnote in computer history. Also, it is likely to gain the Melissa virus writer a nice jail cell.

Viruses and the need to protect against them are inevitable realities in today's world of PCs.

McAfee reports the top ten viruses at their web site. This is a sort of advertising for their products and also helpful to the general PC-owning public. Their site is:

http://vil.mcafee.com/villib/alpha.asp

In the early to middle 1980s, computer viruses didn't exist. Universities were responsible for the first viruses created because they researched the concept of a virus and created the first crude virus programs in the process. In 1987, viruses showed up at universities around the world, including the three most commonly visible viruses Stoned, Cascade, and Friday the 13th.

Actually, we did get the FORM virus on one of our PCs from a nonbootable floppy diskette given to us by a company in Chicago. When we rebooted the PC in our hotel room at the Chicago Hilton, something did not seem quite right. So we immediately powered off the PC and then scanned for viruses. Luckily we caught the FORM virus before it could infect anything. The FORM virus was an early boot sector infecting virus that was the parent of some of the better know viruses identified below.

Viruses versus Trojan Horse/Worm programs

There are several types of programs, each exhibiting a different modus operandi for infecting user PCs. The most prolific programs labeled generally as virus programs are not really virus programs at all but Trojan horse/worm programs that are distributed via Microsoft email products. A true virus program gains entry to the PC by riding on software or disks in an unobtrusive fashion. In contrast, Trojan horse/worm programs are sent most typically as Microsoft Outlook email attachments transmitted across the Internet. The Trojan horse/worm program pretends to do something good while masking its real destructive intent and activity from the PC user. Once the PC is infected, viruses spread themselves to other PCs by copying their code to the boot sectors or program files of other diskettes, thus riding along on these disks to other PCs. Trojan horse/worm programs use the PCs Microsoft Outlook email to send themselves as email attachments on to other nonsuspecting PC users.

VIRUS PROGRAMS

The major characteristic of a virus program is that it is written to intentionally load and run in a PC without a user's knowledge. Viruses attach to files or boot sectors by copying their code into EXE, COM, and other files or into the boot sector. They then disguise this event to hide it from the PC user and virus scanning programs. A virus thus hides itself by making itself become part of other program files. Viruses replicate themselves by this copying process to continue spreading to other PCs. Some viruses do little but replicate. In contrast, other viruses can cause serious damage to a PC's disk files or can significantly slow PC and application program performance.

Viruses can:

- **Remain memory-resident**—A very common virus characteristic is that the virus loads like a "terminate-and-stay-resident" (TSR) program, remaining in memory where it can easily replicate by attaching itself to programs or copying itself into boot sectors.
- **Be nonmemory-resident**—Much less common are viruses that do not remain in memory after the virus host program is closed. They only infect files while the application program is running.

All viruses have a triggering mechanism. This is some action a virus performs that is set off by a date, a particular keystroke sequence, or a Windows or DOS function. Very often the action is a simple message displayed by the PC; sometimes the action is a serious destruction of the data and programs on the fixed disk drive.

Groups tracking virus infections classify viruses as "in the wild" when they cause an infection outside the laboratory. Viruses in the laboratory that have never roamed the real world are referred to as "in the zoo."

TROJAN HORSE/WORM PROGRAMS

In contrast to viruses, worm programs do not attach to other programs in the PC to disguise themselves. They may rename themselves and use other strategies to remain hidden, but they are separate standalone programs. They spread most often today as separate email attachments that are Microsoft Word DOC files or EXE files. Once opened or executed, they infect the PC and propagate themselves by automatically sending more email messages.

One recent EXE file is the HAPPY99.EXE program. This EXE file is not a virus but rather a worm, received through email and newsgroup postings. If the person receiving the program named HAPPY99.EXE in the email or article attachment executes it, it opens a window entitled "Happy New Year 1999!!" showing a fireworks display. This disguised the program that was copying itself as SKA.EXE and that was extracting an SKA.DLL into WIN-DOWS\SYSTEM directory. It modifies WSOCK32.DLL in WINDOWS\SYS-TEM directory and copies the original WSOCK32.DLL into WSOCK32.SKA. The WSOCK32.DLL modification allows the worm routine to run when an Internet connection is made. When the PC is online, the modified WINSOCK32.DLL code loads the worm's SKA.DLL. The SKA.DLL in turn creates a new email or a new article with uuencoded HAPPY99.EXE inserted into the email or article. The email was reportedly sent to the first fifty names in the PC user's email address file or the article was posted, thus replicating the worm program in its entirety.

Similar to worm programs, a Trojan horse program is a complete program that does not hide but rather appears to provide a desirable feature to the PC user. Unlike worm programs, Trojan horse programs do not generally attach and replicate themselves; they just act when some trigger event launches them. Newer variations of Trojan horse program do replicate and distribute themselves via Microsoft Outlook email.

A most recent Worm program that has become well known is ZIPPED_FILES.EXE or EXPLORE.EXE that uses MAPI commands and Microsoft Outlook/Microsoft Exchange to email itself as an attachment to this message:

Hi (A friend's or business associate's name)
I received your email and I shall send you a reply ASAP.
Till then, take a look at the attached zipped docs.
Bye or Sincerely (the friend's or business associate's name)

The attachment is zipped_files.exe which, when executed, copies EXPLORE.EXE to the Windows directory of the PC and modifies WIN.INI to run EXPLORE.EXE. Then EXPLORE.EXE mails itself to other PCs by replying to unread messages in the Microsoft Outlook/Microsoft Exchange Inbox of the infected PC. Additionally, this worm program searches networked drives mapped to that PC and networked machines for Windows installations. Once a mapped drive or accessible networked PC is found, this worm program copies EXPLORE.EXE to the remote PC's Windows directory, then modifies the WIN.INI file to run EXPLORE.EXE. EXPLORE.EXE is a true worm program. In addition to propagating itself, EXPLORE.EXE destroys specific files as designated by the file extension on fixed disk drives, on mapped network drives, and on accessible network machines. EXPLORE.EXE monitors the PC's email Inbox for new messages and uses them to send itself to those PCs from which the email was sent. As you can see, Trojan horse/worm programs can be very sophisticated and insidious.

BOOT-SECTOR-INFECTING VIRUSES

The Michelangelo virus was a boot-sector-infecting virus that became widespread in the early 1990s. Like many boot-sector-infecting viruses, Michelangelo becomes memory resident by loading from a diskette or fixed disk boot sector. It then infects the boot sectors of floppy diskettes accessed by the system or all the fixed disk drives. The Michelangelo virus resides at the top of system memory but below the 640K DOS boundary. CHKDSK could be used to detect the Michelangelo virus because it would report less than 655,360 bytes of total conventional memory in the PC. Similar boot-sector-infecting viruses could also be detected in this fashion.

What made the Michelangelo virus become widespread is that it remained dormant until March 6th each year (Michelangelo's birthday). On that date, the virus would destroy data on the PC's fixed disk and on diskettes. There was no indication of the virus until one hapless PC user's date hit March 6th and their disk drive data was destroyed.

Since boot-sector-infecting viruses are passed from PC to PC using diskettes, it is relatively easy to prevent infection and to clean the viruses from infected PCs.

PROGRAM-INFECTING VIRUSES

Program-infecting viruses originally infected .COM, and .EXE files. Today they may infect .OVL, .DRV, .SYS, or .BIN files or any program file in the PC used by DOS or Windows. They replicate by attaching themselves to other program files. This means that they can travel as program attachments to email. Some program-infecting viruses can be:

- **Stealth viruses**—These viruses hide from detection and cleaning by redirecting disk reads to avoid detection or by altering disk directory data to hide the host program size increase caused by the bytes added by the virus.
- **Encrypting viruses**—These viruses hide by transforming their code into encrypted symbols. These viruses must at some point decode to execute and spread. At that time, the encrypting virus can be detected.
- **Polymorphic viruses**—These viruses mutate by changing code segments to look different from one infection to another. This is the most challenging virus to detect.

Depending on the sophistication of the virus-disguising technique, they may be very difficult to detect. All viruses must decode to continue infecting other files and PCs.

MACRO VIRUSES

Macro viruses are similar to Trojan horse/worm programs that use the macro commands (which are like any other programming language) implemented in spreadsheet or desktop publishing software to infect and distribute viruses to new systems. The Melissa virus is a macro virus that uses Visual BASIC programming because Visual BASIC is supported by most Microsoft products. Melissa was initially distributed as an attachment to an email message that was posted to a newsgroup server. The original message contained a listing of sex sites. When the attachment was opened, the Melissa macro virus executed and disabled the Microsoft macro virus warning. It then sent itself as an email message to addresses listed in the PC's Microsoft Outlook email list. The damage done here was not to individual PCs but rather to corporate email servers, which became overloaded with heavy email volumes generated by the spreading virus.

Visual BASIC, because of its widespread implementation in Microsoft products, is used as one of the programming languages for macro viruses. Microsoft Word files have macros attached that can carry such viruses. However, any popular program (for instance, a Microsoft program) that implements macros can be used to distribute a virus with its macro commands.

Combination macro, boot sector, and program-infecting viruses may combine all distribution mechanisms to widely distribute the next alarming virus.

Sources of Viruses

The most likely means of virus distribution today is the Internet. The viruses can be posted as email or document attachments that when opened infect the PC. The key here is that the document must be opened so that the macro virus (the infecting program) infects the PC. When the file is a program attachment (.EXE file,.COM file, etc.), it must be run to infect the PC. Such virus infections can be received as email or can be downloaded from newsgroup or other software distribution sites.

Several simple precautions can prevent Internet-distributed viruses from infecting your PC and your network. These precautions are:

1. Do not open email attachments unless you know who sent them and you expect them to be a very specific file.

2. Do not download programs from newsgroups. Newsgroup postings were how Melissa and other email viruses were first distributed.

3. Use a more proprietary email program. While Microsoft Outlook and Exchange Server are dynamite products, they are currently the primary means for distributing viruses. Maybe use MS Outlook and Exchange server for internal email and something else for external email.

4. Check McAfee or Symantec virus-reporting sites daily for information on new harmful viruses.

5. Run virus scanning software that checks Internet mail as well as program files for known viruses. Keep your virus data files current (they are updated monthly).

These are some precautions for preventing email infection but other precautions must be observed for diskette-borne viruses. Most people think that the common source of viruses is disks shared by PC users. While viruses are spread in this fashion, most PC users today are cognizant enough to employ virus-scanning software on their PC that make virus transmission from user to user quite uncommon. PC service personnel can easily distribute a virus from user to user because the diagnostic software diskettes they use are in many different PCs. Service personnel must take special precautions to ensure that they do not distribute viruses inadvertently while servicing their users. The simplest precaution of setting diagnostic disks to read only status is quite effective in preventing virus distribution.

Detecting Viruses

There are many ways to spot virus activity before the virus damages a PC's data and program files. Some common virus symptoms are:

- Programs suddenly requiring more time to launch
- Programs failing to run
- Changing program sizes
- File date or time stamps changing or not matching that of other files
- Fixed disks continually running out of free space
- Continual Windows 32-bit illegal operation errors
- Fixed disk drive activity light flashing continually when nothing is being done
- Bad sectors appearing on floppy diskettes
- Booting from drive A preventing access to the fixed disk drive
- Many files or strange files appearing on the PCs fixed disk drive
- Weird sounds and noises coming from the PC and keyboard
- The PC desktop behaving strangely with letters or icons moving

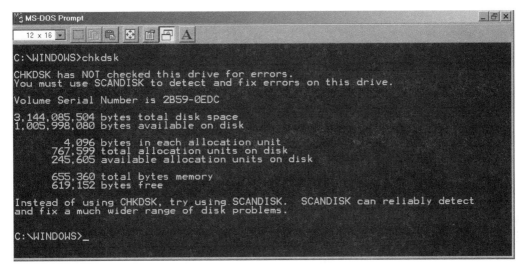

Figure 15–45 *CHKDSK report*

• The PC not retaining CMOS settings even when the battery is fresh

Employing memory-resident virus scanning and detection software like McAfee or Symantec is the best means of detecting and preventing the spread of viruses.

CHKDSK QUICK CHECK

Memory-resident viruses often reduce the conventional memory size as reported by CHKDSK. Thus CHKDSK can provide a quick check for virus infection every time it is run. On several occasions in our PC troubleshooting seminars viruses have been detected using CHKDSK. When CHKDSK is run, it reports the total amount of conventional memory. This total should be 655,360 bytes as shown in Figure 15–45.

When the total bytes free figure is less than 655,360 a memory-resident virus may be the cause. It is possible for some SCSI controllers to cause CHKDSK to report less conventional memory without a virus infection being present.

VIRUS SCANNING PROGRAMS

The best defense is to employ a memory-resident virus scanning and detection program. There are many on the market. It is good to have both DOS and Windows virus-scanning software. Booting into DOS, running SCAN-

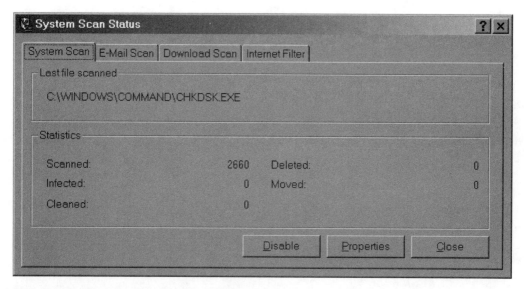

Figure 15–46 *McAfee V-shield control panel*

DISK, and then a virus-scanning program should be the first procedures performed when troubleshooting all PCs. Both McAfee and Symantec virus-scanning programs create DOS bootable disks that check for virus infection. FPROT is another DOS-based virus-scanning program. All these programs can be downloaded from sites on the Internet or from America Online (AOL).

Clean systems should have a Windows virus scanning and detection program installed. Windows 98 comes with virus scanning software from McAfee with several months of virus signature updates. Virus signature updates are downloaded monthly from the McAfee web site. They keep the virus scanning software up to date with the binary patterns (virus signatures) that identify the presence of viruses in any file. See Figure 15–46.

The memory resident V-shield program searches each program as it executes on the PC for viruses, scans email for macro viruses, scans files downloaded into the PC for viruses and filters Internet JAVA and ActiveX applications for virus infections. Downloaded files can be of particular concern because they may be compressed programs containing viruses or documents containing macro viruses. Because they are compressed, the virus scanning software does not see the virus signature unless the file is decompressed and scanned.

Virus Removal Procedure

The first thing in dealing with a virus is to clean the PC of viruses. To clear the viruses or determine that there are none in a PC:

1. First boot from a virus-free DOS diskette that has the virus-cleaning software on it. Be sure the diskette is set to write-protected and that the CMOS of the PC points to booting from the floppy diskette in drive A. Viruses can set the CMOS to boot from C and cause the PC to become infected again, so be sure that the CMOS setup boots the PC from drive A.
2. Booting must be performed from a powered off or cold boot start. The Ctrl-Alt-Del warm boot does not clear viruses from memory and they merely infect the boot diskette unless the boot diskette is set to a write-protect state.
3. As for the software, get the latest Symantec, FPROT, AVP, or McAfee antivirus software that runs from a DOS boot diskette. This should be available from the web or from a local store.
4. Once the PC is booted, run the virus scanning and removal software to clean the virus infection from the PC.

A bootable diskette cannot be created using an infected PC. A boot diskette must be created on a virus-free PC. Get a clean boot diskette from somewhere. Computer retail stores often perform virus removal. PCs can be taken there to have viruses removed.

FPROT and other virus-removing software can be downloaded from Internet web sites or from AOL. In AOL, use the keyword virus, then go to the software libraries to find virus removal software.

If there is a clean boot diskette and the virus is a boot-sector-infecting virus, it may be removed by using FDISK. To remove boot sector viruses, fix the master boot record by using a clean DOS bootable diskette and running FDISK /MBR. It is far more effective to use the latest virus scanning and removal software.

Study Break

Virus Scanning

This study break exercise scans a PC for viruses.

1. Go to a Windows PC and install any popular virus scanning software. Get the trial version off the web sites or from AOL.

2. Create the DOS bootable diskette with the virus scanning software installed on it.

3. Make this diskette read-only by opening the hole in the upper left corner of the diskette.

4. Using this diskette, scan several office PCs by powering them off, then booting using the virus scanning diskette. Find any viruses?

The purpose of this exercise was to illustrate how to check for viruses using virus scanning software installed on a diskette.

■ Summary

This chapter has examined common DOS and Windows software error messages and their cause. Steps to resolve the errors causing the common error messages were covered. Furthermore, other frequent Windows software problems were identified. Resolution of those software problems was presented. DOS and Windows diagnostic programs, problem prevention programs, and troubleshooting utilities were identified. Effective use of these programs was presented. The chapter concluded with a discussion of viruses, virus protection, and virus removal.

▲ CHAPTER REVIEW QUESTIONS

1. *GPF stands for?*
   A. general program fault
   B. a type of Windows software error
   C. general processing format
   D. gross program fault
   Answer: B. a type of Windows software error

2. *When a disk drive activity light suddenly is on continuously, what could cause the problem?*
   A. The diskette is upside down.
   B. The PC has halted.
   C. The PC is infected with a program-infecting virus.
   D. An illegal operation error has occurred.
   Answer: C. The PC is infected with a program-infecting virus

3. *To fix a frozen PC you?*

    A. immediately power off the PC

    B. run CHKDSK

    C. exit Windows to the DOS prompt

    D. hit Crtl-Alt-Del to start the task manager and use it to stop the non-responding application

Answer: D. hit Crtl-Alt-Del to start the task manager and use it to stop the nonresponding application

4. *What maximum conventional memory should CHKDSK report?*

    A. 655,360 bytes

    B. 640K

    C. 1,024K

    D. 1,048,576 bytes

    Answer: A. 655,360 bytes

5. *What PC diagnostic program repairs fixed disk problems?*

    A. MSD

    B. CHKDSK /R

    C. SCANDISK

    D. MSINFO32

    Answer: C. SCANDISK

6. *Fixed disk hardware problems are identified using?*

    A. MSD

    B. the registry scanner

    C. FDISK

    D. CHKDSK

    Answer: C. FDISK

7. *An illegal operation error is an invalid page fault.*

    A. TRUE

    B. FALSE

    Answer: A. TRUE

8. *Viruses infect disk boot records,.COM programs, or.DOC files.*

    A. TRUE

    B. FALSE

    Answer: A. TRUE

9. *Windows startup problems dump Windows into* _____.

    A. virus scanning mode

    B. normal diagnostic mode

    C. safe mode

    D. none of the above

    Answer: C. safe mode

10. *A "permanent swap file is corrupt" message means?*

    A. Windows 98 has crashed

    B. the registry is corrupted

    C. Windows 3.1x cannot find the permanent swap file it expects

    D. none of the above

    Answer: C. Windows 3.1x cannot find the permanent swap file it expects

11. *A missing operating system error is corrected by* _____.

    A. running FDISK

    B. reinstalling the application program

    C. performing the SYS C: command from a bootable floppy

    D. all of the above

    Answer: C. performing the SYS C: command from a bootable

12. *Viruses are always memory resident programs.*

    A. TRUE

    B. FALSE

    Answer: B. FALSE

13. *Virus programs can*

    A. destroy data

    B. replicate themselves

    C. hide as part of other programs

    D. be attached to email

    E. all of the above

    F. none of the above

    Answer: E. all of the above

14. *Stealth viruses*

    A. sometimes redirect disk drive writes to hide

    B. misreport directory information to hide

    C. are not memory-resident

D. are boot-sector-infecting viruses

Answer: B. misreport directory information to hide

15. *SCANDISK does not*

A. fix disk FAT errors

B. scan the disk surface to detect hardware faults

C. help detect viruses

D. correct errors in the disk directory structure

Answer: C. help detect viruses

16. *ERU is*

A. the Emergency Recycle Utility

B. a program that backs up the fixed disk drive

C. the Emergency Reuse Utility

D. a program that backs up key Windows files including the registry

E. none of the above

Answer: D. a program that backs up key Windows files including the registry

Windows Networking

▲ Chapter Syllabus

A+ 16.1 LAN Networking Functions

A+ 16.2 LAN Types and Cards

A+ 16.3 Configuring for Internet Access

This chapter examines networking with DOS and Windows. It presents an overview of LAN and Internet networking using Windows software. Networking is a key PC application. PCs purchased today are used to connect to the Internet. It is the most frequently mentioned reason for purchasing a PC. LANs are an essential part of any business environment. They facilitate the sharing of information, collaboration on work, and email, making work activities more productive than they ever were in the past. Everyone handles the same amount of paper that they did five and ten years ago. However, the amount of information assimilated, analyzed, and disseminated by any worker is 10–100–1,000 times what it was years ago. Networking facilitated this ten-to-one-hundred-fold increase in information handling.

PC networking with Windows is focused in local area networks (LANs) and the Internet. LANs provide a high-speed mechanism for sharing data and multimedia information. The Internet provides access to current information on any topic and a means to publish information on your special interests for anyone to find. Let's examine LAN and Internet networking using Windows software.

A+ 16.1   LAN Networking Functions

Windows provides all needed driver programs and network software to build a LAN. Two types of LANs are supported with the Windows software: peer-to-peer and client-server. Most LANs use both peer-to-peer software and client-server software. Peer-to-peer are simple LANs permitting all PCs to share their disk drives and printers with other networked computers. Security in peer-to-peer LANs is not foolproof. Client-server LANs have central servers providing better overall security and network management capabilities. Both types of LANs provide disk and print sharing capabilities. This means that they permit access to their attached printers and their disk drives from other PCs attached to the LAN. Peer-to-peer LANs are administered at each PC sharing resources on the LAN. Client-server LANs are administered centrally at special primary domain controller (PDC) servers.

Disk Sharing

One of the reasons for having a LAN is that it allows a PC to share disk resources. Disk sharing occurs when either a disk drive on a PC is made available for use by other users, or in a client-server LAN, the server has a shared disk resource for all authorized users.

Disk sharing does not mean that the entire disk is available for use; in fact, in most instances a very specific area of the disk is shared. This is to help organize the people using a shared resource and provide some level of security. Having access to a disk or a server disk does leave a PC open to an attack from unscrupulous employees.

Depending on the type of LAN (peer-to-peer or client-server), there are different access controls. Peer-to-peer can only make a disk or directory read only, full access, and full access password protected. With a client-server LAN, access at the user or group level can be set. This fine-tunes access by providing more access to those who need it and less to those who do not.

With NT, there are other types of sharing beyond just the common storage of a fixed disk. NT also can combine free space on several disks into what appears to be a single logical unit called a *volume set*. Additionally, NT creates logical units that are combinations of several disks, striping the data evenly across each. This is called a *stripe set* or *RAID set*. Each of these units may then be shared out to the network users or populace.

File Sharing

File sharing is a lot like disk sharing, except it is focused on a file. File sharing in definition is very broad. For example, if access to a directory is allowed on a PC in a peer-to-peer network, users on the network are allowed to access those files. The access to the files may be read-only, but they do have access and thus it is considered file sharing. If using a client-server network, then in most cases access permissions can be set at the file level. Access permissions can be set individually for each file in the shared directory. File sharing is tricky to master. With a small network (five to ten users), file sharing and setting permissions is not too difficult. In these types of networks, users tend to be liberal with permissions because they can yell down the hall to see if someone is currently using a shared file. However, in a large network environment, users from all over a facility or the world may be using the shared file, and yelling down the hall does not accomplish much in this case except annoying your neighbors. So in larger networks, complex and carefully planned file sharing is necessary.

Print Sharing

Print sharing is the sharing of a print resource such as a printer or a document center device across the network. This print resource can be attached to any network PC, to a server on a network, or as a node on the network if it has its own NIC and IP address. The advantages are obvious—a good quality printer can be purchased and shared with everyone on the network instead of buying a printer for each person.

Sharing a printer is easy, but there can be some problems. The most common pitfall is that the correct software drivers are required on the PC in order to print to a printer across the network. This means that in most cases the driver software must be installed as if a new printer is being installed. If an NT server is used for print sharing, then that server can load the drivers that the client PC needs for printing. What happens in this case is that when a PC goes to print, that PC downloads the driver from the NT print server and installs it temporarily on the client PC to perform the print job.

Windows 95/98 and NT also allow setting printers out on a network as nodes. There are special jet direct drivers for HP printers that can be loaded on a Windows 95 PC that allow administration and control of printers at though they were directly attached to a client PC.

Print sharing also can have an effect on the machine it is installed on. In order to handle the multiple requests made on the printer, the machine that the printer is attached to has to allow some of its resources to be used in support of printing and have adequate disk space to hold a print queue. This can slow down the machine the printer is attached to when there are heavy printing loads.

Study Break

Identifying Peer-to-Peer and Client-Server LANs

This study break exercise determines what type of LAN you have using Windows 95/98.

1. Use a Windows 98 PC attached to a LAN. Open the network neighborhood desktop icon. Windows should search for network PCs. It should list some PCs and the entire network icon for a peer-to-peer network.

2. Double-click on entire network. This should open a window with some network names. These names are for workgroups of PCs or domains.

3. Double-click on the icons you can see. If the list of computers in the first screen pops up, it is the workgroup to which your PC belongs. The PC names displayed are PCs belonging to a peer-to-peer workgroup.

4. If a "domain is not accessible" error message says domain resources are unavailable, try the icon at least three more times. Sometimes it takes a while before Windows can find the information for the domain.

5. Once the domain information is found, Windows will display a list of the domain servers. These are PCs acting as servers in a client-server network.

6. Double-click on each PC identified to see what disk drives are shared and accessible.

7. Close all windows and right-click on the network neighborhood icon, then select the access control tab. What type of access control is set? Share level access control is used for peer-to-peer networks while user level access control can be used for both client-server and peer-to-peer networks. Click on the cancel button.

This exercise illustrated how to determine the network configuration of a Windows 95/98 PC. It showed some of the setup options for both peer-to-peer and client-server networks.

LAN Types and Cards

Windows supports many different local area network types. In Chapter 8, two network types were identified, Ethernet and token ring. These are the most common LAN boards used, but there are other network types that are supported as well.

By providing Windows with the ability to support multiple LAN types, Microsoft hopes to gain an edge in the LAN market. Windows 95/98 is positioned to become the universal client, able to be used as a workstation operating system on any type of network. NT server does the same thing in an attempt to become the universal server.

Part and parcel of this are the software protocols that are used and how the systems interact with others on the network. This section focuses on the NICs (network interface cards) and examines the different types of cards that are supported. Each card's capabilities are also described.

Ethernet

Ethernet protocol and technology networks are the most common and widely installed networks. Created in the 1960s, Ethernet has used basically the same protocol since its inception. Ethernet protocols have been used in both *broadband* (analog transmission) and *baseband* (digital transmission) communications media. LAN transmission speeds for Ethernet-protocol-based LANs have varied as well, from 1 MBPS to 1 GBPS. This makes it very useful for many organizations.

True Ethernet is a standardized technology. The Institute for Electrical and Electronic Engineers (IEEE) 802 committee sets standards for how Ethernet products operate. These standards include transmission speed specifications. For example, normal Ethernet communicates up to 10 MBPS, Fast Ethernet communicates at speeds of 100 MBPS, and Gigabit Ethernet operates at speeds of 1 GBPS.

The standard also sets what data communications protocol the Ethernet PC board or network interface card (NIC) uses. Ethernet cards employ CSMA/CD or *Carrier Sense Multiple Access with Collision Detection* protocol to transfer data between one card and another across the LAN.

On Ethernet, any device can try to send data at any time. Each device, before it transmits, senses whether the line is idle and therefore available to be used. If the line is idle, the device begins to transmit its first frame. This works great except it is possible to have two devices sense idle on the line and transmit at the same time. If another device has tried to send at the same time, a collision occurs and the frames are discarded. To remove the potential for a second collision, each device then waits a random amount of time and retries until successful in getting its transmission sent.

This protocol is used only with Ethernet cards. That means that an Ethernet board cannot talk to any machines on a token ring network unless a protocol translation device is employed, since the token ring network uses a different protocol.

In order for the Ethernet card to access the network, the operating system of the machine must have the appropriate driver software installed. Windows 98/98 comes with almost all the driver support needed for any Ethernet card. If the correct drivers are not available before installing any NIC, go to the manufacturer's web site and download the driver. These drivers are usually in a zipped file containing the driver and an installation INF file to tell Windows plug-and-play software components how to configure the operating system and operating system registry settings during the install.

Windows 95 and 98 support approximately 76 different manufacturers' NICs. Each of these manufacturers has an average of about four different models of Ethernet cards. In other words, Windows 95/98 supports a huge number of Ethernet cards, easily more than would be practical to list here. A complete list of the supported cards can be found on Microsoft's web site.

Some more notable cards supported would be 3Com cards. These are very popular and in some cases are hardware designed into PC motherboards. Another popular board is the NE2000 compatible board. This is found under the Novell/Anthem manufacturer listing when adding a NIC. This driver is significant in that it is a very universal driver, able to work on many Ethernet cards as an alternative driver to the one that comes specifically with the NIC. See Figure 16–1.

Figure 16–1 *Windows Ethernet NIC support*

Token Ring

Token ring networks are the second most popular networks in use today. The design and implementation is newer than Ethernet, and the data communications protocol is more sophisticated than Ethernet. Despite these characteristics, sales and usage is less than Ethernet due to the cost of equipment required.

Like Ethernet, the IEEE standardizes token ring technology. The 802.5 standard is the token ring standard. The largest developer and implementer of token ring networks is IBM with their IBM Token Ring network. Other technologies use token-passing protocols, although differently. FDDI (Fiber Distributed Data Interface) is an example of a LAN technology using token-passing ring protocols similar in some ways to, but also different from, IBM token ring products. The IBM Token Ring uses a single ring and ring-repairing hubs, while FDDI employs dual counter rotating rings to provide similar ring self-healing capabilities.

Like today's Ethernet networks, token ring networks use baseband transmission. Two PCs cannot transmit at the same time. On a token ring network, all workstations are connected in a true ring (a star-wired topology) and a token-passing scheme similar to polling each terminal is used to prevent collision between two workstations that want to send messages at the same time. In order to ensure no conflicts, empty information frames are continuously circulated on the ring. When a node wishes to transmit, it inserts a token in an empty frame (this is simply a change of a single bit in the frame from a 0 to a 1) and then puts the rest of information including a destination identifier in the frame. Each successive node then views the frame. If the node recognizes that it is the destination for the message, it copies the message from the frame and changes the acknowledgement bits at the end of the frame to 1s. When the frame gets back to the sender, it changes the token to 0, meaning the frame is available to be used by another PC on the ring. The 1s in the acknowledgement bits at the end of the frame designate the message as copied and received. The node removes the message and the acknowledgement bits from the frame. The frame continues to circulate, ready to be taken by a node when it has a message to send.

Although today's token ring networks run at lower speeds than do new Ethernet networks, many token ring drivers are supported by Windows 95/98. See Figure 16–2.

Figure 16–2 *Windows token ring NIC support*

ATM

ATM (Asynchronous Transfer Mode) is a new communications network technology for wide area and local area networks that is being used predominantly by large organizations to combine voice, data, and video communication on the same communications network. In order to do this, high data rates are needed (100 MBPS or greater) as well as the ability to rapidly switch traffic across virtual channels. Data, in and of itself, does not require huge bandwidth because it arrives in bursts. Voice and video, on the other hand, are very sensitive to timing and also hog a constant bandwidth. For that reason, to combine voice, video and data traffic, a technology that can dynamically handle all these types of traffic flows is needed. ATM is a technology that promises to solve such networking problems.

ATM accomplishes the task of transmitting multiple types of transmissions by implementing a dedicated-connection switching technology to organize digital data into 53-byte cells or packets and transmitting them over a medium using digital signal technology. Each cell is processed asynchronously relative to other related cells and is queued before being multiplexed over the line.

This technology is mostly thought of as a wide area technology; however, more and more it is being used as both a local and wide area technology. The high-speed switching makes it ideal in very large/high data throughput LANs. Windows 98 does come with support for Adaptec and other ATM cards. Previous Windows versions would require the driver to be provided by the manufacturer of the card. See Figure 16–3.

Figure 16–3 *Windows ATM NIC support*

ARCnet

ARCnet is an older network type. It enjoyed popularity at one time because of its low cost. Although cheaper in its time than Ethernet and token ring, ARCnet never gathered enough of a following to claim any dominance in the LAN market place.

ARCnet is a local area network technology from the Datapoint Corporation, the originator of the local area network. ARCnet uses a token-bus scheme for managing line sharing among the various devices connected on the LAN. The server continuously circulates empty message frames on a bus (the wire that attaches to every device). When a device wants to send a message, it inserts a token into an empty frame. Then it also inserts a message. When the destination device reads the message, it resets the token for reuse by the other devices. The technology is very effective in high traffic since all devices are afforded the same opportunity to use the shared network.

ARCnet can use coaxial or fiber optic cable with lengths up to 2,000 feet per segment and a total network span of 20,000 feet. ARCnet's bandwidth or information flow capacity is from 2.5 MBPS to 20 MBPS. See Figure 16–4.

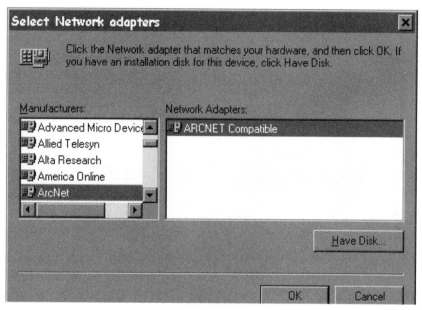

Figure 16–4 *Windows ARCnet NIC support*

NIC Cards

This exercise examines the LAN NIC cards installed in a Windows 95/98 PC. It also illustrates the types of NIC cards that Windows 98 supports.

1. Use a Windows 98 PC attached to a LAN. Right-click on the network neighborhood icon and select properties. Windows 95/98 should display a list of the client software, networking adapters (including LAN NICs), protocols (protocol stacks), and services installed. What type of NIC card is installed in this PC?

2. Double-click on the LAN NIC card. Does it use enhanced mode 32-bit drivers? Generally the NIC cards should use 32-bit drivers.

3. Click on bindings. What protocols is the NIC card bound to? Click on cancel to return to the network panel.

4. Click on add. Select adapter and click add again. After Windows builds a driver information base, scroll through the list of drivers. In Windows 98, which manufacturers offer ATM drivers? There are at least Adaptec, Digital, Efficient Networks, and Olicom. Which type of net-

work has the most support? Ethernet should. Which has the least? Our guess is ARCNet. The goal of this exercise was to illustrate which NIC cards are widely used in PC networks.

A+   16.3   Configuring for Internet Access

One of the most important aspects of networking PCs today is enabling them to connect to the Internet. Since Windows 3.11, TCP/IP has become a part of the Windows interface. This transport protocol and its configuration are critical for connecting to the Internet.

There are two main ways to connect to the Internet using Windows. One of the ways to do this is by connecting through an ISP (Internet Service Provider), using a dial-up connection via modem. Each ISP provides the TCP/IP setup and configuration parameters needed for Windows.

The other way is to connect from an internal local area network to the Internet. This involves careful configuration of the TCP/IP protocol bound to your PC's NIC card. The LAN administrator usually provides these settings for the specific PC. Since dial-up is more frequently used to connect to the Internet, let's examine it first.

Dial-Up Configuration

Dial-up networking is the process of using a modem to connect to and participate on a network. It is most commonly used today as a way to connect to the Internet, but it can also be used as a way to connect remotely to an office network.

Dial-up networking is an installable component under Windows 95/98. Most machines have Windows dial-up networking software components installed when they arrive from the manufacturer. If by some chance a PC does not, then Windows dial-up networking components can easily be installed from the add/remove programs feature in the control panel. See Figure 16–5.

Figure 16–5 *Windows dial-up networking software support*

Once the software components are added, you can begin configuring a dial-up networking connection. Multiple connections can be set up if there are several different connection sites used. To start the process go to the start menu button on the task bar, follow the menus from program files to accessories and then to communications, where dial-up networking is now visible. Selecting it displays the screen shown in Figure 16–6.

Figure 16–6   *Dial-up networking box*

This window contains all the current dial-up networking configurations as well as the Make New Connection wizard. If no connections have been set up then start by double-clicking on the wizard to create a new connection.

Once the wizard is activated, setup is very easy. It asks you to name the connection—for instance, "My ISP." Doing that identifies each connection uniquely when there is more than one. On the same screen it asks for the device that is used to make the connection. Usually, since most machines contain a single modem, this is the only device. Last, it asks for the number to dial. Once the phone number is provided, the dial-up networking phone configuration is complete. A complete networking configuration requires a phone configuration and a network configuration.

To configure the networking side of a new connection, find it in the dial-up networking screen and click the right mouse button while pointing at it. A small pop-up menu appears. Choose properties and the box in Figure 16–7 appears.

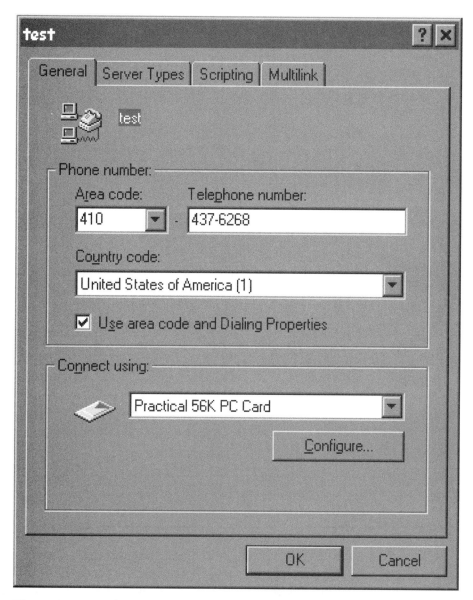

Figure 16–7 *Dial-up network configuration box*

This box configures all the network parameters that are required for a dial-up connection. Several tabs in this box are configured. In most cases, changes to the server type is all that is required.

- **General**—The first tab, general, is used to configure the phone number as well as the modem. Modem settings may include things like memory buffering size, use of terminal screens for logging in, and adding any additional modem strings.

- **Server type**—Server type is used to configure the type of server connection used. Additionally, with the connection different types of logon encryption or security features can be set. A transport protocol is also chosen. If choosing TCP/IP, then there are additional settings to configure with parameters provided by the ISP. Generally with TCP/IP settings, a fixed IP address is not set and a server-assigned IP address is used. Often the ISP has a specific name server. The name server or Domain Name Server (DNS) provides the PC information that supports navigating from Internet site to Internet site.
- **Scripting**—Scripting is used to set any type of automated process or batch process off during logon. This can be used for logon processes that require the user to input information.
- **Multilink**—Multilinking is a function whereby the PC can link more than one phone line and modem together in a communication. This requires that the site to which the PC is connecting to can provide multilink connections.

In almost all cases, the items under the tabs other than server types are accepted as defaults. Under the server tab there are a number of important choices to make. The first thing to choose is the connection type of the server this machine dials into. There are four choices, NRN (NetWare Connect), PPP (Point to Point Protocol), SLIP (Serial Line Interface Protocol, used with UNIX servers), and Windows for Workgroups. The PPP connection type is the most often used; it can use all the different transport protocols (TCP/IP, IPX/SPX, NetBEUI).

Both IPX/SPX and NetBEUI require no special setup with dial-up networking. TCP/IP however, requires some configuration information. This information is obtained from the dial-up ISP. There are a few basic things needed for TCP/IP to work properly. These are:

- First, knowing whether or not the logon server assigns an IP address to the PC or if there is a preassigned address that must be input to the PC as a fixed IP address. Most dial-up providers use server-assigned IP addressing. If this is the case, the configuration job is easy. When configuring dial-up networking for a specific location, the properties—server types—TCP/IP settings may be left at the default settings when dial-up providers assign IP addresses. If not, then an IP address must be provided by the ISP and the "specify IP address" must be set with the exact IP address assigned by the dial-up service provider.

- Second is the name server address assignment. Like the IP address, the dial-up server can assign the name server address. If not, an address for a name server given by the dial-up ISP must be entered into Windows. For dial-up networking to configure a name server address, the properties—server types—TCP/IP settings are used. Similar to the IP address assignments, the name server address settings may be left at the default setting "server assigned name server address" when the dial-up provider's server assigns the name server addresses. Otherwise, the exact name server IP address must be specified using the "specify name server address selection." Entering the information requires clicking on the radio button and then entering the 4-number (for example, 208.80.68.10) IP address. The addresses use the numbers between 0 and 255 for each separate address number. Specifying these addresses correctly is crucial for being able to go out onto the Internet.

For example, if a PC does not have a domain name server (DNS) assigned, then domain lookup errors are displayed when the web browser is used and you may not be able to browse the web at all. If the dial-up service is connected into an office network, not having a Windows Internet Name Service (WINS) server defined prevents finding any of the other servers or peer-to-peer networked PCs on the LAN. See Figure 16–8. Other TCP/IP networking configuration settings are also discussed in Chapter 8 in the study break exercise "Viewing Windows 98 Network Configuration."

Figure 16–8 *Dial-up TCP/IP configuration*

TCP/IP

If the connection to a network is not dial-up, the TCP/IP settings must be configured for the PC's NIC card. When a transport protocol is loaded on a PC, the protocol is bound (linked) automatically to all of the network adapters that are currently installed. Each separate adapter then has to be configured separately for TCP/IP to work properly. Each adapter must have unique TCP/IP settings that identify it on the TCP/IP network. Conflicting IP addresses cause conflicting devices to remove themselves from the LAN. See Figure 16–9.

Figure 16–9 *TCP/IP NIC configuration*

If TCP/IP is not loaded on a Windows 95/98 PC, then this protocol must be added to the PC's current setup. To add it, simply open the Windows

95/98 network control panel item from within the control panel. When the network controls appear, select the add button, select protocols, and the TCP/IP protocol found under the Microsoft list of protocols. This adds and binds TCP/IP to all the adapters the Windows 95/98 PC uses for networking.

To configure the TCP/IP settings for a specific adapter, simply select the TCP/IP binding from the list for that adapter and select the properties button. This brings up a TCP/IP properties box as shown in Figure 16–10.

Figure 16–10 *TCP/IP properties box*

There are several tabs in this configuration window. Only a few are really necessary, so do not become overwhelmed. Most selections remain as default selections. The information on your network needed to complete the PC's network configuration usually is assigned by the LAN administrator. Before we look at the primary items, let's look at what each tab is used to set:

- **IP Address**—This is where a specific IP address is assigned to a PC. LAN administrators generally provide specific IP address assignments. If a specific IP address is not assigned, the network provides the PC an IP address from a DHCP logon server, using the Dynamic Host Configuration Protocol (DHCP). The DHCP server is set up and managed by the network administrators. If the PC is on a Windows NT network, then a Windows NT server is very likely running DHCP. If the LAN has a Windows NT server using DHCP, then IP address configuration is easy. The DHCP server automatically sets up all the required fields in this configuration screen.
- **WINS Configuration**—The WINS (Windows Internet Naming Service) is a server on a LAN that dynamically translates NETBIOS names into TCP/IP addresses. NETBIOS names identify the shared resources of the network. As an example, we have a drive we share called DRC. If a PC looks at a TCP/IP address for a share named DRC, it has a hard time finding it unless another machine tells it where to look. That is where WINS comes in. If a Windows NT server is using DHCP, then this can be automatically assigned, but if not, the TCP/IP address of the WINS server must be provided and set as a parameter in the Windows TCP/IP configuration.
- **Gateway**—The gateway or default gateway is the router that allows communications outside a local area network. This can be a router internally to other segments of the network, or a router out to the Internet. Without a router, a PC is restricted to communicating on a single logical network segment and not on a internetwork of logical network segments.
- **DNS Configuration**—DNS is a service that resolves domain names like dialanerd.com to TCP/IP address. This, like the WINS server, can be assigned through the DHCP server. If a DNS server is not assigned, then the IP address of a DNS service must be entered in Windows. This is crucial for using an office intranet or the Internet. Without a DNS server, an Internet name like dialanerd.com is meaningless.

- **Bindings**—Bindings show the services and client types that the protocol is using. This should be bound to all client types and services automatically.
- **Advanced**—Advanced settings permit viewing any advanced setting selected. Additionally, TCP/IP can be selected to be the default protocol for this adapter. This makes TCP/IP the first protocol bound to the adapter, which can result in a minor increase in network performance for that specific PC.
- **NetBIOS**—Allows NetBIOS to piggyback itself across the TCP/IP protocol. This makes NetBIOS calls across TCP/IP possible.

Of all these parameter settings, the IP address and the default gateway settings are the most important. However, do not neglect to find out whether or not a DNS or a WINS server address is needed and available. Generally, in any large organization the network system administrator has the detailed information needed. When signing up with an ISP, they provide the needed DNS and IP address setup information.

On our network we prefer to use DHCP to set this up for the PC clients. We find it easier to input the needed information once into the DHCP server and have it set this up for each machine as they log on. The DHCP server must be set up by the network administrator before it can be used to automatically assign IP addresses. Some typical problems with DHCP servers are:

1. Placing standard network IP addresses in the scope (range of address numbers—208.80.68.0 to 208.80.68.255) of addresses administered by the DHCP server. For example, the 208.80.68.0 address designates the subnetwork and must not be included in the DHCP scope or if included it must be identified as a preassigned address. This problem is fixed by identifying the standard network-assigned IP addresses as not available for dynamic DHCP assignment.

2. Not identifying the server and special function PCs having fixed addresses properly in the DHCP scope. Consequently, the DHCP server thinks that it can use those addresses for dynamic assignment. This causes conflicts in IP addresses on the network. This problem is fixed by identifying all servers and their fixed IP addresses as not available for dynamic DHCP assignment.

3. Having more PCs on a network than available IP addresses in the DHCP address range (scope). This problem may be solved by shortening the IP address lease period. When a DHCP address is assigned to a PC at logon, it is leased from the DHCP server for a predetermined

time. Making this time an hour can potentially free up IP addressees for reuse by other active PCs.

4. Having the DHCP server down when PCs are starting and attempting to log on to the network. Since the DHCP server is down, no IP addresses can be assigned and error warning messages are issued the PCs as they logon to the network. The PCs may attempt to use old DHCP assigned addresses to communicate and this may work, but some PCs will be locked out of the network until the DHCP server is operational. Make the DHCP server very reliable or install the NETBEIU nonroutable protocol stack on the networked PCs as well as TCP/IP. With the NETBEUI protocol stack installed, the networked PCs can perform some network communications although the entire network's resources may not be available to them.

These are some potential problems and solutions using DHCP servers. Most solutions are implemented by the network administration personnel at the DHCP server.

The World Wide Web (WWW)

The World Wide Web (WWW) is a standardized way of representing information in text and graphics linked together on computers. The World Wide Web is implemented by software running in computers connected to the Internet. The Internet is the planetwide communications network using TCP/IP that interconnects WWW and other computers together for the purpose of exchanging data, image, voice, and video information. The World Wide Web uses the HyperText Mark Up Language (HTML) and the HyperText Transfer Protocol (HTTP) to send information from WWW servers to client PCs running web browser software for display across TCP/IP-based networks.

The information is referenced through hyperlinks to other documents on the Web. The hyperlinks employ Universal Resource Locators (URLs) to identify and connect to other computers on the Web. Special programs, called "browsers," such as Microsoft's Internet Explorer and Netscape's Navigator, are used to access the information on the Web.

Prior to the World Wide Web, information on the Internet was presented primarily in ASCII Text. Such text information was searched using ARCHIE and VERONICA software. Some was set up in an indexed, more searchable form. One such form was called GOPHER space. However, the free form hypertext links of the World Wide Web have now become the dominant form for presenting information on the Internet.

Universal Resource Locators (URLs)

A Universal Resource Locator (URL) is the text string that identifies the location of information (web pages) on the Internet. A typical URL is: http://www.dialanerd.com.

Note that this URL jumps immediately to the Dial-A-Nerd web page. Use URLs to go directly to any information displayed on the Internet. Generally, web browsing software jumps to the INDEX.HTML file at each web site.

HyperText Markup Language (HTML)

HyperText Markup Language is the ASCII text codes that are used by web browsing software to translate the plain text files with the embedded HTML markup into the interesting text and graphics displays presented on our client PCs.

An HTML view of text is shown in Figure 16–11.

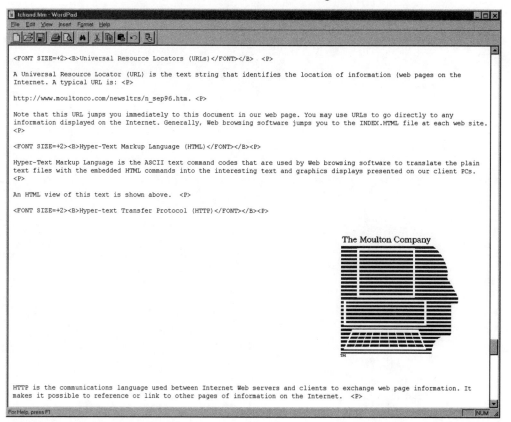

Figure 16–11 *Raw HTML*

HyperText Transfer Protocol (HTTP)

HTTP is the communications language used between Internet web servers and clients to exchange web page information. It makes it possible to reference or link to other pages of information on the Internet.

File Transfer Protocol (FTP)

File Transfer Protocol transfers text and binary files across the Internet. There are special standalone FTP programs and FTP software built into web browsers that make it easy to download software from across the Internet.

Domain Names (Web Site Designations)

Domain names are text representations of registered Internet IP addresses. For each domain, there is a specific registered IP address. Domain name servers (DNS) translate the text domain name into a routable IP address. Routers in the Internet to direct traffic between the PC client and the server supporting the domain name, then use the IP address. That server provides access to the domain's web site files.

A domain server is a PC system that runs a UNIX or a Windows NT operating system. On its disk drives reside the files for the web sites that are for one domain or are part of a larger domain. For example, we have two domains running on one Internet domain server. They are MOUL-TONCO.COM and DIALANERD.COM. Each domain has a specific IP address. The moultonco.com IP address is 209.8.195.52, and the dialanerd.com IP address is 209.8.195.51. The kickoff file for each domain is index.html. This is the same as the kickoff file for any web site. When someone on the Internet accesses the index.html file using a web browser, the website-opening page is displayed on their web browser. (At one time they were routed to the MDConnect.net ISP's Windows NT or UNIX domain server from the MAE-East NAP through a feeder network.) The web browser software and the index.html files makes our domain sites part of the world wide web (WWW). Web browser software does not present the detailed commands used to produce the web page displays. The web browser software only presents the web page display. A web site is comprised of linked HTML files on the server assigned to a domain name that has a registered (official) Internet IP address.

Domain names have extensions depending upon their use. Some current extensions are:

1. .GOV are for government

2. .NET are for network providers
3. .MIL for military organizations
4. .EDU for educational organizations and universities
5. .ORG for nonprofit organizations
6. .COM for commercial enterprises

New domain extensions have been planned for a while, but the U.S. Government has caused a delay in their release. Some of the planned high-level domain name extensions are:

1. .firm
2. .info
3. .shop
4. .arts
5. .rec
6. .nom
7. .web

These proposed new domain name extensions are to better identify the type of enterprise behind the domain.

Domain names make it easy for people to find web sites. It is much easier for us to identify and remember moultonco.com than it is to identify and remember 209.8.195.52. To assure that each domain name correlates with a single domain and IP address, domain names must be unique. No organization can share the same domain name.

This has produced some legal issues for people registering domain names that are commercial trademark names. In one case, the YAHOO-2000 name case, the person who originally registered the name was forced legally to give it up because YAHOO had established YAHOO as a trademark.

Internet Service Providers (ISPs)

An Internet Service Provider (ISP) is an organization offering access to the Internet for a fee. They may be a feeder network provider reselling high speed Internet access to smaller Internet Service Providers. The smaller ISPs in turn sell Internet Access to individual Internet users. We purchase Internet access from MDconnect.net and AOL. Both offer access to the Internet. AOL provides nationwide service while Mdconnect.net is local to Baltimore, Maryland. Our web site information resides on MDconnect.net's Internet server.

In the Internet food chain, an Internet user sits at his office PC and connects through a dial-up line using a modem to his local ISP. Telephone company switching equipment routes his call to the ISP's Server. At the server, the web browser finds the files that comprise the web site. The Internet is literally thousands and thousands of these information pages located on ISP Server disk drives accessible to anyone connected to the Internet.

Email

A major application of networking and the Internet is email. Internet electronic mail is messages sent between systems, including PCs, connected to the Internet. Mail servers and gateways are used to deliver the mail to the addressed PCs.

Email today can be text messages, binary images or pictures or binary file attachments such as programs and other data.

Email started from several different origins. There was:

1. Host-based
2. PC LAN-based
3. Internet-based including:
   a. BITnet
   b. ARPAnet
   c. CompuServe
   d. MCI Mail

Early host-based email systems were PROFS and ALL-IN-ONE software packages that ran on IBM and DEC mainframe computers. PC LAN-based packages are cc:Mail, Word Perfect Office, and Microsoft mail, which run on PC LANs. Internet mail systems were supported by several types of mail software systems that ran on different mainframes, each with a specific audience, but interconnected in such a way that they form a cohesive mail system for all connected computers. For example, BITnet (Because It's Time net) provides email support for the academic community. ARPAnet (Advanced Research Projects Agency in the Department of Defense) is email for organizations performing Federal Government research and other work. MCI mail is a commercial service aimed at businesses.

In 1985 our early email experiences were with MCI mail and DEC. One time we were developing seminar notes for an Advanced Data Communications seminar with DEC. MCI mail was just starting and they laser printed their messages with four hour delivery to the destination. We thought that it would make an impression and show that we were using the latest technology if we sent the new course notes to DEC via MCI mail.

It cost only $0.33 per page to print the pages on their laser printers. Our notes were only about 300 pages or about $100 to print the notes. The surcharge for four hour delivery was only $25 (After spending the $100, what is an additional $25 for four hour delivery!). So we sent the notes via MCI mail.

This meant that we needed to format the pages to 53 lines per page, and to make the drawings with "-", "=", and "+" characters. Once complete, we transmitted the notes at 1,200 BPS to MCI Mail.

Whenever employing new technology for the first time it is difficult to understand its practical limits. For example, we requested instant four-hour delivery, but it required more than four hours transmission time to send the data to MCI mail. Also there was no error correction, so every error required that we stop transmission and restart at a point prior to the error.

Once the message was received in its entirety by MCI mail, we rechecked the destination address by requesting it be played back (or so we believed) because it is bad to send a $125 message to an incorrect address. Nothing came back, so we reentered the destination address and requested another play back. Again nothing. The procedure was repeated with identical results, so we carefully entered the correct address and quickly sent the message before it was accidentally dropped into the electronic bit bucket. Then we played back the message that had been sent only to discover that we had transmitted four identical messages and spent $500!

When something like this happens you quickly attempt to correct the mistake. We did so by immediately contacting MCI mail. They tried to cancel the message only to discover that it had overloaded their system (it wasn't designed to handle 300 page messages) and had to be purged. Consequently, we were not charged the $500.

Today virtually all ISPs provide email as part of Internet service.

To set up a PC to use email, an email program like Microsoft Outlook is used. Outlook must be installed on the user's PC. Once installed, Outlook is pointed to an email server such as a Microsoft Exchange server. The email server acts as the post office for email. Mail sent to the user is stored on it until the users log into the email server and retrieve their email. Outlook manages the receipt and display of the email messages. PCs that are used on AOL need no special email software beyond the proprietary AOL software. Email is built into the standard AOL software. It uses AOL servers as the email post office.

There is no payment for email other than the fees paid for normal Internet access. Some Internet email services provide fee service with the proviso that the subscribers be subject to on-screen advertising while they send and retrieve email. Furthermore, email message formats are standardized to the point that any email system can exchange email with any other email system worldwide.

HTML Documents

This exercise illustrates the formatting and display of HTML documents using Microsoft's Internet Explorer.

1. Use a Windows 98 PC attached to the Internet. Open Internet Explorer and open the http://www.moultonco.com/ web page.

2. Select view source. This shows the HTML tags added to text that creates the web page display on the browser. Similar commands are used in Netscape to edit web page source code. Sometimes the edit source command opens Microsoft Word. In that case you would need to view the HTML source to see the HTML tags added to the text.

3. Return to the IE menus and select view—Internet options (for IE4) or tools—Internet options (for IE5). This opens the setup and controls for the Internet Explorer. Select connections and view the dial-up and LAN connections for IE.

4. Click on LAN settings. If the PC connects to the Internet through a LAN, this shows whether a proxy server is used to route the network traffic to the Internet. A proxy server is a special server that represents a LAN to the Internet as a typically single IP address. It filters packets and routes them to the appropriate connected LAN that is browsing the World Wide Web.

5. Click on cancel, then on the security tab. What security level is set? The default for Windows in general is medium security for Internet access.
The goal of this exercise is to illustrate HTML code for web pages and to show some of the Microsoft Internet Explorer settings for connecting to the Internet using a LAN. There are similar settings for Netscape, but different menu selections are used to access them. We use IE as our example here; it is likely found on most Windows 95/98 PCs, whether it is used to access the Internet or not.

■ Summary

This chapter has examined local area network functions and types of LANs. Windows software supports both disk sharing and printer sharing for peer-to-peer and for client-server network types. Network interface cards (NICs) driver software is provided with Windows for Ethernet, token ring and ARC-net cards. Newer Asynchronous Transfer Mode (ATM) cards also have software support provided by Windows. The dominant NICs are likely to be

Ethernet and ATM because they are operating at high speeds and they provide capabilities to handle newer voice and video data streams. Finally, the chapter discusses configuring PC and Windows for Internet access. This involves setting up Windows TCP/IP software for dial-up network and LAN Internet access.

▲ CHAPTER REVIEW QUESTIONS

1. *LAN means?*

    A. Limited Area Network

    B. Locally Arranged Network

    C. Limited Access Network

    D. Local Area Network

    Answer: D. Local Area Network

2. *LANs can be _____*

    A. peer-to-peer or client-server

    B. ARCnet

    C. Ethernet

    D. token ring

    E. Asynchronous Transfer Mode

    F. all of the above

    Answer: F. all of the above

3. *The oldest LAN technology is_____*

    A. Ethernet

    B. ATM

    C. Token ring

    D. FDDI

    Answer: A. Ethernet

4. *Which LAN technologies are most likely to prevail in the next millennium?*

    A. Ethernet and ATM

    B. Ethernet and token ring

    C. ARCnet and token ring

    D. FDDI and token ring

    Answer: A. Ethernet and ATM

5. *What Windows software is needed for Internet access?*

A. special display drivers

B. communications software

C. TCP/IP software components

D. dial-up networking software

Answer: c. TCP/IP software components

6. *TCP means*

A. Transmission Control Properties

B. Transfer Control Protocol

C. Transmission Centric Protocol

D. Transmission Control Protocol

Answer: D. Transmission Control Protocol

7. *CSMA/CD means*

A. Collision Sense Multiple Access with Carrier Detection

B. Carrier Sense Multiple Access with Common Detection

C. Carrier Sense Multiple Account with Carrier Detection

D. Carrier Sense Multiple Access with Collision Detection

Answer: D. Carrier Sense Multiple Access with Collision Detection

8. *Which network uses CSMA/CD?*

A. Token ring

B. Ethernet

C. ATM

D. ARCnet

E. FDDI

Answer: B. Ethernet

9. *Ethernet and token ring are?*

A. networking software

B. Windows components

C. NICs

D. wide area networking technologies

Answer: C. NICs

10. *Modems support _____*

A. LANs

B. voice communications

C. dial-up communications

      D. access to AOL only
      Answer: C. dial-up communications

11. *An ISP* _____
      A. hosts web sites
      B. provides email services
      C. connects dial-up users to the Internet
      D. all of the above
      E. none of the above
      Answer: D. all of the above

12. *HTTP means* _____
      A. HyperText Transmission Protocol %
      B. HyperText Transfer Procedure
      C. Hyperlink-Text Transfer Protocol
      D. HyperText Transfer Protocol
      Answer: D. HyperText Transfer Protocol

13. *HTML is used to* _____
      A. transfer data across the Internet
      B. install windows Internet software
      C. build web browsers
      D. format web site files
      E. none of the above
      Answer: D. format web site files

14. *A URL is*
      A. a list of web sites
      B. used by TCP/IP
      C. a link to another web site
      D. Unique Resource Location
      Answer: C. a link to another web site

15. *Domains can have* _____
      A. .COM and .GOV name extensions
      B. unique IP addresses
      C. HTML files
      D. all of the above
      E. none of the above
      Answer: D. all of the above

16. *Servers are* _____
    A. devices that route data
    B. PCs connecting LANs to the Internet
    C. web site browsers
    D. network diagnostic computers
    E. all of the above
    F. none of the above
    Answer: F. none of the above

Customer Satisfaction

▲ Chapter Syllabus

A+ 17.1 Communicating with the Customer

A+ 17.2 Understanding Customer Problem Descriptions

A+ 17.3 Communicating at the Appropriate Technical Level

A+ 17.4 Establishing Customer Rapport

A+ 17.5 Professional Conduct

A+ 17.6 Responding to and Closing Service Calls

A+ 17.7 Handling Customer Complaints

A+ 17.8 Empathy for Customer Problems

Customer service is the most important part of PC support. This chapter deals with customer service and satisfaction issues. It covers personal interactions with the customer, professional conduct, projecting confidence and winning credibility with the customer, and keeping a perspective and sense of humor when solving customer problems. Getting reliable information from the customer and PC user is a key step in troubleshooting and resolving PC problems. Understanding customer needs and perspectives is important in providing PC support. See Figure 17–1. When a customer's PC is not working properly, it often means that your customer cannot perform assigned tasks and productivity suffers.

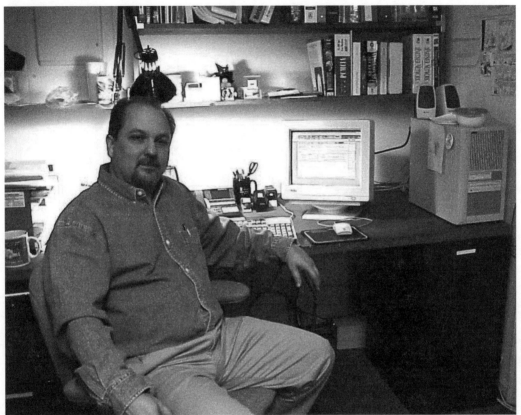

Figure 17–1 *Typical customer with PC problem*

A+ 17.1 Communicating with the Customer

Just fixing a PC problem does not necessarily solve the customer's problem. For example, a business owner had a problem with the FAX software on his Windows machine. A service person got the software to start and then placed it in the *Windows\Programs\Startup* folder so that it was launched each time the PC was started. This was not helpful to the customer; he only needed it on the desktop so that it could be reliably launched when he needed to fax. The customer spent a full day trying to figure out how to stop the fax from automatically launching when the PC was powered on. Having the fax software act reliably when he needed it was vital to his international trade business. He lived or died by being able to fax to suppliers and customers. The service technician never understood the importance of faxing to the customer and as a result misconfigured the fax software on the PC.

There are two primary forms of customer communication. They include face-to-face and telephone communications. Another form of customer communication is solving problems via e-mail, as we do as part of our broadcasts on radio and TV. E-mail is very difficult because you never get all the facts or see the actual PC. So there is a lot of reading between the lines. Answers usually start people down the path that reveals how to solve the problem, but may not directly correct the problem itself. Let's examine the other forms of customer communications.

Face-to-Face

The ability to communicate effectively with customers face-to-face is essential to being successful in solving problems efficiently. Accurate, complete information from the customer saves a great deal of time making each service call more productive. Factors that are unique in face-to-face communications are:

1. Appearance—The first impression that customers receive from service personnel is visual. A neat, well-groomed, professional appearance inspires confidence and helps to alleviate anxiety. Wrinkled clothes or scuffed shoes are not the mark of a competent professional.
2. Demeanor—Act calm. Customers will almost always be upset. To get clear and accurate information, they must be relaxed. Slow down the rate of your speech and speak at a lower, relaxed pitch. If a customer does not follow suit, ask them to slow down.
3. Eye contact—Look at customers and maintain eye contact. This assures them that you are listening and are just as concerned as they are with the problem. When customers have problems, they want undivided attention. This gives them confidence that their problem will be solved.
4. Take notes—It is impossible to remember every detail that a customer describes. Taking notes ensures that every bit of information available is at your disposal and reassures the customer that you are listening and understanding what they say.
5. Explain everything—Teaching the customer what happened and why prevents reoccurrence of the same problem. It also builds confidence in your solution and helps uncover additional troubleshooting information.

Following these five factors can greatly improve customer communications and aid in finding the root cause of most PC problems.

Telephone Communications

Telephone communications are plagued by unique problems. These unique problems are caused by not being able to see the customer and the customer's PC. Further, the customer cannot see you, so the confidence-building visual demeanor cannot be conveyed. However, utilizing a few simple techniques can create an image of professionalism and competence. These techniques are:

1. Project a professional image—Speak clearly and distinctly. Observe the rules of proper grammar and express questions or comments in complete sentences. Avoid technical jargon and slang words or phrases. Speak in descriptive terms and, if possible, analogies that are clearly understood rather than vague phrases or technical acronyms that may be misinterpreted. NEVER EAT OR DRINK WHILE SPEAKING WITH A CUSTOMER. Always be polite and smile when on the phone because a smile has a surprising effect on any presentation.
2. Demeanor—Remain calm, just as with a face-to-face conversation. The customer will be upset and must become relaxed if you are going to get clear and accurate information. As with face-to-face communication, slow down the rate of speech and speak at a lower, relaxed pitch. When a customer does not follow suit, ask them to slow down.
3. Clarify and confirm—Frequently summarize what has been heard and ask the customer to confirm that they have been understood correctly. This step reassures customers that someone is listening and interested in their problem. This also ensures that any information received has not been misinterpreted.
4. Take notes—Take accurate and complete notes to preserve all the important details that have been expressed by the customer. It is impossible to remember every detail. Calling a customer back for clarification may make a service representative look much less knowledgeable and helpful.
5. Explain everything—As with face-to-face contact, explaining to a customer what happened and why prevents problem reoccurrence. Explaining how and why helps uncover additional troubleshooting information and builds confidence in the problem solution.

Since telephone conversations often cannot directly fix PC hardware malfunctions, documenting the symptoms and verifying what is failing is critical to the service personnel following up the telephone call. Missing the root cause of the problem because of a failure to carefully explore all symptoms with the customer on the telephone, often results in the need for a follow-up repair call by the field personnel. Following these five techniques improves customer telephone information and symptom gathering. Acting highly knowledgeable as opposed to being very interested in discovering new information can limit the effectiveness of telephone communications. The primary goal here is to discover all the symptoms and describe them accurately. Only then can the problem be solved.

Study Break

Communicating with the Customer

List three ways that you personally can improve your skills.

1. Think over your interaction with a PC user in the last month. What could you have done differently to make them feel less stress?

2. What could you have done to cause them to laugh without making them feel the object of ridicule?
   The goal here is to think of better ways to interact with the customer.

A+ 17.2 Understanding Customer Problem Descriptions

All service calls, whether in person or by telephone, start with a verbal description of the problem provided by a customer. This initial conversation provides valuable information if time is taken to understand the customer's description of the problem and symptoms.

The key technique to understanding your customer is active listening. Active listening is a technique which encourages your customer to "tell you all about it" while you guide the description in the most productive direction through the use of questions. (In psychology this is called reflecting the other person's statements.) The following are the guidelines for active listening:

1. **Do not assume**—Many technicians instantly begin to diagnose a problem based on the limited description that is given when the service call is dispatched. They often fail to listen to added details given by customers. Listen objectively to the customer and then determine the best

course of action to resolve or further diagnose the problem based on the facts.

2. Don't interrupt—Allow the customer to describe the problem completely without interruption. Most customers forget important details and become confused when repeatedly stopped to answer questions. Customers also appreciate courtesy. Courtesy and patience in handling customer communications increases their confidence in the technician's ability to help them solve their PC problem.

3. Clarify with questions—After hearing the complete problem description, ask questions to clarify the problem description or to verify your hypothesis as to the root source of the problem. These questions should require a yes or no or specifically detailed answer. They should directly relate to the description. For example, if the customer says that a PC is running slowly, a question to ask is "Does it run slow all day or only at just some specific times?" If the slowdown only occurs during peak activity on a network or the Internet, the problem could be excessive network traffic and have nothing to do with the PC hardware or software components. Ask "Did you attempt this? Or Did you try to … ?"

4. Summarize and confirm—After you have completed questioning a customer, summarize the problem and obtain confirmation from the customer that you have all of the details. It is very important that the customer confirms the understanding of the problem. If there is any discrepancy between the understanding and the customer description, repeat step number three, Clarify With Questions. Ask "Why is this important to them?" or "What is important to them?"

Active listening is a technique for extracting the maximum amount of information from the customer during the troubleshooting process. When performed properly, active listening helps to clarify what exactly is important to the customer as well as provides the clues essential to resolving the problem.

Verbal and Nonverbal Cues

We have discussed how to uncover verbal cues to the root source of PC problems. Next we need to examine briefly some nonverbal clues.

Being observant and attending to nonverbal cues helps identify key troubleshooting information. People often provide valuable facts without even knowing that they are doing it. For example, if the user is running Windows 95 but keeps referring to the Explorer function as the File Manager, he or she may be a new Windows 95 user who has not been properly trained on

Windows 95. The problem may be operator error due to inadequate training. A great deal of time could be wasted investigating a hardware or system problem that doesn't exist.

Nonverbal cues are also helpful. Problems that are caused by faulty hardware but not by software glitches are indicated by overloaded power outlets; a lack of a surge protectors; poor ventilation; coffee stains on carpets or desks; lots of loose paper clips; excessive dust; dry conditions and wool carpets; and filled ash trays.

Helping with Problem Identification

Helping with problem identification is based upon postulating tests that verify problem symptoms and hypothesized solutions. Based on customer descriptions, suggest simple tests that can verify the problem description or solution. Does the difficulty happen repeatedly under the same set of circumstances or is it more intermittent. What patterns can you spot and verify. Which general area is the problem in—hardware, software, or network. Explain the why of each question to the customer to encourage them to further describe what happened and what changed in their system prior to this specific problem arising. One helpful thing to do is have the user walk you through the process; have the user show you what causes the error, what steps are taken, and how the problem manifests itself.

Study Break

Understanding Customer Problem Descriptions

List three ways that you personally can improve your ability to zero in on PC problems when talking with a user.

1. Describe the symptoms of a typical customer problem to a friend or another student and see if they can identify the problem.

2. Do you think that your customers are better able to describe problems than you? The goal here is to think of better ways to identify problems as described by customers.

A+ 17.3 Communicating at the Appropriate Technical Level

Customers are usually anxious to help by answering questions and giving a description of the problem. It is important, however, to recognize the level of technical knowledge and savvy of the customer. Asking questions that are beyond the capability of the customer to understand because they contain technical jargon wastes time, and embarrasses and angers customers. Communicating at a mismatched technical level can often provide inaccurate information that hinders problem resolution. If the contact is not capable of answering specific questions (e.g. the PC configuration description and installed options), use PC diagnostic tools to gain new insight into the problem, request assistance from another person, or perhaps contact the technical support person originally responding to the call.

When you find the appropriate contact, involve them in the process and be sure to recognize their knowledge and contribution to the solution. People, especially technical personnel, want to know that their knowledge is respected and appreciated. They are much more willing to assist resolving a PC problem if they receive credit for their efforts.

Study Break

Communicating at the Appropriate Technical Level

A customer is complaining of extremely slow performance and prolonged pauses in the operation of their PC.

1. List three questions that you would ask the nontechnical user to try and diagnose the cause of the problem.

2. List three questions that you would ask the support manager to try and diagnose the cause of the problem.
The goal here is to understand the difference in the way technical and nontechnical people communicate.

A+   17.4   Establishing Customer Rapport

Many people have an incorrect understanding of the concept of customer rapport and assume that they should become friends with their clients. Good customer rapport is established when a working relationship is developed which allows for the efficient delivery of service satisfying the needs of both the customer and the provider. Always remember that a relationship with a customer is based on their need for services and that nothing should interfere with the efficient resolution of their problems.

Ways to encourage good customer rapport are:

1. Learn the name and title of all contacts.
2. Determine the standards of service that a customer expects and then meet those standards.
3. Keep all promises.
4. Do not make promises contingent upon factors outside of your immediate control.
5. Keep customer contacts and other involved parties informed.
6. Periodically ask the customer if they are happy with the service and how might the service be made better.

Following these simple guidelines keeps customers and other parties involved in the service effort happy.

Study Break

Establishing Customer Rapport

Describe what you plan to do to establish good customer rapport.

1. What would you do to learn the name and title of all contacts?

2. What would you do to determine the standards of service?

3. What would you do to keep promises?

4. What would you do to not make promises contingent upon factors outside of your immediate control?

5. What would you do to keep customers informed?

6. How would you check on customer satisfaction?
   The goal here is to explicitly identify tangible things that can be done to establish customer rapport.

A+ 17.5 Professional Conduct

Professional conduct is always associated with the best organizations in any industry. IBM set the standard for service in the data processing marketplace by insisting on professional conduct by everyone in the organization. This lesson was learned by H. Ross Perot when he founded EDS and grew it to be the premier service organization in the US. During his tenure at EDS, all EDS employees worked in suits. This action set a standard for professional service and support conduct industrywide.

The following actions help set up recognition of the service person as a true professional.

1. Put your customer's interest first—A self-serving act may be profitable in the short term; however, an honest concern for the welfare of the client establishes and maintains a long and mutually rewarding relationship.

2. Maintain a neat appearance—Clothing should be neat and clean, shoes polished or brushed, and personal hygiene maintained. Clothes make the PC service person. Many companies have dispensed with neckties as part of the dress code for their service engineers and technicians; however, all clothing should be appropriate for a business environment.

3. Be punctual—Arriving on time or slightly early always sets the customer up in a good mood. Arriving late shows lack of concern about their problem.

4. Be honest—State facts clearly and concisely and never exaggerate the good or bad aspects of a situation.

5. Respect your customer's time—Focus on the task at hand and do not spend excessive amounts of time socializing with customers or customer contacts; everyone has work to do so do not waste their time and yours.

6. Never flirt with or make suggestive comments to customers or their employees.

7. Focus on the job at hand—Do not become involved in internal company politics or personal matters outside of the responsibilities as a service provider.

These actions can become habits. When they do, the service personnel practicing them look highly competent and professional.

Punctuality

Always be on time. Excessive lateness, or failing to arrive as promised, undoes all of the goodwill accumulated. When you know that there will be a delayed arrival, call the customer and advise them of the arrival status. The customer can then decide whether to work with the late arrival or to reschedule the service call.

Late arrival without extraordinary circumstances implies that the customer's problem is unimportant. It may be less important to the service personnel, but it is critical to the customer because their business depends on PCs working properly.

Avoiding Conflicts

Computers are a critical component of almost all business operations. Any interruption of service is considered a major problem. It is inevitable that situations will escalate to a point of producing some conflict between the service person and the client. Many of these conflicts can be avoided if two rules are observed: (1) Stick to the facts, and (2) The customer has the final word (really the "customer is always right" rule).

A clear understanding of all of the facts is most important when there is a potential conflict. Most of us are good at getting details; however, in this situation the summarize and confirm step of understanding the customer's problem description must be stressed and followed. If everyone can agree on the problem, it becomes much easier to agree on the solution. If there is a disagreement regarding the problem description, go back and revisit the questions and clarify the details before again trying to reach agreement on the problem description.

If a conflict remains after agreeing on the problem, it is probably due to a disagreement regarding the solution. All options should be explained completely to the customer, along with their implications. If it is appropriate, recommend a solution. But the customer determines the course of action. Their first choice may not be the technician's recommendation, but the customer makes the final decision. If the customer insists on a course of action that is inappropriate, or impossible to deliver, explain the reasons why their wishes cannot be fulfilled. When the customer wishes cannot be met, escalate the matter to management.

It is an unfortunate fact of life that "They cannot all be won." However, professional conduct is possible even in the worst conflicts. Always maintain a professional demeanor and never offend the customer. Clearly state the facts and offer the best possible solution. Never get caught up in emotional arguments or personal attacks. Finally, never agree to any detail or solution that is not correct, workable, and in the best interest of the customer. A customer may be unhappy with the turn of events but they always in the long term respect integrity and professionalism. That respect is usually enough to earn a second or third chance when the next problem occurs.

Professional Conduct

Describe the last encounter that you had with a service technician or sales person who acted professionally.

1. Would you deal with them again?

2. How could you act more like them?

3. What did they do that made them seem professional?
   The goal here is to determine what makes a service person appear professional.

A+ 17.6 Responding to and Closing Service Calls

When responding to a call, observe the following steps:

1. Determine the urgency of the situation if the dispatcher does not automatically volunteer that information.
2. Contact the customer in a timely fashion and advise them of the assignment to their call. Tell them when they should expect arrival at their site.
3. Be on time. Make sure that arrival at the site is within the time committed to the customer.
4. Upon arrival at the site, go directly to the contact and confirm the nature of the problem.

After you have identified the problem and implemented the repair, you should close out the call as follows:

1. Thoroughly test all repairs to make sure that the problem has been resolved.
2. Advise the customer of the successful completion of the call and explain the steps that were taken.
3. Obtain confirmation from the customer that the problem has been fixed and they are satisfied.
4. Call dispatch and advise them of the time of completion and your status.
5. If the problem cannot be resolved, advise the customer that further effort is required. Give them a clear description of why the problem can-

not be fixed now and let them know when someone will return to complete the repair.

Responding to and Closing Service Calls

List three mistakes that could be made when responding to a service call.

1. How could these mistakes be averted?

2. How could these mistakes be corrected?

3. Who is responsible for correcting the mistakes?

4. Who pays for correcting the mistakes?
   The goal here is to determine how to avert and correct common mistakes.

A+ 17.7 Handling Customer Complaints

The process required for effective resolution of customer complaints may be summed up in five steps: maintain a professional demeanor, listen and empathize, clarify, repeat and confirm, and present a solution. Let's examine these steps in detail:

1. **Maintain a professional demeanor**—Your customer is already upset; it is your job to instill confidence by speaking calmly and letting your customer know that they have your full attention by maintaining eye contact.

2. **Listen and empathize**—Allow the customer to explain the problem their way and at their pace. It may be tedious to listen to nonessential details; however, an interruption may cause the customer to forget important information that you need.

   Frequently reassure the customer that their problem is important to you and empathize with them and the difficulties that they have incurred.

3. **Clarify**—Ask specific questions to clarify details of the information that you are being given. Try to pick an appropriate time to ask clarification questions so as not to interrupt the customer. Take notes, you cannot be expected to remember everything without writing it down.

4. Repeat and Confirm—Finally, summarize the facts as they have been told to you and solicit confirmation from the customer that you have an accurate understanding of their complaint.

5. Present a solution—Outline a plan of action that resolves the problem to the satisfaction of your customer. As always, make sure that the customer verifies that they will be satisfied with your solution when it is implemented.

Handling complaints without anger goes a long way to building a long-term customer relationship. Remember we all make mistakes. It is always the best policy to immediately admit the mistake, take responsibility for what was done and then determine a solution to rectify the problem that satisfies the customer within the limits of the business environment.

Study Break

Handling Customer Complaints

Describe the way that you were treated the last time that you filed a customer complaint.

1. Were you pleased with the outcome?

2. How could the person that you talked to have done a better job?
   The purpose of this exercise is to illustrate how to handle customer complaints.

A+ 17.8 Empathy for Customer Problems

When customers have a problem, they can often feel responsible in some way or they may feel that no one else is having such difficulties. It is important to let the customer know that their problem is understood and that their frustration is recognized. The customer now has a partner in the effort to find a solution. One way to show empathy is to recount similar circumstances in which you were involved and how the problem was resolved or fixed. Expressing the frustration and other emotions involved in the troubleshooting and problem resolution process may help with customer empathy.

Be empathetic when a customer feels that they have caused the problem or are not capable of understanding the technical complexities of the situation. Assure them that computers and LANs are complex and that you have undergone extensive training to be able to provide support. Assure the customer that their contribution is important and that both of you are in this together.

Sense of Urgency

When a customer's system is down, their only desire is to have the problem solved and the system functional as quickly as possible. It is essential to demonstrate an understanding of their priorities and let the customer know that their urgency is shared. Demonstrate concern in the following ways:

1. Respond to the call quickly.
2. Be on time.
3. Get right to the point, do not waste time with idle conversation or funny comments.
4. Do not make jokes about the seriousness of the situation.
5. Keep the customer contact informed of progress as the problem is being solved.
6. Reassure the contact that everything possible is being done.
7. Where appropriate, request assistance to speed up the diagnosis and solution implementation.

Not every problem is an emergency. But solving a problem and moving on to the next problem with decided speed builds customer confidence and respect for the service personnel as technical professionals.

Flexibility

Rigidly following company policies when working on customer problems can result in conflicts. These conflicts can easily escalate into something that can be more costly than bending the rules to quickly solve a customer problem.

For example, customer induced problems (such as not knowing that you have to turn on the power switch on the surge protector) are chargeable under the warranty period. Taking five minutes to educate the customer and waiving the charges of the call can assure you of a satisfied and loyal customer. On the other hand, repeated customer-induced errors cannot be forgiven, due to the cost of this support.

Company policies are guidelines for conduct that should be followed when they make sense. However, they are written by managers that are probably not working and may not ever have worked in the field with customers. A customer never wants to hear the word "no." Bending rules to solve a problem that saves the customer and the service organization money always makes more sense than following the rules exactly.

Study Break

Empathy for Customer Problems

List three ways to demonstrate empathy for the customer's problem.

1. How do these ways help the customer feel that you are empathetic?

2. How can this help solve the customer's problem?
   The purpose of this exercise is to examine ways to be empathetic with a customer.

■ Summary

The service engineer or technician is the most important person in the relationship between the service organization and the customer. Their actions and words form the image of the service organization and are the only criteria that the customer has to assess the value of the service provided.

For example, accurately documenting service calls and keeping accurate records reassure the customer that you are providing them with the best possible support. This attention to detail, and focus on the customer, will make you a partner rather than a vendor.

The professional technician that is perceived as honest, knowledgeable, and willing to put the customer first is always a valuable asset to any organization.

▲ Chapter Review Questions

1. *Which of the following factors are part of good telephone communications?*
   A. speaking clearly
   B. frequently summarizing what you have been told.
   C. taking notes.
   D. all of the above.
   Answer: D. all of the above.

2. *Active listening is a key technique for understanding customer problem descriptions. Which of the following best describes active listening?*

A. Tell the customer what you think the problem is and get their agreement.

B. Encourage the customer to "tell you all about it" while you guide the description in the most productive direction through the use of questions.

C. Ask closed-ended or descriptive questions.

D. Frequently summarize the description and get confirmation from the customer.

Answer: B. Encourage the customer to "tell you all about it" while you guide the description in the most productive direction through the use of questions

3. *An example of a verbal cue is:*

A. Learning the contact's name and title.

B. The customer states that their PC is running slow.

C. Remain calm and speak at a slower speed.

D. The customer refers to Windows Explorer as the file manager.

Answer: D. The customer refers to Windows Explorer as the file manager

4. *Which of the following statements regarding avoiding conflicts is false:*

A. All conflicts can be resolved to everyone's satisfaction.

B. Getting agreement on the nature of the problem can help avoid conflicts.

C. An unresolved disagreement does not always result in a lost customer.

D. There may be more than one solution to a problem.

Answer: A. All conflicts can be resolved to everyone's satisfaction

5. *An example of a non-verbal cue is:*

A. The computer fails to power up.

B. There are stains on the desk from spilled coffee.

C. The customer states that the fan in the PC is not running.

D. The problem is the result of a power failure.

Answer: B. There are stains on the desk from spilled coffee

6. *Which of the following statements describe professional conduct?*

A. Maintain a neat appearance.

B. Be punctual.

C. Never flirt with, or make sexually suggestive comments to your customer or their employees.

D. All of the above.
Answer: D. All of the above

7. *Good customer rapport can best be described as:*

   A. The customer is always right.

   B. A good technician is the customer's best friend.

   C. A working relationship allowing efficient delivery of services that satisfies the needs of both the customer and the provider.

   D. A happy customer.

   Answer: C. A working relationship allowing efficient delivery of services that satisfies the needs of both the customer and the provider.

8. *Which of the following is not one of the five steps for handling customer complaints?*

   A. escalate the problem

   B. maintain a professional demeanor

   C. listen and empathize

   D. clarify

   E. repeat and confirm

   F. present a solution

   Answer: A. escalate the problem

9. *Which of the following is not part of the process for understanding customer problem descriptions?*

   A. do not assume

   B. do not interrupt

   C. clarify with questions

   D. present a solution

   Answer: D. present a solution

10. *Why should you communicate at the appropriate technical level?*

    A. You may waste your time.

    B. You may embarrass or anger your customer.

    C. To avoid obtaining inaccurate information.

    D. All of the above.

    Answer: D. All of the above.

Y2K and Other PC Tales

▲Chapter Syllabus

| A+ | 18.1 | PCs and Y2K |

Other PC Tales

If you have read this far it is time to have some fun. This chapter concludes the book with some tales of what you can do to act like the TV hero MacGyver in a pinch and become a PC hero. The chapter first examines the impact of the Y2K change on PCs. It then presents some PC repair tales.

PCs and Y2K

The Y2K computer problem is caused by computer systems using software that sets dates using only the last two numbers of the year. For example, 81 is used instead of 1981. This creates a potential problem when the year ends in 00. Since 00 can represent 1900 or 2000, computers viewing 00 as 1900 can potentially cause failures in date-stamped information used by any PC, computer, or anything containing an embedded computer chip, like elevators or even automobiles.

The Y2K impact is projected to be anything from Armageddon to little or no noticeable impact at all. What must be done to PCs to make them Y2K compliant? After all weren't all of them designed and built in the last twenty years with the impact of Y2K in mind? More importantly, with the constantly changing technology aren't most of the PCs in use built in the last three or at most five years? Won't most of them be already Y2K compliant?

Yes Virginia, the over hyped Y2K bug can indeed affect PCs. However, many Y2K related problems are easy to fix. Both hardware and software vendors already offer Y2K patches and fixes. If these patches fail, third-party vendors are providing other software and hardware fixes to solve the problems.

Our belief is that PCs used at home and in business will largely become Y2K compliant in advance of 1/1/2000. Key financial and operating system software sold commercially for PCs have updates or patches that fix any Y2K compliance issues.

It is only a matter of finding the software patches and installing them on the appropriate PCs. For example, Windows 98 has already had software updates to fix Y2K compliance issues with it, and Microsoft published Windows 95 software updates in April 1999. The new Windows 95 patch allows users to achieve Y2K compliance without upgrading to Windows 98. Previously, Microsoft provided Windows 95 patches that made the Windows 95 Y2K compliant with minor issues. These patches and others probably issued before the end of 1999 should make all Microsoft Windows products fully Y2K compliant. The patches are provided free at the Microsoft website.

BIOS Compatibility

When BIOS doesn't handle 00 dates properly, no application software will properly handle dates as well. The BIOS code in read-only memory (ROM) holds basic start-up information for your computer. When a PC is booted, the BIOS retrieves the date and time from an internal real-time clock, and passes it along to the operating system. The operating system, in turn, passes the date and time to the applications.

Internal clocks using a two-digit century field on January 1, 2000 give BIOS a 01/01/00 date. Newer PC's BIOSs automatically change the 00 to 2000. Some can still misinterpret 00 as 1900. Even if a BIOS makes errors, Windows NT 3.51 with Service Pack 5, Windows NT 4.0, Windows NT 5.0 (Windows 2000), and Windows 98 operating systems can correct this problem automatically. These operating systems still have other minor problems to resolve to make them fully Y2K compliant.

To be sure that a PC sets the date correctly, use a test program. There are free test programs that can be downloaded from the Internet to test PCs for Y2K compliance. These test programs conduct both a date-forward test by setting the BIOS date to near midnight on December 31, 1999, then letting it run forward and a reboot test to determine if the new date is stored after restarting. Some programs change the date to beyond 2000 to ensure the PC's date and time information is correctly maintained by the BIOS. This procedure can be performed manually as well as by using a test program.

Tests produce one of three results:

1. **The PC BIOS is Y2K compliant**—The PC hardware is ready for 2000 and beyond.
2. **The PC BIOS is noncompliant but can be upgraded using a software update**—Flashing (using a PHLASH.EXE program) the BIOS performs these upgrades. First contact your PC's manufacturer to find the proper BIOS upgrade. They provide free upgrades or they can direct you to third-party vendors who sell patches. There are third-party download software libraries providing BIOS upgrades. Most all PCs are fixable. Only very old PCs with no CMOS setup are unfixable.
3. **The PC BIOS requires a workaround to be Y2K compliant**—This requires workaround software. Once installed the PC's date must be manually set on 01/01/2000 for the workaround software to correctly set the date. To manually reset a PC's system date:

    a. Close all open applications and documents.
    b. Go to the PC's DOS prompt. For Windows 95, click on the start button and select run, then enter COMMAND.
    c. Once a DOS window is opened or DOS is booted to the DOS prompt, enter DATE.
    d. The current date appears along with a request to enter a new date.
    e. Type in the date 01-01-2000 and press Enter.

Once the date is set for the workaround software, the PC should work fine from that date on, no matter how many times it is rebooted.

Some Y2K test programs cause applications to act strangely, lose data, or expire. A good precaution is to close date-sensitive programs and make backups of crucial data and applications before running Y2K compliance tests.

Operating System Compatibility

The Microsoft operating systems all have Y2K problems. Most Windows Y2K bugs are relatively easy to correct. Windows 3.1 and Windows for Workgroups require more work and Windows 95/98 and Windows NT are almost compliant out of the box. Some things to watch for are:

The **Windows 3.1x** file manager that is **installed with Windows 95** cannot display file dates beyond the 12/31/1999 without a patch. Microsoft provides update files on its Y2K web site that correct these and other problems. The Microsoft web site link is listed below. This link has changed several times, but a search for Y2K on the Microsoft site usually leads to the correct page.

Some Y2K bugs are specifically related to the version of Internet Explorer used with the OS, and those can only be fixed by upgrading to Internet Explorer version 4 or version 5.

The **Windows 95** Explorer recognizes four-digit dates only when the regional settings in the control panel are changed.

Windows 98 is touted to be Y2K compliant with a couple of adjustments. The control panel's regional settings must be set to work with four-digit entries for the year. If the Microsoft Wallet stores credit card numbers, they have to be entered as four-digit years in the expiration date field. Version 2.1.1383 or later of the Microsoft Wallet corrects this.

Windows NT Workstation 4.0 requires the latest Service Pack and additional downloaded fixes to bring it into full compliance. Otherwise, there are problems with the find files feature and the user manager.

Applications Compatibility

Applications are the most difficult Y2K problems to resolve. Applications that have potential Y2K problems are:

- spreadsheet programs
- database programs
- financial programs
- scheduling programs

- office organizers
- email programs
- and other programs that rely heavily on dates, such as transaction processing software.

Keep in mind, too, that, even if your application is Y2K compliant, it is still possible to create noncompliant spreadsheets or other documents. Also, macros can have noncompliant dates and functions in them. If you rely on a particular program and use special macros, test them as early as possible to give you time to find and install a fix, if necessary.

Some applications interact with others or with public information sources. If one application creates a 1900 date as opposed to the correct 2000 date, then applications working with that application can get the 1900 date and create errors in spite of being Y2K compliant themselves.

Most major application program manufacturers have patches or revised application releases versions that are Y2K compliant. Macros, plug-ins, and shareware may not be Y2K compliant, which could possibly cause problems. Since each PC has a unique combination of installed applications, application compliance checking for each PC is different. Some Y2K testing applications claim to find and fix noncompliant application software. We believe that this is a limited capability. Manual testing or checking the application program's web site for Y2K fixes are more effective in resolving Y2K problems.

ROLL-AHEAD TESTING

Roll-ahead testing looks into the future to see how an application behaves using Y2K dates. Roll-ahead testing is performed by setting the DOS clock ahead in time to dates after 1/1/2000. Before performing this test make backup copies of all key data because any Y2K problems that pop up that cannot be solved could potentially corrupt the application's data files. Using the backup data and turning the clock back to 1999 should restore normal operation until a more permanent fix is found.

Rolling over the date into the year 2000 can cause some shareware programs time duration licenses to expire or may cause them to stop displaying how much time remains before the license expires. Contacting shareware vendors to determine whether their shareware is Y2K compliant prevents these problems. Make a backup copy of all shareware before performing Y2K roll-ahead testing.

MICROSOFT APPLICATIONS

Microsoft provides compliance details on its products and what must be done to fix noncompliant software at its Y2K website,

http://www.microsoft.com/year2000/
or the U.S. site:
http://www.microsoft.com/technet/year2k/

The site permits you to search for a software product and download patches for that product from one place.

Office 97 is in good shape. Office 97 versions of Excel, Word, Access, and Outlook were roll-ahead tested and no problems were found. Intuit's Quicken 98 was also roll-ahead tested, and all transactions worked fine. Custom macros using dates could require editing to make them work as expected.

INTERNET APPLICATIONS

The Internet was developed from technology designed to operate a network that could survive war and natural disasters. Y2K shouldn't impact it, either. The Internet Engineering Task Force (IETF) that oversees development and operation of Internet technology and architecture has studied Y2K's impact on basic Internet protocols including FTP, HTTP, and MIME. It found them to be Y2K compliant.

Some portions of the Internet could experience Y2K problems and some parts of the Internet may crash. PC's connected to a crashed portion of the Internet can rest assured that the remaining Internet is working fine. Online financial, e-mail, and other traffic may have problems because of the computers supporting them.

Major companies including AT&T, Cable and Wireless, PSInet, World-Com (UUNet), and Sprint own the networks that make up the Internet backbone. These companies must identify and repair potential Y2K hardware and software problems. Millions of lines of code must be examined. Older routers, bridges, proxy servers, and firewalls must be repaired or replaced. These Internet backbone companies have detailed Y2K strategies in place and claim to be on or ahead of schedule. The Internet backbone and local ISPs are often separated by several layers of interconnected hardware. Bridge, router or server failure at any level could cause the Internet to be inaccessible. Most servers and Internet computers run Unix, which has relatively few Y2K problems. But other hardware problems may hurt smaller ISPs because these components may fail in Y2K.

Both Microsoft's and Netscape's web browsers had no particular problems when roll-ahead testing was performed. Problems may be encountered when a browser accesses Y2K errors on old servers, in old software, or in date dependent ActiveX or JavaScript programs. The safest strategy for avoiding trouble is to upgrade to the latest generation of browsers in November or December of 1999.

General Y2K Protection

Y2K computer problems can impact products at home and at work. Here are a few steps that can help avoid problems:

1. Test home PC hardware and software as described above. It is never too early to begin the testing process. Start by going to your computer manufacturer's home page; all of the major ones have Y2K information about their computers available. Also testing can take more time that you expect—start early.
2. For businesses, test all PCs and network servers for compliance.
3. Monitor news reports and contact banks, brokers, suppliers, and others with whom you do business to ensure there will be minimal disruption in business activities. There are also online magazines and newspapers that allow you to receive via email any article that matches your request.
4. At home and at work, keep paper records of all transactions in case electronic data gets corrupted or lost. Make backups of data regularly.

Following simple precautions should make the transition to the next millennium just a hiccup for most computer systems and computer-related activities.

Study Break

Y2K Compliance Test

This exercise tests the Microsoft products installed on your PC for Y2K compliance.

1. 1. Use a Windows 95/98 PC connected to the Internet to access the Microsoft Y2K website. At the Microsoft site select the Microsoft Year 2000 Product Analyser. (http://www.microsoft.com/technet/year2k/pca/pca.htm)

2. 2. Go to the installation guide section of the page and double-click on Intel Build to download the compliance test program.

3. Download and install the program on your PC.

3. 4. Run the compliance test to determine the work that must be done to your Microsoft products to prepare the PC for Y2K.
The goal of this exercise is to show the steps needed to make PC software Y2K compliant in 1999 and in 2000.

Other PC Tales

We have completed the more serious work in this book, so it is time to tell a few tall PC tales. You know the kind, the ones field engineers tell after they have had several beers around the campfire, burning a 286 PC. We look at PC tools in a pinch and some what-happens-when tales. You have gotten this far so let's have fun!

Tools in a Pinch

You are out at a cocktail party and attacked by the host and asked to fix their home PC. You have no tools. When you are naked (without tools) what kind of tools can be employed to fix PCs in a pinch? Certainly Swiss Army knives are effective but somewhat cumbersome PC repair tools. The multifunction pliers in a single unit tool works as well. However, we have from time to time found it necessary to use whatever was at hand to perform PC troubleshooting and repair tasks.

Our personal favorite tool is a Sears magnetic screwdriver. Either the ratchet or nonratchet model works fine. They have multiple tips (or bits) that work on flat, cross-point or Torx bolts. Once in a seminar we were asked if our Sears magnetic screwdriver caused any problems with the PC. We said, no, it never had. And just to really drive home the concept we waved it across a running PC CPU chip and main logic board components like a magic fairy wand. The PC continued to run. Next we waved it across the fixed disk drive. The PC continued to run as before. We entered the command DIR C: only to have the PC display "Sector not found." Oops! Since the metal casing around the disk drive was aluminum, it permitted the magnetic flux from the screwdriver to corrupt the data on the fixed disk drive.

Electric screwdrivers are also considered a gift from heaven because they make PC disassembly and reassembly much quicker and easier. Some other tools we have used are:

- Superglue
- Chewing gum
- Flash light bulb and wire
- Old LEDs

- Lamp
- AM radio
- Finger—heat sensor
- Nose
- Floor
- Paper clips
- Other PC components

Superglue is good for repairing broken plastic parts in rental PCs. It holds them just long enough for the rental technicians to complete testing with the diagnostic programs. Once the plastic component is touched for a second time, it breaks again. By that time the equipment has been returned to the rental facility and no one can pinpoint where it was broken. Superglue is great for fixing broken main logic board memory mounts and leaving no hint that they were ever broken.

Chewing gum is an excellent tool for repairing broken SIMM or DIMM mounts. It is flexible and moulds to just about any shape. When dry, it is harder than iron. Although the concept of memory held in place by chewing gum is somewhat gross, it works.

Most PC voltages are low voltages—3-volts, 5-volts, or 12-volts. Only inside the power supply are dangerous voltages. An effective tester for the presence of electrical power is a **flash light bulb** soldered to two wires. This is used as a probe to test for the presence of low-voltage DC power. It can be used to test power supply output (5-volts and 12-volts) and other low-voltage power sources.

Similarly an old **light-emitting diode (LED)** can also act as a voltage tester. LEDs only light up when current flows in one direction. This means that, to perform a thorough test, the connecting wires must be tested by connecting contact A to contact B and then by connecting B to contact A.

Any old **lamp** can also serve to verify that a PC is plugged into a live wall socket. There have been some occasions where a PC would not power on because the wall socket was dead, not the PC. It is always good to start troubleshooting by verifying that a facility has electrical power. It is most embarrassing to discover that lack of power is the source of a PC failure.

AM radios are good tools for finding high RF fields. When tuned down to the bottom or tuned up to top of the AM frequency band, they should make no noise because there are no stations broadcasting in those frequencies. Moving the AM radio close to a monitor, PC or any other electrical device causes it to emit from its speaker white noise static. Any place the radio produces white noise static has a high RF field that could cause the PC to malfunction.

An ancillary benefit of using the AM radio is that it makes for great nerd party entertainment. Just open the case on any PC. Power off the PC and place the AM radio on top of or next to the CPU chip. Next power up the PC and listen to the sounds the radio makes as the POST tests memory and loads the OS from the disk drives. You can by just listening almost tell what the PC is doing. OK, OK this is a real nerdy party joke.

The **index finger** is also a good diagnostic tool. Generally bad or failed components are shorted out internally and generate a lot of heat. By feeling the components on a board, the bad components or a bad board can be spotted. When one component is much hotter than the other components (chips) it indicates a failed component.

The **nose** can also be used to locate failed components. Burnt components have a cooked polyvinyl chloride smell. Just think of it as "the smell" because it is very distinctive and unforgettable. Components having "the smell" are likely failed components. They are easy to locate when you follow your nose.

Once in a seminar a student brought his luggable Compaq PC (an 8086 chip unit) to the class to work on some exercises at night. When he checked in to the flight (on a crop duster plane) he asked the US Air people whether he should carry on his PC or check his PC as baggage. They of course being helpful airline people replied "Check it as baggage." When he was settled in the hotel the night before the seminar, he powered on the PC only to discover nothing happened. Soon he smelled the smell and knew something was drastically wrong. He was so panicked that he removed the outside plastic case from the Compaq using his bare hands. This was a feat of super human strength. Of course once the plastic was off he could go no further without tools to open the metal chassis.

We disassembled the PC after the seminar was over and discovered that a memory expansion board had popped up in its connector and shorted the edge connector 5-volt power lead directly to the ground lead. This shut down the PC. It also heated up the circuit connection (or run) on the memory board so much so that the gold plating melted off and the copper forming the connection lifted off the fiberglass. Once the memory board was removed from the PC, it worked just fine. If we had had super glue so that the copper edge connection could have been reattached to the fiberglass board we could have probably fixed it as well.

The **floor** can be used to sometimes fix disk drives. Sometimes disk drives would have their heads land on the disk surface and stick there. They would stick to the surface with such force that the disk drive motor could not rotate the disk. We have had this happen to at least four IDE drives and perhaps more. The solution is to hit the disk drives with a severe physical jolt.

We tried hitting them with a screwdriver handle without success. The next step was to drop them two feet to the floor. Our success rate was not outstanding with this tool. One drive was fixed and several others were destroyed (of course they were not working anyway). The one that was repaired reported in a SCANDISK surface scan that a bad spot had developed on the surface of the disk drive. No kidding!

Paper clips are excellent gender menders for female-to-female connectors. They can also be used to create test plugs for COM port interfaces. A connection from pin 20 Data Terminal Ready (DTR) to pin 5 Clear To Send (CTS) changes the status of the port from disabled to enabled. Paper clips can also be used to eject stuck floppies and CDs.

They can also substitute for a cable in a pinch. Once we had bid to set up the communications for a $10 million government contract. This involved PCs, terminals and multiplexing equipment connected using RS-232 cables. To assure the RS-232 connections were made exactly correct so that the devices would communicate, we performed a pilot test. This involved going to a government facility one morning around 11:00 AM when we had to fly from Baltimore airport at 6:00 PM. We brought all the RS-232 test equipment we could carry. This included cables, break out boxes, modems, switch boxes, etc. At the site we set up to do the test with the multiplexing equipment, a terminal, an A-B switch, and a modem. The government personnel were all excited to see the new equipment they would soon work with in action.

We made all the needed connections to perform the test except one between the terminal and the A-B switch. When we went to make this final connection, we found that we needed to connect together two 25-pin female RS-232 connectors. So two words came instantly to mind ... not the two words that pilots say just before they crash their plane but rather Radio Shack.

Radio Shack has gender menders and other RS-232 components that can solve almost any RS-232 connection problem. But there was no way that we would be able to leave the facility, find a Radio Shack, get some stuff, return, perform the tests, and catch our plane at BWI at 6:00 PM. So the next natural thought was ... you guessed it ... paper clips. So we were given paper clips that we promptly straightened out and stuck between the two female connectors. However, the test still did not work. We noticed that some paper clips were touching other paper clips creating undesired connections. So insulation was needed. We thought paper would do and requested some. A pad of yellow paper was produced which we immediately tore into strips and placed between the paper clips.

Just envision what these poor government workers are saying now. Another low bid job. We appeared to the government workers to be just like the person in Central Park NYC crumpling up paper and flattening the paper out again. When asked what they were doing, the reply was keeping away tigers and elephants. When informed that there were no loose tigers or elephants around, they replied "Effective isn't it."

In spite of our effort to insulate with the paper, the test still did not work. So the next step was to disassemble the terminal and examine the inside for any glitches or deliberate traps set by the previous contractor. We powered off and disassembled the terminal only to find no obvious problems. At this point we believed that we had failed with our paper clips. So we reassembled the terminal and were about to pack up our equipment and reschedule the test, when we noticed that **it worked**! We asked ourselves later "What did we do to make it work?" After some intensive reflection we remembered that when the terminal was disassembled and reassembled it had been powered off. Powering the terminal off reset the RS-232 configuration and permitted our paper clip cable to work. Always remember when troubleshooting that the best starting point for any test is from the powered off position.

Other and old **PC components** act as the best test equipment. The old boards that seem useless can effectively help diagnose a variety of problems. Old video boards can as a temporary fix replace nonfunctioning boards to pinpoint a video problem. External modems with lights act as COM port testers. Old Adaptec SCSI controllers with their CTRL-A SCSI select ROM utility make excellent SCSI bus and drive testers.

Just remember that anything can act as a tool for testing and repairing PCs.

What Happens When?

Most PCs we treat with respect, but there have been those few occasions when frustration outweighed common sense and we have treated a PC badly. Liquids and magnets bring to mind some stories.

PCS AND LIQUIDS

In our first PC repair seminars back in the days when Apple outsold IBM we were lecturing on PC maintenance for the American Management Association and one of the students was real excited because they had something to contribute to the lecture. This person was Leo. He was 65 and owned a foundry. So we called on him for his contribution. He related that about once a month on Friday night he would remove all the boards from his PC system (an 8-bit rack-mount computer, at that) and carry them home. At home he would run a sink full of the hottest water he could stand and put in some Woolite. Next he washed off all his boards.

About that time we were thinking, "Oh, this was a good idea."

But he continued on to report that the next step was to place the boards into a 200-degree oven to heat them and dry them. Then on Monday morning he placed the cleaned boards back into the PC. He had been repeating this process for some time. Of the steps above, heating the boards to 200-degrees is definitely not recommended. Any dry air will dry out wet components sufficiently.

He started this process because the foundry air was filled full of dust that contained metallic particles. Eventually the metallic particle dust build up on the PC's circuit boards shorted out the electrical connections causing the PC to fail. By cleaning the boards periodically, the failures were averted. However, he could have used some safer cleaning solution designed for electronics as opposed to washing the boards.

When should boards in a PC be washed? When the PC has been in a flood.

At a training conference we did a PC troubleshooting presentation. In the presentation, the plan was to disassemble and then reassemble a PC to illustrate how easy PC repair could be performed. The sacrificial PC in this case was a new IBM PS/2. It was not a 1987 PS/2 but a non-MCA (Micro Channel Architecture) version. Unfortunately for us, this PS/2 required a bolt holding the floppy disk drive in place to be removed to complete the disassembly. The stubborn bolt would not come loose. It was as though IBM knew and had super glued the bolt to the chassis. Being trainers, the attendees were not tolerant of presentation miscues. Soon eggs, tomatoes and other vegetables were flying from the audience up to the speaker's platform. There was no disassembling the PC so we removed the RAM SIMMs and used them for swizzle sticks in a glass of water. We were so frustrated at that point that we used both ends of the SIMM to make sure it was thoroughly wet. We then returned the SIMMs to the PS/2, powered it on and **it worked**!

Similarly with our first TV appearance—we wanted to make a splash so we used the PC on a block of wood in the basement, as shown in Figure 18-1.

Figure 18–1 *Block of wood PC*

It is always good to have a block of wood PC in the basement just in case. At any rate, the TV shot setup was to have us washing a PC board off in the basement bathroom sink, place the wet board into the block of wood brand PC, then power it on to show that it worked OK. We ran a test prior to the show using the video board only to discover that the wet board produced no video. It required several hours of drying before the display again operated properly. So we next used a serial port board which worked just fine. The TV shot went as planned.

PCS AND MAGNETS

Our other favorite PC abuser is a magnet. This can result in all kinds of fun things. Try placing a powerful magnet in the center of a high-resolution monitor. It makes all kinds of strange colors and patterns. And yes they do eventually return to normal operation. Several degaussing procedures may be needed to return the display to normal.

BAD POWER

It is often possible to misconnect the power connections into a PC. On at least one occasion we have switched the main logic board P8 and P9 connectors. The operating rule there is that the black (ground) wires go side by side. This just caused the PC not to work. Fortunately nothing was damaged or rendered inoperable. We have on other occasions misconnected power to the main logic board and as yet caused no damage.

In almost all instances, the PC just would not start. There was no display. Once we misconnected the power connector on a 3.5-inch floppy drive. Just a single pin to the right or left and the 5-volt power is connected directly to the PC ground. This caused the PC to not start when a second before it had started. We kept turning it on and then off, attempting to find the source of the problem. When nothing could be found, we just turned it on and left it on until … smoke came out the top. The power supply did not have an automatic overload feature so it just kept providing power and heating up the power cable to the floppy drive. When the cable reached the correct temperature, the insulation began to smoke and catch fire. We found the problem then.

IMPACT

There are many tales we can relate about PCs and physical shock. One customer told us he had a PC that fell off the back of a truck. We thought that this PC may have been delivered at night by friends one does not mention to the police, but it really had been dropped off the back of a truck. The chassis was all dented. It was a Panasonic 386 SX PC. When we opened it up to see if we could make it run, we found the disk drive had some rails along the outside that were bow legged (like a cowboy that has ridden a horse for a month straight). When the PC was powered on, strange noises came from the disk drive and DOS did not see it. So we replaced it and the PC worked. Of course the case was dented beyond belief. There was no chance of someone stealing it because it was such an ugly computer.

PCS AND X-RAYS

The one question that most travelers have is do I pass my machine through the x-ray machine or do I endure the strip search at the airport. For years back in the early '80s when portable PCs were luggable Compaq suitcases, we always passed our PC around x-ray. Of course those bulky Compaq PCs would not have fit through most x-ray machines any way. This lasted up into the Compaq III machines. Then in one seminar we met a student that was a

West Point graduate. He carried information around on removable fixed disk drives (for security purposes) and always passed them through the x-ray machine. So we thought why not and have not been strip-searched since. The x-ray machines have never caused a problem with any of our PCs. Many airports, including San Francisco International—in the heart of the Silicon Valley, now ask you to turn on your computer even if you send it through the x-ray. This is an interesting problem as the emissions from the drive belt motors on the x-ray machines can actually do potentially more harm than the x-rays themselves.

Study Break

Mission Accomplished

If you have arrived at this point, you definitely have earned a reward. This exercise is to have fun and exchange a tall tale or two.

1. The tall tale: A Digital field service engineer in the 60s assigned to servicing the first PDP-11 computers got a call from a University research lab to repair their PDP-11. The field service engineer arrived at the University lab around lunch time so no one was there. He found what appeared to be the PDP-11 and ran a memory diagnostic. Unknown to him at the time was that the lab was performing behavior research on animals. The PDP-11 computer he tested was attached to electrodes installed in a monkey's brain. Needless to say the monkey's brain did not pass the memory diagnostic, nor did the monkey for that matter. This is certainly a sick but true tale.

2. Do you have any fun PC stories? We would like to hear them. Send them along to help@dialanerd.com along with your snail mail address.

3. In exchange we will send you an official DialANerd pocket protector.
   The goal of this exercise is to have some fun and reward those dedicated readers who have read this far.

■ Summary

This chapter examined Y2K issues with PCs. Although potential glitches exist, they are relatively minor and can be resolved by 1/1/2000. Microsoft provides a web site dedicated to assuring its key products are Y2K compliant before the year is out. Other hardware and software manufacturers provide similar fixes and patches to their products. Finally, we had some fun. If you read this far we hope you enjoyed the tales as well. Remember the truth is always better than fiction.

▲ CHAPTER REVIEW QUESTIONS

1. *PCs are all Y2K compliant.*
   A. TRUE
   B. FALSE
   Answer: b. FALSE

2. *Which type of test is performed with PC applications to assure Y2K compliance?*
   A. roll-back testing
   B. BIOS testing
   C. roll-ahead testing
   D. patch testing
   Answer: C.roll-ahead testing

3. *Y2K problems potentially impact*
   A. PC BIOS
   B. Windows
   C. PC application programs
   D. all of the above
   E. none of the above
   Answer: D. all of the above

4. *PC BIOS tests can tell_____*
   A. the BIOS is Y2K compliant
   B. the PC BIOS is absent
   C. the BIOS was created after 1985
   D. this PC was built before 1985
   Answer: A. the BIOS is Y2K compliant

5. *X-ray machines*
   A. destroy data on PC disk drives
   B. erase diskettes
   C. have no impact on PCs
   D. destroy PC CPU chips
   Answer: C. Have no impact on PCs

6. *The most difficult Y2K problems to solve involve*

    A. the fixed disk

    B. the PC BIOS

    C. Windows

    D. applications programs and the Internet

    Answer: D. applications programs and the Internet

7. *When would you use water to clean a PC?.*

    A. when it gets dusty

    B. when the power is turned off

    C. when it has been in a flood

    D. once a month

    Answer: C. when it has been in a flood

8. *Y2K problems are all fixed by entering 2000 as the year instead of 00.*

    A. TRUE

    B. FALSE

    Answer: B. FALSE

A

A20CONTROL:ON|OFF, 144
abrasive cleaning compounds, 206
AC adapter, laptop PCs, 373-375
Accelerated Graphics Port (AGP), 281-282
active heat sinks, 270-271
active partitions, 637-638
administrative functions, Windows 95/98, 582
advanced graphics port bus, 308-309
age, fixed disk drives and, 151-152
air ionizers, 235
alcohol cleaning compounds, 207-209
AM radios, as a PC tool, 929-930
ANSI.SYS, 490
antistatic, chairs/mats/floors/floormats, 234-235
application does not load or start error message, 829-830
application errors
    programs hang, resolving, 182-183
    troubleshooting, 182-183
application management
    DOS, 470-471
    Windows 3.X, 500-505
    Windows 95/98, 578
applications architecture, Windows 3.X, 503-505
archive file attribute, 616-617
ARCnet, 878, 879f
Asynchronous Transfer Mode (ATM), 877
ATM (Asynchronous Transfer Mode), 877
ATTRIB.EXE, 840
audio beep error codes, troubleshooting and, 131-132
AUTOEXEC.BAT file
    DOS, 484-486
    role of, 52
    Windows 95/98, 595-597

average power and limiting exposure time, defined, 225

B

bad or missing COMMAND.COM error message, 811-812
bad or missing HIMEN.SYS error message, 812
bandwidth loss, network, 453-454
base memory size, CMOS setup and, 321
Basic Input/Output System (BIOS), 10-11
BAT files, editing, DOS, 620-621
battery
    disposal of, 230
    laptop PCs, 371-373
    troubleshooting, 138-139
binary versus text tiles, 608-616
bindings, TCP/IP and, 890
BIOS (Basic Input/Output System), 10-11
    troubleshooting, 136
    upgrading, 119-120
    Y2K and, 922-924
blackouts, 217
BMP files, defined, 531
BNC LAN cable, installing/upgrading, 100
board versus IP address, LAN, 449-452
boot settings, CMOS setup and, 317-319
bootable diskette
    DOS, creating, 766-767
    formatting, 727-728
    troubleshooting, 172
    Windows 95/98 diagnostic tool, 775-778
booting procedures, 764-781
    DOS, 764-768
        versus MS-DOS command and prompt in Windows, 780-781
    Windows 3.X, 768
    Windows 95/98, 768-781
        function keys and, 778-780
        to safe mode, 780

bootlog.txt file, 775, 776f
boot-sector-infecting viruses, 858
branch prediction, CPU chips, 254-255
brownouts, 217
"buffers" parameter, DOS, 480-481
bus architecture, 301-313
    advanced graphics port bus, 308-309
    clock speeds, 302t
    connectors, 302f
    Extended Industry Standard Architecture
      (EISA), 305
    IEEE 1394/FireWire, 312-313
    Industry Standard Architecture (ISA), 303-
      304
    micro-channel, 306
    PC card/PC-MCIA bus, 309-310
    Peripheral Component Interconnect
      (PCI), 307-308
        hot-pluggable, 308
        small form-factor, 308
    Universal Serial Bus (USB), 311-312
    VESA local bus (VL bus), 306
    zoomed video, 310-311
bus termination, SCSI and, 109
bus topology, network cabling, 414-415
byte, defined, 719

C

C:\DOS\SMARTDRV.EXE, 489
cable pin connections, 94-95
cabling. *See* specific type of cabling
cache
    CPU chips,
        AMD/Cyrix/Motorola/Alpha, 272, 275
        Intel, 260-261
cache memory, 7
    upgrading, 121
cannot find a device file needed to run Windows
    error message, 816-817
cannot log onto network error message, 831-
    833
cartridges, replacing, 356
cathode ray tubes (CRTs), disposal of, 230-231

CD-Recorders, 21
CD-ROM (Compact Disc-Read Only Memory),
    20-21
    drives,
        laptop PCs, 378-379
        removing/adding, 71-72
        troubleshooting, 161-162
Central Processing Unit (CPU), 6-8
    chip, removing/adding, 73-75
    memory summary, 8t
CGA display, 33
chairs, antistatic, 234
charge plate analyzer, 235
chassis cover
    main, 3-4
    removing, 61-62
chewing gum, PCs and, 929
chip set configuration, CMOS setup and, 321-
    322
CHKDSK, virus check with quick check, 861
CHKDSK/CHKDSK messages, 652-654
clamping time, defined, 218
clamping voltage, defined, 218
cleaning, PCs, 199
cleaning compounds, 200-203
    abrasive, 206
    alcohol/volatile, 207-209
    special, 203-206
    water-based, 205-206
cleaning devices, 203-204
cleaning supplies, disposal of, 231
client-server versus peer-to-peer networks, 420-
    441
    NetWare, 437-441
    Windows 95/98, 428-431
    Windows 311, 421-428
    Windows NT, 431-437
clock speeds
    bus, 302t
    versus RAM, 283t
clocking problems, laptop PCs, 389
clothing, ESD protective, 234

CMOS (Complementary Metal Oxide Silicon), 11
  date/time settings, 315
  set up, 313-324
    advanced chip set configuration, 321-322
    basic settings, 314-315
    boot settings, 317-319
    event logging configuration, 323-324
    floppy drive types and, 315
    IDE controller settings, 316-317
    peripheral configuration, 319-321
    plug-and-play configuration, 323
    power management configuration, 322
  troubleshooting, 136-138
coaxial network cabling, 415-416
code compatibility, LAN, 397-399
color inkjet printers, 37
COM files, defined, 531
COMMAND.COM
  DOS, 477-478
  Windows 95/98, 595-597
communication
  with customer, 904-907
    at appropriate technical level, 909-910
    face-to-face, 905-906
    telephone communications and, 906-907
  networks, troubleshooting, 164
  ports, main logic boards and, 297-298
complaints, handling customer, 915-916
complimentary Metal Oxide Silicon (CMOS), 11
components
  electrical, storing, 222
  high voltage, safety precautions, 226-228
  replacement summary, 58-60
  Windows 95/98 management, 578
conduct
  professional, 911-914
    conflict avoiding, 913
    punctuality, 912-913
CONFIG.SYS, 478-480

memory control statements, 676
  role of, 52
configuration problems, laptop PCs and, 386
configurations/components, laptop PCs, 368-371
connectors, cleaning, 213
contacts, cleaning, 213
control panel
  Windows 3.X, 523-524
  Windows, 845-846
conventional memory, 667-668
coolers, Peltier, 271-272
cooling, CPU chips, 268-272
core operating system, Windows 95/98, 586
CPU, 6-8
  buses, 261-263
  cache memory, 7
    upgrading, 121
  chip,
    removing/adding, 73-75
    summary, 8t
  clock speed versus RAM, 283t
  memory summary, 8t
  modes, 251-253
  mounting, 249-251
  packaging, 265-266
  sockets, 299
  troubleshooting, 141-142
  upgrading, 120
CPU chips
  AMD/Cyrix/Motorola/Alpha, 272-275
  bandwidth, 263t
  characteristics of, 244-276
  Intel, 245-272
    buses and, 261-263
    cooling, 268-272
    instruction sets, 245, 248-249
    L1 and L2 cache, 260-261
    modes, 251-253
    mounting, 249-251
    multiprocessing and, 263-264
    out-of-order execution, 255
    packaging, 265-266

register renaming, 255
size, 256-258
sockets/number of pins, 266-268
speculative execution/branch prediction, 254-255
speeds, 259-260
summary of, **246-247**
superpipelining, 253-254
superscalar architecture, 253
voltages, 258-259
write buffers, 255-256
CPUCLOCK:ON|OFF, 144
CRTs (cathode ray tubes), disposal of, 230-231
customer
communicating with, 904-907
at appropriate technical level, 909-910
face-to-face, 905-906
telephone communications, 906-907
empathy for problems of, 916-918
handling complaints of, 915-916
problem identification with, 909
professional conduct with, 911-914
conflict avoidance, 913
punctuality, 912-913
rapport, establishing, 910-911
satisfaction, 903-938
service calls, responding to, 914-915
understanding problem descriptions, 907-909
verbal/nonverbal clues, 908-909

D

data
format compatibility, LAN, 397-399
loss, network, 454-455
swapping, Windows 3.X, 503
transmission, full versus half duplex, 411
date/time settings, 315
DB-25/DB-9 for serial com interfaces, 95-98
installing/upgrading, 95-98
dedicated cache bus, 261-262
DEFRAG, 654-655, 656f, 837-839
defragmenting, disk management, 643

design defects, fixed disk drives and, 150
desktop, Windows 95/98, 628-630
detergents, disposal of, 231
DEVICE=, DOS, 482
device addresses, SCSI, 110-111
device controllers, removing/adding, 77
device drivers
DOS and, 782
loading/adding, 782-790
plug-and-play, 789
special hardware, 783-788
Windows 3.X and, 782
Windows 95/98, 583, 584f, 782-783
DEVICEHIGH=, DOS, 482
dial-up Internet configuration, 880-885
digital versatile disc (DVD), 21-22
DIMM sockets, 299
DIN connector designation, 103-104
DIP (dual inline package), 265
DIR command, FAT and, 652
direct memory access channels, 89
directory, disk management and, 638-640
directory layout
Windows 3.X, 737-737, 738f
Windows 95/98, 746-750
DirectX diagnostic tool, 848
dirt, computers and, 188
disk access functions
Windows 32-bit, 506
fast disk, 506-509
disk caching, Windows 3.X, 525
disk drives
partitioning, strategies, 721t
removing/adding, 66
disk management
DOS, 465-468
FAT system, 638-40, 719, 720f
procedures, 636-644
defragmenting, 643
formatting, 641-642
partitioning, 636-641
repairing, 643
utilities, 644-657

CHKDSK/CHKDSK messages and, 652-654

DEFRAG, 654-655

FAT system, 650-654

    DIR command and, 652

FDISK, 644-647

FORMAT, 647-648

SCANDISK, 648-650

SYS, 656

Windows 3.X, 505-514

Windows 95/98, 576-577

disk preparation, 718-728

disk sharing, LAN, 870-871

display

    controller, 35-37

    problems, laptop PCs, 388-389

    upgrading, 118-119

DLLs

    defined, 531

    Windows 3.X, 526

    Windows 95/98, 586-587

DNS configuration, TCP/IP and, 889

docking stations, laptop PCs, 379-380

domain names, 893-894

DOS

    8.3 format, 609, 612

    boot files, required, 766

    bootable diskette, creating, 766-767

    booting, 764-768

        errors, 178-179

    commands,

        C:\DOS\SMARTDRV.EXE, 489

        DEVICE= and DEVICEHIGH=, 482

        DOS=HIGH,UMB, 483

        editing, 620t

        LH C:\DOS\DOSKEY, 489

        LH C:\DOS\MSCDEX.EXE/

        D:MSCD001/M:10, 488

        MODE, 489-490

        PATH

        C:\DOS;C:\WIN;C:\PE;C:\UTIL;C:\NET, 485

        PROMPT $P $G, 486-488

        SET TEMP=D:\TEMP, 486

        SHARE, 483

    components, 43, 473-476

    file operations, 620-623

    functions, 462-473

        applications management, 470-471

        disk management, 465-468

        file management, 469

        system management, 465

    history of, 461-464

    installation procedures, 728-729

    key system files, 476-492

        ANSI.SYS, 490

        AUTOEXEC.BAT, 484-486

        COMMAND.COM, 477-478

        CONFIG.SYS, 478-480

        EMM386.EXE, 491

        files, buffers, stacks, and, lastdrive, 480-483

        HIMEN.SYS, 490-491

        MSDOS.SYS, 477

    loading/adding device drivers, 782

    memory setup, 696-707

    partitions, primary/extended, 637

    utilities, 835-854

    versions of, 462-464

    versus Windows memory conflicts and, 678

DOS=HIGH,UMB, 483

dot matrix printers, 37, 337-338

drag-and-drop operations

    Explorer, 633

    Windows, 626

DRAM (dynamic RAM), 277

driver programs

    Windows 3.X, 525-526, 737-740

    Windows 95/98, 750-751

DRV files, defined, 531

dual inline package (DIP), 265

DVD (digital versatile disc), 21-22

dye sublimation printers, 333

Dynamic Link Libraries (DLLs). *See* DLLs

E

EDIT.COM, 843
EDO (extended data out) RAM, 278-279
EIDE disk drives, 14
    installing, 107-108
    main logic boards and, 298-299
    troubleshooting, 155-157
EISA (Extended Industry Standard Architecture), 144
    bus architecture and, 305
electric components, storing, 222
electro-magnetic interference, computers and, 188
electrostatic discharge (ESD) procedures, 232-237
    damage, 233-234
    environments, 236-237
    protecting from, 234-236
electrostatic field meters, 235
email, 895-896
emergency recovery utility, 722-723, 850-852
emitted light wavelength, defined, 225
EMM386.EXE, 491, 693-695
EMS, 673-674
encrypting viruses, 858
end user license agreement (EULA) dialog box, 743, 744f
Enhanced IDE, 14
environmental hazards, 215-223
equipment, high voltage, safety precautions for, 223-230
error codes, observed symptoms and, 186
error in CONFIG.SYS line xx, 810-811
error indicators, printer, 350
error messages, 804-819
    bad or missing,
        COMMAND.COM, 811-812
        HIMEN.SYS, 812
    cannot find a device file needed to run windows, 816-817
    error in CONFIG.SYS line xx, 810-811
    incorrect DOS version, 808-809
    missing HIMEM.SYS, 812-813

    missing operating system, 809-810
    swap file, 813-816
    video, troubleshooting, 132
    Windows safe mode and, 804-808
error writing, from a fixed disk drive, 180
ERU.EXE, 722-723, 850-852
ESD (electrostatic discharge)
    damage, 233-234
    environments, 236-237
    procedures, 232-237
    protecting from, 234-236
Ethernet
    CSMA/CD protocol, 408
    LAN, 873-874
EULA dialog box, 743, 744f
event logging configuration, CMOS setup and, 323
exabyte, defined, 719
EXE files
    defined, 531
    Windows 95/98 and, 587
executable programs (EXEs). *See* EXEs
exit, CMOS setup and, 324
EXPAND.EXE, 842
expanded memory (EMS), 673-674
expansion slots, 11-13
Explorer
    drag-and-drop operations, 633
    editing TXT files with, 633-634
    launching programs with, 634
    searching for files with, 633
    Windows 95/98, 631-633
Extended data out RAM, 278-279
Extended Industry Standard Architecture (EISA), 144
    bus architecture and, 305
extended memory (XMS), 669
EXTRACT.EXE, 841-842

F

fast page mode, 278
FAT-16, 716
    versus FAT 32, 636

FAT-32, 716
FAT system
    compared with NTFS, 720t
    directories and, 650-654
    disk management and, 638-640, 719, 720-721f
FDISK, 644-647, 724-727, 835
feature compatibility, LAN, 399
fiber optic cable
    loose, printer problems and, 352
    network cabling and, 417-419
field replaceable units. *See* FRUs
file allocation tables. *See* FAT
file attributes, 616-617
    changing, 617
file management
    DOS, 469
    Windows 3.X, 514-516
file manager, Windows 3.X, 624-635
file sharing, LAN, 871
file system
    basics of, 608-619
        archive, 616-617
        binary versus text files, 608-616
        changing file attributes, 617
        file attributes, 616-617
        hidden, 616
        read only, 616
        system, 616
    installation procedures, 716-718
File Transfer Protocol (FTP), 893
filenames, long, 612-616
files
    managing, Windows 95/98, 576-577
    parameter, DOS, 480
    searching for,
        Explorer, 633
        Windows, 625-626
FireWire bus, 312-313
firmware, 11
fixed disk drives
    controllers, 13-16
    laptop PCs, 380

partitioning, 724-727
removing/adding, 67-69
troubleshooting, 150-162
upgrading, 118
flash light bulb, as a PC tool, 929
flatbed scanners, 39
floor, as a PC tool, 930
floormats, antistatic, 234-235
floors, antistatic, 234
floppy drive, 17-19
    CMOS setup and, 315
        interfaces, 319
    controllers, main logic boards and, 298-299
    removing/adding, 69-71
    troubleshooting, 149-150
floppy drives, 17-19
FON files, defined, 532
font managers, Windows 3.X, 521-523
formatting
    disks, 641-642
        bootable, 727-728
FRUs (field replaceable units)
    pin one rule, 62-63
    removing/adding, 60-83
        CD-ROM drives, 71-72
        CPU chip, 73-75
        device controllers, 77
        disk drives, 66
        fixed disk drives, 67-69
        floppy drives, 69-71
        I/O cards, 77
        LAN cards, 79-80
        main logic board, 64
        mistakes made during, 81-82
        modems, 77-78
        power supply, 72-73
        RAM, 76-77
        removing chassis cover, 61-62
        SCSI controllers, 80-81
        sound cards, 78-79
        video capture cards, 81
FTP (File Transfer Protocol), 893
fuser, printer problems, 353-355

G

gateway router, TCP/IP and, 889
general protection faults, 679-680
GLD.EXE
　　Windows 3.X, 527-528, 562
　　Windows 95/98, 586
grounding, service personnel, 234

H

hard drives. *See* disk drives
hardware components. *See* PC hardware components
hardware configuration parameters, 83-90
　　common I/O port addresses, 84-86
　　direct memory access channels, 89
　　standard IRQ settings, 86-87
　　upper memory used by PC hardware, 87-89
hardware device drivers, loading/adding special, 783-788
hardware errors, critical, 829
hardware failures, fixed disk drives and, 154-155
hardware requirements, operating system, 714t
hazardous waste disposal, 230-232
heat sinks, active/passive, 269-271
hidden file attribute, 616
high memory (HIMEN), 669-670
high voltage
　　components, safety precautions with, 226-228
　　equipment, safety precautions for, 223-230
HIMEM.SYS, 689-690
　　troubleshooting and, 144-146
HIMEN, 669-670
HIMEN.SYS, 490-491
　　troubleshooting and, 144-146
HKEY_CURRENT_CONFIG, 589
HKEY_CURRENT_USER, 589
HKEY_DYN_DATA, 589
HKEY_LOCAL_MACHINE, 589
HKEY_USERS, 589
HLP files, defined, 532
HMAMIN=m, 144
hot-pluggable PCI, 308

HP LaserJet 4 set up operations, configuring, 520
HTML (HyperText Markup Language), 892
HTTP (HyperText Transfer Protocol), 893
HyperText Markup Language (HTML), 892
HyperText Transfer Protocol (HTTP), 893

I

I/O
　　cards, removing/adding, 77
　　port addresses, 84-86
I/O cabling/connectors, 90-107
　　DB-25/DB-9 for serial com interfaces, 95-98
　　installing/upgrading,
　　　　BNC LAN cable, 100
　　　　DB-25/DB-9 for serial com interfaces, 95-98
　　　　integrated disk electronics, 104
　　　　parallel port cables, 99-100
　　　　PS-2 mini-din and, 103-104
　　　　RJ for modems, 103
　　　　SCSI, 104-106
　　　　serial versus parallel cables, 93
　　　RJ-45 or MOD-8 LAN cable, 100-103
　　　selected cable pin connections, 94-95
　　　serial versus parallel cables, 93
IBM numeric error codes, troubleshooting and, 133-134
ICO files, defined, 531
IDE disk drives, 14
　　CMOS setup and, 316-317
　　　　interfaces, 319
　　devices per channel, 108
　　electronics, 104
　　installing, 107-108
　　main logic boards and, 298-299
　　troubleshooting, 155-157
IEEE 1394, 312-313
illegal operation errors, 679-680
incorrect DOS version error message, 808-809
index finger, as a PC tool, 930

Industry Standard Architecture (ISA), bus architecture and, 303-304
INF files, defined, 531
infrared link, printer configuration/connections and, 345-347
INI files, Windows 3.X, 532
inkjet printers, 37, 336-337
installable file system, Windows 95/98, 585-586
installation procedures
    operating system, 715-754
    disk preparation, 718-728
    DOS, 728-729
    file systems, 716-718
    Windows 3.X, 729-740
    Windows 95/98, 740-753
INT15=xxxx, 145
Integrated Drive Electronics (IDE), 14
Intel chips. *See* CPU chips
interface, types/characteristics, 15-16t
interleaving, memory banks and, 282-284
Internet access
    dial-up configuration, 880-885
    domain names, 893-894
    email, 895-896
    File Transfer Protocol (FTP), 893
    HypeText Markup Language (HTML), 892
    internet service providers, 894-895
    LAN, 441-445
    TCP/IP, 886-891
    Universal Resource Locators (URLs), 892
    World Wide Web (WWW), 891
Internet applications, Y2K and, 926-927
Internet Service Providers (ISP), 894-895
invalid working directory error message, 827-828
IO.SYS
    DOS, 476-477
    Windows 95/98, 592-594
IP address, TCP/IP and, 889
IRQ settings, 86-87
ISA (Industry Standard Architecture), bus architecture and, 303-304
ISA LFB size, CMOS setup and, 321

ISO seven-layer model, network compatibility, 400-402
ISP (Internet Service Providers), 894-895

J

JAZ drive technology, 16-17
jumpers, network interface cards and, 445-446

K

kernel, Windows 3.X, 526-527
keyboard, 30-31
    installing, 114
        PS-2 mini-din and, 103-104
        troubleshooting, 148-149
KRNKxxx.EXE, 564-565

L

L1 and L2 cache, 260-261
labels, static awareness, 235-236
LAN
    adapters, 24-26
    board versus IP address, 449-452
    boards, troubleshooting, 166-168
    cards, removing adding, 79-80
    code compatibility, 397-399
    data format compatibility, 397-399
        code compatibility, 397-399
        feature compatibility, 399
        operational compatibility, 399
        printer connection/configuration and, 343-344
        protocol compatibility, 399
    drivers, Windows 3.X, 525-526
    full versus half duplex, 411
    installing/configuring network interface cards, 445-453
        jumpers, 445-446
        Windows 3.X, 446-449
        Windows 95/98, 449
        Windows NT installation, 449
    Internet access, 441-445
    network cabling, 411-419
        bus topology, 414-415

coaxial, 415-416
fiber-optic, 417-419
ring topology, 415
star topology, 413-414
twisted pair, 416-417
network functions, 870-873
disk sharing, 870-871
file sharing, 871
network interface cards, 405-407
network problems, 453-456
bandwidth loss, 453-454
data loss, 454-455
slow networks, 455-456
network protocols, 407-410
collisions and network types, 410
Ethernet CSMA/CD, 408
token-passing ring, 409-410
networking compatibility, 400-402
ISO seven-layer model, 400-402
peer-to-peer versus client-server, 420-441
NetWare, 437-441
Windows 3.11, 421-428
Windows 95/98, 428-431
Windows NT, 431-437
print sharing, 871-872
printer connection/configuration and, 343-344
types and cards, 873-880
ARCnet, 878
Ethernet, 873-874
token ring, 875-876
types of, 402-405
laptop PCs
AC adapter, 373-375
battery, 371-373
CD-ROM drives, 378-379
configurations/components, 364-384
liquid crystal display (LCD), 368-371
docking stations, 379-380
fixed disk drive, 380
network cards, 381
PC card bus, 375-377
problems, 384-389

clocking, 389
configuration problems, 386
connector damage, 388
displays, 388-389
dropping the computer, 385
power management, 388
temperature extremes, 385-386
Windows configuration, 387
X-ray exposure, 386
RAM, 382-384
laser
classifications, 225
safety, 224-226
laser printers, 37-39, 332-336
cleaning drum of, 335-336
Laser Servo-120 drives, 19
laser shutter, malfunctioning, 352
laser toner cartridges, disposal of, 231
"lastdrive", DOS, 481
latency times, CMOS setup and, 322
LED (light-emitting diode), as a PC tool, 929
LH C:\DOS\DOSKEY, 489
LH C:\DOS\MSCDEX.EXE\D:MSCD001 / M:10, 488
LIB files, defined, 531
light-emitting diode (LED), as a PC tool, 929
liquids, computers and, 189-190, 932-934
Local Area Network (LAN). *See* LAN
logical drives, DOS partitioning, 637
lost files, fixed disk drives and, 152-154
low resources, resolving, 823-826
LS-120 drives, 19

M

MACHINE:xxxx, 145
macro viruses, 859
magnetism, computers and, 190
magnets, PCs and, 934
Main chassis, 3-4
main logic board, 4-6, 289-301
AT style, 292-293
ATX style, 294-296
baby AT style, 294

buses, 303t
communication ports, 297-298
components, 296
CPU sockets and, 299
floppy controllers and, 298-299
form factor features, 291t
IDE/EIDE fixed disk drives and, 298-299
L2 cache and, 300
parallel ports and, 298
PC/XT style, 292
removing/adding, 64-65
SIMM/DIMM sockets and, 299
troubleshooting, 136
types of, 290-292
universal serial bus (USB) ports and, 298
make compatibility utility, 852
Master versus slave designation, 107
mats, antistatic, 234
maximum energy dissipation, defined, 218
maximum surge current, defined, 218
maximum surge voltage, defined, 218
megabyte, defined, 718, 719
MEM.EXE, 839
MEMMAKER, 686-689, 729
memory
    addressing, 261-263, 262
    banks, interleaving and, 282-284
    bus, 285
    check program, 839
    configuration, DOS, 261-263, 729
    control statements, CONFIG.SYS, 676
    data bus, 262
    DOS setup, 696-707
    management, Windows 3.X, 525
    ROM assignments, 672-673
    types of, 664-677
        conventional, 667-668
        expanded, 673-674
        extended, 669
        high memory, 669-670
        shadow ROM, 674
        upper memory blocks (UMBs), 670-672
        virtual, 675-676

        video usage, 673
    memory conflict resolution, 678-696
        DOS versus Windows, 678
        EMM386.EXE and, 693-695
        general protection faults, 679-680
        HIMEM.SYS and, 689-690
        illegal operating errors, 679-680
        MEMMAKER and, 686-689
        SMARTDRV and, 690-692
        upper memory blocks and, 693-695
        Windows,
            resolving problems of, 680-685
            system monitor, 685-686
            system resource meter, 686, 825
metal oxide varistor (MOV), defined, 218
mice, installing, 114
micro-channel bus architecture, 306
microphones, 41
Microsoft applications, Y2K and, 926
missing CD-ROM error message, 826-827
missing floppy error message, 826-827
missing HIMEN.SYS error message, 812-813
missing operating system error message, 809-810
MKCOMPAT.EXE, 852
MMO (mobile module), 266
mobile module (MMO), 266
MODE command, DOS, 489-490
modems, 26-28
    data compression, 28t
    installing, 115-116
    removing/adding, 77-78
    RJ-11 for, 103
    transmission speeds, 27t
    troubleshooting, 164-166
Modified Frequency Modulation (MFM) interfaces, 14
monitor, 32-35
    installing, 114-115
    troubleshooting, 146-148
    voltages, safety and, 229
mother board, 4-6
mouse, 29-30

installing, 114
PS-2 mini-din and, 103-104
troubleshooting, 148-149
MOV (metal oxide varistor), defined, 218
MS system configuration utility, 850
MSCONFIG.EXE, 850
MSD.EXE, 844-845
MSDOS.SYS
DOS, 477
Windows 95/98, 594
MSINFO32.EXE, 847-848
multifunction units, 39
multimeter, as troubleshooting tool, 174
multiprocessing, 263-264

N

narrow SCSI bus transfers, 110
NetBIOS, TCP/IP and, 890
NetWare client-server software, 437-441
network, Windows. *See* Windows networking
network cabling, 411-419
bus topology, 414-415
coaxial, 415-416
fiber optic, 417-419
ring topology, 415
star topology, 413-414
twisted pair, 416-417
network cards, laptop PCs, 381
network interface cards, 405-407
installing/configuring, 445-453
jumpers, 445-446
software setup, 446-449
troubleshooting, 154, 164
network printer offline, 351
network problems
bandwidth loss, 453-454
data loss, 454-455
slow networks, 455-456
network protocols, 407-410
Ethernet CSMA/CD, 408
token-passing ring, 409-410
type collisions, 410
networking, Windows 95/98, 581-582

networking compatibility, 400-402
NICs. *See* network interface cards
noise attenuation, defined, 218
non-DOS partitions, 638
nose, as a PC tool, 930
NTFS (New Technology File System), 717
FATS compared with, 720-721t
NUMHANDLES=n, 145
NVRAM, troubleshooting, 136-138

O

on-board controllers, 11
operating hazards, 215-223
operating system
hardware requirements, 714t
installation procedures, 715-754
disk preparation, 718-728
DOS, 728-729
file systems, 716-718
Windows 3.X, 729-740
Windows 95/98, 740-753
Y2K compatibility and, 924
operational compatibility, LAN, 399
optical rewritable drives, 17
option will not function error message, 829
OS/2 HPFS (High Performance File System),
716-717
out-of-order execution, CPU chips, 255

P

Page printers, 332-336
paper feed and output, printer problems and,
348
paper feeders, 338-340
paper jams, 349-350
parallel cables, versus serial cables, 93
parallel port
cables, installing/upgrading, 99-100
main logic boards and, 298
printer configuration/connections and, 341
troubleshooting, 139
parity, as error checking mechanism, 285-286
partitioning

disk drive, 636-641
    strategies, 721t
    fixed disks, 724-727
passive heat sinks, 269-270
passwords, CMOS setup and, 323
PATH
    C:\DOS;C:\WIN;C:\PE;C:\UTIL;C:\NET,
    485
PC
    bad electric power and, 935
    boot process, 50-52
    cleaning, 199
        contact/connector, 213
        dust, 214-215
        letter, 198
        process, 209-213
    component replacement summary, 58-60
    hazards, operating environmental, 215-223
    liquids and, 189-190, 932-934
    magnets and, 934
    physical shock and, 935
    power problems, 216-217
    tools and, 928-932
    troubleshooting, 130-134
        cooling, 187-188
    upgrading, 117-121
    X-rays and, 935-936
PC bus architecture. *See* bus architecture
PC card bus
    architecture and, 309-310
    laptop PCs, 375-377
PC components
    core, 2
    Windows 3.X, 505-514
PC file systems, 651t
PC hardware components, 2-42
    CD-Recorders, 21
    CD-ROM, 20-21
    controller, 35-37
    digital versatile disc (DVD), 21-22
    disk drive summary, 22
    fixed disk drives, 13-16
    floppy disk drives, 17-19

        3.5 inch, 18-19
        5.25 inch, 18
        super disk, 19
    JAZ drive technology and, 16-17
    keyboard, 30-31
    local area networks (LAN) adapters, 24-26
    main chassis, 3-4
    main logic board, 4-13
        BIOS, 10-11
        CPU, 6-8
        expansion slots, 11-13
        on-board controllers, 11
        RAM, 9-10
        ROM, 8-9
    microphones/speakers, 41
    modems, 26-28
    monitor, 32-35
    mouse, 29-30
    optical rewritable drives, 17
    power supply, 13
    printers, 37-39
    scanners, 39
    sound cards, 23-24
    tape drives, 23
    video, 32
    video camera, 40-41
    ZIP drives, 19-20
PCI (Peripheral Component Interconnect)
    bus architecture, 307-308
    CMOS setup and, 322
PC-MCIA bus, 309-310
peer-to-peer versus client-server networks, 420-
    441
    NetWare, 437-441
    Windows 3.11, 421-428
    Windows 95/98, 428-431
    Windows NT, 431-437
Peltier coolers, 271-272
Peripheral Component Interconnect (PCI)
    bus architecture, 307-308
    CMOS setup and, 322
peripheral devices
    configuration, CMOS setup and, 319-321

installing, 114-116

peripheral port connector types/cabling, 91-93

permanent swapfiles, 502-503

petabyte, defined, 719

PGA (pin grid array), 265

phase change printers, 334

physical shock, PCs and, 935

PIF files
    defined, 531
    Windows 3.X, 565-566

pin grid array (PGA), 265

pin one rule, 62-63

pins, number of, CPU chips and, 266-268, 273-274t

plug-and-play
    components, Windows 95/98, 752-753
    configuration, CMOS setup and, 323
    device drivers, 789

polymorphic viruses, 858

POST (Power-On Self-Test), 50
    troubleshooting and, 130-131

power connections, PCs and, 935

power management problems, laptop PCs, 388

power problems, 216-217
    troubleshooting, 187

power spikes, 216

power supply, 13
    removing/adding, 72-73
    safety, 228-229
    troubleshooting, 135

Power-On Self-Test (POST), 50
    troubleshooting, 130-131

preventive maintenance
    abrasive compounds, 206
    alcohol/volatile compounds, 207-209
    cleaning compounds, 200-206
    contact/connector cleaning, 213
    PC cleaning, 199
        process, 209-213
    products/procedures for, 199-215
    removing dust, 214-215

print
    files, corrupted, 351

quality, 353-354

sharing, LAN, 871-872

printer drivers, Windows 3.X, 521

printer ports, CMOS setup and, 320-321

printers, 37-39
    configuring,
        in Windows 3.X, 518-520
        in Windows, 791-796
    connections/configurations of, 340-347
        infrared link, 345-347
        LAN, 343-344
        parallel port, 341
        serial port, 342-343
    dot matrix, 37, 337-338
    inkjet, 37, 336-337
    laser, 37-39, 332-336
        cleaning drum of, 335-336
    paper feeders for, 338-340
    problems of, 347-355
        corrupted print files, 351
        error indications, 350
        failed electronic components, 351-353
        fuser problems, 353-355
        network printer offline, 351
        paper feed/output, 348
        paper jams, 349-350
        printer timeout, 351
        printing to wrong printer, 350
    resolution summary, 349t
    safety considerations, 354-355
    servicing/preventative maintenance, 355-357
    Windows use of, 520-521

printing, problems with, 330-332

printing management
    Windows 3.X, 516-524
    Windows 95/98, 580-581

professional conduct, 911-914
    conflict avoiding, 913
    punctuality, 912-913

PROGMAN.EXE, 563-564

PROGMAN.IOI, 563-564

program-infecting viruses, 858-859

programs
    launching,
        DOS, 621
        Explorer, 634
        Windows, 627-628
PROMPT $P $G, 486-488
protected mode, defined, 252
protocol compatibility, LAN, 399
PROTOCOLINI File, 422-423
pulsed lasers, classification of, 225

R

radio frequency interference (RFI), 221-222
radio frequency (RF), computers and, 188
RAM (random access memory), 9-10, 276-289
    laptop PCs, 382-384
    operating characteristics/parameters, 282-288
        memory banks/interleaving, 282-284
        memory bus, 285
        passive versus nonparity, 285-286
        single in-line memory module
        (SIMMS), 287-288
    removing/adding, 76-77
    troubleshooting, 142-146
    types of, 276-282
        EDO, 278-279
        fast page mode, 278
        SDRAM, 279-280
        static versus dynamic, 277
        VDRAM, 280-282
        WRAM, 282
    upgrading, 117-118
    versus CPU clock speeds, 283t
random access memory (RAM), 9-10, 276-289
    laptop PCs, 382-384
    operating characteristics/parameters, 282-288
        memory banks/interleaving, 282-284
        memory bus, 285
        passive versus nonparity, 285-286
        single in-line memory module
        (SIMMS), 287-288

removing/adding, 76-77
troubleshooting, 142-146
types of, 276-282
    EDO, 278-279
    fast page mode, 278
    SDRAM, 279-280
    static versus dynamic, 277
    VDRAM, 280-282
    WRAM, 282
    versus CPU clock speeds, 283t
RDISK.EXE, 723-724
read only memory (ROM), 8-9
    assignments, 672-673
    shadow, 674
read-only files, 616
real mode, defined, 251-252
REGEDIT.EXE, Windows 95/98, 597
register renaming, CPU chips, 255
registry
    checker, 849-850
    Windows 95/98, 587-591
resource heaps, Windows 3.X, 528-529
RF (radio frequency), computers and, 188
RFI (radio frequency interference), 221-222
ring topology, network cabling, 415
roll-ahead-testing, Y2K, 925
ROM (read only memory), 8-9
    assignments, 672-673
    shadow, 674

S

safe mode
    properties box, 806f
    Windows, 780, 804-808
safety
    high voltage components, 226-228
    laser, 224-226
    monitor voltages, 229
    power supply, 228-229
SCANDISK, 836-837
scanner cables, printer problems and, 352-353
scanners, 39-41
SCANREG.EXE, 849-850

SCR files, defined, 531
SCSI (Small Computer System Interface), 14-16
    bus termination, basics of, 109
    bus types, 110
    cabling, 111-112
    controller cards, 104-106
    controllers, removing/adding, 80-81
    device addresses, 110-111
    installing/configuring, 108-113
    switches/jumpers, 112-113
    troubleshooting, 157-161
SDRAM, 279-280
SEC (single-edge contact), 265-266
security, CMOS setup and, 323
serial cables, versus parallel cables, 93
serial port
    CMOS setup and, 319-320
    printer configuration/connections and,
     342-343
    troubleshooting, 139-141
service calls, responding to, 914-915
service personnel, grounding, 234
SET TEMP=D;\TEMP, 486
SETUP.EXE
    Windows 95/98
     running, 742-746
SFC.EXE, 849
shadow ROM, 674
SHADOWRAM:ON|OFF, 145
SHARE command, DOS, 483
sheet-fed scanners, 39
signature verification tool, 849
SIGVERIF.EXE, 849
SIMMS (single in-line memory modules)
    detected, CMOS setup and, 322
    random access memory and, 287-288
    sockets, 299
single in-line memory modules (SIMMS)
    random access memory and, 287-288
    sockets, 299
single-edge contact (SEC), 265-266
single-inline memory modules (SIMMS),
    detected, CMOS setup and, 322

size, AMD/Cyrix/Motorola/Alpha CPU chips,
    272, 275t
slot covers, troubleshooting, 168-169
Small Computer System Interface. *See* SCSI
small form-factor PCI, 308
SMARTDRV, 690-692
smocks, ESD protective, 234
sockets
    CPU chip,
     AMD/Cyrix/Motorola/Alpha, 273-274t
     Intel, 266-268
     main logic boards and, 299
    SIMMS and, 299
software components, 42-49
    DOS, 43
    Windows, 44-48
    Windows NT, 48-49
software error messages. *See* error messages
software problems
    resolving, 829-834
     application program errors, 820-822
software upgrades, 754-764
    DOS to Windows 95/98, 760
    procedures, 757-759
    system requirements, 756-757
    to Windows, 98, 760-763
    Windows 3.X,
     to Windows, 95, 760-761
     to Windows 95/98, 760
solid ink jet printers, 334
solvents, disposal of, 231
sound cards, 23-24
    removing/adding, 78-79
    troubleshooting, 162-163
speakers, 41
specialty scanners, 39
speculative execution, CPU chips, 254-255
speeds
    CPU chips, AMD/Cyrix/Motorola/Alpha,
     272, 275
    CPU chips Intel, 259-260
SRAM (static RAM), 277
stacks, DOS, 481

star topology, network cabling, 413-414

Start Menu, Windows, 748, 750f

startup files, bypassing, 767

static awareness labels, 235-236

static dissipating, mats/chairs/floors/floormats, 234

static electricity, computers and, 188

stealth viruses, 858

Super Disk, 19

Superglue, PCs and, 929

superpipelining, CPU chips, 253-254

superscalar architecture, CPU chips, 253

surge suppressors, specifications/terminology, 217-223

surges, 216

    suppressing, 217

swap file error messages, 813-816

swapfiles, 502-503

SYS command, 656

SYS files, defined, 531

SYSEDIT.EXE, 843, 844f

system

    board, 4-6

    file attribute, 616

    file checker, 849

    files, DOS. *See* DOS, key system files

    freezing, resolving, 822-823

    management, DOS, 465

    monitor, Windows, 685-686

    resource meter, Windows, 686, 825

SYSTEM.DAT, Windows 95/98, 597-598

SYSTEM.INI

    Windows 3.X, 542-544

        selected, 544-561

T

tape carrier packaging (TCP), 266

tape drives, 23

taskbar, Windows 95/98, 630-631

TCP (tape carrier packaging), 266

TCP/IP, Internet access and, 886-891

temperature, laptop PCs and, 385-386

temperature shock

    computers and, 189

    fixed disk drives and, 151

temporary swapfile, Windows 3.X, 502

terabyte, defined, 719

TESTMEM:ON|OFF, 14

text versus binary files, 608-616

thermal dye transfer printers, 333

thermal wax transfer printers, 333-334

32-bit shell, Windows 95/98, 586

386files, defined, 532

token ring, LAN, 875-876

token-passing ring protocol, 409-410

Trojan horse programs, 856-858

Trojan horses, versus viruses/worm programs, 855

troubleshooting

    application errors, 182-183

    audio beep error codes and, 131-132

    battery, 138-139

    BIOS, 136

    CD-ROM, 161-162

    CMOS, 136-138

    communication networks, 164

    CPU, 141-142

    determining problem source, 129

    diskettes, 172

    DOS boot errors, 178-179

    fixed disk drive, 150-162

        writing errors, 180

    floppy drives, 149-150

    guidelines, 128

    IBM numeric error codes and, 133-134

    IDE/EIDE disk drives, 155-157

    LAN boards, 166-168

    main logic board, 136

    modems, 164-166

    mouse/keyboard, 148-149

    network interface cards, 164

    NVRAM, 136-138

    parallel ports, 139

    PC cooling, 187-188

    power problems, 187

    power supply, 135

power-on self-test, 130-131
procedures/practices, 176-191
    problem isolation/determination proce-
      dures, 177-178
RAM, 142-146
SCSI drives, 157-161
serial port, 139-141
slot covers, 168-169
sound cards, 162-163
tools, 170-176
video error messages and, 132
video and monitor, 146-148
viruses, 184-185
WAN, 164
Windows boot problems, 181-182
TTF files, defined, 532
Tweak User Interface, 852, 853f
twisted pair network cabling, 416-417
TXT files
    editing,
        DOS, 620-621
        Explorer, 633-634
        Windows, 626-627

U

ultra wide SCSI, 110
UMBs, 670-672
uninterruptible power supplies (UPS), 220-221
unit sizing, allocating, 637t
Universal Resource Locator (URL), 892
Universal Serial Bus (USB), 311-312
    main logic boards and, 298
upgrades. *See* software upgrades
Upper memory, used by PC hardware, 87-89
upper memory blocks (UMBs), 670-672, 693-
   695
UPS (uninterruptible power supplies), 220-221
URL (Universal Resource Locator), 892
USB (Universal Serial Bus), 311-312
    main logic boards and, 298
USER.DAT, Windows 95/98, 598-599
USER.EXE
    DOS, 586

Windows 3.X, 527-528, 561
utilities, DOS/Windows, 835-854

V

VA bus, 306
VCMUI.EXE, 850
VERBOSE, 146
version conflict manager, 850
VESA local bus, 306
VFAT (virtual files allocation table), 640-641
VGA display, 33
vibration
    computers and, 189
    fixed disk drives and, 150-151
video, 32
    troubleshooting, 146-148
video camera, 40-41
video capture cards, removing/adding, 81
video card
    installing, 114-115
    memory usage, 673
video error messages, troubleshooting and, 132
video palette snoop, CMOS setup and, 321
video ram (VRAM), 280-282
virtual 8086 mode, defined, 252-253
virtual files allocation table (VFAT), 640-641
virtual machine manager, Windows 95/98, 585
virtual memory, 675-676
virtual real mode, defined, 252-253
virus programs, 856
viruses
    boot-sector-infecting, 858
    CHKDSK and, 861
    detecting, 860-861
    macro, 859
    program-infecting, 858-859
    removing procedures, 863
    scanning program, 861-862
    sources of, 859-860
    troubleshooting, 184-185
    versus Trojan horse/worm programs, 855
        VL-bus, 306
voice rejection, defined, 218

volatile cleaning compounds, 207-209
voltage
    blackouts, 217
    brownouts, 217
    CPU chips,
        AMD/Cyrix/Motorola/Alpha, 272, 275t
        Intel, 258-259
    monitor, safety and, 229
    sags, 216-217
    surges, 216
        suppressing, 217
VRAM (video ram), 280-282

W

WAN, troubleshooting, 164
water-based cleaning compounds, 205-206
wax jet printers, 334
web site designations, 893-894
Wide Area Network. *See* WAN
wide SCSI, 110
WIN.COM
    defined, 531
    Windows 3.X, 562-563
    Windows 95/98, 599
WIN.INI
    Windows 3.X, 532-534
        understanding, 534-542
Windows
    boot problems, 181-182
    components, 44-48
    configuration, 790-796
        changing installed options, 790-791
        laptop PCs and, 387
        printers, 791-796
    control panel, 845-846
    files operations, 623-635
    fonts, 334f
    launching applications in, 797-798
    memory conflicts,
        resolving, 680-685
        versus DOS, 678
    RAM, 282
    safe mode and, 780, 804-808

Start Menu, 748, 750f
system monitor, 685-686
system resource meter, 686, 825
utilities, 835-854
Windows 3.X
    booting procedures, 768
        required files for, 770-775
    components, 524-529
        DLLs, 526
        kernel, 526-527
        resource heaps, 528-529
    control panel, 523-524
    described, 497-498
    directory layout, 736-737, 738f
    driver programs, 525-526
        installing, 737-740
    file manager, 624-635
    functions, 498-524
        managing applications, 500-505
        managing disks, 505-514
        managing files, 514-516
        managing PC components, 505-514
        managing printing, 516-524
    GDI.EXE, 527-528
    installation procedures, 729-740
    key system files, 529-566
        GLD.EXE, 562
        INI files, 532
        KRNLxxx.EXE, 564-565
        PROGMAN.EXE, 563-564
        PROGMAN.INI, 563-564
        selected SYSTEM.INI file parameters,
        544-561
        SYSTEM.INI, 542-543
        SYSTEM.INI FILE sections, 543-544
        USER.EXE, 561
        WIN.COM, 562-563
        WIN.INI, 532-542
    loading/adding device drivers, 782
    network interface cards, 446-449
    peer-to-peer versus client server networks,
    421-428
    USER.EXE, 527-528

Windows 95/98 versus, 571-575
Windows 32-bit
   disk access, 506-509
      blocking, 511-512
      functions, 506
      switched on, 509-510
   file access, 512-514
Windows 95/98
   bootable diskette diagnostic tool, 775-778
   booting procedures, 768-781
      function keys and, 778-780
      to safe mode, 780
   components, 583-591
      32-bit shell, 586
      core operating system, 586
      device drivers, 583, 584f
      DLLs, 586-587
      EXEs, 587
      installable file system, 585-586
      virtual machine manager, 585
   desktop, 628-630
   directory layout, 746-750
   driver programs, 750-751
   ERU.EXE, 722-723
   Explorer, 631-633
   functions, 576-583
      administrative, 582
      applications management, 578-580
      disks/files management, 576-577
      networking, 581-582
      PC components management, 578
      printing management, 580-581
   installation procedures, 740-753
   key system files, 592-600
      AUTOEXEC.BAT, 595-597
      COMMAND.COM, 595-597
      IO.SYS, 592-594
      MSDOS.SYS, 594
      REGEDIT.EXE, 597
      SETUP.EXE, 592, 742-746
      SYSTEM.DAT, 597-598
      USER.DAT, 598-599
   loading/adding device drivers, 782-783

network interface cards, 449
networking with, 428-431
options section parameters, 594-595t
paths section parameters, 594t
plug-and-play components, 752-753
registry, 587-591
taskbar, 630-631
WIN.COM, 599
Windows 3.X versus, 571-575
Windows networking, 869-901
   internet access configuring, 880-897
      dial-up configuration, 880-885
      domain names, 893-894
      email, 895-896
      File Transfer Protocol (FTP), 893
      HyperText Markup Language (HTML), 892
      internet service providers, 894-895
      TCP/IP, 886-891
      Universal Resource Locators (URLs), 892
      World Wide Web (WWW), 891
   LAN, 870-873
   disk sharing, 870-871
      file sharing, 871
      print sharing, 871-872
      types and cards, 873-880
      Windows NT
   features/components, 48-49
   network interface cards, 449
   networking with, 431-437
   RDISK.EXE, 723-724
Windows for Workgroups, 421-428
WINS configuration, TCP/IP and, 889
World Wide Web (WWW), 891
worm programs, 856-858
   versus viruses/Trojan horses, 855
WRAM (Windows RAM), 282
write buffers, CPU chips, 255-256
WWW (World Wide Web), 891

X

xerographic printing, 37-39

XMS, 669
X-rays
    laptop PCs and, 386
    PCs and, 935-936

Y

Y2K
    BIOS compatibility and, 922-924
    Internet applications and, 926-927
    Microsoft applications and, 926
    operating system compatibility and, 924
    protection, 927
    roll-ahead-testing, 925

Z

Zip drives, 19-20
zoomed bus, 310-311

Other curricula available from CBT Systems:

- Cisco
- Informix
- Java
- Marimba
- Microsoft
- Netscape
- Novell

- Oracle
- SAP
- Sybase
- C/C++
- Centura
- Information Technology/
  Core Concepts

- Internet and Intranet
  Skills
- Internetworking
- UNIX

CBT SOFTWARE LICENSE AGREEMENT

IF YOU DO NOT AGREE WITH THESE TERMS AND CONDITIONS, DO NOT INSTALL THE SOFTWARE.

This is a legal agreement between you and CBT Systems Ltd. ("Licensor"), the licensor ("Licensor") from whom you have licensed the CBT Group PLC courseware (the "Software"). By installing, copying or otherwise using the Software, you agree to be bound by the terms of this License Agreement (the "License"). If you do not agree to the terms of this License, the Licensor is unwilling to license the Software to you. In such event, you may not use or copy the Software, and you should promptly contact the Licensor for instructions on the return of the unused Software.

1. **Use.** Licensor grants to you a non-exclusive, nontransferable license to use Licensor's software product (the "Software") and accompanying documentation in accordance with the terms and conditions of this license agreement ("License") License and as specified in your agreement with Licensor (the "Governing Agreement"). In the event of any conflict between this License and the Governing Agreement, the Governing Agreement shall control.

You may:

a. (if specified as a "personal use" version) install the Software on a single stand-alone computer or a single network node from which node the Software cannot be accessed by another computer, provided that such Software shall be used by only one individual; <u>or</u>

b. (if specified as a "workstation" version) install the Software on a single stand-alone computer or network node from which node the Software cannot be accessed by another computer, provided that such Software shall be used only by employees of your organization; <u>or</u>

c. (if specified as a "LAN" version) install the Software on a local area network server that provides access to multiple computers, up to the maximum number of computers or users specified in your Governing Agreement, provided that such Software shall be used only by employees of your organization; <u>or</u>

d. (if specified as an "enterprise" version) install the Software or copies of the Software on multiple local or wide area network servers, intranet servers, stand-alone computers and network nodes (and to make copies of the Software for such purpose) at one or more sites, which servers provide access to a multiple number of users, up to the maximum number of users specified in your Governing Agreement, provided that such Software shall be used only by employees of your organization.

<u>This License is not a sale. Title and copyrights to the Software, accompanying documentation and any copy made by you remain with Licensor or its suppliers or licensors.</u>

2. **Intellectual Property**. The Software is owned by Licensor or its licensors and is protected by United States and other jurisdictions' copyright laws and international treaty provisions. Therefore, you may not use, copy, or distribute the Software without the express written authorization of CBT Group PLC. This License authorizes you to use the Software for the internal training needs of your employees only, and to make one copy of the Software solely for backup or archival purposes. You may not print copies of any user documentation provided in "online" or electronic form. Licensor retains all rights not expressly granted.

3. **Restrictions.** You may not transfer, rent, lease, loan or time-share the Software or accompanying documentation. You may not reverse engineer, decompile, or disassemble the Software, except to the extent the foregoing restriction is expressly prohibited by applicable law. You may not modify, or create derivative works based upon the Software in whole or in part.

1. **Confidentiality**. The Software contains confidential trade secret information belonging to Licensor, and you may use the software only pursuant to the terms of your Governing Agreement, if any, and the license set forth herein. In addition, you may not disclose the Software to any third party.

2. **Limited Liability**. IN NO EVENT WILL THE LICENSOR'S LIABILITY UNDER, ARISING OUT OF OR RELATING TO THIS AGREEMENT EXCEED THE AMOUNT PAID TO LICENSOR FOR THE SOFTWARE. LICENSOR SHALL NOT BE LIABLE FOR ANY SPECIAL, INCIDENTAL, INDIRECT OR CONSEQUENTIAL DAMAGES, HOWEVER CAUSED AND ON ANY THEORY OF LIABILITY, REGARDLESS OF WHETHER LICENSOR HAS BEEN ADVISED OF THE POSSIBILITY OF SUCH DAMAGES. WITHOUT LIMITING THE FOREGOING, LICENSOR WILL NOT BE LIABLE FOR LOST PROFITS, LOSS OF DATA, OR COSTS OF COVER.

3. **Limited Warranty**. LICENSOR WARRANTS THAT SOFTWARE WILL BE FREE FROM DEFECTS IN MATERIALS AND WORKMANSHIP UNDER NORMAL USE FOR A PERIOD OF THIRTY (30) DAYS FROM THE DATE OF RECEIPT. THIS LIMITED WARRANTY IS VOID IF FAILURE OF THE SOFTWARE HAS RESULTED FROM ABUSE OR MISAPPLICATION. ANY REPLACEMENT SOFTWARE WILL BE WARRANTED FOR A PERIOD OF THIRTY (30) DAYS FROM THE DATE OF RECEIPT OF SUCH REPLACEMENT SOFTWARE. THE SOFTWARE AND DOCUMENTATION ARE PROVIDED "AS IS". LICENSOR HEREBY DISCLAIMS ALL OTHER WARRANTIES, EXPRESS, IMPLIED, OR STATUTORY, INCLUDING WITHOUT LIMITATION, THE IMPLIED WARRANTIES OF MERCHANTABILITY AND FITNESS FOR A PARTICULAR PURPOSE.

4. **Exceptions**. SOME STATES DO NOT ALLOW THE LIMITATION OF INCIDENTAL DAMAGES OR LIMITATIONS ON HOW LONG AN IMPLIED WARRANTY LASTS, SO THE ABOVE LIMITATIONS OR EXCLUSIONS MAY NOT APPLY TO YOU. This agreement gives you specific legal rights, and you may also have other rights which vary from state to state.

5. **U.S. Government-Restricted Rights**. The Software and accompanying documentation are deemed to be "commercial computer Software" and "commercial computer Software documentation," respectively, pursuant to DFAR Section 227.7202 and FAR Section 12.212, as applicable. Any use, modification, reproduction release, performance, display or disclosure of the Software and accompanying documentation by the U.S. Government shall be governed solely by the terms of this Agreement and shall be prohibited except to the extent expressly permitted by the terms of this Agreement.

6. **Export Restrictions**. You may not download, export, or re-export the Software (a) into, or to a national or resident of, Cuba, Iraq, Libya, Yugoslavia, North Korea, Iran, Syria or any other country to which the United States has embargoed goods, or (b) to anyone on the United States Treasury Department's list of Specially Designated Nationals or the U.S. Commerce Department's Table of Deny Orders. By installing or using the Software, you are representing and warranting that you are not located in, under the control of, or a national or resident of any such country or on any such list.

7. **General**. This License is governed by the laws of the United States and the State of California, without reference to conflict of laws principles. The parties agree that the United Nations Convention on Contracts for the International Sale of Goods shall not apply to this License. If any provision of this Agreement is held invalid, the remainder of this License shall continue in full force and effect.

8. **More Information**. Should you have any questions concerning this Agreement, or if you desire to contact Licensor for any reason, please contact: CBT Systems USA Ltd., 1005 Hamilton Court, Menlo Park, California 94025, Attn: Chief Legal Officer.

IF YOU DO NOT AGREE WITH THE ABOVE TERMS AND CONDITIONS, DO NOT INSTALL THE SOFTWARE AND RETURN IT TO THE LICENSOR.

About the CD-ROM

The enclosed CD-ROM contains the following computer-based training (CBT) course module:

Technical Support: PC Diagnostics and Repair

The CD can be used on Windows 95, Windows 98, or Windows NT systems. To access the CBT course, launch the SETUP.EXE file. For further information about installation, read the README.TXT file on the CD. At the Start menu, select Run and type in D:/readme.txt (where D is your CD-ROM drive).

Technical Support

For issues regarding bad media or replacement software, please contact Prentice Hall at:

disc_exchange@prenhall.com

For issues relating to running CBT Systems software, please contact CBT Systems Technical Support at:

Support@CBTSYS.COM